WHAT IS AN EXCHANGE?

WHAT IS AN EXCHANGE?

The Automation, Management, and Regulation
of Financial Markets

RUBEN LEE

OXFORD
UNIVERSITY PRESS

OXFORD

UNIVERSITY PRESS

Great Clarendon Street, Oxford OX2 6DP

Oxford University Press is a department of the University of Oxford.
It furthers the University's objective of excellence in research, scholarship,
and education by publishing worldwide in

Oxford New York

Athens Auckland Bangkok Bogotá Buenos Aires Calcutta
Cape Town Chennai Dar es Salaam Delhi Florence Hong Kong Istanbul
Karachi Kuala Lumpur Madrid Melbourne Mexico City Mumbai
Nairobi Paris São Paulo Singapore Taipei Tokyo Toronto Warsaw

with associated companies in Berlin Ibadan

Oxford is a registered trade mark of Oxford University Press
in the UK and in certain other countries

Published in the United States
by Oxford University Press Inc., New York

British Library Cataloguing in Publication Data

Data available

Library of Congress Cataloging in Publication Data
Lee, Ruben.
What is an exchange?: the automation, management,
and regulation of financial markets/Ruben Lee.
p.   cm.
Includes bibliographical references.
1. Stock exchanges—Management.   2. Futures market—Management.
I. Title.
HG4551.L345   1998
332.64'2'068—dc21   98–20655
ISBN 0–19–828840–9 (hbk.)
ISBN 0–19–829704–1 (pbk.)

5 7 9 10 8 6 4

Printed in Great Britain
on acid-free paper by
Bookcraft (Bath) Ltd,
Midsomer Norton, Somerset

To Swee Kheng and Tian Mei, my darlings
To Mom, Dad and Geoff
To Paul and Deirdre
To Aman and Rachna

ACKNOWLEDGEMENTS

A great amount of help was given to me in writing this book. I would like to give a special thank you to the people who read through the full text, or substantial parts of it, and provided many fascinating insights. They are Alden Adkins, Corinne Bronfman, Geoffrey Butcher, Gillian Bull, Andrea Corcoran, Ian Domowitz, James Moser, James Overdahl, Deborah Sabalot, Hyun Shin, Susan Singleton, David Westbrook, Fields Wicker-Miurin, and Mark Young. Nothing in the book is the responsibility of any of these people or the institutions at which they work.

Very many other people have provided documents, assistance, and advice. While many have preferred to remain anonymous, I would like to thank by name: Robert Aber, Steven Abrams, Michael Aitken, Mike Alex, Antonella Amadei, David Andrews, Janet Angstadt, Louise Anstead, Clive Archer, Paul Arlman, Doug Atkin, Michael Atkin, Robert Austin, James Baillie, Leonard Baptiste Jr., John Barrass, Roger Barton, Peter Beales, Brandon Becker, Peter Bennett, Hans Berggren, Daleep Bhatia, Julia Black, Belinda Blaine, Keith Boast, Richard Britton, Saul Bronfeld, Gregg Browne, Phillip Bruce, Michael Burnett, Alan Cameron, Eudald Canadell, Ann Carlson, John Carson, Edmundo Castellanes, Carrie Catlin, Alger 'Duke' Chapman, Vary Coates, Jack Coffee, Thomas Coleman, David Colker, Josephine Cottey, Geoffrey Creighton, Nancy Crossman, Michael Dalby, Tom Davin, Didier Davydoff, Michael Deveney, Rhys Dogan, Peter Donnelly, James Doty, James Duffy, Jeffrey Duncan, Fionnuala Earley, Scott Early, Peter Farmery, Kevin Fogarty, Yasuyuki Fuchita, Michael Gallagher, Kristen Geyer, Stuart Gill, Frederick Grede, Tom Haley, Mark Harding, John Hart, Cathy Haugh, Gérard Hertig, Charles Hood, Pamela Hughes, Lynton Jones, Jonathon Kallman, Hideki Kanda, Jane Kang, Roberta Karmel, Richard Ketchum, Jeffrey Knight, Andrew Kolinsky, Howard Kramer, Jeffrey Kuhn, Edward Kwalwasser, Paul Laux, John Lawton, Bruno Lederer, Sheree Levine, Ulph Lindgren, Craig Long, Eugene Lopez, Simon macLachlan, Graham Mansfield, John Martin, Joan McCarthy, Neil McGeown, Joanne Medero, Leo Melamed, Sam Scott Miller, John Moore, Barbara Muston, Paul Nelson, Sheila Nicoll, Alan Norrie, Janet O'Connor, Sadakazu Osaki, Gerrit de Marez Oyens, Derek Parker, Randee Pavalow, Fred Perkins, Todd Petzel, Bill Picken, Norman Poser, Bernard Rashes, Graeme Reid, Howard Rhile, John Ridler, Ivers Riley, Aidan Robertson, Amanda Rogers, Carl Royal, David Ruder, Ian Russell, Bengt Rydén, Michael Sanderson, Jamie Scarlett, Jeffrey Schaefer, James Shapiro, Brad Sherman, Michael Simon, Sheila Slevin, Paul Smee, Daniel Soffin, Benn Steil, Giles Stimson, Leslie Stratford, Harvey Tanzer, Patrick Thompson, Ruth Thompson, Shane Tregillis, Jean Tricou, David Van Wagner, Giles Vardey, Edward Waitzer, Consuela Washington, Jane Welch, John Whitmore, Andrew Whittaker, Barbara Wierzynski, Keith Woodbridge, and Steven Wunsch. Again, nothing in this book is the responsibility of any of these people or the institutions at which they work. To anybody I have missed, I apologize.

I would like to thank Robert Merton for permission to reproduce several paragraphs from his article 'Operation and Regulation in Financial Intermediation: A Functional Perspective' (1993), and Patrick Thompson for permission to reproduce several paragraphs from the 'Joint Proxy Statement' by NYMEX and COMEX (1994). I would also like to give a big thank you to David Musson of Oxford University Press for all his patience and support, and to Sarah Dobson for her efficiency and hard work.

The book draws on much previous work of mine, including most importantly an article I wrote for the Capital Markets Forum of the International Bar Association in 1992, also entitled 'What is an Exchange?', which inspired my interest in the topic. Chapters 4, 6, and 9 draw on, reproduce, and extend some of the analysis I presented in a book entitled *The Ownership of Price and Quote Information: Law, Regulation, Economics, and Business* (1995). Chapter 12 draws on, reproduces, and extends an article I wrote with Ian Domowitz entitled 'The Legal Basis for Stock Exchanges: The Classification and Regulation of Automated Trading Systems' (1996). A small section of the article is also used in the introduction. I would like to thank him for allowing me to use it here.

Five technical points are noteworthy. First, the intention is to allow for an uninterrupted reading of the book. Only summary details of references are therefore provided in the text and in the notes to each chapter. The notes themselves and full references are provided at the end of the book. Second, each chapter, apart from the first, comprises a brief introduction, some substantive sections, and then a conclusion with a summary of the key issues discussed in the chapter. Third, dates are cited in the English fashion, so that the day of the month, is followed by the month, which is followed by the year (i.e. 1/8/97 represents the first of August 1997). Fourth, for the most part Oxford English spelling conventions are used. Given, however, that much of the literature comes from the USA, some of the spelling uses American conventions. Finally, no information arising after January 1998 is used in the book.

I enjoyed writing this book. I hope you enjoy reading it.

CONTENTS

ABBREVIATIONS

ADR	American Depository Receipt
AFEIS	Australian Futures Exchange Information Services Pty. Ltd. (Australia)
AIM	Alternative Investment Market (UK)
AMEX	American Stock Exchange (USA)
AP	Associated Press (USA)
APT	Automated Pit Trading (UK)
ASC	Australian Securities Commission (Australia)
ASX	Australian Stock Exchange (Australia)
ASXO	Australian Stock Exchange Operations Ltd. (Australia)
AZX	Arizona Stock Exchange [previously known as WASI] (USA)
BBC	British Broadcasting Corporation (UK)
BBO	Best Bid and Offer
BDC	Botswana Development Corporation (Botswana)
BDTS	Broker–Dealer Trading System (USA)
BEACON	Boston Stock Exchange Automated Communication and Order-routing Network (USA)
BOTCC	Board Of Trade Clearing Corporation (USA)
BSE	Boston Stock Exchange (USA)/Botswana Stock Exchange (Botswana)
BTP	Buoni de Tesoro Poliennali (Italy) (Italian Treasury Bonds)
CAES	Computer Assisted Execution System (USA)
CBB	Chicago Board Brokerage (USA)
CBOE	Chicago Board Options Exchange (USA)
CBT/CBOT	Chicago Board of Trade (USA)
CCOS	Clearing Corporation for Options and Securities (USA)
CDPA	Copyright, Designs and Patents Act (UK)
CDT	Chicago Day Time
CEA	Commodity Exchange Act (USA)
CFI	Court of First Instance of the European Communities (EU)
CFR	Code of Federal Regulations (USA)
CFTC	Commodity Futures Trading Commission (USA)
CJEC	Court of Justice of the European Communities [sometimes ECJ] (EU)
CME	Chicago Mercantile Exchange (USA)
COB	Commission des Opérations de Bourse (France) (Exchange Operations Commission)
COMEX	Commodity Exchange (USA)
CQ	Consolidated Quotation (USA)
CQS	Consolidated Quotations System (USA)
CSCE	Coffee, Sugar and Cocoa Exchange (USA)

CSE	Cincinnati Stock Exchange (USA)
CTA	Consolidated Tape Association (USA)
CTCD	*Chambers Twentieth Century Dictionary*
DGOC	Delta Government Options Corporation (USA)
DIE	Designated Investment Exchange (UK)
DTB	Deutsche Terminbörse (Germany) (German Futures Exchange)
DTI	Department of Trade and Industry (UK)
EASDAQ	European Association of Securities Dealers Automated Quotation system
EC	European Community (now referred to as European Union)
ECC	Executive Committee Chairman
ECJ	European Court of Justice (sometimes CJEC)
ECN	Electronic Communication Network (USA)
ECU	European Currency Unit
EOE	European Options Exchange (Netherlands)
ET	Exchange Tiering
ETH	Electronic Trading Hours (USA)
EU	European Union
EWM	European Wholesale Market
FCM	Futures Commission Merchant
FESE	Federation of European Stock Exchanges [previously known as FSEEC]
FEX	First European Exchange
FIA	Futures Industry Association (USA)
FIBV	Fédération Internationale des Bourses de Valeurs (International Federation of Stock Exchanges)
FISD	Financial Information Services Division [of IIA] (USA)
FLEX	Flexible Exchange options
FMA	Floor Members' Association (USA)
FSA	Financial Services Act (UK)
FSEEC	Federation of Stock Exchanges in the European Community [now known as FESE]
FT	*Financial Times* (UK)
FTSE	*Financial Times* – Stock Exchange index (UK)
GAO	General Accounting Office (USA)
GATT	General Agreement on Trade and Tariffs
GCC	GLOBEX Control Center (USA)
GLOBEX	Global Exchange (USA)
GNMA	Government National Mortgage Association (USA)
HMT	Her Majesty's Treasury (UK)
IBA	International Bar Association
IBIS	Integriertes Börsenhandels- und Informations-System (Germany) (Integrated stock exchange trading and information system)

IDB	Inter-Dealer Broker
IDIS	Inter Bourse/Stock Exchange Data Information System (EU)
IFAC	International Federation of Accountants
IIA	Information Industry Association (USA)
IMM	International Monetary Market division, CME (USA)
IOM	Index and Option Market division, CME (USA)
IOSCO	International Organisation of Securities Commissions
INS	International News Service (INS)
IPUG	Information Providers Users Group (UK)
ISD	Investment Services Directive (EU)
ISE	International Stock Exchange [now known as LSE] (UK)
ISMA	International Securities Market Association [previously known as AIBD]
ISSRO	International Securities Self-Regulating Organization (UK)
IT	Information Technology
ITP	Independent Television Publications (UK)
ITS	Intermarket Trading System (USA)
JDS	Joint Exchange Computers Data Service (Australia)
JECNET	Joint Exchange Computers Network (Australia)
JV	GLOBEX Joint Venture L.P. (USA)
LCE	London Commodities Exchange (UK)
LIFFE	London International Financial Futures Exchange (UK)
LSE	London Stock Exchange [previously known as ISE] (UK)
MATIF	Marché À Terme International de France (France) (International Futures Market of France)
ME	Montreal Exchange (Canada)
MONEP	Marché des Options Négociables de Paris (France) (Traded Options Market of France)
MONSTER	Market-Oriented New System for Terrifying Exchanges and Regulators
MOU	Memorandum Of Understanding
MRRP	Merger Recognition and Retention Plan (USA)
MSE	Midwest Stock Exchange (USA)
MSRB	Municipal Securities Rulemaking Board (USA)
NASD	National Association of Securities Dealers (USA)
NASDAQ	NASD Automated Quotation system (USA)
NBA	National Basketball Association (USA)
NMS	National Market System (USA)
NoMS	Normal Market Size (UK)
NQDS	National Quotation Data Service (USA)
NSC	Nouveau Système Cotation (France) (New Quotation System)
NYCE	New York Cotton Exchange (USA)
NYMEX	New York Mercantile Exchange (USA)
NYSE	New York Stock Exchange (USA)

OCC	Options Clearing Corporation (USA)
OECD	Organisation for Economic Co-operation and Development
OED	*Oxford English Dictionary*
OFT	Office of Fair Trading (UK)
OHT	Off-Hours Trading
OM	Options Marknad (Sweden) (Options Market)
OMLX	OMLX, The London Securities and Derivatives Exchange [previously OM London] (UK)
OPRA	Options Price Reporting Authority (USA)
OSC	Ontario Securities Commission (Canada)
OTC	Over-the-Counter
ÖTOB	Österreichische Termin und Optionenbörse (Austria) (Austrian Futures and Options Exchange)
PHLX	Philadelphia Stock Exchange (USA)
PIPE	Price and Information Project for Europe
PMT	Post-Market-Trading (USA)
POSIT	Portfolio System for Institutional Trading
PTS	Proprietary Trading System (USA)
REE	Rational Expectations Equilibrium
RFS	Reuters Futures Services Inc.
RIE	Recognised Investment Exchange (UK)
RHCD	*Random House College Dictionary*
RMJ	RMJ Options Trading Corporation (USA)
ROIE	Recognised Overseas Investment Exchange (UK)
RTE	Radio Telefis Eireann (Ireland)
SBB	Stock Brokers Botswana (Botswana)
SBF	Société des Bourses Françaises (France) (French Exchanges Company)
SBL	Section on Business Law
SEA	Securities and Exchange Act (USA)
SEAQ	Stock Exchange Automated Quotation system (UK)
SEAQi	SEAQ International (UK)
SEATS	Stock Exchange Automated Transaction System (Australia)
SEC	Securities and Exchange Commission (USA)
SEIS	Stock Exchange Information System (Hong Kong)
SFA	Securities and Futures Authority (UK)
SFE	Sydney Futures Exchange (Australia)
SIA	Securities Industry Association
SIAC	Securities Industry Automation Corporation (USA)
SIB	Securities and Investments Board (UK)
SIMEX	Singapore International Monetary Exchange (Singapore)
SIP	Securities Information Processor (USA)
SOFFEX	Swiss Options and Financial Futures Exchange (Switzerland)
SPNTCO	Security Pacific National Trust Company (USA)

SRO	Self-Regulatory Organisation
SSE	Spokane Stock Exchange (USA)/Stockholm Stock Exchange (Sweden)
STATS	Sports Team Analysis and Tracking Systems (USA)
TALISMAN	Transfer Accounting Lodgement for Investors/Stock Management for principals (UK)
TCCD	*Twentieth Century Chambers Dictionary*
THS	Transactions Hors Séance (France) (After-Hours Trading)
TIFFE	Tokyo International Financial Futures Exchange (Japan)
TOPIC	Teletext Output of Price Information by Computer (UK)
TPA	Trade Practices Act (Australia)
TRIPs	Trade Related aspects of Intellectual Property Rights
TSE	Toronto Stock Exchange (Canada)/Tokyo Stock Exchange (Japan)
WASI	Wunsch Auction Systems Inc. [now known as AZX] (USA)
WIPO	World Intellectual Property Organization
WTIND	*Webster's Third New International Dictionary*

1

Introduction

QUESTIONS

The existence and nature of exchanges used not to be controversial. They were easily identified and characterized. New technology, however, has led to the birth of a previously unknown type of institution, the 'MONSTER' (a Market-Oriented New System for Terrifying Exchanges and Regulators), which has meant that this is no longer true.[1] What is, and what is not, an exchange is now unclear. This book aims to resolve the enigma.

The question of what an exchange is may be interpreted in a variety of ways, only some of which are examined here.[2] It may be understood as a question of existence, to be answered by identifying those institutions unambiguously recognized as exchanges. A list of the world's exchanges, however, is not presented here.[3] Rather than merely pointing to exchanges to show their existence, the question may also be addressed by describing the attributes and characteristics of exchanges. This descriptive approach may be further extended using a functional perspective. The question of what an exchange is, then turns on what an exchange does.

Three types of functional responses to the enigma may be attempted. The first is to identify and analyse some key attributes and functions of organizations accepted as exchanges. Such an approach is undertaken here. Attention is focused on the role of exchanges as providers of 'trading systems'. At the most general level, a trading system may be thought of as a forum for executing a trade. Though different for different markets, the standard trade cycle is composed of many activities, including consideration of pre- and post-trade information, order routing, order execution, matching, clearing, and settlement.[4] A trading system is defined here to be a mechanism that delivers the first three of these functions, namely data dissemination, order routing, and order execution. Data dissemination is the act of transmitting pre- and post-trade data, about quotes and trades respectively, to market participants.[5] Order routing is the act of delivering orders from their originators, such as investors and financial intermediaries, to the execution mechanism. Order execution is the process whereby orders can be transformed into trades. A market's structure or architecture is the full set of rules governing these three components.

This definition of a trading system is quite general in many ways. It places no restrictions: first, on the type of organization that may operate a trading system— which may be an individual financial intermediary, an investor, a data vendor, or an association of intermediaries; second, on the types of items that may be traded on a trading system—which may include commodities, foreign exchange, futures, options, or securities; third, on the corporate status of a trading system— which be organized on a nonprofit, a cooperative, or a for-profit, basis; or, fourth, on the regulatory classification of a trading system. The definition does, however, exclude the functions of matching, clearing, and settlement.[6] The reason for this is not because it is believed that these functions are unimportant, on the contrary, but because to have included them would have required the examination of many questions that are beyond the scope of this book to address.[7]

Rather than prejudging which institutions are exchanges and which are not, the analysis discusses three fundamental issues relevant for the creation, development, operation, and management, of all trading systems, whether they are believed exchanges or not. These are the manner in which they are governed, the way in which they compete and cooperate with each other, and their policies towards the dissemination of their price and quote information. No attempt is made in the book to summarize, let alone describe, the full range of existing trading systems. Appendix 1 does, however, contain a brief outline of some ways of categorizing trading systems, and also descriptions of the market architectures of three specific systems. Other issues related to the provision of trading systems, including most significantly an evaluation of the merits of different order execution algorithms are not addressed in depth here.[8]

A second functional response to the question of what is an exchange is to try to identify the key characteristics and activities by which to determine whether an institution should be considered an exchange or not. By itself, this strategy is of limited use. Opinions differ as to what the relevant attributes and functions of exchanges should be, and unless the reasons for identifying which institutions should be specified exchanges are made explicit, the selection of which attributes or functions should be deemed conclusive is either arbitrary or a matter of preferences. More importantly, the choice of what the relevant attributes and functions are, is often made by studying institutions unambiguously recognized as exchanges. By construction, however, such an approach cannot assess whether new trading systems with non-traditional attributes and functions should be considered exchanges or not. This strategy is not undertaken here.

A third functional interpretation of the question of what is an exchange may be asked in a practical, if not commercial, manner by exchanges. As such, the question is normally based on several assumptions. First, it is acknowledged that some of the services which used to be provided by exchanges in the past without question, and indeed which frequently used to be thought essential to their functioning, may now be supplied more efficiently by sources external to the exchange. Second, it is accepted that exchanges' previous ways of operating may be outdated or inefficient. Finally, it is recognized that in the face of competition, exchanges must take action so as to survive. In such circumstances, the question of what an exchange is, becomes a strategic issue of what it should do in order to prosper. Sometimes the question takes on a reductionist air, so that it is asked what is the minimum that an exchange should do while at the same time enhancing the external provision of those services no longer to be provided internally. Different responses are called for in different situations. A range of strategies that exchanges might employ in order to thrive in a competitive environment is evaluated in this book.

Yet another way in which the question of what is an exchange may be answered is by examining how the term is defined. Dictionary definitions of the word are interesting because they provide an indication of its widely accepted meanings. As a survey presented in Appendix 2 of the definitions of an 'exchange', a 'stock exchange', a 'futures exchange', and a 'market', illustrates, however, there is a wide diversity in the accepted meanings of these words.

It is in the legal and regulatory domain that the definition of the term 'exchange' becomes critical, given the central role that exchanges have historically played in the regulation of trading markets. The current confusion about what the term means has undermined the theoretical foundations for the regulation of markets, and led to some bruising legal and regulatory conflicts. In order to resolve them, the question of what is an exchange needs to be interpreted, at the most general level, as asking which institutions are required to undertake what regulatory obligations in trading markets. As important as the identification and elucidation of the existing law and regulation governing exchanges, is the question of whether the current legal and regulatory framework is appropriate. A further crucial interpretation of the question what is an exchange, is thus the policy question of what should be an exchange. The analysis and critique of the law and regulation governing exchanges, principally with regard to the development, operation, and management of their trading systems, are pivotal issues examined here.

THEMES

Four broad themes run through the book. The first is that the answer to the question of what is an exchange is complex. Not only does the question need to be interpreted in many ways, responses to each of these interpretations require intuitions and expertise from many different spheres of knowledge and experience, including those of business, economics, law, and regulation. Each of these different arenas has its own complexities and puzzles, and is constantly changing. Furthermore, there are many subtle ways in which these various fields interact with each other.

The second theme is the need to balance an understanding of a range of broad abstract topics with an appreciation of the minutiae of many variegated contexts. On the one hand, there are some conceptual issues central to the operation of all trading systems that transcend national, temporal, and physical, boundaries. On the other hand, the specificity of a particular exchange's market architecture, of its historical and institutional background, of the types of items traded on the market, and of the legal and regulatory environment within which it operates, can all be determinative factors in effecting outcomes at the exchange. Different approaches are used throughout the book to address different problems, with some broad analytical exegesis examining the conceptual issues, combined with various case studies detailing the particularities of specific exchange situations and decisions.[9]

The third theme is the importance of technology in understanding the nature and role of exchanges and trading systems. Progress in automation has had a range of important effects. It has made possible the construction of new types of dealing facilities which would otherwise have been difficult, if not impossible, to build. It has allowed organizations to compete selectively with exchanges by choosing to offer some, but not all, of the services that historically only exchanges provided. It has eliminated the need for the person-to-person contact required by traditional market mechanisms such as trading floors or telephone networks. It has reduced the costs of establishing new trading systems, thereby making it easier for new entrants to enter the market for markets. It has increased the power of the buyers of the services offered by trading systems, and in the case of low cost systems such as those that operate via the internet, has democratized access to the trading environment. Finally, it has meant that orders and market data can be routed and manipulated more easily, and transmitted both more quickly and to a much larger group of participants, than was previously feasible. These effects, in turn, have encouraged the development of new products, the process of disintermediation, and the growth of cross-border trading.

The final theme running through the book is the struggle between what is believed to lie in the public domain and what is thought to be a matter solely of private concern. Not only is this conflict at the heart of many regulatory issues, it underpins a central dilemma that the individual participants in a market frequently face: should they agree to limit their freedom of action in order to benefit the market as a whole, and thereby potentially and indirectly benefit themselves? or, should they view such constraints as damaging to their self-interest, and therefore reject them?

IMPORTANCE

There are currently about 250 institutions recognized as exchanges in the world, and both individually and collectively they play a critical role in most national economies and also at the global level. They provide cash, futures, options, and other forms of derivatives, markets for almost all the major commodities and assets traded in the world, including agricultural goods,[10] energy-related products,[11] financial products,[12] metals,[13] precious metals,[14] soft commodities,[15] securities, and other miscellaneous items.[16] These markets perform a wide range of economic and political functions. They offer fora for trading, investment, speculation, hedging, and arbitrage. They serve as mechanisms for price discovery and information dissemination. They provide vehicles for raising finance for companies. They are frequently pivotal elements in the success of financial centres. They are used to implement privatization programmes, and they often play an important role in the development of emerging economies. The effective delivery of all these market functions depends upon the sound operation and regulation of the exchanges organizing the relevant markets, and the ways in which these goals can be achieved are central issues examined here.

Different aspects of the question of what is an exchange investigated in the book are of concern to different audiences. The full range of issues is clearly of critical importance to exchanges themselves. There are several key topics that are crucial for those market participants most closely associated with exchanges, namely their members and owners, and also to the wider group of market participants who consume or use the goods and services offered by exchanges, including commodity producers, financial intermediaries, investors, and issuers. The key questions that affect them are: What price and quote data might exchanges be expected to provide, and at what cost? How is it possible to influence exchanges' actions? How do exchanges react to competition? and, How can the legislative and regulatory environment concerning exchanges be interpreted and influenced to further their own advantage? These issues are also of great consequence both to the sponsors of trading systems that compete with exchanges, and also to the data vendors that obtain, manipulate, and sell, exchanges' price and quote data. The topics of how exchanges and trading systems both are, and should be, regulated are of pivotal concern to those people charged with serving the public interest in the context of trading markets, including primarily legislators, government staff, and regulators. Finally, many of the issues examined here will be of interest to those engaged in the academic analysis of exchanges and trading systems, including business and organizational theorists, economists, finance scholars, and lawyers.

CONTENTS

The book is composed of eleven chapters in addition to the introduction. In the first five, the nature and conduct of exchanges and other forms of trading systems are described and analysed. Chapter 2 examines the governance of exchanges. Four key questions are explored: What does governance mean in the context of an exchange? Why are particular governance structures adopted by exchanges? How does an exchange's governance affect its behaviour? and finally, Why do governance structures change? In order to illustrate the considerations that are important in affecting exchange governance, Chapter 3 presents five case studies of various situations in which the governance structure of different exchanges has been at issue. Chapter 4 discusses the nature of competition and cooperation in the context of exchanges. Four broad issues are addressed: What does it mean to say that an exchange faces competition? What are the factors that give rise to such competition? How do exchanges react to such competition? and, When, why, and how do they attempt to cooperate with, rather than compete against, each other? In order to illustrate the factors that influence how and why exchanges cooperate with each other, Chapter 5 presents some case studies of various cooperative linkages, joint projects, and also one merger, between diverse stock and futures exchanges. Chapter 6 investigates the importance to exchanges of the dissemination of their price and quote information. The main questions examined are: What types of price and quote information do exchanges release, when, and to whom? What rights do they claim in the data they publish? and, What pricing policies do they employ for the sale of these data?

The next three chapters describe the law and regulation governing some key aspects of the operation of exchanges and trading systems. Chapter 7 examines the law and regulation that specify how trading systems should be classified, and how those elements of their market structure apart from the dissemination of their prices and quotes should be controlled. The relevant American, British, and European Union law and regulation are summarized. In Chapter 8, six key branches of law and regulation that are important for the dissemination of price and quote information in various jurisdictions are described. They govern, respectively, copyright, a new *sui generis* right in databases, misappropriation, confidentiality, competition, and the securities markets. Chapter 9 studies the American federal law and regulation that affects the governance and self-regulation of both securities and futures exchanges. The three-way separation presented in Chapters 7, 8, and 9 of the law and regulation affecting first classification and market structure, second information dissemination, and third governance, is by necessity somewhat arbitrary.

Chapter 10 presents a survey of the current state of knowledge of the role that the dissemination of prices and quotes plays in the functioning of markets, as examined in the economics literature. Two broad topics are examined: the informational role of prices in equilibrium models, and the effects of disseminating different amounts of price and quote information in a broad spectrum of theoretical, empirical, and experimental, market contexts.

The last two chapters contain some policy analyses and recommendations. Chapter 11 examines various key issues concerning information and competition. Some general comments are presented on the nature and role of regulation in financial markets, and in particular on the function that competition policy should play in the regulation of exchanges and trading systems. Two broad questions are then addressed: Should the dissemination of price and quote information be mandated by regulation? and, How, if at all, should the price of such information be regulated? Chapter 12 addresses the issue of how trading systems should be classified and governed. The criteria the American Securities and Exchange Commission (SEC) has historically employed to identify whether a trading system should be classified as an exchange or a broker are identified. A range of flaws with the traditional exchange/broker distinction is discussed. Finally, various approaches to regulating exchanges and trading systems, including the newest suggestions by the SEC, are analysed and criticized. One approach, namely the separation of the regulation of market structure from the regulation of other areas of public concern, and the employment of competition policy to regulate market structure, is recommended as the best way of classifying and regulating trading systems.

2

Governance

To understand the behaviour of an exchange, it is insufficient to think of it merely as a black box.[1] Approaches which ignore the inner structure of exchanges, such as those viewing an exchange solely as a trading system (in the language of microstructure financial economists), a reduced-form production function (in the language of neoclassical economists),[2] or an impersonal instrument guided by its managers (in the language of organizational theorists),[3] are not rich enough in detail or subtlety to be able to explain the nature and conduct of exchanges. To do so, it is necessary to analyse who has what power at an exchange, how and why they obtain it, and how and why they exercise it. An initial analysis of some of these issues, which may collectively be referred to as governance, is presented in this chapter. Four key questions are explored: What does governance mean in the context of an exchange? Why are particular governance structures adopted by exchanges? How does an exchange's governance affect its behaviour? and finally, Why do governance structures change?

Several aspects of the analysis presented here should be noted. First, all the questions to be examined are closely interrelated, and it is thus not easy to address one of them without simultaneously addressing others. The choice of what governance structure an exchange adopts, for example, is critically dependent on the effects that different structures have on exchange behaviour. Second, the governance of an exchange will be affected both by the formal and legal constructs within which the exchange operates, such as its constitution and any contractual arrangements it has made, and also by a range of informal, non-constitutional and non-contractual factors. Both types of influences are examined here.

Third, notwithstanding the fact that the nature of governance is defined above in terms of the power wielded at an exchange, the analysis of governance provided in this chapter draws for the most part on several strands of the theory of the firm. These include the 'nexus of contracts', 'property rights', and 'principal–agent' methodologies, and most importantly the 'transaction cost' approach.[4] All four methodologies, but especially the transaction cost approach, may be characterized not simply as economics, but rather as interdisciplinary studies combining legal, economic, and organizational perspectives. Both sociological and political explanations of how exchanges are governed, however, are for the most part ignored.[5]

The key tenet of the transaction cost approach, following Hansmann (1980; 1996), is that the governance structure adopted by an organization will be the one which minimizes the combined costs to all 'patrons' of dealing with the organization. The meaning of patrons in this context is very broad, and includes amongst others, the institution's owners, members, controllers, management, staff, consumers, suppliers, and financiers.[6] Two key elements of governance are the assignment of ownership and control. Cost-minimization requires that the sum of the costs of ownership and control incurred by those patrons who are an organization's owners or controllers, and the costs of contracting with the organization incurred by those patrons who are not its owners or controllers, are together minimized. In order to assess the relative efficiency of different institutional forms, a comparison of the total costs they each give rise to is required.

A fourth noteworthy aspect of the analysis provided in this chapter is that its prime aim is to present an understanding of a range of conceptual issues. Many specific examples, however, are used to illustrate the conceptual points discussed. Some of these are drawn from the case studies on exchange governance examined in the next chapter.

Finally, it is important to stress that attention is focused here on those aspects of governance which are not subject to legal or regulatory intervention specific to the securities or futures markets. Such intervention may affect an exchange's governance, either directly by constraining the organizational structure of the exchange, or indirectly by limiting the choices that an exchange and its board may take concerning the exchange's operations and activities. The mere threat of such interference may also be an influential factor determining exchange governance. The impact of this type of legal and regulatory intervention on exchange governance is examined in Chapters 9 and 12.

The chapter is composed of three sections. In the first, a preliminary analysis is presented of the three archetypal organizational structures that have most commonly been adopted by exchanges: the nonprofit, the consumer cooperative, and the for-profit forms. The relative costs of adopting each archetype are also examined. In the second section, the variety and complexity of different exchanges' governance structures are discussed, and some additional costs associated with the three archetypal forms are identified. The assumptions underlying the three archetypes are also scrutinized and relaxed. In the third section, two important ways in which the governance of an exchange may come under pressure to change are analysed.

ARCHETYPAL BUSINESS AND LEGAL FORMS: PRELIMINARY ANALYSIS

The three archetypal organizational structures that have most commonly been adopted by exchanges are the nonprofit, the consumer cooperative, and the for-profit forms. Although historically most exchanges have been nonprofit firms, there have been some consumer cooperative exchanges, and, recently, there has been a trend for exchanges to incorporate themselves as for-profit entities. This section contains an initial analysis of the essential elements of these three archetypes, and of the relative costs to financial intermediaries of adopting each of the organizational structures in the establishment of an exchange.

There are four connected reasons why the analysis presented here should be viewed as preliminary. First, only the most basic governance elements of each archetype are examined. Second, it is assumed that associated with each of the three organizational structures is a simple and well-defined objective function that is maximized by any organization adopting the relevant form. Third, when assessing the relative costs of an exchange adopting each archetypal form, attention is focused only on the costs that would be incurred by the market participants who are normally most closely identified with an exchange, namely the financial intermediaries who trade on, and are consumers of the services offered by the exchange. The behaviour of, and incentives facing other types of patrons of the exchange are ignored. Finally, it is assumed that all the financial intermediaries trading on an exchange may be modelled by a single representative firm. The importance of relaxing these assumptions is examined in subsequent sections.

One further point about the analysis presented here is noteworthy. The fact that the three governance archetypes are examined here, does not necessarily imply that one or other of them is the most economic in terms of costs for financial intermediaries, or indeed for a broader group of patrons. While this may be so, the only way to assess this would be to compare the costs arising from each of the three archetypes with those arising from any other institutional arrangements deemed relevant. There is in fact one particularly important relevant institutional arrangement which is ignored here, but discussed in later chapters. It is when no exchange is established, and the participants in a market either execute all their transactions internally, or seek to find counterparties with whom to trade without the establishment of any exchange or similar institutional structure to help them do so.

The Nonprofit, Consumer Cooperative, and For-Profit Structures

The precise implications of an exchange adopting each of the three governance archetypes—the nonprofit, the consumer cooperative, and the for-profit forms—will depend on the applicable jurisdiction. Nevertheless, several essential elements associated with each legal form may be identified. The central characteristic of the governance structure of a nonprofit firm is that it is restricted from distributing any profit or surplus that it earns, outside the firm. In order that any such surplus is not distributed to the firm's management, a nonprofit firm is also typically only allowed to pay a 'reasonable compensation' to its management. Following Hansmann (1980), the simplest characterization of an exchange as a nonprofit firm is as a 'commercial mutual' nonprofit.[7] 'Commercial' refers to the fact that a nonprofit's income derives primarily from providing goods or services for a fee to its customers. In the case of an exchange this is taken to mean offering financial intermediaries a marketplace on which to deal.[8] 'Mutual' refers to the fact that the agents who are the prime source of a nonprofit's income also control the organization. For an exchange, this means that the financial intermediaries who trade on the exchange also control it.[9] Given that a commercial mutual nonprofit firm is controlled by and run for the consumers of the firm, that it cannot distribute any profits, and that it cannot operate if its cumulative losses exceed its cumulative gains, the idealized vision of the objective function of such a firm is that it maximizes consumer surplus subject to breaking even.[10]

The governance structure of a consumer cooperative revolves around the notion of membership. The key attributes of a cooperative are that the services it provides and goods it offers are mainly for the use of its members, and that membership is limited only to those agents who consume the cooperative's goods and services.[11] The formal control of a cooperative, namely the assignment of voting rights at such an organization, is allocated solely to members. Typically, this is done on an equal basis, so that each member has only one vote regardless of the number of shares he owns or the amount of equity he has in the cooperative. The economic benefits associated with membership may also be allocated on an equal basis or on the basis of members' patronage of the cooperative. They are normally not allocated according to the amount of equity a member has in the cooperative. Other aspects of the governance of a cooperative are common. Although outside equity may be issued, it may have no voting rights attached to it, and may sometimes be restricted to earn a maximum rate of return.[12] Transfer of ownership interests is normally prohibited or limited. The initial investment in a cooperative is normally paid by the initial membership, either on an equal basis or in an amount proportionate to the amount of patronage a member is expected to bring. Net earnings are often used to retire the investments of cooperative members, with the oldest outstanding shares normally retired first via a system of revolving finance.

Despite the key difference between consumer cooperatives and commercial mutual nonprofits, namely that the first type of organization may make distributions in cash to its owners while the second is only allowed to do so in kind, the similarities between the two organizational archetypes are more evident than the differences. Furthermore, nonprofits and cooperatives are not always carefully distinguished in the law.[13] The idealized vision of the objective function of a consumer cooperative is that it maximizes consumer surplus plus producer surplus, with profits being distributed to the members of the cooperative.[14]

Although the governance structures of for-profit firms are typically extremely complex and varied, it is sufficient initially to characterize them by contrasting them with those of the commercial mutual nonprofit and consumer cooperative forms. In particular, the central constraints binding nonprofit and consumer cooperatives are not imposed on for-profit firms. Unlike nonprofits, therefore, for-profit firms are not required to retain all profits within the firm, and such profits may be, and normally are, distributed to equity holders. Similarly, unlike consumer cooperatives, for-profit firms may allow market participants other than customers and non-market participants to have voting rights, and may also allow non-members to be their customers. Indeed, the notion of membership is not easily applicable to a for-profit firm. The idealized goal that a for-profit firm is assumed to follow is the maximization of the present value of profit or producer surplus.

It is important not to exaggerate the differences between the nonprofit and for-profit forms in the exchange context. Although nonprofit exchanges are not allowed to distribute any profits they earn, they can effect a similar result by lowering the fees they charge members for the various services that they offer, or by offering rebates to their members. While the payment of a dividend by a for-profit exchange will primarily benefit the large owners of the exchange, however, the reduction of fees or the payment of rebates at a nonprofit exchange will primarily benefit the large users of the exchange's services. The importance of this distinction depends critically on whether the two groups are congruent or not.

Transaction Cost Comparison

When adopted by an exchange, each of the archetypal governance forms imposes different costs on the financial intermediaries trading in a market. Five sources for such costs are briefly discussed in turn. They concern, respectively, monopoly, the inevitability of incomplete contracts, horizon problems, the difficulty of diversifying the risk of holding shares in nonprofit and cooperative firms, and various miscellaneous factors.[15]

Monopoly

A monopolistic for-profit firm will maximize producer surplus by raising prices and reducing output compared to the competitive outcome. This will not be optimal for the customers of the firm who would rather that the lower price and higher output competitive outcome obtains. As observed by Hansmann (1980: 44), both the nonprofit and the cooperative forms may, however, be able to deliver the preferred outcome:

The nonprofit producer, like its for-profit counterpart, has the capacity to raise prices . . . without much fear of customer reprisal; however it lacks the incentive to do so because those in charge are barred from taking home any resulting profits.

Hansmann (1981: 508) similarly notes that,

Cooperatives tend to arise . . . in situations in which the organization's customers feel a need to maintain control of prices set by the enterprise—as, for example, when the enterprise occupies a position of natural monopoly.

In order for the nonprofit or the cooperative form to be adopted by a monopolistic producer, the costs to customers of exercising control over the firm by switching to one of these governance structures must be lower than those they would incur by contracting via the market with the monopolistic for-profit firm.

Traditionally there have been two sources of monopoly with which the financial intermediaries in a market have been concerned. The first is in the provision
of trading systems. Consider a situation where there is only one such system,
where this system is operated on a for-profit basis, and where it is not owned and
controlled by the financial intermediaries. Its owners would then be able to raise
the prices paid by the financial intermediaries for their use of the system, and
restrict the amount of services available, compared to what would obtain if there
were many such systems competing with each other. In such circumstances, the
financial intermediaries might seek to operate the trading system as a nonprofit or
consumer cooperative, assuming the costs of exercising control over it were not
too high.

The second source of monopoly with which financial intermediaries have
historically been concerned is the provision of broking and dealing services to
investor-clients. By restricting competition between themselves, typically by
limiting the number of brokers and by charging minimum commissions, financial
intermediaries have been able to exploit some monopoly power over their
customers.[16] This situation may be viewed as a monopolist operating in an
upstream market who provides an indispensable factor of production to a downstream market. The exchange is the monopolist, the indispensable factor of
production is the trading system, and the downstream market is the one for
broking and dealing services provided by financial intermediaries. The owners of
the exchange can refuse to sell use of the trading system to those brokers who are
not members of the cooperative, thereby reducing unwanted competition. The
governance structure of an exchange may thus help the brokers sustain such a
cartel by limiting access to the exchange. It is paradoxical that on the one hand
the cooperative governance structure may be employed by intermediaries to miti-
gate the effects of a monopoly which they face for the provision of trading
systems, while on the other hand the same governance structure may be used to
bolster the cartel which they operate for the provision of broking services.

The claim that exchanges are organized as cooperatives because a cooperative
is an effective mechanism for sustaining a cartel amongst brokers has been
contested by Hart and Moore (1994).[17] They note that an outside owner could
implement the same outcome by similarly restricting the numbers of brokers and
raising commissions. This argument, however, ignores the issue of how any
monopoly profits that arise are to be distributed. The outcomes at a monopolistic
for-profit exchange and at a monopolistic consumer cooperative exchange may be
indistinguishable from an investor's point of view, in that the same (relatively
limited) number of brokers would be operating and they would be charging the
same (relatively high) fees to investors. The two different governance structures
are likely, however, to have markedly different effects on the distribution of
profits. At the for-profit exchange, the owners of the exchange may seek to appropriate the monopoly profits by charging the intermediaries a high transaction fee,
which the intermediaries would in turn pass on to investors. At the consumer
cooperative, in contrast, the intermediaries may look to obtain this money via

relatively high commissions, and setting themselves a relatively low transaction fee.

Further evidence of the importance of governance may be seen by considering whether a monopolistic exchange would be willing to grant access to its trading system directly to investors. A nonprofit or cooperative monopolistic exchange whose members were financial intermediaries would be loath to do so, as this might lead to the financial intermediaries being disintermediated, and thereby imperil the livelihood of the members whose very welfare the exchange existed to serve. A monopolistic for-profit non-member-owned system, on the other hand, would have no such qualms, as it would not have to satisfy the preferences of the financial intermediaries trading on its system.

Incomplete Contracts
All real contracts are necessarily incomplete for two reasons: first, because it is costly to specify how a contract should operate under all circumstances, and second, because not all outcomes can be anticipated in advance. As noted by Hart (1991), the presence of incomplete contracts may affect the most efficient alloca-tion of ownership. Williamson (1975; 1979; 1985), and Klein, Crawford and Alchian (1978) argue that this may be especially important when the parties to a business relationship make sunk investments. As summarized by Holmstrom and Tirole (1989: 68–9),

> [Williamson's] standard paradigm is one in which partners are locked into a relationship *ex post* because of investments that have substantially higher value within the relationship than outside of it. To the extent that one cannot specify *ex ante* how the surplus should be divided between the two, i.e. if one cannot write a comprehensive contract, the division will depend on *ex post* bargaining positions. Bargaining positions in turn will depend on the organizational context. Where relationship-specific investments are large, Williamson argues against the use of market exchange, because parties will fear that they will be unable to appropriate the returns from their investments in an *ex post* non-competitive bargaining environment. Bringing the transaction within the firm will offer safeguards against opportunistic behavior.[18]

An instance of this may arise if the customers of a firm have to make investments that are specific to that firm. In order to avoid the possibility that the firm may seek to exploit these customers, it may be cost-efficient for the firm to be governed by its customers, via a nonprofit or cooperative structure for example. There clearly are sunk costs to a financial intermediary of being associated with a particular exchange. In particular, if the exchange has a physical trading floor, an intermediary will incur the costs of establishing and maintaining appropriate floor space. Similarly, if the exchange employs an automated trading system, an intermediary will need to implement the necessary electronic links. Nevertheless, the costs to an intermediary of switching its order flow from one exchange to another do not generally appear to be so high that once it has become a member of the first exchange, it is effectively locked into dealing on that exchange. Relatively cheap alternatives are typically available, either by leasing space on the second exchange if it operates a trading floor, by hiring electronic capacity to deliver orders to the second exchange if it operates an automated trading system, or by routing orders through a member of the second exchange and paying the required brokerage fees.

The notion and importance of ownership in the context of incomplete contracts has been formalized by Grossman and Hart (1986). They define ownership as the set of residual rights of control associated with an asset, where residual means the set of rights that have not been pre-specified contractually. Once again, the possibility that bargaining about the returns to an asset may occur after an initial contracting period, may make it optimal for ownership to be allocated to those participants who have made investment decisions specific to the asset. Hart and Moore (1990) extend this analysis to note that agents' importance as trading partners may be as significant a determinant of the optimal allocation of ownership rights as agents' investment decisions. In particular, when an agent is identified as being *indispensable* to an asset, it may be optimal to grant ownership to him.[19] If this is not done, the possibility of bargaining outcomes obtaining which are not efficient is again increased. To the extent that the financial intermediaries in a market have historically been the only agents who could usefully employ the services offered by exchanges, their indispensability may have been one of the factors making their ownership of exchanges relatively cost-efficient. Given that other market participants can now use an exchange's services, however, the importance of this determinant of exchange governance is likely to have been reduced.

Horizon Problems
As Porter and Scully (1987) note, a horizon problem may arise when an owner's claim on the net cash flow generated by an asset of his is shorter than the productive life of the asset. When this happens, and when the market for the asset is not competitive, the return to the owner will be less than the return generated by the asset, and there will be under-investment in such assets compared to the situation where such horizon problems were not present. This may occur in nonprofit and cooperative exchanges. In nonprofits, claims to incremental net earnings cannot be bought and sold. In cooperatives, the capitalization and transfer of future net earnings is likely to be only partially effective at best: even though outside equity may be issued, members' equity can only be transferred by relinquishing trading rights. In both types of exchanges, therefore, horizon problems may obtain. Members reducing their use of an exchange's services will undervalue investment assets compared to the discounted cash flows the investments are expected to yield. They will not want to pay more fees now for benefits they may not see in the future. In contrast, those members for whom patronage is expected to grow over the life of an investment will place a higher value on the asset. This may create control problems at exchanges where all members are required to make the same investments, given that investment incentives may differ between members.

The for-profit form may lead to a different type of horizon problem for an exchange. Claims to net earnings can be capitalized and transferred in for-profit exchanges, and therefore the financial potential of the long-term investments necessary for exchange marketing and product development, can be appropriately evaluated by such exchanges' owners. It is sometimes argued, however, that the shareholders of for-profit exchanges may be more 'short-termist' than those of nonprofit and cooperative exchanges.[20] In particular, pressure on for-profit firms to pay dividends rather than retain their earnings for investment, may allow nonprofit and cooperative exchanges to make longer term but more profitable investments than for-profit exchanges.

Non-Diversifiability of Risk
The ability of the members of a nonprofit or cooperative exchange to diversify their investments in their exchange, while still retaining the right to trade on the exchange, is limited. This is not only because the shares of such exchanges cannot easily be bought and sold while retaining trading rights. In addition, as remarked by Davidson (1994: 6), 'seat ownership is a particularly illiquid form of wealth . . . [and] next to no one in his right mind will accept a futures exchange membership as collateral for a loan'. Even if this statement is an exaggeration, the volatility of seat prices will make bankers cautious to take a seat as collateral for a loan of an amount close to the seat's market value. Members of nonprofit and cooperative exchanges will therefore be unlikely to be able to arrange their invest-ment portfolios so as to reflect their personal preferences for risk, and this may make them demand a greater return on their investments, or make less of an investment, than their counterparts in for-profit exchanges.

Miscellaneous
Three other cost differentials associated with the various organizational arche-types are noted here. The first concerns financing. A for-profit firm may issue dividend-paying and voting equity to anybody, whereas a cooperative may only issue dividend-paying but non-voting equity to non-members, and a commercial mutual nonprofit may only issue non-voting and non-dividend-paying equity to non-customers. The for-profit firm may therefore be able to raise finance more cheaply than the other two organizational structures. A second cost advantage may arise as a result of legal constraints. In contrast with for-profit firms, the functions which nonprofits are allowed by law to undertake may be restricted. They are, however, typically allowed to establish trade associations, a category in which exchanges may often be classified.[21] Some jurisdictions similarly limit the activities of cooperatives, in some instances only allowing agricultural associa-tions to incorporate as cooperatives.[22]

The third cost advantage concerns certain legal benefits. In the USA, for exam-ple, nonprofits have advantages over for-profit corporations in many areas of federal legislation.[23] These include various aspects of the treatment of social security, unemployment insurance, the minimum wage, securities regulation, bankruptcy, antitrust, unfair competition, copyright, and postal rates. Some nonprofits, though not exchanges, also receive an exemption from paying federal income tax. The value of these, and other, legal benefits should not, however, be over-emphasized: many older exchanges adopted the nonprofit form prior to the establishment of any of the legal benefits currently associated with it.[24]

VARIETY AND COMPLEXITY

The governance structures of actual exchanges are extremely diverse and compli-cated. So much so, indeed, that the assumptions on which the three archetypal models presented above are based, are so far from representing how exchanges operate in practice, that the models themselves are not realistic. This section explores the implications of such variety and complexity, and studies the ramifi-cations of relaxing the assumptions previously made. In particular, the intricate detail of exchanges' constitutional structures is recognized; the simplicity of the objective functions pursued by exchanges adopting each of the three organiza-tional forms is questioned; the transaction costs incurred by market participants other than financial intermediaries are investigated; the implications for exchange governance of the behaviour of these other types of patrons are discussed; and, the heterogeneity of the participants trading on an exchange is acknowledged. The section is composed of two parts. Various factors that complicate exchange governance are described first of all. The manner in which these factors affect the transaction cost comparison, and thus the relative efficiency, of the different orga-nizational structures is then examined.

Description

Two ways in which the actual governance structures of exchanges are more complicated than those indicated by the archetypal forms previously identified are discussed here. The detail of the formal governance structures adopted by exchanges is briefly illustrated, and then the simultaneous pursuit by exchanges of multiple objectives and the endemic nature of conflict in exchange governance is scrutinized.

Formal Structures
In order to specify the formal governance structure of an exchange, it is necessary to identify the constitutional rights and duties that are allocated to the key partic-ipants at the exchange, including its owners, members, traders, board, commit-tees, and management. Such a specification typically requires addressing questions such as: What types of shares in an exchange are available? What rights and duties, most particularly concerning voting, trading and representation, are associated with the different types of shares? How may such rights and duties be varied? Who may own which shares? How may shares be transferred? Who may be appointed to the board? What are the powers of directors? How may managers

be appointed and fired? and When are decisions of the exchange required to be put to a ballot? These questions have been answered in varied ways at different exchanges.

Ownership structures of exchanges differ. There may be up to five broad classes into which the owners of a stock exchange may typically be classified: intermediaries, issuers, investors, management, and the state. Other classes are common at futures and commodities exchanges, including floor brokers, floor traders, futures commission merchants (FCMs), and producers. The voting rights associated with being an owner vary. At some exchanges, each member is granted one share and one vote in general meetings of the exchange;[25] at others, members who do more business have been granted more shares, and correspondingly more votes, than their smaller counterparts.[26] Some exchanges issue several classes of shares with different rights or duties attached to them. This often occurs at futures exchanges with more than one trading pit, where different classes of shares are issued, associated with each of which are the rights to trade in different pits.[27] The different types of memberships are frequently designed to attract new participants to an exchange in order to trade new products.

Board representation also differs across exchanges. In some stock exchanges, for example, investors are granted access to the board; in others they are not. The manner of selecting the chairman of an exchange also varies. Sometimes he is elected by the board of directors,[28] sometimes by the full electorate of all members of the exchange,[29] sometimes he is appointed by the state.

The internal organization of the London Stock Exchange (LSE) exemplifies the complexity of the formal governance structure typical of many exchanges. Its Memorandum of Association lays down thirty 'objects' for the company, the first eight of which are the most relevant for its activity as a stock exchange. They state that it is the purpose of the exchange:

(1) To carry on the business of an investment exchange and clearing house; to provide, manage and regulate markets in, and clearing and settlement services with respect to transactions in, investments of all kinds, whether direct or derivative, including financial instruments and currencies; and to provide facilities for the transaction of the businesses of broking, dealing, market-making, stocklending, investment management and advice and other businesses in the field of financial services.

(2) To act as an authority for the admission of investments to be traded or dealt in on any exchange or market and to maintain any official list for the time being required or recognised by the law of any country.

(3) To provide information, depository and nominee services.

(4) To provide, maintain and operate systems for and in connection with the evidencing and transfer of investments without a written instrument and to regulate the use thereof.

(5) To act in any statutory, supervisory, regulatory or public capacity pursuant to statute or otherwise in relation to investments or financial matters of any kind or any market relating thereto.

(6) To enter into arrangements of any kind and to co-operate and share information with governmental and non-governmental authorities, bodies and persons in any part of the

world, and in particular with those having responsibility for the supervision or regulation of financial services.

(7) To promote high standards in the financial services industry and in particular to make, administer, monitor and enforce rules governing access to and use of any services and facilities provided by the Company [i.e. the exchange] and the qualification and conduct of persons engaging in the financial services industry or any part thereof, and to make arrangements for the investigation of complaints in respect of business transacted by means of the Company's services and facilities.

(8) To establish and maintain, by the levying of contributions, by insurance or otherwise, compensation schemes for the benefit or protection of the public or of any class of person.[30]

The exchange has designated itself a nonprofit institution. In particular, its net revenues can only 'be applied . . . towards the promotion of the objects' of the exchange, and no portion of these revenues can be paid directly or indirectly to its members.[31]

The Articles of Association specify how the exchange is to be controlled.[32] Only members of the exchange may be shareholders of the exchange, and all members of the exchange must become shareholders.[33] There are, however, effectively no restrictions on the number of shares that may be issued.[34] The rights attached to shares may, in general, be changed either with the consent in writing of three-quarters of the nominal amount of issued shares, or with the sanction of an extraordinary resolution passed at a separate general meeting of such holders. The transfer of shares is generally restricted.[35] Each shareholder has the right to attend and vote at any general meeting of the exchange. Every shareholder is allowed one vote on a resolution which is put to a show of hands at a general meeting, if personally present, and one vote on a resolution which is put to a poll at a general meeting, if present either in person or by proxy. Resolutions may be passed on a show of hands or on a poll by a majority of the votes, subject to there being a quorum. In the case of a tie, the chairman is entitled to a casting vote.

The exchange must normally have between twelve and twenty-five directors. Directors may be appointed either on the recommendation of other directors, or by a member representing at least one tenth of the total voting rights of all members. Every annual general meeting one third of the directors must retire. The directors may recommend a person for appointment only if he is already a director retiring by rotation, or if he is approved by the chairman. The directors are empowered to manage the exchange. Although not required constitutionally, since 1991 representatives of investing institutions and listed companies have been invited on to the board of directors of the LSE, giving them some influence over the control, if not the ownership, of the exchange.

The chairman, one of the deputy-chairmen, or any three directors may call a directors' meeting. Each director has one vote on any issues put to a vote in such a meeting, and in the case of equality, the chairman has a casting vote. In general, the quorum necessary to hold a vote in a directors' meeting is ten people, of

whom not less than five must be non-executive directors. The directors may elect
or remove the chairman and the deputy-chairmen.

An application for membership may be made by a partnership or body corporate.[36] In order to be a member, a firm must conduct business on the exchange,
must be suitable to do so (namely it must be technically competent, have sufficient knowledge and experience, and have adequate systems and controls), and
must be appropriately authorized by a Self-Regulatory Organization (as discussed
in Chapter 7). The exchange's rules outline the types of business that may be
conducted on the exchange. The main categories of firms allowed to become
members are agents, principals, market makers, execution-only brokers, inter-
dealer brokers, clearing firms, and introducing brokers.[37] Although there are no
restrictions on investors being members and having direct access to the
exchange's trading systems, to date no investors have chosen to take up this
option.[38]

Multiple Objectives and Conflict

Any attempt to explain an exchange's behaviour by seeking to isolate a single
parameter which the exchange seeks to maximize is likely to be flawed. As noted
by Jensen and Meckling (1976: 311),

viewing the firm [in the abstract] as the nexus of a set of contracting relationships among
individuals . . . serves to make it clear that the personalization of the firm implied by
asking questions such as 'what should be the objective function of the firm' . . . is seriously
misleading. *The firm is not an individual.* It is a legal fiction which serves as a focus for a
complex process in which the conflicting objectives of individuals . . . are brought into
equilibrium within a framework of contractual relations. In this sense the 'behavior' of the
firm is like the behavior of a market; i.e., the outcome of a complex equilibrium process.
We seldom fall into the trap of characterizing the wheat or stock market as an individual,
but we often make this error by thinking about organizations as if they were persons with
motivations and intentions.[39]

Whether exchanges are seen as firms or as markets, their behaviour is also best
viewed as the 'outcome of a complex equilibrium process'. Furthermore, it is not
only the contractual relationships at an exchange that determine its governance
structure. Both an exchange's constitutional arrangements, and some relationships determined by neither contractual nor constitutional factors, can be critical
in influencing its nature and behaviour. The very multiplicity of these relationships means that conflict is endemic to exchanges. Some of the many ways in
which such multiplicity and conflict can emerge are now described.

Different ownership groups may attempt to promote their own competing
interests. They may, for example, seek to minimize the particular fees that they
are required to pay. Some of an exchange's members may also be its competitors,
and these participants are likely to pursue different goals than those followed by
non-competitors. Many financial intermediaries in the cash markets, for example,
operate their own internal order matching systems in competition with the
exchange of which they are a member. Some of an exchange's members may

themselves have internally conflicting interests, and these conflicts may affect the exchange as well as the firms themselves. The large member firms of an exchange, which pay most of the revenues to the exchange, may wish to wield greater power than the exercise of their voting rights at the exchange would grant them given the relatively small number of votes that they typically own.

Particular types of conflicts may arise at futures exchanges, especially if they operate trading floors. Such exchanges' different types of members typically have divergent goals. The locals want to keep their contract expenses down, and want as much trading and information infrastructure as possible placed on the floor. The floor-brokers are concerned about the fact that their customers often pay a significantly higher fee per contract than that paid by floor members. If the price discrimination factor gets too big, the customers of the floor-brokers will choose to buy their own seats and obtain their own dedicated traders, rather than trading through the brokers. The futures commission merchants want their customers' fees to be as low as possible in order for the exchange to remain competitive with alternative trading arenas. They also obtain little direct benefit from systems which enhance the floor.

It is widely accepted that the board, the management, and some committees at different exchanges, each play a vital role in exchange governance. The nature of their roles and their relative importance are, however, difficult to gauge. Not only is it hard to obtain relevant information, given that board and committee minutes and management memoranda are almost always kept confidential, but also the power of the three institutional structures appears to differ sharply across exchanges. A full analysis of the roles of an exchange's board, management, and committees, is therefore not attempted here. Some brief comments are, nevertheless, provided on the way in which their behaviour both contributes to, and reflects, the complexity of exchange governance.

The fact that an exchange's board is standardly granted the constitutional authority to decide a wide range of issues is often taken as evidence to confirm that the board plays a critical role in the exchange's governance.[40] A rather different perception of the board's role is also, however, possible. The growing complexity and value of the services provided by exchanges has meant that only the most political of issues are now being referred to the governors of large exchanges, and the managements of exchanges are therefore *de facto* gaining more power at the expense of their boards. This may be particularly relevant for nonprofit exchanges. As Middleton (1987: 152) observes, the notion that the boards of nonprofit firms in general, of which nonprofit exchanges are an example, are 'policy-making, goal-evaluating organisational units', is frequently not borne out in practice.

Most of the data indicate that boards do not formulate policy but rather ratify policy that is presented to them by staff. The executive committee in concert with top management may be the only place within the board structure where policy is designed. Certain situations (such as organizational transformations) may increase the likelihood that boards enact policy, but as a rule they do not. Instead, they are used more or less effectively for external linking functions.

The extent to which the committees established at an exchange have either any formal power delegated to them by the exchange's board, or any informal power vested in them, varies considerably. One exchange at which committees have been very powerful is the Chicago Board of Trade (CBT).[41] An analysis of the merits of this exchange's committee structure illustrates the complex manner in which committees can influence exchange governance. In a review of the exchange's organization, three main benefits were identified with its committee system: it provided a mechanism through which the owners of the exchange could influence its activities and business direction, it allowed the knowledge and expertise of the membership to be captured for the benefit of the exchange, and it served as a vehicle for building consensus and communicating with the broader exchange membership.[42]

Five costs of the system were also noted: there was an unbalanced representation of different membership groups on the various committees, with agricultural traders generally over-represented; the committees' decision-making processes were slow, and often *ad hoc*; there was over-involvement by the committees in detailed operations creating diffused responsibility and accountability; participation in committee work was time-consuming for management and members; and finally, priorities for the exchange were generated from the bottom up, and not within a strategic framework. The significance of these costs and benefits in this context is not that they allow an assessment to be made of the merits of the committee system at the CBT, but rather that they show that attempting to characterize the role that committees play in exchange governance is not simple.

The role of management in exchange governance is similarly complex. An indication of the multiplicity of goals which a nonprofit exchange may follow, for example, is mirrored in the capacities that are believed appropriate for its executives. The ideal model for the chief executive officer of a nonprofit organization has been identified not as 'the political wheeler-dealer, the capitalist venturer and marketer, the disciplined technical manager, or the master of interpersonal relations—but [as] a special mix of all these things'.[43] Similarly, the perfect candidate for the position of the chief executive of the London Stock Exchange has been identified as 'a diplomat and intelligent and a businessman'.[44] To the extent that chief executives of exchanges meet these standards, they evidently need to reconcile competing interests. Different characteristics have also been thought appropriate at different times by various exchanges, depending both on the stage of growth of the exchange, and the nature of the issues that it faces. An important quality necessary to found an exchange or to establish a new trading environment, for example, is a dynamism often associated with an autocratic tendency in an individual. Once such projects have been implemented, however, exchange boards have frequently sought to find a new management that is better able to operate through consensus.

Amongst the types of market participants who may be able to affect an exchange's governance via their contractual relationships with the exchange, even though they have no constitutional role in the exchange's governance, are its lenders, partners, and suppliers. The role Reuters played in GLOBEX, as discussed in the next chapter, is an example of this.[45] Reuters was initially seen as merely the provider of the hardware and software for GLOBEX, in contrast to the participating exchanges which were viewed as the creators and sponsors of the markets trading on GLOBEX. The convoluted history of the system's development meant, however, that Reuters became progressively more involved with its governance in addition to being responsible for the efficacy of its operations. The 'end-investors', or the customers of the financial intermediaries on an exchange, may also have a strong influence on exchange governance even if they have no direct constitutional rights at, or contractual agreements with the exchange. Their power lies in the possibility of their diverting order flow away from exchanges the governance of which they believe not to be in their interest.

Even if it is hoped to ascribe a single objective function to a nonprofit exchange, and it is assumed that this should be the maximization of consumer surplus, the manner in which this objective should be interpreted has been conceived in several ways. Saloner (1984) presents a model in which a nonprofit exchange seeks to maximize the profits of its members by granting just that number of memberships which leads to a profit-maximizing bid–ask spread. Black (1986) suggests that exchanges seek to maximize their members' utility by maximizing total trading volume. In addition, at least three other goals have been proposed for the goals that nonprofit firms, including exchanges, seek to achieve. They have been assumed to maximize the quality of goods and services that they offer, the quantity of goods and services that they offer, or their annual budget, all subject to the constraint that revenues equal costs.[46] Quality maximization may be pursued by a nonprofit firm run by professionals who derive strong satisfaction from the provision of good services, independent of the needs or desires of their customers. Quantity maximization might be imputed to managers who are empire builders or who seek to serve as broad a segment of the public as possible. Maximization of a firm's budget may be followed because it enhances the importance of, or justifies a higher salary for, the firm's managers.

One way of gauging what objectives exchanges seek to maximize is to examine how they have been valued when issuing new shares.[47] Unsurprisingly, a diversity of valuation methods have been employed. In addition to an exchange's balance sheet and income statement, other relevant criteria have included seat prices, trading volume, open interest, average daily volume, assets of the exchange such as any proprietary technology or any contracts it has developed that have a use outside the exchange, and the extent to which trading on the exchange is vulnerable to competition by other exchanges or OTC trading.

Conflict between the objectives that an exchange seeks to realize is often both evident in, and caused by, the goals that the exchange publicly states that it seeks to pursue. The objectives that nonprofit firms officially follow are normally not the financial returns they achieve, but those reflected in their 'mission statements'. These objectives are often both ambiguous in nature and difficult to measure. Most nonprofit exchanges, for example, identify the 'efficiency' and 'integrity' of their markets, both of which are extremely nebulous concepts, as being key objectives. As Kanter and Summers (1987: 155) state, nonprofits are often thought to 'have many goals, . . . [which] can be inconsistent, contradictory, or incoherent; [and] it is often unclear even at what level or with respect to what units the attainment of goals should be measured'. Ambiguity in, and conflict between, the objectives pursued by a nonprofit firm can create opportunities for internal politics, for goal displacement, and for a decoupling between the firm's official mission and the goals it actually follows. Nonprofit firms are thus frequently seen as 'temporary alliances of separate groups, each interpreting the organization's purpose a little differently'.

Tension between the official goals of an exchange and those it actually pursues is not limited to nonprofit exchanges. Like many for-profit firms, for-profit exchanges are progressively also defining the goals they pursue in much wider terms than simply the returns that they achieve. For-profit exchanges often have mission statements similar in nature to those pursued by nonprofit exchanges.[48] The assumption that the maximization of profits is the prime, let alone the sole goal of such exchanges is therefore also open to question.

Discussions at the CBT provide an example of the ambiguity typical in the aims of an exchange. In 1993 a committee examining strategic planning at the exchange, prepared a 'vision statement' to describe what it believed the exchange needed to become. This stated that,

the Chicago Board of Trade will be the premier, innovative, aggressive, global venue for the risk transfer and clearing of commodities, securities, financial instruments and other products. Trading opportunity will be maximized by focusing on satisfying customer needs. Ownership returns will be maximized by professionally managing the Chicago Board of Trade as an efficient and profitable business.[49]

'Trading opportunity' was defined to mean 'not just volume of contracts but a breadth and depth of potential possibilities and courses of action'. 'Ownership returns' was defined to mean 'not just "seat value" but a variety of ways in which to derive earnings based upon business performance'. Notwithstanding the intent to provide flexibility to the exchange in its choice of action, the goals that this vision statement promotes are clearly ambiguous.

The internal politics and the personalities at an exchange can also be critical factors in affecting an exchange's governance. As the case studies of the Chicago Mercantile Exchange, the LSE, and Stockbrokers Botswana presented in the next chapter highlight, both the specific identity of important participants at an exchange, and the manner in which arguments are presented at an exchange, may be as, if not more important, in determining why an exchange chooses one amongst a range of options, than the economic costs associated with each choice.

Transaction Cost Comparison: Additional Factors

There are many ways in which the factors complicating exchange governance described above may affect the relative efficiency of the different organizational forms for an exchange. Three are examined here. The first arises because the assumption that the decisions taken by an exchange reflect the preferences of a single market participant is in general not believable. An exchange must thus adopt a more complicated collective choice rule than that of a dictatorship, and this may bring with it various costs. The second occurs because the management of an exchange cannot be assumed simply to follow the desires of its owners or customers, and this, together with the presence of asymmetrical information, may result in a principal–agent problem. Finally, a brief comment is made on the possibility that different governance structures might be cost-efficient for an exchange at different stages of its development.

Collective Choice

Once the assumption that an exchange follows the dictat of a single market participant is dropped, and it is accepted that it is impossible to write a complete contract covering all the decisions that an exchange might need to take, the manner in which decisions are reached at an exchange needs to be specified in order to assess its governance structure. A formal way of characterizing such a decision-making process is to view it as a collective choice rule, namely an algorithm which determines how decisions are taken for the exchange as a whole, given the preference functions of all the owners of the exchange. Many algorithms are possible, such as those of granting each owner one vote on relevant issues, and then specifying either that the option with the highest number of votes wins, or that a majority, a super-majority (66.66% of all votes cast), or unanimity, is required. The collective choice rule adopted can affect the substance of the decisions taken, and can also lead to the imposition of different costs on the various patrons of the exchange.[50]

The costs of collective decision making may be high, particularly if the ownership of an exchange is heterogeneous and one group of patrons seeks to use the collective choice mechanism to maximize its own welfare by exploiting other groups or customers to the extent permitted by competition.[51] When this is possible, there is a strong incentive to form coalitions to capture the available benefits, and much may be spent on the creation of such coalitions. As Hansmann (1988: 279) notes, however, even where patrons' interests diverge considerably, the costs associated with collective decision making will not necessarily be large, especially if there is a simple and pertinent criterion for balancing their interests. Where it is easy to account separately for the net benefits bestowed on an organization by each individual patron, for example, dividing up the net returns according to such a procedure may be uncontroversial.

Different voting structures may be cost-efficient for different types of decisions at an exchange. Zusman (1992) models an environment in which a collective choice rule has to be chosen for a cooperative. Two criteria for selecting a collective choice rule are used: it should minimize bargaining costs between members, and it should maximize the possibility of effecting an outcome in which the spread of utilities obtained by the different members of the cooperative is minimized. A wide spread of utilities amongst members is viewed as undesirable because members do not know in advance of choosing the collective choice rule how successful they are going to be, and therefore wish to ensure that if they are not successful the collective choice rule adopted will not harm their interests too adversely. Bargaining costs are assumed to decrease as the number of agents participating in the decision-making process is lowered. The more centralized the decision-making process, however, the more likely will it be that members have strongly divergent preferences over the outcomes that are chosen. In such circumstances, it may be optimal to give to a single person the power to make decisions that only affect members to a small extent. For more important policy issues, however, it may be better that decisions are decided by a majority (i.e. 50%) of the membership; and for the most important decisions, such as constitutional amendments, it may be appropriate to require a super-majority (i.e. 66.66%) or even unanimity.

Hart and Moore (1994) compare the merits of a cooperative exchange whose members take decisions democratically on a one-member one-vote basis, with an exchange owned by 'outsiders' who simply maximize profits and do not consume the services offered by the exchange. The drawback of the cooperative structure is that collective decision making may be inefficient because the views of the decisive, or median, voter in the exchange, do not represent those of the membership at large, or its average voter. When the distribution of traders becomes more skewed, namely when the 'distance' between the preferences of the median voter and the average voter increases, the attractiveness of the cooperative solution is reduced.[52] On the other hand, in the absence of competition the outside owners will act monopolistically, raising prices and restricting supply, and thus excluding too many traders from the exchange compared to the most efficient competitive outcome. An increase in the skewness of the distribution across membership does not affect the incentives facing outside ownership. The analysis is critically dependent on the median-voter theorem.[53] If traders have objectives which are not easily collapsible into a single dimensional measure, however, the median-voter theorem either breaks down, or only holds under very un-intuitive circumstances.

A further cost may arise in nonprofit or cooperative exchanges, because their owners' shares cannot be traded and because a separation of voting from trading rights may not be allowed. Any single member of such an exchange cannot therefore easily influence the decisions taken by the exchange by buying the votes of other members. It is also normally expensive to buy a large enough number of seats to exert control, and in any event doing so is likely to reduce the liquidity on the exchange, and thus the value of controlling the exchange. The only way to exert pressure, therefore, is via the democratic process which suffers from a 'free-rider' problem. Any single voter will only be able to obtain a small part of the gains realized by his actions, even though he will have to incur all the costs necessary to undertake such activities. Costly actions designed to increase the value of an exchange are therefore less likely to be undertaken in nonprofit or cooperative exchanges than in for-profit exchanges, where claims can be concentrated.

This is not true, however, for all nonprofit or cooperative exchanges. In particular, in some exchanges, such as the Chicago Mercantile Exchange (CME), an owner of a membership is allowed to lease his membership to somebody else.[54] In that case, the owner will retain the voting rights, while the lessee will keep the trading rights. An individual member can thus acquire a number of seats for investment purposes and retain the voting rights associated with those memberships. If votes are allocated on the basis of one per membership owned, rather than one per member, concentration of voting claims will then be possible. The costs of doing so will be dependent on the cost of buying a membership, the opportunity cost of the sunk capital, and the revenues obtainable from leasing out seats.

Principal–Agent Concerns and Asymmetric Information[55]

The owners of a firm typically do not run the firm themselves, but employ a management group to act as their agents in doing so. When the management has preferences that are not identical to those of the firm's owners (the principals), and when it is also able to advance its own interests at the expense of those of the owners, a principal–agent problem is said to arise. A central factor that allows principal–agent problems to occur is the presence of asymmetrical information between management and owners. This may happen when the owners are unable to monitor directly the performance of the management, and thus cannot evaluate whether self-interested actions by their agent are occurring. In assessing the effects of principal–agent problems on the relative efficiency of the nonprofit, cooperative and for-profit structures for an exchange, the important issue is whether such concerns give rise to different costs for the different organizational forms.

There are various ways in which principal–agent problems may be mitigated. One is to establish an incentive scheme for management so as to align its interests as far as possible with those of the owners. In for-profit firms, this typically involves paying the management a salary dependent on the returns earned by the firm. Notwithstanding the difficulties with employing this approach in the for-profit firms, there are two reasons why such a solution may be neither possible nor appropriate for nonprofit exchanges. The first is that by law, management is not allowed to share in the residual earnings of nonprofit firms. The management of nonprofit firms may therefore face a reduced incentive to seek cost efficiency than would be present in similar for-profit firms.[56] There are, however, ways around this constraint at an exchange. The CME, for example, has a bonus plan for staff which is based on volume increases. Although compensation packages are also subject to the discretion of the exchange's membership, they may therefore be closely linked to the residual earnings of the exchange.

The second problem is that, as discussed above, the objective function of a nonprofit exchange may be more ambiguous and multi-faceted than that of a for-profit exchange. It may thus be harder to construct an appropriate incentive scheme for management, even if the law allowed the incentive scheme to be implemented. This may give the management of a nonprofit exchange the opportunity to advance its own interests, again imposing greater transaction costs on such an exchange than would be placed on for-profit exchanges.

Principal–agent problems may also be alleviated via the market for corporate control. If the management of a for-profit firm becomes inefficient, a predator can take over the firm, install a new manager who maximizes value, and thereby possibly realize an arbitrage profit. In contrast, the market for control of both nonprofit and cooperative firms is likely to be limited. The purchasers of such firms cannot reap the benefits of any enhanced efficiency achievable as a result of a takeover via an increase in earnings. This may again, therefore, reduce the incentive for management to act efficiently, given that it is not subject to outside scrutiny. The fact that the rewards of improved efficiency cannot be reaped via enhanced earnings, however, does not mean that there is no market for control of nonprofit or cooperative firms. If the customers of such firms are able to gain the benefits of any efficiencies that could be effected by a takeover, via lower fees for example, they will have an incentive to encourage such takeovers. Indeed, there have been several mergers between nonprofit exchanges for this reason, amongst others. The question of whether the market for corporate control does in fact limit managerial inefficiency is in any event controversial.[57]

Another way in which the organizational structure of an exchange may affect the relative costs imposed by principal–agent problems concerns the information available to the exchange's owners about its performance. On the one hand, the owners of a nonprofit or cooperative exchange will have less external information available to them to evaluate the performance of their management than would the owners of a similar for-profit exchange, given that the shares of nonprofit and cooperative exchanges are not readily tradable. On the other hand, as customers of an exchange's services, the financial intermediaries trading on an exchange may have better information about management performance than would any outside owners, given that they take direct receipt of the services provided by the exchange, and can therefore monitor the services' quality relatively cheaply.[58]

The need for the owners of an exchange to monitor management will be lessened if the exchange faces competition. The opportunity for management inefficiency will be reduced in such circumstances.

Development
Different governance structures may be appropriate for an exchange at different stages of its development. The situation at Stockbrokers Botswana, described in the next chapter, is an instance where the formal governance structure of a trading system allowed for the possibility that market participants might easily be exploited by the owners of the system. In particular, given that there was effectively only a single individual who controlled all aspects of trading, investors might have felt vulnerable both to overpricing and to the possibility that any information they released to this individual might be used against them. The good

reputation of the individual in question, and the relatively high costs of establishing any alternative governance structure, however, probably meant that patrons were willing to forgo any potential benefits that might be obtained under a different governance structure in favour of the *status quo*.

CHANGE

Two important ways in which the governance of an exchange may come under pressure to change are analysed in this section. The first relates to the desirability and consequences of transforming an exchange from a nonprofit into a for-profit organization, and the second concerns the notion of 'ungovernability'.

For-Profit Transformations

Over the past few years, there has been a trend amongst exchanges to consider alternative governance structures to the traditional nonprofit or cooperative models. In addition to the growing number of new for-profit trading systems being developed in the securities markets, many stock exchanges that have historically been operated on a nonprofit or cooperative basis are either contemplating transforming themselves into for-profit companies, or have already done so. This is occurring, for example, in Australia, Denmark, Finland, Greece, Italy, the Netherlands, Sweden (as described in the next chapter), and the UK.[59] This trend in the securities markets has not been matched by a similar trend in the futures markets. It is believed that no other for-profit futures exchanges have been created apart from those operated by the OM Group. Furthermore, many of the major futures exchanges, including the CBT (again as described in the next chapter), CME, the New York Mercantile Exchange (NYMEX), and the London International Financial Futures Exchange (LIFFE), have rejected the option of transforming themselves into for-profit entities.[60]

The main reason for this divergence between cash and futures exchanges is that competition is much more intense in the market for providing trading systems in the cash than in the futures markets. Similar trading system technology is evidently available to both types of exchanges. Unlike in the futures markets, however, where several jurisdictions explicitly grant exchanges a legal monopoly for the trading of particular contracts, the possibility of competition between exchanges in the securities markets has been widely sanctioned.[61]

In addition, and more importantly, centralization of order flow on a single futures exchange yields the advantage that all contracts traded are fungible, as they can be offset against each other through a single clearinghouse. If competition between futures exchanges obtains without appropriate agreement between the relevant clearinghouses, such fungibility is impossible. This increases both the costs and the risks of trading in competing contracts.[62] Apart from a few notable exceptions, once a contract has been listed on a particular futures exchange, trading has tended to centralize on that exchange.[63] As discussed in Chapter 4, however, it is also the case that OTC products may provide competition to exchange-traded contracts.

The greater pressure of competition in the cash markets than in the futures markets has important implications for the balance of the costs and benefits of for-profit governance structures in the different types of markets. The costs of collective decision making in a nonprofit or cooperative stock exchange are likely to be relatively burdensome compared to those that would be incurred in a for-profit stock exchange. Furthermore, the benefits to financial intermediaries of having a nonprofit or cooperative exchange in a stock market are likely to be relatively low given the difficulty of obtaining any monopoly profits. In contrast, in a futures exchange there will be less pressure to reduce the costs that arise as a result of collective decision making given the relative lack of alternative trading venues. In addition, the costs that might arise as a result of having a for-profit exchange may be higher. As noted by Davidson (1994: 6), one key aim of the proponents of transforming a futures exchange into a for-profit company 'is to utilize the exchange's ability to extract monopoly rents from clearing members and distribute these rents to individual members'.

To date, it has typically only been when a particular subset of the members of a futures exchange has a proportionally greater voting power at the exchange than the amount of business they bring to the exchange, that they have sought to transform the profitable status of the exchange. In particular, only in the USA, where locals and floor-brokers have a majority of the votes at several exchanges, have there been strong campaigns to switch to for-profit status.[64] This has not occurred outside the USA, where the fastest-growing exchanges are controlled mostly by the institutional market. If a futures exchange becomes able to exploit customers other than merely its membership while retaining its effective monopoly position, however, the entire membership of the exchange may seek to transform the exchange into a for-profit company. Given the extent to which exchanges are trying to obtain revenues from the users of their price and quote data who are not solely exchange members, this may be more likely in the future than before.

A further source of competition in the securities markets, but not in the futures markets, is that it is now relatively cheap for investors to deal directly with each other, thus doing away with the need for financial intermediation in securities markets. The nature of the consumers of the services provided by stock exchanges is therefore changing: while before they used only to be intermediaries, progressively they now include investors as well. This may lead to a problem for stock exchanges owned by financial intermediaries. As noted in the *Financial Times* (1996),

the survival of any exchange depends increasingly on expensive investment in large scale technology. Yet the investment usually also brings about changes in dealing practice which transfer the benefit of the resulting efficiency gains from the practitioners who financed it to other market users. The practitioners are thus reluctant to update their technology, even in the face of increasing competition.[65]

The benefits to financial intermediaries of operating a nonprofit stock exchange are therefore diminishing. Even if an intermediary-owned nonprofit stock exchange were believed to maximize consumer surplus, the identities of the exchange's consumers are changing. Both the magnitude in number and the diversity of the end-investors on a stock exchange, also mean that any benefits that might accrue to these participants of owning and operating an exchange are likely to be dwarfed by the costs of collective decision making in such circumstances.

As discussed above, it is difficult for the members of a nonprofit or cooperative exchange to diversify the risk they face in holding a seat on the exchange. This is particularly so for the floor-brokers and locals at futures exchanges which operate pit-trading mechanisms. Membership for them is usually a personal investment, and often a substantial part of their individual net worth. Many locals also bought their exchange seats before the large rises in seat prices associated with the huge growth of the futures markets over the past two decades, and would thus be liable to pay significant amounts of capital gains tax should they choose to sell their seats.[66] These locals therefore have a great interest in enhancing the return on their investment without actually selling their seat, and often see the transformation of their exchange from a nonprofit to a for-profit status as a way of doing this.

There are various ways in which the transformation of a nonprofit exchange to a for-profit status may be effected. Members could share in the profits an exchange obtains from its core business, through dividends or distributions. An exchange could create for-profit subsidiaries or affiliated business entities for the provision of certain specific services.[67] Dividend-paying shares may be issued free or sold to members, or indeed to other market participants.

Requiring dividend payments at a membership-exchange is likely to lead to a redistribution of either profits, or of power, at the exchange. The members who pay the most to an exchange are those members who most use the services provided by the exchange. If the transformation of the exchange is such that each member receives the same number of dividend-paying shares, there will be a redistribution of revenue from the large to the small users of the exchange. One way of avoiding this is to allot shares to members according to the amount of revenues that they pay the exchange. If voting rights are kept allied with dividend rights, however, the smaller firms will find their power diluted. One way to resolve this issue is to separate membership from ownership. This may be hard, however, under applicable law. Even if it is not, it may lead to conflict between the members and the owners of the exchange, with regard to how the exchange should be run, and may also make management more independent. The perceived merits of these different options depend on the precise circumstances in which an exchange operates, and the preferences of its various stakeholders.[68]

Allowing the shares of an exchange to be freely transferable may affect the intensity of competition in the market for the services provided by an exchange.

An institution which perceives that an exchange with tradable shares may be a potential competitor may buy up the exchange's shares in order to pre-empt such competition. This may have occurred in Sweden, where OM built up a significant shareholding in the Stockholm Stock Exchange (SSE) and subsequently merged with it.[69] One reason for this was probably to limit the possibility of the SSE competing with OM in the derivatives market, a possibility which the SSE had publicly considered prior to OM's buying the shareholding. The fact that OM held a large block of the SSE's shares before the merger did not necessarily mean, however, that it would either choose or be able to restrict competition. Several major Swedish investing institutions also held large shareholdings in both OM and the SSE, and they may have exerted a restraining influence on any anti-competitive behaviour on the part of either institution which might have damaged their interests.

Ungovernability

The notion that an exchange might be 'ungovernable', if not widely accepted, is at least becoming common currency.[70] The concept of ungovernability at an exchange is, however, difficult to define. At a minimum it would seem to require that the interests represented on an exchange are too diverse for a single forum to be able to reconcile them. But as previously discussed, the presence of conflict-ing goals is endemic to the nature of nonprofit and cooperative exchanges, and therefore cannot be sufficient for an exchange to be called ungovernable. Exchanges have never been able to realize the goals of all the various patrons of their markets. It may nevertheless be argued that in particular circumstances, such as at the LSE in 1996 as discussed in the next chapter, the range of preferences that market participants reveal concerning an exchange's decisions becomes so diverse, and the strength with which they express their views about these deci-sions becomes so powerful, that application of the term 'ungovernability' is reasonable.

   Even then, however, it is questionable whether the idea of ungovernability is a useful notion. The most important reason why market participants have become more vocal than before about revealing their views on an exchange's decisions, is probably that they feel they can affect the exchange's decisions by doing so. The development of relatively cheap technology now allows small groups of market participants, and even single traders, to develop their own dealing systems to satisfy their own trading preferences. If an exchange is no longer able to satisfy the preferences of such market participants, they can divert their order flow away from the exchange more easily than before, and this therefore gives them some leverage in trying to affect the decisions of the exchange. The fact that an exchange cannot satisfy all its constituencies' preferences, that their differences of opinion may be very vocal, and that the exchange may lose business because various interests are not adequately represented on its governance structure, should not, however, be taken as a sign that the exchange is 'ungovernable'. A more useful response is to question whether the governance structure of the exchange is still cost-efficient for some of the exchange's patrons.

CONCLUSION

The key questions explored in this chapter are: What does governance mean in the context of an exchange? Why are particular governance structures adopted by exchanges? How does an exchange's governance affect its behaviour? and finally, Why do governance structures change? The chapter is composed of three sections. In the first, the nature of the three archetypal organizational structures that have been adopted by exchanges are described. These are the nonprofit, the consumer cooperative, and the for-profit forms. An initial analysis is also presented of the relative costs to financial intermediaries of adopting each of these organizational structures for the establishment of an exchange.

In the second section, the diversity and complexity of the governance structures of exchanges is explored. Five assumptions made in the first part are scrutinized. In particular, the intricate detail of exchanges' constitutional structures is recognized, the simplicity of the objective functions pursued by exchanges adopting each of the three organizational forms is questioned, the transaction costs incurred by market participants other than financial intermediaries are investigated, the implications for exchange governance of the behaviour of these other types of patrons are discussed, and, the heterogeneity of the participants trading on an exchange is acknowledged. The manner in which these factors affect the transaction cost comparison, and thus the relative efficiency, of the different organizational archetypes is examined.

In the third section, two ways in which the governance of an exchange may come under pressure to change are analysed. The first relates to the desirability and consequences of transforming an exchange from a nonprofit into a for-profit organization, and the second concerns the notion of 'ungovernability'.

3

Governance: Case Studies

INTRODUCTION

In order to illustrate the considerations that are important in determining exchange governance, five case studies of instances at different exchanges where the nature and development of their governance structures have come under scrutiny are described in this chapter. A summary of the transformation ('companization') of the Stockholm Stock Exchange (SSE) into a for-profit firm is provided first.[1] Next, a members' referendum that proposed to turn the Chicago Board of Trade (CBT) into a for-profit organization, but was defeated, is discussed. In the third part, a referendum that failed to transform the governance structure of the Chicago Mercantile Exchange (CME) is described. In the fourth part, the establishment of Stockbrokers Botswana (SBB) and the Botswana Stock Exchange (BSE) is outlined. Finally, a debate at the beginning of 1996 about the governance of the London Stock Exchange (LSE) is examined.

There are three main reasons for presenting these case studies. First, they illustrate a range of key issues discussed in the previous chapter. These include the differences between nonprofit and for-profit exchanges, the incentives that different types of exchange participants have to seek different governance structures, the endemic nature of conflict at exchanges, the possibility that diverse governance structures might be appropriate at different stages of development at an exchange, and the question of ungovernability at an exchange. It is not intended here to repeat the analysis of these issues provided in the last chapter. The focus is therefore on describing, rather than analysing, the relevant exchange situations.

The second purpose of presenting the case studies is that they highlight a crucial general point concerning the governance of exchanges not explored in the previous chapter, namely that the specificity of an exchange's particular circumstances greatly influences the outcomes that obtain at the exchange. No apology is therefore made for the fact that a richness of detail about each case is provided.

The final reason for including the case studies is simply that it is extremely difficult to obtain descriptions of situations where the governance of exchanges is at issue. Available public information about them is sparse. Of the two important primary sources of relevant information, the minutes of board meetings of exchanges are for the most part unavailable, and conversations with, and reflections of, participants from exchanges and other interested parties suffer from the standard problems of memory distortion and historical revisionism.[2] The veracity of secondary sources, including primarily media commentary, is also frequently open to question. Given these problems, it is not claimed that the accounts presented here are either complete or accurate.[3] They are, however, viewed as the best available descriptions of the relevant exchange situations.

COMPANIZATION OF THE STOCKHOLM STOCK EXCHANGE

On 1 January 1993, the monopoly that had previously been granted to the SSE to operate the sole stock exchange in Sweden was rescinded.[4] At around this period, the exchange also decided to change its corporate status from the legal form under which it had historically operated to one of a limited liability company.[5] The process by which the exchange transformed its status was to issue shares in the exchange to those parties deemed relevant. Half the new shares were offered to the members of the exchange, namely the banks and other securities institutions entitled to transact on the exchange, and half were offered to the companies or other organizations that had issued financial instruments listed on the exchange. The subscription rights were offered to the members of the exchange in proportion to the amount of annual fees they had paid over the preceding five years, and to the issuers in proportion to the entrance and listing fees they had similarly paid. All the shares in the new company were of the same type.[6]

Both the intermediaries and the issuers were offered shares to reward them for creating the exchange, and also in the hope of retaining their loyalty, in case other organizations began competing with the exchange in the provision of trading systems. The decision as to how to allocate the shares between the intermediaries and the issuers, and also why not to offer shares directly to investors, was justified by the President of the exchange, as follows.

The Stock Exchange defined its members, issuers and investors as the central interested parties. It was possible to trace the amount of fees that had been paid to the exchange by members and issuers. The issuers had paid the largest amount of fees to the core Exchange business, but the members emphasised that the Stock Exchange was their place of work. Both groups were willing to take the whole responsibility. The investors did not have a natural association or channel for their views, but might have claimed that they were really the ones who had paid every cent that the members had been credited with. As some issuers are also major investors in the market, it can still be said that institutional investors have been given a *de facto* place on the board of directors.[7]

The SSE chose to become a limited liability company for several interrelated reasons. In the five years before the exchange's transformation, it had been subject to intense competition from the LSE, via the SEAQ International trading system, which had successfully attracted a large percentage of the trading volume in Swedish stocks. The migration of trading occurred not only because it was possible to execute large transactions more easily in London than in Sweden, but also because of the imposition of a tax on trading executed in Sweden.[8] In the face of this and potentially other competition, the new governance structure was believed to be more 'suitable for efficient decision-making and flexible management of operation' than the old.[9]

After the post-war period the Swedish government had progressively increased its influence on the exchange's board of directors at the expense of market participants. Prior to the exchange's companization, its board was composed of twenty-two directors and deputies, fourteen of whom were elected by the government, and four each by the members and issuers respectively. The President of the exchange claimed that the board at that time had become 'both large and fragmented by different interests', and that it 'functioned more as a parliament than as an effective body for decision-making. It [therefore] became increasingly evident that this form of organisation was becoming anachronistic'. Following the transformation, the size of the board was reduced to eight members, comprising the chairman, the chief executive, and six representatives of intermediaries and issuers.

In addition to concerns over the size of the board, the exchange also argued that the reformed governance structure would provide 'the opportunity for active owner participation'.[10] The President of the exchange stated that this possibility was viewed as very important by the exchange's members who 'saw privatisation [of the exchange] as a process that would increase their influence'. He also noted, however, that,

by consistently separating ownership of the Exchange from use of the members and issuer services provided by the Exchange, an increased clarity in the various roles and responsibilities is achieved. Each interested party can only play one role at a time. In other words, the membership interests become a commercial 'customer issue' in the same way that the issuers are viewed as a customer group.

More bluntly, he stated that,

the business strategy was based on the view that the Exchange's different customer groups have different needs. The work has made clear that the long-term interests of the Exchange do not necessarily coincide with the interests of the members or issuers.

Three other factors also contributed to the exchange's decision to become a limited liability for-profit firm. The first was that such an organizational structure was judged to be the most suitable for raising the capital deemed necessary for the long-term development and expansion of the exchange. The second was that the existence and success of OM, the Swedish futures and options exchange that had been created and was operated on a for-profit basis, acted as a role model for the SSE.[11] Finally, the political climate in Sweden at the time was such that the private sector was seen as critical in furthering the national interest, and thus the effective privatization of what was previously a national asset was not only conceivable but also politically attractive.

FOR-PROFIT REFERENDUM AT THE CHICAGO BOARD OF TRADE

On 22 September 1994 the CBT (sometimes also referred to as the CBOT) held a member's referendum on the issue of whether the exchange should be transformed into a for-profit institution. The referendum was held following a proposition submitted by one of the exchange's members, who proposed that it be operated on a for-profit basis, and that a goal of at least 15% rate of return per annum on members' equity be set.[12] The other elements of the proposal were that the number of shares to be allocated to each class of membership (and each membership interest) be fixed at an amount proportional to the last sale price of each membership as of a pre-specified date; that all shares belong to, and be inseparable from, the membership to which they were allocated; and that the issuance of the new shares not alter the voting capacity of each membership.

Three advantages of the plan, in addition to enhancing the rate of return earned by members, were put forward. Firstly, it was suggested that 'any dividend paying plan would be reflected by an increased value in the asset (the seat)'. Secondly, it was argued that although 'there are some opinions in the FCM community that a better way to share profits is to reduce fees', 'Any reduction in fees would be a difficult formula since there is no fee that applies evenly to all classes of members'. Finally, it was maintained that the transformation would 'put into place a much higher level of accountability than presently exists'.

The proposal was unanimously opposed by the Board of the exchange for a range of reasons. It believed that,

a 'for profit' emphasis at the Exchange level would detract from the goal of maximizing members' own profits. It should remain an important CBOT goal to continue offering a low-cost trading environment in which members as individuals and registered firms are able to optimize their own respective profit opportunities.[13]

The Board disputed the claim that the transformation would enhance accountability, stating that,

the CBOT is, and has been, prudently managed on a business basis . . . The CBOT is the lowest-cost exchange in our industry; has the fewest employees of any comparable exchange; has waived dues for every quarter for the last five years; has reduced member transaction fees; has a virtually unparalleled occupancy rate for CBOT buildings; and has enjoyed a minimum overall increase in operating expenditures despite major expenditures undertaken for significant projects.

In order to achieve the proposed rate-of-return goal, the Board noted that,

[the] CBOT would either have to increase revenues, decrease costs, or both. Exchange costs have already been subject to stringent reductions. Further cuts would likely impair the Exchange delivery of vital members' services. Exchange revenues can only be increased by increasing member and/or non-member fees.

The Board also claimed that the proposed transformation would reduce the competitive advantage of the exchange, stating that,

[it] would significantly increase the costs of access to our markets at a time when competitive, unregulated markets offer virtually fungible instruments. The potential for driving business away from our markets cannot be overlooked.

The Board maintained that an emphasis on dividends would 'imperil' important growth projects, the most important of which was the construction of the CBT's expanded trading floor. According to the exchange's chairman, the four local banks that had 'tentatively agreed to bankroll construction would have walked away from their commitments if cash rich exchange coffers were to be earmarked to meet dividend payouts to shareholder members'.[14] The board argued in addition that the proposed transformation would lead to double taxation of exchange profits at both the corporate and member levels, would have 'unprecedented' legal complications, and might lead to increased regulation. There was also concern that the creation of profits at the exchange might tempt the government to establish a futures transaction tax, a proposition which the legislature had recently discussed.[15] The proposal was defeated in the ballot by 731 votes to 162.[16]

TRANSFORMATION REFERENDUM AT THE CHICAGO MERCANTILE EXCHANGE

On 10 October 1994, a proposal by the board of the CME to reform the exchange's governance structure was put to a vote of the membership of the exchange. The proposal involved merging the exchange's two largest divisions, and changing the trading rights associated with the different types of memberships at the exchange.

Prior to the proposed merger the exchange was composed of three divisions, each of which had its own category of member.[17] The divisions were the CME division, the International Monetary Market division (IMM) and the Index and Option Market division (IOM). It is important to stress that the CME division was only part of the exchange, itself also called the CME. The CME division had 625 members, each of whom was entitled to six votes at members' meetings on 'core' issues.[18] CME division members elected twelve of the twenty-four elected members of the full exchange's board of directors, and had the right to trade all contracts listed on the exchange, including the exclusive right to trade most of the agricultural contracts. A CME division membership conferred in addition an important right concerning clearing. In order for a firm to be recognized as a clearing member of the exchange, and thereby enjoy lower transaction fees, it was required to own, or have assigned to it, at least six memberships. At least two of these had to be CME division memberships, two or more could be IMM memberships, and at most two could be IOM memberships.[19] For the period prior to the referendum, the price of CME seats had varied from between $40,000 to $70,000 more than those of IMM seats.

The IMM division was composed of 813 members. Each member had the right to two votes at members' meetings on 'core' issues. IMM members elected eight of the twenty-four elected members to the board, and had the right to trade all

contracts at the exchange other than the agricultural contracts. The most important of these were the financial futures contracts. The IOM division was
composed of 1,287 members. Each member had the right to one vote at members'
meetings on 'core' issues. IMM members elected four of the twenty-four elected
members to the board, and had the right to trade index and option contracts, and
other contracts assigned to their division by the Board.

In the merger proposal, the board recommended that the CME and IMM divisions be combined to form a single division with 1,438 members. All members of
this division would have equal voting, trading, and representation rights. The new
CME/IMM division would be entitled to elect twenty of the elected directors to
the board, and the IOM division four. On core issues, CME/IMM divisional
members' votes would be multiplied by a weighting factor of two, while IOM
votes would be counted on a one for one basis.[20] For a firm to be a clearing
member, it would need at least four CME/IMM seats and two IOM seats.[21]

In order to compensate CME members for giving up their access and voting
rights to IMM members, and also to recognize 'their long time contribution', the
exchange agreed to pay $60,000 to each CME member.[22] In addition, IOM
members were to be offered the opportunity to purchase trading rights on the agricultural pits for a specified period by paying $10,000. CME members would be
entitled to a proportional amount of all such fees paid by IOM members. If all
IOM members exercised the proposed rights, each CME member would receive
an additional $20,592.

Three reasons for the merger were put forward by the board. The first was to
satisfy the traders in the financial markets who wanted a greater say in how the
exchange was run.[23] As the board noted,

in 1976 when the IMM was merged into the CME and the basic divisional structure of the
Exchange was established, the differential trading, voting and representational rights in
favor of the CME division members were entirely consistent with the volume of business
transacted in each division's principal products. However, since 1976, there has been a
major revolution in the futures industry which is reflected in the volume of business transacted at the Chicago Mercantile Exchange. Financial products traded in markets open to
IMM members now account for more than 95% of the Exchange's business.[24]

The second reason in favour of the proposal was to create a more homogenous
membership than that then prevailing at the exchange. In particular, the board
stated that,

the Exchange [i.e. its board] has determined that it is necessary to unify its two principal
divisions in order to insure the solidarity of interest and purpose requisite for adopting and
implementing business and strategic plans to carry the Exchange into the next century. The
Exchange has observed the adverse impact of disunity and the perception of unjustified
political disparity at other exchanges. The Exchange must act now to eliminate the potential for divisiveness and to preserve its leadership role as an innovator.

Finally, the board claimed that the merger was necessary in order to bolster trading in the agricultural contracts. The board claimed that,

the combination of low trading volume in the agricultural sector of the Exchange's business, plus the high cost of CME memberships which afford traders access to those agricultural products, creates a serious impediment to the growth of Exchange business. The high membership price creates a difficult barrier to entry into the agricultural futures sector on which the Exchange was founded. The Exchange does not believe that it can eliminate that barrier so long as the distinctions between CME and IMM memberships remain intact. Absent the elimination of barriers to entry to agricultural futures products, the alarming trend toward loss of volume and member participation that has been experienced over recent years is certain to continue. The Exchange needs to implement a program that will lower the entrance cost and attract new members to trade agricultural products.

Several factors contributed to the perceived merits and disadvantages of the transformation plan. A crucial source of disagreement arose because of the nature of the different types of owners of the CME and the IMM division memberships. Many CME seats were owned by individual traders who operated primarily within the agricultural complex, who had bought their seats before the establishment of the IMM, who were older than many financial futures traders, and who leased out their trading rights for IMM contracts to other market participants. In contrast, the growth of the markets and the rise in seat prices meant that many owners of IMM seats, as well as some newer purchasers of CME seats, were major financial institutions. Some CME seatholders did not accept the argument that because the major financial institutions provided most of the exchange's revenues they should also be able to dominate the voting structure of the exchange. Some CME members thought that $60,000 was not enough compensation for the loss of their voting rights. The general transformation of the exchange to a forum for the major financial institutions was also not liked by some individual traders, who resented the influence of the large business interests on the social nature of the exchange.

There was argument both about the causes of the low levels of trading in the agricultural contracts, and the board's response to the situation. Some members accepted that the high price of CME seats had turned away young traders from the agricultural pits because the heavy volume in financial markets offered a better opportunity to make a profit on seat leases. Others believed that the fact that there was an ageing population trading the agricultural contracts 'contributed to stagnant volume'.[25] Yet others argued that business was slow due to a lack of outside customers. Some agricultural traders were also concerned about sanctioning increased competition to their activities.

The issue of the profitable status of the exchange also affected perceptions of the proposed reforms. In 1993, the exchange chairman had suggested turning the exchange into a for-profit corporation. By 1994, however, he acknowledged that a for-profit move had moved to 'back-burner' status,[26] and at the time of the proposed merger, the board noted that it had considered and rejected the option of converting the CME to a for-profit institution.[27] Notwithstanding this, it was reported that the issue of a for-profit conversion was 'the keystone to the merger talk'.[28] There was little enthusiasm on the part of the major financial institutions for changing the exchange's status to a for-profit corporation that would have provided large dividend payouts to the CME division members who were not the major contributors to the exchange's revenues.[29] To the extent that the transformation plan limited this possibility, the institutions strongly supported it.

Although the reforms were supported by the full board of the exchange, the proposed referendum was closely associated with the exchange's chairman, Jack Sandner. The focal source of opposition to the transformation plan was Leo Melamed, a central figure in the governance of the exchange. Melamed was the founder of the IMM, a former chairman of the exchange, the exchange's chairman emeritus, and viewed by many members as a charismatic leader. Melamed, a one-time mentor to Sandner, had, however, allegedly become 'an intense Sandner rival'.[30]

Melamed (and Tamarkin, 1996: 430) believed the proposed reforms were 'nonsensical', and argued strongly against them. He contended, first, that the superior voting rights of CME members, their 'birthright', should be preserved because it was they who initially underwrote the launch of the IMM division. Second, he saw the plan as unnecessarily threatening to agricultural traders, asking 'Can anyone imagine what would happen to the ag pits if they lose voting control? The financial community will overwhelm them.'[31] He claimed, third, that there was no driving force demanding the proposed changes, and that the proposed plan was therefore creating a rift between members where none had existed before. He noted, as confirmed by the exchange's board itself, that the results of the 6-2-1 voting arrangements had never been different from that which would have occurred had a 1-1-1 voting system been in place.[32] He also argued that IMM members could be given equal representation on the board of the exchange with a board vote, rather than by changing the exchange's constitution, stressing that this method had been used before to increase IMM representation on the board. Melamed maintained, fourth, that rather than depleting the treasury at the exchange to equalize voting rights, the money should be used for the next emergency in the futures markets. Finally, he believed that the plan was unlikely to enhance trading in agricultural products.

The transformation proposal was put to a vote of the combined membership of all three divisions. The motion was classified as a core issue which meant that the votes of the members of the three divisions were weighted accordingly, and that at least a two-thirds majority was required for the motion to pass. Although the percentage of weighted votes in favour of the proposal was 57.6% with 42.4% against, the two-thirds majority was not obtained, and the proposal was thus defeated.[33] Quite apart from the merits of the arguments he put forward, the personal intervention by Melamed was cited by many participants as being a determinative factor in the result.

STOCKBROKERS BOTSWANA AND THE BOTSWANA STOCK EXCHANGE

The Botswana share market started trading on 19 June 1989, in response to a desire by the Botswana Development Corporation (BDC), a development company owned by the government.[34] The BDC was created in order to help found small companies in Botswana. It had no interest in managing these companies, and transferred part of its equity stakes to its wholly owned subsidiary Sechaba Investment Trust. The shares owned by Sechaba Investment Trust were then sold to the public so as to expand public ownership. Stockbrokers Botswana Ltd. (SBB) was created to facilitate secondary market trading. It was incorporated as a public company, but its shares were not quoted on a market. It was initially owned 53% by the BDC, 20% by Barclays Bank of Botswana (a commercial bank), 20% by Edwards and Co. (a Zimbabwean stockbroker), and 7% by Standard Chartered Bank Botswana (a commercial bank). The management of SBB reported to its board, which contained representatives of its shareholders, and three outside directors.

SBB was the only broker in the market, and it undertook most of the functions necessary for the operation of the market. It made prices, recorded turnover, and issued contract notes to buyers and sellers. Prices were quoted daily between 9.00 and 12.00 at the offices of SBB, where informally there was a rule that a small order would always be filled before a big one was executed. SBB acted solely as an agent, and did not take any principal positions for itself. It charged a fixed handling fee for every trade, and per-share commissions that were also fixed at predetermined levels and that declined with the size of the trade (in line with rates from the Zimbabwe Stock Exchange). SBB also advised on listings, takeovers, and mergers, and the chief executive of the company wrote a weekly report and analysis of the market. Barclays Bank of Botswana and Standard Chartered Bank Botswana offered custodian services for overseas investors.

In order to encourage foreign investors to Botswana, an Interim Stock Exchange Committee was set up in October 1990 with representatives from the public and private sector, including the secretary of the Zimbabwe Stock Exchange, the chief executive of SBB, the permanent secretary of the Ministry of Finance, and the Deputy Director of Bank Supervision. The Committee had the power to list and de-list a stock, and was also charged with ensuring that the BSE traded ethically. SBB was also required to submit its accounts to the Committee. In 1994, a Stock Exchange Act was passed which formally established the Botswana Stock Exchange (BSE).[35] The exchange was to be a limited company run by a governing Committee with members appointed by both the government and brokers, and to be subject to surveillance by a Registrar of the exchange, and if necessary, by the Ministry of Finance. The possibility of there being more than one broker in the market was sanctioned. Prior to the Act, all buyers booked their trades with SBB, as did all sellers. After the Act, the method of booking trades was formally changed so that each buyer booked his trade with SBB, who in turn booked it with the BSE, which in turn booked it again with SBB, who in turn booked it with the seller. In reality, however, SBB still executed all trades. It was anticipated that when South African investors were permitted to invest on the BSE following exchange control liberalization, a number of South African-based stockbroking companies might become members of the BSE.

The market remained fairly illiquid for the first years of its operation, during which time local buyers and sellers dominated the market. Volumes tended to start high after a new issue, and then fall as the institutions took stock out of the system. A Mr Bill Picken was the first chief executive of SBB, followed by a Mr Alan Norrie. That the system worked was credited by most market participants to the fact that both men were absolutely trustworthy.

GOVERNANCE OF THE LONDON STOCK EXCHANGE

In 1996 an unusually public and charged debate concerning the governance structure of the London Stock Exchange took place. The debate was initiated by two linked events. The first was that, following the widely publicized sacking on 4 January 1996 of the exchange's then chief executive, Mr Michael Lawrence, the Treasury Select Committee of the House of Commons held some hearings to 'examine the need for reforms to the way the Exchange operates, its internal regulatory and management structure, the prospects for the Exchange and its competitive position'.[36] The second was that on 12 January 1996 the exchange issued a consultation paper on the desirability of establishing some form of public limit order book to complement or replace its existing market making structure.[37] Many market participants submitted responses to the consultation paper, and for the first time the exchange published full contents of most of the responses received, together with a statistical analysis of the responses.[38] Summaries of three issues raised in the debate are presented here. They concern, respectively, the diversity of opinion about the merits of the exchange establishing a public limit order book, the appropriate way of governing the exchange, and the reasons why the chief executive was sacked.

Diversity

Prior to the chief executive's dismissal, a central issue being examined at the exchange was whether, and how, to establish a public limit order book or 'order-driven' system, to complement or replace the exchange's then operating market maker or 'quote-driven' system.[39] The board of the exchange was reported to have rejected on 28 September 1995 proposals put forward by the exchange's executive to transform the trading structure, so as to allow both a quote-driven and an order-driven market to be operated simultaneously on a single screen.[40] The option of employing some form of order-driven system was not, however, rejected at that meeting, and the board met again on 30 November 1995 to discuss this possibility.[41] It was decided then to postpone taking a decision on the establishment of such a system until the exchange had consulted with all its members on a range of alternative proposals.[42]

In its consultation document the exchange outlined three main options for its future market structure: an order book for all stocks with an associated block trading mechanism, an order book for some stocks and a quote book for others, and both a quote and order book for some or all stocks.[43] A range of questions concerning the possible implementation of such systems were also asked.[44] The response rate to the document was high, with 95% and 87% of the membership represented, in terms of the value and volume they traded respectively, and 38 institutional investors representing 38% of the UK equities under management also replying. In the statistical analysis of the replies, respondents were classified into seven groups: large and small market makers, large and small brokers, large institutional investors, other investors, and a miscellaneous group of others. The responses were notable both for their diversity, and for the strength with which they were expressed. The diversity was evident not only between different types of institutions, but also amongst institutions classified in the same group, and even between different divisions of the same firm. The range of responses on three issues is indicative of this.

The question of whether an order-driven system was desirable or not, was not asked directly by the exchange. Nevertheless, just over 20% of the respondents felt that the Exchange had either failed to prove adequately the case for operating a public limit order book or had allowed too little time for a decision to be reached. Several of the major market makers were outspoken in their rejection of the desirability of a new system,[45] and some institutional fund managers and private clients also denied the need for change.[46] One stated, for example, that 'the thought of added costs to an already over-burdened cost centre sends shivers of fear down the spine of the private client stockbroker if order driven trading and its associated technology is made mandatory'.[47] In contrast, some of the foreign intermediaries indicated a strong preference for a new system,[48] many investors, both large and small, advocated change, and some market makers were also open to the possibility that change might be desirable.[49] Some firms were internally conflicted on the issue. While Schroder Securities, for example, recommended that a public limit order book should be made available for all UK stocks,[50] Schroder Investment Management, the fund management division of the same firm, stated that they felt 'the case for change ha[d] yet to be made'.[51]

Of those respondents who responded to the question of whether different trading mechanisms should be used for different stocks, 49% by number said they should, and 51% said they should not.

When asked whether they believed that order matching in the most liquid stocks would reduce liquidity, 60% of the respondents said they did not, while 40% said they did. The split in the exchange's membership on this issue was however quite different: 47% of the membership, weighted by the value of shares they traded, did not believe that order matching in the most liquid stocks would reduce liquidity, while 53% did. The different categories of membership also appeared to be almost evenly split on the issue: of the 47% who believed liquidity would not be reduced, 42% were market makers and 5% brokers; while of the 53% who believed liquidity would be reduced, 47% were market makers and 6% were brokers.

Optimal Control Structure

In the hearings before the Treasury Select Committee, three distinctive sets of opinions were set out concerning the optimal way in which the exchange should be governed and the appropriate role of the board of the exchange. The first perspective, advanced by two of the largest market makers, was that,

the Exchange should take a stance which properly represents the views of its members. If this does not happen, given the extremely competitive environment member firms are in, they may well be tempted to examine the benefits of transacting business away from the Exchange.[52]

The threat to set up an alternative market-making organization to the LSE had indeed already been considered by several market makers.[53] The two market makers believed in addition that their views, as major users of the exchange, should have more weight than other market participants. They noted that,

the commitment level of Members differs widely, thus one Member one vote does not in this case reflect the reality of the market structure. This point is equally valid if the Exchange deems its Members to be its customers and thereby wishes to operate a customer/supplier relationship. The Exchange's 'best customers' must expect the service to be tailored to their needs.[54]

The view put forward by Mr Lawrence for the best way of governing the exchange differed from the market makers' approach in two key ways. He believed that account needed to be taken not only of the views of the market makers, but also of other types of market participants. He accepted that,

if the Exchange is to remain the dominant market, it requires securities houses and the broking community to co-operate willingly and to invest their money in building systems that interface with those of the Exchange. Such organisations will quite properly be reluctant to make such a commitment . . . unless they can exercise significant control over the Exchange. In that sense the existing ownership structure of the Exchange, supported by its practitioner committees, is wholly appropriate.[55]

At the same time he argued that,

the Exchange's influence over aspects of the market, which can have important consequences for investors and companies, is substantial. The present structure is therefore only likely to be tolerated in the longer term if the Exchange demonstrates that it is capable of taking other interests fully, and sensitively into account. During my tenure at the Exchange, I found that other market participants or outside agencies were not convinced that this is the case.[56]

Lawrence also believed that the executive of the Exchange should have more power than that envisaged by the market makers. When he arrived at the exchange he did in fact obtain board approval for two changes in governance to effect this. These were:

The creation of an Executive Committee, of the senior management of the Exchange under my [*sic*] Chair, with full delegated responsibility for the management of the Exchange's day-to-day affairs, and responsible for developing policy for Board approval.

The chair of policy-making practitioner committees, but not appeal committees, to be taken by members of the Executive to increase accountability.[57]

A key instance of the problem of practitioner control identified by Lawrence concerned the possibility of the exchange competing with its own members. He claimed that on his appointment as chief executive,

[he] inherited an unwritten policy that the Exchange should not compete with its members, and in defining this policy the interpretation seemed to be any single member irrespective of the collective good. Such a proposition renders the Exchange's position untenable in the long term as it reduces the Exchange's role to only supplying services that no member is prepared to undertake in the field of securities trading, and is likely to deny the Exchange the ability to plan long-term developments for the general improvement of its market.[58]

Lawrence identified two examples of such competition.[59] The first was the possibility of the exchange providing an integrated electronic order routing and trading system, which could compete with BZW's Trade system and Kleinwort's Best system for the retail market. Lawrence argued that if the exchange did not do this, other firms would provide similar systems and the market would fragment. The second was the possibility of the Exchange offering an order-driven system to act as an IDB for market makers. He noted that the potential savings of such a system could be the £25 million that was then earned by the four IDBs in the market, but that as members of the exchange they resisted any move by the exchange to provide such a facility.[60]

A third view of the appropriate way of governing the exchange and of the role of the board of the exchange, was presented by one of its two Deputy Chairmen, Mr Plenderleith. The role of Plenderleith was important, not only because he was an Executive Director at the Bank of England, but also because he, together with the other Deputy Chairman, had been asked by the Chairman to examine whether the governance structure of the exchange needed reforming. Two elements of his view are noteworthy. The first concerned the nature of his role. When asked whether he was at the exchange 'to ensure that the wider national interest of having an efficient Stock Exchange is not actually lost in the in-fighting between members and the Exchange?', he replied, 'that is the role of the board, and I am a member of the board'.[61]

The second important element of his view of governance concerned the relationship between executive and membership control. When asked whether there was 'something irreconcilable' in the conflict that 'on the one hand the Stock Exchange should be a professionally run business and on the other hand you have got this large number of committees, lots of different people, lots of different views, all of which have to be placated?' he responded, 'not at all'.[62]

Plenderleith expanded on this by noting the 'important balance' that needed to be met when deciding how exchange committees should be chaired.[63] He believed on the one hand that 'the executive must be able to run the exchange in a business-like way, they must be able to get input to the policies they want to develop and propose to the Board based on practitioners' input'. On the other hand, he commented that 'you also need the committees to be able to communicate to the Board that has got to decide on the policy proposal when it comes up, the Board needs to know are the people whose businesses are going to be affected by this happy with this proposal'. He thereby implied that intermediation by the executive might hinder direct communication between practitioner committees and the Board. He concluded, however, that 'the formal arrangements are not as important as long as you have got some dynamic working that ensures both [i.e. the executive and the Board] are properly informed'.

Reasons for Dismissal of Chief Executive

Immediately after the dismissal of Lawrence, the Chairman of the Stock Exchange, Mr Kemp-Welch, stated that,

The Board, having lost confidence in its chief executive, has required his resignation with immediate effect. While Mr Lawrence's departure reflects the loss of confidence in him, it does not imply any change in the Stock Exchange's policy. This erosion of confidence took place gradually. A combination of incidents made his situation untenable.[64]

That it was the board's lack of confidence in Lawrence personally that was the reason for his dismissal, was repeated at the parliamentary hearings both by Kemp-Welch, and by Mr Brydon, a fellow board member who was also Deputy Chief Executive of BZW.[65]

The issue of Lawrence's personality had been widely discussed in the press, prior to his dismissal. In particular, he had been reported as having antagonized a broad range of interests at the exchange.[66] His determination to press ahead with an order-driven system had angered the major market-making firms. He had further upset the exchange's member firms by suggesting that the exchange should in some circumstances compete directly with them. He had annoyed company directors by insisting on tightening up the terms of the Greenbury report on corporate governance. He had been criticized for leaking a letter to HM Treasury, which effectively accused the government of insider dealing during the sale of its stakes in National Power and Powergen at the time. He had threatened to sue an exchange member over its plans to provide an Internet share dealing system, without prior approval from the Board, and then climbed down. He had irritated private client broking firms by apparently backing the interests of big institutions against those of the private investor.[67] In addition, he apparently had a bad relationship with the Bank of England, which was developing Crest, the alternative to the exchange's failed settlement system, Taurus. Comments on Lawrence's character in the press had also been vitriolic.[68]

Notwithstanding these reported antagonisms, Lawrence argued that there was an inconsistency in the Chairman's statement that he had been sacked due to a lack of confidence in him by the board.[69] He maintained that the key policy proposal he had been advancing, namely that of consulting the market before seeking to reform the market structure of the exchange, had been both communicated to, and approved by the board, most recently at the board meeting on 30 November 1995. Against this Brydon noted that 'the issue of Mr Lawrence's departure is not to do with order-driven against quote, that is Mr Lawrence's interpretation, it certainly is not mine and never has been'.[70]

The central reason put forward by Lawrence for why he had been dismissed was that he was ousted in a 'classic coup' by one or two powerful market makers.[71] He argued that,

the real issue was the fact that we [i.e. the management] were increasingly managing the Exchange in a professional and commercial way and moving away from the old system of a high level of practitioner control. One market maker actually remarked to me in December, 'The whole world thinks that we control the Exchange except us.' I believe that the major market makers were very surprised by the Board's decision on 30 November. I think they decided following that meeting that it was time for them to re-exert their own control over the Exchange. I believe that they saw me (and I would probably tend to agree with this) as a potential impediment to going back to the old method of control.[72]

Again in contrast, Brydon stated that 'the suggestion that there was a market makers' coup is absolutely wrong'.[73] He maintained that, 'were any one or two or three members of the Board able to mount a coup on the Board I think the entire Board should be extremely uncomfortable with that and be considering their position on it. It simply could not be.'[74]

CONCLUSION

In order to illustrate the considerations that are important in determining exchange governance, five case studies of instances at different exchanges where the nature and development of their governance structures have come under scrutiny are described in this chapter. The case studies describe, respectively: the companization of the Stockholm Stock Exchange into a for-profit firm; a members' referendum that proposed to turn the Chicago Board of Trade into a for-profit organization, but was defeated; a referendum that failed to transform the governance structure of the Chicago Mercantile Exchange; the establishment of Stockbrokers Botswana and the Botswana Stock Exchange; and finally, a debate in 1996 about the governance of the London Stock Exchange.

4

Competition and Cooperation

INTRODUCTION

If there is one single factor that is universally accepted as being the most important determinant of both exchange behaviour and market structure, it is competition. The ubiquity of the term has not meant, however, that its nature is clear. On
the contrary, its meaning remains extremely ambiguous. The aim of this chapter
is to scrutinize several key aspects of the concept in the context of exchanges. The
following broad questions are addressed: What does it mean to say that an
exchange faces competition? What are the factors that give rise to such competition? How do exchanges react to competition? and in particular, When, why, and
how, do they attempt to cooperate with, rather than compete against, each other?
As will become evident, a Manichean view of exchanges either competing or
alternatively cooperating, is too simplistic to represent usefully how exchanges
actually relate to each other.

The chapter is composed of two sections. The nature of competition in the
context of exchanges and markets is examined first. In the second section, some
general comments on the nature of exchange cooperation are made. A range of
case studies illustrating various aspects of cooperation between exchanges is
presented in the next chapter.

THE NATURE OF COMPETITION

The notion of competition may be decomposed into a range of distinct but
closely related concepts, following Bork (1978: 44–53), Bronfman, Lehn, and
Schwartz (1994: 53–5) and Abolafia (1996: 201, footnote 7). It may imply, first,
that there is a rivalry between the participants in a particular economic arena in
their pursuit of the same goal. Second, it may imply that the market is fragmented in some manner, often because there is no single or dominant participant in the economic arena. Third, it may imply that the participants in the
market are each individually too small to affect the prices established in the
market, and also that they do not act together in order to achieve such an effect.
Fourth, it may imply a lack of restrictions on market participants, and a corresponding freedom for these agents to choose their own actions. Fifth, it may
imply that different legal and regulatory constraints are not placed on different
participants who undertake the same activities. This is sometimes referred to

as a 'level playing field', or a lack of discrimination. Finally, it might refer to an outcome in which the economic benefits available from the activity undertaken in a market, sometimes referred to as social welfare, are maximized.

Attention is focused here on the two most complicated facets of competition, namely rivalry and fragmentation. An analysis of the applicability of these concepts to the behaviour of exchanges is presented, and some ways in which exchanges respond to these forms of competition are discussed. The presence and the absence of the other elements of competition are examined in subsequent chapters. The section is composed of four parts. In the first, the types of rivalry that may exist between exchanges are analysed. In the second, the manner in which a market may be fragmented is described. Various factors that give rise to these types of competition between exchanges are identified in the third part. The extent to which the relationship between exchanges and financial intermediaries may be thought of as one of rivalry is studied in the last part.

Rivalry

The standard interpretation of the notion of rivalry is that it is a contest between different agents for the pursuit of the same goal. It is tautologous to note that the primary goal of all exchanges and trading systems is to attract order-flow. The nature of the rivalry that exists between competing systems to attract orders is, however, often not simple. Market participants have a range of criteria by which they assess the quality of a market and accordingly where to route their orders.

The core objective that all types of traders seek from a trading system is to minimize their costs of trading. If it cost nothing to find an appropriate counterparty and to exchange assets, there would in many circumstances be no need to establish institutions like exchanges in order to achieve these goals. The direct costs of trading typically include exchange fees and brokerage commissions. There are also various indirect costs that traders seek to minimize, the presence of which in a market is normally characterized by the concept of 'illiquidity'. This concept, and analogously that of its converse, namely 'liquidity', is extremely elusive.[1]

One conception of a perfectly liquid market is that of a forum where it is possible to buy and sell an infinite amount of the asset being traded, at the same time, without any delay, and at the same price. As is self-evident, this definition is composed of several distinct components. The difference between the bid and the ask price for small-sized orders, or the 'width' of the spread, is one measure of liquidity. Another is the 'depth' of the market, a gauge of the manner in which the spread widens or narrows as the size of a transaction becomes larger. A further element of liquidity is the market's 'immediacy', namely whether there will immediately be a price at which it is possible to execute trades. Another aspect of a market related to liquidity is the speed at which orders can be executed, or analogously the expected time market participants need to wait before an order on the other side of the market appears. Yet a further element of the liquidity of a market relates to the dynamic properties of transaction prices, and in particular the extent to which transaction prices diverge from and revert to equilibrium prices, or the so-called 'resiliency' of a market.

There are many other attributes of trading systems that may be attractive to diverse groups of investors. Some traders wish to remain anonymous, others wish to reveal their identities. Some traders wish to trade on continuous markets, others are happy to deal on batch or periodic markets. To the extent that the structure of a trading system may affect the price volatility of the items traded on the system, some traders wish to use systems that stabilize prices, while others prefer volatility. Different exchanges and trading systems choose the structure of their markets to cater for different sets of market participants. Those exchanges that attempt to deliver the same constellation of criteria by which market participants assess where to route their orders, are most likely to consider each other rivals.

Establishing the extent to which rival trading systems are successful in their goal of attracting order flow is not always easy. Statistical measures of the amount of trading executed on an exchange both vary and are also sometimes obscure in nature. Steil (1996: 52–3) notes a divergence among European exchanges between the 'regulated environment' view and the 'trading system' view of measuring trading volume.[2] Under the first approach, the amount of trading quoted on an exchange is that which is reported to an exchange for regulatory reasons; under the second, the amount of trading quoted is that which passes through an exchange's dealing system. There are other ways in which the definition of trading volume may vary: it may include the number of trades on a market over a specified period, the total number of shares traded, or the total value of the shares traded.

The attraction of orders is not only a central objective of all trading systems *per se*, it also affects, both directly and indirectly, the attainment of a second key goal of theirs, namely the need to obtain revenues. The direct effect is due to the fact that an exchange's receipts for transaction services are dependent on the trades it executes which in turn depend on the order flow it attracts. The indirect effects arise because the volume of trading reported on an exchange, again critically dependent on the amount of orders attracted to the exchange, is regularly used both as a marketing tool to attract new listings to the exchange, and sometimes as a determinant for how much the exchange receives from the sale of its price and quote data. Although the flow of revenues to an exchange is strongly dependent on trading volume, however, the two goals are not the same.

Historically, stock exchanges' main sources of income have been fees for transaction-related services, listing, clearing, and settlement services, charges for the provision of company news and other market-related information, most importantly prices and quotes, and membership subscriptions. Derivatives exchanges have also had similar revenue flows, though they do not obtain fees for the provision of company news or listing, and sometimes have to pay for the right to list particular contracts. The advent of cheap automation and the application of pro-competitive regulatory policies have meant that all these sources of income have come under threat. The situation at the LSE in 1997 provides a typical example.

In the 1990s the LSE faced several different types of competition for the provision of transaction services. One direct competitor for trading in stocks listed on the LSE, Tradepoint, was established in 1995. It operated an automated auction market, in contrast with the quote-driven system historically run by the LSE.[3] Following the establishment of the LSE's own auction trading system in 1997, dealing through Tradepoint appeared, however, to diminish.[4] Trading in LSE-listed stocks executed on the LSE may also have been reduced by the growth in the trading of American Depository Receipts outside the UK. Competition to provide trading facilities for stocks listed on exchanges outside the UK but traded on the LSE was also intense. While the LSE was successful in attracting a substantial amount of trading in European stocks following the 'Big Bang' in 1986, much of this trading was subsequently repatriated back to the stocks' domestic markets. Although the revenue the exchange received from trading in foreign stocks was lower than for domestic stocks, the decline in this trading nevertheless still reduced the income received by the exchange.

Revenue from the listing function offered by the LSE was at risk in various ways. Issuing companies could choose to list their shares on another exchange. A company might do this for many reasons, including to reduce its direct listing costs, to obtain a wider international exposure, or if it believed that an alternative market could deliver greater liquidity for its shares, with the consequence that its cost of capital would be cheaper.[5] At that time, however, few British companies had de-listed their shares from the LSE and moved to another exchange. The creation of EASDAQ (the European Association of Securities Dealers Automated Quotation system), although not intended to be a direct competitor of the LSE's market for new companies, the AIM (the Alternative Investment Market), may, however, have offered a plausible alternative to the exchange as a listing agent for companies that were listing for the first time.[6] Other exchanges, notably the New York Stock Exchange (NYSE), also sought to attract listings in non-domestic (i.e. non-British and non-American) stocks. In addition, the possibility was raised that the statutory role of the LSE as a Competent Authority for listing could also be transferred to another body.[7] Without such an official sanction, it would have been difficult for the LSE to obtain any revenue from listing UK shares.

Unlike the situation at many other stock exchanges, the settlement of shares listed on the LSE was provided by a company that was not fully owned by the LSE. Following the demise of the proposed TAURUS system in 1993,[8] the Bank of England established a new company to manage the settlement of UK shares that was only partly owned by the LSE.[9] The replacement of the old TALISMAN settlement system by its successor, CREST, thus led to a further diminution of the revenues received by the exchange from settlement. The costs associated with the provision of TALISMAN were, however, also reduced.

The receipts from the dissemination both of company news, and of price and quote information, had been under pressure at the LSE as well. In 1990, the

Director General of the Office of Fair Trading concluded that the exchange's practices in the market for real-time company news were anti-competitive, given that it was the sole source of news for domestic companies.[10] The government subsequently ruled that the then-existing arrangements at the LSE constituted an abuse of competition law, and ordered that listed companies should be free to pass announcements to commercial news vendors at the same time as they did so to the exchange.[11] Following this, the exchange stopped selling company news.

In 1993 the LSE also stopped selling dedicated terminals on which market participants could see its price and quote information.[12] It did, however, still sell its data to end-users via the data-vending community. The sole source of revenue for the LSE from information sales was thus as a wholesaler of prices and quotes. The exchange's ability to raise significant revenue from this activity was, however, likely again to have been circumscribed as a result of anti-monopoly considerations. When considering what would be a fair price for the dissemination of information, for example, the Director General of the OFT had stated his general view that,

any organisation with monopoly control over information which stems from the collective actions of market participants has a responsibility to exercise that control fairly and without discrimination and should ensure that such information is available as widely and cheaply as possible.[13]

The final source of income to the LSE was its membership fees. Given that its competitors, such as Tradepoint, did not impose such charges, however, the exchange faced pressure to keep these charges low, or abandon them altogether.

Fragmentation

There is much confusion both about what the term 'fragmentation' means, and about the four concepts that are usually taken to refer to its opposite, namely 'concentration', 'consolidation', 'centralization', and 'integration'.[14] At the most general level, a market is normally described as fragmented if it is split or divided in some manner, frequently because there is no single or dominant participant operating in the market. There are, however, five reasons why ambiguity about the definition of fragmentation obtains in the context of exchanges and markets.

A central source of confusion is that the term may be applied either to the market for exchanges and trading systems, or to the market for securities. Though associated, the two are not identical. A second reason why ambiguity may occur is that it is unclear whether in order for a market to be designated 'non-fragmented' or consolidated, it is necessary that the market be appropriately unified, or whether it is sufficient that the disparate aspects of the market merely be closely linked together. A third complication may arise because when fragmentation is used to refer to the structure of a market, it may refer to the extent to which each of the three key elements of the market—the information dissemination, order routing, and order execution mechanisms—are provided in a unified manner or are split.

A fourth factor complicating the notion of fragmentation may occur if there are any substitutes for the items traded in a market, such as associated options or futures contracts. Their presence may mean that traders view the trading systems on which the substitutes are traded, as viable alternatives to the trading systems on which the underlying items are traded. The derivative markets may then be thought of as fragmenting the market for the underlying items. A further confusion may arise because fragmentation is sometimes used not only to describe a market that is split or divided in some manner, but also to imply that the performance of a market is impaired as a result of such a split or division. This use is viewed as inappropriate here, as the term is taken to be applicable solely to market structure and not to market performance. Indeed, many forms of fragmentation may be beneficial for market performance.

Although there is no single dimension by which to evaluate the extent to which both the organization of exchange activity and the structure of a market are fragmented, a partial ranking is nevertheless possible. At one end of the spectrum it is possible to envisage a market in which there is a single exchange with a single order execution mechanism on which all securities are traded, with a single order routing facility via which all orders are routed to the order execution mechanism, and with a single data dissemination mechanism. Such a trading system clearly faces no competition, and may be described as a completely consolidated market. Allowing for the possibility of more than one exchange, it is still possible for all the order flow in a particular security to be consolidated, namely for all the trading in the security to be executed on a single trading system. Once a security is listed on a specified trading system, it will then not be traded on other systems, but there will be competition between systems to determine which securities are traded on which systems. The market for each security will thus remain consolidated, while the market for exchanges is fragmented. It is also possible to conceive of an environment in which the market for exchanges is consolidated, in that there is only one exchange, but in which the market for each security is fragmented, in that order-flow is not concentrated on a single trading forum, perhaps because the exchange operates several trading systems.

Once the three different elements of the structure of a securities market are considered, many more types of fragmentation are conceivable. Most cannot be ranked against each other in terms of their level of fragmentation. Consider the market for a single security. There may be more than one order execution mechanism on which it may be traded, but all the competing systems may be linked together via both some form of order routing mechanism, and a single data dissemination mechanism. Even if there is no order routing mechanism, the presence of arbitrageurs dealing on the telephone, may be viewed as an informal order routing system that effectively links the execution systems together. There may be a single order execution mechanism, a single data dissemination mechanism, but many order routing systems. There may be many order execution mechanisms, with many order routing systems, but data from all the competing systems may be consolidated together in some manner. The most fragmented market is one in which there are many trading systems, and no formal linkages between any of the three elements of their market architectures.

Influential Factors

Six factors that influence the extent to which agents will choose to compete with an exchange for the provision of alternative trading systems are briefly noted here. They are the potential of profits, a diversity of trading objectives, legal impediments, economies of scale, network externalities, and enhancements in order routing facilities. Given the previous discussion, the first two factors may be simply stated. The possibility of obtaining sufficient profits will provide an inducement for private firms to compete with an exchange in the provision of some of its functions. A diversity of preferences amongst investors for different trading objectives will give an incentive for market participants to develop different trading systems to satisfy these diverse preferences.

The intensity of competition between trading systems may also be influenced by the presence of legal impediments. At the extreme, the law may require that all trading be undertaken on a particular exchange, as used to be the case with the Paris Stock Exchange. Less stringently, it may stipulate that all trading take place on a particular type of institution. Trading in futures contracts in the USA, for example, is forbidden unless executed on an institution recognized as a 'board of trade', and designated by the relevant governmental regulator, the Commodity Futures Trading Commission (CFTC), as a 'contract market'.[15]

Economies of scale arise in the management of a trading system if the cost per trade of operating the system declines as the number of trades executed on the system increases. The presence of economies of scale will reduce the incentive for market participants to compete with an exchange. It used to be the case that the establishment of an exchange required relatively high fixed costs, such as the building of a trading floor, but relatively low variable costs. Exchanges with high trading volumes were therefore able to charge lower fees per transaction than were exchanges with low volumes. Advances in technology, however, have lowered the costs of building trading systems. This is reducing the cost advantage available to large exchanges as a result of economies of scale, and making it easier for new entrants to enter the market for trading systems. Falls in the cost of establishing new systems do not necessarily mean, however, that existing exchanges with high historical costs are at a competitive disadvantage. New technology has not reduced all the ongoing costs of exchanges, and the marginal cost of executing a trade on one of the old floor or pit exchanges may still be equal to, or lower than, that of dealing on a new automated system.

Existing exchanges are also likely to benefit from a positive 'network externality'.[16] This is an advantage an already-operating network has over potential competitors, and also a benefit that accrues to the users of such a network, which is dependent on the fact that other participants are already using the same network. In the context of an exchange such an externality may arise in the provision of its order execution facility. In particular, the likelihood of a trader receiving an execution of his order on an exchange is higher if other traders already send their orders to the exchange. Order-flow attracts order-flow, and a trading system with a large number of orders therefore has an advantage over other trading systems to which only a relatively small number of orders are submitted. This spatial network externality is matched by a similar temporal network externality: there is an inducement for traders to send their orders to a trading system all at the same time, and thereby again increase the likelihood that these orders will each be executed.

A trading system that already attracts a large amount of orders will have an advantage over any new competing systems.[17] Even if all investors appreciated that a particular new system would be unequivocally better than the already-existing one, *if* it could attract all the orders currently flowing to the incumbent system, the new system still might not succeed in attracting much order-flow. While it would be better for the market as a whole to move to the new system, it still might be individually rational for each market participant to submit his orders to the old system until everybody else submitted their orders to the new system. This is precisely because it is to the already-existing system that order-flow is currently directed. Such a network externality will not necessarily be affected by technological advances. The fact that a new system is more automated or operates more cheaply than an existing one will not reduce the network externality available to the first one.[18]

A further network externality is normally relevant for futures exchanges. An advantage of using a single clearinghouse to settle futures transactions is the associated reduction in counter-party risk. It may be difficult to create fungibility between functionally similar derivative instruments that are traded on different futures exchanges, unless there are mutual off-set arrangements between the competing exchanges' clearing-houses. This does not, however, mean that competition between futures exchanges is impossible if there is no fungibility between contracts. The instances of competition between LIFFE and the DTB for the trading of the bund contract, and similarly between SIMEX and the Osaka Securities Exchange for Japanese equity index contracts, provide counter-examples. Off-exchange products, such as OTC derivatives, can also be substitutes for on-exchange contracts, and the fora on which these products are traded can thus provide alternative trading venues to traditional exchanges.

Not all elements of market architecture benefit from network externalities. For example, the presence of one order on an order routing system does not make it more attractive to send other orders on the same order routing system. If 'peak-loading' is a problem, so that the rapidity of the order routing system slows down as the number of orders routed on the system increases, it will be advantageous to use another order routing system, if one is available, with a smaller number of orders being routed on it.

Enhancements in order routing facilities also affect market participants' willingness to establish trading systems that compete with an exchange. As the direct switching costs to investors of diverting their order-flow away from an incumbent market to a newly developed one become lower, with advances in information technology, so investors become more disposed to consider using alternative trading systems. Improvements in the ease of submitting contingent orders to many markets may have the same effect. In particular, as it becomes easier to submit the same order to several markets, on the condition that if one of the orders submitted is executed, all the orders on the other markets are cancelled, so the likelihood of using different markets increases.

The Exchange–Intermediary Relationship

A complex rivalry may exist between exchanges and intermediaries. Interpretations of the creation of exchanges, prior to the evolution of cheap information technology, tend to portray their development as the formalization of informal associations of brokers.[19] The primary aim of an exchange has thus traditionally been seen as the furtherance of the interests of its broker members. The possibility of rivalry between an exchange and the financial intermediaries who both trade on the exchange and are members of the exchange, is therefore at first sight implausible. Such a rudimentary notion of an exchange does not, however, capture the conflicts that inevitably obtain between an exchange and its members.

The members of an exchange always have divided loyalties. On the one hand, they benefit from the existence of the exchange by having a forum on which they are likely to be able to find a counter-party for any orders which they want executed. On the other hand, the more successful a member is in obtaining orders, the more likely it will be able to internalize the execution of these orders, and the more that the duties of being a member of the exchange become onerous. The two obligations that are typically most burdensome to the members of an exchange are the transaction fees that the exchange charges, and the order execution rules of the exchange that may hinder the possibility of a member internalizing order flow.

If a member of an exchange does internalize order flow, for example via the operation of an automated trading system, there are several reasons why the member and the exchange are still not likely to see each other purely as opponents, each of whom can gain only at the expense of the other. It is true that all orders internally executed by members will not be submitted to the exchange's order execution mechanism, and that the quality of the market provided by the exchange's trading system will consequently probably not be as good as it could have been had the orders been so submitted. Members sometimes argue, however, that a requirement to submit all orders to their exchange's trading system, would mean that the orders they internalize would not then be routed to them at all. In addition, members often pay exchange fees for all orders they execute, whether they are internalized or not. They also normally report all internally executed trades to their exchange for surveillance and information dissemination purposes.

An exchange may thus obtain the additional benefit of increasing the amount of trading reported on its trading system by not discouraging the internal execution of orders by its members.

Other factors may complicate the nature of the rivalry that exists between an exchange and its financial intermediary members. The fact that the chief executives of the member firms of an exchange typically sit on the governing board of the exchange, limits the actions that the exchange may take. Attempts by an exchange either to restrict off-exchange trading by its members, or to provide services that directly compete with these members, may therefore be vetoed by the exchange's member directors.[20] Also, if an exchange has a for-profit governance structure, the dependence between the exchange and the intermediaries trading on its system may be weaker than that which obtains under the traditional nonprofit or cooperative structures. This is unsurprising given that a for-profit governance structure typically reduces the power of membership, and may even sever the link between the ownership and trading rights at an exchange.

The situation where an exchange and a financial intermediary are most likely to view each other as rivals is when both operate order execution mechanisms for exactly the same set of assets or commodities, and when the intermediary is not a member of the exchange. The intermediary may prefer to trade off-exchange because his dealing spreads are less transparent, and possibly wider, than those quoted on the exchange. Even then, however, the intermediary may still use the exchange both as a source of prices, and as a means of locating balancing transactions for that portion of his order flow which he is not able to off-set internally. The intermediary may also have access to a set of customers who do not submit any orders to the exchange. In addition, the intermediary may still use and pay for the settlement services operated by the exchange, even if the exchange's order execution mechanism is bypassed.[21] The more that the assets traded by the intermediary become complementary to those traded on the exchange, rather than direct substitutes, the less likely that the exchange and the intermediary are to see each other as rivals. For example, intermediaries may hedge their trades in OTC derivative products by effecting appropriate trades in the associated exchange-listed contracts. An increase in OTC trading may thus lead to an increase in on-exchange trading.

A dynamic perspective on the way in which the relationship between an exchange and financial intermediaries is more than merely adversarial has been identified by Merton (1993: 21–4). He focuses on the development of new financial products, first noting that,

financial markets . . . tend to be efficient institutional alternatives to intermediaries when the products have standardized terms, can serve a large number of customers, and are well-enough 'understood' that transactors are comfortable in assessing their prices. [In contrast] intermediaries are better suited for low-volume products. Some of these products will always have low volume either because they are highly customized or because of fundamental information asymmetries. Others, however, have low volume only because they are new. Among those, the 'successes' are *expected* to migrate from intermediaries to markets.

That is, once they are 'seasoned,' and perhaps after some information asymmetries are resolved, those products are structured to trade in a market. Just as venture-capital intermediaries that provide financing for start-up firms expect to lose their successful customers to capital-market sources of funding, so do the intermediaries that create new financial products.

Instead of gauging the extent of the rivalry between markets and intermediaries by assessing the characteristics of the products that they trade, however, Merton argues that,

following the particular time path of a particular financial function instead of a product leads to a very different pattern of competition between intermediaries and markets. Instead of a secular trend away from intermediaries towards markets, it is more cyclical— moving back and forth between the two.

In particular,

intermediaries help markets to grow by creating the products that form the basis for new markets and by adding to trading volume in existing ones. In turn, markets help intermediaries to innovate new more-customized products by lowering the cost of producing them. In sum, financial markets and intermediaries are surely *competing* institutions when viewed from the *static* perspective of a particular product activity. However, when viewed from the *dynamic* perspective of the evolving financial system, the two are just as surely *complementary* institutions, each reinforcing and improving the other in the performance of their functions.

While Merton's characterization of the relationship between financial intermediaries and exchanges is insightful, two market developments illustrate how this relationship may be more complicated than he posits. Both are briefly described, and then their implications assessed. The first one was the creation of so-called FLEX options by the Chicago Board Options Exchange (CBOE).[22] These contracts were designed to 'broaden institutional investor demand for customized derivative products', but to be traded on the exchange. FLEX options are similar to standard listed options except that many more of their parameters (including their exercise price, expiration date, and the exercise style) may be tailored by purchasers and sellers, than those on standard options.

The CBOE has argued that trading in a FLEX option has several advantages over dealing in an OTC customized contract with the same terms. First, unlike in the OTC market where the counter-parties to a trade expose themselves to each others' credit risk, trading in FLEX options is cleared through the CBOE's clearinghouse, the Options Clearing Corporation (OCC). Given that this has the highest credit rating available, credit exposure is minimized. The second purported advantage of FLEX options is that price discovery takes place on a competitive auction market operated by CBOE, rather than via a bilateral search process in the OTC market. Finally, the CBOE has claimed that it may be administratively more convenient for investors to trade in listed options than in OTC contracts.

The second relevant market development is Chicago Board Brokerage, Inc. (CBB). Rather than describe the full evolution of this project, which has had a tortuous history with varying market participants being involved at successive stages in different organizational structures, a snapshot of the system as it was proposed in March 1997 is presented.[23] At that time, CBB was intended to provide an automated system for trading US Treasury instruments, overnight repurchase agreements and basis trades (arbitrage trades between the cash and the futures markets).[24] CBB was to be owned 51% by the CBT, and 49% by Hudson Holdings, which itself was a company jointly owned by two interdealer-brokers in the cash markets, Prebon Yamane and Liberty. The clearing of all trades executed through CBB was to be undertaken by the Clearing Corporation for Options and Securities (CCOS), a company owned by the Board of Trade Clearing Corporation (BOTCC).

Several characteristics of the proposed system were believed beneficial. First, it was hoped that CBB would allow CBT members easier and cheaper direct access to the cash and OTC markets than was currently available to them. Second, the project was intended to let traders in the cash markets swap their exposure to each other's counter-party risk with exposure to CCOS, and ultimately BOTCC. Given BOTCC's perceived high credit standing, it was thought that this would encourage more participation in the market, in particular by the lower-rated market participants. Without the intervention of the clearinghouse, these participants found it difficult to persuade higher-rated participants to deal with them. Third, the project was designed so that a clearing member firm of the CBT who took a position in both the futures and cash markets could off-set the margin of one position he was required to put up by the exchange, against the margin of the other position. This would thus reduce the total margins the firm would need to be put up.

The main implications of both CBOE's FLEX options and CBB for an understanding of the relationship between intermediaries and exchanges are similar. Both projects attempted to provide a derivatives exchange access to an OTC cash market. Rather than an exchange seeing an OTC dealer market as a source of competition, the financial intermediaries in the OTC market were therefore seen as a potential source of business, to be courted by the exchange. Both exchange projects also probably caused several types of divisions in the views of the financial intermediaries trading in the market. Those intermediaries who already had a significant presence in the relevant OTC markets, some of whom also had their own internal trading mechanisms, may have seen the exchange projects as being competitive to their own activities. Those intermediaries, on the other hand, who did not, might have thought they would benefit by being able to respond to orders of which they would previously have been unaware.

The aim of both systems to immunize market participants against the credit exposure of lower-rated counter-parties by ensuring that all trades clear through a clearinghouse, probably also received a mixed reception amongst financial intermediaries. The lower-rated companies would have seen such a development as advantageous as it would allow them to deal with higher-rated companies without paying a premium for doing so. In contrast, the higher-rated intermediaries would probably have been antagonistic, precisely because they had higher credit ratings and wanted to use these as a competitive advantage against their lower-rated rivals. A further split in the views of financial intermediaries about the merits of the projects might have occurred between members and non-members of the relevant exchanges. To the extent that either project was successful, the owners of the exchange developing the project, namely its members, would have received indirect benefits as a result of increased revenues to the exchange from the increased levels of trading and clearing on the exchange. Non-members would not have benefited in this manner. Had the projects been failures, of course, the members would have effectively lost their investments in them, while the non-members would have lost nothing.

THE NATURE OF COOPERATION

There are many ways in which an exchange can effect a linkage, joint venture, or merger with another exchange. Any subset of the various functions undertaken by the two exchanges can be shared, including their marketing, listing, order routing, information dissemination, order execution, matching, clearing, settlement, and administration services. There are also different contractual procedures by which shared delivery of these services can be implemented. For example, one exchange can purchase the services from another exchange, both exchanges may agree to sub-contract delivery to a third party, the first exchange can buy the second exchange, or vice versa. Given their diversity, a general comparison of market linkages and other joint projects between exchanges is therefore not useful, let alone feasible. Four important and closely associated aspects of such schemes are, however, common to many of them.

The first concerns their goals. A prime aim of an exchange in entering any linkage, joint venture or merger, is normally to reduce costs, and thus gain an advantage over its competitors. The relevant costs are not simply those incurred by the exchange, but also those borne by all the patrons of the exchange. As before, the meaning of the term patron should be understood in broad terms to include, amongst others, the exchange's owners, members, controllers, management, and consumers. Cost savings can arise from different sources.

An exchange may establish an order routing mechanism or joint clearing arrangement with another exchange in order to offer some of its products to members of the other exchange, without requiring them either to buy a seat on its market, or to deal through a local intermediary. This may allow traders who are not members of the first exchange cheaper access to its products than would otherwise be available. The presumed cost advantage of an exchange-sponsored linkage may, however, be less than anticipated. If an individual firm at one exchange does enough business at another exchange, it may pay the firm to establish its own dedicated link to the second exchange, rather than deal via any exchange-sponsored linkage. If a sufficient number of firms do this, the exchange-sponsored linkage will not attract enough order-flow to cover its costs. Similarly, if the firms trading on one exchange that has a linkage with another exchange, are bought by larger firms which have direct access to both markets, they may have no need for a link between the two exchanges. Internal linkages may be sufficient.

Many other types of efficiencies may be realized by two or more cooperating exchanges. Economies of scale may be available to both exchanges, if their shared costs in any joint facilities are less than the sum of their separate costs would otherwise be.[25] This may occur in investment not only in physical facilities but also in such intangible items as marketing, education, and product development.[26] A link between two markets that operate sequentially in different time zones may reduce the risks incurred by market participants. The ability for traders with positions at one exchange to liquidate their positions on the other exchange, means that they will face lower timing risks than if they were not able to liquidate their positions on the second market, and had to wait till the first one was open again to do so. Linkages between futures markets may reduce the costs of maintaining off-setting positions on both exchanges, such as the need to pay two margin requirements. A linkage may also allow cooperating exchanges to benefit from the network externality associated with the attraction of order-flow. If the linked exchanges are able to combine the order-flows they receive for similar products in a manner that is unavailable without a linkage between them, they may together be able to achieve a more liquid market than either would be able to realize separately.

A second critical element common to most shared exchange initiatives is the central role that technology plays in their development. Its significance is unsurprising given its importance as one of the primary costs incurred by exchanges. Domowitz (1994) has argued that an exchange's choice of whether to adopt an electronic or a floor-based trading system, is affected by the enhanced network externality the exchange may obtain by establishing a market linkage between itself and other exchanges. The central feature of an exchange that is believed to determine the scope of its trading network is the compatibility of its trading system technology with those of other exchanges. The adoption of a floor-based trading system by an exchange is assumed to preclude the possibility of it linking with other exchanges, given limitations of space. The scope of the trading network any floor-based exchange will be able to develop is thus limited to the set of traders who have direct access to its trading system. In contrast, it is assumed that the establishment of an electronic trading system by an exchange will mean that it has a technology compatible for linking with other exchanges that also employ electronic trading systems.

The incentives for adopting an electronic trading system versus a floor-based one therefore increase as the possibilities for increasing liquidity via market linkages increase. In a dynamic setting, Domowitz discusses the possibility that even if the immediate costs of an electronic system are higher than a floor-based system, the automated option may still be chosen because it will allow for the possibility of achieving a larger network and thus greater liquidity in the longer term. Several shortcomings with the theory may, however, be identified. As noted by Domowitz, not all electronic trading systems are cheaply compatible with each other.[27] The characterization of the technology adopted by an exchange as either being floor-based or as being electronic may also be too simplistic to be useful. Exchanges have automated various aspects of their order routing, order execution, and information dissemination functions, and many different types of linkages between these diverse elements have been attempted.

Another related problem is that the assumption that only by being automated can an exchange take advantage of the network externality associated with combining its liquidity with that of other exchanges may be too strong. There have been automated market linkages between two exchanges both of which employ, at least partially, floor-based specialist systems, such as the ME/BSE link discussed in the next chapter. There has also been at least one linkage, even though ultimately it failed, between a fully automated exchange, OMLX, and a floor-based exchange, EOE, again discussed in the next chapter. A further weakness of the theory is that arbitrage between competing exchanges, even in the absence of any exchange-sponsored linkages, may reduce the relative benefits of the positive network externality obtainable as a result of an exchange-sponsored linkage.

A third important aspect common to most cooperative exchange projects is the pivotal influence that governance has both on their development and on their success. Linkages, joint ventures or mergers, are never neutral in terms of their effects on the various patrons of the participating exchanges. As a result, one or more constituencies at exchanges potentially cooperating in a joint initiative frequently fear that it, or they, may be worse off if such a project were established. The governance structures of the collaborating exchanges determine how any benefits obtained by the scheme will be distributed, and whether those constituencies which believe their interests might be harmed have the power to change or obstruct its implementation.

The adoption of the technology necessary to implement a market linkage by an exchange is frequently associated with a reform in the exchange's operating structure, and typically with the elimination of floor-trading. In such circumstances, conflict may arise between traders based on the floor of the exchange, who are typically relatively small in capitalization, and the larger firms which have offices in many locations and are members of many exchanges. Floor members may worry about the possibility of business either moving from the floor to the electronic system, on which they believe they will lose their privileges, or worse, migrating to the other exchanges participating in the linkage. In contrast, the institutional members of the exchange may believe that significant benefits will accrue to them.

Sometimes, the resolution of such conflicts is in favour of those members whose welfare is most closely linked to the functioning of the exchange, namely the floor traders, rather than the other groups whose interests are not so integrated with those of the exchange. This often occurs when the governance structure of the relevant exchange grants each member only one vote, and when the exchange has a relatively large number of floor members. In other circumstances, the larger, wealthier members triumph, normally because it is they who are required to fund the necessary investments for any modernization of the exchange. Sometimes the wealthier members can succeed in buying off the resistance of the smaller members, by reimbursing them for the future losses which they believe they will incur.

Joint ventures may give rise to conflict both within a particular exchange participating in such a scheme, and between the exchanges supposedly working together on the project. The resolution of these conflicts may be dependent not only on the contractual agreements signed between the relevant parties, but also on their relative commercial power. One development in the history of GLOBEX, as discussed in the next chapter, provides an acute example of this. The first two GLOBEX Joint Venture Agreements expressly forbade participating exchanges from using electronic trading facilities other than the GLOBEX system. Indeed, when the CBT decided not to stop implementation of its own electronic system, Project A, this exclusivity requirement appeared to be one of the determinative factors causing the eventual departure of the CBT from the venture. A different result occurred, however, when MATIF, another GLOBEX partner, decided to pursue the creation of an electronic trading link between itself and the DTB outside of GLOBEX. It was able to do so, while still remaining a partner exchange in GLOBEX, because it was at the time contributing 80% of the business to GLOBEX, and thus had the commercial power effectively to ignore or re-negotiate its contractual obligations.

Notwithstanding the ever-present potential for conflict, there are several ways in which tension between cooperating exchanges may be reduced. The simplest occurs where the ownership configurations of the participating exchanges are exactly the same, as in the link between OM Stockholm and OMLX, again discussed in the next chapter. In such circumstances, the success of the link is primarily dependent on whether the combined trading volume of both exchanges increases as a result of the link. The benefits of any growth in trading volume that occurs at either exchange will accrue to the same people, namely the shareholders of both exchanges, and there are thus few concerns about the distribution of any benefits obtained as a result of the link.

A similar instance may arise if both the governance structures of the linking exchanges are dominated by their members, and if there is a large overlap in membership between the participating exchanges. If the member firms of the exchanges are indifferent where they conduct their business, they will not be concerned about movements in trading volumes between the exchanges, and the intensity of competition between the cooperating exchanges will again be attenuated. This often occurs when the regional exchanges in a country merge to form a single linked exchange, as has taken place in Australia, France, Italy, and Switzerland. Conflict between cooperating exchanges may also be diminished if the exchanges operate in different time zones. One of the reasons why the CME/SIMEX link prospered may have been that the floor traders in Chicago did not believe that they were losing business when they saw a significant volume of trading in Singapore. While SIMEX was open, the Chicago traders would rather have been sleeping.

Given the historical prevalence of the nonprofit and the cooperative governance structures among exchanges, the phenomenon of the hostile takeover in the market for markets has not yet occurred. It could only happen at an exchange with tradable shares. To date the only context where such a possibility has even been raised is in Sweden where at one stage the OM Group mooted the potential takeover of the Stockholm Stock Exchange against the wishes of the management of the SSE. An agreed merger was subsequently consummated.

A fourth noteworthy aspect of market linkages is the difficulty of creating credible contractual commitments between the cooperating partners. To achieve this, not only do such agreements have to be initially beneficial for the participants, they have to continue to be so even in a changing environment. If material circumstances vary, as often occurs, one or more of the participating exchanges may decide that the original contractual agreement is no longer appropriate. It is normally then hard for the other participating organizations to insist that the dissenting exchange honour its original agreement, as is evident in GLOBEX's development. The costs of enforcing any such contract are typically too high to warrant any legal attempt to do so, particularly in an international environment. More importantly, however, even if a participating exchange could be forced into an action it perceived as unfavourable, the traders which the exchange typically represents cannot be compelled to trade on the linkage. There would thus be little point in forcing an unwilling exchange to continue honouring its initial participation agreement without the active support of its members.

CONCLUSION

The aim of this chapter is to scrutinize the concepts of competition and cooperation in the context of exchanges. The following broad questions are addressed: What does it mean to say that an exchange faces competition? What are the factors that give rise to such competition? How do exchanges react to competition? and, When, why, and how, do they attempt to cooperate with, rather than compete against, each other?

The chapter is composed of two sections. In the first, the nature of competition in the context of exchanges and markets is examined. The types of rivalry that may exist between exchanges are analysed. The ways in which a market may be fragmented are described. Various factors that influence the extent to which agents will choose to compete with an exchange for the provision of alternative trading systems are noted. Finally, the extent to which the relationship between exchanges and financial intermediaries may be thought of as one of rivalry is studied.

In the second section, some general comments on the nature of exchange cooperation are made. An analysis is presented of the reasons why such cooperative schemes have been proposed, and the difficulties that exchanges have had in concluding and in maintaining agreement between themselves regarding such projects. Four central aspects of such projects are discussed. They are first, the fact that the prime aim of most exchange linkages, joint ventures and mergers, is to reduce costs; second, the importance of new technology in achieving this; third, the role of exchange governance in affecting both the development and success of such projects; and fourth, the difficulty of creating credible contractual commitments between cooperating exchanges.

5

Cooperation: Case Studies

INTRODUCTION

Of the many attempts at cooperation between exchanges that have been proposed, few have been implemented; of those that have been realized, most have failed. A range of case studies illustrating various aspects of cooperation between exchanges is presented in this chapter.

The case studies are examined for two general reasons similar to those discussed in Chapter 3: they confirm that the specificity of an exchange's particular circumstances greatly influences the outcomes that obtain at the exchange, and they provide descriptions of joint ventures between exchanges that are otherwise extremely difficult to obtain. They also illustrate a range of factors specific to cooperative projects. These include the multiplicity of ways in which exchanges can effect joint ventures, the pivotal role that technology plays in their development, the fact that a prime aim of exchanges in entering joint ventures is to gain an advantage over their competitors frequently by reducing costs, and the difficulty of creating credible contractual commitments between cooperating exchanges. In addition, the case studies highlight the ever-present nature of conflict in exchange governance, and provide a vivid background for evaluating the extent to which different interest groups are able to influence the governance of exchanges, given that cooperative projects frequently threaten existing vested interests at the potentially cooperating exchanges.[1] Finally, they illustrate how joint schemes can affect market architecture by changing important aspects of the order routing, order execution, or information dissemination components of a market.

The chapter is composed of two sections. In the first, a series of market linkages and joint ventures proposed and undertaken by various stock exchanges are described. These include various European projects (IDIS, Euroquote, and Eurolist), three American–Canadian order routing linkages (between the AMEX and the TSE, the MSE and the TSE, and the BSE and ME), and two Anglo-American projects (between the PHLX and the LSE, and the NASD and the LSE). In the second section, several cooperative schemes pursued by diverse futures exchanges are discussed. These include the mutual-offset link between the CME and the Singapore International Monetary Exchange (SIMEX), GLOBEX, three European linkages—between DTB and MATIF, between OM and OMLX, and the FEX proposal, and finally the merger between NYMEX and COMEX. As with the case studies previously presented, it is not claimed that the accounts presented here are either complete or accurate. They are, however, viewed as the best available descriptions of the relevant joint ventures. It is also important to stress, again as before, that the focus in this chapter is on describing rather than analysing the various exchange situations.

LINKS BETWEEN STOCK EXCHANGES

A range of market linkages and joint ventures proposed and undertaken by various stock exchanges is described in this section. Some European schemes and then some American projects are discussed in turn.

Europe

The first attempt at cooperation between European stock exchanges took place in the late 1970s. The InterBourse/Stock Exchange Data Information System (IDIS) project was established in order to disseminate share prices between the floors of the various European stock exchanges.[2] The project was abandoned mainly because at the time, continuous computer-assisted trading was not yet available, and the exchanges did not have the means to make the project operational. Nevertheless, the project was seen as a useful indicator of what could be achieved by cooperation, not only by the exchanges themselves and their trade association, which was then called the Federation of Stock Exchanges in the EC (FSEEC), but also by the European Commission.[3]

From the middle of the 1980s, three connected trends began to accelerate in the European equity markets, all of which influenced the manner in which stock exchanges perceived the value of linkages between themselves.[4] The first was an increase in international competition on several different levels: between financial intermediaries, between exchanges, and between financial centres. This competition intensified when the London Stock Exchange created a vehicle in 1985 for trading non-UK equities, SEAQ International (SEAQi). Over a period, this forum attracted significant percentages of the trading in equities listed on the major continental stock exchanges.[5] The second trend was the modernization of the technology supporting exchanges' operations following the Big Bang in London in 1986. Prior to this, most of the European stock exchanges had little or no computer infrastructure supporting their trading facilities, and most trading was undertaken via a single price fixing rather than on a continuous basis.

The third trend affecting European equity markets in the mid-1980s was the process of deregulation, both at a national level, where the laws governing the financial markets in various countries were reformed, and at an international level, with the European Community initiating its Single or Internal Market programme in 1985. The European Commission intended the Single Market programme to be a vehicle for liberalizing trade in most areas of economic activity, including the capital markets. The Commission believed that some form of linkage between stock exchanges would help further such competition, and encouraged its development. Indeed, in its White Paper setting out the goals for the Single Market, the Commission noted that:

Work currently in hand to create a European securities market system, based on Community stock exchanges, is also relevant to the creation of an internal market. This work is designed to break down barriers between stock exchanges and to create a Community-wide trading system for securities of international interest. The aim is to link stock exchanges electronically, so that their members can execute orders on the stock exchange market offering the best conditions to their clients. Such an interlinking would substantially increase the depth and liquidity of Community stock exchange markets, and would permit them to compete more effectively not only with stock exchanges outside the Community but also with unofficial and unsupervised markets within it.[6]

Against this background, the FSEEC decided to pursue again the possibility of establishing some form of linkage between its member exchanges. In October 1988 it presented an introductory paper to its members, summarizing what might be achieved if they cooperated in creating an information network.[7] The association proposed that a system be established first to deliver information from the regulated securities markets in the EC, with the possibility of disseminating regulated company information, third party commercial information services and databases, and even member–firm research, at a later stage. Several advantages were seen as arising from such cooperation. Most importantly, it was believed that participating exchanges could avoid wasting time and money by not replicating each other's activity in the provision of market information delivery networks, and by standardizing technology. It was also argued that the establishment of a shared network would make the European markets more efficient, transparent, liquid, and actively used, and that such benefits could accrue both to financial intermediaries and to the industry as a whole.

In order to validate the first paper's recommendations, a survey of a representative group of exchange members and other potential users was undertaken. This study concluded that there was a demand for an 'integrated regulated information service' which would carry not just price information but also company news, stock events, and other important market information throughout the EC. Respondents to the survey indicated that they believed that a regulated quality source of both price and news information was not being adequately delivered by the commercial vendors. The research did, however, identify a lack of confidence that the European stock exchanges would be able to cooperate effectively. It was felt that this difficulty could best be solved by exchanges working together 'at the level of the lowest common denominator, [in] the provision of a consolidated source of strategic equities market information for the European region'.[8]

Following the survey, the members of the FSEEC agreed in September 1989 to pursue the creation of such an information network, and the Price and Information Project for Europe (PIPE) was formally launched. The twelve founder shareholders subscribed seed-capital of ECU 2.7 million with the London, Paris, Frankfurt, and Madrid stock exchanges each holding approximately 15% of the equity. A

competitive 'Invitation to Tender' for the supply of facilities and services for the
network was issued in January 1990, and following a selection process, awarded
in March 1991 to General Electric Information Systems.[9] In order to develop the
project, a joint venture between the twelve exchanges was officially signed in May
1990 in Copenhagen, and a company was established to run the project in Belgium
in June 1990. The company was called Euroquote, rather than PIPE.

By the time the company was formally established, the goals of the project had
widened beyond that of being solely an information provider. In particular,
Euroquote's objectives were stated to be, subject to commercial viability:[10]

1. To provide an authorised, recognised source of strategic equities market information for
the European region. 2. To maximise the visibility of European equities markets by providing a 'window' on them on a global basis. 3. To reduce the costs associated with access to
information from European markets. 4. To enhance the quality of information available to
market users. 5. To provide the basis for a common trading platform for the European
region.[11]

The intention was to implement Euroquote in three phases:

1. An information capture and dissemination system for real time information throughout
Europe. 2. Provision of interactive access to systems operated by the company and
exchanges. 3. Provision of a central point for automated trade execution, trade confirmation, and settlement message routing.[12]

It was not the aim of Euroquote to compete with commercial data vendors.
Rather, it was intended that subscribers would have the choice of buying an integrated feed of information directly from Euroquote, or of subscribing to it indirectly through commercial vendors, or of doing both. It was believed that the
service offered by Euroquote would differ from others then available commercially in three ways: by offering a single consolidated official source of information, by having a 'utility' pricing structure that would benefit all market
participants, and by providing equal access to information throughout Europe. It
was also believed that such an information system would in the long run obtain
the necessary profits to recover the initial capital investment, that it would stimu-
late competition between national markets,[13] and that it would serve the
'European ideal'.

There were, however, differences of opinion about the development of
Euroquote. In May 1990, a London Stock Exchange official stated that 'the business case for the system had not been made',[14] and in November 1990, another
London official noted that 'we shall support the Euroquote project, so long as it
continues to add up commercially, and allows us to offer our services more
widely and effectively'.[15] In May 1990, a German official commented that securities firms and investment banks would only be willing to bear the costs of PIPE
if they were presented with an overall plan that was 'future-oriented': 'this means
that PIPE should not be allowed to become just a European price information
system but must develop into a trading system in its own right with integrated
settlement facilities'.[16] In contrast, in February 1991 the Chairman of the

Amsterdam stock exchange asserted that 'Euroquote can contribute to the efficiency and visibility of the emerging European financial marketplace, and thus create an attractive instrument for investment from both inside and outside Europe'.[17] Similarly, in February 1991 one of the promoters of Euroquote claimed that 'co-operation amongst market centres is required to achieve a safer more efficient system of market places to facilitate investment in Europe'.[18]

The debate concerning Euroquote was complicated by the proposal in 1990 of two other possible forms of cooperation between the European stock exchanges: the European Wholesale Market (EWM) and Eurolist. The EWM was promoted by the LSE, and was intended to provide a 'one-stop-shop' professional market for international intermediaries and investors, in order to allow them to trade leading European and non-European equities quickly and efficiently without onerous rules and regulations. It was believed that a separate and thirteenth market, which transcended national boundaries and was not tied to any exchange floor, would attract large-size off-exchange business on to a single orderly market, and thereby pool liquidity. The EWM was intended to be a self-financing, nonprofit organization, with significant participant influence in the governance of the market. The LSE argued that the liquidity of national markets would not be impaired by the addition of such an international market.[19] Furthermore, it asserted that linkages between exchanges were not desirable for three reasons: they would be expensive; many different types of links would be required given the many different national systems; and there were different requirements for retail business, which would largely be done on the national markets, from those for professional business, which could better be handled on the EWM. Most of the continental exchanges viewed EWM as a potential competitor, proposed by the LSE to further its competitive advantage, and nothing came of it.

EuroList was a proposal to allow the largest companies to be officially and simultaneously listed, and thus traded, on all EC stock exchanges. It was argued that this would be advantageous to issuers because they would gain a 'European' status by being showcased on such a list. It was anticipated that companies would be required to pay a listing fee for multiple listings, in addition to their national listing fee, and that each country would choose the domestic companies that it wished to quote on the European list.[20] It was also claimed that trade would be made easier for investors, thanks to multiple market access and increased liquidity.[21] Investors would be able to trade on their national stock exchange, with which they were familiar, and there would be some system of linkages between the various national exchanges. Prices of multiply-listed issues would be quoted in their domestic currency, in the currency of the national exchange on which they were quoted, and possibly also in ECU. Eurolist was seen by London as an attempt by the French, Belgians, and Italians, in particular, to buttress the positions of their national exchanges.[22] Despite this, however, the FSEEC and participating exchanges did continue working on Eurolist. A central element of the project involved the creation of a network enabling a company to give information to the domestic exchange on which it was listed, which could then transmit the information instantly to the other exchanges on which the company's share was listed.

It was at the Athens semi-annual meeting of the FSEEC on 23–4 May 1991, that the discussions concerning the future of Euroquote reached a climax. After the initial project appraisal and the appointment of the contractor, ECU 12.3 million of new capital was needed to continue the development of the project.[23] Both London and Frankfurt declined, however, to participate in the fund raising. Although there was a clause in the Articles of Association which allowed the other shareholders to take up the British and German equity, the balance of exchanges did not pursue it. When the Board of Euroquote proposed a smaller capital increase of ECU 9.5 million to its shareholders at a meeting on 5 July 1991, London and Frankfurt again refused to participate, the project was abandoned, and the company dissolved.

There are a range of different reasons why the project failed. The LSE stated publicly that it was not convinced that an adequate business case had been made for the project, even as purely an information network. This is probably because it believed that, notwithstanding any claims to the contrary, Euroquote would be in direct competition with Reuters, and that in the assumptions underlying the business case for the project no provision had been taken of any possible price reaction that Reuters might take in response to Euroquote's establishment. It is also likely that the LSE was concerned that by sponsoring Euroquote, it might be encouraging an institution which could challenge the success of its own information dissemination system, TOPIC, and perhaps also of its international price quotation mechanism, SEAQi.[24] Indeed, it was probably for this very reason, namely in the hope of repatriating some of the trade in the equities listed on their exchanges, that some of the continental Europeans supported Euroquote in the first place.

A different interpretation of why the LSE retracted its support for the project, which was not confirmed in public, may have been due to a change in the exchange's management. When the idea of Euroquote was first mooted, rather than seeing it as a venture which might threaten SEAQi, it was in contrast reportedly viewed by the exchange as a way of capitalizing on the success of SEAQi. Euroquote was effectively seen as an instrument by which SEAQi might triumph as the trading system for institutional dealing in equities throughout Europe. With a change in the management of the LSE in 1989, however, such a view was apparently repudiated.

The Frankfurt Stock Exchange believed that there was no need to create a new system purely for the delivery of information, and argued that it was essential that Euroquote become both a joint clearing and settlement system and a trading system.[25] At the time, the Germans were already in the process of developing their own national system for the trading and settlement of stocks, which was reputedly over budget. By insisting that Euroquote should become a fully integrated information, trading, and settlement system, the Germans probably thought they would ensure one of two outcomes. The most likely one, and indeed the one that occurred, would be that the project would fail, given the likelihood that the other shareholders of Euroquote would not agree to it. This would be good for the German banks, the major shareholders of the Frankfurt Stock Exchange, as they did not want to sink any more money into large automated projects with uncertain returns, and believed in any event that they should build their own national system first, and then move to the international arena. Alternatively, it might have been the case that the other shareholders of Euroquote might have agreed with Germany, in which case the German system might well have been used as the basis for Euroquote itself.

There are two other more subjective factors that also probably contributed to the failure of the project. Throughout its development, great stress was placed on the value of providing a source of information which was officially authorized by the regulated markets in the EC. The view that an exchange was an officially sanctioned public body, and that information arising from such a source would be more valuable than information arising from 'non-regulated' markets, was a concept common on continental Europe. It was not accepted, however, by all the exchanges participating in Euroquote, particularly by the LSE. In addition, in the late 1980s, the LSE had lost a regulatory battle concerning whether it should remain the sole official source of information about company news in the UK.[26] The LSE might therefore both have doubted the value of 'officially' sanctioned information, and also been wary of becoming involved in a project to promote such information internationally, when it had just lost the power to promote such information domestically.

The other factor which may have contributed to the downfall of Euroquote, related to the concept of 'Europe' itself. Some of the continental exchanges were motivated to join Euroquote because they believed that they would be furthering the cause of European integration by linking up, and thought that doing so would benefit the people of Europe as a whole. In general, London was sceptical about this vision.

America

In the mid-1980s five linkages between various stock exchanges in the USA and elsewhere were proposed. Of these, three were order routing linkages between an American and a Canadian exchange. The most ambitious was between the American Stock Exchange (AMEX) and the Toronto Stock Exchange (TSE). It was between two primary markets, it was intended to involve trading in different currencies, and it joined two trading floors with many dissimilar trading procedures, including different market making systems, different priority rules for the execution of orders, and somewhat different concepts of agency and principal transactions.[27] Amongst the anticipated benefits of the link were that it would give investors in both countries an opportunity to obtain the best prices in either country for dually listed stocks, faster executions, more cost-effectiveness, and greater liquidity.[28]

The linkage started with a pilot scheme that allowed orders to be sent from the floor of the TSE to the floor of the AMEX for execution. Although it was also intended to facilitate a northbound flow of orders from the AMEX to the TSE, this was delayed because the TSE did not initially have the ability to provide a currency transaction at the same time as a northbound stock trade was executed through the linkage. Each exchange displayed on its trading floor the quotes distributed by the other exchange in the linkage stocks. Quotes on the AMEX were in US dollars, while those in Toronto were at first in Canadian dollars. Orders were transmitted between the two trading floors using the existing auto-mated routing systems of the two exchanges. Initially, only 'marketable' limit orders were sent over the linkage. These were orders for which the price was equal to, or better than, the quote then being displayed at the receiving exchange. Such orders were treated as 'immediate or cancel' orders, to be promptly executed or cancelled depending on whether they were marketable when received by the relevant market maker at the receiving exchange. Agency orders were guaranteed an execution up to a minimum amount of shares. It was planned to accommodate 'away from the market orders', namely orders whose prices were worse than the best available quote at the receiving exchange, at a later date. The linkage was initially available only for dually-listed stocks, namely stocks traded on both the AMEX and the TSE. Transactions were cleared and settled through an interface between the American National Securities Clearing Corporation and the Canadian Depository Service.[29]

The AMEX/TSE link began operating on 24 September 1985. Six stocks were listed on the link to begin with, though this number later increased to twenty. A similar linkage between the Midwest Stock Exchange and the Toronto Stock Exchange started operating on 16 June 1986.[30] All orders on this linkage were initially southbound, though again it was intended to accommodate northbound orders once the TSE became capable of simultaneous currency transactions. The link was to be implemented in two phases: in the first it was to be available for the trading of the seventeen dually-listed issues on both exchanges, and in the second was to include non-interlisted issues.

Both the AMEX/TSE links and the MSE/TSE links were perceived as obtaining a minimal order flow, most of which was between the specialists on the two exchanges' floors.[31] The average ratio of southbound to northbound transactions was approximately 5:1. A TSE report noted that although such a ratio might be 'interpreted as a loss of market share by the TSE to AMEX . . . any such interpretation should take into account that some southbound order flow may have been a result of offsets for TSE trades. As such, a trade on the AMEX may not necessarily take away an opportunity for a trade on the TSE but take place only because a trade was done on the TSE.'[32] Two obstacles were believed to have restricted the northbound flow of orders in the MSE/TSE link-age. The physical layout of the MSE trading floor apparently precluded easy access to the entry of northbound orders, and the absence of guarantees of execution for professional orders acted as a disincentive for professional traders to use the link. Both linkages were discontinued at the end of 1988 as being uneconomical to run.

The third order routing linkage established at the time was between the Boston Stock Exchange (BSE) and the Montreal Exchange (ME). The link went through several stages of development. In 1984, a connection was established to allow a southbound flow of marketable orders in the roughly forty Canadian stocks listed in the USA, or trading pursuant to unlisted trading privileges in the Intermarket Trading System (ITS).[33] Members of the ME could direct orders to the floor of the BSE via electronic terminals located on the floor of the ME. In the second phase, the list of stocks eligible to be traded on the link was enlarged to include most of the 2,000 ITS stocks that were traded in Boston.[34] In 1989 the ME joined its order routing system to the BSE's automated order routing network, BEACON.[35]

By 1992 members of the ME could access the link in three ways: they could route orders via a 'Montreal Direct Access' terminal, they could use their own internal order management systems if appropriately connected, or they could telephone orders through to the floor of the ME.[36] At that time, specialists on the BSE guaranteed an execution at the best price quoted on all US exchanges for all orders up to 1,299 shares routed over the linkage, and in the most actively traded stocks, for up to 2,599 shares. In 1994, northbound order traffic between the BSE and the ME was allowed for those Canadian securities listed on the BSE, or trading pursuant to unlisted trading privileges in the ITS.[37] The linkage was still in operation in 1996. Three key benefits of the linkage were identified: the savings to brokers of using the link rather than having to deal directly with another broker at the other exchange, the rapid turnaround time in which orders were executed on the link and notifications of execution were received, and the reduction in errors associated with cross-border trading.

The other two linkages proposed in the mid 1980s were between an American stock exchange and the LSE. One, between the Philadelphia Stock Exchange (PHLX) and the LSE, was never implemented.[38] The goal was to allow certain foreign currency options traded on both exchanges to be fungible. The mechanism suggested for achieving this was to require that the relevant options be issued by a single organization, the Options Clearing Corporation, which would also clear and settle them. A trader would thus have been able to take a position in Philadelphia, and then close it out on the LSE by taking an off-setting position. Quote and trade information from each exchange were also to have been disseminated on the floor of the other exchange.

The PHLX decided not to go ahead with the linkage when some of its brokers became aware that it would be possible to avoid the PHLX crossing requirements by trading in London.[39] Philadelphia had a rule that required a broker who wished to execute his customers' buy and sell orders against one another, to bring such trades to the PHLX floor and 'expose' the crosses to the crowd. This provided an opportunity for the orders in a cross to receive a better price than that initially suggested, and also gave Philadelphia traders a chance to 'break up' the cross and trade against part of it should they wish to do so. The Philadelphia traders realized that if the same cross were executed in London, where there was no exposure requirement for crosses, their ability to participate in such trades would have been restricted.

The other Anglo-American link was between the LSE and the NASD. Both exchanges agreed to disseminate information about the quotes on each other's markets for a two-year pilot period.[40] NASDAQ was to display the quotes from the top 100 LSE shares included in the FT-SE index, and for 180 other stocks for which there was an active London market off the exchange floor. SEAQ was to display the quotes for 200 companies listed on NASDAQ and seventy-five non-UK companies whose ADRs were also traded on NASDAQ.[41] Only a few of the 550 stocks covered by the data link were dually traded on both exchanges. There was no intention that the information linkage should develop into any form of joint order routing or order execution mechanism, and after operating for several years, the link was abandoned, primarily because neither exchanges' members expressed a strong demand for its existence.

LINKS BETWEEN FUTURES EXCHANGES

The development of a range of linkages and joint ventures, and one merger, between various futures exchanges are described in this section. They are respectively, the mutual off-set agreement between the CME and SIMEX, GLOBEX, three linkages between various European exchanges, and finally the merger between the New York Mercantile Exchange (NYMEX) and the Commodity Exchange (COMEX) in the USA.

CME/SIMEX Mutual Off-Set Arrangement

The first linkage created between futures exchanges was the mutual off-set arrangement activated between the CME and SIMEX on 7 September 1984.[42] The link allows a trader taking a position on one exchange to reverse the position on the other exchange. A trade executed on SIMEX by a CME clearing member, for example, can be transferred to the CME's account at the SIMEX clearing organization, which in turn results in the establishment of an identical position on the CME for the CME clearing member. CME traders can thus effectively use SIMEX as an extension of the CME trading floor after the CME has closed. An analogous arrangement allows SIMEX traders to use the CME while SIMEX is closed.

The primary reason why the CME established the link was as a weapon to help it compete internationally against LIFFE, which was then battling against the CME to establish itself as the dominant forum for trading Eurodollar contracts. Given LIFFE's perceived advantage in being closer to the Asian time zone than the CME, a link with SIMEX was viewed as providing a valuable foothold for the

CME in the Far East. The CME also identified several benefits of the link for its members and their clients. The advantages noted for FCMs were that it gave them the ability to offer clients something closer to 24-hour trading at low cost, and that it reduced the costs and risks they incurred in trading on a foreign market. CME member firms also gained the ability to increase business by acting as executing agents for those SIMEX member firms which wished to have their trades cleared through the CME. The benefits of the link anticipated for members' clients were as follows: they gained the ability to manage the risk of potential price movements overnight; the link expanded the number of trading hours available for active traders; it reduced transaction costs by requiring only a single margin structure; it assured clients the ability to offset a position taken on SIMEX on what they knew to be a liquid market—namely the CME; finally, it gave clients reassurance because their positions, whether initiated in Singapore or on the CME, could be held in Chicago on the books of the CME.

The link was initially agreed for a ten-year period in 1984. Although the contractual details of the scheme were not released, there was apparently no financial aspect to the original CME/SIMEX agreement. The CME thus saw the main goals of the linkage to be to increase order flow to its members, and to forestall LIFFE's attempts to trade Eurodollar contracts. The system did indeed succeed in doing this, as LIFFE's share of trading volume dwindled following the opening of the link, until LIFFE finally de-listed its Eurodollar contract in 1996.[43] When the mutual off-set agreement was re-negotiated in 1994, a financial element to the contract was established.[44] In particular, if one exchange was a net transferor of contracts to the other exchange, the first exchange agreed to pay a pre-specified fee per contract to the other exchange.

The main tactical benefit of establishing the link for Singapore was to build a financial centre to rival Hong Kong. The link was the foundation on which SIMEX was created and gave the exchange access to a contract for which there was already a pool of liquidity in the USA with a reputable exchange, and for which demand had already been identified. It thus gave the new exchange a good chance of being successful.

GLOBEX

It is extremely difficult to describe the evolution of GLOBEX for several reasons: it was a complicated technical system; its governance structure and underlying contractual basis were both intricate and changed several times; not only did the publicly stated goals of the various participants in the system evolve over time, they also did not always reflect their private intentions; and finally, many aspects of its history have not been disclosed. Notwithstanding these problems, GLOBEX remains the most ambitious joint venture implemented between futures exchanges to date, and an attempt is therefore made to describe its development.

In the mid-1980s the CME, lead by Leo Melamed, became concerned to protect its position as a leading world market against competition by foreign exchanges. Given that it was relatively easy for a foreign exchange to create a contract that mimicked those listed on the CME, the CME decided that a pre-emptive response to such potential competition was to create an after-hours computerized trading system. In 1987 it therefore established a joint venture with Reuters, the data-vending and information technology company, to develop such a system.[45] The hardware and software were to be produced by, and belong to, Reuters, while the creation of market liquidity was to be the CME's responsibility.

The joint venture was formalized in an agreement on 20 June 1988 between the CME, Reuters, and PMT (Post-Market-Trade).[46] PMT was a limited partnership, in which the CME was the general partner, and its members, membership interest holders, and clearing-member firms, were the limited partners. Each of the CME's members and clearing members was invited to join PMT, but was under no obligation to do so.[47] The CME retained those partnership interests which exchange members declined to purchase, with the intention of offering to sell them to any subsequent purchaser of those members' seats. PMT was created to provide a mechanism whereby profits and losses from the automated system could be passed directly through to CME members. Any profits obtained by PMT were to be split 70% to the members, 20% to the clearing members, and 10% to the exchange for running the system.[48] While PMT remained the name of the limited partnership, the name of the project was changed early in its development from PMT to GLOBEX.

Although the agreement between the CME, PMT, and Reuters was not made public, it is believed to have included the following provisions:[49]

(1) Up until 30 July 1990 the CME would not be allowed to use any electronic network for trade execution for any CME contract, other than GLOBEX or another system operated by Reuters. After that date Reuters would essentially have a right of first refusal to carry any CME contract that the exchange wanted to trade over an electronic trade execution system.

(2) Up until 27 months after 30 July 1990, Reuters was not allowed to use GLOBEX or any other trading system to provide trade execution services for any non-CME futures or options contracts. After this time, Reuters would be allowed to provide trade execution services for certain energy-related contracts. It would not, however, be allowed to facilitate trading in any contracts which were defined as 'competitive' in the agreement, without the consent of the CME. Any contract based on a major world currency, or on an interest rate denominated in one of these currencies was deemed to be competitive. The agreement stipulated that 'the CME should weigh the overall benefit to GLOBEX against the competitive detriment to itself and its members when considering whether to waive its right to exclude non-CME contracts from the system'.

(3) The duration of the agreement was to be 12½ years, unless it was either terminated earlier for due cause by one of the parties, as per a series of

pre-specified termination clauses, or unless the CME and Reuters together agreed to an extension. The agreement allowed both parties to negotiate successive five-year extensions, but did not oblige them to do so.

(4) Only clearing members, individual members, and certain affiliates and parents of clearing members, were guaranteed access to GLOBEX terminals. In addition, an 'Institutional Access' programme was established to grant a maximum of fifty institutional traders direct access to GLOBEX terminals.[50]

(5) Reuters was to build the system at its own cost, and to be paid a monthly transaction fee based on the volume of contracts traded through GLOBEX.

(6) As a data vendor, Reuters would not obtain any preferential treatment over its competitors with regard to the information arising from the trading on GLOBEX. In particular, it would receive such information at the same time as all other competing data vendors.

Over the period from 1988 to 1992, the organizational structure and objectives of GLOBEX changed in two important ways. First, in 1989 the CME convinced the Marché à Terme International de France (MATIF) to join the system. MATIF wanted to replace its own after-hours trading system, the THS (Transactions Hors Séances), and saw in GLOBEX a way of doing this. It therefore agreed, at this time, to use the system for 12 years.[51] MATIF was, however, the sole exchange that decided to join the system during this period. Despite several overtures by the CME to LIFFE to see if it wished to join GLOBEX, LIFFE chose not to do so. The key reasons were, as noted by Kynaston (1997: 211–12), that 'as a sub-licensee LIFFE would not be a party to the CME/Reuters agreement, whose terms could therefore be changed without reference to LIFFE, and furthermore not only would limitations be imposed on the expansion of LIFFE's membership but also the GLOBEX board, on which the CME would have a controlling interest, would be responsible for setting all GLOBEX fees, admitting new exchanges and approving all system changes'. There was also a view that the automated after-hours trading system that LIFFE itself had developed, APT, was technologically superior to GLOBEX. Finally, there were concerns about the credibility of the system, given that its implementation was continually being delayed.

The second significant development in GLOBEX over the period from 1988 to 1992 was the participation of the CBT. During this time, the CBT began to develop an electronic system to simulate pit-trading, called AURORA. This was done for reasons similar to why the CME initiated GLOBEX, namely 'to protect domestic daytime markets and to exploit 24-hour international customer demand'.[52] After much internal debate, the CBT held a referendum of its members to vote on whether it should become part of GLOBEX.

The main perceived advantage to the CBT of joining GLOBEX, as opposed to pursuing AURORA, was the anticipated cost savings of doing so. There was also a view that actually implementing the technology for AURORA would prove difficult. In addition, both the CBT and the CME hoped to allow foreign exchanges access to GLOBEX, and thus enhance international cross-exchange access, whereby each market offered some of its products to members of the other participating markets on a reciprocal basis. It was believed that this would give exchange members the opportunity to diversify and internationalize their activities, without having to buy a seat on each of the participating exchanges. It was further hoped that cooperation might allow the founding exchanges to provide a technical infrastructure that other markets would be willing to pay for in order to get access to a fully interconnected global system. Given that together the CME and the CBT had more than half of the total global trading volume in futures contracts at the time, the creation of a single trading system for both exchanges was seen as a magnet that might draw in other exchanges who wished to use an automated trading system.

Although the vote at the CBT went in favour of joining GLOBEX, support for the proposal was not unanimous. While the large member firms voted in favour, some locals at the CBT regarded GLOBEX as an encroachment on their territory. In addition, given the long history of feuding between the two rival Chicago exchanges, there was concern about the CBT going into partnership with the CME. To Reuters, there was the hope that it would gain more revenue from GLOBEX through increased amounts of trading on the system by sanctioning the CBT's entry, and hopefully the entry of other exchanges at a later date.

After much negotiation between the three potential partners, the CBT finally joined GLOBEX.[53] The original agreement between the CME and Reuters was revoked, and a new 'GLOBEX Joint Venture Agreement' was drawn up, and signed on 7 April 1992.[54] A complicated structure was created to allow the various participants to the agreement to pursue their different roles. The Joint Venture Agreement was between Reuters Futures Services Inc. (RFS), a wholly-owned subsidiary of Reuters Ltd. and the GLOBEX Joint Venture L.P. (JV).[55]

The JV was a limited partnership, in which J.V. Management Inc. was the general partner owning 1% of the equity, and PMT Limited Partnership and Ceres Trading Limited Partnership were the two limited partners, each owning 49.5% of the equity. J.V. Management Inc. was owned by PMT and Ceres, each with 50% of the equity. Ceres was a limited partnership, similar to PMT, except that the CBT was its general partner, and the members and clearing members of the CBT were its limited partners. The board of the JV was composed of seven representatives each from the CME and the CBT, and two representatives from the Futures Industry Association. The chairmanship of the JV was to alternate between the CME and the CBT. The first chairman was Melamed, who, discussing the board's composition, noted that,

the representatives to the JV [board] were chosen by the Merc and CBOT boards in the first place; a majority of them had to be directors of their respective exchanges; they served the JV at the pleasure of their exchange chairmen. Consequently, their actions were, in effect, always controlled by the exchange boards and there was no need for further controls.[56]

The GLOBEX Corporation was also established, as a wholly-owned subsidiary of JV, to provide a forum in which participating exchanges could have a voice and a vote in GLOBEX affairs, including marketing, the admission of new exchanges, and the allocation of rights to list new products. The intention was to allow other exchanges to trade their contracts on the system, without participation in its ownership, but with some participation in its control. MATIF was not party to the GLOBEX Joint Venture Agreement, although it did apparently sign a 'side-letter' to the contract.

The Joint Venture Agreement was not made public, but it is believed to have included the following provisions:

(1) For the first three years, most decisions of the JV would require the consent of both Ceres and PMT, and even after this period some decisions would still require unanimity. For example, GLOBEX's order execution algorithm could only be modified if all the participating exchanges were unanimous in wanting the change.

(2) Each participating exchange had the right to approve which of its products were listed for trading on GLOBEX. At the same time, participating exchanges had some form of affirmative obligation to list their premium products on GLOBEX.

(3) Once a contract had been assigned to a particular exchange on GLOBEX, that exchange was given 'exclusivity' for the contract, so that no other exchange was allowed to trade it or a competitive contract on GLOBEX. Furthermore, the CME or the CBT could individually veto the trading of any contract deemed potentially competitive with any contract it might want to trade. Each exchange, however, also had a duty to weigh the over-all benefit to GLOBEX against the competitive detriment to itself and its members when considering whether to waive its right to exclude contracts from the system.

(4) A committee was established to decide how new products should be assigned to participating exchanges. The committee was composed of one representative from each participating exchange, each of whom had one vote. Decisions were to be taken by majority vote. The committee had a series of non-binding guidelines for how to assign a new contract. The following questions had to be answered: Which exchange had dominance in the trading of the contract? Which exchange invented the contract? Did any exchange trade any related products to the new product? and, Did any exchange have a particular 'affinity' for the new product, for example by being based in the home country of the assets underlying the contract? If there was no exchange which clearly satisfied the guidelines, the commit-tee could decide not to allocate the new contract to any exchange, or alter-natively to allocate it to more than one exchange. Neither the JV nor RFS had any formal say in the allocation of new products.

(5) The JV promised to use GLOBEX as the sole electronic system for trading

futures contracts during GLOBEX hours (6.00 pm to 6.00 am Chicago time). The exchanges remained free, however, to employ open outcry from 6.00 am to 10.30 pm, or even after 10.30 pm if necessary to meet a competitive threat.

(6)   The JV agreed to offer the GLOBEX system to other exchanges on a fair basis that brought a flow of revenue to the JV and did not jeopardize the products of the CME and the CBT.

(7)   The members of each exchange would be allocated the profits from the transaction revenues generated by that exchange's products. Profits obtained by the JV that were generated from transactions in contracts of other participating exchanges would be shared equally between CBT and CME members. All operational costs would be divided in proportion to revenues, and until cumulative profits were generated, equally.

(8)   For the most part, only members of participating exchanges, and affiliates, parents and subsidiaries of such members, were to be given access to GLOBEX terminals. The CME did, however, continue its Institutional Access programme, and also created a so-called ETH (Electronic Trading Hours) programme, that allowed individuals and Commodity Trading Advisors access to GLOBEX terminals under specified circumstances.[57]

(9)   Reuters was to be paid a monthly transaction fee based on the volume of contracts traded through GLOBEX.

(10)   Reuters would not obtain any preferential treatment should it choose to act as a data vendor for information arising from the trading on GLOBEX.

(11)   The agreement would last 20 years, although each of the parties to the agreement would be allowed to terminate the agreement on certain grounds. There were many termination provisions. The JV or RFS could end the agreement if the system did not operate successfully, or if one of the other parties failed to perform its duties. The JV could terminate the contract: (i) if at any time after the first four years it sustained a recurring net operating loss, and if RFS did not agree to adjust the financial structure; or (ii) if at any time after the first four years, the JV notified RFS of a more efficient system and if the RFS failed or refused to match such a system within two years. RFS could terminate the agreement: (i) if at any time after the first four years it was unable to earn a commercially reasonable operating income, and if the JV did not wish to modify the financial terms; (ii) if the combined total of active GLOBEX terminals from both Chicago exchanges was less than 500 by a pre-specified date; or (iii) if the combined volume of contracts traded on GLOBEX by both Chicago exchanges was less than 50,000 per day during the three-month period beginning 18 months after the GLOBEX start.

GLOBEX started trading on 25 June 1992, with terminals in Chicago, New York, London, and Paris.[58] It reportedly cost Reuters $100 million to build.[59] Different strategies were employed to attract trading to the system, particularly by the

CME. The range of contracts listed on GLOBEX was progressively widened, to include the CME's major currency and interest rate products. The period for which GLOBEX operated was progressively lengthened, so that by November 1993, trading operated on a 'seamless' continuous basis from 2.30 pm to 6.00 am Chicago time on the CME for its currency products, and from 3.00 pm to 6.00 am Chicago time for its interest rate products. The GLOBEX fees of approximately $1 per trade were initially waived by the CME and Reuters, though not by the CBT. Market makers were given incentives to operate on GLOBEX in order to stimulate liquidity. Notwithstanding all these attempts, however, the volume of contracts traded on the system remained only a small percentage of the volume traded on the partner exchanges, and the system was not viewed as a success. The enthusiasm of the CME for GLOBEX was not mirrored at the CBT, which refrained from putting its most liquid contracts on to the system.

The GLOBEX JV talked to many exchanges about the possibility of their joining the system, including the AMEX, the Chicago Board Options Exchange (CBOE), the COMEX, the Coffee, Sugar and Cocoa Exchange, the Deutsche Terminbörse (DTB), LIFFE, the New York Cotton Exchange, the New York Futures Exchange, the NYMEX, the Sydney Futures Exchange (SFE), SIMEX, and the Tokyo International Financial Futures Exchange (TIFFE). Apart from MATIF, however, which established its link with GLOBEX prior to the establishment of the JV, no other exchanges joined the system. Trading in MATIF's contracts on GLOBEX started on 12 March 1993, and grew relatively rapidly so that by September 1993 MATIF volumes represented about 80% of the global contract volume on GLOBEX.[60] The very success of its contracts on GLOBEX, however, highlighted a major problem for MATIF: although it provided most of the revenues to GLOBEX, it had little control over how the system was run.

GLOBEX's discussions with LIFFE were complicated by the fact that LIFFE was interested both in linking with the CBT and in joining GLOBEX. The discussions were interdependent. In October 1992 the possibility of introducing a fungible link between LIFFE and the CBT, like that in operation between the CME and SIMEX, was raised.[61] It was intended that the CBT's ten-year T-note futures and options and LIFFE's Bund futures and options and BTP (Italian government bond) futures and options contracts could be traded on both exchanges through a mutual off-set arrangement.[62] These discussions were, however, abandoned in June 1993 for three reasons: first, LIFFE believed the prospective agreement was unbalanced, in that while it was prepared to put its high volume Bund contract on to the link, the CBT was not prepared to reciprocate by offering its high volume T-Bond contract; second, there was a fear that trading activity might move from London to Chicago, especially during overlap periods; finally, there was concern that there might be a 'migration of clearing business from LIFFE members, as North American clients sought to have business cleared in the US'.[63]

LIFFE's discussions with GLOBEX were similarly unsuccessful. LIFFE's preconditions for joining included that the trading of its products on GLOBEX should take place only outside the European trading day of 7.00 am to 7.00 pm, during which time LIFFE would have full control of its products. LIFFE insisted as well that it be allowed to continue using APT, but this conflicted with GLOBEX's previous policy.[64] Six other aspects of GLOBEX also proved problematical.[65] Most importantly, the CBT insisted on an exclusive right to list the Bund contract on GLOBEX, thus stopping LIFFE from listing its Bund contract, one of its most successful products, on the system.[66] MATIF similarly refused to withdraw its pre-emptive right to list ECU-related products on GLOBEX.[67] Second, Reuters wanted LIFFE to sign up for a long time, perhaps for a twelve-year period similar to MATIF, while LIFFE only wanted to join for one year. Third, the governance of GLOBEX continued to look unattractive to London. LIFFE's chief executive officer noted that 'GLOBEX is designed to attract business to Chicago. The people who run it, own it and control it, are the Merc [i.e. CME] and the Board of Trade [i.e. CBT]. Any non-Chicago exchange is going to think seriously about that. We don't particularly want to see our business going to Chicago.'[68] Fourth, there appeared to be a limited demand for after-hours or 24-hour trading.[69] Fifth, LIFFE believed that participation in GLOBEX would deny the exchange its 'preferred linkage strategy', which included negotiations with Japan's TIFFE. Finally there was a division between different members of LIFFE as to whether it should move to an automated trading system or remain an open-outcry market.[70]

LIFFE's decision whether to participate in GLOBEX was also dependent on the relationship between the CME and the CBT in GLOBEX, which in turn was dependent on the internal politics at both exchanges. Initially one person, Leo Melamed, was chairman of both the CME and the GLOBEX JV. This changed, however, when Jack Sandner became chairman of the CME. Friction between the two people arose as a result of a policy Sandner pursued.[71] Sandner reportedly demanded that all decisions by the JV board be referred back to both exchanges' boards before implementation. Melamed saw this as a recipe for disaster, believing that it effectively gave each exchange's chairman a veto on developments at GLOBEX, thereby reducing the power of the JV board. Sandner was also unhappy with allowing the CBT to pursue a mutual off-set link with LIFFE, while it continued to be part of GLOBEX; Melamed, in contrast, viewed this essentially as irrelevant. There were several arguments in favour of allowing the CBT to continue its planned mutual off-set agreement with LIFFE, including that the linkage would be hard to implement, that the CME already had a similar arrangement with SIMEX, and therefore could not reasonably ask the CBT not to undertake such an agreement, and that the successful participation of the CBT on GLOBEX would reduce the incentive it faced to create a link with LIFFE.

For its part, the CBT wanted to pursue the off-set link with LIFFE, and thus became progressively less willing to participate in GLOBEX the more this opportunity was blocked. The CBT's lack of commitment to GLOBEX, and the widely publicized disarray in the governance of GLOBEX, reduced LIFFE's incentive to join the system, given that a major reason for its doing so was precisely that GLOBEX was a system used by the two largest futures exchanges in the world. LIFFE therefore decided again not to participate in GLOBEX.

LIFFE's exit led to further friction between the partners in the Joint Venture Agreement. Reuters stated in a letter to the CBT that 'we believe the position on bund contracts you have taken with LIFFE is inconsistent with the GLOBEX agreement'.[72] The CBT replied that 'in considering the best interest of the GLOBEX system, the Board of Trade is not required to ignore its own best interests'. This tension was exacerbated in late 1993 by several other factors, all stemming essentially from the low volumes being executed on the system.[73] Reuters apparently made four demands of the CBT: first, that it immediately list its agricultural contracts on GLOBEX; second, that it refrain from marketing its Project A electronic trading system, a local area network it had developed for trade execution, at the expense of GLOBEX; third, that it retract disparaging remarks made by its chairman about GLOBEX; and fourth that it introduce a seamless trading session on GLOBEX, beginning at 2.30 pm Chicago time.[74]

Although the CBT was reported as making several differing responses to Reuters' demands, the nub of its policy appeared to be threefold: first, it refused to list its agricultural contracts on GLOBEX;[75] second, it stated it would not stop the development of its Project A; and third, it indicated that while it was willing to introduce seamless trading on GLOBEX, it would not do so in place of its existing evening trading session which was a substantial source of business for its main bond contracts.[76] Reuters then wrote another letter to the CBT asserting that as a result of its actions, the CBT has 'put the GLOBEX Joint Venture in breach of material obligations under the 1992 Agreement'.[77] The CBT's policy was not uncritically received in Chicago. Some exchange members attacked the CBT for being unwilling to broaden access to GLOBEX by other exchanges, believing that the CBT had not been 'acting in good faith', and that its strategy was being constrained by a 'cabal of guys in the grain pits operating on their own agenda'.[78] The CBT nevertheless withdrew from GLOBEX on 15 April 1994.

A new organizational structure was then established for the joint venture with the incorporation of the GLOBEX Corporation. The corporation's shareholders were the exchanges which used the GLOBEX trading system, and did not include Reuters, which as before simply provided services to the company. Associated with the corporation, it is believed that a new 'GLOBEX Consortium' was also established. This consortium was responsible for various activities: representing the interests of the shareholder exchanges in negotiations with potential new participants; joint marketing and international regulatory efforts, such as securing terminal access in particular countries; reaching decisions on the shareholder exchanges' positions with regard to technical uniformity and other system issues; negotiating such issues with Reuters; and the allocation of new products to Consortium members. Similar restrictions were placed on Consortium members as on previous exchange participants in GLOBEX. They were not allowed to introduce new contracts that were 'identical' to those already traded on the system, they had to guarantee a minimum trading volume, and they were not allowed to develop other linkages with other exchanges.

After two further years of attracting relatively small amounts of trading, the corporate structure of GLOBEX was changed yet again on 30 April 1996, at which time a new, and again unpublished, contract extending the joint venture for two years was signed. The intention this time was to make the trading system more of a 'utility' that could be accessed by a wider group of exchanges, but that was not controlled by any particular group of exchanges. The parties to the new contract were the CME, MATIF, and Reuters. Under the old contract, GLOBEX could only be used as an after-hours trading system, whereas under the new one it could be used all day. The fee schedule was also changed significantly. Under the new contract, there were no transaction fees, but each terminal user paid Reuters a monthly subscriber fee of $800 for access to either MATIF or CME contracts on his terminal, or $1,200 for access to both exchanges' contracts.[79] In addition, each exchange paid Reuters a flat annual fee for the right to have a pre-specified amount of 'capacity' on GLOBEX. This capacity was measured not only by the volume of the exchange's contracts traded on the system, but also by the number of the exchange's instruments that were traded on the system, and the extent to which the key stations, the network, and the host computers were used.

The new contract allowed an exchange two ways of accessing the trading system. Previously, if an exchange wanted to have its contracts traded on the system, it was required to join the GLOBEX Consortium. Under the new contract, while it was still allowed to do this if it so desired and if the other Consortium members assented to its joining, the new exchange could also simply use the system without joining the Consortium. Amongst the benefits of being in the Consortium were access to the 'GLOBEX Control Center' (GCC), and participation in joint marketing, legal, and regulatory initiatives. Any exchange using the trading system was required to have some form of control centre to undertake various duties, including 'permissioning' users, and setting the last settlement price. Thus if a new exchange did not join the Consortium, it was required to establish a control centre by itself.

The new contract also placed no restrictions either on what other automated trading systems or linkages any participating exchange was allowed to use, or on the exchanges to which Reuters was allowed to sell the system. There was still, however, a prohibition against identical contracts from different exchanges being traded on the same dedicated terminal. Identical contracts from different exchanges were, however, allowed to be traded on different terminals, and contracts from different exchanges were allowed to be traded on the same terminal as long as they were not identical. Although none of the joint venture agreements were ever released, it is believed that the 1996 contract was both simpler and less complete than the earlier ones.

On 24 January 1997, MATIF announced that it would adopt a new trading system, called Nouveau Système Cotation (NSC), developed and used by the Société des Bourses Françaises (SBF—the French stock exchange), to replace the GLOBEX system.[80] It was noted that the then current contract linking MATIF, the CME, and Reuters, was to end in April 1998. Like GLOBEX, NSC was to be used for transactions outside floor-trading hours and as a back-up system should open outcry sessions be interrupted. This announcement was effectively the public statement of the end of GLOBEX as it had previously been operating. On 13 February 1997 Reuters stated that it would stop providing the computer system for GLOBEX in 1998.[81] On 20 February 1997, the CME, NYMEX, MATIF, and the SBF, announced that they had signed a letter of intent saying that the American exchanges would adopt the NSC trading system in return for the Paris markets adopting the Clearing 21 system developed jointly by the CME and NYMEX.[82] Upon 'implementation' of the NSC system, the name GLOBEX would continue to be used to refer to the after-hours electronic trading system of the CME and MATIF. The name, however, would be the only part of the original system that remained.

European Linkages

The evolution of three linkages between various European futures exchanges is summarized in this section. They are respectively, a joint project by MATIF and DTB discussed between 1992 and 1996, a link between OM and OMLX, and a multilateral network proposed between various exchanges called the First European Exchange (FEX). Only the second of these projects was successfully implemented.

DTB/MATIF

A proposal to link the DTB and MATIF was agreed by the two exchanges before Christmas 1992, and formally announced on 29 July 1993.[83] The intention was to implement the project in several phases.[84] In stage one, initially intended to be completed by the middle of 1994, and actually started on 16 September 1994, DTB screens were to be installed at MATIF, giving MATIF members direct access to trade selected DTB products and to settle them via DTB clearing members. In stage two, initially intended to be completed by the middle of 1995, MATIF was to install its own host and trading software, bought from the DTB, and list two of its contracts on the system. Trading of these contracts using the open-outcry method would then be stopped, but access to these products would be restricted to MATIF members. In the third stage, initially intended to be achieved by the end of 1995, MATIF and DTB were to give their respective members reciprocal access to some of each other's contracts. Finally in the last stage, there would be joint product development between MATIF and DTB, with the possibility of both exchanges using the same market mechanisms, including that of fully automated clearing. It was anticipated that other exchanges might also be given access to the link.

The two exchanges were believed 'more complementary than competitive in nature' because of their complementary range of products, and their numerous structural parallels, such as the number and magnitude of their members, and the quality and financial strength of their clearing members.[85] The link had three main objectives: commercial, operational, and strategic. Commercially, the deal was aimed at giving members of the two exchanges direct access to each other's products, thus enlarging the spectrum of products in which they could trade. At the beginning, MATIF's members would have access to DTB's Deutschemark interest rate contracts, and DTB members would have access to MATIF's ECU contracts. Operationally, both markets would be equipped with the DTB electronic trading system. This would allow MATIF to buy into an electronic trading system which it controlled and thereby reduce pressure on its floor space, and also let the DTB sell a copy of the software it had developed, and thus share the investment it had made. Strategically, it was hoped that cooperation between the two exchanges would help attract the world's leading financial traders, and would improve the competitive position of both exchanges versus LIFFE. It was also believed that with over twenty different exchanges in Europe, there was a need to standardize systems in order to reduce costs. At a later date an exchange executive expanded on this, noting,

when monetary union occurs there will be a reduction in business and of the number of viable exchanges. By building a platform that incorporates a business and technical strategy, we will be able to offer a package with economies of scale when times get difficult.[86]

Initial agreement on the linkage was made relatively easy because the two exchanges were not in competition on technology, products or membership: they would share the technology investment; they traded different contracts; and only two of MATIF's more than 80 members were firms whose parent companies were German, while only four out of DTB's almost 90 firms had French origin. The MATIF chairman stated that the link would have no impact on MATIF's commitment to GLOBEX in that the DTB link would be used during the day, while GLOBEX would continue to be used at night.

Several factors militated against the success of the link. Some German traders remarked that they were not given access to the high-volume French contracts, while in contrast they had granted the French access to their high-volume contracts. In addition, the DTB amended its rules to allow foreign traders to have direct access to the exchange via terminals located outside Germany, thus reducing the need for any formal link between exchanges to obtain direct foreign participation. From the French point of view, there was much concern by the floor traders over the advisability of transferring their liquid 'notionnel' contracts on to an entirely automated system.[87] When LIFFE stated that it saw an opportunity to gain trading volume at the expense of MATIF in the contracts which were to be transferred completely from the open-outcry system to the electronic one, the chairman of MATIF retracted his previous statements and said that the choice by MATIF to link with the DTB was not a statement that it would stop using open-outcry.[88] He commented that MATIF was still investing in new trading pits, and that its commitment to both pit and electronic trading indicated the exchange's pragmatism, and was testimony to MATIF's success in that it could afford to invest in both.[89] He also said that the ultimate decision as to whether a contract would trade by open outcry or on the computerized link would remain with the users of the exchange.

The nature of the agreement between DTB and MATIF was significantly changed on 30 October 1995, when a letter of intent was signed between MATIF, DTB, SBF, and the Marché des Options Négociables de Paris (the French options market) for enlarged cooperation. Such cooperation was hoped to include the creation of a double Franco-German technology platform, based on the SBF's system for the cash markets and the DTB system for the derivatives markets. Deutsche Börse then put out a tender for a supplier to provide an electronic system for trading in the cash market in Germany, one of the bidders for which was SBF. When Deutsche Börse decided not to purchase the SBF's trading system, the linkage between DTB and MATIF was effectively abandoned.[90] Subsequent to its abandonment, however, a new joint venture between MATIF, MONEP, SBF, Deutsche Börse, and the Swiss Exchange, was proposed in 1997.[91]

OM/OMLX

The first exchange that OM Gruppen established was OM Stockholm, a futures and options market and clearing house based in Stockholm. In 1989, OM Gruppen launched another exchange based in London called OM London, the full name of which is now OMLX, the London Securities and Derivatives Exchange.[92] The contracts listed on both OM London and OM Stockholm were identical, and were traded via a linkage between the two exchanges. All orders submitted to both exchanges were placed on one central electronic order book, were ranked by the same priorities, and could match against each other. Clearing, however, was effected locally.

Both exchanges established a system of market makers to ensure liquidity in the contracts traded on their exchanges. Such market makers had an obligation to quote, continuously or upon request, firm bid and ask prices, with certain maximum spreads and minimum volumes, for the series of contracts for which they were responsible. Market makers were granted a discount on clearing fees. Although OM Stockholm and OMLX used the same technical systems, which made establishing the link between them technically relatively simple, and although the link was gauged a success in that there was 'a significant increase in turnover and better liquidity than the Swedish market alone could achieve', there were problems with its operation.[93]

Differences arose between participants on the two exchanges because of the divergent nature and customs of the markets in Sweden and the UK. The major members of OM Stockholm were universal banks, which sometimes transacted business between each other away from the exchange, and then used the exchange merely as a place to cross these orders. This practice angered the traders on OMLX, because it stopped them from having the chance to participate in these trades, and possibly to offer better prices than those agreed by one side of the already-completed transactions.

The customer bases of both markets were also quite different. In 1996, OM Stockholm had approximately 35,000 customers, while OMLX had about 500, and the traders on OMLX were almost all professionals, and market makers. Not only did this mean that the styles of trading in both markets differed, it also meant that OMLX received relatively low revenues compared to OM Stockholm, because the market makers had a relatively high share of London's trading, and their fees were substantially lower than for brokers' customer transactions. The perception of the success of OMLX and its trading link with OM, may therefore have been tempered by the view that OMLX had not been a major income generator.

FEX

The First European Exchange (FEX) was originally intended, when formed in 1992, to be a grouping between OM Stockholm, OMLX in London, the European Options Exchange (EOE) in Amsterdam, and the Swiss Options and Financial Futures Exchange (SOFFEX) in Switzerland.[94] The Österreichische Termin-und Optionenbörse (ÖTOB) in Austria later joined the group, via a bilateral agreement with SOFFEX.[95] The aim was to provide a vehicle whereby the distribution of each participating exchange's products could be enhanced by linking with other exchanges throughout Europe, and possibly also by establishing an intra-European clearing link. It was anticipated that such cooperation would give greater strength to its members together, than if they remained separate at a time of great exchange competition. Bilateral or multilateral cooperation agreements between exchanges were proposed in order to give access to contracts listed on one exchange to members of another, through a central order book maintained on each contract's domestic market.[96] This form of linkage was believed both superior to multiple listing which it was argued would fragment markets, and cheaper for an exchange than building its own electronic network or even opening a new exchange in new territory.[97] The added value to an exchange of distributing its products through a linkage was identified as:

Increased liquidity in own products distributed through other exchanges. Increased fee income from greater volume of trading. Low additional cost for introduction of new products (i.e. other exchanges' products). Increased membership fees (where applicable) due to new members being attracted by the growing product mix and growing liquidity of existing products. Increased service level to members by larger assortment of financial products.[98]

The added value to an exchange's membership of product distribution through a linkage was identified as:

Increased liquidity for distributed products. Single trading interface for own and distributed products. Single clearing arrangement for own and distributed products. Cheaper cost of execution. Cheaper clearing fees. Ability to give up costs of overseas memberships and correspondent relationships. Access to foreign exchanges without dependency on intermediaries.

The trading and clearing link between OMLX and EOE, launched on 29 January 1993, was the first and only FEX link to be made operational.[99] The link allowed members of EOE to trade on OMLX directly without going through an OMLX member, by trading on one of the OMLX automated trading screens placed on the floor of the EOE. Although OMLX members were also allowed to trade directly on the EOE, they still had to telephone orders to an EOE floor-broker, as the EOE did not have an electronic trading system, unlike the other potential participants in FEX.[100] The advantage to OMLX's members was that they could trade and clear EOE products without becoming a member of EOE. Clearing was to be carried out through a common member of the OMLX clearinghouse, and EOE's European Options Clearing Corporation subsidiary, the International Derivatives Clearing Corporation. Initially 5–7% of the turnover on OMLX came from the EOE, and this was viewed as 'new' business, given that there was no evidence before that business was coming from Amsterdam. The flow of business from London to Amsterdam over the link was, however, small. After operating for a couple of years, the OM/EOE element of FEX was discontinued.

The link between OMLX and the EOE was contentious in Amsterdam.[101] Some members of the EOE saw the exchange as aiming 'too low' in terms of its partners for the future, and preferred that it should ally itself with one of the bigger European exchanges, such as LIFFE or DTB. Other Dutch traders were concerned that the link would take away the commissions they had previously earned from foreign investors who, with the establishment of the link, would no longer need to go through a broker based in Amsterdam to trade on the EOE. This argument was refuted by an EOE director who believed that a system which required customers to pay two commissions, one to their domestic brokers and one to Dutch brokers, actually discouraged investors from trading on the EOE. Some brokers on the floor of the exchange also believed that FEX was an excuse for the EOE management to push through the creation of an automated system to replace the floor. In addition, the linkage appeared to conflict with the efforts of some of the larger member firms of the EOE which were clearing members of both exchanges, and which offered to clear customer business globally.

Neither the Swiss nor the Austrian ties in FEX were ever implemented. Although the Swiss link initially appeared to progress smoothly, SOFFEX decided in July 1993 to put its decision to join FEX on hold.[102] The reasons for this delay arose because at the same time as the proposed link between SOFFEX and OMLX was being developed, not only were the three regional Swiss stock exchanges in the process of creating a single electronic bourse, which was to be merged with SOFFEX, but also the legislation governing the financial markets was being reformed. Publicly, the SOFFEX board members stated that they were concerned that the futures exchange linkage was moving too fast for the stock exchange project, and that it would be appropriate to wait for the reform of the legislation before cementing any international linkages.

Other reasons for the delay were, however, suggested. Apparently prior to the merger of the stock exchanges, the then-existing big three Swiss banks had a dominant role in the futures market, but not in the cash market. They might have seen the reform of the cash market, and the linkage between the cash and the futures markets, as an opportunity to assert their dominance in the cash market. The banks may also have been concerned that an international link in the futures market might bleed away trading from Switzerland's stock market to London. Finally, it was indicated by some Swiss market participants that SOFFEX should have been looking to link with the DTB rather than OMLX, given both that the DTB system was originally based on a design bought from SOFFEX, and that DTB was viewed as a better potential ally than the FEX grouping. The Austrian link was not pursued probably because ÖTOB's members were wary of allowing the large UK firms into their small market, and because, from OMLX's point of view, there did not appear to be much demand for trading in Austrian products in the UK.

The NYMEX/COMEX Merger

On 3 August 1994, NYMEX merged with COMEX by buying all the equity interest in COMEX. Two aspects of the merger are described here: the offer which NYMEX made to COMEX, which was later accepted, and the arguments put forward both in favour of and against the proposed terms.

The Offer

Prior to the merger, NYMEX traded a range of energy and platinum-group metals futures and options contracts, while COMEX traded various gold, silver, and copper futures contracts, together with some other futures contracts based on aluminium and the Eurotop 100.[103] NYMEX's offer envisaged that COMEX would become a Division of NYMEX (to be called New COMEX), that the equity interests in COMEX would cease to exist, and that the voting members of COMEX, its Regular Members, would become COMEX Division Regular Members. The three main elements of the offer concerned the proposed trading rights of COMEX Regular Members after the merger, the payments that these members would receive for selling their exchange, and the governance rights that COMEX Division Members would have in the merged exchange.

NYMEX envisaged that COMEX Division Members would retain the right to trade the gold, silver, copper, and Eurotop 100 contracts, and also indicated it would take all reasonable steps to ensure that these contracts were traded on its automated trading system, ACCESS.[104] COMEX Division Members would also obtain certain other trading privileges, including: (i) the right to trade in all 'New Metals Contracts';[105] (ii) some non-transferable proprietary trading rights for 'New Products Contracts', where 'proprietary' meant that members were only allowed to take a position for their own books, and not on behalf of any customers;[106] (iii) proprietary trading rights in 'New Energy Contracts', if any were established, and in the platinum/palladium contracts;[107] (iv) proprietary trading rights on the floor of NYMEX, for a period of 5 years, in all contracts listed on NYMEX ACCESS; and finally (v) the right to trade on NYMEX ACCESS. Other participants in COMEX would retain trading privileges similar to those they held on COMEX, and also potentially the right to trade on NYMEX ACCESS in various contracts. NYMEX Division Members would also be given proprietary trading rights in the COMEX replacement contracts.

NYMEX proposed that a range of different types of cash payments be made to COMEX Regular Members. Immediately after the merger, an initial cash payment of $30 million (approximately $39,000 per Membership, assuming 768 memberships) would be paid proportionately to each member.[108] A deferred cash payment of $20 million plus interest, would be payable in instalments of $5 million each, plus interest, on the first four anniversaries of the merger. So-called 'ticker based' payments of up to $20 million, would be payable in instalments of up to $5 million, again on the first four anniversaries of the merger. The amount of the ticker based payments would depend on the extent to which the COMEX Division's revenues from the sale of its real time price data to customers exceeded $18 million. Given similar revenues in 1995 as in 1994, it was predicted that the ticker-based payments would be approximately $4 million, or $1 million a year. Should NYMEX make an initial public offering of shares in the exchange, each COMEX regular member would also receive an amount of $12,953 to give a total of $10 million. NYMEX was not allowed to issue any memberships on COMEX that would reduce the payments to be made to any COMEX Division Regular Members. On conclusion of the merger, NYMEX also agreed to make a special distribution of $21 million to its regular members, to give approximately $25,735 per membership.

The governance structure of NYMEX was to be reformed in a variety of ways following the merger. A Board of Directors for New COMEX would be estab-lished, in addition to the Board of Directors of NYMEX. COMEX Division Regular Members would not have the right to vote and participate in NYMEX's corporate governance, nor to receive dividends or distributions, nor to vote and participate in New COMEX's corporate governance (unless they were members of NYMEX). The New COMEX Division's Board of Directors would consist entirely of NYMEX designees, and initially would be the same as NYMEX's Board of Governors. A new COMEX Governors Committee would be established to represent COMEX Division Members, but it would act primarily in an advis-ory capacity. Initially this committee would consist of the Board of Governors of COMEX but within 90 days it would be reconstituted as a thirteen-member committee. Ten of its members would be elected by the COMEX Division Regular Members (one chairman, one representative from each of the trade group, the commission house group and the floor group, and six additional COMEX Division Regular Members). The remaining three would be appointed by the COMEX Governors Committee from the members of the NYMEX Division, at least two of whom had to be serving as Directors of NYMEX.

The New COMEX By-Laws and Rules could be amended by the Board of Directors of COMEX Division, except those subject to certain veto rights or special matters. These included any rules concerning the gold, silver, copper, or Eurotop futures and options contracts, and any trading privileges of

COMEX Division Members. Action with regard to these matters could be taken by the Board of New COMEX only with the consent of the COMEX Governors Committee. Even if the COMEX Governors Committee approved such rules, COMEX Division Regular Members had one further form of recourse against such actions. If holders of 20% or more of the COMEX Division Regular Members requested a special meeting to vote on such actions, and then voted against them by a majority of 66.66%, they could veto the proposed actions.

Debate

The NYMEX Board of Directors voted unanimously to recommend the merger proposals. Although the details of its deliberations were not released, the broad factors it considered were identified publicly. These included the nature of its business, the operations, financial condition, assets, liabilities, business strategy, and prospects of NYMEX, and the current state and prospects of the commodities and futures markets generally.[109] Various 'synergistic' advantages of combining the two exchanges were identified including: reduced costs for the exchanges achieved through economies of scale and elimination of duplicative operations; reduced costs for joint member firms through the possibility of combined or uniform systems, procedures and operations; reduced costs for market users due to greater market efficiency; a wider appeal of NYMEX ACCESS through the addition of the gold and silver contracts; a greater global presence; an increased flexibility in its decision to relocate its premises; and a potential increase in NYMEX's institutional profitability from ticker and other revenues, a potentially important factor were the combined exchange to consider converting itself to a for-profit status corporation.

The COMEX board voted in favour of recommending the merger by a margin of 18 to 6. Of these votes, the independent governors were in favour of the merger by a margin of 8 to 2. Eleven reasons were put forward publicly for why the Board supported the merger:

i) the Merger Consideration [i.e. the various payments made by NYMEX to COMEX Regular Members] is fair to the COMEX Regular Members;

ii) the combined trading products and resources of COMEX and NYMEX would result in a financially stronger and more stable exchange than if COMEX remained independent;

iii) the Merger will ensure that COMEX Regular Members retain their existing trading rights, enable them to continue to trade on a preeminent exchange, and provide them with certain, significant additional trading rights;

iv) the rights of COMEX Division Regular Members are sufficiently protected since the most important New COMEX Rules and New COMEX By-Laws cannot be changed without the consent of at least a majority of either the COMEX Governors Committee or the COMEX Division Regular Members;

v) COMEX Division Regular Members will have input into the operations which affect COMEX Division Regular Members' interests through their guaranteed representation on certain NYMEX committees;

vi) the required funding of the COMEX MRRP for a specified period of time is beneficial to many COMEX Division Regular Members and offers greater protection than is available under the current MRRP;[110]

vii) the combination of the financial resources of NYMEX and COMEX will encourage greater efforts at marketing and new product development than can currently be undertaken by COMEX alone, and thus, may lead to increased participation in products currently traded on COMEX and lead to the introduction of trading in new products in which COMEX Divisions Regular Members will have trading privileges;

viii) [the] combination of the two exchanges increases the possibility that all of the New York commodities exchanges and clearinghouses will merge and move together to a new facility, which could provide economies of scale and, therefore, reduce the operating costs of Futures Commission Merchants doing business on all of these exchanges and the costs to customers, which, in turn, would enhance the competitive position of the COMEX Division products internationally;

ix) a combined exchange will have greater resources to effect policy changes on regulatory issues than either constituent exchange;

x) the combined exchange will have greater standing on a world-wide basis; and

xi) the adequacy of the limitations on NYMEX's ability to change COMEX's existing culture and trading environment, which are critical to COMEX's ability to remain the world's most active precious metals market.[111]

The governors who voted against recommending the merger did so for one or more of the following reasons:

i) a belief that the Merger Consideration is inadequate relative to the COMEX's current earnings and projected future earnings;

ii) a belief that remaining an independent exchange could deliver greater value to COMEX Regular Members through the development of new revenue streams and the distribution to COMEX Regular Members of income derived from both these new sources and existing revenue streams, which, in turn, could result in enhanced seat values while enabling COMEX Regular Members to retain all of their existing rights and privileges;

iii) a belief that the Merger does not offer COMEX Regular Members sufficient additional trading privileges and that, in the future, NYMEX will place the highest priority on developing New Energy Contracts, which offer COMEX Regular Members no business (i.e. brokerage) opportunities and only short-term Proprietary Trading opportunities.

iv) a belief that the rights of individuals owning only COMEX Division Regular Memberships ('COMEX-only' Regular Members) are not adequately protected after the Merger. The Merger Agreement permits amendments of New COMEX By-Laws and Term Sheet Rules to be made by majority vote of the COMEX Governors Committee, even if six of the ten members of the COMEX Governors Committee elected by the COMEX Regular Members—a majority of the COMEX-elected Governors—oppose the amendment, so long as the three NYMEX representatives and four of the COMEX Division representatives on the Committee support the change. Moreover, since the Merger Agreement requires representation of the Trade and Commission House Groups on the Committee, it is possible that at least two of the ten COMEX Division representatives on the COMEX Governors Committee will be dual members (i.e. individuals owning both a COMEX Division Membership and a NYMEX Division Membership), who may have interests which are divided between the COMEX Division and the NYMEX Division; . . .[112]

v) a belief that COMEX Division Regular Members will be unable to influence NYMEX's decisionmaking process or require the NYMEX Board to address issues affecting COMEX Division Regular Members, since they would not have petition rights or Board representation; and

vi) ... [a concern] about the lack of any express protections for COMEX Division Regular Members concerning the selection and development of new trading technologies for use on the COMEX Division and how the cost of developing or acquiring these technologies will be financed.

Various other arguments against the merger were also informally put forward, the most important of which was that COMEX should look for a larger partner exchange than NYMEX.[113]

CONCLUSION

Various case studies of cooperation between exchanges are presented in this chapter. In the first section, a range of market linkages and joint ventures proposed and undertaken by various stock exchanges are described. These include: various European projects—IDIS, Euroquote, and Eurolist; three American–Canadian order routing linkages—between the AMEX and the TSE, the MSE and the TSE, and the BSE and ME; and two Anglo-American projects— between the PHLX and the LSE, and the NASD and the LSE. In the second section, several cooperative schemes pursued by diverse futures exchanges are discussed. These include: the mutual-offset link between the CME and SIMEX; GLOBEX; three European linkages—between DTB and MATIF, between OM and OMLX, and the FEX proposal; and finally the merger between NYMEX and COMEX.

6

Information

The publication of price and quote information is a pivotal component of all exchanges' operational strategies. The determination of the optimal policy an exchange should adopt is, however, both complex and controversial. A range of questions must be answered, including: What types of price and quote information should the exchange release, when, and to whom? What rights should it claim in the data it publishes? and, What pricing policy should it employ for the sale of these data?[1] The factors influencing how, and the manner in which, different exchanges have addressed these issues are examined in this chapter.

Some terminological clarification is necessary before beginning. A 'quote' or an 'order' is an indication of a willingness to deal on the part of a market participant.[2] Each quote typically contains information about the price and size at which a market participant is willing to deal in the future, either on the bid side of the market for a bid quote, or on the offered side for an ask quote. Information relating to transactions or trades relates to orders that have already been executed. Although historically the term 'quotes' used to refer both to the bid and offer prices in a market and to the prices of executed trades, it is used here only to denote the prices of unexecuted orders. The term 'transparency' is used here generically to refer to the extent to which information about prices and quotes is publicly disseminated. Sometimes it is used to refer specifically to whether information about the prices and quantities of trades are published immediately after they have been respectively submitted to, or executed on, the relevant market. The 'reporting' of trade information refers to the act of reporting it to the relevant regulatory authorities. Reported information may or may not be published subsequent to having been reported. In the USA, the phrase 'last-sale reporting' has been used to refer to the situation where the prices and quantities of trades are published immediately.

The chapter is composed of three sections. In the first, the determinants and nature of an exchange's information dissemination policy are examined. In the second, the rights that exchanges have claimed over the data they publish in a world of 'closed systems' technology are surveyed. In the third, the initial development of a new business and contractual model for the dissemination of data in an 'open systems' environment is described.

DETERMINANTS AND NATURE OF INFORMATION DISSEMINATION

The information dissemination policy an exchange chooses to adopt is dependent on several main factors, including most importantly the market architecture of the exchange, the competition for the orders flowing to the exchange, and the governance structure of the exchange. The significance of these, and a group of other miscellaneous, factors is explored here in turn. One important determinant of exchanges' dissemination policies, namely the 'symbology' problem, is ignored.[3]

Market Architecture

The choice by an exchange of what price and quote information to release is a central element of the wider decision as to what market architecture to adopt. Not only are there substantial differences between the types of data about prices and quotes that trading systems choose to release, there are also differences in the types of information that trading systems are able to deliver. Amongst the data that may be disseminated are:[4]

(1) price of last trade;

(2) quantity of last trade;

(3) time of last trade;

(4) identities of parties to last trade;

(5) high, low, opening, and closing, trade prices;

(6) aggregate price data and price indices;

(7) cumulative trade volume;

(8) best bid and ask prices;

(9) quantities at best bid and ask prices;

(10) identities of parties who placed those orders;

(11) bid and ask prices behind the best prices;

(12) quantities at those prices;

(13) identities of parties who placed those orders;

(14) high, low, opening, and closing, mid-quote prices;

(15) requests for quotes;

(16) identities of parties who requested quotes;

(17) number of individuals logged onto system;

(18) identities of those individuals.

In no trading system are all these categories of price and quote information published. Indeed, the strategic non-disclosure of some types of price and quote information is a central element of all market architectures. For some of the information categories, the reason is a matter of confidentiality. In most markets, for example, investors are unwilling to countenance releasing information about what their trading policies have been or will be. The identities of market participants submitting quotes and participating in trades are therefore normally not publicly released. Sometimes, however, identities are concealed for commercial reasons. For example, although the identities of traders on Instinet were initially released, Instinet later decided against allowing this.[5] By releasing the identities of the counter-parties willing to trade on its system, market participants were able to advertise their trading interest on Instinet, but conduct their business off Instinet thus avoiding the payment of commissions. In order to stop this, Instinet required traders to maintain anonymity on its system.

Some trading systems, such as POSIT, allow the practice of 'sunshine' trading, whereby traders on the system are offered the choice to release information about the trades they want to undertake, what type of trader they are, and in some instances, their identities.[6] A trader may wish to do this both to attract the other side of the trade, and to convince other market participants that he does not have any inside knowledge about the stocks in which he wants to trade. By releasing information about his identity, the trader hopes to lower his costs of trading by not having to pay a premium either for immediacy, or for the possibility that he might be an informed trader.

Many electronic trading mechanisms allow different types of trading information to be concealed, for example by permitting the input of hidden orders, as on the AZX.[7] Increased transparency may reduce market participants' willingness to submit orders to a trading system. Some institutional investors choose not to reveal much information about their orders, because they believe that doing so makes execution of their orders more difficult, by 'moving the market' against their intentions. In a similar manner, many market makers claim that immediate disclosure of any trades they undertake is likely to mean that other market participants will act in a manner costly for market makers, and ultimately for the market. If, for example, a market-maker sale is reported, investors may want to buy more stock because they believe somebody has some good information about the stock, and this will make it more expensive for the market maker to cover his initial sale. Market makers may thus widen their bid–ask spreads in more transparent markets to avoid being 'picked off'. A discussion of the effects of transparency on market performance is presented in Chapter 10.

Competition

There is a conflict at the heart of the question of how much price and quote information an exchange will choose to release. On the one hand, an exchange must disseminate some price and quote information in order to attract trading.[8] Not to do so would make it hard to attract order-flow, given that market participants will not normally send their orders to a trading arena without some knowledge of the quotes and prices on the exchange. On the other hand, the very dissemination of such information makes off-exchange trading easier. There are two main incentives for trading off an exchange: to avoid the charges associated with trading on the exchange, and to escape any exchange rules that might hinder the execution of trades. If an exchange is providing pricing information, there will also be no need for a market participant trading off the exchange to incur the burden of establishing its own system to generate this information. If a trading system is relatively opaque, it gives traders who use it an informational advantage over those who do not. Traders on its system will be able to see its data plus those available from other markets, whereas traders not using its system will not have access to its data.[9]

Off-exchange trading reduces the transaction fees that the exchange receives, and may also decrease the value of the data which the exchange sells, if alternative sources of data about the trading in the relevant assets become available. Competition by alternative trading systems will, however, affect an exchange's attempt to exploit the demand for its information to a lesser extent than it will affect the other two elements of its market architecture, namely its order routing and order execution facilities. While many new trading systems have been established to compete with existing exchanges, it is hard to find a new trading system that has ousted an already-operating exchange from being the primary source of price and quote information about the assets traded on the exchange.[10] Most such dealing systems price their trading passively in a derivative manner off the first exchange's pricing mechanism.[11] This means that an exchange is likely to be able to exploit the demand for its information to some extent, even if new execution facilities compete for the trading in the assets dealt on the exchange.

The establishment of alternative trading mechanisms to an exchange is relatively easy if the exchange is required to disseminate full details of the prices and quotes arising on its trading system. In both the USA and the UK, for example, quote-matching systems have been established, such as Madoff Securities and TRADE, on which the quotes originating on the primary market for a particular security, the NYSE and the LSE respectively, are used as the basis for automatic execution of small trades.[12] Typically a market maker agrees to purchase a flow of orders from a broker in return for paying the broker a commission. He then guarantees to execute any orders submitted to him at the best publicly disseminated bid and ask quotes, and sometimes at better prices. There are two main attractions to the market maker of doing this. First, the traders submitting orders to him are unlikely to be more informed than him. Second, the risks of taking on a particular position are low, both because of the small size of each trade, and because of the high likelihood of receiving a balancing order on the other side of the market in a relatively short period. The advantage to a client of allowing his order to be executed on such a system is that he is guaranteed an execution, and is able to queue-jump any secondary exchange priorities that may hinder the execution of his order. Such trading systems may be operated both by members of the primary exchange and by non-members.

Governance

There are two areas concerning the dissemination of price and quote information in which the governance structure of an exchange critically influences the decisions made by the exchange: access to the exchange's quotes and prices, and the level of fees charged by the exchange for the information. A few instances of how different governance structures can affect these issues are now provided.

The release of price and quote information is a key determinant of who is relatively better informed in a market, and this in turn influences market participants' profits. A membership-governed exchange will in most instances be unwilling to publish information so as to disadvantage its members. The LSE, for example, has historically been loath to release information about executed trades, in the belief that were it to do so, the trading positions of its market-making members would be jeopardized, and liquidity on the exchange would suffer accordingly. Similarly, the NYSE does not disseminate the full information about all the orders on the specialists' books, in the belief that to do so might undermine the specialists' ability to undertake their affirmative market-enhancing duties.[13] It is true that the effects of these different aspects of pre- and post-trade transparency differ (as discussed in Chapter 10), and also that investors associated with the trades on the LSE and with the orders on the NYSE may prefer that the relevant information not be publicly released. The importance of the LSE's and the NYSE's positions in this context, however, is that both exchanges argue that what is good for their members is also good for their markets. It is not the validity of these statements that is at issue here. Rather, it is the explicit recognition by the exchanges that they seek to protect their members' interests in the decisions that they take.

Sometimes the nature of an exchange's membership may make it difficult for an exchange to reach a consensus on its policy towards the dissemination of its information. This is particularly evident when the individual members of the exchange have internally conflicting interests. One instance of this was the response of LIFFE to the question of what level of transparency should obtain on the London Stock Exchange. LIFFE publicly adopted a pro-transparency approach.[14] Many members of LIFFE were, however, also members of the London Stock Exchange. As derivatives traders they wanted as much transparency as possible on the underlying cash market, but as market makers on the stock exchange they wanted to restrict such transparency in order to protect their cash positions.

Each ownership group at an exchange will attempt to minimize the particular fees that it is required to pay, and the power that the governance structure of the exchange allots each group will therefore influence the level of fees demanded. One typical result of this is that an exchange may charge different prices to its members than it does to non-members. In particular prices and quotes may be provided free to members as part of an exchange's automated trading system, while non-members may be charged.

Whether an exchange is owned by its members or not may also affect how it charges for its information in a different way. Consider the following analysis. Suppose there are two for-profit exchanges operating in identical environments with different governance structures. The first is owned and operated by a group of investors who have the sole aim of maximizing their profits. The second is owned and operated by its members, and has the aim of maximizing their profits.

Suppose also that no competition to either exchange is allowed, so that all trading must be carried out on the exchange in each environment, and that all profits at each exchange come from the sale of price and quote information and from the sale of trading services. The first exchange will seek to maximize the sum of profits from the sale of information and from the sale of trading services. The second will seek to maximize this sum plus the total profits received by its members, assuming that all profits earned by the exchange are distributed back to the members.

Assume each exchange has two key policy variables: the price for information and the price for trading services. The first exchange will evaluate the profits it receives from both information and trading services, and will choose a profit-maximizing balance between the two. This balance will take account of the fact that there may be cross-elasticity effects between the demands for information and for trading services. For example, the more information sold, the more likely market participants are to want to trade. Similarly, the more trading undertaken on the exchange, the more valuable the information emanating from the exchange will be.

The membership-owned exchange is likely to choose a different price for each service than the non-membership-owned exchange because, in general, the price constellation that maximizes the profits obtainable solely from information and trading services sales, will not equal the price constellation that maximizes this sum plus the profits earned by the exchange's members. Typically the membership-owned exchange will be likely to sacrifice some of its direct profits, by charging a lower amount for both its information and trading service sales than the non-membership-owned exchange. By doing so the exchange is likely to be able to increase the profits of its members by a larger amount than it would lose by not choosing the prices that maximize the sum of its profits from trading and information sales. This would not only have the direct effect of reducing members' information costs, it would also indirectly increase the level of trading, due to the wider dissemination of the exchange's information.

The extent to which the members of an exchange form a large subset of the market participants who wish to receive its price and quote information and to use its trading facilities, may also affect the membership-owned exchange's pricing decisions. Suppose that all members of the exchange were on the floor of the exchange, and therefore had no need to buy any price and quote information, as they could see it all directly. The membership-owned exchange might then seek to charge a higher price for its information, which would be paid by non-members, and a lower price for trading services, which would be paid by members, than would the non-membership-owned exchange.

A theoretical model of how an exchange may decide to charge for the information it releases is presented in Bronfman and Overdahl (1992). They assume that an exchange acts as a member-owned cooperative, and thus maximizes the expected sum of the profits earned both by its members, who are financial intermediaries, and by itself. The profits of intermediaries are assumed to be the average bid–ask spread on the market times the volume transacted on the market. The revenues of the exchange are assumed to be the sum of the transaction fee charged to members per trade times the volume transacted on the market, plus the per-transaction revenue earned from information production and distribution times the volume transacted on the market. The costs of the exchange are assumed to be a variable per transaction cost and a fixed cost.

The width of the spread is assumed to be such that each member covers his costs and makes a competitive rate of return. It is also assumed that the volume traded on the exchange is a function of the spread, that the spread on the exchange is a function of the volume traded, that the competitive rate of return earned by a member is a function of the volume traded, and that the per-transaction revenue earned on information sales is dependent on the expected level of trading.

Bronfman and Overdahl argue that if the per-transaction information charge is fixed, any increase in the fixed or variable costs of the exchange must be counterbalanced either by an increase in the spread or by a decrease in the returns earned by intermediaries. Such a decrease in returns will reduce the willingness of intermediaries to participate in the market, thereby also reducing the liquidity in the market. They further argue that if an exchange were able to contract with other exchanges for the provision of its information, then any reduction in fees it suffered as a result of losing transactions to the competing systems could be compensated for, at least in part, by an appropriate fee structure for the information provided to the relevant competing systems. It is questionable, however, whether such a policy would be sustainable in the long run. The more successful a competing trading system became, the more likely it would be to oust the original exchange as the primary source of information about the trading in the relevant assets.

Miscellaneous Factors

The decision as to how an exchange charges for its price and quote data and what proportion of its income an exchange seeks to obtain from information sales, is typically dependent on a range of factors, including the nature and size of its other sources of income, the costs which the exchange faces, and the nature of the demand for its information. Exchanges do not necessarily seek to maximize the amount of revenue that they receive from the dissemination of their price and quote data. On the contrary, they typically see the information decision as part of the larger strategic question of how they want to position themselves competitively.

A brief examination of various exchanges' strategies, including a survey of seventeen exchanges' practices in 1996, suggests several stylized facts concerning their information sale policies.[15] First, the sale of price and quote information is a significant source of revenue for many exchanges, with the average proportion of total income arising from information sales at the surveyed exchanges being 21%. Second, in many instances it is the largest source of revenue at an exchange. Third, there is a wide disparity across exchanges in the proportion of total income arising from information sales. In 1996, for example, this proportion was 0% at the Warsaw Stock Exchange, 1% at the Sao Paulo Stock Exchange, 2% at the OM Group, 2% at the Stock Exchange of Singapore, 10% at the SSE, 12% at LIFFE, 14% at the Stock Exchange of Hong Kong, 15% at the NYSE, 15% at the New Zealand Stock Exchange, 22% at the CME, 29% at NYMEX, 30% at the CBT, 32% at the LSE, 35% at the Tel Aviv Stock Exchange, 43% at the American Stock Exchange, 45% at the Winnipeg Commodity Exchange, and 57% at the Santiago Stock Exchange.[16] These levels do not appear to be correlated with the size of the exchange, however this is measured, with the nature of the items traded on the exchange, or with the jurisdiction in which the exchange operates.

The proportion of revenues received from information sales at any particular exchange may also change over time. Bronfman and Overdahl (1992) note that over the period from 1968 to 1981, the CME received less than 5% of its total revenues from information sales.[17] By 1982, this figure had risen to above 10%, and by 1989 it broke 20%. Since then it has stayed relatively constant at this level. This trend matched a period of sharp internal growth at the exchange, and also a period in which the dissemination of price and quote data was revolutionized by the emergence of new communications and computer technology. There are other exchanges, however, that have also been subject to similar factors, but for which the proportion of revenues arising from information sales has not changed in the same manner.

There are three main criteria by which market participants informally determine the value of a set of price and quote data disseminated by an exchange. The first is the contents of the data themselves. The more types of information that are released, the higher the value that will be placed on the exchange's information. The second is the timeliness of the information. In most circumstances, the faster the information is disseminated the more valuable it is. The third major determinant is the extent to which the exchange's data are thought to reflect accurately the market for the assets in question. This will be dependent upon the absolute amount of trading undertaken on the exchange, the amount of trading undertaken on the exchange relative to the total amount executed elsewhere, and the extent to which the exchange contributes to the price discovery mechanism. The larger both these absolute and relative amounts, the higher the value that will be placed on the data.

CLOSED SYSTEMS CONTRACTS

An exchange will seek to claim as many property rights as possible over the price and quote data it disseminates, in order to protect both its authority to choose what types of information it publishes, and the value of this information as a source of revenue. This section aims to identify and describe those rights claimed by exchanges that most directly affect the structure and development of their markets.[18]

There are three basic types of contracts employed to govern the flow of data disseminated by exchanges: those that operate between an exchange and a vendor, those that operate between an exchange and an end-user, and those that operate between a vendor and an end-user. Contracts between exchanges and vendors are referred to here as 'vendor contracts'. Some of the exchanges which distribute their data only to vendors, and all exchanges which sell directly to end-users, require such participants also to sign a contract directly with the relevant exchange. These contracts are referred here to as 'exchange-subscriber' agreements. Finally, vendors require that their customers sign a contractual agreement with the vendors themselves. These contracts are referred to here as 'vendor-subscriber' agreements. Attention is focused on vendor contracts. These contracts are, however, mostly similar to the other two types of contracts.

A comparison between the contractual rights claimed by different exchanges is difficult for many reasons. First, it is hard to analyse the importance of selected rights and obligations in a vendor contract, without evaluating the nature of the full contract. Second, the terminology employed in different contracts is not standardized. Third, in any jurisdiction, a contract for the provision of information may be subject to a range of conflicting branches of law. Fourth, the supply of market data typically crosses national jurisdictions, the laws of which may vary and also may conflict. Fifth, although English is the international language of business, the language of record of many contracts is not English. Notwithstanding these problems, however, it is notable that many of the key rights claimed in various vendor contracts that affect the structure and development of markets, appear to transcend specific contractual, national, and indeed temporal, boundaries.

The property rights that exchanges claim with regard to the price and quote information they disseminate are dependent on the nature of the available technology. Contracts are thus continuously being revised in an attempt to keep pace with new technological developments. For an extended period up until relatively recently, the technological model which all vendor contracts implicitly embraced was that of a 'closed systems' world. Under such a model, it was believed that there was an identifiable source and an identifiable end-point for the flow of price and quote information. The source was seen as the relevant exchange. End-users were thought to be investors or financial intermediaries. The key assumption underlying the technological model was that information was transmitted from the source down a wire to a terminal at the end-user's location, either directly or via intermediary institutions, and that once at the end-user, it was not possible to re-distribute the information electronically. Although the perceived technological model for the dissemination of information is currently changing so as to embrace the widespread adoption of open systems technology, as discussed below, the various contracts examined here all assume a closed systems technology.

The section is composed of six parts. Contracts from twenty-five commodities, futures, options, and stock exchanges from around the world are surveyed in order to assess different exchanges' approaches to six topics relevant to the structure and development of markets.[19] The topics are classified under the following categories:

definitions, copyright and the redistribution of data, confidentiality, pricing strategies, trading restrictions, and discrimination. Other contractual issues that do not
influence the structure and development of exchanges and markets are ignored,
including those concerning jurisdiction, indemnification of licensees versus third
party claims, exclusion of liability for data, programme licences, indemnities,
warranties concerning quality of data, and suppliers' warranties concerning performance of the services they provide.[20]

Definitions

The terminology used in vendor contracts varies considerably. Furthermore, even
when the words are the same, they do not always refer to the same things.
Consider, first, the terminology used to denote the participants in the data industry. Organizations which buy data and then re-sell them, are variously called 'data
vendors', 'distributors', 'information providers', 'licensees', 'quote vendors',
'redistributors', 'subscribers', 'vendors', and 'wholesalers'. Organizations which
buy data and then do not re-sell them, are variously called 'customers', 'clients',
'end-users', 'purchasers', 'recipients', 'subscribers', and 'users'.

A distinction is normally made between 'real-time' or 'live' data on the one
hand, and 'historical' data on the other. The phrase 'real-time' is essentially used to
denote data which are available for viewing immediately after being created.
Historical data, in contrast, may only be viewed after a period of delay. The sale of
historical data is mostly ignored here for two reasons. First, for most exchanges the
revenues from real-time data are significantly greater than those from historical
data, which in many instances have to date actually been set at zero.[21] Second, the
dissemination of historical data does not affect the extent to which trades are undertaken on or off a particular exchange, given that all the information they provide is
historical, which by definition yields no indication of the prices at which trades
may *currently* be executed. Some markets define all data about transactions as
'historical', even if published immediately, given that the transactions are already
completed by the time the data about them are disseminated. According to this view
only quote data can be called 'real-time'. Other markets have different definitions
of what constitutes 'historical' data, with different delays being applied.

Copyright and Redistribution

Attempts by an exchange to enforce contracts governing the sale of its information are likely to be productive only to the extent that the exchange can monitor
its co-contractants' actions. If an exchange has a large number of end-users
receiving data world-wide, ensuring that its contractual provisions are being
complied with is difficult. Furthermore, it may be the case that many end-users
of the exchange's data have no privity of contract with the exchange, because
they are at the end of a long chain in the data dissemination process. In the
absence of privity of contract, reliance by an exchange on the law of contract to
enforce the substance of its vendor or subscriber contracts on these remote market

participants will then be impossible. It is for this reason that exchanges almost always attempt to claim rights which extend beyond privity of contract. One critical such right is that of copyright, which is a right versus 'all the world'.

The central element of all vendor contracts is a requirement by the exchange distributing its price and quote data that forbids the unauthorized redistribution of these data.[22] Most exchanges do not 'sell' their data to vendors, but rather grant the vendors a 'licence' to distribute the data to the vendors' clients. Such a licence normally allows vendors to redistribute the data to end-users, while stating that the exchange still reserves property rights in the data. The most important of these is that the vendors' clients are not allowed to redistribute the data to other market participants, or, if they do wish to do so, are themselves required to sign a vendor contract with the exchange. In an attempt to prevent unauthorized redistribution occurring, not only are vendors obliged to assure the exchanges that their clients do not redistribute data, but frequently those clients also are required in their subscriber contracts to confirm this directly with the exchange. Vendors are normally also required to ensure that they do not employ data for any purpose other than the maintenance, development, control, and demonstration of their databanks. If a vendor does use data for other purposes, it is typically required in addition to sign a subscriber agreement.

Some exchanges specify in great detail what vendors and end-users may do with the data they receive. The Tokyo Stock Exchange, for example, insists that vendors deliver its data to their clients on a terminal, and not via an electronic datafeed from which redistribution is relatively easy.[23] In addition, vendors are prohibited from acting as wholesalers to other vendors. The NYSE allows professional end-users, such as registered broker-dealers or investment advisers, to furnish limited amounts of market data to their customers, clients, and branch offices in the regular course of their securities business.[24]

There are two central aspects of price and quote data over which exchanges assert property rights: the actual contents of the data, and the manner in which they are presented. Although almost all exchanges claim copyright and other property rights in the data which they generate and sell, there are subtle differences in the contractual provisions to which they require vendors to agree. The Société des Bourses Françaises states that it is the 'owner' of the stock exchange data bank,[25] because it is its 'creator and author' as per the law in France.[26] Similarly, the Hong Kong Stock Exchange requires data vendors to acknowledge that they have 'no entitlement to any proprietary rights including rights of copyright in and to the Information or the presentation of the Information, which rights are owned by the Exchange'.[27] The Brussels Stock Exchange requires its subscribers to acknowledge its 'exclusive ownership . . . over all data relating to assets quoted on the Brussels Stock Exchange', implying that data about the assets quoted on the exchange, even if they derive from trading off the exchange, are the property of the exchange.[28] The London Stock Exchange requires its subscribers to acknowledge that 'any copyright or other intellectual property rights of whatever nature which subsist or may subsist in the presentation of the information comprised in the Service or in the Information itself . . . shall remain the property of Exchange absolutely'.[29] This formulation does not unequivocally state that there are any copyright or other intellectual property rights which subsist in the data and their presentation.

There is less uniformity across exchanges concerning the property rights they assert over the presentation of their data. The London Stock Exchange does not allow a data vendor to 'display composite Pages made up of Information from different parts of the Service, or mix Information with data supplied by third parties, except with the Exchange's prior written consent'.[30] Furthermore, 'quotations from non registered market makers may not be mixed with SEAQ market maker prices'.[31] The Stockholm Stock Exchange requires that it 'be set out as the source of the Information on dissemination thereof. Should the Information be disseminated in processed form, those responsible for such processing shall be set out in conjunction with presentation of such information'.[32] The NASD allows vendors to change the display format without prior approval, provided that 'such change is not misleading to Subscribers', and that the vendor 'notify NASDAQ, describing such change in reasonable detail'.[33] The Amsterdam Stock Exchange 'recognizes the (prospective) proprietary rights of Data-vendor[s] with respect to adaptations carried out as a result of upgrading or any other actions performed by the Data-vendor[s]'.[34] The possibility that vendors might therefore modify the data, and by doing so obtain some property rights in them, is therefore explicitly admitted.

Confidentiality

Many exchanges seek to impose an obligation of confidentiality on the purchasers of their data so as to constrain them from being able to disclose the data without the exchanges' permission. The Hong Kong Stock Exchange, for example, specifies that the 'Licensee shall at all times treat the [price and quote] Information and any information ancillary thereto obtained . . . as confidential and shall not disclose such Information to any third party other than to a Subscriber [i.e. one of the vendor's duly recognized clients], irrespective of whether it is in the same format as supplied to Licensee by the Exchange'.[35]

Some exchanges attempt to impose this obligation of confidentiality also on to the end-users of their data, by requiring that an appropriate clause be inserted either into a subscriber agreement the end-user is obliged to sign with the exchange, or into the contract the subscriber signs with the vendor from whom it receives the exchange's data. LIFFE, for example, requires all subscribers who receive its data from a vendor via a digital feed to sign a subscriber agreement directly with itself. This agreement requires the subscriber to undertake that 'during the term of the Agreement and thereafter it will keep confidential and save as expressly provided in this Agreement will not without the prior written consent of LIFFE disclose to any third party any and all information of a confidential nature (including without limitation the Outgoing Market Ticker [i.e. the electronic signal containing the exchange's information]) which may become known from LIFFE'.[36]

Some exchanges note the circumstances when the obligation of confidentiality lapses. LIFFE, for example, states that a party receiving any confidential data from the exchange shall not be required to keep it confidential if 'such information is public knowledge or already known to such party at the time of disclosure or subsequently becomes public knowledge other than by breach of this Agreement or subsequently comes lawfully into the possession of such party from a third party'.[37] Although no examples were found in the contracts examined, it is believed that some exchanges specify the time limit for which a duty of confidentiality should hold.

Trading Restrictions

Three instances were found of exchanges restricting the trading uses to which the data they sell may be put. The Stockholm Stock Exchange states that all clients are 'entitled to process the Information to the extent that such processing is not harmful to the Stock Exchange'.[38] In particular, clients are 'not entitled to utilize the Information, in either processed or unprocessed form, in an electronic or other system for direct or indirect matching of bids and offers leading to closure'.

The Hong Kong Stock Exchange states that 'no Subscriber shall use the Information or any part thereof to establish, maintain or provide or to assist in establishing, maintaining or providing an Off Market'.[39] An 'Off Market' is defined as 'a trading floor or dealing service where trading in Securities listed on the Stock Exchange or of a type capable of being so listed or any other Securities or Futures Contract is being undertaken otherwise than at or through the Stock Exchange'.[40]

The Copenhagen Stock Exchange restricts access to its dealing system. It requires that if a stockbroker receives its data and redistributes them to a third party, the stockbroker 'shall secure that there is no technical link-up between the information clients of the company (third parties) and the system linked to the trading systems of the Copenhagen Stock Exchange. Thus none of the clients of the stockbroking company shall be able to place orders direct in the trading systems of the Stock Exchange, but the stockbroking company in question will have to handle the matter manually'.[41]

Pricing

It is difficult to describe the pricing policies that exchanges employ for the sale of their price and quote data for several reasons. First, there are almost as many different policies as there are exchanges. Second, many of these policies are confidential. Third, the prices for the different goods and services offered by some exchanges are bundled together in such a way that their underlying composition is not transparent. In such circumstances, the amount an exchange charges specifically for the use of its information is therefore unclear. Fourth, changes in technology are continually bringing changes in pricing strategy. Rather than attempt to present an exhaustive description, therefore, a brief note on the most important types of such policies is provided.[42]

Almost all exchanges charge end-users for their price and quote data, rather than data vendors who are viewed purely as intermediaries. Under the closed systems approach, exchanges typically charge customers on an 'entitlement' basis according to which a fee is demanded for each 'device' or 'physical' unit on which the relevant information is received. Although the relevant definitions vary, a physical unit is normally identified by being connected by wire to the exchange or by having a relatively permanent address. Amongst the types of such devices are a hard-wired desk unit—such as a terminal; a hard-wired display unit—such as a quoteboard; a hardware controller; a site or location—such as an office or a building; a device which may not be hardwired but still automatically reports the identity of the user of the data—such as a laptop computer or pager; and a foreign port or electronic gateway.

In addition to any differences in the way exchanges both classify and count such units, there is also a wide variety in the pricing strategies they employ. Five different strategies actually employed illustrate this diversity. They are: a constant per-unit fee; an average fee for every unit, which declines with higher volumes of units; a lump-sum fee to a vendor for all distribution to terminals outside of the exchange's home country;[43] different prices for terminals inside and outside the exchange's home country;[44] and finally, different fees for professional and non-professional or retail users.[45] Exchanges' attempts to exploit the value of their information have meant that to a greater extent than before they are trying to segregate between the different types of information services they provide. For example, some exchanges now charge differently for snapshot as opposed to continuous feeds of data, and for historical as opposed to real-time data.

The fees charged by exchanges also vary considerably. Furthermore, the formula by which an exchange receives income for the information it disseminates is a pivotal element of its pricing policy. In the US equity markets, for example, the revenue which each exchange receives from the sale of its quote and price information comes to it via its participation in the Consolidated Quote System (CQS) and the Consolidated Tape Association (CTA) plans. The revenue an exchange receives from each plan is calculated as the total number of last sale trades, or quotes, originating from its trading system, divided by the total number of such trades, or quotes, times the total net income for the network. This may be one of the reasons why the larger exchanges opposed allowing the AZX entry into the CTA plan. If a large number of trades on AZX were reported via the CTA, the revenues the existing participants in the CTA obtained would be diluted, unless total revenues rose proportionately.

Discrimination

Most exchanges would contend that they do not discriminate between different purchasers of their data, and some even make a contractual statement to this effect. The Amsterdam Stock Exchange declares, for example, that it 'does not make any distinction amongst/between Purchasers . . . with respect to the availability, sequence, timeliness, accuracy, usefulness, identifiability, integrity and completeness of the Information'.[46]

The position of the Sydney Futures Exchange (SFE) is similar, but more complicated. It agrees 'not to . . . discriminate against the Vendor in relation to: . . . variations in the fees and charges payable by such persons [i.e. end-users] provided always that SFE and AFEIS [the Australian Futures Exchange Information Services] shall not be in breach of this paragraph merely through the varying of fees and charges due to special relationship, preferred customer or bulk purchase arrangements or other bona fide commercial practices'.[47] The charging of different fees to different types of customers, irrespective of the costs of providing the services, is thus not seen as being discriminatory.

Most exchanges which discriminate between different purchasers make no mention of it in their vendor contracts. There are, however, some exchanges which do discriminate between purchasers, and which also recognize this explicitly. The Tokyo Stock Exchange, for example, stipulates that the dissemination of quotes from the exchange through data vendors is allowed only to the offices of securities firms located in Japan. The reason given for this is that,

in order to avoid confusion among investors and occurrence of trouble between securities firms and investors, dissemination of quotations should be limited to the offices of securities companies in Japan where there are appropriate persons who understand the characteristics of such information and the trading method of the Exchange correctly, and can explain them to investors.[48]

A NEW BUSINESS MODEL

The technological assumption on which most vendor contracts have to date been based, namely that the flow of price and quote information around a market has an identifiable source and an identifiable end-point, is no longer appropriate. Advances in computer and data transmission technology now mean that it is relatively cheap for market participants to take in a digital real-time feed of financial information, manipulate the data from the feed in a manner that adds value so as to produce 'derived data', and then re-distribute the enhanced feed both internally and to other market participants. In this new 'open systems' world, the routing of price and quote information thus typically follows a much more labyrinthine path than that implied by the closed systems model. This has led to difficulties both in monitoring the usage of data, as the historical approach of counting devices has lost its meaning, and in enforcing previously accepted contractual conditions, such as forbidding users of exchanges' data from re-distributing them. Together these changes are undermining the usefulness of the traditional contractual approach, and indeed the very commercial basis by which exchanges disseminate their data.

In a survey conducted in 1993 of American securities firms, 40% of the respondents stated that they would like to re-distribute outside their own organization the real-time market data that they received.[49] The reality now is that many do. It is common knowledge that re-dissemination of price and quote information does occur in electronic form, even though such an activity is still almost always prescribed by contract. At the same time, however, exchanges have mostly been unwilling either to sue the market participants they have caught undertaking unauthorized re-dissemination, or to cut off the supply of data to the relevant parties. Instead, they have preferred to seek some form of commercial recompense by requesting the relevant parties either to pay some form of penalty or to increase their subscription levels.[50]

There are several likely reasons for why exchanges have not sought legal redress. When an exchange discovers one of its own members re-disseminating information without permission, it may not feel it wise to prosecute the member given that a key goal of the exchange is likely to be precisely to further the interests of its members. Similarly when an exchange discovers a non-member undertaking unauthorized re-dissemination, it may be unwilling to go to court, not only because it wants the customer to carry on being a customer, but also because it does not want to frighten off its other customers. Informal solutions may be seen as preferable to public exposure of the problem. Exchanges may also be uncertain as to whether their contractual agreements forbidding unauthorized re-dissemination would actually be upheld in court.

The identification of an exchange as being the ultimate source for, and thus the owner of, the market data emanating from its trading system has also come under question. Exchanges still provide mechanisms by which quotes are collected and translated into trades, and still disseminate information about these quotes and trades to the market. Developments in automation have made it clearer, however, that the quotes arriving at an exchange are not spontaneously created, but rather are submitted by an array of broker-dealers, market makers, and investors. Any trades that arise on an exchange are furthermore dependent on an interaction of a minimum of two quotes on both sides of the market. The growing perception that exchanges themselves are only intermediaries in the flow of information has made market participants less willing to agree to, and abide by, the rights claimed by exchanges in their data.

The notion that information flows in a two-way process is more transparent in markets that consist entirely of contributed prices. In these markets, there are no institutions designated exchanges. Participants are simply invited by a system-provider to advertise or provide their services on technology controlled by the system-provider. There is a continuous interaction between the information emanating from the market and the supply of information to the market. In the foreign exchange market, for example, banks submit their prices to data vendors; this information is then instantaneously disseminated, and may lead to trades in the market; and this in turn may lead to the initial quotes being revised, and so on.

The evolution of open systems technology, together with increases in the number of participants in the market data industry, in the range of services being offered, and in the rapidity with which it is possible to enter new markets, has also lead to a blurring of the commercial strategies of market participants. The fact that many companies are now undertaking different roles in the market for price and quote information, is leading them to pursue divergent, and sometimes conflicting, objectives simultaneously. On the one hand, data recipients do not want to be constrained about how they may manipulate the price and quote information they receive, nor to whom they are allowed to re-distribute it, nor how and what they may charge for it.[51] On the other hand, and in a diametrically opposed manner, information providers want to be able to capture as full a value as possible for whatever services they offer in their manipulation of price and quote information. As a result, they, in the same manner as exchanges have historically done, also want to constrain whomsoever receives their data from re-disseminating them without their permission, and without due compensation.

The conflict between these two objectives is well illustrated by considering the following four commercial positions which Reuters and various of its affiliate companies have espoused at different times:

(1) Reuters reportedly complained informally to the EU Commission in 1989 that the data dissemination affiliate of the Brussels Stock Exchange, Bourse Data Beurs, was disseminating the five best bid and ask prices to members of the Exchange, while only the single best bid and ask prices were made available to the public and commercial data vendors.[52] As a data vendor, Reuters presumably wanted as much information as possible disseminated from the exchange.

(2) Instinet, a subsidiary of Reuters, argued that the NASD should charge for its information so as to cover only its costs.[53] Instinet presumably wanted the fees which it paid the NASD for price and quote data to be minimized.

(3) Reuters made an arrangement with Cantor Fitzgerald such that the data arising from the operation of Cantor's IDB in Canada would be supplied on an exclusive basis to Reuters, who would thus be the sole vendor disseminating them.[54] As a data vendor, Reuters presumably wanted the data published by the IDB trading system to be disseminated solely by itself, in order presumably to exploit their full value.

(4) Reuters used to be paid a monthly transaction fee based on the volume of contracts traded through GLOBEX.[55] It did not, however, obtain any preferential treatment when acting as a data vendor for information arising from the trading on GLOBEX, and in particular, received such information at the same time as all other competing vendors. All vendors received details about the price and quantity of the best bid and offer in each contract, and the price and quantity of the last executed trades.[56] Brokers with a GLOBEX terminal, however, obtained details of the ten best bids and offers rather than just simply the best. This put a premium on subscribing to a terminal, for which Reuters received a fee. It also made it more difficult for other exchanges which traded competing contracts, to price their contracts off the information available from GLOBEX. As a trading system owner, Reuters presumably pursued this strategy because it wanted to limit the

dissemination of information from GLOBEX in order to enhance and protect its investment.

What is important to note from these various examples is not the legal status of Reuters' positions, nor the fact that it was Reuters which took these positions, as indeed many other companies have taken similar stances, but rather the fact that the goals which the company pursued in one context conflicted with those it pursued in other contexts. The conflicting objectives that arose internally in Reuters mirror those occurring both inside, and between, other companies in the market data industry.

Other factors have also been undermining the closed systems contractual model. As previously noted, if an exchange does not have a direct contractual relationship with a subscriber to its data, it typically requires the vendors who deliver its data to the subscriber to act as policemen on its behalf so as to ensure that the subscriber pays it the correct fees. This is costly for both vendors and subscribers to administer, and both types of market participants have put pressure on exchanges to reduce these costs. A more important worry of vendors is that it is no longer technologically feasible to enforce the closed systems contractual model. In an open systems world, a vendor cannot control the flow of an exchange's data once the vendor's digital feed reaches its customers. As a group, vendors have thus become anxious that they are being held responsible for circumstances beyond their control. Advances in information storage technology have raised a further contractual concern for exchanges. Given the use of exchanges' data as inputs to historical analysis, exchanges have been anxious to capture some of this value for themselves, in addition to that available from the use of real-time data.

No consensus has yet been reached on what business and contractual model exchanges should adopt in an open systems environment. An association of vendors has suggested that a combination of technological developments together with appropriate internal controls by users of data, and external monitoring of such control structures, may allow a freer use of data on the part of data recipients while still providing sufficient security and revenue for exchanges as information providers.[57] Various alternatives to pricing data on an entitlement basis have also been made, including charging on a 'logical' basis, a 'usage' basis, a 'bulk' or 'wholesale' basis, a 'site licence' basis, or a 'firm licence' basis.

Logical units identify people or processes who or which may be unrelated to any physical device. For example, a software application or a data feed, may each be classified as a logical unit. Some logical units redistribute data after having processed it. Charging for data on a 'usage' basis is done by measuring the 'amount' of data 'used'. For example, the time for which a customer has access to a particular database may be measured, or the number of quotes or transactions which are viewed by the customer may be counted. 'Bulk' or 'wholesale' charging is the practice whereby an exchange sets a total amount which it agrees to charge a particular vendor. Once the vendor has paid this fee, the vendor is then allowed to distribute the exchange's data to whomever the vendor wants. 'Site-charging' is when a customer is charged a flat rate for the data he receives at a particular location, and is allowed to re-distribute the data wherever he wants at that location. 'Firm-charging' is when a customer is charged a flat rate for the data it receives, and is allowed to re-distribute the data wherever it wants inside its firm. None of these pricing strategies have yet been widely adopted.

One of the first exchanges to develop a new information charging policy in response to the changing technology has been the CBT. In April 1997, it established a charging policy that depended on whether a datafeed/network client operated a controlled or an open environment for using the CBT's data.[58] The notion of a controlled environment was one in which access to data was monitored and supervised in an enforceable manner. More specifically it was defined as 'an environment at a location where technical controls report on receipt of market data by devices that are connected to the network'. Charges for data usage in a controlled environment depended on a specific device count. In particular, two fees were set: a monthly location fee of $50, and a monthly fee of $10 per device that actually received the exchange's data. In an open environment, three types of charges were set: a similar $50 monthly location fee; a monthly fee of $10 for each device that could receive the exchange's data, whether or not the data were actually used on these devices (so-called 'authorized' devices); and finally, an open datafeed/network surcharge of $100 per month to customers with between 11 and 100 devices that could access CBT market data, and $250 per month for customers with more than 100 such devices. A fee for delayed data was also established.[59]

CONCLUSION

The aim of this chapter is to examine how exchanges answer some key questions central to their determination of what information dissemination policies they adopt. These include: What types of price and quote information should they release? What rights should they claim in the data they publish? and What pricing policy should they employ for the sale of these data? The chapter is composed of three sections. In the first, the determinants and nature of an exchange's information dissemination policy are examined. Four main factors affecting such policies are identified and discussed. They are, respectively, the market architecture of the exchange, the governance structure of the exchange, the nature of the demand for the exchange's price and quote information, and the competition for the orders flowing to the exchange.

In the second section, the pivotal rights that exchanges claim in their vendor contracts over the data they disseminate are surveyed. Only those rights that most directly affect the structure and development of exchanges and their markets are examined. All the vendor contracts studied implicitly assume a closed systems technology world. Although a comparison between the rights asserted by different exchanges is difficult for many reasons, it is notable that the key rights claimed are common to almost all exchanges. The most important is that all exchanges forbid the unauthorized re-distribution of the price and quote data emanating from their trading systems. Most exchanges also claim some form of copyright in the data they generate and sell. There is less uniformity concerning the property rights exchanges assert over the presentation of their data. Many exchanges seek to impose an obligation of confidentiality on the purchasers of their data so as to constrain them from disclosing the data without the exchange's permission. A few exchanges restrict the trading uses to which their data may be put. Almost all exchanges charge end-users for their price and quote data on an 'entitlement' basis, by counting the number of devices on which their data is displayed at the clients' offices. Many different pricing strategies are, however, employed. Most exchanges do not explicitly discriminate between different purchasers of their data.

In the third section of the chapter, various factors that are rendering the closed systems contractual model no longer appropriate are discussed. The initial development of an alternative business and contractual model for the dissemination of data in an open systems world is also described.

7

Classification and Market Structure: Law and Regulation

INTRODUCTION

The legal and regulatory classification of exchanges and trading systems has to date been indissolubly linked with the regulation of market structure. The aim of this chapter is to provide an introduction to how various legal and regulatory structures both classify trading systems and exchanges, and regulate their market structure. Questions concerning the dissemination of price and quote information are, however, for the most part discussed in the next chapter. Attention is focused on the securities markets in the USA, the UK, and the EU. These jurisdictions are chosen for a variety of reasons. Many difficult regulatory issues have arisen in them. Their statutory and regulatory approaches have been used as models in other locations. They differ from each other in important ways. Finally, the EU is the only region where a supranational law governing the regulation of the securities markets is in force.

The chapter is composed of three sections. In the first, the American law and regulation affecting trading systems and exchanges in the securities markets is outlined. In the second, the relevant British law and regulation are described. In the third section, relevant European Union law is summarized.

USA

The statutory approach governing the regulation of trading systems in the USA may be termed 'institutional' in nature. The Securities and Exchange Act 1934 (SEA), the primary legislation covering the securities markets, defines a range of categories of market participants. It specifies that an institution acting in a manner covered by one of the definitions, must for the most part either obtain registration in that category from the SEC, or where appropriate seek exemption from registration, again from the SEC.[1] The Act then details the duties that each type of market participant must undertake. Further obligations on the different types of market participants have also been imposed by the SEC itself, in various of its orders, rules, and regulations.

This section is composed of four parts. In the first, the definitions of the key statutory categories relevant for trading systems are presented. In the second, the main duties associated with the two most important of these categories, those of an 'exchange' and a 'broker', are summarized. In the third part, the SEC's 'no-action' procedure, whereby a trading system may be excused from the need to register in a particular category, is outlined. In the fourth part, the nature and development of the National Market System (NMS) is examined. A revised approach for classifying and regulating trading systems and exchanges, proposed by the SEC in 1997, is examined in Chapter 12.[2]

DEFINITIONS

There are four main categories into which a trading system may be classified: a 'securities exchange', a 'broker', a 'dealer', and a 'national securities association'. An 'exchange' is defined as,

any organisation, association, or group of persons, whether incorporated or unincorporated, which constitutes, maintains, or provides a market place or facilities for bringing together purchasers and sellers of securities or for otherwise performing with respect to securities the functions commonly performed by a stock exchange as that term is generally understood, and includes the market place and the market facilities maintained by such exchange.[3]

An exchange's facilities are defined as,

[its] premises, tangible or intangible property whether on the premises or not, any right to the use of such premises or property or any service thereof for the purpose of effecting or reporting a transaction on an exchange (including, among other things, any system of communication to or from the exchange, by ticker or otherwise, maintained by or with the consent of the exchange), and any right of the exchange to the use of any property or service.[4]

A 'broker' is defined as,

any person engaged in the business of effecting transactions in securities for the account of others, but does not include a bank.[5]

A 'dealer' is defined as,

any person engaged in the business of buying and selling securities for his own account, through a broker or otherwise, but does not include a bank, or any person insofar as he buys or sells securities for his own account, either individually or in some fiduciary capacity, but not as a part of a regular business.[6]

There is no formal definition of what constitutes a national securities association, other than it being an association of brokers and dealers.[7] Currently only one association has registered as a national securities association, namely the NASD. All exchanges and national securities associations are classified as 'self-regulatory organizations' (SROs).[8]

Duties

The main duties imposed on exchanges and on broker-dealers as of October 1997 are summarized in this section. Those imposed on registered national securities associations are not described in detail, as they are similar to those placed on registered exchanges.[9]

Exchanges

An institution which falls within the Act's 'exchange' definition is obliged to follow one of two regulatory paths. It must either register as an exchange with the SEC, or seek exemption from such registration, again from the SEC. Exemption may be granted only if, in the opinion of the Commission,

by reason of the limited volume of transactions effected on [the] exchange, it is not practicable and not necessary or appropriate in the public interest or for the protection of investors to require . . . registration.[10]

Prior to 1996, the SEC had not been given authority to exempt exchanges from only parts of the statute.[11] It could, however, impose conditions on the exemption. The SEC exempted seven exchanges from 1935 to 1936, and since then the only other exemption granted has been to the AZX in 1991.[12] As described in Appendix 1, the AZX is an automated trading system which allows institutional and broker-dealer participants to trade US stocks directly with each other in a single price auction. The SEC imposed relatively few requirements on the AZX as conditions for its low volume exemption, the main ones being that the various corporate components of the AZX and the shares traded on the system remain adequately registered, that sufficient trading data be made available to the SEC, that appropriate surveillance by the AZX of its employees and participants be undertaken, and that adequate capacity, security, and contingency plans be maintained on a continuous basis.

  In contrast, a registered exchange has many duties. It must enforce compliance by its members with federal rules and with its own rules.[13] It must allow broker-dealers or persons associated with registered broker-dealers to become members.[14] It must assure fair representation of its members in the selection of its directors and in the administration of its affairs, and it must allow one or more of its directors to be representative of issuers and investors.[15] It must ensure that its dues are reasonable and equitably allocated among its members, issuers, and other persons using its facilities.[16] Its rules must be designed,

to prevent fraudulent and manipulative acts and practices, to promote just and equitable principles of trade, to foster cooperation and coordination with persons engaged in regulating, clearing, settling, processing information with respect to, and facilitating transactions in securities, to remove impediments to and perfect the mechanism of a free and open market and a national market system, and, in general, to protect investors and the public interest.

Its rules must not 'permit unfair discrimination between customers, issuers, brokers, or dealers'.[17] It must provide fair disciplinary, approval, censorship, and rescission procedures for its members.[18] Its rules must 'not impose any burden on competition not necessary or appropriate in furtherance of the purposes' of the Act.[19] Proposed rule changes must be filed with the Commission and published for notice and comment. In general, the SEC must approve or disapprove a proposed rule change within thirty-five days of publication. In certain circumstances, this period may be extended up to ninety days, and in others the rule change may become effective immediately upon filing.[20] The SEC may also rescind or add to any rule of a registered exchange.[21] A registered exchange is subject to the Automation Review Policy, a request by the Commission that it have formal capacity, security, and contingency plans for any automated systems it operates.[22] It is subject to various other conditions concerning short selling,[23] unlisted trading privileges,[24] a limitation on trading by its members for their own account,[25] and record-keeping and reporting requirements.[26]

Some of these provisions are applicable to transactions executed on exempt, as well as registered, exchanges.[27] An exchange is not allowed to seek exemption from any regulatory burden on behalf of any automated trading systems that it operates, given that any such system would be classified as a facility of the exchange.

Broker-Dealers

All brokers and dealers are required to register with the Commission and with an SRO.[28] The duties of registered brokers and dealers are different from, and more limited than, those of exchanges, whether or not they operate a trading system. The chief aim of the SEC's regulation of broker-dealers is to protect the customers of those broker-dealers.[29] They are obliged to comply with a range of requirements including those concerning supervision of employees,[30] financial responsibility rules,[31] suitability, mark-up and other ethical obligations contained in the rules of SROs, customer confirmation requirements,[32] and general anti-fraud and anti-manipulation rules.[33]

Broker-dealers are supervised by their SRO. They are not required to enforce the securities laws, have no members, and have no limitation on the number of OTC stocks that they can trade. A trading system classified as a broker-dealer is typically not obliged to undertake real-time market surveillance, or show that it has adequate capacity, security, and contingency plans. Historically, the broker-dealer regulatory framework made no requirements concerning system access criteria, terms of trade execution, or the dissemination of prices and quotes.[34] As discussed below, however, the rules the SEC implemented in 1996 concerning the order execution obligations of brokers, and the execution of their orders on electronic communications networks, changed this. Some record-keeping and reporting requirements have also been imposed by the SEC on trading systems designated 'Broker-Dealer Trading Systems' (BDTSs).[35]

The SEC's No Action Approach

In order to provide legal comfort for an institution concerned about its regulatory status, the SEC has developed a procedure whereby such an institution may request a 'no-action' position from the SEC staff. The company requesting the relief submits a letter to the SEC describing its nature and manner of operations, and outlining why it believes it need not register under one or more of the Act's statutory classifications. On the basis of this description, SEC staff may then decide not to recommend enforcement action against the company if it operates without registering under the relevant portion of the Act. The SEC staff typically impose certain conditions on the company before confirming the no-action position. There is no public notice and comment period in the no-action process, and no-action letters are not subject to judicial review. One of the institutions which has been granted a no-action letter is Instinet, the market structure of which is described in Appendix 1. Instinet was allowed to register as a broker, and not obliged to register as a securities exchange.[36]

A brief history of Instinet's regulatory status in the USA provides an illustration of how the no-action procedure operates. When Instinet began operating in 1969, the Commission decided that Instinet could be appropriately regulated as a broker-dealer based on four reasons:

1) Instinet, unlike other registered exchanges, operated on a for-profit basis with no members; 2) Instinet had no market participants, such as market makers or floor brokers; 3) customers furnished all quotes and orders themselves, through the Instinet facilities; and 4) Instinet did not seem to fit within the statutory scheme contemplated for exchanges.[37]

To confirm this regulatory status, and to protect itself from enforcement action by the SEC, Instinet applied in 1986 for a no-action position from the SEC staff concerning Instinet's non-registration as a national securities exchange, a national securities association, and a clearing agency.[38] Following a submission by Instinet of a detailed description of its trading system to the SEC, the SEC staff agreed to take a no-action position concerning Instinet's non-registration in all three categories.[39] The SEC staff did, however, impose several conditions on Instinet. They requested that Instinet provide data on a quarterly basis about: the operations of the System; the number and identity of the subscribers in the system; the number of applicants or subscribers who have been denied participation or have withdrawn from the system, and the reasons for these events; and the number of money defaults or failures to deliver, and the company's response, if any. The SEC staff also required that Instinet provide trading volume data, information concerning the kinds of securities traded through the system, and copies of all rules, regulations, contracts, and other similar documents. It was stipulated in addition that Instinet provide thirty days' prior notice to the SEC of any contemplated material changes in the operation of the system.

The National Market System

The concept of the NMS may be viewed either abstractly as a set of objectives which Congress mandated the SEC to pursue, or more concretely as the institutions that have been established in order to deliver these objectives. Three aspects of the NMS are described here: first, the objectives and development of the NMS; second, some key rules concerning the dissemination of prices and quotes initially passed by the SEC to implement the NMS goals in 1975, together with an important amendment to one of these rules made in 1996; and finally, the main institutions established in order to deliver the NMS objectives. The SEC has imposed many other obligations on exchanges and other market participants to implement the NMS that are not discussed here.

Objectives and Interpretation

The NMS came into existence as a result of a set of amendments made to the SEA in 1975. The amendments established as a purpose of the Act the need to 'remove impediments to and perfect the mechanism of a national market system for securities',[40] and directed the SEC to 'facilitate the establishment of that system'.[41]

Congress found that,

(A) The securities markets are an important national asset which must be preserved and strengthened.

(B) New data processing and communications techniques create the opportunity for more efficient and effective market operations.

(C) It is in the public interest and appropriate for the protection of investors and the maintenance of fair and orderly markets to assure–

(i) economically efficient execution of securities transactions;

(ii) fair competition among brokers and dealers, among exchange markets, and between exchange markets and markets other than exchange markets;

(iii) the availability to brokers, dealers, and investors of information with respect to quotations for and transactions in securities;

(iv) the practicability of brokers executing investors' orders in the best market; and

(v) an opportunity, consistent with the provisions of clauses (i) and (iv) of this sub-paragraph, for investors' orders to be executed without the participation of a dealer.

(D) The linking of all markets for qualified securities through communication and data processing facilities will foster efficiency, enhance competition, increase the information available to brokers, dealers, and investors, facilitate the offsetting of investors' orders, and contribute to best execution of such orders.[42]

The Act then directed the Commission,

having due regard for the public interest, the protection of investors, and the maintenance of fair and orderly markets, to use its authority . . . to facilitate the establishment of a national market system for securities (which may include subsystems for particular types of securities with unique trading characteristics) in accordance with the findings and to carry out the objectives set forth [i.e. as above].[43]

The concept of an NMS was first mooted by the SEC in 1971 when it stated that,

a major goal and ideal of the securities market and the securities industry has been the creation of a strong central market system for securities of national importance, in which all buying and selling interest in these securities could participate and be represented under a competitive regime.[44]

The SEC defined such a system,

> as a system of communications by which the various elements of the marketplace, be they exchanges or over-the-counter markets, are tied together. It also includes a set of rules governing the relationships which will prevail among market participants.[45]

After the Act had been amended, the SEC identified in 1978 four broad sets of market reforms which were necessary for the establishment of the NMS:

> (i) implementation of a nationwide system for disclosure of market information designed to make price and volume information in all markets universally available; (ii) elimination of artificial impediments to dealing in the best available markets created by exchange rules or otherwise; (iii) establishment of terms and conditions upon which any qualified broker-dealer could negotiate access to all exchanges; and (iv) integration of third market firms and exchanges into a national market system, subjecting them to appropriate market responsibilities and other regulatory requirements commensurate with the benefits they would realize in such a system.[46]

In view of the Congressional belief that it was 'best to allow maximum flexibility in working out specific details' of what should be elements of a national market system, the 1975 Amendments neither defined the term 'national market system' nor mandated specified minimum components of such a system.[47] In this regard, a Senate Committee examining the NMS stated that,

> The Committee considered mandating certain minimum components of the national market system but rejected this approach. The nation's securities markets are in dynamic change and in some respects are delicate mechanisms; the sounder approach appeared to the Committee, therefore, to be to establish a statutory scheme clearly granting the Commission broad authority to oversee the implementation, operation and regulation of the national market system and at the same time charging [the Commission] with the clear responsibility to assure that the system develops and operates in accordance with Congressionally determined goals and objectives.[48]

Despite not specifying in detail the components which should comprise the NMS, Congress did identify several principles which should underlie it. The first was that auction-type trading was believed advantageous for several reasons: public limit orders could be executed ahead of those of market professionals, and ahead of those at inferior prices; also public limit orders could compete with, and better, the prices quoted by a dealer.[49] The second principle was that the securities to which the principles governing the NMS should apply, which were called 'qualified securities', should be selected primarily according to their characteristics, for example their trading volume or number of shareholders, rather than by where they happened to be traded. A third principle was a refusal to abolish over-the-counter trading in listed securities in order to sanction a nationwide centralized auction-type market for qualified securities, unless the Commission found that 'the maintenance or restoration of fair and orderly markets in such securities may not be assured through other lawful means'.[50] The dealers operating in the third market were believed to provide valuable competition to the exchange specialists.

The SEC identified two major problems that the NMS was aimed at resolving. The first, defined as 'market fragmentation', was the existence of multiple, geographically separated fora in which trading in the same security occurred. The second, defined as 'institutionalization', was the trend by which the major investing institutions had come to own a progressively larger percentage of the tradable shares.[51] These two issues were believed to give rise to many problems, amongst the most important of which were:

(i) the need to perfect existing mechanisms for the disclosure of information concerning all completed transactions in multiply-traded securities; (ii) the absence of a comprehensive, composite quotation system displaying buying and selling interest in those securities from all markets (whether on an exchange or over-the-counter); (iii) the inadequacy of existing means available to brokers for routing orders to and among markets in pursuit of the most favorable execution opportunities; (iv) the lack of a mechanism to provide nationwide agency limit order protection, affording time and price priority to such orders regardless of geographical location; (v) impediments to effective market maker competition for orders of relatively small size; and (vi) the need to integrate block transactions more effectively into the normal course of securities trading.

Rules

The SEC initially passed three key rules to implement the NMS goals with regard to the dissemination of price and quote information: the 'last sale rule', the 'quote rule', and the 'display rule'. The last sale rule requires that a report be published of all trades in 'national market securities'.[52] Such securities include all exchange-listed stocks and the largest NASDAQ stocks.[53] The price and volume of the transaction and the marketplace where each transaction is executed must be reported. No vendor may be prohibited from re-transmitting the data available from a transaction reporting plan, provided it pays the appropriate fees.

The firm quotation or quote rule requires each broker or dealer to communicate promptly to its exchange or association its best bids and offers and associated quotation sizes for all relevant securities, and also that each exchange or national association make available to quotation vendors, the highest bid and the lowest offer for the relevant securities, plus the associated quotation size or aggregate quotation size.[54] This must be done at all times the exchange or association is open for trading, except during a trading suspension of the relevant security. The aggregate quotation size is the sum of the quotation sizes of all responsible brokers or dealers. Each exchange or association must also be able to identify and disclose to other members of that exchange or association, the brokers or dealers making the relevant quotes.

An important amendment to the quote rule was made on 28 August 1996, when the SEC passed a series of rules and rule amendments in order to improve the handling and execution of customer orders by brokers and dealers.[55] The rules were aimed primarily at exchange specialists and OTC market makers in listed securities on whom three requirements were imposed. They had, first, to publish quotations for listed securities where the market maker traded more than 1% of the aggregate trading volume for that security. They were obliged, second, to quote to the public any prices that they quoted privately, through certain so-called 'electronic communications networks' (ECNs), that were better than their publicly displayed prices. Finally they were required to display customer limit orders that were priced better than their own quotes. Attention is focused here on the second of these requirements, concerning ECNs.

An ECN is defined as,

any electronic system that widely disseminates to third parties orders entered therein by an exchange market maker or OTC market maker, and permits such orders to be executed against in whole or in part; except that the term electronic communication network shall not include:

i) Any system that crosses multiple orders at one or more specified times at a single price set by the ECN (by algorithm or by any derivative pricing mechanism) and does not allow orders to be crossed or executed against directly by participants outside of such times; or

ii) Any system operated by, or on behalf of, an OTC market maker or exchange market maker that executes customer orders primarily against the account of such market maker as principal, other than riskless principal.[56]

The amendment obliges brokers and dealers to include the bids and offers they place on ECNs in determining the best bids and offers that they communicate to their exchange or association. If an order a broker-dealer displays is for his own account, he is required in most circumstances to execute transactions at the prices he quotes on an ECN in any amount up to the minimum quotation size specified by his exchange or association. If the displayed order is for the account of a customer, the broker-dealer is required to deal up to the full size of the quote. Although a customer is allowed to insist that a dealer handling its order not display the order publicly, once a customer has allowed the order to be displayed on an ECN, the order must then be displayed on the full quote tape.

The rule also specifies that the duty of a broker-dealer to communicate promptly the prices and quotes that he places on an ECN to his exchange or association, can be satisfied if the ECN itself disseminates these prices and provides access to other broker-dealers to trade at these prices. This alternative is called the ECN alternative. In order to achieve this, an ECN has to provide to an exchange or association the prices and sizes of the best bids and offers entered into it by any broker-dealers.[57] It also has to offer other broker-dealers the same ability to trade against these bids and offers that they would have obtained if the bids and offers had been directly disseminated by the exchange or association to which the ECN provided the quotes. In addition, the ECN has to ensure an execution for orders up to the size of the cumulative total of orders entered at the relevant prices by any market makers. If a quote from an ECN is disseminated to the public, the disseminated price has to be identified as originating either from the market maker originally quoting it, or from the ECN. The market maker providing the quote may thus retain his anonymity. He must, however, be willing to deal up to the full size for which he is quoting on the ECN.

The third key rule created to implement the NMS, the display rule, requires that if a vendor disseminates last sale data for securities subject to mandatory trade reporting, it must distribute the 'consolidated' price, the 'consolidated' volume, and an identifier indicating the market centre where trades occur.[58] If a moving ticker identifies the location of one last sale report, it must identify the location of all last sale reports. Similarly, a vendor disseminating quotation information, must distribute consolidated quotation information which must include, the 'best' bid and offer for such a security, the quotation size or 'aggregate quotation size' associated with the best bid and offer, and identifiers indicating the market centres which reported these quotes, or a 'quotation montage' from all other reporting centres. The identity of individual market makers does not have to be identified.

The 'consolidated' price and volume are respectively the price and volume of the most recent transaction from all reporting market centres. The cumulative consolidated volume is the sum of the volume for all transaction reports from all reporting market centres, that is to say all exchanges, and all market makers reporting to a national association. The 'best' bid and offer for listed securities are the highest bid and lowest offer quoted amongst all reporting centres, with bids and offers of equal values ranked first by size, and then by time, for exchange-listed securities. For NASDAQ securities, the 'best' bid and offer are calculated solely using the priorities of price and then time. A 'quotation montage' shows best bids and offers from all market centres.

Institutions

Three key institutions were developed to bring about the NMS: the Consolidated Quotation System (CQS), the Consolidated Tape Association (CTA), and the Intermarket Trading System (ITS). Each system was developed according to an operating plan, in which the main exchanges and the NASD participated.

The CQS was established to implement the firm quotation rule.[59] It is a mechanism for making available to data vendors, information about the bid and offer quotations and associated volumes, for eligible securities from the markets which participate in the NMS. The bid and ask quotes from all the plan participants (i.e. the registered exchanges and the NASD), are combined to obtain a consolidated Best Bid and Offer (BBO). The CQS disseminates both the BBO and all the quotes provided by all the participants. The source of each quote, namely the relevant exchange or the market maker on NASDAQ, is also identified.

Administration of the system is undertaken by an operating committee which is composed of one representative from each 'plan participant', each of whom has one vote on the committee. Amendments to the CQS Plan require unanimity. Each participant provides information about quotations in their market to a central processor, operated by the Securities Industry Automation Corporation (SIAC). The participating exchanges and the NASD, rather than SIAC, are liable for the content of the information distributed. The participants share in the income and expenses associated with publishing the quotation information. There are two networks associated with the plan: Network A and Network B. Network A contains information about NYSE-listed stocks, and Network B contains information about AMEX listed stocks, and other regional stocks which meet criteria similar to the AMEX listing requirements.[60]

Any net income from the sale of the CQS information is divided up proportionally between the different participants according to their relative 'annual shares'. The 'annual share' of a participant for any calendar year is essentially the total number of last sale prices of the network's eligible securities reported by the participant divided by the total number of reported last sales.

The CTA was established to consolidate the last sale reporting of all trades in exchange-listed securities.[61] Information about each trade is reported to SIAC which then releases it for public dissemination. Various types of trades are excluded from reporting, for example odd lots, or transactions agreed at a price unrelated to the current market for the security. Trade reports by participants must be made promptly, so that under normal conditions not less than 90% of such prices must be reported within one and a half minutes. When there is a trading halt or suspension in the primary market for a security, transmission of last sales will not be reported on the consolidated tape. The operation of financial matters is separate for Network A and Network B securities. Administration of the CTA is undertaken by a similar committee to that running the CQS.

When a stock is listed on an exchange, the CQS and the CTA govern the dissemination of all information about the trading in it, even when the stock is also traded over the counter. Similarly, for all NASDAQ stocks, the NASD governs the dissemination of all relevant information, even if such a stock is traded on an exchange via the 'unlisted trading privileges'.[62] Various other organizations have also been developed to facilitate the dissemination of information about the trading in other types of securities, not all of which were established as a result of a direct regulatory mandate. The Options Price Reporting Authority (OPRA) disseminates information about prices and quotes in the markets for standardized options.[63] The NASD has created a quotation display system for non-NASDAQ stocks traded OTC called the OTC Bulletin Board,[64] and also a system for disseminating information about the trading in high yield fixed income bonds called the Fixed Income Pricing System.[65] The Municipal Rule Making Board also created a pilot programme for enhancing transparency in the municipal bond market.[66]

The purpose of the ITS is to provide an intermarket communications linkage by which a member of one participant market may trade with a member from another participant market, provided that the first participant market furnishes continuous two-sided quotes in the security.[67] Operation of the ITS presupposes the existence of the CQS, in that members of the participant markets must be able to see which market is quoting the best price in the security in which they are interested. The quotes a broker or dealer submits to the CQS are considered to be firm, unless he has notified his exchange that he is changing the price, or has just completed a transaction in the security, but has not yet changed the price. A member of a participating market wishing to trade at a price quoted on another market, can send a 'commitment to trade' to the other market. A 'commitment to trade' is a firm order which is good for a pre-specified period of either one or two minutes. If the quote is still available at the market to which the commitment to trade is sent, or if a better price is available, and if the market rules permit an execution at that price, the market must accept the commitment and execute the order. If executed, the order is reported to the CTA processor by the market whose member executes the trade, and also reported back to the originating market. If the commitment is not accepted within the specified time-frame, it is automatically cancelled. Partial executions may occur.

All the registered exchanges and the NASD participate in the system. When an order is sent from an exchange to the NASD, it passes through an electronic linkage to the NASD's Computer Assisted Execution System (CAES) on which market makers guarantee to execute trades automatically at the prices quoted. When an order is sent to the Cincinnati Stock Exchange (CSE), it is routed electronically to the National Securities Trading System. When an order is sent to one of the other exchanges it is routed to the specialist's post.

In most circumstances, 'trade-throughs' are not allowed on the ITS. A trade-through occurs when a participant either buys a security at a higher price than the lowest offer quoted among the participating markets, or sells a security at a lower price than the highest bid quoted among the participating markets. The trade-through rules do not apply to block transactions, and are not binding during trading halts and suspensions. A block trade is a trade of 10,000 or more shares, or a trade with a value of $200,000 or more. Participating markets have also agreed to 'continue their efforts to define and develop an additional Application that will address the trading of blocks of System securities so as to further enhance protection of public limit orders'.[68] Although nothing has so far been developed to achieve this, participating markets are obliged to ensure that if a block is executed at a price worse than the BBO on the CQS, the participating member is required to send a commitment to trade at the block price in order to 'clean up' any orders through which the block trade was traded. In addition to the operation of the ITS through the trading day, it is also used for the Pre-Opening Application. This allows a market maker for a specific security in a participant market to access the interest in other markets for the same security prior to the opening of the market.[69]

UK

Following the creation of the Financial Services Authority in 1997 to supersede the Securities and Investments Board (SIB), the legislative and regulatory structure governing trading systems in the UK has been in a state of flux. Until the new structure is formally established, however, the Financial Services Act 1986 (FSA) remains the primary legislation governing the regulation of such systems. Its central thrust is that,

No person shall carry on, or purport to carry on, investment business in the United Kingdom unless he is an authorised person . . . or an exempted person.[70]

A trading system wishing to operate in the UK may choose between a range of statutory and regulatory options. If it carries on investment business, and if it does so in the UK, it may select either to be authorized or to be exempted under the FSA. If a trading system does not carry on investment business, or if it carries on such business outside the UK, it may avoid the need for regulation under the FSA. The various ways in which such authorization and exemption may be obtained or avoided, are outlined in turn in this section. Two ways in which a trading system may obtain regulatory approval to operate in the UK under EU law are described in the next section.[71] To avoid confusion, the regulator is referred to as the SIB.

Authorization

A person may be authorized under the FSA either indirectly, by being a member of an SRO, which in turn is recognized by the SIB, or directly via the SIB. If a person wishes to be a member of an SRO, he must satisfy the rules of the SRO. If he wishes to be regulated directly, he must normally satisfy the SIB's Conduct of Business Rules.[72]

The Securities and Futures Authority (SFA) is the SRO governing firms that operate in the UK securities and futures markets. A primary goal of the SFA's rules is to 'deliver high standards of investor protection' by ensuring, amongst other things, that the firms it regulates are fit and proper, financially sound, and safeguard investors' assets.[73] Various automated trading systems have chosen to obtain authorization by being a member of the SFA including, BEST, Instinet, POSIT, and TRADE.[74] All these firms have also chosen to be members of the LSE. As such they are required to satisfy the rules of the exchange, and to pay any fees charged by the exchange.

If a person wishes to be directly regulated by the SIB, he must in most circumstances satisfy the SIB's Conduct of Business Rules. Such direct regulation has been discouraged, however, and to date few firms are so regulated. The SIB has, however, established a non-statutory regulatory category called a 'Service Company', to allow it to waive the application of many of its Conduct of Business Rules to companies which 'arrange deals in investments' where compliance in its view would be unduly burdensome.[75] Such companies must only provide services to the following types of people:

(i) a business investor generally and not merely by virtue of being a professional investor; (ii) a person who is in relation to those services an experienced investor, or (iii) a person for whom the firm was currently providing services when this instrument was made.[76]

A Service Company need only obey a small subset of the SIB's Conduct of Business Rules.[77] The firm must submit a business plan to the SIB. It must ensure that if there is a complaint relating to the conduct of its investment business, the complaint is investigated promptly and thoroughly, and that appropriate action is taken. It must also remind the complainant that it is open to him to report the matter to the SIB, and that if he is dissatisfied with the outcome of the firm's investigation of the complaint, he may ask the SIB to investigate the complaint. If the SIB determines that an independent investigation is warranted, the firm must co-operate with the investigator by providing him with all relevant information and documents, and all assistance it is reasonably able to provide.[78] In addition the firm must establish adequate supervision of its employees, must provide for the protection of its customers in the event of it ceasing to do business, must advise the SIB of *force majeure* situations, and must follow the SIB's rules concerning advertisements.

The SIB has also published some guidelines concerning Service Companies.[79] These state that Service Companies must have adequate financial resources, that they must obey the SIB's 'Unsolicited Calls' regulations, and that they must ensure that a range of matters is specified in their contractual agreements with each of their customers. Three are particularly important. The Service Company must establish:

(iii) the division of responsibilities between the customer and the organisation for the accuracy and timeliness of the data processed by these services with special attention paid as to which party fulfils the requirements of market regulations and whether the service organisation is responsible to highlight possible regulatory breaches and to whom;
(iv) the ownership of the data being processed and its protection;
(ix) the duties and responsibilities of the service organisation in the event of their being unable to provide the service and the fall back and disaster recovery arrangements.

Following the SIB's report on the regulation of the UK equity markets in 1995, the status of the Service Company regime has been under review.[80] At that time the SIB suggested the Service Company regime should no longer be available to trading systems (or 'market service providers'), and that it 'would hope and expect' that trading systems should thus either seek recognition as a Recognized Investment Exchange, or should become members of an SRO.

Exemption

There are three regulatory categories relevant for trading systems that grant exemption from authorization under the FSA: 'Recognized Investment Exchanges', 'Recognized Overseas Investment Exchanges', and 'International Securities SROs'. The value of obtaining an exemption to a trading system is that it thereby avoids the need to be authorized and to satisfy the full panoply of the SFA's or the SIB's rules.

Recognized Investment Exchanges
Any body corporate or unincorporated association may apply to the SIB to become a Recognized Investment Exchange (RIE).[81] The Act does not contain a

definition of what an RIE is, nor does the SIB have any duty to regulate any particular types of organizations as RIEs. What the Act does, however, is to specify the requirements that an institution must satisfy in order for it to be recognized as an RIE.[82]

In particular, the institution must have sufficient financial resources. Its rules and practices must ensure that business undertaken on it is conducted in an orderly manner and affords proper protection to investors. It must limit dealings on its facilities to investments in which there is a proper market; and where relevant, require issuers to publish proper information for determining the current value of their securities. It must have appropriate arrangements for ensuring the performance of transactions effected on its systems, including default and settlement procedures, and for recording information about these transactions. It must have effective arrangements to monitor and enforce compliance with its rules and any clearing arrangements made by it. It must have effective arrangements for the investigation of complaints made in respect of business transacted on its facilities. It must be able and willing to promote and maintain high standards of integrity and fair dealing in the carrying on of investment business and to cooperate with other appropriate regulatory authorities.

The Act also declares that the Chancellor must not recognize an investment exchange unless he is satisfied that the rules, guidance, arrangements, regulations, and practices of the exchange, and any practices of persons who are members of, or otherwise subject to the rules made by, the exchange,

do not have, and are not intended or are likely to have, to any significant extent the effect of restricting, distorting or preventing competition, or if they have or are intended or likely to have that effect to any significant extent, that the effect is not greater than is necessary for the protection of investors.[83]

Before the Chancellor makes a ruling on an application by a trading system to become an RIE, the Director General of the Office of Fair Trading (OFT) is required to consider whether the application is anti-competitive. The Director General must report on whether he believes competition will be affected by the application, and if so what its effect on competition is likely to be. He is also required to review the conduct of an exchange on an on-going basis. As a result of the inclusion of this automatic referral to the OFT for the rules and practices of all RIEs, the FSA exempts exchanges from various other aspects of competition law.[84] The Chancellor or the SIB can revoke recognition of an investment exchange once it has been granted, if the RIE fails to comply with any obligations it has under the Act, and may also direct an RIE to change its rules if they do not satisfy the purposes of the Act.

Although the SIB has not published details of what it expects an applicant to supply in its application to become an RIE, it has set out some guidelines it would use for recognizing RIEs. The SIB noted that it 'appreciate[d] that the widely differing nature of the investment products traded on Exchanges will to a considerable extent necessitate the adoption of an individual approach to each individual Exchange'.[85] It stated that 'whilst the overall requirements . . . applicable to all Exchanges must be satisfied, it will be necessary for SIB to apply its criteria differently in certain detailed respects to take into account the characteristics peculiar to different investment products and their applicable trading, clearing and reporting systems'. The SIB considered that 'the specialised skills of [exchanges'] members and practitioner-based staff will play a particularly important part in its relationship' with them. It also noted that in addition to the notification requirements applicable to all exchanges, the SIB will establish reporting requirements which 'will vary between Exchanges dependent upon the type of investments traded on such an Exchange'.[86]

Recognized Overseas Investment Exchanges
An institution with a head office outside the UK which wishes to carry on investment business in the UK and which applies to become a recognized investment exchange for the purposes of exemption, is required to apply for recognition as a Recognized Overseas Investment Exchange (ROIE).[87] Unlike with RIEs, the power to recognize ROIEs lies with HM Treasury, and not with the SIB. The requirements for recognition as an ROIE are different from those necessary to become an RIE. They are that,

(a) the applicant is, in the head office country, subject to supervision which together with the applicant's rules and practices is such that investors in the United Kingdom are afforded protection in relation to the applicant at least equivalent to that provided by the Act in relation to recognised investment exchanges . . . whose head offices are situated within the United Kingdom;
(b) the applicant is able and willing to co-operate, by the sharing of information and otherwise, with the authorities, bodies and persons responsible in the United Kingdom for the supervision and regulation of investment business or other financial services;
(c) adequate arrangements exist for such co-operation between those responsible for supervising the applicant in the head office country and the appropriate supervisory and regulatory authorities . . . in the United Kingdom;
(d) . . . the rules and regulations . . . do not have, and are not intended or likely to have, any significant anti-competitive effect (other than the minimum such effect which may be necessary to protect investors).
(e) the rules and practices of the applicant, together with the law of the head office country must be such as to provide adequate procedures for dealing with the default of persons party to market contracts connected with the applicant.[88]

An institution wishing to become an ROIE must also submit details of its operations, including its financial resources, of the categories of investments traded on the exchange, of any arrangements for the provision of clearing services, and also its rules and regulations. When considering an application, the Chancellor may 'have regard to the extent to which persons in the United Kingdom and persons in the head office country have access to the financial markets in each other's countries'.[89] This criterion is used by HMT as a means of obtaining reciprocal access for UK firms and exchanges in a foreign jurisdiction, similar to that which is granted in the UK to foreign firms and exchanges. Once an application has been granted, the Chancellor may revoke recognition under several circumstances, primarily if any of the above conditions are not met on an on-going basis. He may also withdraw recognition if such 'revocation is desirable in the interest of investors and potential investors in the United Kingdom'.[90]

ROIEs are essentially allowed to function by their own rules, and their home regulators are allowed to be their principal regulators. The Treasury notes that because it relies substantially on the supervisory and regulatory arrangements in the country where the applicant's head office is situated, recognition as an ROIE reduces intervention by the UK authorities in the day to day affairs of an overseas investment exchange.[91]

International Securities Self-Regulating Organizations

A third way in which a market participant is able to obtain exemption from the FSA is to become an International Securities Self-Regulating Organization (ISSRO). In order to be classified as an ISSRO, an organization must have its head office outside the UK; it must not be able to become an ROIE because the participants trading on it will not receive investor protection equivalent to that available in the UK; adequate arrangements for cooperation between those responsible for supervising the organization and the UK authorities must not exist; and finally the organization must facilitate and regulate the activities of its members in undertaking 'international securities business'.[92] 'International securities business' is defined as including the trading in investments,

which by their nature, and the manner in which the business is conducted, may be expected normally to be bought or dealt in by persons sufficiently expert to understand any risks involved, where either the transaction is international or each of the parties may be expected to be indifferent to the location of the other, and, for the purposes of this definition, the fact that the investments may ultimately be bought otherwise than in the course of international securities business by persons not so expert shall be disregarded.[93]

It is the Chancellor who grants approval to an ISSRO. He may do so to any body or association satisfying the above criteria,

if, having regard to such matters affecting international trade, overseas earnings and the balance of payments or otherwise as he considers relevant, it appears to him that to do so would be desirable and not result in any undue risk to investors.[94]

There is currently only one ISSRO, namely the International Securities Market Association (ISMA).[95]

Participants outside the Remit of the Act

There are two types of market participants that operate trading systems in the UK which may be excluded from coverage of the FSA: 'overseas persons', and organizations which do not 'deal in' or 'arrange deals' in investments. The non-statutory regulatory category of a 'Designated Investment Exchange' is ignored here.[96]

Overseas Persons

A person is defined as carrying on investment business in the UK, if he:

(a) carries on investment business from a permanent place of business maintained by him in the United Kingdom; or (b) engages in the United Kingdom in one or more of the activities [prescribed in the Act as conducting investment business] and his doing so constitutes the carrying on by him of a business in the United kingdom.[97]

A person who does not satisfy either of these two criteria is classified as an 'overseas person'. The Act states that its definition of 'dealing in investments' does not apply to any transaction by an overseas person, with or through 'an authorised person' or 'an exempted person acting in the course of business in respect of which he is exempt'.[98] An instance of a trading system which obtained classification in 1991 as an overseas person is IBIS, an automated trading mechanism then operated by the Frankfurt Stock Exchange.[99] In October 1991 Bayerische Hypotheken-und-Wechsel Bank (HypoBank) in London installed one IBIS screen in its London office.[100] The SIB decided that IBIS did not need to be directly regulated as an ROIE, as an RIE, or indeed at all, for two reasons.[101] The first, and most important, was that the Frankfurt Stock Exchange did not maintain a permanent place of business in the UK. The second was that the Frankfurt Stock Exchange had not come into the UK in order to sell IBIS screens. Rather, HypoBank, a member of the SFA, had decided by itself to install the screen in its offices. The Frankfurt Stock Exchange could therefore not be construed as carrying on a business in the UK. HypoBank, however, did have to be regulated in the UK, and in fact, was already regulated as a member of the SFA. As such it was required to follow the SFA's rules, and, in particular, to report any transactions via IBIS to the SFA, and to obtain best execution for its customers.[102] No restrictions were placed on the manner in which the IBIS screen operated, or on the underlying trading system which could be accessed via the screen.

Participants Who Do Not Undertake Investment Business

The FSA identifies two main activities that constitute carrying on 'investment business' and that are relevant for trading systems: 'dealing in investments' and 'arranging deals in investments'.[103] 'Dealing in investments' is defined as,

buying, selling, subscribing for or underwriting investments or offering or agreeing to do so, either as principal or as agent.[104]

'Arranging deals in investments' is defined as,

making, or offering or agreeing to make, (a) arrangements with a view to another person buying, selling, subscribing for or underwriting a particular investment; or (b) arrangements with a view to a person who participates in the arrangements buying, selling, subscribing for or underwriting investments.[105]

Trading systems that do not 'deal' or 'arrange deals' in investments (and also do not undertake the other forms of investment business specified in the Act), do not require either authorization or exemption under the FSA. The provision of such services as trade matching, confirmation, information display, and custody of securities are not viewed as 'dealing' or 'arranging deals' in investments.[106] Furthermore, so long as a company is not offering to trade in investments as a counter-party or an agent it will probably avoid the need to be authorized. For example, a telephone company or mail service via which trades are conducted may not require authorization. However, if a 'modern telecommunications network' is specifically created to serve investment market users, it may 'cross the line from unregulated public infrastructure to regulated investment business', and then be required either to be authorized, or exempted from authorization, under the FSA.

Although there has been no public record of the deliberations concerning applications to become ROIEs, an off-the-record comment concerning the CME's application to operate GLOBEX in the UK is important in this context. In assessing the CME's application, a critical question appeared to be whether what the CME was proposing to undertake constituted investment business. If it did not, then recognition was not required for it to establish itself in the UK. Three factors were reportedly investigated by the DTI to assess whether the CME was going to conduct investment business: the range of information provided by the CME system, the extent to which information was transmitted on a real-time basis, and the variety of different types of transactions it was possible to effect in response to the information received. Based on the proposed level of interaction with the market, it was decided that the CME was going to conduct investment business, and as such that it was required to seek exemption.

EU

EU law provides two ways in which a trading system may obtain regulatory approval to operate throughout Europe. In order to evaluate them, the aims and legal basis underlying the 'Single Market' in the EU are briefly described, and then the relevant elements of the Investment Services Directive, the applicable EU law, are outlined. Other EU laws that impinge on the regulation of exchanges are ignored.

The Treaty Basis and the Single Market

The legal basis governing the EU, laid out in the Treaty of Rome, establishes the fundamental European freedoms of movement and of establishment.[107] The freedom of movement of services gives nationals who are established in one Member State the right to provide services in other Member States—the so-called European 'passport'.[108] The freedom of establishment includes the right for a natural or legal person from one Member State, to set up and manage a firm in another Member State, under the conditions laid down for the nationals of the second Member State.[109] A third critical element of the Treaty, discussed in the next chapter, is that competition should not be inhibited in an inappropriate manner.

The freedoms of movement and establishment are not completely without limits. Member States are allowed to impose restrictions on both these freedoms on various grounds, including that of 'public policy'.[110] In addition, the European Court has recognized a series of so-called 'mandatory requirements' which Member States may impose in the absence of Community rules, even if such impositions obstruct or stop the exercise of the European freedoms.[111] These mandatory requirements include ensuring the effectiveness of fiscal supervision, the fairness of commercial transactions, and the defence of the consumer.

The aim of the EU's Single (or Internal) Market programme is to effect the freedoms established in the Treaty, namely to make the EU 'an area without internal frontiers in which the free movement of goods, persons, services and capital is ensured'.[112] Although these freedoms are guaranteed in the Treaty itself, the Single European Act, which amended the Treaty and initiated the Single Market programme, was passed for several reasons. Amongst these were that it was believed that reliance on appeals to the European Court to uphold the Treaty would be costly, time-consuming, and uncertain in their outcome, and that the obstacles to the establishment of the Single Market could best be removed by direct legislation. The Single European Act mandated the Commission to draft a programme of secondary legislation to remove the many technical and other barriers which restricted the European freedoms.

Investment Services Directive

The Investment Services Directive (ISD) is one element of the European legislation aimed at realizing the Single Market in financial markets. The Directive is based on three linked legal strategies: the harmonization between EU Member States of the minimum standards for the prudential supervision of financial institutions; the mutual recognition by each Member State of the competence of the supervisory bodies for the governance of these minimum standards in each other Member State; and finally the assignment of the control and supervision of financial institutions to the home country of the institution in question, in those areas which have been harmonized between Member States.[113]

The Directive provides two regulatory routes by which a trading system operating in one EU Member State may offer its services freely throughout the EU. The first is for institutions classified as 'investment firms', such as brokers or dealers. Essentially, if an investment firm is appropriately authorized in its home Member State, the ISD allows the firm to offer its services in all other Member States without the need for further authorization. The Directive also stipulates that authorized investment firms must be allowed to become members of, or be given access to, all 'regulated' markets, as defined below, in any host Member State. National restrictions on the number of members of such 'regulated' markets must be eliminated.

The Directive stipulates a range of conditions that must be satisfied by an investment firm for it to make use of its European passport. These include that the firm have an adequate initial level of capital, that its directors be sufficiently experienced, that it have appropriate measures for administrative and accounting procedures, for safeguarding clients' securities and funds, for record-keeping, that it minimize conflicts of interest, and that its employees act fairly and honestly.

The second regulatory route by which a trading system is allowed to offer its services throughout the EU under the ISD is applicable to so-called 'regulated' markets. The Directive says that a Member State must allow the regulated markets of other Member States to provide 'appropriate facilities' within its territories, in order to enable its investment firms to become remote members of, or have access to, the other Member States' regulated markets.[114] A trading system classified as a regulated market that operates without the need for a physical presence, should therefore be allowed to place its automated facilities in Member States of the EU other than the one in which it is based, without the need for any regulatory recognition other than that required by its home Member State.

In order to be classified a regulated market, an institution must satisfy a range of criteria.[115] It must be recognized as a regulated market by its home Member State. It must function regularly. It must have regulatory approval for the manner of its operations, for the manner in which access to it is granted, and for the listing or eligibility conditions for the securities traded on its system. Finally, it must satisfy the reporting and transparency provisions laid out in the Directive. The reporting provisions specify how information about trades must be reported to the appropriate regulatory authorities. The transparency provisions stipulate the minimum data, concerning prices, quotes, and volumes on the market, that must be disseminated publicly.

Given the importance of the transparency provisions, they are quoted in full. The Directive states that,

The competent authorities shall require for each instrument at least:

(a) publication at the start of each day's trading on the market of the weighted average price, the highest and the lowest prices and the volume dealt in on the regulated market in question for the whole of the preceding day's trading;

(b) in addition, for continuous order-driven and quote-driven markets, publication:

– at the end of each hour's trading on the market, of the weighted average price and the volume dealt in on the regulated market in question for a six-hour trading period ending so as to leave two hours' trading on the market before publication, and

– every 20 minutes, of the weighted average price and the highest and lowest prices on the regulated market in question for a two-hour trading period ending so as to leave one hour's trading on the market before publication.

Where investors have prior access to information on prices and quantities for which transactions may be undertaken:

(i) such information shall be available at all times during market trading hours;

(ii) the terms announced for a given price and quantity shall be terms on which it is possible for an investor to carry out such a transaction.

The competent authorities may delay or suspend publication where that proves to be justified by exceptional market conditions or, in the case of small markets, to preserve the anonymity of firms and investors. The competent authorities may apply special provisions in the case of exceptional transactions that are very large in scale compared with average transactions in the security in question on that market and in the case of highly illiquid securities defined by means of objective criteria and made public. The competent authorities may also apply more flexible provisions, particularly as regards publication deadlines, for transactions concerning bonds and other forms of securitized debt.[116]

CONCLUSION

The aim of this chapter is to provide an introduction to how various legal and regulatory structures both classify trading systems and exchanges, and regulate their market structure. The chapter is composed of three sections. In the first, four aspects of the American statutory and regulatory approach are described. The definitions of the key statutory categories relevant for trading systems are presented. The main duties associated with the two most important of these categories, those of an 'exchange' and a 'broker', are summarized. The SEC's 'no-action' procedure, whereby a trading system may be excused from the need to register in a particular category, is outlined. Finally, the nature and development of the National Market System is examined.

In the second section, the various statutory and regulatory options available under the Financial Services Act (1986) to a trading system wishing to operate in the UK are discussed. A trading system must be 'authorized', 'exempted', or avoid the need for regulation altogether. Authorization may be obtained either indirectly from the Securities and Futures Authority, or directly from the Securities and Investments Board now replaced by the Financial Services Authority. A trading system may obtain exemption if is classified in one of three statutory categories: a Recognized Investment Exchange, a Recognized Overseas Investment Exchange, or an International Securities Self-Regulating Organization. Finally a trading system may avoid the need for regulation altogether, if it does not carry on 'investment business', or if it carries on such business outside the UK.

In the third section, the relevant EU law is examined. The nature and importance of the Single Market is outlined, and then two ways in which a trading system may obtain regulatory approval under the Investment Services Directive to operate throughout the EU are described. The first is for institutions classified as 'investment firms', such as brokers or dealers, and the second is applicable to 'regulated' markets.

8

Information: Law and Regulation

INTRODUCTION

Not only is the concept of ownership generally not simple, it is even more complex and opaque than normal when applied to the price and quote information emanating from an exchange or market. Following Honoré (1961), it may be viewed as the bundle of rights and obligations associated with the purchase and sale of such information. The aim of this chapter is to identify and describe the key legal and regulatory authorities that determine these rights and obligations.

This is extremely difficult to do for a range of reasons. It is first necessary to identify the exact nature of the relevant quotes and prices. As noted by Bull (1997), 'data produced by modern markets are electronic messages which may be grouped into four mutually exclusive categories': a single event or datum, a group of consecutive or batched events or data, a single value-added event or datum, or a compilation of value-added data. In determining the relevant property rights, it is also necessary to consider three other message components of which the data may be composed: a software program, a search procedure, and various structure and layout specifications. Different bodies of law are relevant for all these different elements of electronic messages.

Consider one problem, not examined in detail here, that has arisen as a result of the transition being made in the market data industry from an analogue to a digital world.[1] It is widely accepted that copyright does not subsist in a work unless and until it has been recorded in writing or otherwise, and that mere facts may not be protected by copyright. Many jurisdictions do, however, allow computer programs to be protected by copyright. In a digital environment, programs (which are sets of instructions) and copyright works, both of which are artefacts, cannot be distinguished from acts, namely transactions. It is therefore difficult to establish whether a single digital trading datum on the one hand should *not* be protected by copyright, because it is a mere fact, or on the other hand *should* be protected by copyright, because it can be characterized as a program.

The next problem in determining the relevant rights and obligations is that in any one jurisdiction there are normally many relevant legal and regulatory authorities. In the USA, for example, the law and regulation governing contracts,[2] copyright, trade secrets, 'hot news' and commercial misappropriation, the securities markets, and in the future, possibly also database protection,[3] are all pertinent. In the UK, other areas of legislation may be relevant for assessing the legality of a particular data dissemination contract. Some information contracts specify details of the sale or lease of goods, such as a publication containing price and quote information. These contracts are subject to the Sale of Goods Act 1979. Some contracts concern the supply of a service, such as the provision of a terminal on which data are displayed, or the supply of an electronic datafeed. Such contracts are subject to the Supply of Goods and Services Act 1982. All contracts are also subject to the Unfair Contract Terms Act 1977. Almost all the different relevant bodies of law and regulation are also the subject of great controversy. In addition, many are currently subject either to legislative revision, regulatory interpretation, or judicial clarification, processes that can be particularly volatile and difficult to predict. Further complications arise because there may be conflict between the different relevant legal and regulatory authorities, and it is not always clear which takes priority.[4]

In the international context even more problems are present, because the law and regulation governing the same topics can differ substantially, and because conflict between different jurisdictions' laws is common. Consider, for example, the area of intellectual property rights. There are two widely accepted international agreements which cover such rights: the Berne Convention for the Protection of Literary and Artistic Works, and the GATT Agreement on Trade-Related Aspects of Intellectual Property Rights (TRIPs).[5] Notwithstanding these agreements, however, substantial differences remain between different countries' legal approaches to authors' and creators' rights. One area where this is important is the divergence between the civil law jurisdictions, for example in continental Europe, and the common law jurisdictions such as the UK. In continental Europe, the *droit d'auteur* concept is an essential element of copyright law. Put at its most abstract, this concept aims to protect the creative spirit and moral rights of human authors. One of its central implications is that copyright subsists only in personally authored works. Commercial considerations are important, if at all, only on a secondary level. In contrast, in the UK copyright has been used as a key tool to protect commercial investment in intellectual property.

Another factor which leads to confusion concerns language. There are many instances where the same word means different things to different people, and where use of a word in a particular context may either be misinterpreted or viewed as nonsensical. This is not merely a problem of terminology, but also one of substance. Consider, for example, the distinction sometimes drawn in legal theory and in information-provider contracts between the terms 'data' and 'information'. 'Information' is typically defined as the *contents*, namely the set of quotes, prices, volumes, identities, etc., which an exchange transmits to its clients in some particular *form*. In contrast, 'data' is defined to be the combination of both the *contents* and the *form*, be it in written, electronic or some other medium, in which the relevant information is transmitted. Use of the terms 'purchase', 'sale', 'buyer', 'seller', and even 'ownership', is controversial when applied to price and quote information in a legal context.

In contrast to the legal approach, it is notable that in the economics and regulatory literature, no distinction is standardly made between the terms 'information' and 'data', and the terms 'purchase', 'sale', 'buyer', 'seller', and 'ownership' are frequently applied to prices and quotes. Any discussion of the literature on price and quote information which transcends the boundaries of one discipline is therefore likely to give rise to terminological inconsistencies. In order to be able to use language which encompasses a range of concepts from different disciplines, no single terminology is employed uniformly here. Where ambiguity arises, the meanings of the relevant terms are specified, and where particularly important, for example in the discussion of intellectual property rights, the language of one particular discipline is adopted, in this instance that of the law. The possibility of employing inconsistent terminology is accepted as a price worth paying in order to be able to address the concerns of different subject areas.

Six branches of law and regulation that are important for the dissemination of price and quote information in a range of jurisdictions are described in consecutive sections of the chapter. They govern, respectively, copyright, a *sui generis* right in databases, misappropriation, confidentiality, competition, and the securities markets. Rather than attempting to provide a definitive exegesis of any of these branches of law and regulation for one, let alone all, jurisdictions, key elements are selected and discussed.

COPYRIGHT

The owner of a copyright in a 'work' typically has the right to prevent unrestricted copying or use of the work for a specified period.[6] Most exchanges therefore claim copyright in the price and quote data they disseminate, in order to restrict copying of such data other than on a historical basis. This section examines whether compilations of an exchange's price and quote data may be protected by copyright law. The relevant copyright law in the UK and the USA is described in turn. A description of the conflict between copyright law and competition law in the EU is presented in the section on competition.

UK[7]

Copyright in the UK is governed by the Copyright, Designs and Patents Act (CDPA) 1988. Although the CDPA identifies many types of 'works' in which copyright may subsist, the works which are relevant for price and quote data are those defined as 'original literary works'.[8] All written documents are 'literary works', including tables and compilations.[9] The owner of a copyright in a work has the exclusive right, amongst other things, to copy the work, to issue copies of the work to the public, to broadcast the work, to adapt the work, or to do any of these acts in relation to an adaptation.[10] A person who does any of these acts, or authorizes another person to do so, without the licence of the copyright owner, infringes the owner's copyright.[11] None of these acts may be done 'in relation to the work as a whole or any substantial part of it'; 'either directly or indirectly; and it is immaterial whether any intervening acts themselves infringe copyright'.[12] Privity of contract is therefore not required to enforce a copyright claim.

The owner of a copyright may transfer the rights associated with ownership in two main ways. First, he may sell the copyright to another person. Second, he may issue a licence to another person, allowing this person to exercise all the rights that the owner is allowed to exercise, except that of selling the copyright to somebody else.[13] If the owner grants an exclusive licence to one particular person, only that person is allowed to exercise the rights associated with owner-ship of the copyright, bar that of being able to sell the copyright.

There is no statutory definition of what makes a work 'original', and it is on this concept that much of the judicial analysis has concentrated. A seminal judg-ment stated that,

The word 'original' does not . . . mean that the work must be the expression of original or inventive thought. Copyright Acts are not concerned with the originality of ideas, but with the expression of thought, and, in the case of 'literary work,' with the expression of thought in print or writing. The originality which is required relates to the expression of the thought. But the Act does not require that the expression must be in an original or novel form, but the work must not be copied from another work—that it should originate from the author.[14]

A work may be original, even if the author has drawn on common knowledge, or has used already existing material.[15] If an author has made use of existing subject-matter, however, there must be more than an exact reproduction to secure copyright: there must be 'some element of material alteration or embellishment which suffices to make the totality of the work an original work'.[16]

The main judicial criterion that has been developed to assess whether a work should be deemed original is whether sufficient 'labour, skill and capital' have been expended by the author in creating it.[17] The kinds of skill or labour relevant to make a compilation able to be protected by copyright include the selection and arrangement of the subject-matter of which the compilation is composed. Although there have been instances where copyright protection has been refused because the labour of selection has been thought negligible,[18] a wide range of compilations have been deemed protected by copyright.[19] Since 1895 following *Exchange Telegraph Co. v. Gregory and Co.*, it has been assumed that a list of stock exchange prices exhibits sufficient 'originality' to warrant copyright protec-tion.[20]

The facts of the case were as follows. Exchange Telegraph Co. (Extel) was a company which entered into an agreement with the London Stock Exchange to collect information concerning the prices of stocks and shares on the exchange. Extel distributed this information to its subscribers, via newspapers and the tele-graph, on condition that it be used only in the office or place where it was deliv-ered, and not be communicated to non-subscribers. After a time, the exchange decided to stop brokers who acted outside the exchange, including Gregory, from receiving the information. Before the change in the exchange's policy, Gregory had received the exchange's information from Extel, but this stopped in March 1894, when the contract between Extel and Gregory came to an end and was not renewed. Gregory then successfully approached certain of Extel's clients to obtain the exchange's information throughout the day, and posted the information up on boards in its office. When Extel discovered this, it sought an injunction to stop Gregory both from copying the information published in its newspapers and via the telegraph, and also from copying or exhibiting any information obtained from its subscribers.

In an initial judgment, it was found that Extel 'had a right of property at common law in the information so collected'. This was confirmed on appeal, where it was ruled that the 'information is a thing which can be sold. It is property, and, being sold to the plaintiffs, it was their property'. The rationale for this was stated as follows,

The Stock Exchange belongs to certain persons, and is managed by a committee. The persons admitted there are bound to submit to the terms imposed upon them. It is a valuable thing to a member to know what is being done there at intervals during the day. That is a valuable thing, and the Stock Exchange have a right to deal with the matter as they please. . . . In the present case they gave valuable information to the plaintiffs, who paid for it. The committee of the Stock Exchange say, however, that they will not give the information to persons who do outside the Stock Exchange what stockbrokers do within it— that is to say, to outside brokers. They have, of course, a perfect right to say so.

Even if an exchange does have copyright in the data it disseminates, however, the extent to which it will be able to restrict the re-dissemination of the data is questionable. Most market participants wishing to re-disseminate an exchange's data, do much more than simply re-transmit the data. Typically they also expend significant labour, skill and capital, in manipulating, formatting and presenting, the data, in their own unique way, and believe that they add value to the original data. Even data vendors who simply re-transmit an exchange's data, are required to 'massage' and 'clean' the data, an expensive activity, before re-transmission. It is likely, therefore, that even if exchanges do have copyright in the data which they release, most other market participants would themselves also be able to claim copyright in any derived data which they disseminate.

USA[21]

The source of federal copyright law in the USA is the Constitution which authorizes Congress,

to promote the progress of science and useful arts by securing for limited times to authors and inventors the exclusive right to their respective writings and discoveries.[22]

This has given rise to a series of Copyright Acts, the latest of which was passed in 1976. The central thrust of the Act is that,

(a) Copyright protection subsists in . . . original works of authorship fixed in any tan-gible medium of expression, now known or later developed from which they can be perceived, reproduced or otherwise communicated, either directly or with the aid of a machine or device . . . (b) In no case does copyright protection for an original work of authorship extend to any idea, procedure, process, system, method of operation, concept, principle, or discovery, regardless of the form in which it is described, explained, illustrated, or embod-ied in such work.[23]

The most relevant category of works into which the data emanating from an exchange might fall is that of a 'compilation'.[24] This is defined as,

a work formed by the collection and assembling of preexisting materials or of data that are selected, coordinated, or arranged in such a way that the resulting work as a whole consti-tutes an original work of authorship. The term 'compilation' includes collective works.[25]

Copyright in compilations only extends, however,

to the material contributed by the author of such work, and does not imply an exclusive right in the preexisting material. The copyright in such work is independent of, and does not affect or enlarge the scope, duration, ownership, or subsistence of, any copyright protection in the preexisting material.[26]

The basic rights of a copyright holder include those of reproduction, the prepara-tion of derivative works,[27] distribution, and public display.

The statute does not define the term 'original', and thus interpretation of what it means has to rely on the courts. Two quite distinctive standards have been developed to assess the originality of a work: the 'industrious collection' or 'sweat of the brow' approach, and the 'creative selection' approach. Under the 'sweat of the brow' theory, copyright protection is granted as long as the compi-lation is the product of meaningful effort, no matter how mechanical the selection or presentation of facts in the compilation. The approach was most clearly expressed as follows:

the right to copyright a book upon which one has expended labor in its preparation does not depend upon whether the materials which he [the author] has collected consist or not of matters which are publici juris, or whether such materials show literary skill or originality, either in thought or in language, or anything more than industrious collec-tion. The man who goes through the streets of a town and puts down the names of each of the inhabitants, with their occupations and street numbers, acquires material of which he is the author. He produces by his labor a meritorious composition, in which he may obtain a copyright, and thus obtain the exclusive right of multiplying copies of his work.[28]

Under the 'creative selection approach', in contrast, copyright exists in a compil-ation only if it exhibits a minimal amount of creativity in its selection and arrangement of facts. The expenditure of labour, capital or other assets, in the production of the compilation is irrelevant for assessing whether it is protected by copyright or not.

In a seminal case in 1991, *Feist Publications Inc. v. Rural Telephone Service*

Company, Inc., the US Supreme Court declared that only the second of these approaches was valid.[29] The Court confirmed that,

facts, whether alone or as part of a compilation, are not original and therefore may not be copyrighted. A factual compilation is eligible for copyright if it features an original selection or arrangement of facts, but the copyright is limited to the particular selection or arrangement. In no event may copyright extend to the facts themselves.[30]

It also stated that this,

inevitably means that copyright in a factual compilation is thin. Notwithstanding a valid copyright, a subsequent compiler remains free to use the facts contained in another's publication to aid in preparing a competing work, so long as the competing work does not feature the same selection and arrangement.[31]

The background to the case is as follows. Rural Telephone was a public utility providing telephone services to several communities in Kansas. As part of its regulatory duties, it was required to publish a white pages listing of all its subscribers. It obtained the information necessary for its white pages directory from its subscribers. Feist was a company which provided area-wide telephone directories for areas much larger than that covered by Rural Telephone. Feist requested Rural Telephone for a licence to incorporate Rural's telephone listings into its own white page directory, and when Rural refused to grant such a licence, took the information without Rural's consent.

The Supreme Court ruled that Rural's white pages were not entitled to copyright by assessing the measure of their originality. It declared that,

originality is not a stringent standard; it does not require that facts be presented in an innovative or surprising way. It is equally true, however, that the selection and arrangement of facts cannot be so mechanical or routine as to require no creativity whatsoever. The standard of originality is low, but it does exist.[32]

The selection, co-ordination, and arrangement of Rural's white pages were ruled not to satisfy the minimum standards for copyright protection, in that they 'could not be more obvious'. The 'sweat of the brow' theory was explicitly dismissed, and the Court observed that 'Rural expended sufficient effort to make the white pages useful, but insufficient creativity to make it original'. When considering the minimum standards of originality, it stated that,

there is nothing remotely creative about arranging names alphabetically in a white pages directory. It is an age-old practice, firmly rooted in tradition and so commonplace that it has come to be expected as a matter of course. . . . It is not only unoriginal, it is practically inevitable.[33]

It is arguable that a list of exchange prices and quotes does not exhibit sufficient 'originality' to warrant copyright protection in the USA, given that the selection and arrangement criteria used to create such a list also 'could not be more obvious'. If an exchange does disseminate any data, it is practically inevitable that it disseminates the last-sale prices and volumes, and the best bid and offer quotes.

A compilation of such data is therefore likely to satisfy neither the selection nor the arrangement criteria, and thus would not contain sufficient originality to be protected by copyright. Furthermore, even it were to do so, copyright would only subsist in its selection and arrangement. Other market participants would therefore be allowed to employ the data of which the compilation was composed, and re-package and re-distribute them as they saw fit. As a result of a tension between copyright law and the law of misappropriation, discussed below, the CME has paradoxically been willing to deny the existence of copyright in its price and quote data, asserting that 'financial exchanges' real-time price quotations fall squarely within the rule of *Feist*' and that such information is not a work of authorship.[34] This was done so as to allow claims about what are perceived to be unfair uses of an exchange's data to fall within misappropriation law as described below.

There are, however, other selection and arrangement criteria that an exchange may use to justify its claim for copyright in the price and quote data it disseminates. In particular, a stock exchange may claim that the prices and quotes it publishes are dependent on the choice of which companies are listed or traded on the exchange. This choice is not mechanical or obvious, and indeed, companies can be de-listed. Similarly, both cash and futures exchanges may claim that the prices and quotes they disseminate are dependent on the market surveillance facilities they operate, which in turn are dependent on human intervention. Exchanges have the power, and sometimes use this power, to force quotes or transaction prices to be changed, if for example they are viewed as being manipulative in nature. Finally, an exchange may claim that the quotes and trade prices it publishes are opinions, given that they arise as a result of decisions taken by the participants on its market.[35] An exchange may then claim copyright in them as opinions, a possibility that would be excluded if they were merely facts.

SUI GENERIS RIGHT

The establishment of a *sui generis* right to protect databases of information is a new phenomenon. The development of such a right in the EU's Database Directive is briefly described here. A similar right under consideration in the USA is ignored.[36]

In March 1996 the EU passed a Directive to harmonize the legal protection of databases. Several reasons were given for why the law was believed necessary. The diversity of national legislation in the EU governing the protection of databases, most importantly in the area of copyright law, together with the fact that in some Member States databases were not clearly protected, were seen as major impediments to the achievement of the Single Market.[37] It was also argued that the development of electronic databases required considerable investment, that they could often be cheaply copied and accessed, and furthermore that 'in the absence of a harmonized system of unfair-competition legislation or of case-law, other measures [were] required in addition to prevent the unauthorized extraction and/or re-utilization of the contents of a database'.[38]

The Directive decreed that if a database were to be protected by copyright, the sole criterion for determining whether copyright subsisted in the database was similar to the creative selection criterion employed in the USA, namely, 'that the selection or the arrangement of the contents of the database [was] the author's own intellectual creation'.[39] The contents of a database would not be protected by copyright under the Directive.[40] The Directive also created a new intellectual property right, the so-called *sui generis* right. The goal of this right was to ensure that the creator of a database could protect his investment against any harm, misappropriation, or copying, that did not infringe whatever copyright that might exist in the arrangement of the database. A database was defined as,

a collection of independent works, data or other materials arranged in a systematic or methodical way and individually accessible by electronic or other means.[41]

The maker of a database was given the right 'to prevent the extraction and/or re-utilization of the whole of or a substantial part, evaluated qualitatively and/or quantitatively, of the contents of that database'.[42] This right was to apply to data-bases, irrespective of whether they or their contents were eligible for protection by copyright or other rights. The term of the *sui generis* right in a database was set at fifteen years from the date of completion of the making of the database.[43] The Directive also allowed the term of protection of a database to be extended if the database were changed in an appropriate manner. It stated, in particular, that,

any substantial change, evaluated qualitatively or quantitatively, to the contents of a data-base, including any substantial change resulting from the accumulation of successive addi-tions, deletions or alterations, which would result in the database being considered to be a substantial new investment, evaluated qualitatively or quantitatively, shall qualify the data-base resulting from that investment for its own term of protection.[44]

Notwithstanding the creation of the new *sui generis* right, a central objective of the European Commission when it proposed the Directive was to promote compe-tition between suppliers of information products and services. In order to prohibit the *sui generis* right from being used to bolster a monopolistic position, the Directive therefore also stipulated that,

protection by the *sui generis* right must not be afforded in such a way as to facilitate abuses of a dominant position, in particular as regards the creation and distribution of new prod-ucts and services which have an intellectual, documentary, technical, economic or commercial added value; . . . therefore, the provisions of this Directive are without prej-udice to the application of Community or national competition rules.[45]

The importance of the Database Directive is precisely that it may offer exchanges the possibility of protecting their price and quote data under the *sui generis* right, in addition to any copyright that may subsist in the compilations of their data. While an exchange will typically claim that it makes a significant investment in producing its price and quote data, it is arguable that what exchanges are investing in are systems to execute trades, and therefore that any data that emanate from such systems are simply by-products.[46] As such compilations of them would not be eligible for protection under the *sui generis* right, given the lack of investment in them. Even if the new right were applicable to an exchange's price and quote data, the term of the protection would be unclear. The contents of such databases are constantly being added to as new bits of information, namely prices and quotes, are created by the exchange. It is, however, debatable whether a substantial enough investment could be considered to be made on a continuous basis so that the term of protection could also be constantly extended forwards.

Given that many trading systems have a monopolistic position with regard to the dissemination of their price and quote data, they are likely to be required to license the use of these data on fair and non-discriminatory terms. This view was indeed suggested in the explanatory memorandum to the Commission's first proposal for the Directive, where the situation of an exchange disseminating its information was explicitly used as an example of a possible information monopoly. The Commission stated that if a 'Stock Market refused to supply [its closing] figures to more than one applicant [i.e. vendor], remedies under competition rules might have to be sought to deal with that issue'.[47]

MISAPPROPRIATION

One protection in the USA against the misappropriation of a property right in price and quote data may be provided by the law of unfair competition. The nature and importance of this body of law is, however, controversial for several reasons. First, given that it is a doctrine developed in state case law, and thus has no statutory backing, the manner in which it may be applied is relatively flexible. Its relevance to a particular case therefore depends critically on the precise details of the case. Second, there has been recent support to eliminate entirely the tort of misappropriation.[48] Most importantly, it is a matter of great debate whether the law of unfair competition is pre-empted by federal copyright law, and if so, to what extent. As of mid-1997, the tension between federal copyright law and state misappropriation law in the context of the dissemination of time-sensitive news was the subject of a highly disputed case, *National Basketball Association v. Sports Team Analysis and Tracking Systems Inc. (NBA)*, subsequently called *National Basketball Association v. Motorola Inc.*. While an initial judgment in the District Court gave a broad interpretation of the validity of state misappropriation law,[49] the Appeals Court provided a much more limited vision of the sort of claims that fit within this law.[50] It is expected that the case will be appealed to the Supreme Court. The debate about the nature and applicability of state misappropriation law is summarized here.

Prior to *NBA*, there were a range of cases concerning the misappropriation of time-sensitive or 'hot' news.[51] A seminal one was *Board of Trade of the City of*

Chicago v. Christie Grain and Stock Company.[52] At the time, the CBT disseminated its quotes, and required recipients of these data to pay appropriate fees and
to sign a contract promising to keep the data confidential. Christie Grain obtained
the CBT's quotes without signing a contract with the exchange or paying the
appropriate fees. It used these quotes to set up an off-exchange trading business,
or in the language of the day a 'bucket shop'. The CBT then sought an injunction
to stop this. The Court found that,

the plaintiffs' [i.e. CBT's] collection of quotations is entitled to the protection of the law.
It stands like a trade secret. The plaintiff has the right to keep the work which it has done,
or paid for doing, to itself. The fact that others might do similar work, if they might, does
not authorize them to steal the plaintiffs'. . . . The plaintiff does not lose its rights by
communicating the result to persons, even if many, in confidential relations to itself, under
a contract not to make it public, and strangers to the trust will be restrained from getting
at the knowledge by inducing a breach of trust, and using knowledge obtained by such a
breach.

The contract the Board of Trade used to govern the dissemination of its information was described as 'simply a restraint on the acquisition for illegal purposes of
the fruits of the [exchange's] work'.

Another key case for the commercial misappropriation doctrine with regard to
hot news was *International News Service v. Associated Press (INS)*.[53] Associated
Press (AP) was a cooperative news service which, through its expenditure of
money, skill, and effort obtained news. This was then passed to AP's members
who in turn published it in their newspapers. INS managed to obtain a source for
this news by copying it from pre-publication sources or early editions of AP
members' newspapers, and then sold the news in competition with AP.[54]

In examining whether INS's actions were legal, the court recognized that,

the peculiar value of news is in the spreading of it while fresh; and it is evident that a valuable property interest in the news, as news, cannot be maintained by keeping it secret.[55]

The court then argued that in taking the news from AP and selling this news as its
own, INS had been 'endeavoring to reap where it has not sown', and thus appropriate to itself, 'the harvest of those who have sown'.[56] The defendant's practice
was seen as nothing more than,

an unauthorized interference with the normal operation of [AP's] legitimate business
precisely at the point where the profit is to be reaped, in order to divert a material portion
of the profit from those who have earned it to those who have not.

This was viewed clearly as an act of unfair competition, despite the fact the AP
could claim no copyright in its new bulletins. The court therefore granted AP
injunctive relief in order to stop INS's misappropriation. The scope of AP's property right was, however, limited in two ways, as discussed by Overdahl (1997:
16). First, it was only effective against AP's direct competitor, INS, and not
against the public at large.[57] Second, the duration of the right could only last as
long as the information contained in AP's wire service had commercial value.

The question of whether federal copyright law preempts the state law of unfair competition in the context of the dissemination of hot news is controversial. The Copyright Act preempts state protection of rights if two conditions are satisfied.[58] The first requires that the relevant state law must vindicate 'legal or equitable rights that are equivalent' to those within the 'general scope' of copyright law. The second requires that the work that it is sought to protect under state law must be of a type within the 'subject matter' covered by the Copyright Act. The legislative history of the Act also states, however, that,

'misappropriation' is not necessarily synonymous with copyright infringement, and thus a cause of action labeled as 'misappropriation' is not preempted if it is in fact based neither on a right within the general scope of copyright . . . nor on a right equivalent thereto. For example, state law should have the flexibility to afford a remedy (under traditional principles of equity) against a consistent pattern of unauthorized appropriation by a competitor of the facts (i.e., not the literary expression) constituting 'hot' news, whether in the traditional mold of INS . . . or in the newer forms of data updates from scientific, business or financial data bases . . . The proprietor of data displayed on the cathode ray tube of a computer terminal should be afforded protection against unauthorized printouts by third parties (with or without improper access), even if the data are not copyrightable.[59]

As of mid-1997, the conflict between copyright law and state misappropriation law was under consideration in *NBA*. The background to the case is as follows. The NBA produced and promoted basketball games, and sold licenses for the broadcast and reporting of real-time information about these games. The commercial value of the NBA games was vast, and the NBA's most valuable asset was the excitement of a game in progress, an asset that could only be realized by the dissemination of real-time information. In transmitting this information, the NBA imposed a range of restrictions on its customers, most importantly that they were not allowed to disseminate similar information to that the NBA itself disseminated without due compensation. Similar restrictions were placed on people who viewed the NBA games from sports arenas.

Motorola manufactured and marketed a portable beeper device, SportsTrax, on which statistics about various sports were relayed to its clients. Sports Team Analysis and Tracking Systems (STATS) supplied the game information that was transmitted to these pagers. STATS entered into negotiations with the NBA to carry information about the NBA's games. When these negotiations broke down, STATS began disseminating information about the basketball games, which was obtained by reporters watching the NBA's games on the television or listening to them on the radio. NBA then filed suit against STATS.

In the initial judgment on the case, the District Court first determined that the NBA games themselves were not copyrightable, because they were not 'works of authorship', and thus did not fall within the subject matter of copyright law. Although the court accepted that the NBA's broadcasts were copyrightable as motion pictures or other audiovisual works, it also determined that STATS had not violated this copyright in its actions, as what it had done, at most, was to copy the idea of the games and the facts from the broadcasts.

The court then discussed whether the Copyright Act preempted the relevant state law in this context. In discussing the general-scope requirement, it noted that state laws had been held not to establish rights equivalent to the Copyright Act if they required proof of an 'extra element' that changed the nature of the action so that it is qualitatively different from a copyright infringement claim.[60] Among the claims which were stated as satisfying the extra element test were 'unfair competition claims based upon breaches of confidential relationships, breaches of fiduciary duties and trade secrets'. The court also noted that many common law misappropriation claims had been held to be preempted by the Copyright Act. In this case, the court asserted that the NBA had not identified any material extra element, and that the general-scope requirement for copyright law to preempt a misappropriation claim was therefore satisfied with regard to both the NBA games and the NBA broadcasts.

In considering whether the subject-matter criterion necessary for preemption was satisfied, the court determined that because the NBA's *broadcasts* were copyrightable, the NBA's misappropriation claim was preempted to the extent that it relied on property rights in these broadcasts. In contrast, however, because the NBA's *games* were not copyrightable, the NBA's misappropriation claim was not preempted to the extent that it relied on property rights in its games. Whether a work attracted copyright protection was therefore not determinative in assessing whether copyright law preempted state misappropriation law. Rather, what was important was whether a work was of a type that could in some circumstances attract copyright, but for its lack of originality, or a failure to meet a technical requirement. The judge acknowledged that,

it is difficult to imagine a misappropriation of a broadcast (which is preempted) which is not also a misappropriation of the underlying event (which is not preempted). And yet this partial preemption—of the broadcast but not the games—is an inevitable consequence of adhering to the distinctions which the Copyright Act requires.[61]

Having thus determined that the relevant state law was not preempted by the Copyright Act, the court then assessed whether STATS and Motorola had in fact engaged in unfair competition by misappropriating the NBA's property interest in its games. Citing *Metropolitan Opera Association v. Wagner-Nichols Recorder Corp. (Metropolitan Opera)*, the court argued that the law of unfair competition was developed to respond both to the 'ethical as well as the economic needs of society', that it had evolved as a broad and flexible doctrine with a capacity for further growth to meet changing conditions, and that there was no complete list of activities which constituted unfair competition.[62] The court noted that the concept was initially applied to the activity of palming off, namely the fraudulent representation of the goods of one seller as those of another. Such activity was actionable because of the two wrongs inflicted thereby: '(1) the deceit and fraud on the public; and (2) the misappropriation to one person of the benefit of a name, reputation or business good will belonging to another'. The court argued that the doctrine of unfair competition had subsequently been extended beyond cases of palming off to grant relief 'in cases where there was no fraud on the public, but only a misappropriation for the commercial advantage of one person of a benefit or "property right" belonging to another'.

The breadth of the commercial misappropriation doctrine was stated as being evidenced by the absence of a requirement of 'actual competition between parties'. Instead, again quoting *Metropolitan Opera*, the court asserted that,

[the] modern view as to the law of unfair competition does not rest solely on the ground of direct competitive injury, but on the broader principle that property rights of commercial value are to be and will be protected from any form of commercial immorality, and a court of equity will penetrate and restrain every guise resorted to by the wrongdoer. The courts have thus recognized that in the complex pattern of modern business relationships, persons in theoretically non-competitive fields, may, by unethical business practices, inflict as severe and reprehensible injuries upon others as can direct competitors.

In addition to the news gathering and dissemination context, it was noted that the property rights of those who invest the time and money into the creation of sports events and their broadcasts have been repeatedly protected through the doctrine of commercial misappropriation, by limiting the permissible uses which others may make of information regarding ongoing sports events.

The court summarized its view by noting that the NBA games had tremendous commercial value, and that STATS and Motorola did not contribute in any manner to this value. It therefore concluded that the defendants had attempted to reap profits where they had not sown any effort, and thereby misappropriate NBA's rights in the NBA games.

This decision was reversed in the Court of Appeals. The Appeals Court did confirm the decision of the District Court that the underlying basketball games did not fall within the subject matter of federal copyright protection because they did not constitute original works of authorship. Similarly, it confirmed that, while the NBA broadcasts were copyrightable, Motorola and STATS had not infringed NBA's copyright because they had reproduced only facts from the broadcasts, and neither the expression nor the descriptions of the game that constituted the broadcasts.

The Appeals Court argued, however, that,

although game broadcasts are copyrightable while the underlying games are not, the Copyright Act should not be read to distinguish between the two when analyzing the preemption of a misappropriation claim based on copying or taking from the copyrightable work.[63]

Adoption of the partial preemption doctrine proposed by the District Court was therefore rejected, in that it 'would expand significantly the reach of state law claims and render the preemption intended by Congress unworkable'.[64]

The Appeals Court also disagreed with a further aspect of the District Court's conclusion concerning the preemption claim. While it accepted the District Court's analysis of the general-scope criterion, it disagreed with the District Court's conclusion that the subject-matter criterion was not met. In particular, the

Appeals Court noted that the District Court 'relied on a series of older New York misappropriation cases involving radio broadcasts that considerably broadened *INS*'. Citing a series of more recent cases, most importantly *Financial Information, Inc. v. Moody's Investors Service, Inc.*, the Appeals Court held that much of this older law went 'well beyond' hot-news claims and was therefore bad law.[65] Claims regarding 'commercial morality' or society's 'ethics' were viewed as 'virtually synonymous for wrongful copying', were 'in no meaningful fashion distinguishable from infringement of a copyright', and should therefore be preempted.[66]

The Appeals Court concluded that only a narrow 'hot-news' INS-type misappropriation claim could survive preemption by copyright law. The Court identified five criteria all of which such a claim had to satisfy:

(i) a plaintiff generates or gathers information at a cost; (ii) the information is time-sensitive; (iii) a defendant's use of the information constitutes free-riding on the plaintiff's efforts; (iv) the defendant is in direct competition with a product or service offered by the plaintiffs; and (v) the ability of other parties to free-ride on the efforts of the plaintiff or others would so reduce the incentive to produce the product or service that its existence or quality would be substantially threatened.[67]

After assessing Motorola's and STATS' actions against the above criteria, the Appeals Court determined that their transmission of real-time NBA game scores and information tabulated from television and radio broadcasts of games in progress did not constitute a misappropriation of any property of the NBA. The Court identified three different informational products: first, generating the information by playing the games; second, transmitting live, full descriptions of those games; and third, collecting and retransmitting strictly factual information about the game. The first and second products were viewed as NBA's primary business. The Court believed that the NBA had 'failed to show any competitive effect whatsoever from SportsTrax on the first and second products and a lack of any free-riding by SportsTrax on the third'.[68] SportsTrax was viewed as bearing its own costs of collecting factual information on NBA games, and therefore not as a free-rider.

Whether the above five criteria are sufficient to determine that a party taking price and quote data from an exchange without due compensation could be held liable under misappropriation law is debatable. Clearly the precise circumstances of any particular claim are critical. The second criterion will almost always be satisfied. Exchanges' prices and quotes are time-sensitive. Determination of whether the other criteria are satisfied may, however, be controversial.

As far as the first criterion is concerned, it is highly debatable whether exchanges do generate their prices and quotes at cost.[69] By analogy to the Appeals Court decision with regard to the third criterion, a party copying data from a vendor and then retransmitting them might be viewed not as a free-rider, given that it had to bear the costs of collecting these data. Satisfaction of the fourth criterion would depend on exactly what service the plaintiff was providing. If it acted as a data vendor, it might be said not to be in competition with the exchange. The fifth criterion is also problematic. Whether an exchange would cease to exist, or would reduce the quality of the price and quote information it published, were third parties not to pay for its data is debatable given the other sources of income to exchanges. Unsurprisingly, the CME has argued that 'a substantial portion of financial exchanges' revenues, and thus their viability as financial markets, depends on the sale of its real-time quotations'.[70]

CONFIDENTIALITY

An obligation of confidentiality arises when one party imparts to another party secret information, on the understanding that the information is to be used only for a restricted purpose. Most exchanges attempt to impose a contractual obligation of confidentiality upon all parties receiving their information, including data vendors, not to divulge it in a proscribed manner. The nature of such obligations under UK law is discussed here.[71]

Three criteria must be satisfied for a breach of confidence to be actionable.[72] First, the information in question must 'have the necessary quality of confidence about it': it must be confidential, and must not be public property or public knowledge.[73] Although no statutory or formal standards have been established to assess whether information is confidential or not, the courts have tended to evaluate the confidentiality of commercial information by assessing whether any special economic effort would be necessary to reproduce the information.[74] Another important issue determining whether information should be considered confidential is the question of how much revelation of the information is required before it is deemed to be in the public domain. This is not a new problem. In *Exchange Telegraph Co. Ltd. v. Central News Ltd.*, the judge stated that the fact that some information was available at a particular location, did not make it a matter of public knowledge. Although the legal response to the question of when any 'relative secrecy' disappears has been seen to be dependent on the technology currently available,[75] it has also been noted that the 'widespread use of the information drives a hole into the blanket of confidence'.[76]

The second criterion that must be met for a breach of confidence to be actionable, stipulates that the person receiving the information should have done so 'in circumstances importing an obligation of confidence' on him.[77] A confidant will thus be subject to an obligation of confidentiality if he is aware of the obligation, or if he is in a position where he ought to be aware of the obligation. The law also imposes an obligation of confidentiality on third parties, that is to say on people who obtain confidential information indirectly as a result of a breach of confidentiality on the part of a direct confidant, as soon as such third parties become aware that they received the information as a result of an initial breach of confidentiality.

The third criterion that must be met for a breach of confidentiality to be actionable requires that the confidant must make an unauthorized use of the information, possibly to the detriment of the party initially confiding the information. Both elements of this criterion are sometimes difficult to prove. In particular, it is not always easy to confirm that an unauthorized use of information has taken place, and even if this can be demonstrated, proving that commercial damage has been inflicted on the confidant may be hard to show.

Although the case of *Exchange Telegraph Co. Ltd. v. Central News Ltd.* is almost one hundred years old, and thus the reasons presented for the judgment are not necessarily valid today, it does provide an insight into the judicial reasoning concerning breach of confidentiality with regard to information similar to price and quote data.[78] As well as disseminating stock exchange news, the Exchange Telegraph Co. also disseminated horse-racing results to its subscribers, subject to certain conditions. One of these conditions stated that,

the news supplied by the company is to be used only in the newspaper, or posted only in the club, news-room, office, or other place at which it is delivered. No copy of it shall be made for any other purpose than for such publication and it shall not be transmitted, communicated, or delivered to any other party or parties by messenger, telegraph, telephone, or otherwise, nor shall the subscriber assign the benefit of the whole or part of this agreement, nor let upon hire the instrument or the right to use it, nor in any way part with the possession of the instrument, without the written consent of the company.

In 1897, Extel discovered that one of its competitors, Central News, together with a closely connected company, the Column Printing Telegraph Syndicate, was disseminating almost exactly the same information as Extel itself was disseminating. In particular, Extel found on four occasions that errors and corrections which it had announced, were published almost verbatim by its competitors. Extel then sought an injunction to stop Central News and, at a later date, the Column Printing Telegraph Syndicate, from copying the information which Extel communicated to its subscribers, and from communicating this information to their subscribers.

Three key facts were established:

the communications made by the plaintiffs to their subscribers were the results of the labour of persons employed and paid by them, the names of winners having been denoted by figures posted on a board at the racecourse at Manchester, and being thence telephoned by agents of the plaintiffs to London;
information of an erroneous or misleading character published by the plaintiffs was within a very short time published by the defendant companies in consequence of information received at the office of the syndicate . . . from an unknown person;
the messages received . . . came from some source which, as the manager of the syndicate was conscious, could not be enquired into and could not honestly be made use of by the syndicate.

There were three central elements to the judgment. In response to a claim by the defendants that 'the information had become public to the world at Manchester', the judge stated that on the contrary, 'the information was not made known to the whole world; it was no doubt known to a large number of persons, but a great many more were ignorant of it'. The judge noted, secondly, that 'by their expenditure of labour and money, the plaintiffs had acquired [the] information, and it was in their hands valuable property in this sense, that persons to whom it was not known were willing to pay, and did pay, money to acquire it'. As such, the judge concluded that 'the plaintiffs were at full liberty to communicate that information upon such terms as they saw fit'.

Finally, the judge examined the question of obligation and breach of contract. He recognized that it had previously been established that 'a subscriber who communicated the information to third parties contrary to the terms [of a contract] would commit a breach of contract, and might be restrained by injunction from so doing', and also 'that a third party who induced a subscriber to break his contract, and in that way acquired and published information, might also be restrained by injunction from so doing'. The defendants claimed, however, that in this case 'all persons who received information through the plaintiff's machines were not, or might not be, under an obligation to abstain from publishing it'. They argued therefore that somebody could have legally read the news supplied by the plaintiff, and then communicated this news to the defendant.

The judge did not rule on whether such an action would have been legal or not. He did state that in the circumstances, however, this was unlikely, and therefore that the Syndicate must have acquired the information 'from or through some subscriber with knowledge or notice on the part of their manager that it was acquired contrary to the terms imposed on the plaintiff's subscribers'. The judge therefore issued an injunction to restrain the defendants from 'surreptitiously obtaining or copying' information from the defendant.

The question of whether an exchange's price and quote data can be considered confidential depends on the precise circumstances under examination. Consider the situation of a vendor re-distributing an exchange's price and quote data, having signed a confidentiality clause requiring it to treat the data it receives as confidential, and thus not to disclose them to any third party other than to an authorized subscriber. Suppose the vendor distributes the data to an unauthorized subscriber. The question of whether such an action is an actionable breach of confidence depends on whether the three relevant criteria are satisfied.

The main criterion which has been established to determine whether commercial information is confidential, is whether any special economic effort would be necessary to reproduce the information. If it is argued that the production of price and quote information, via the establishment and maintenance of an exchange, takes a great deal of labour, expense, and time, such information is likely to be classed as confidential. If, alternatively, it is claimed that the price and quote information emanating from an exchange is merely a by-product of the trading system operated by the exchange, the information would probably not be classed as confidential.

The question of the relative secrecy of the information may also stop the information from being judged confidential. When an exchange disseminates its information, it has the express aim of disseminating it as widely as possible, for the appropriate fees. In contrast to the American decision taken in *Board of Trade of the City of Chicago v. Christie Grain and Stock Company*, it can also be argued that for an exchange to attempt to classify its price and quote information as confidential, when its aim in releasing the information is to publicize it as much as practicable, may be considered perverse. The very act by an exchange of offering to sell or license its prices and quotes to whomever is willing to buy them, may dispel any notion of confidentiality imposed on the purchasers of the information. Historical price and quote data will not be regarded as confidential, given that they have already been publicly disseminated.

The second criterion is likely to be easier to prove. Given the presence of a confidentiality provision in the vendor contracts, all vendors should know that they have an obligation of confidentiality. Furthermore, if an exchange requires either that vendors insert a confidentiality clause in their subscriber contracts, or that the clients of the vendors sign a contract directly with the exchange in which there is also a confidentiality clause, then the vendors' subscribers should also know that they have an obligation of confidentiality. If neither of these conditions hold, however, then it may be difficult to expect the clients of the vendor to be aware of their supposed obligation of confidentiality. This may occur if the information distribution chain were more extended than the three-stage one initially posited, and if an exchange did not have direct contractual relationships with all the downstream users of its information.

In the case of a vendor distributing an exchange's data without the exchange's permission, it is likely to be simple to establish whether the vendor's use of the information is authorized or not—the third criterion for an actionable breach of confidence. The vendor will have a list of authorized clients, and if the subscriber receiving the information is not on the list, the vendor's use of the information will be unauthorized. Such distribution by the vendor will also be to the detriment of the exchange, which would receive less revenue from the sale of its information than if the client had been duly authorized. In the case of a more extended information chain, however, it may once again be more difficult to prove that the dissemination of data was unauthorized.

In sum, it may be difficult to prove the three criteria that must be satisfied for a breach of confidence to be actionable, in the context of a vendor which redistributes an exchange's price and quote data to an unauthorized subscriber, having signed a standard confidentiality clause. Provisions in an exchange's contract which prohibit a vendor from disseminating the exchange's data without its permission as an obligation of confidentiality, may thus be hard to enforce.

COMPETITION

If an exchange captures a large percentage of the trading in an asset or a commodity, or if it is granted any intellectual property rights in the information it disseminates, it may become the dominant or even the sole source of information about trading in the asset or the commodity. Such an exclusive position may bring the exchange within the remit of anti-trust legislation and regulation. The manner in which competition policy affects the dissemination of price and quote information is discussed in this section. The importance of EU competition law, and the conflict between competition and copyright law in the EU, are examined first of all. Next, an Australian court case between the Australian Stock Exchange and Pont Data is summarized. The case concerned the extent to which the exchange breached the domestic anti-monopoly legislation in its policies concerning the release of market data.

EU

In order to give an indication of how the dissemination of an exchange's prices and quotes may be affected by European Union competition policy, the general legal framework governing such policy is outlined, and the conflict between EU competition law and intellectual property law is examined.

General Framework[79]

One of the prime activities of the EU is 'the institution of a system ensuring that competition in the common market is not distorted'.[80] The most important Articles in the Treaty of Rome explicitly aimed at regulating competition are Articles 85 and 86. Article 85 prohibits agreements and concerted practices between undertakings which have as their object or effect the restriction of competition within the EU, and which affect trade between Member States. Article 86, the central legal instrument established to control monopolistic behaviour, states that,

Any abuse by one or more undertakings of a dominant position within the common market or in a substantial part of it shall be prohibited as incompatible with the common market in so far as it may affect trade between Member States. Such abuse may, in particular, consist in: (a) directly or indirectly imposing unfair purchase or selling prices or unfair trading conditions; (b) limiting production, markets or technical development to the prejudice of consumers; (c) applying dissimilar conditions to equivalent transactions with other trading parties, thereby placing them at a competitive disadvantage; (d) making the conclusion of contracts subject to acceptance by the other parties of supplementary obligations which, by their nature or according to commercial usage, have no connection with the subject of such contracts.[81]

Article 86 is a directly applicable Treaty provision, and is thus enforceable in proceedings in national courts and takes precedence over national law. The initial implementation of Article 86 is undertaken by the Commission. Its decisions may be appealed to the Court of First Instance (CFI), and the CFI's decisions may be appealed, on points of law, to the European Court of Justice (ECJ). Both private and public institutions are subject to Article 86.

The assessment of whether an undertaking holds a dominant position is usually undertaken in two stages: first by ascertaining what the relevant market is, and then by evaluating the undertaking's power in that market. When evaluating what constitutes the relevant market, the geographical extent of the market is examined in order to determine with what other undertakings it is in competition. In addition, the product market is defined in such a manner that where goods or services can be regarded as interchangeable, they are viewed as being within the same market. Generally each Member State is viewed as a 'substantial part' of the EU, and the inter-state trade clause is typically interpreted in a broad manner.[82]

The court has stated that,

[a] dominant position . . . relates to a position of economic strength enjoyed by an undertaking which enables it to prevent effective competition being maintained on the relevant market by affording it the power to behave to an appreciable extent independently of its competitors, customers and ultimately of its consumers.[83]

No definitive criteria are established in the Treaty for assessing when an undertaking has a dominant position, so a range of indicative standards has been developed. These include whether the undertaking has a statutory monopoly, whether there are any legal provisions granting it exclusivity such as intellectual property rights, what its market share over time is, and whether there are any barriers to entry in the undertaking's industry, such as superior technology, economies of scale, vertical integration, a well-developed distribution system, product differentiation, or the undertaking's overall size and strength.

Although it is not an offence for a firm to have a dominant position, the ECJ has stated that a firm in a dominant position 'has a special responsibility not to allow its conduct to impair undistorted competition on the common market'.[84] The Treaty itself identifies four instances of abusive conduct by an undertaking in a dominant position. Of critical importance is the conduct of a monopolist who reduces his output and increases the price of his goods above the competitive level. The assessment of when a pricing strategy is excessive has, however, proved, both conceptually and practically, fraught with difficulty.

Amongst the questions which the Commission has addressed are: Should you add an acceptable profit margin to the actual cost of producing the goods to obtain the hypothetically competitive price? What is the actual cost of producing the goods? Should costs be measured historically, or at their present day value? How should fixed costs be allocated? How should the presence of risk be assessed? and, How should the costs of a multi-product firm be apportioned in assessing whether an undertaking is making an unreasonable profit in one particular market? The presence of large profits at an undertaking is not definitive in determining abusive conduct: they may be due to efficiency, rather than any monopoly status. Where appropriate, the price of similar goods elsewhere is used as a basis for comparison.[85]

Many types of conduct, in addition to excessive pricing, have been found to be abusive. These include price discrimination, contractual tie-ins, a refusal to supply, conduct in one market stifling competition in an adjacent market, selling at below cost, discounting practices, selective distribution of goods, and exclusive dealing. As a practical matter, it is important to note both that the Commission does not want to become a price setter, and that the resources it has available for competition investigations are extremely scarce. The Commission has therefore focused its investigations on instances which have as wide a relevance as possible.

Article 85(3) specifies some situations when anti-competitive agreements or concerted practices between undertakings may escape the attention of EU competition law, if they have some compensating benefits. No similar forms of exemption are allowed in Article 86, however, for the behaviour of an undertaking in a dominant position. Formally, therefore, Article 86 does not allow any issues other than an assessment of competition, to be taken into account when assessing whether a particular conduct is abusive or not. In some instances, however, the ECJ and the Commission have interpreted the term 'abuse' in a rather wide manner, and have developed the concept of an 'objective justification' which might excuse the conduct of an undertaking which at first sight may appear abusive. If there is an *objective justification* for the conduct of a dominant undertaking, the Court has also asked whether the undertaking behaved in a 'proportional' way in defending its legitimate interests. In particular, an undertaking is not allowed to take more restrictive measures than are necessary to achieve its objectives.

Decisions of the Commission on competition matters are made public, but complaints to the Commission are not. There have, nevertheless, been unofficial reports that the Commission investigated the data dissemination policy of the information vending arm of the Brussels Stock Exchange after an informal objection by Reuters in 1989. No confirmation that such a complaint was made, nor any decision on it, has been issued by the Commission.

In addition to Articles 85 and 86, the Treaty is also concerned to reduce barriers to trade, and to establish and promote the European 'freedoms of movement'. In particular, Articles 30 to 36 prohibit quantitative restrictions on the import and export of goods between Member States of the EU, and all measures having equivalent effect. Similarly, Articles 59 to 66 prohibit restrictions on the freedom to provide services between Member States of the EU. In certain circumstances when such restrictions arise, they may be viewed as being anti-competitive. Only national measures and not the behaviour of private parties are the subject of the case law argued under these Articles.[86]

Intellectual Property[87]

The assignment of an intellectual property right, which grants exclusivity over the right to license the reproduction of a particular 'work', by its very nature conflicts with competition law, the general aim of which is to dismantle exclusive arrangements. This conflict has proved particularly acute in the EU for two reasons. First there is little harmonization of EU copyright law, and thus for the most part it is national legislation which determines copyright.[88] The diversity of such national legislation has been thought to obstruct trade between Member

States in the EU and thus to act as an impediment to the development of an inte-grated market. The competition and freedom of movement provisions in the Treaty of Rome have therefore been employed as a tool to attenuate the perceived adverse effects of such diversity.

The second reason why the conflict between competition and intellectual property rights has been so intense in the EU is that there is a tension between different elements of the Treaty itself. The right to move goods freely throughout the EU is subject to several exemptions, the most important of which, in this context, is that it not be allowed to prevent prohibitions or restrictions on 'the protection of industrial and commercial property'.[89] Intellectual property has been taken to be included in such industrial and commercial property. The same article in the Treaty also states, however, that such prohibitions or restrictions are not allowed to 'constitute a means of arbitrary discrimination or a disguised restriction on trade between Member States'. In addition, these prohibitions often conflict directly with the Treaty's competition provisions, Articles 85 and 86. The question of which part of the Treaty is pre-eminent, and of whether the protection of industrial and commercial property on the one hand, or the pursuit of compe-tition or free trade in the EU on the other, should dictate policy, has therefore had to be resolved in the courts.

A brief summary of the jurisprudence of the ECJ on this conflict is now presented, followed by an analysis of the seminal case in which this conflict has been reviewed by the Court, namely *RTE v. EC Commission (Magill)*.[90] The factual and legal background to the case, and the final judgment by the ECJ, are discussed in turn.

Jurisprudence: A key conceptual approach that the ECJ has used to resolve the conflict between competition and free trade law on the one hand and intellectual property law on the other hand, has been to draw a distinction between the *exis-tence* and the *exercise* of an intellectual property right. It noted that,

Whilst the Treaty does not affect the existence of rights recognized by the laws of Member State in matters of industrial and commercial property, yet the exercise of those rights may nevertheless, depending on the circumstances, be restricted by the prohibitions contained in the Treaty.[91]

A significant difficulty, however, has been to identify the existence of a right which is separable from its exercise. The existence of a right has also been linked to another key juridical concept developed by the ECJ which relates to the *specific subject-matter* of the right. Only if an intellectual property right granted by a national law falls within the area recognized by the ECJ as the specific subject-matter of the right, is a prohibition on the free movement of goods by the national law deemed compatible with Community law. 'If a national law's protection reaches beyond this limit, its restriction on the free movement of goods becomes impermissible'.[92] There are no standards estab-lished in the Treaty for what constitutes an intellectual property right's specific subject-matter, and the Court has therefore attempted to define such standards on a case by case basis.

No undertaking is viewed as being dominant simply because it has an intellectual property right. Furthermore, the exercise by a dominant firm of its intellectual property rights is not of itself an abuse, in particular if it 'is justified for the purposes of safeguarding rights which constitute the specific subject matter of such property'.[93] The Court has, however, noted that,

the exercise of an exclusive right . . . may be prohibited by Article 86 it if involves, on the part of an undertaking holding a dominant position, certain abusive conduct . . . , provided that such conduct is liable to affect trade between Member States.[94]

The Court's use of the *existence/exercise* distinction and the *specific subject-matter* concept has not resolved all ambiguity about when particular conduct may be viewed as abusive. In one case, a car manufacturer invoked its design rights to prevent the manufacturing and marketing of spare parts by an independent third party.[95] The ECJ refused to impose a compulsory licence on the owner of the design rights, stating that the nature of the exclusive right in the design was to prevent third parties from manufacturing and selling or importing products incorporating the design. An obligation on the proprietor to grant a licence to third parties, even for a reasonable royalty, was viewed as depriving the proprietor of the substance of his design right. The refusal to grant a licence was thus not taken as an abuse of a dominant position. The ECJ did, however, provide three examples where the enforcement of an exclusive right by a dominant firm might violate Article 86: the charging of prices at an unfair level, an arbitrary refusal to supply the spare parts, or a decision no longer to procure spare parts although cars of that model were still in circulation.[96]

Magill: Factual and Legal Background: The conflict between intellectual property rights on the one hand and competition and free trade law on the other came to a head in *Magill.* The case arose because three television broadcasters refused to sanction the use of information about their individual programme schedules by a publisher who wished to produce a combined listing schedule. It was the subject of an initial Commission decision, an appeal to the CFI, and finally an appeal to the ECJ.

The case concerned three television broadcasters, and their publication arms, from the UK and Ireland: the British Broadcasting Corporation (BBC), Independent Television Publications (ITP), and Radio Telefis Eireann (RTE). Each broadcaster used to prepare a schedule of programmes for broadcasting which was finalized about two weeks before transmission. Copyright under the programmers' national law subsisted in the listings, and belonged to the broadcasters. For a long time, the weekly programme schedules had been released to third parties, who were permitted to publish them, but only a day at a time or for both days of the weekend. Such third parties were, however, forbidden to publish the full week's listings a week in advance. This right was reserved for the broadcasters' own in-house weekly television publications.[97]

In 1986 Magill TV Guide Ltd. (Magill), an Irish publisher, began to publish a comprehensive weekly guide, including the schedules from all three companies. The three companies then obtained an interim injunction in Ireland stopping Magill from any further publication which infringed their copyrights, a decision which was later upheld in a judgment of the Irish High Court.[98] In April 1986, Magill complained to the European Commission on the grounds that the broadcasters' refusal to license the joint publication of their weekly schedules breached Article 86 of the Treaty.

In its decision on the matter the Commission agreed.[99] The Commission identified three separate product markets: daily listings by each individual TV station, weekly listings by each individual TV station, and comprehensive weekly TV magazines. The Commission found the TV companies to be dominant in their individual weekly listings. In addition, it claimed that experience in other countries where weekly magazines were available proved that a demand for comprehensive weekly information existed and that consumers would not regard the stations' limited listings and a comprehensive listing to be interchangeable. As a result third parties wishing to publish weekly programme schedules were in a position of economic dependence on the broadcasters. Preventing the introduction of a comprehensive weekly guide, and thus attempting to preserve a 'derivative' market for themselves, was found to constitute an abuse of the broadcasters' dominant position. The Commission said that the copyright had been used as an instrument of abuse in a manner outside the specific subject-matter of the intellectual property right claimed. It therefore ordered the broadcasters to make their programme schedules available to third parties on non-discriminatory terms, against payment of a licence fee, if desired.

The BBC, ITP, and RTE appealed to the CFI to annul the Commission's decision.[100] The CFI upheld the Commission's decision in all significant respects. The relevant market was identified as being the publication of weekly listings, and the publication of television magazines was found to be a commercial activity unrelated to the broadcasters' main activity of broadcasting. The broadcasters were found both to have, and to have abused, a dominant position. The court considered as indicative of abuse, the use of copyright to prevent the emergence on the market of a new product for which there was a significant consumer demand. The broadcasters were viewed as using their copyright in the programme listings market to secure a monopoly in the derivative market of weekly television guides. A key element of the judgment stated,

while it is plain that the exercise of the exclusive right to reproduce a protected work is not in itself an abuse, that does not apply, when, in the light of the details of each individual case, it is apparent that the right is exercised in such ways and circumstances as in fact to pursue an aim manifestly contrary to the objectives of Art. 86. In that event, the copyright is not exercised in a manner which corresponds to its essential function, within the meaning of Art. 36 of the Treaty, which is to protect the moral rights in the work and ensure a reward for the creative effort, while respecting the aims of, in particular, Art. 86. In that case, the primacy of Community law, particularly as regards principles as fundamental as those of the free movement of goods and freedom of competition, prevails over any use of a rule of national intellectual property law in a manner contrary to those principles.[101]

Following the CFI's judgment, ITP and RTE appealed to the ECJ to overturn the CFI's decision.[102] A preliminary opinion about the case by Advocate General Gulmann was then presented to the ECJ.[103] Although he argued that copyright laws did not confer unrestricted exclusive rights on copyright owners, he believed that 'in principle, where copyright law confers an exclusive right, that must be respected by competition law'. He proposed that the exclusive rights granted to copyright owners may be restricted only when an infringement of a copyright owner's right of exclusive reproduction did not interfere with its essential function, namely to protect the moral rights in the work and ensure a reward for the creative effort. He then determined that there were no such special circumstances in *Magill*, and therefore recommended overturning both the Commission's original decision and the CFI's judgment.

Magill: Final Judgment: The essence of the ECJ's final judgment on Magill was brief.[104] The Court confirmed that mere ownership of an intellectual property right was not sufficient to confer a dominant position in a market.[105] It noted, however, that RTE, ITP, and the BBC enjoyed a *de facto* monopoly over the information necessary to produce listings for the television programmes, given that it was only they who produced the television programmes. The Court argued that this *de facto* monopoly allowed them to prevent competition in the market for weekly television magazines, and therefore meant that they did occupy a dominant position.[106]

The Court then found three reasons why the actions of RTE, ITP, and the BBC were abusive under Article 86 of the Treaty.[107] First, their refusal to provide the listing information prevented the appearance of a new product which they did not offer, and for which there was a potential consumer demand. Second, there was no justification for such a refusal, either in the activity of television broadcasting or in that of publishing television magazines. Finally, by denying Magill access to their listing information, which was the raw material indispensable for the compilation of a weekly television guide, the appellants reserved to themselves the secondary market of weekly guides by excluding all competition on that market. Given these abuses, the Court maintained it was unnecessary to examine the conflict between national intellectual property rights and the freedom to trade between Member States enshrined in Article 36 of the Treaty.[108] No analysis of the *existence/exercise* distinction and the *specific subject-matter* concept was undertaken. The Court concluded that the Commission's decision to impose compulsory licensing on the appellants was appropriate, given that it was the only way of bringing the abuses to an end.

Interpretation of the relevance of the judgment for questions about market data ownership is controversial. One view is that it is a seminal ruling for exchanges concerning the dissemination of their price and quote data. Given that most exchanges operate a *de facto* monopoly as the sole source for the price and quote data emanating from their trading systems, they are likely to be seen as having a dominant position in the market for the provision of these data. Any refusal by an exchange to license the use of its data, notwithstanding any copyright claimed in the data, will therefore probably be viewed as abusive.

An alternative view, espoused by Bull (1997: 85) is that the *Magill* judgment is essentially irrelevant for questions about market data ownership. She takes this position for two reasons. First, the judgment is regarded as focusing on new or secondary products, whereas in contrast the market for raw or value-added data is believed to be clearly established as a primary market. Second, the issue of monopoly intellectual property rights, the subject matter of those rights, and the dominant position they give an IPR owner, was not analysed by the ECJ. Bull believes that the national courts of EU Member States still have to decide between applying *Magill*, or continuing to adhere to the Berne Convention on copyright.

Australia: Pont Data v. Australian Stock Exchange

In February 1990, the Australian Stock Exchange (ASX) was taken to court by Pont Data Australia Pty. Ltd., a commercial data vendor, for conducting business against the Trade Practices Act 1974 (TPA), the anti-monopoly legislation in Australia. The exchange was accused of charging too much for the data arising from its operations, and of discriminating in favour of its own data vendor over the commercial vendors who were in competition with it.[109] After an initial ruling that was substantively in favour of Pont, an appeal was lodged by the ASX. The judgment in the appeal considerably modified the lower court's ruling, this time much in favour of the ASX. The case was finally settled out of court in a secret agreement. Three aspects of the dispute are described: the background to the case, the initial judgment, and the appeal.

Background[110]

In 1986 the ASX and its subsidiary ASX Operations Pty Ltd. (ASXO) had a division, the Market Information Services Division, which disseminated price and quote information electronically. The Market Information Services Division provided a data service, the JEC (Joint Exchanges Computers) Data Service (JDS), which delivered five electronic signals containing differing amounts of information. Signal C was the general ASX trading signal. It was transmitted on a real-time basis, contained information about the trades, quotes, and indices, from all the subsidiary exchanges of ASX and the Stock Exchange Automated Trading System (SEATS), and was the sole source of such data. One of the recipients of Signal C was Pont Data (Pont), the Australian subsidiary of Pont International, a world-wide supplier of information to the financial services market. In addition to supplying its electronic feeds through JDS, ASXO also operated a retail information service, JECNET (Joint Exchanges Computers Network), which delivered price and quote information via a screen-based network to end-users of information.

At that time the ASX charged for Signal C on a per-terminal basis.[111] In a strategic plan presented to the ASX in September 1986 it was stated that it was 'essential that ASX achieve a monopoly on the wholesaling of its market information in order to establish one integrated Australian market and to leverage profits from third parties who provide value-added services with this information'.[112] The ASX subsequently introduced three new contracts for the provision of Signal C: the 'dynamic', the 'non-dynamic', and the 'international' contract. The term 'dynamic' refers to an information service in which information is automatically updated on the client's screen. In contrast, in a 'non-dynamic' service information is only updated if the client specifically requests it by pushing the appropriate key on his terminal. The international contract is ignored here.

Three types of parties were required to sign the dynamic contract: ASXO, a party called the 'Carrier' (i.e. the vendor), and another party called the 'Licensee' (i.e. the end-user). The contract specified that ASXO supply the ASX Signal on a real-time basis to the Carrier for transmission to the Licensee. The Carrier was licensed to transmit the data to the Licensee, and the Licensee was licensed to receive them. There were several key conditions in the agreement. The Carrier was not allowed to 'publish, show or make available the Information to any other person'.[113] The Licensee was not allowed to 'publish, show or make available the Information to any other persons except by way of fair dealing for the purpose of research, private study, criticism or review'. The Carrier was not permitted to store the information beyond the day on which it was first transmitted to the Carrier, unless an 'Unrestricted Licence Fee' had been paid. The Carrier was not allowed to 'supply the Information or any part thereof to any other person on terms that would allow that person to do any act or thing that either the Carrier or the Licensee [had] hereby agreed not to do'. The non-dynamic agreement was similar in most aspects to the dynamic one, but did not require that the ultimate user be a signatory to the agreement.

The proposed fee structure was that a Carrier would pay a monthly licence fee of A$150 for the first terminal of every Licensee, together with a further A$75 for each subsequent terminal of a Licensee. In addition the Carrier had to pay a licence fee of A$15,000 for the non-dynamic contract, or an unrestricted licence fee of A$60,000 for the dynamic contract.

By 2 September 1988 only three subscribers had signed the new agreements, and the manager of the Market Information Services Division wrote to the other subscribers saying that unless they signed the new agreements by 9 September 1988, the ASX would terminate the supply of Signal C to them. Pont signed the agreements on 9 September 1988, but stated that it was doing so only because of the 'commercial coercion' that the ASX exerted on it. Pont stated that it had 'little alternative' to doing so, if it wished to remain commercially viable.[114] Following the signing of the three agreements, Pont asserted that the ASX was in breach of the Trade Practices Act 1974 (TPA). Three of Pont's claims, concerning respectively sections 45, 46, and 49 of the TPA, are examined here.

The relevant part of section 45 essentially declared that a corporation shall not make a contract or arrangement, or arrive at an understanding, which had the purpose, or would have or be likely to have the effect, of substantially lessening competition. The relevant part of section 46 declared that a corporation that had a substantial degree of power in a market shall not take advantage of that power for the purpose of preventing the entry into, or deterring or preventing competitive conduct in, that or any other market. The relevant part of section 49 essentially declared that a corporation shall not discriminate between purchasers of goods of like grade and quality.

Initial Judgment and Relief

The judge ruled in favour of Pont with regard to all three of these claims. When applying section 46 to any particular case, the judge stated that the first question that arises is the definition of the relevant market or markets. From previous case history, he noted that the 'definition of the market and evaluation of the degree of power in that market are "part of the same process and it is for the sake of simplicity of analysis that the two are separated" '.115 He stated that 'if the defendant is vertically integrated, the relevant market for determining [the] degree of market power will be at the product level which is the source of that power'.

The judge accepted that there were two markets in Australia relevant to Pont's claims: the first being 'a market for the provision of facilities for public trading of stocks and securities (a "stock exchanges market")' and the second being 'a market for the supply of information about activities on stock exchanges (an "information market")'.116 He observed that the ASX did not have a monopoly in the stock exchanges market, as a number of other stock markets had been allowed to operate in competition with it. Notwithstanding this, the judge noted that the 'competition provided by [these] exempt stock markets would appear to be minimal' and therefore argued that the ASX had a substantial degree of power in the stock exchanges market. He also agreed with Pont's claim that the ASX and ASXO had substantial control over the information market.

Following the determination that the ASX had a substantial degree of market power, the judge then considered the exchange's purpose in establishing the three agreements. He concluded that the ASX's actions were informed throughout by the aim, presented in its strategic plan, of achieving a monopoly in the wholesaling of its market information. The judge stated that the 'evidence clearly show[ed] that it was a purpose of the respondents to prevent anyone else entering the stock exchanges market. . . . Similarly, it was at all times a purpose of ASXO to prevent the material supplied by it being wholesaled by others'. Given that the objective of the contracts was to prevent competition by others with JDS in the wholesale information market, and to deter competition with JECNET in the retail market, he judged that the respondents had breached section 46.

The judge accepted that in 'finding that the respondents had the purpose of preventing the entry of somebody into a market or deterring or preventing a person engaging in competition in a market, the Court would necessarily have found that ASXO had the purpose of substantially lessening competition'.[117] This proved the section 45 claim.

The judge also found that ASXO did discriminate between subscribers according to the number of end-user terminals they took, whether they supplied dynamic and non-dynamic data, and whether they stored the data. He noted that these differences had 'nothing to do with the nature of what ASXO supplie[d], but rather with the use to which subscribers . . . put the signal'.[118] He therefore judged that the section 49 claim was also established.

In assessing the extent of relief he should award Pont, the judge decided he had the power to alter the contracts so that Pont could continue to receive Signal C on 'reasonable' terms. Pont had argued that as the ASX had 'failed to establish that the provision of Signal C to subscribers occasion[ed] any cost which it would not otherwise incur, [the ASX] ought to be compelled to provide that signal at a nominal price'.[119] In contrast, the ASX had argued that it was unreasonable for the Court to 'compel it to give away its asset' as 'Signal C [was] a valuable resource which [the ASX was] entitled to exploit'.[120] The judge decided that satisfactory criteria for deciding what was commercially reasonable would be to evaluate the cost, and the normal profit margin, associated with delivering such a service. He accepted the price was 'likely to be low, compared with the fees charged in the . . . [new] contracts. But that [was] because the cost of supply [was] low. In a competitive situation that low cost would be reflected in a low price.'

The judge decided that as no evidence was available to show that the ASX suffered any costs attached to the supply of Signal C which it would not otherwise incur, a nominal charge of A$100 per year should be made by the ASX for the provision of Signal C to Pont.[121] He also reconfirmed that the basis on which the trial and judgment had been conducted, was that,

regardless of Signal C, ASX would operate a computer system. In other words, [he said] if Signal C close[d] down today there would remain a need for a computer system for the satisfaction of the other functions of the exchange. The question of the cost of Signal C ha[d] to be approached by reference to that underlying fact. The relevant cost [was] the extra cost which [was] incurred by ASX because of the need to supply real time information to the subscribers to Signal C.[122]

The court also changed the terms of the agreements between ASXO and Pont so as to remove all the provisions opposed by Pont, which the court held contravened the Act, and ordered that ASX be restrained from refusing to supply Signal C on terms similar to those that had been struck out of the agreements.[123]

Appeal and Subsequent Relief

The ASX and ASXO appealed against the initial judgment, complaining principally about the orders reformulating the agreements and imposing upon Pont and ASXO an inappropriate fee structure. The appeal judges overturned substantial parts of the initial decision.[124] They ruled that the ASX and ASXO had not discriminated between purchasers of goods of like grade and quality (the section 49 claim). They argued that what Pont purchased from the ASX and ASXO could not be described as 'goods', and that the Act was only applicable to the purchase of 'goods'. Although electricity was defined as 'goods' in the Act, the judges determined that this was not what Pont purchased from the appellants.

The judges decided that the ASX and ASXO had also not prevented entry into, or deterred competitive conduct in, the stock exchanges market (the section 46 claim). They argued that the evidence which Pont had adduced showed that what the ASX and ASXO had done was to prevent the unlawful establishment of a stock exchange in Australia and the establishment of an off-shore exchange dealing in Australian securities. Neither of these activities were, however, prohibited by the TPA.

The judges further determined that the ASX and ASXO had not contravened section 45, by reason of having provisions in the contracts having the *purpose* of substantially lessening competition.[125] The judges examined the purposes of the ASX and ASXO both in the stock exchanges market and in the information market. They argued that, given their finding with regard to section 46 concerning the stock exchanges market, the ASX and ASXO must be successful in their appeal against section 45 concerning the stock exchanges market. Furthermore, the judges decided that the first judgment had not made the 'necessary factual findings to lay the ground' to conclude that the ASX and ASXO actions had or were likely to have the *effect* of substantially lessening competition in the stock exchanges market. The appeal was therefore upheld with regard to section 45 concerning the stock exchange market.

The judges also argued that it 'was not possible to infer a purpose of substantially lessening competition' in the information market. The judges did, however, determine that the provisions in the agreements which required the provision to ASXO by subscribers of their own commercial information and which prohibited wholesaling, were likely to have the effect of substantially lessening competition in the information market. The initial judgment in Pont's favour was therefore upheld concerning section 45 with regard to the information market.

The initial judgment in Pont's favour was also upheld with regard to section 46 in the information market. The judges determined that the ASX and ASXO had taken advantage of their power in the information market for the purpose of preventing competition in the wholesale market, and deterring competition with JECNET in the retail market.

The appeal judges dismissed the relief provided by the lower court judge concerning the dynamic and the non-dynamic agreements. They accepted ASX's argument that the lower court judge had erred in stating that, 'once it was accepted that ASXO "was not entitled to misuse its monopoly position", it ought not to be regarded as unfair to compel it to supply Signal C to Pont at a price which reflected the cost together with a low margin of profit'. Both the dynamic and the non-dynamic agreements were ruled void *ab initio*. Although the judges noted that the Court had the power to vary the contract in question, they believed that 'the Court must be slow to impose upon the parties a regime which could not represent a bargain they would have struck between them'.[126] They therefore ordered that the pre-9 September 1988 contract, which had been entered into willingly between ASXO and Pont, should be reinstated.[127]

SECURITIES MARKETS

The manner in which the legislation and regulation governing securities markets affects the dissemination of price and quote information is examined in this section. Although attention is focused on the USA, one aspect of the UK environment is described. Two preliminary comments are important. First, and as already noted, the separation of the law and regulation governing trading systems from that affecting the dissemination of information is not always clear cut. For example, the statutory and regulatory basis governing exchanges, national associations, and the NMS in the USA, and the transparency provisions of the ISD in the EU, also govern the dissemination of price and quote information in their respective jurisdictions. These were discussed in the previous chapter. Second, although the main laws, regulations, cases, and decisions, relevant for the dissemination of information are discussed in this section, there are many others not examined here.

The section is composed of six parts. In the first, the American law and regulation governing securities information processors and exclusive processors is described. The next four parts contain descriptions of four American judicial and regulatory cases and decisions. In part two, the settlement of a dispute between two data vendors, Bunker Ramo and GTE, and the Options Price Reporting Authority (OPRA), concerning whether information on options transactions could be charged for, is outlined. In the third part, a court case concerning the price that the NASD was allowed to charge for the information arising from the trading on its system is examined. The SEC's regulatory analysis of the importance of transparency on two trading systems, the NYSE Off-Hours Trading (OHT) Sessions and NASDAQ International, are summarized in parts four and five. In the final part, two reports by the UK's Office of Fair Trading (OFT) on transparency on the London Stock Exchange are discussed.[128]

Securities Information Processors and Exclusive Processors

A 'securities information processor' (SIP) is defined in the SEA as,

any person engaged in the business of (i) collecting, processing, or preparing for distribution or publication, or assisting, participating in or co-ordinating the distribution or publication of, information with respect to transactions in or quotations for any security (other than an exempted security) or (ii) distributing or publishing (whether by means of a ticker tape, a communications network, a terminal display device, or otherwise) on a current and continuing basis, information with respect to such transactions or quotations.[129]

An 'exclusive processor' is defined as,

any securities information processor or self-regulatory organization which, directly or indirectly, engages on an exclusive basis on behalf of any national securities exchange or
registered securities association, or any national securities exchange or registered securities association which engages on an exclusive basis on its own behalf, in collecting,
processing, or preparing for distribution or publication any information with respect to (i)
transactions or quotations on or effected or made by means of any facility of such
exchange or (ii) quotations distributed or published by means of any electronic system
operated or controlled by such association.[130]

All SIPs and exclusive SIPs have to be registered with the SEC, unless the SEC
exempts them from registration. Such exemptions must be 'consistent with the
public interest, the protection of investors, and ... the maintenance of fair and
orderly markets in securities and the removal of impediments to and perfection of the
mechanism of a national market system'.[131] Although the SEC thus has jurisdiction
over all SIPs, for the most part it has not seen the need to regulate non-exclusive SIPs
(except via the display rule). The central thrust of its attention has been on exclusive
SIPs, those SIPs which have monopolistic control over a market's data.

When granting the registration of an exclusive SIP, the SEC must find that it
operates 'fairly and efficiently'.[132] If an SIP 'prohibits or limits any person in
respect of access to services offered, directly or indirectly', the SIP must notify
the SEC for review of such a prohibition or limitation.[133] If the Commission
subsequently finds that the person has been 'discriminated against unfairly', or
that the SIP's prohibition or limitation is inconsistent with the provisions of the
Act and the rules and regulations made thereunder, or that the SIP's prohibition
or limitation 'imposes any burden on competition not necessary or appropriate'
for the furtherance of the purposes of the Act, the SEC must set the prohibition
or limitation aside.

The legislative history behind the development of the law on SIPs and exclusive SIPs gives an insight into why the statutes were passed. When considering
the legislative proposals, the Senate noted that,

any exclusive processor is, in effect, a public utility, and thus it must function in a manner
which is absolutely neutral with respect to all market centers, all market makers, and all
private firms. Although the existence of a monopolistic processing facility does not necessarily raise antitrust problems, serious antitrust questions would be posed if access to this
facility and its services were not available on reasonable and nondiscriminatory terms to
all in the trade or if its charges were not reasonable.[134]

With respect to quotations for, and transactions in, the majority of securities, the
purposes of the Act's regulation of SIPs are stated to be:

(A) [to] prevent the use, distribution, or publication of fraudulent, deceptive or manipulative information ... ;
(B) [to] assure the prompt, accurate, reliable, and fair collection, processing, distribution
and publication of information . . . and the fairness and usefulness of the form and content
of such information;

(C) [to] assure that all securities information processors may, for purposes of distribution and publication, obtain on fair and reasonable terms such information . . . as is collected, processed, or prepared for distribution or publication by any exclusive processor of such information;

(D) [to] assure that all exchange members, brokers, dealers, securities information processors, and, subject to such limitations as the Commission, by rule, may impose as necessary or appropriate for the protection of investors or maintenance of fair and orderly markets, all other persons may obtain on terms which are not unreasonably discriminatory such information with respect to quotations for and transactions in such securities as is published or distributed by any self-regulatory organization or securities information processor;

(E) [to] assure that all exchange members, brokers, and dealers transmit and direct orders for the purchase or sale of qualified securities in a manner consistent with the establishment and operation of a national market system;

(F) [to] assure equal regulation of all markets for qualified securities and all exchange members, brokers, and dealers effecting transactions in such securities.[135]

Bunker Ramo and GTE Corporation v. OPRA

In 1978, the SEC ruled on a dispute between two quote vendors, Bunker Ramo and GTE Corporation, on the one side, and OPRA on the other.[136] The conflict arose when OPRA decided to charge a fee to vendors, news services and others, for having access to its high speed transmission of options last sale reports. This was done in order to recoup the costs of developing and operating the consolidated options reporting system. The SEC analysed three issues related to the dispute, only one of which is examined here. This was the question of whether OPRA was allowed to charge vendors a fixed access fee for receiving information about options transaction reports.

The SEC ruled that although the charging of such a fee by an exclusive SIP, like OPRA, was a limitation on access, it was nevertheless, consistent with the Act. The Commission expressly ignored the question of 'whether the costs incorporated by OPRA into the access fee represent limitations on access which are permitted under the Act, or whether the level of the fee charged by OPRA [was] reasonable'. The fee was not deemed unfair or discriminatory, given that it was charged equally to all subscribers, and it was also not viewed as imposing a burden on competition.

Bunker Ramo asserted in its verbal testimony that,

the imposition of a fixed access fee on vendors would impose a burden on competition which [was] not necessary or appropriate since a vendor, to be on an equal footing with other vendors, would need the same number of customers as other vendors in order to spread its fixed costs over the same number of units. . . . If a vendor had fewer customers, but [paid] the same access fee, it would be forced either to decrease its profitability by absorbing some of the cost or to pass a higher proportional share of the access fee along to its smaller number of customers.

In response the SEC noted that 'although OPRA might have chosen alternative means to derive revenues equivalent to those derived from the access fee, the

Commission cannot determine that any particular alternative would have been more appropriate than that chosen by OPRA'.

NASD v. SEC and Instinet

Following the introduction of the quote rule, a disagreement arose between the NASD on the one hand, and the SEC and Instinet on the other hand, concerning the price the NASD could require Instinet to charge its subscribers for receiving quote information arising from the trading on NASDAQ. After several reviews, the SEC rejected the fees that the NASD proposed that Instinet require its customers to pay for the NASD's National Quotation Data Service (NQDS) as being excessive. The dispute culminated in a court case in 1986. The background to the case, the arguments presented in the SEC's ruling and in the briefs to the court, and the judgment, are summarized in turn.

Background

At the time of the case, the NASD provided market information in four forms: the Level 1, Level 2, and Level 3 services, and the NQDS. The Level 1 service contained information about the best bid and offer for each security traded on NASDAQ in the form of an electronic data feed. It was available to data vendors who then distributed it to subscribers. Subscribers to Level 1 were required to pay a monthly fee of $8.75 per computer terminal to the NASD, in addition to the fees the data vendors charged. The Level 1 service was viewed as being wholesale in nature.

The Level 2 service contained information about all market maker bids and offers for all NASDAQ securities, and also contained a 'query function' which allowed subscribers to obtain the most recent bids and offers. The NASD distributed the Level 2 service directly to subscribers for a monthly fee of $150 per computer terminal. The Level 3 service had the same information as that in the Level 2 service, but also allowed new quotes to be entered into the NASDAQ system. It was therefore solely for the use of market makers. As with the Level 2 Service, the Level 3 service was provided solely by the NASD, and cost $150 per month per terminal. Both the Level 2 and Level 3 services were viewed as being retail in nature, because they were supplied directly to the end-users. The fourth service, the NQDS, contained the same information as that in the Level 2 service. Instead, however, of being marketed directly to subscribers by the NASD, it was provided in the form of an electronic feed to data vendors who processed the data delivered in the feed and then re-distributed them to subscribers.

The NASD started the NQDS as a result of the SEC's quote Rule. At the outset of the proposals to establish the NQDS, Instinet was the only data vendor which indicated an interest in being a subscriber to it. Instinet wanted to use the NQDS to provide a service that was in competition with the NASD's Level 2 service. Following a break-down in negotiations between the NASD and Instinet to determine the terms on which the NQDS would be supplied, the NASD proposed a fee schedule to the SEC in June 1983. Under this schedule, Instinet was to be charged a $3,200 per month 'vendor fee', to cover the cost of transmitting the data from the NASD to Instinet, and Instinet's subscribers were to be charged a monthly 'subscriber fee'.

The NASD argued that its fees should be based on the value of the service provided to Instinet. It proposed to base the subscriber fee on the $150 per terminal fee paid by its Level 2 and Level 3 customers, but to discount this amount to reflect the fact that Instinet subscribers would receive quotations for only NMS securities rather than all securities traded through NASDAQ. The discount was to be in rough proportion to the percentage of total NASDAQ trading volume not consisting of NMS securities. Instinet responded to the NASD's proposals by claiming that the NASD, as both an SIP and an exclusive processor, had proposed fees at a level and on terms that inappropriately limited and prohibited Instinet's access to information available from the NQDS.[137] Instinet argued that because the NASD was a public utility, its fees should be based on the costs it incurred in collecting the NQDS data.

SEC Ruling and Briefs for the Court
The SEC determined that the NASD's pricing structure constituted a denial of access to Instinet to the information arising from the NASD's system. The SEC then assessed whether such a denial by the NASD was inconsistent with the Act and subsequent regulations. The SEC believed that all subscribers to NASDAQ information, whether receiving the information through NASDAQ Levels 1, 2, or 3, or via the NQDS, could 'be expected to pay to support those aspects of the NASDAQ system used to provide services to them'.[138] It argued, however, that,

because Instinet seeks to distribute certain NASDAQ quotation information in competition with the NASD, which is an exclusive processor of that information, the proposed fees must be cost-based and calculated by allocating the percentage of system use of each quotation service offered by the NASD . . . , to ensure the neutrality and reasonableness of the NASD's charges to Instinet and its subscribers.[139]

The SEC contended that the NASD should recover only those costs that it would incur if it operated a pure 'pass through' system—a system that collected information and passed it on to vendors. It should not be allowed to recover any costs related to its own competing vendor service, such as the costs of storing quotations for inquiry purposes and of responding to inquiries.[140]

The Commission maintained that 'value-of-service' ratemaking was a price-discrimination device, used either to maximize a monopolist's profit or to subsidize certain interests.[141] It argued that the NASD's method of computing the subscriber fee would effectively require Instinet's customers to pay for services that they did not receive from the NASD. The SEC noted that the subscriber fee which the NASD charged for its Level 2 and Level 3 services covered the cost of the query function which was not available in the NQDS service, and which

Instinet had to provide at its own expense and therefore charge for in its fees. The SEC argued therefore that if the NASD were allowed to charge Instinet's customers the subscriber fee, they would be forced to pay twice for the query function which they only received once.

The SEC approved the $3,200 vendor fee, but ruled that the $150 subscriber fee was inconsistent with the SEA.[142] It found that the best indication of the cost to the NASD of providing the NQDS was the $8.75 per month fee that the NASD charged for its Level 1 service, given that it was the only NASDAQ service which related to a pass-through service. The SEC argued that the information provided in the Level 1 service was a refined form of the NQDS data, as only the best bids and offers were provided in Level 1 whereas all bids and offers were provided in the NQDS. The Commission did, however, note that there might be other costs which could properly be allocated to the NQDS of which it was not aware.

The NASD gave two key reasons for why it should not be required to separate out the costs of the query function from the costs of providing the NQDS. It argued, first, that because the NASDAQ system was highly integrated, the SEC was not permitted to require the NASD to separate out the cost of one element of the system, in particular the query function for Level 2 and 3 services. The NASD believed that any attempt to isolate the cost of the query function alone could only be done on an arbitrary basis that bore no relationship to any functional analysis.[143]

The SEC responded that,

the NASD apparently believes that simply because its computer system performs functions other than providing quotation information to Instinet, the Act requires the Commission to permit the NASD to charge Instinet for all services offered by its computer system 'as is'. Such a result is neither compelled by the statutory language, as the NASD claims, nor is it appropriate.[144]

The NASD also argued that because market makers must examine market conditions before updating their quotations for particular securities, the query function was integral to NQDS data collection. The NASD explained that market makers could not update their quotations without knowing the bids and offers of other market makers, and the only way for them to obtain this information was through the Level 2 and 3 query function. In response the SEC argued that there was no requirement that market makers should retrieve NASDAQ quotation information through NASDAQ terminals.

Judgment

The Court ruled that the NASD's position was 'obviously untenable' and affirmed the SEC's decision. It accepted that the NASD should recover only those costs it would incur if it operated a pure 'pass through' system, and determined that the NASD's proposed fees were greater than could be justified by such a pass through system. It concurred with the SEC's view that the NASD's proposal would force Instinet's subscribers to pay NASD retail rates for a wholesale service, thereby making Instinet's services uncompetitive with the NASD's Level 2 service.[145] The Court did not rule on whether the fees should be cost-based or value-based, given that during the proceedings the NASD had conceded that the NQDS fee should be cost-based. It did, however, dismiss both of the NASD's arguments for allocating the query function costs to NQDS subscribers.

The Court maintained that the fact that it was difficult to allocate costs of common or integrated facilities among different groups of customers, did not provide the NASD with an excuse for refusing to do so. It argued that even in cases involving highly integrated facilities, cost allocations required by a governmental agency would be upheld if they were not arbitrary and were supported by a reasoned analysis. In particular, the Court stated that the avoidance of cross-subsidization of services was a legitimate, non-arbitrary, reason for requiring difficult cost allocation. The Court therefore accepted the SEC's argument that Instinet's subscribers should not subsidize Level 2 subscribers by paying the costs of the query function.

The Court also dismissed the NASD's argument that because market makers must examine market conditions before updating their quotations for particular securities, the query function was integral to NQDS data collection. It accepted the SEC's statement that 'while NASDAQ now may be the primary source for market makers to inquire as to the full quotation stream in a stock, there is no reason why that has to hold true for the future'.[146] The Court also agreed that because,

some, most, or even all market makers do not use the Instinet service does not mean that Instinet subscribers may by forced to subsidize the query service used by those market makers.[147]

The SEC's initial orders were therefore affirmed. The NASD's proposed $3,200 vendor fee to Instinet was upheld, but the $150 per month subscriber fee proposed by the NASD for providing the NQDS was ruled as excessive, and instead the $8.75 per month fee, the figure that the NASD charged for its Level 1 wholesale service, was viewed as appropriate.

NYSE OHT Crossing Sessions

On 1 November 1990 the NYSE filed with the SEC a series of proposed rule changes to allow it to implement its Off-Hours Trading (OHT) facilities—the Crossing Sessions I and II.[148] Following publication of the proposed rules and receipt of some comments, the SEC issued a release on the proposed rule changes in May 1991.[149]

Crossing Session I was intended to provide a facility for NYSE members to attempt to have their orders executed at the closing price of the NYSE's regular trading session. Crossing Session II was intended to provide a facility for NYSE members to cross multiple stock orders based on aggregate prices. Only two-sided orders that had already been matched were allowed to participate in this

Session. The NYSE sought to obtain relief for the two Sessions from various requirements of the SEA, including that of last-sale reporting. For Crossing Session I, it proposed that the only information disseminated about trading should be the closing price and aggregate volume for all orders executed. For Crossing Session II, it proposed that trades should be consolidated into a total dollar value and total number of shares traded, and that these data would then be included in the reported total volume for the day. The NYSE therefore requested that it not be required to disseminate last-sale reports in the individual stocks that comprised the aggregate-price executions. It argued that an 'appropriate balance had been struck between the disclosure necessary to meet market regulatory needs and the anti-disclosure pressures attendant to the recapture of overseas order flow and the competition presented by domestic off-exchange markets'.

The SEC identified two main benefits of the proposed Sessions. The first was that they would provide a service which was not then provided elsewhere in the USA. The second was that they were intended to attract the order-flow currently being executed overseas back to the USA with the attendant benefits of the Commission's and the NYSE's oversight. While the SEC recognized that the 'Crossing Session II [did] not provide an auction market for portfolio trades', it argued that 'the reality of the marketplace . . . [was] that these portfolio trades currently [were] being effected off-exchange and, frequently, overseas'. It maintained that 'bringing institutional trades that currently [were] being exported overseas for execution within the purview of U.S. regulatory bodies and subject to transaction reporting [would] benefit the marketplace overall, as well as help to protect the investing public'.

The Commission stressed its belief in the long-standing policy encouraging the dissemination of consolidated market data, stated that it did not believe that the NYSE had provided convincing evidence to depart from this practice, and expressed its view that real-time reporting of programme trading data was important. The Commission did, however, believe that there might be 'significant timing and implementation difficulties involved in establishing the systems necessary to accomplish this goal', and it therefore allowed the NYSE a one-year exemption from the last-sale reporting Rule on condition that the NYSE examine how next-day reporting could be undertaken within a period of four months.

The order approving the OHT rules was not unanimous. A dissenting opinion was delivered by Commissioner Fleischman about the rules relating to the Crossing Session II. He stated that,

Undifferentiated reporting, solely in gross, deprives all market participants, other than those directly involved, of crucial market information and mocks what has become one of the fundamental tenets of American market regulation.

He also argued that,

The American securities markets, in my view, do and will compete with foreign markets for trades on the basis of the unrivalled fundamental strengths of the American markets: Liquidity, transparency, ease of entry, and breadth of participation. To sacrifice one of those strengths—transparency—and thereby to diminish the others is for me too high a price to pay to accomplish the laudable purpose of furthering the domestic markets' role in international market competition.

NASDAQ International

On 27 June 1991 the NASD filed with the SEC a proposed rule change to allow it to establish NASDAQ International in London for a pilot period of two years.[150] The system was to be a market-maker based trading mechanism, similar to that operated by the NASD in the USA. Although the SEC granted the NASD permission to operate NASDAQ International for the trial period, the extent to which last-trade reporting should be required of the system again gave the SEC particular concern.[151]

The NASD requested that trade reports only be completed within three minutes, as opposed to within the ninety seconds required in the USA. It also requested that publication of trades should be obligatory within three minutes, only if the security was both a UK American Depository Receipt (ADR) and a NASDAQ/NMS security subject to real-time reporting in the USA, and was being quoted by at least two market makers. For all other securities the NASD requested that there be no real-time publication of trade reports. The reason these exemptions were sought was that information dissemination from the LSE, NASDAQ International's primary competitor, was regulated in this fashion. The NASD did, however, propose publishing information about the aggregate volume, and the high, low, and closing transaction prices, at the end of each European Session of NASDAQ International, information which was not published by the LSE. The NASD asserted that for the SEC to demand more regulation of NASDAQ International than the LSE would impose a competitive handicap on NASDAQ International.

The SEC agreed to the NASD's various requests for the relaxation of the last-sale reporting rule, accepting the NASD's claim that its new service 'would not be a viable competitor [with SEAQi] if its rules were dramatically more stringent than those of its primary competitor'. The Commission also believed that 'if NASDAQ International [was] successful, it [would] return order flow currently being executed overseas back to the scrutiny of U.S. regulators, with the attendant benefits of Commission and SRO oversight'. The Commission agreed in addition that no simultaneous publication would be required for those securities on NASDAQ International in which there was only one market maker. The SEC took this position because it believed that without it, sole market makers would be 'picked off', and because the LSE had a similar rule. The SEC also agreed to allow the NASD to disseminate market data through NASDAQ facilities, rather than through the CTA. By doing so, the SEC accepted that the volume effected during the early NASDAQ International trading sessions need not be consolidated with the trading in the same securities when the American market was open.

The Commission justified its rulings by noting that,

[it] has stated numerous times, transparency is crucial to the efficient and fair operation of our capital markets. Market transparency has been an essential aspect of the Commission's efforts to facilitate the establishment of a national market system. Market transparency, in the form of trade and quotation information, enhances liquidity in the marketplace and provides investors with the opportunity to ensure the best execution of their orders. The lack of widespread availability of transaction information, therefore, has an adverse impact on the efficiency of the market. Nevertheless, in recognition of the desirability of repatriating order flow, the Commission, on occasion, has adopted a flexible approach in interpreting regulatory requirements during the start-up phase of proposals that the Commission believes will bring some benefit to the markets.[152]

As in the NYSE OHT ruling, however, the Commission was not unanimous in its decision. Commissioner Fleischman again dissented from the majority opinion, noting that 'the Commission preaches transparency to the Congress and to the securities world, but . . . it fails to require trade transparency when proposed marketplace rules afford it the opportunity to do so'.[153] He argued that the 'transparency needs for particular securities should be assessed on a global basis in order to avoid a flight to opacity'.[154] In response to the other Commissioners' belief that these rules were to be viewed as an initial-stage concession, to be replaced after a time by trade-by-trade reporting, he replied that,

[the] sacrifice of transparency for competitive reasons is a mistake from the beginning; competitive pressures to maintain opacity, and to attract participants back to local-market opacity, will be no less compelling in six months, a year or longer.

Transparency on the LSE

Although the power of the Office of Fair Trading (OFT) is only advisory in nature, it plays an important role in determining regulatory policy in the UK. Two of its reports, both of which directly examine the issue of transparency on the LSE, are therefore discussed in turn.[155]

OFT 1990

The OFT's first examination of the LSE's information dissemination policy was in response to a series of rule changes that the exchange proposed in the early part of 1989.[156] Prior to the rule changes, trades in the 'alpha' stocks, the most actively traded ones, had to be reported to the exchange in five minutes, and were then immediately and publicly disseminated; trades in the 'beta' stocks, the second tier of stocks, were not published. The rule changes proposed that there would be immediate publication of trades in beta stocks, for deals valued up to £50,000. For trades in beta stocks with a value above £50,000, however, and for trades in alpha stocks with a value above £100,000, there would be a delay of twenty-four hours before such information would be published. There was a further rule change which removed the obligation on market makers to deal with each other at the prices and in the sizes they quoted on SEAQ.

The exchange made the rule changes in the context of a sharp reduction in trading volume and a widening of spreads after the Crash in 1987, which had been preceded by a large rise in trading volume following Big Bang in 1986. There had also been a large rise in the number of market makers following Big Bang, but no reduction in their number following the 1987 Crash. The exchange noted that 'highly efficient and effective member firms reported greater difficulty in providing the large investor with narrow quotes for block trades, and many announced losses on their UK equity business'.[157]

The exchange argued that immediate publication of large trades meant that a market maker taking on a position could often be identified by the rest of the market, and then 'spoiled' by other market participants. It stated, in particular, that,

[a] substantial purchase by a market maker published at a price significantly below the prevailing touch [meaning in this context the best quoted bid] will cause other market makers to lower their prices in order not to be hit by the market maker who has made the purchase.[158]

Such reactions led, the exchange maintained, to price volatility that was 'spurious' because it arose as a result of transactions which were 'liquidity' trades motivated simply by a need to realize an investment rather than by any new information about the stock. This activity made it increasingly difficult for market makers to undertake large transactions at a profit and they became reluctant to take on large deals, or did so only by demanding a size premium to compensate them for the added risk. The exchange argued that this in turn led to business not being done, to institutions moving business off-exchange, and to an increase in 'protected' business, whereby one side of a transaction was confirmed only when the other side was confirmed. The exchange maintained that ending immediate publication for the large alpha trades would improve liquidity and market depth by minimizing the size premia for large deals, that it would reduce the cost of using the market, and that it would improve the quality of prices by dampening such 'spurious' volatility.

The Director General of the OFT dismissed most of the LSE's arguments. He noted that it was difficult to 'isolate the effect of the delay in trade publication and of the other rule changes from the effect of other factors at work in the market', and that given this empirical difficulty, his conclusions were 'based primarily on *a priori* analysis of the likely effect on competition of the rule changes'.[159] He contended that, with on average fourteen market makers for each alpha stock, it would be difficult to identify which market maker had taken on a position. He also believed that 'spoiling' could not be successful, because it unbalanced the position of the spoiler. If, for example, a market maker sold stock to another market maker, he would have to repurchase the stock at a later date. In the case of pure liquidity trades, the Director General believed that such trading could neither be sustained nor profitable.[160]

In the case of informationally motivated trades, he believed such activity should more properly be viewed as 'legitimate market reaction, rather than spoiling'. In his view 'most trades reflect[ed] a revised view of a company's future prospects and [were] therefore information based'.[161] 'Keeping trade details from the market [would] therefore impair the ability of market makers to adjust their prices speedily and accurately so reducing pricing efficiency.' Noting that spreads appeared to arise as a result of inventory risk and information risk, the Director General argued that delaying trade publication would increase the information risk with the attendant consequences of increasing spreads, increasing transactions costs, reducing market liquidity, and possibly declining trading volume.

The Director General accepted that the period before the rule changes had been a 'difficult time' for market makers.[162] He believed, however, that the origin of these difficulties 'lay not in the rules, but more in the excess market making capacity which [had] still to be eliminated'. His analysis suggested that the delay in publication of large trades denied to the market two kinds of information relevant to the valuation of a security: details about the trades occurring, and the information that might be implicit in the trades about the prospects of the particular company. These effects were viewed as important, both because he believed that most trades had some information content, and because over 78.5% of the volume of all trading in alpha stocks, and 55% of all trading, were in deals about which information would be withheld.

The Director General argued that a delay in trade publication would mean that a market maker involved in an undisclosed trade would generally possess information relevant to the evaluation of the share price not available to other market participants. This information asymmetry was thought likely to mean that larger unpublished business benefited at the expense of smaller transparent business, because the delay in publication allowed the larger investor to obtain a price better than he would otherwise get. The market maker taking on the position would be likely to unwind it against a series of smaller deals, who would be trading in ignorance of the information obtained by the market maker. The information asymmetry would also give a market maker executing a trade an advantage over its rivals, who might therefore widen their spreads to protect themselves.

The effect of delayed last-trade publication on competition in market making was also thought to depend on whether large order business, and hence the trading opportunities created by the information asymmetry, was evenly distributed. The Director General noted that there was a wide variation between market makers in the average size of transaction which they undertook, and that eight market making firms accounted for 70% of all domestic equity trading. He believed that those firms which did more of the institutional business would benefit more from the rule change than their competitors. This advantage was viewed as a distortion to competition because it was not the result of superior efficiency, and was also a barrier to entry given that new firms would be likely to start off with small market shares. Unpublished information would also give an advantage to market makers who executed large trades over broker dealers who did not know about them. The Director General finally argued that there might also be adverse effects on the London Traded Options Market and LIFFE, since market participants in possession of unpublished information about equity trades might be able to take advantage of it to the disadvantage of traders in the derivatives markets. He concluded that the delay in the publication of large trade details was 'likely to have to a significant extent the effect of restricting and distorting competition'.

OFT 1994

The OFT re-examined the question of transparency on the LSE in 1994. The re-examination was undertaken both in light of the exchange's new publication rules established in 1991 and 1993, and to assess the available empirical evidence.

In February 1991 the exchange again changed the rules according to which it released transaction information.[163] Rather than using its previous alpha, beta, gamma, and delta, categories, the exchange re-classified all stocks according to a measure called 'Normal Market Size' (NoMS), which was based on the average transaction size for each stock. The NoMS was intended to be a proxy for the liquidity of a stock, and twelve NoMS bands were established. Information about almost all trades smaller than three times a share's NoMS was required to be published immediately. For trades larger than this size, however, information about both the prices and volumes was subject to a ninety-minute delay. In December 1993, a further change was made allowing market makers to delay the publication of information about trades seventy-five times larger than NoMS for either up to five working days, or until 90% of the original transaction had been unwound, whichever occurred first.[164]

In examining these rules, the Director General identified several potential benefits of transparency. He first enunciated his general view that,

subject to cost, . . . it is important that consumers in all markets are well informed. Without adequate information about the product, or the circumstances in which they are buying or selling, consumers may well make poor decisions and competition can be distorted.[165]

He noted that the 'timely and extensive release of information ensures that all investors are treated as fairly and equally as possible'. He also cited the efficient markets hypothesis as an economic justification for transparency in quotes and prices, stating that an implication of it was that,

immediate last-trade publication can contribute to pricing efficiency if details of past trades convey information to the market.[166]

Three possible effects of large trades on prices and spreads were identified, arising respectively from price pressure, inventory costs, and information. Price pressure was said to occur when a large trade led to a temporary imbalance in supply and demand, and prices therefore changed. Inventory costs were posited as arising because a large trade took a dealer's inventory away from his desired position, and he therefore demanded a premium for taking on such a trade. Finally an information effect was said to exist when the existence of a large trade conveyed information. The first two effects were stated as leading only to a temporary effect on prices, while the third effect was thought to give rise to a permanent effect.

The Director General argued that if large trades did not contain information and price effects were temporary, then delayed publication might reduce the risks that market makers faced, and therefore make them prepared to offer better prices, leading to narrower spreads and less volatility. In contrast, if large trades were thought to contain information, and price effects were permanent, then delayed publication might lead to two effects. The first would be that dealers narrowed their spreads for large trades in order to attract business, and thereby capture the information. The second effect would be a general widening of spreads, given that market makers would be aware that other dealers might be better informed than they were, and would therefore seek to protect themselves when trading with a potentially better informed competitor. In such circumstances, it was argued that immediate last-trade publication would lead to a narrowing of spreads.

In order to assess which of the above theories were most relevant, the Director General evaluated the available empirical evidence, including some research by Gemmill (1994) which the OFT had specially commissioned.[167] The Director General drew four main conclusions from Gemmill's analysis. First, large trades were found to convey information because price levels changed permanently under all the exchange's publication regimes. Second, there was no evidence that delayed publication led to any reduction in price volatility. Third, pre-trade quotes were a poor indicator of actual transaction prices, as evidenced by the fact that many trades were executed at prices inside the touch, namely the best bid and ask quoted prices. Fourth, large trades did benefit at the expense of small trades. The justification for this last position was that the average large-trade spread was relatively smaller than the average small-trade spread in circumstances of reduced publication. This was seen as 'consistent with the existence of a cross-subsidy from small to large trades under delayed publication'.[168]

Two other secondary conclusions were drawn by the Director General. The first was that prices tended to move before large trades were executed. It was thought that this implied that Gemmill's results understated the impact of large trades. Second, it was noted that the price adjustment after large trades was quite quick. The Director General did not agree, however, with Gemmill's conclusion that the relevant information 'seeped out' too quickly into the market for dealers to exploit it.

Other relevant empirical analysis of trading on the London market was also examined. It was noted that several comparisons of the dealing costs in equities traded both on the London and the Paris stock exchanges, showed that the costs of executing small transactions were lower in Paris than in London, while the costs of executing large transactions were lower in London than in Paris.[169] The Director General accepted that there were many differences between the two markets, but noted that an important one was that the Paris bourse required immediate publication while the LSE did not. Another study comparing transactions on the LSE during two periods, one with immediate and one with delayed publication, confirmed similarly that spreads were narrower on small trades and wider for large trades with full publication.[170] Despite the reservations the Director General made concerning the applicability of these findings, he maintained that 'delayed publication is likely to result in a cross subsidy from those executing small trades to those executing larger trades'.[171]

The main conclusions drawn in the previous OFT study concerning the competitive effects of delays in trade publication were then re-examined in light of the new evidence and arguments available to the Director General. He identified the exchange's two key arguments as being first, that most large trades are liquidity motivated so that price changes resulting from such trades are temporary and represent spurious volatility, and second, that the publication of post-trade information is not necessary in a dealership market where pre-trade quotations are published. The Director General rejected both these arguments as being contradicted by the evidence. In his view large trades were associated with permanent price movements, and thus with the presence of information, and pre-trade information was not sufficient to inform investors properly about the state of the market.

Several arguments against full transparency presented by Franks and Schaefer (1990) were also analysed by the Director General. The first concerned the regulatory implications and problems of enforcing transparency. While it was accepted that some market makers might break any transparency rules that were implemented, this was regarded as a problem of enforcement, rather than one concerning the nature of the rule. The Director General also examined the argument that full transparency would lead to an increase in off-exchange business and in matched trades. With regard to off-exchange trading, he noted that the ideal solution would be to require that all trading, whether on- or off-exchange, be subject to the same transparency requirements.

The question of matched trades was viewed as a more complicated issue. A matched trade occurs when a market maker agrees to a trade with a client, but does not complete the trade until he has found a counter-party for the other side of the trade. Franks and Schaefer maintained that such trades were a way of evading the requirement for immediate publication. The Director General identified three different types of matched deals, where:

(i) The market maker agrees in principle to trade at a particular price but does not take on the deal until it has made provision for rebalancing its inventory. No-one is committed to the trade until the market maker has found sufficient counter-parties to take some or all of the trade. This arrangement reduces the market maker's risk.

(ii) Unlike (i), a minimum price is agreed and the market maker tries to do better after its search for counter-parties. Again, no-one is committed until the trade is actually executed.

[or] (iii) The market maker commits to dealing at a particular price but does not execute the trade until the position has been partially or fully laid off.[172]

The Director General gave several reasons why he believed that even if such trades occurred or their number increased, it was not a matter of competitive concern, and immediate last-trade publication was still a desirable policy. He argued that the information content of the first two types of trades was 'reduced', because there is no guarantee until they actually go through that 'the trade will be a real trade'.[173] He claimed that 'the ability to trade on information ahead of publication is therefore reduced'. As for the third classification, the Director General believed that market makers would be under pressure to off-load such trades as quickly as possible so as to reduce their price risk, and therefore the information delay would be minimal. Finally, the Director General questioned whether many large trades would in fact be matched under a full-transparency regime.

The other argument Franks and Schaefer put forward against full transparency, was that dealing was concentrated in a small number of dealers on SEAQ, that market makers' books were therefore more evident to their competitors in London than elsewhere, and that last-trade reporting was therefore more of a problem in London than elsewhere. Against this, the Director General first asserted that there was a large enough number of market makers in the liquid stocks that it would be difficult to discover which one had taken on a trade. Furthermore, the market had become less concentrated in 1993, than in 1990 when the argument was actually made. Also the Director General questioned why the identity of the market maker was important, noting that market makers would react to the existence of a large trade, whoever had participated in it. Although so-called 'spoiling' would be easier with the knowledge of who executed the trade, such activity was either 'irrational', or the 'legitimate market adjustment of quotes'.[174] Finally, the Director General claimed that the more concentrated a market is, the greater will be the harmful effects of delayed publication on spreads. In less liquid stocks, market makers not involved in large trades will be more likely to be at an informational disadvantage, and therefore to widen their spreads.

Given the above analysis, the Director General re-confirmed his prior findings that delayed publication would be likely to restrict and distort competition both because it gave those market makers executing more large trades an information advantage over those undertaking fewer large trades, and because it created a cross-subsidy from small to large trades.

CONCLUSION

The aim of this chapter is to describe some important elements of the law and regulation governing the dissemination, purchase, and sale of price and quote data. The law and regulation from a range of jurisdictions governing copyright, a *sui generis* right in databases, misappropriation, confidentiality, competition, and the securities markets, are examined respectively in the six sections of the chapter. The main conclusions are as follows.

The primary statutory criterion by which it is assessed whether a compilation of data may attract copyright in the UK is whether the compilation exhibits sufficient originality. The central judicial criterion that has been developed to assess whether a work should be deemed original is whether sufficient labour, skill, and capital have been expended by the author in creating it. The value of a copyright in a compilation may be limited, however, as it may not take much embellishment to obtain copyright in a slightly modified work. Although the primary statutory criterion for the assignment of copyright is also that of originality in the USA, judicial interpretation of the term there has been quite different than in the UK. In particular, it is the 'creative selection approach' that has been confirmed as the key test of originality in the USA. Copyright subsists in a compilation only if it exhibits a minimal amount of creativity in its selection and arrangement of facts. The expenditure of labour, capital or other assets, in the production of the compilation is therefore irrelevant for assessing whether it is protected by copyright or not.

Under the EU's Database Directive, the creator of a database may be able to protect his database under a *sui generis* right. An exchange may be able to claim this right for the price and quote data it produces. If applicable, the *sui generis* right would give the maker of a database the right to prevent the unauthorized extraction or re-utilization of the database or its contents. If, however, the creator had a monopolistic position with regard to the information in the database, competition law would probably require him to license the use of the database on fair and non-discriminatory terms.

One protection in the USA against the misappropriation of a property right in price and quote data may be provided by the law of unfair competition. The nature and importance of this body of law is, however, controversial for several reasons. Given that it is a doctrine developed in state case law equity and thus has no statutory backing, the manner in which it may be applied is relatively flexible. Its relevance to a particular case therefore depends critically on the precise details of the case. In addition, it is a matter of great debate whether the law of unfair competition is preempted by federal copyright law, and if so, to what extent. As of mid-1997, the tension between federal copyright law and state misappropriation law in the context of the dissemination of time-sensitive information was the subject of a highly disputed case. To date, the Appeals Court has confirmed that only a limited set of claims may fit within state misappropriation law.

Most exchanges attempt to impose a contractual obligation of confidence upon the agents receiving their information so as to stop them from divulging it without their permission. In order for a breach of confidence to be actionable in the UK, three criteria must be fulfilled. First, the information in question must have the necessary quality of confidence about it, meaning that it must not be public property or knowledge. Second, the receiver of the information should know that he has an obligation of confidence placed on him, given the circumstances in which he received it. Finally, it must be shown that the confidant breached this obligation by making an unauthorized use of the information, possibly to the detriment of the party initially confiding the information.

If an exchange captures a large percentage of the trading in a commodity, or if it is granted any intellectual property rights in the information it disseminates, it may become the dominant or even the sole source of information about trading in the commodity. Such an exclusive position may bring the exchange within the remit of anti-trust legislation and regulation. Two instances of whether conduct by an exchange concerning the dissemination of its information is anti-competitive have been examined in Australia. They concern whether the Australian Stock Exchange charged too much for the information which it sold, and whether it favoured a data vendor which it operated over other competing commercial vendors. It is controversial whether competition law or copyright law takes precedence in the context of an exchange disseminating its data. The conflict between competition policy and copyright law has been acute in the EU.

The most detailed legislation and regulation supervising the dissemination of price and quote information in securities markets has been developed in the USA. The Securities and Exchange Act lays out a complex hierarchy of objectives which the SEC is obliged to pursue. At the most general level, it is required to further the public interest, to protect investors, and to maintain fair and orderly markets. Other subsidiary objectives, concerning the operations of the National Market System, exchanges, national associations, securities information processors, and the general process of the dissemination of information are also specified. The category of an exclusive Securities Information Processor (SIP) is defined, and duties requiring exclusive SIPs to operate fairly and efficiently are imposed. Any form of discrimination practised by an SIP is forbidden if it imposes a burden on competition not necessary or appropriate. Exclusive SIPs are viewed as monopolists, and their conduct is closely scrutinized by the SEC.

The SEC has made a series of important rulings concerning who has a right to receive what information at what price. The most important is that transparency is required. In particular, the prices, sizes and locations of all trades and all quotes in the largest listed and NASDAQ equities must be published rapidly. Despite this general policy, however, and in an attempt to repatriate order flow to the USA, the SEC has in certain restricted circumstances relaxed the amount of price and quote information that an exchange is required to disseminate. With respect to the price that may be charged for price and quote information, the SEC has ruled that an exclusive SIP may set a fixed access charge for the information which it sells. The Commission has, however, also determined, and has been backed judicially, that an exclusive SIP that also retails its information, should only recover those costs it would incur if it operated a pure 'pass through' system, when setting its charges.

Regulatory examination of transparency on the London Stock Exchange has been undertaken twice by the Office of Fair Trading. Successive Director Generals have come to a similar conclusion that a delay in the publication of large trade details is likely to restrict and distort competition significantly. In one report, based on *a priori* reasoning, the Director General argued that delaying trade publication would increase the information risk associated with taking on a trade, with the attendant consequences of increasing spreads, increasing transactions costs, reducing market liquidity and possibly declining trading volume. In a second report, the Director General claimed that the available empirical evidence also supported these conclusions.

9

Governance: Law and Regulation

INTRODUCTION

The question of who should have what power at an exchange has long been a matter of public concern. The aim of this chapter is to identify and describe the main legal and regulatory factors that affect the governance of exchanges in the securities and futures markets. The analysis is limited in three important ways. First, attention is focused on what are believed to be the two aspects of exchange governance of most public significance, namely board representation and conflicts of interests on the boards of exchanges.[1] A range of other topics is thus ignored, such as the placing of limits on the monetary liability of the directors of an exchange, and the indemnification by an exchange of its directors.[2] Second, the discussion concentrates on the American environment, because it is there that the legal and regulatory concerns about exchange governance have been explored in most detail.[3] Finally, only the relevant federal law and regulation in the USA is examined. State law is viewed as being of secondary importance, and is thus not considered.[4]

In order to understand the nature of the law and regulation that affects exchange governance in the securities and futures markets in the USA, it is critical to appreciate the costs and benefits of self-regulation, a concept that underpins the entire American approach to the regulation of financial and commodities exchanges.[5] There is a range of arguments in favour of self-regulation. First, only self-regulation may be able to monitor effectively many types of conduct and activity that lie beyond the reach of the law.[6] Second, market participants may have a direct and strong interest in maintaining the integrity of the markets on which they trade. Third, the presence of market practitioners as 'self-regulators' may enhance the knowledge, expertise and experience of the regulatory authorities. Fourth, market practitioners may learn about the regulatory process by participating in it, and thereby enhance their firms' internal compliance with their regulatory duties. Fifth, rules imposed by industry peers may carry more legitimacy with market participants than those imposed by an external regulator.

Sixth, it may be difficult for governments to pay the same wages, or attract the same calibre of people, as private regulators are able to do. Seventh, self-regulation is typically funded from private sources, whereas regulation by a public body needs to be financed by some form of tax. Eighth, policies determined by self-regulation may be less susceptible to political whim than those determined by a public regulator. Ninth, the alternatives to self-regulation, for example those of direct regulatory intervention, or of an institutional layer of regulation between a regulatory commission and an SRO, may not be cost-effective. Finally, self-regulation may be more flexible and informal in its decision-making procedures than the alternatives.

The tensions inherent in self-regulation have, however, been widely recognized. SROs are simultaneously 'quasi-governmental bodies implementing the federal securities laws as well as their own rules', 'membership organizations' that 'represent the economic interests of their members', and also 'marketplaces concerned with preserving and enhancing their competitive positions'.[7] The most important conflict that has been thought to arise from the multi-functional roles of SROs, is that as membership organizations they may regulate the markets they operate to their own advantage, and thereby prejudice the delivery of the public interest.[8] Sometimes this may lead to anti-competitive situations.[9] As noted by the Department of Justice, while 'self-regulation can be a useful supplement to government regulation in disciplining members for fraud and dishonest commercial activities since in such cases the interests of almost all of the members [of an exchange] are likely to be coincident with the public interest', the same coincidence of interest 'is not likely to exist with respect to situations involving economic conflicts between members or with non-members'.[10]

A further problem is that an SRO may be required to supervise traders who have no interest in the commercial markets which the SRO itself operates. Conflicts of interest, this time between participants on the SRO-sponsored market and non-participants, may again not be easily resolved by a self-regulatory process. An important instance of this arises at the NASD. There are many broker-dealers who are required to register with the NASD, but who do not trade on NASDAQ, the market operated by the NASD. Yet another difficulty with self-regulation is that if there are several SROs with overlapping jurisdictions, their independent market surveillance and enforcement activities may duplicate each other, and thereby force market participants to incur unnecessary costs.

Notwithstanding its disadvantages, self-regulation has been accepted as a central component of the American regulatory structure for both the securities and futures markets.[11] The problems that arise as a result of it are thought to be manageable with sufficient statutory, regulatory, and judicial, oversight of SRO practices, and it is this oversight in the context of exchange governance that is examined here.

The chapter is composed of two sections. In the first, the federal law and regulation that affects the governance of securities exchanges is analysed. A similar analysis for futures exchanges is presented in the second section.

SECURITIES EXCHANGES

The statutory constraints on the governance of securities exchanges, and the regulatory interpretation of these requirements, are examined here in turn.

Statutory Basis

The SEA imposes four major obligations on exchanges concerning their governance structures. The first two are that an exchange,

assure a fair representation of its members in the selection of its directors and administration of its affairs and provide that one or more directors shall be representative of issuers and investors and not be associated with a member of the exchange, broker or dealer.[12]

The fair representation requirement is believed to act as a barrier against the possibility that one segment of an exchange's membership may dominate the decisions the SRO takes. It also ensures 'that modifications or improvements in the way in which SROs function may be initiated from within'.[13] The requirement that one or more of an exchange's directors be representative of issuers and investors is thought to provide a counter-weight to the inevitable promotion of members' viewpoints on commercial and regulatory matters.

The third statutory constraint is that, subject to certain exceptions, only brokers and dealers may become members of an exchange. The Act requires that,

a national securities exchange shall deny membership to (A) any person, other than a natural person, which is not a registered broker or dealer or (B) any natural person who is not, or is not associated with, a registered broker or dealer.[14]

A member is defined as:

(i) any natural person permitted to effect transactions on the floor of the exchange without the services of another person acting as broker, (ii) any registered broker or dealer with which such a natural person is associated, (iii) any registered broker or dealer permitted to designate as a representative such a natural person, and (iv) any other registered broker or dealer which agrees to be regulated by such exchange and with respect to which the exchange undertakes to enforce compliance with the provisions of this title [i.e. the Act], the rules and regulations thereunder, and its own rules. For purposes of sections . . . of this title, the term 'member' when used with respect to a national securities exchange also means, to the extent of the rules of the exchange specified by the Commission, any person required by the Commission to comply with such rules pursuant to section 6(f) of this title.[15]

This section states that,

the Commission . . . may require—(1) any person not a member or a designated representative of a member of a national securities exchange effecting transactions on such exchange without the services of another person acting as a broker, . . . to comply with such rules of such exchange as the Commission may specify.[16]

The SEC has noted that these combined definitions do not require an entity to participate in the ownership of an exchange in order to be considered a statutory member of the exchange.[17]

The issue of whether the SEA does actually prohibit a registered exchange from granting membership and also direct trading access to participants who are not broker-dealers is controversial.[18] The history of the Act and the standard reading of the above provisions imply that a registered exchange is not permitted to grant direct trading access to market participants other than brokers or dealers. This was confirmed by the Court of Appeals which stated that,

the statute requires that an exchange be controlled by its participants, who must in turn be registered brokers or individuals associated with such brokers.[19]

Section 6(f)(1) implies, however, that the possibility that exchanges might sanction direct institutional participation was accepted by Congress when formulating the Act.

To date, all registered exchanges have only allowed broker-dealers to be members, and have granted fair representation to these members. While it is true that the AZX does grant direct trading access to institutional investors, does not grant fair representation in its governance to the traders who participate on its system, and was deemed by the SEC to satisfy the 'exchange' definition, the AZX has not yet had to register as such with the SEC as a result of its limited volume exemption. The statute has no requirement that a registered exchange be owned either by its members or by any other types of market participant. While the registered exchanges are owned by their members, the AZX, in contrast, is not owned by the market participants who trade on it.

The fourth statutory constraint on exchange governance is that the rules of an exchange must be 'designed . . . in general, to protect investors and the public interest'.[20] The Act does not, however, make any direct requirement regarding the minimum representation of the public on the boards of exchanges, nor does it specify how such representation should be effected.

Regulatory Interpretation

The SEC has influenced the governance structures of securities exchanges in two main ways. Under the formal authority granted to it, it has both approved and disapproved a series of rule changes by various exchanges concerning their governance structures. Informally, it has also influenced exchanges' governance structures, most importantly by encouraging, sometimes with the threat of direct regulatory action, increased public representation on exchange boards. Attention is focused on the SEC's formal approval and disapproval process.

A seminal ruling of the Commission concerned the inappropriateness of allowing a single constituency at the Chicago Board Options Exchange (CBOE) to dominate the exchange's governance. The SEC examined this issue in its analysis of two rule changes proposed by the exchange.[21] Prior to the proposals, the Board of the CBOE was composed of twenty-one directors. Fifteen of these had to be members or executive officers of member organizations of the exchange, and were elected by the membership. Four directors were appointed by the Chairman of the Board to represent the public, and could not be members. The remaining two seats were occupied by the Chairman and the President. Of the fifteen member directors, at least six were required to be executives of member firms that conducted primarily a non-member public customer business. These executives were also individually not allowed to be primarily engaged in business activities on the exchange floor ('off-floor directors'). Another six had to be members who individually either owned or directly controlled their memberships, and who also were primarily engaged in business on the floor of the exchange ('floor directors'). The remaining three were allowed to be members who functioned in any recognized capacity ('at-large directors'). Traditionally these at-large directors had come from the floor, and not from firms engaged primarily in public customer business.

The Executive Committee Chairman (ECC) was the highest ranking official at the exchange. He presided at meetings of the Executive Committee, could appoint standing committees and special committees with the approval of the board, and was responsible for the coordination of the activities of all exchange committees. The constitution of the exchange required that the ECC be a director who owned or directly controlled his own membership on the exchange, and that he be elected annually by a majority of the directors. From 1978 to 1982 an informal nominating committee of the nine floor representatives on the Board, namely the six floor directors and the three at-large directors, had nominated a candidate from amongst themselves for this position, and the candidate was confirmed by the Board. In 1983, the nominating committee split, and the issue was submitted to the board for discussion.

In order to resolve this, the exchange proposed two rule changes. The first stated that if there were more than one candidate for the ECC, the position was to be filled by a majority vote of the CBOE members in an election held at an annual meeting of the membership, rather than by the directors of the exchange.[22] The second proposal was that the Board of directors should be increased from twenty-one to twenty-four members, eighteen of whom would be members or executives of member organizations of the exchange, four of whom would be public directors, and the other two of whom would be the Chairman and the President. Of the eighteen member directors, the minimum number of floor directors would be increased from six to nine, at least six would be off-floor directors, and the other three would be at-large directors.[23] Both these rule changes were proposed by a membership petition and approved by a membership vote, over the opposition of the Board of directors.

The election proposal for the ECC was believed by the SEC to raise questions concerning the statutory fair representation criterion, as it appeared that representation of member firms which did public business would be eroded if the proposed rule change were approved. This was because members serving public customers had considerably fewer seats on the CBOE than they did on the Board, and thus would have considerably less influence on who was selected as ECC in a membership vote than in a vote of the Board. The SEC also noted that,

retail firm input may be especially important on options exchanges because, so long as those exchanges retain exclusive franchises on certain individual options, retail firms and public investors have no choice but to do business on those exchanges or forego entirely using standardized options on certain securities.[24]

The Commission argued that the rule change concerning floor member representation on the Board of directors would lead to floor members becoming the dominant group on the Board, most likely controlling twelve out of the twenty-four seats, via the nine designated floor directors and the three at-large directors. The Commission was worried that,

> this numerical dominance may cause the floor directors, acting in concert as a voting block, to focus on the particular interests of the floor membership rather than act in their fiduciary capacity as representatives of the broader public interest, or the CBOE as a whole. The Commission [was] also concerned that the floor directors may effectively prevent the Board from enforcing those rules of the Exchange which the floor members do not favor.[25]

The SEC also believed that the proposal might discourage persons from serving as public representatives on the Board, as they might feel that they had no meaningful voice in the administration of the exchange. In addition, it questioned whether, because of the fiduciary duties their firms owed to their public customers, off-floor directors might not represent the interests of public investors to a greater degree than would floor members, who did not conduct a substantial public customer business.

The principal proponent of the rule amendments, the CBOE Floor Members' Association (FMA) maintained that the members, as owners of the exchange, had a right to determine how and by whom they should be governed.[26] The FMA argued that an increase in floor representation on the Board was warranted because under the then-existing rules the floor membership was 'not properly nor proportionately' represented on the Board. The two other commentators in favour of the rule proposals rejected the notion that the floor directors had a 'pro-floor, anti-firm, anti-public' bias, and would as a result act in their own best interests to the detriment of the exchange's other constituencies. They claimed that the trading floor population of any exchange had 'a vested interest in satisfying the public customer . . . [because otherwise] he will either go elsewhere or stop trading options'. They also argued that the floor traders had 'everything to lose and nothing to gain, including their livelihood, if CBOE does not offer the investing public a fair and open market place'. The Board of the exchange, in contrast, opposed the proposed rule changes. In its opinion, the amendments were not in the best interests of the exchange as a whole, and would have a negative effect upon the Board's ability to oversee the management of the exchange and to carry out the purposes of the SEA.

The SEC vetoed the rule change that proposed increasing the number of directors as being inconsistent with both the fair representation requirement and the requirement that the rules of an exchange be designed to protect investors and the public interest. The election rule for the ECC was however approved. Although the Commission was concerned that the proposal was undesirable because it raised the possibility that floor members might be successful in controlling the selection of the ECC, the Commission believed that the proposal was not literally inconsistent with any specific section of the Act. It also believed that the power of the ECC was sufficiently circumscribed by the considerable authority vested in the CBOE Board, and the continuing balance of representation on the Board. The SEC also noted its awareness that the previous rules had sanctioned the likelihood that the ECC would be a floor member, and that this would remain the case whatever the rules for election.

The Commission expressly avoided ruling on the question of whether the principle of 'one seat, one vote' would in all circumstances constitute fair representation of the membership of an exchange. It did, however, note that,

direct election of exchange officials may not, in all cases, appropriately ensure fair representation of the exchange membership, or adequately protect the interest of investors. Specifically, a simple count of member firms does not adequately reflect that in contrast to floor members, public member firms account for the vast majority of order flow sent to an exchange.[27]

Other instances where the SEC has been concerned not to allow a single constituency at an exchange to obtain dominance on the board of the exchange include the Philadelphia Stock Exchange,[28] the AMEX,[29] the Cincinnati Stock Exchange,[30] and the Midwest Stock Exchange.[31] In addition, the Commission has promoted a diversity of representation on the nominating, the audit, and other types of exchange committees, as well as on the boards of clearing agencies.[32] The Commission has also noted that clearing agencies may satisfy the fair representation requirements in different ways, including by:

(1) solicitation of board of directors nominations from all participants; (2) selection of candidates for election to the board of directors by a nominating committee which could be composed of, and selected by, the participants or representatives chosen by participants; (3) direct participation by participants in the election of directors through the allocation of voting stock to all participants based on their usage of the clearing agency; or (4) selection by participants of a slate of nominees for which stockholders of the clearing agency would be required to vote their share.[33]

One example of the SEC's concern about a single constituency at an exchange gaining excessive power occurred when the SEC sanctioned a change of policy by the Boston Stock Exchange (BSE) concerning its review of the concentration of specialist units at the exchange.[34] The BSE's Specialist Concentration Policy established standards for reviewing proposed mergers, acquisitions, and other combinations between specialist units at the exchange. In 1995, the BSE proposed that this policy should be implemented by members of the Executive Committee of the exchange who were not affiliated with a specialist organization. Four criteria were to be used to assess a proposed combination of specialist units:

(1) specialist performance and market quality in the stock subject to the proposed combination; (2) the likelihood that the proposed combination would strengthen the capital base

of the resulting organization, minimize the potential for financial failure and negative consequences of any such failure on the specialist system as a whole, and maintain or increase operational efficiencies; (3) commitment to the Exchange market, focusing on whether the constituent specialist organizations engage in business activities that might detract from the resulting specialist organization's willingness or ability to act to strengthen the Exchange agency/auction market and its competitiveness in relation to other markets; and (4) the effect of the proposed combination on the overall concentration of specialist organizations.

The reason why the BSE wanted to limit specialist concentration was that it believed that,

if specialist units were permitted to aggregate control or dominate activity on the Floor of the Exchange: the potential for increasing order flow would be diminished seriously; a disproportionately large number of top quality stocks could be handled by one or a small number of specialist firms; the barriers that new entrants to the specialist business face may increase; the Exchange could become dependent upon one firm for a disproportionately large portion of its revenues; the influence of the larger firms over the policies or direction of the Exchange would increase significantly; competition among specialists for new stock allocations would be reduced; the integrity of the entire stock allocations process would be undermined; and, in general, the incentives for quality markets and higher standards of performance would be reduced.

The SEC approved the proposal noting its belief that excluding affiliated Executive Committee members from participating in the decision-making process should allow 'the Exchange to avoid a potential conflict of interest situation and result in a fairer decision'.

The voting procedures of other exchanges, and similarly the NASD, have also been the subject of SEC inquiry. For a long period of time the NASD, for example, required that certain of its rules be submitted to the membership for their approval as part of the rule-making process. In 1994, however, the SEC allowed the NASD to eliminate this requirement, agreeing that it was not necessary in order to give the NASD's members fair representation. This was despite the fact that at least one commentator thought the new process was undemocratic.[35] The NASD argued that the rule changes would simplify and render more effective its rule-making process. It noted that its members had access to this process through several means other than membership votes, most importantly by participating in the NASD's various committees, through the NASD's election process, and through the regular publication and comment process on its rules.

Various other aspects of exchanges' governance structures have been examined by the SEC. The Commission allowed an exchange to permit a single individual to act simultaneously as its chairman and its president, where the Commission believed that the operations of the board of the exchange placed sufficient checks and balances on the authority of both positions for the combination not to present a problem.[36] It gave approval for an exchange to permit selected governors to serve three consecutive terms, if the individuals in question had made 'an extraordinary contribution to the exchange'.[37] It also ruled on the appropriate length of terms of office that an exchange official might serve, and on the period after which officials may seek re-election.[38]

The most controversial aspect of exchange governance that the SEC has influenced has been the issue of public representation on exchange boards. Although the SEC has no direct statutory mandate to require such representation, other than its duty to ensure that the rules of exchanges protect investors and the public interest, it has sought throughout its history to increase the presence of the public on exchange boards. Typically the path by which this has been achieved at a particular exchange has followed a convoluted political process taking several years. Frequently it has occurred after a scandal at the exchange, and has been realized as much by action from within the exchange itself, sometimes with the external threat of regulation from the SEC, as by direct regulatory command from the Commission. The board structures of the NYSE,[39] the NASD,[40] and the AMEX,[41] have all been reformed in this manner. Despite the complexity of the processes by which these changes have been effected, however, the regulatory rationale for such changes has been both simple and constant. Essentially the goal has been 'to create an organization which . . . will strengthen self-regulation and answer the prevalent criticism that member firms . . . cannot be expected to discipline themselves'.[42] Enhanced public representation has been hoped to temper the conflicts of interests that are an inescapable result of employing self-regulation.

The precise nature of who may represent the public on the board of a securities exchange has not been an issue of major regulatory concern. The characteristics of the twelve non-member directors of the NYSE's board of governors illustrate the flexibility with which such representation has been interpreted. Historically, six to eight of these directors have usually represented non-financial NYSE-listed companies, two or three have represented securities investors, and the remaining positions have been filled by persons who are not associated with either listed companies or financial institutions, and who are knowledgeable about financial markets—such as academics, foundation presidents, and former government officials.

FUTURES EXCHANGES

The American federal law and regulation that affects the governance of futures exchanges is examined in this section. Factors influencing the composition of exchanges' governing boards, and the management of conflicts of interests on such boards, are analysed in turn.

Board Composition

Two statutory constraints on the composition of the governing boards of futures exchanges were made by Congress in 1992. It stipulated, first, that,

each contract market shall . . . provide for meaningful representation o
board . . . of a diversity of interests, including: (i) futures commissior
producers of, and consumers, processors, distributors or merchandise
commodities traded on the board of trade; (iii) floor brokers and traders
pants in a variety of pits or principal groups of commodities traded on tl

It also required that,

each contract market shall . . . provide that no less than 20 per cent of the regular voting
members of such board be comprised of nonmembers of such contract market's board of
trade with—(i) expertise in futures trading, or the regulation thereof, or in commodities
traded through contracts on the board of trade; or (ii) other eminent qualifications making
such persons capable of participating in and contributing to board deliberations.

In order to achieve the diversity requirement, the CFTC proposed that each SRO
should have the latitude to establish a board composition that was most appropriate to that SRO. It also suggested, however, that,

any scheme must establish, by rule, some fixed form of categorical representation which
will ensure that the various interests which could be affected by the decision-making of an
SRO governing board will be fairly represented on the board.[44]

Two criteria were proposed to assess whether a person satisfied the 'nonmember'
requirement. Such people would be required to show that they,

(i) Are knowledgeable of futures trading or financial regulation or are otherwise capable
of contributing to governing board deliberations, and
(ii) (A) Are knowledgeable of futures trading or financial regulation or are otherwise capable of contributing to governing board deliberations, and (B) Are not and for the prior
year have not been registered with the Commission in any capacity, and (C) Are not receiving and for the prior year have not received more than ten percent of their income as
compensation for work performed for any self-regulatory organization, self-regulatory
organization member or Commission registrant.

The CFTC noted that its intention was,

to ensure board representation by persons who will be sufficiently independent to represent and protect the public interest. In defining what constitutes a governing board public
member, the Commission has attempted to exclude persons whose interests might be so
closely aligned with a particular SRO, registrant or SRO member as to be considered
unrepresentative of the general public interest.[45]

In their comments on the diversity requirement, most of the futures exchanges
argued that the CFTC had limited excessively the manner in which they should
ensure meaningful representation. In its final rule, the CFTC stressed that its
requirement did not necessarily oblige each SRO to establish either a quota
system or proportional representation for the different types of membership and
other interests that had to be represented on the board. The CFTC also stated that
the representation requirements were to apply only to the full governing board,
and not to specific meetings of the board, so long as all relevant parties on the

board had been advised with adequate notice of any board meeting. It also permitted exchanges to use a single director to meet more than one governing board
composition requirement. In a subsequent analysis of how its rules had been
implemented, the CFTC recognized that the fact that a governor who was
intended to represent one membership interest appeared to have strong ties to
another membership interest as well complicated the question of what 'meaningful' representation should mean.[46] It found, for example, several representatives
of futures commission merchants who appeared in addition to engage in floor-
related activity.

The futures exchanges also criticized the CFTC's proposals about who should
be allowed to be a 'nonmember'. Although there was no definition for the term
nonmember in the statute, the term 'member' was defined to be,

an individual, association, partnership, corporation, or trust owning or holding membership in, or admitted to membership representation on, a contract market or given members'
trading privileges thereon.[47]

The CME argued that qualifications for nonmember participation should be
strictly limited to persons who were not members of the relevant SRO, given that
exchanges had clearly defined rules separating members from nonmembers.[48]
The proposed restriction that nonmembers should not have registered with the
CFTC within the prior year was claimed as excluding the bulk of potential participants who would have both the necessary expertise and sufficient independence.
The CBT maintained that the 'general public' and nonmembers were not the same
class of persons although they did overlap.[49] COMEX concluded that 'the mere
fact that an individual either previously was or currently is employed or otherwise
compensated by an industry participant should not automatically disqualify him
from board service'.[50] Another criticism of the CFTC's proposals was that the
limits on the earnings of a potential nonmember board participant were unnecessary because they would limit highly qualified individuals from serving, would
skew the selection process to high income individuals, and would also require
exchanges to monitor the income of their board of governors.

The CFTC's final rule took account of some of these criticisms. It retracted
both its suggestion concerning the earnings of potential nonmember persons, and
also the proposed criterion concerning Commission registration. It continued,
however, to exclude persons who were salaried employees of the SRO, as well as
persons who primarily performed services for the SRO in a capacity other than as
a member of its governing board. In addition, the CFTC continued to restrict SRO
members and their employees from satisfying the nonmember status, concluding
that,

there is no principled regulatory scheme which could effectively and reliably distinguish
between employees of a member of an SRO who could and could not be expected to serve
as independent and contributing non-member representatives to that SRO's governing
board. The Commission believ[ed] that this view [was] consistent with the basic tenet of
agency law that an agent's acts or knowledge may be imputed to its controlling principal.[51]

Conflicts of Interests[52]

There is no commonly accepted definition of what a 'conflict of interests' is in the context of the behaviour of the governors of an exchange. Furthermore, the phrase frequently 'calls up preconceptions based on legal standards in other fields and, indeed, raises the implication of misconduct'.[53] Notwithstanding these difficulties, the phrase is used here to describe a situation where an exchange board member is in a position knowingly to incur a benefit or a detriment from an action on which he is called to vote, and where his judgement may be influenced by this benefit or detriment.[54] No implication of misconduct is indicated by use of the phrase.

Conflicts of interests occur in a particularly acute form on futures exchanges, unlike on securities exchanges, when they are confronted with an emergency situation, such as a sharp movement in the price of one of the contracts traded on their market. In the face of such an emergency, an exchange's board typically has to take action to resolve the situation immediately. This may include halting all trading, or requiring that all outstanding contracts be liquidated at a specified price. A conflict of interests may then arise if some of the members of the exchange's board have open trading positions for their own accounts, their families or related persons, or similarly if some of the members' firms have open positions for their own accounts or those of their customers. When this obtains, there may be complaints that the 'conflicted' board members either acted, or failed to act, so as to further their own interests or those of their firms at the expense of the interests of the market as a whole.

A series of judicial and administrative proceedings have examined a range of emergency situations at futures exchanges in which just such complaints have been made.[55] The decisions have developed a standard of conduct for directors of exchanges according to which they are presumed to have obligations to the public. These obligations are quite distinct from the duties of the directors of other types of companies, which normally are owed primarily to the shareholders of the relevant companies. Only if a director of an exchange acts in 'bad faith', namely in a manner contrary to the presumed public obligations, can he be held liable for his actions.

When first passed, the Commodity Exchange Act (CEA) formalized the public duties of exchanges, though not initially those of exchange governors.[56] Two duties of exchanges are particularly relevant for the issue of conflicts of interests on exchange boards. Exchanges are required to 'provide for the prevention of manipulation of prices and the cornering of any commodity by the dealers or operators upon such boards',[57] and to demonstrate 'that transactions for future delivery in the commodity for which designation as a contract market is sought will not be contrary to the public interest'.[58] Each exchange has rules specifying the terms on which delivery of a commodity may be made or taken, or cash settlement may be made, under the futures contracts traded on that exchange. In addition, each has rules governing both the manner in which those contracts are executed and the trade practices of exchange members.

The CEA specifies that most exchange rules are subject to review, and in many cases prior approval, by the CFTC. In the event of an emergency, however, the CEA allows the board of an exchange to vote by a two-thirds majority to place into immediate effect a temporary rule dealing with the emergency without prior Commission approval.[59] Emergencies may include actual or attempted market corners, squeezes or manipulations. If an exchange does declare a temporary emergency, it is allowed to undertake any actions 'necessary or appropriate to meet the emergency'.

It was only in 1992 that the first statutory provisions governing the public duties of exchange directors with regard to the management of conflicts of interests on futures exchanges' boards were introduced. Although the CFTC has proposed some rules to implement these provisions, and public comments on them have been solicited and received, the implementing rules had not been finalized by mid-1998.

Summaries are now presented of the case law developing the notion of bad faith and some associated regulatory analysis of the issue, and then of the statutory provisions directly aimed at preventing conflicts of interests on exchange boards, together with the regulatory interpretation of these provisions.

Case Law and Associated Regulatory Analysis
The seminal case examining a conflict of interests on an exchange's board was *Daniel v. Board of Trade of the City of Chicago*.[60] On 5 May 1946 the US Government Office of Price Administration gave notice to the CBT that wartime price ceilings on grain would be raised substantially. In response to this emergency, the CBT forbade the trading in certain grain futures contracts and ordered the liquidation of positions at or below the old price ceilings. Thereafter, trading in the affected contracts was reinstated under the new price ceilings. Two weeks later, to the plaintiffs' detriment, the CBT ordered the termination of outstanding contracts and required them to be settled at prevailing market prices. The plaintiffs then brought suit against the CBT (referred to as the 'Board' by the Court), its clearing organization (referred to as 'Clearing' by the Court), and the directors, governors, and officers of the Board and Clearing for having acted 'wilfully, maliciously, and for their own personal gain through profits accruing to them through their individual brokerage houses'. When their case was dismissed by the District Court, the plaintiffs appealed.

The Court of Appeals stated that the actions of the CBT were within its rules, that the plaintiffs, as members of the CBT, were bound by these rules, and that the plaintiffs were therefore obliged to abide by the CBT's actions, unless the conduct of the exchange amounted to fraud. The Court then set forth a standard of conduct that would become critical in assessing what would constitute fraud in such circumstances by an exchange's board. The Court stated that,

because of the Board's relation to the public, it must . . . act with utmost objectivity, impartiality, honesty, and good faith. It owes that duty not only because it is affected with the public interest, but because of the complete confidence reposed in it by its members, and the further fact that the directors, governors, and officers of the Board and Clearing may themselves be members of the market, and as such have to act where their own private interests are concerned.

It follows as a natural corollary that if the individual defendants, the directors, governors, and officers of the Board and Clearing, did not act in good faith, but acted to further their own selfish interests and for their personal gain, the corporate defendants' action cannot be bona fide, since the Board and Clearing can act only by their directors, governors, and officers. If the directors, governors, and officers were unfaithful to their responsibilities, the action taken by the Board and Clearing is bound to be tainted with such conduct.[61]

The concept of bad faith was upheld in an administrative proceeding examining the emergency actions of the CME concerning the July and August 1973 pork belly futures contracts. The judge there similarly concluded that 'if . . . the Governors of the board acted in their own private interest for personal gain, this would justify a finding of bad faith and that such actions are null and void'.[62] In order to assess whether the governors had acted in their own self-interest, the judge examined the long and short positions of each governor and of their firms. He found that the six governors who voted for the emergency did so against the interests indicated by the holdings of their firms. He then asserted that while the positions of a governor's firm may not necessarily reflect the private interests of the governor, he accepted that this was the case in this context, and therefore that the directors had not acted in bad faith. The fact that a board member or his firm held an open position and voted for an action favourable to that position, was thus accepted as a factor determining whether or not the governor acted in good faith. The existence of such a position was not, however, taken to be sufficient to determine that the relevant governor acted in bad faith.

In *P.J. Taggares Co. v. New York Mercantile Exchange*, the notion of bad faith was defined as 'ulterior motive, for example, personal gain'.[63] In addition, the Court remarked that an exchange and its officials were entitled to the benefit and protection of the 'business judgment' rule in the discharge of their statutory and regulatory duties, absent allegations of bad faith. This rule has been characterized as 'embodying a judicial reluctance to impose liability upon corporate directors or officers simply for bad judgment'.[64]

A range of relevant cases followed the crisis in the silver market in the period from 1979–80. In *Gordon v. Hunt*, Gordon initially alleged common law fraud on the part of COMEX and the CBT, arguing that they had 'failed and refused to maintain an orderly market in the trading of silver futures because of their boards of directors' own self-interests'.[65] The Court dismissed this complaint, holding that it could not sustain an allegation of fraud because the complaint did not allege that the exchanges had acted with an intent to deceive. Gordon was, however, allowed to re-plead, and he did so, this time alleging that COMEX and the CBT 'intentionally, recklessly or negligently, out of their own self-interest, failed to maintain an orderly market in silver futures contracts', and that 'the Exchanges' failure to act was motivated by an intent to profit from the increased volume of trading resulting from the manipulation'.[66] The Court denied the exchanges' motion to dismiss this complaint, noting that Gordon's allegations were sufficient to satisfy the *Taggares* definition of bad faith, namely ulterior motive. If proved, this would have meant that both the positions of the relevant governors and whether the governors benefited from any increase in the total amount of trading in the market, would have to be considered in determining bad faith.

Several further refinements of the bad faith standard were developed in *Bishop v. Commodity Exchange*. Bishop held a long position in the January 1986 silver futures contract, and complained that the promulgation by COMEX of a 'liquidation only rule' constituted bad faith on the part of the COMEX Board of governors, in that the governors who enacted the rule did so 'in order to derive direct financial benefit and to advance their own individual and/or corporate interests'.[67] The judge again upheld the principle that,

exchange actions motivated by ulterior motives such as personal gain are not consistent with the exchange's duty to prevent manipulation, nor are they in accord with the responsibility to protect the public interest, which . . . is a 'primary function of an exchange'.[68]

When the exchange argued that the plaintiffs' complaint should be dismissed because the action of the exchange was reasonable in the circumstances, the judge stated that,

in view of the exchange's duty to act with 'utmost objectivity' in the public interest, we conclude that if an exchange enacted a rule for the sole purpose of advancing the private interest of its members, and if the rule damaged the plaintiff, it would not be a defense for the exchange to allege that the rule was reasonable.[69]

The judge also stressed, however, that if a governor voted in favour of a rule 'in the belief that the rule served the public interest, even if also in the expectation and hope that it would serve his personal interest, his behavior would not give rise to liability'. In addition, the judge rejected the business judgment rule as an appropriate criterion for assessing exchange boards' actions, noting that COMEX was 'not merely a private corporation whose board of directors is responsible primarily to its shareholders'.[70]

The notion of bad faith was elucidated in *Sam Wong v. New York Mercantile Exchange*, an appeal case concerning the emergency actions taken by NYMEX regarding the March, April, and May 1979 Maine potato futures contracts, and alleged conflicts of interests on the part of the exchange's governors.[71] The Court asked 'can defendants in such a case [namely the exchange and its directors] be found liable if their action was prompted in part by self-interest or animosity but still was within the range of discretion accorded them by the regime of exchange self-regulation?'[72] It noted that the *Daniel* opinion,

seems to speak with two different voices. On the one hand . . . a complaint must be dismissed 'in the absence of an averment of bad faith amounting to fraud'—more colloquially that in order for defendants to be found liable, they must have acted very badly indeed. On the other hand . . . the governors must 'act with the utmost objectivity, impartiality, honesty, and good faith'—more colloquially that in order for defendants to escape liability, they must have acted very nobly . . . despite—or even because of—the fact that they must often act 'where their own private interests are concerned'.[73]

The Court then observed that with the exception of *Bishop*, the cases following *Daniel* offered little guidance on the issue of whether 'the self-interest or ulterior motive of the governors of an exchange must be the sole or at least a dominant factor in the exchange's action or whether it suffices that such factor may have played a not insignificant part'. The Court reconfirmed the *Bishop* decision that if an exchange's action was taken to further the public interest, its governors could not be held liable, even if the decision had the 'incidental effect of advancing their private interest or damaging someone who they do not like'.[74] Nevertheless, the Court did decide that granting summary judgment against the plaintiff was wrong, because he had alleged personal animosity towards him on the part of the NYMEX governors, and he was entitled to discovery on that issue. The Court thus suggested that personal animosity could be sufficient ulterior motive to constitute actionable bad faith.[75]

Several refinements of the bad faith standard were developed in *Jordon v. New York Mercantile Exchange*. The standard was stated as being even more protective of exchange actions than was the business judgment rule concerning the decisions of the officers and directors of a profit-making corporation.[76] Three reasons put forward by an earlier Court for the judicial reluctance to impose liability upon corporate directors for bad judgment, were said to be applicable to the emergency actions of an exchange. These were first, that 'stockholders voluntarily undertake the risk of bad business judgment [by choosing stock ownership in a particular corporation]'; second, that 'courts recognize that after-the-fact litigation is a most imperfect device to evaluate corporate business decisions'; and third, that 'because potential profit often corresponds to potential risk, it is very much in the interest of shareholders that the law not create incentives for overly cautious corporate decisions'. In addition the Court noted that,

unlike the officers and directors of a profit-making corporation, an exchange board is called upon to exercise quasi-governmental regulatory authority in situations where its decisions will necessarily favor the interests of one group over another.

The Court also noted that,

the bad faith standard can be satisfied only by substantial evidence supporting more than mere suspicion or speculation about a Board's ulterior motives for taking emergency action. Inasmuch as a system of self-regulation inevitably will provide dis-satisfied traders with some evidence consistent with self-interest, the existence of bad faith must be tested by an objective standard, rather than a subjective standard that would permit trial on the issue of board members' state of mind virtually without regard for the insubstantiality of the objective, circumstantial evidence of ulterior motive.[77]

The Court concluded that,

In order, therefore, to create an issue of fact concerning exchange bad faith, a plaintiff must demonstrate the existence of a conflict of interest substantially greater than that which inevitably 'taints' the decisions of self-regulatory exchange boards.[78]

In the absence of such evidence, the Court asserted that 'only a demonstration of reckless and virtually irrational exchange behavior could conceivably be permitted to raise independently an issue of fact concerning bad faith'.[79]

In *Minpeco, S.A. v. Hunt*, the Court re-affirmed its commitment to the bad faith standard, rejecting the use of a negligence-based standard. It stated that,

to apply [such] a lesser, negligence-based standard in a claim against an exchange 'would conflict with the Congressional scheme of exchange self-regulation' and would 'force a court to substitute its judgment for that of experts on the exchange,' aided 'neither by specific statutory standards nor by any particular financial expertise'.[80]

The Court's analysis of the two reasons put forward by the plaintiffs for why COMEX had purportedly acted in bad faith was also instructive. The plaintiff claimed first that the exchange's actions were irrational, arguing that 'COMEX's failure to control the silver market "reflects a complete and total abdication of responsibilities for no apparent rational reason," from which bad faith can be inferred'.[81] While the Court accepted the possibility that such exchange behaviour might constitute bad faith, it asserted that there was insufficient evidence to find that COMEX's actions constituted the kind of reckless and virtually irrational exchange action that might independently support an inference of bad faith.[82]

The second argument of the plaintiffs was that there was evidence to support the inference that self-interest, and specifically the expectation of either personal or corporate financial gain, was the substantial motivating factor of COMEX's actions and inaction. The Court noted that the presence of the 'troika' organization of the COMEX Board—whereby metals firms, commission houses, and floor traders were equally represented on the Board, with the three general members representing the public at large—tended to prevent any one particular interest from dominating the Board. The Court also stated that,

plaintiffs can not defeat this summary judgment motion simply by pointing to evidence of personal conflicts of interest on the part of various board members. Plaintiffs must make a showing first, that these potential conflicts actually influenced the votes of the board members, and if so, that any instances of bad faith on the part of individual members could 'be deemed to taint the entire Board's actions,' . . . by influencing the outcome of Board votes or otherwise swaying the Board's course of action.[83]

In order to determine whether such circumstances existed, the Court analysed the trading positions held by the various governors and their firms in order to determine whether potential conflicts existed. Even when they did, however, the Court required that it be determined that such interests were the sole or motivating force behind the members' votes and actions as COMEX governors. This was done by examining the minutes and other records concerning who lobbied or voted for the relevant emergency actions. The Court determined that there was 'insufficient evidence of record that any of the potentially conflicting business affiliations actually influenced the actions of any COMEX governor. Nor was there any evidence of record that any alleged conflict of interest, even if proven to exist, tainted the actions of the Board as a whole'.[84]

The presence of conflicts of interests on exchange boards has been examined several times by the CFTC, even prior to the establishment of the statutory provisions directly examining the topic.[85] The most exhaustive such analysis was in a study by the Commission's Division of Trading and Markets on the silver market crisis over the period 1979–80. Although the Division found that certain members of the COMEX board had voted in a manner consistent with their personal financial interests, it determined that neither the COMEX nor the CBT had acted in bad faith during the period.[86] Several factors mitigating the conflicts of interests facing these governors were identified. These included that only a small minority of the governors had been so conflicted, and that they were therefore unlikely to have dominated the board's thought processes; that the board's actions were supported by governors who held neutral interests, or whose interests were harmed by the decisions; and that the actions chosen by the board were in the public interest, and generally in line with indications of the policy preferences of the CFTC.

A range of comments on the appropriate way of managing conflicts of interests on exchange boards was also made in the report. The Division concluded that,

the events of 1979/1980 silver, particularly at COMEX, argue strongly that financially interested or industry-affiliated directors are often uniquely qualified to participate in emergency-related exchange decision-making because of their day-to-day experience in the market, and that it would be bad public policy to exclude these officials from board deliberations simply because of their market affiliation.

A key reason for this was that,

each [governor] had an incentive to assure that the silver market as an institution remained viable and effective, totally apart from any potential short-term gains or losses on immediate price movements, and this long-term interest, coupled with the sizeable expertise of these particular directors, enabled them to act as opinion leaders for the boards as a whole.[87]

The Division believed that 'to have barred these potentially "interested" directors from participation would likely have significantly weakened the quality of decision-making'. It was also sceptical about the value of board members recusing themselves from decisions on which they were conflicted, noting that,

abstention is not always the appropriate response for board members holding significant, relevant market interest where mitigating factors are present. Service on an exchange governing board carries with it a responsibility to make decisions on ultimate questions on exchange policy. An abstention, without justification, is a direct abdication of this

decision-making function, a formal expression of 'no opinion'. In a controversial setting
. . . where the major substantive issues of position limits and liquidation only trading
were at stake along with exchange credibility, this 'duty to decide' was significant.

More succinctly, the Division stated that,

somebody had to take responsibility for making an emergency decision in a dangerous
market situation, and that responsibility properly rested with the Exchange Board of
Governors.

The Division believed that protections other than abstentions,

such as position disclosure and balanced board structures, are sufficient to prevent any
undue bias in exchange decision-making at the board level, and actual disqualification of
the member from voting or participating in Board deliberations is unnecessary.

It also identified,

the extreme difficulty of developing a single, uniform definition which can accurately
and consistently distinguish between which market holdings create an interest in price
movements sufficient to taint a director's motivations on a given board vote and which
do not.

Statutory Requirements and Regulatory Interpretation

In 1992 Congress enacted the first statutory requirement that futures exchanges
establish procedures to avoid the occurrence of conflicts of interests on their
governing boards.[88] Four demands were made of exchanges. First, any member
of a governing board was obliged to abstain from confidential deliberations and
from voting on any matter, where the named party in interest was the member or
a person with whom the member was affiliated. Second, any member of a governing board was required to abstain from voting on any significant action that would
not be submitted to the CFTC for its prior approval, if the member knowingly had
a direct and substantial financial interest in the result of the vote. Third, the trading positions of the members of an exchange's governing board and those of their
firms, had to be reviewed prior to relevant deliberations of the board. Finally, the
governing board had to reflect in the minutes of its meetings the exist-ence of
such reviews, and the occurrence of any decisions for a member to abstain from
deliberating or voting on a matter before the board.

    In its initial rule-making proposal for how to interpret these statutory obliga-
tions, the CFTC recognized that the requirement not to act in bad faith had
become the central judicial standard for assessing the behaviour of exchange
governing boards with regard to the management of conflicts of interests. It
claimed that,

by including more specificity in the factors to be considered with respect to barring
persons with potential financial or personal interests from deliberating and voting on
committee decisions, the proposed rulemaking should reduce the potential for collateral
attack of such committee decisions on the grounds that they were made in 'bad faith'.[89]

The rules were intended to apply to two types of exchange decisions that would not normally be submitted to the CFTC for prior approval, namely actions addressing emergencies, and margin changes made in response to extraordinary market conditions.

The CFTC recommended that board members abstain from deliberating and voting on any matter in which they had a significant relationship with the matter's named party in interest.[90] Such relationships would include being the named party, being part of his immediate family, being his employer or employee, or maintaining a significant on-going business relationship with him. Acting to clear the member's trades, or being part of the same broker association, would also constitute having an on-going business relationship with the member, but acting solely to execute his trading orders would not.[91]

The Commission also proposed that board members abstain from deliberating and voting on any matter in which they had 'a direct and substantial financial interest'.[92] The criteria for assessing whether an interest was 'direct and substantial' would consist of whether the individual would be exposed to market risk, the absolute size of his positions, their size relative to the market, whether or not they were market neutral, and their potential effect on his firm's capital. The CFTC recommended that exchange staff should review the positions of the member, his immediate family (excluding non-dependants and non-residents), his firm and his customers. The positions to be examined would include all relevant gross positions, and his firm's and customers' net positions. The types of contracts that would need to be examined were also specified by the CFTC, but it left open what size position warranted a member's abstention.

SRO staff were also to be required to make abstention decisions and to keep a record of various information so as to demonstrate the propriety of any abstentions made at governing board meetings. It was proposed that such information include the names of all members who attended the meeting or were present by electronic means, the names of any members who voluntarily recused themselves, the names of the position reviewers, the details of members' positions, and the names of members asked to abstain. The Commission proposed that board members be required to disclose relevant positions that 'are known or should be known' to their exchange's staff. It recommended that the failure to disclose such information be a direct violation of the rule prosecutable by the Commission, and that the member should bear the burden of providing evidence of his lack of knowledge.

In a limited number of circumstances the Commission proposed that a board member be allowed to participate in the deliberations on a particular matter, even though he not be allowed to vote on it. To allow this, a board would need to believe that it had insufficient expertise, knowledge or experience to consider a particular matter, that it needed the counsel of a member who would otherwise be excluded from participation by a conflict of interest, that it would not be able to deliberate meaningfully without him, or that it would not have a quorum without him. The CFTC proposed that such a decision be made by the board itself, and not by SRO staff, and that all such exceptions should require the approval of all the 'public' members of the board who were present when the determination was made.

The CFTC's initial proposals were widely criticized. The Coffee, Sugar and Cocoa Exchange (CSCE) argued that the Commission's approach of requiring the abstention of a board member from voting on any matter in which he had a direct and substantial financial interest would ultimately be a disservice to every exchange, by 'excluding from important deliberations the very committee members whose knowledge and expertise was needed'.[93] The CBT put this view more bluntly stating that under the proposal, 'self-regulation and its underlying concept of knowledgeable participants governing the markets terminates'.[94]

The CSCE also contended that excluding interested parties would go against the diversity requirements the CFTC had already required of governing boards, and that the exceptions to the conflict proposals would not remedy this bias. 'Eliminating the normal interplay among diverse committee members holding differing positions and "interests" may result in only one point of view being aired, depending on which experts are requested to deliberate under the exception'. The CSCE claimed that a proper balance between ensuring that exchange boards made well-informed decisions and minimizing the influence of a board member's self-interest, could be made by having board members' biases disclosed to all other board members, and then allowing the members who made such disclosures to participate in the deliberations. It did recommend, however, that voting should only be allowed, if the relevant positions were *de minimis*. The CME maintained that the requirement that all public members of a board agree to the presence of a particular conflicted person in emergency deliberations should be eliminated, arguing that to allow one member of a board to veto a decision with which he disagreed was not justified by the CEA or in corporate law.[95]

The New York Cotton Exchange (NYCE) recommended that the direct and substantial interest test be applied using a so-called 'but for' test. This would require assessing whether or not the board member or his firm would gain or lose a 'substantial' financial amount but for the vote.[96] If the gain or loss would occur anyway, there would be no need to recuse the Board member. The NYCE also noted that conflicted members who did not participate in deliberations could still make their feelings known before the relevant meetings. The CBT recommended that the decision of whether a member had a significant financial interest should remain within the discretion of an exchange.

There were many objections to the CFTC's proposed procedural and information requirements. NYMEX argued that developing dense information obligations would 'impede swift and effective regulation with regards to emergency actions, at exactly the time when such action [was] needed'.[97] The CSCE said that they would impose too large a duty on members, who might be held responsible for knowing about positions of which they had no knowledge. The CBT claimed that the positions held by a member's firm were in many instances unknowable, and the CME similarly stated that an SRO would have no direct access to positions held by a member outside of its own market. It maintained that the requirement to obtain such information would not only take a long time, but would also discriminate against exchange-traded products, the positions of which were more easily identified than off-exchange instruments. The CSCE noted that most members would not know about the gross positions of their customers, and the CME added that there was in any event no need for a review of customer positions in assessing potential conflicts of interest.

Several exchanges together with the Futures Industry Association opposed the need for creating a risk of personal and institutional liability by requiring disclosure by board members of that which 'should have' been known, both to members and to SROs. They argued this would result in exchange members declining to serve on governing boards or recusing themselves in any emergency situation, again denying the market and the exchange the benefit of their insights and judgements. The Commission's proposal was said to place unnecessary burdens on the member and the SRO in evaluating the propriety of members' participation in governing board deliberations. It was also argued as creating 'footholds for litigation that . . . [would] serve to chill the participation of such members, and therefore deny the process valuable input and judgment from members of a governing board'.[98] The CBT asserted that 'a member who is not actually aware of a financial interest cannot be motivated by that interest, and is therefore incapable of affecting the deliberations or voting improperly. That member should not be afraid to participate and vote. A member whose conduct is subject to attack after the fact will be well-advised to abstain in every case.' The CME recommended that the CFTC drop the presumption of knowledge by members, and rely instead only on what the member actually knew.

The impositions the proposed rules placed on exchange staff were also attacked. The CSCE commented that it might not be easy for an exchange's staff to be aware of the relationships that existed between members, and argued that the staff should therefore not be held responsible to know about them. The CBT noted that the very act of seeking to obtain information about members' positions might alert the market to the possibility of emergency action, and that any abstention decisions should be made by the board involved, and not by exchange staff. It also believed that exchange staff might find it hard to direct members to act in a certain way, and should therefore not be required to implement the requirements.

In response to the CFTC's hope that the proposed rules might reduce the potential for judicial attack on exchange boards' decisions on the grounds of bad faith, the CBT noted that even prior to the new rules, it had been 'advised by counsel that any emergency action . . . was deeply problematic'. It stated that it was therefore unlikely to invoke its emergency powers in a crisis, preferring rather to consult with the Commission, and to defer to the Commission in addressing such situations. It believed that the new rules would only increase this likelihood.

Following receipt of the various comments on its initial rule-making proposal for how to reduce conflicts of interests on SRO governing boards, the CFTC put forward a revised proposal incorporating many of the suggestions it had received.[99] Amongst the most important of the revisions were the following.

The new proposal required an SRO to base its conflict of interest determinations upon information provided by board members themselves, and any other sources of information that were reasonably available to it. Board members were required to disclose to SRO staff whether they had any relevant relationships with a matter's named party in interest, or whether they had a direct and substantial financial interest in any significant action being considered. Relevant positions held by an SRO board member both at, and outside of, his SRO would have to be examined. Board members were, however, required to disclose to their SROs only the relevant position information that was known to them, and not any information that they should have known.

The revised proposal required SROs to make a determination as to the existence of conflicts of interest, but it did not identify any particular SRO personnel or committee that must make these determinations. Each SRO was thus allowed to allocate the responsibility for such determinations as it saw fit, and could do so to its staff, its board, or some other party. The new proposal stated that in reviewing position information an SRO should examine any positions that it reasonably expected could be affected by the significant action. An SRO would, however, only have to base determinations on certain limited sources of information specified in the proposal. The new proposal also provided that an SRO may take into consideration the exigency of the significant action, when making conflict of interest determinations. This was believed to allow SROs the flexibility to make such decisions in an expeditious manner while not preventing SRO boards from promptly handling significant actions.

The new proposal retained a provision that allowed an SRO under certain conditions not to exclude a board member from relevant deliberations if he faced a conflict of interests. It required, however, that when an SRO board determined whether to grant such an exception, the board must consider all of the position information which served as the basis for the member's conflict of interest in the matter. The requirement that any deliberation exception be approved by all public members of the board who were present when the board made such a determination was deleted.

One point not addressed by the CFTC in either its initial or its revised proposed rulemaking on conflicts of interests was whether the review of an exchange board's decisions by the CFTC itself should affect whether these actions should be open for judicial review or not. This issue had, however, been addressed by the Commodities Committee of the New York Bar Association in 1980. It argued that an action taken by an exchange board should not be subject to being set aside by the courts solely on the grounds that a conflict of interests existed on the board, if the action had been approved by the CFTC. The reason given was that the Committee believed that, exchange actions should be afforded finality where CFTC oversight is available to assure that the action is lawful. Otherwise, whenever there is controversy over a particular exchange action, the marketplace would be left in a state of uncertainty as to whether the particular action would stand, and such uncertainty would be a detriment to the entire trading public.[100]

The Committee did not believe, on the other hand, that,

CFTC approval or review should necessarily immunize an exchange or its board members from civil liability if there is a showing of bad faith . . . Otherwise, the CFTC might consider itself obligated to investigate whether a conflict of interests existed with respect to every significant action submitted to it for review. This would add an enormous, unjustified burden to the review process, which Congress did not intend. The Committee believed that Congress intended the courts to decide whether conflicts of interests rise to the level of bad faith.

CONCLUSION

The aim of this chapter is to describe the main factors that affect the governance of exchanges in American federal law and regulation. Attention is focused on what are believed to be the two aspects of exchange governance of most public significance, namely board representation and conflicts of interests on the boards of exchanges. Following a summary of the costs and benefits of self-regulation, the chapter is composed of two sections.

In the first, the federal law and regulation that affects the governance of securities exchanges is analysed. The Securities Exchange Act imposes four major obligations on exchanges with regards their governance structures. An exchange must assure fair representation of its members in the selection of its directors; it must ensure that one or more of its directors are representative of issuers and investors and are not associated with a member of the exchange; subject to certain exceptions, only brokers and dealers may become members of an exchange; and finally, an exchange must ensure that its rules are designed to protect investors and the public interest. There are no statutory requirements regarding the minimum representation of the public on the boards of exchanges, nor on how such representation should be effected.

A prime concern of the SEC has been to ensure that no single constituency at an exchange dominates the exchange's governance. It has thus required that there be sufficient diversity of representation on exchange boards to ensure this, and has made similar requirements of clearing agencies' boards, as well as of different types of exchange committees. Although the SEC has no direct statutory mandate to require public representation on exchange boards, it has sought throughout its history to increase such representation. Other aspects of exchanges' governance structures have also been the subject of regulatory inquiry in the securities markets.

In the second section of the chapter, the American federal law and regulation affecting the governance of futures exchanges is discussed. Two statutory constraints have been imposed on the composition of exchanges' governing boards. An exchange is first required to guarantee that various interest groups are each given meaningful representation on its governing board. In interpreting this rule, the CFTC has allowed much leeway to each exchange to establish a board composition that the exchange believes is most appropriate to its market. The Commission has also not insisted that exchanges establish either a quota system or proportional representation for the different types of membership and other interests that need representation. Exchanges have furthermore been allowed to use a single director to meet more than one governing board composition require-ment. The second statutory constraint imposed on exchanges is that they must ensure that no less than 20% of the regular voting members of their boards are 'nonmembers'. The CFTC has excluded from this capacity of people, exchange members and their employees, previously salaried employees of exchanges, and people who have primarily performed services for the exchange in a capacity other than as a member of its governing board.

A series of regulatory and judicial decisions about the behaviour of futures exchanges in emergency situations, have developed a standard of conduct for the directors of exchanges according to which they are presumed to have obligations to the public when faced with a conflict of interests. Only if a director of an exchange acts in 'bad faith' can he be held liable for his actions. In order to avoid acting in bad faith, a director must essentially not act purely to further his own gain or an ulterior motive. Substantial evidence is required to prove bad faith, given the existence of conflicts of interests that inevitably taint the decisions of self-regulatory exchange boards. Even if there is evidence of bad faith on the part of some directors, it must also be shown that their actions were sufficient to taint the actions of the board as a whole. In 1992 Congress enacted the first statutory requirement that futures exchanges establish procedures to avoid the occurrence of conflicts of interests on their governing boards. In 1996 the CFTC issued an initial rulemaking proposal for how these statutory obligations should be inter-preted. Following widespread criticism of this proposal, it put forward a revised proposal in 1998.

10

Information: Economics

INTRODUCTION

Although it is widely accepted that the dissemination of prices and quotes plays a central role in the functioning of markets, the nature of that role is the subject of much controversy and ignorance. An understanding of this topic is vital in order to develop a reasoned regulatory response to the issue of transparency. The aim of this chapter is to survey the current state of knowledge on the subject as examined in the economics literature.

The chapter is composed of two sections. The first contains a discussion of the informational role of prices in equilibrium models. These models attempt to explain how goods are allocated and prices are determined in an economy. The next section focuses on the market microstructure literature, a body of work that examines how the detailed structural elements of markets affect their performance. The effects of disseminating different amounts of price and quote information are examined in a range of contexts.

EQUILIBRIUM

Equilibrium models are essentially abstractions or reduced-form descriptions of how markets work, and as such do not specify either a detailed price formation mechanism or an explicit game between market participants. In such models, producers and consumers interact with each other in the market, they act rationally to maximize their desired objectives, and markets clear, in the sense that the amount of a good produced at its equilibrium price is exactly equal to the amount of the good demanded at that price. Although equilibrium models are not designed specifically to assess the importance of the dissemination of price and quote information, as distinct from other types of information, they do nevertheless contain important implications for the informational role of prices.

This section is composed of three parts. In the first, the Classical or Walrasian model of competitive equilibrium is discussed. In the second, various types of rational expectations equilibrium models are described. The section concludes with some comments on the social value of information in the context of these models.

The Walrasian Paradigm[1]

The notion of Classical or Walrasian equilibrium is important for three reasons. It is the foundation on which almost all competitive equilibrium models have been constructed, it explains one particular role that prices play in a market, and it is frequently used to justify welfare recommendations concerning the operations and value of markets. One of the most important insights of Walrasian economics is that in certain circumstances, markets can lead to a Pareto optimal or efficient allocation of resources in an economy. On the consumption side of an economy, such an outcome is one in which it is impossible to make anybody better off without making somebody else worse off. On the production side of an economy, it is one in which it is impossible to re-allocate the input factors of production, and thereby increase the total output of the economy.

The institutional structure on which the Walrasian model is constructed is premised on the existence of a notional auctioneer whose role is to conduct a series of hypothetical auctions for each good in the economy. He posts a price for the particular good in question, and then sees whether there is any excess demand or supply for the good. If there is excess supply, he lowers the price; if there is excess demand, he raises the price. Under the Walrasian assumptions, it is possible to prove both that a price exists which clears the markets for each good, and that this price is unique.

The role of prices in the model is critical. They show the terms of trade between goods, and in equilibrium also reflect the various marginal rates of substitution and production in the economy. They therefore signal to producers whether they should reduce the use of, or increase the production of, scarce resources. Similarly, they signal to consumers whether they should consume more or less of particular costly goods. Each individual agent in the economy need only examine the relevant price, which he takes as given, in order to decide what his optimal actions are. He need not attempt to acquire information about the tastes, endowments and technology of other market participants; all relevant information is incorporated in the price.

The Walrasian model has two central conclusions relevant for determining the importance of price and quote information. The first is that prices convey all the information necessary for market participants to make optimal decisions, and the second is that the equilibrium outcome is allocationally efficient. There are several reasons, however, why great care should be taken in accepting either that these conclusions are valid, or that they are important, for real financial markets.

The first concern arises because of the existence both of uncertainty about the future, and of asymmetric information. In an environment in which the future is unknown, market participants will attempt to forecast future states of nature and to predict how these states will affect other market participants. Typically each market participant will have access to his own private information or signal about the future state of the world, and in general, the information each agent has will differ. Asymmetric information is said to arise when market participants are differentially informed.

Three types of environment may then be considered: the first in which no agent has yet received his private signal about the future state of the world, the second in which each agent has received this private signal, but has not made it public, and the third in which all agents' private signals are made public. In general, an efficient allocation of resources will require the third state of affairs. For example, the producers of wheat need to know *now* what consumers of wheat are likely to want to consume in the future, in order to take current action so as to avoid feast or famine in the future. In the absence of any form of publication, however, information about each consumer's future desires is privy to that consumer.

The Walrasian auctioneer is a simple construct which is extremely unlike the workings of most real markets. The construct is not rich enough in institutional detail to be able to capture the possibility that individual agents may be differentially informed about future states of the world, nor can it describe how agents may behave strategically towards each other in their submission of orders to the market, nor can it examine how the heterogeneous information of individual agents may be aggregated via some form of public revelation. In the Walrasian model, prices do convey all relevant information about the tastes, technology and endowments of market participants. They do not, however, signal individual agents' information about future states of the world, and as such do not therefore necessarily contain all relevant information needed to effect a Pareto efficient outcome in a world with uncertainty and asymmetric information.

A second concern about the Walrasian model arises as a result of the assumptions necessary for the allocational efficiency conclusions to be drawn. Amongst the many such assumptions are, first, that there are no externalities, and, second, that all the markets in the economy are perfectly competitive. An externality is where the consumption or production of a particular commodity by one agent in the economy, affects another agent's consumption or production possibilities. If there are externalities, and the possibility of Coasian bargaining is too costly, or if the markets in an economy are not perfectly competitive, the Walrasian outcome will not necessarily be Pareto efficient.[2] The outcome might indeed be far from the second best available.

A third weakness of the Walrasian model is that even if it did accurately describe the workings of an economy, the equilibrium may not be thought socially desirable. Although the outcome will be Pareto efficient, this is a weak criterion by which to judge what is in the public interest as it takes no account of how goods are distributed in the economy. Pareto efficiency is frequently viewed, therefore, only as a minimal requirement towards what is believed to be socially optimal.

Rational Expectations[3]

In contrast to the Walrasian paradigm, rational expectations equilibrium (REE) models are specifically designed to describe a world in which market participants do have diverse information about an uncertain future. In such models, agents learn of each other's information by observing prices, and change their actions according to the prices that they see. By doing so, the diverse information available in an economy about future states of the world may be partially or fully aggregated into a single price.

Typically in an REE model, each agent observes some private information which allows him to deduce something about the statistical distribution of the relevant future price. Each market participant also infers that prices transmit information about other agents' beliefs about future values, and this information may in turn lead him to revise how much of the relevant assets he wants to hold. For example, if the offered price of an asset is relatively low, a consumer may believe that other consumers know something that reflects badly on the asset. He may therefore revise downwards his demand for the asset. Conversely, if the offered price is relatively high, the consumer may deduce that other market participants know something positive about the value of the asset, and he may revise his valuation upwards.

In equilibrium, each consumer acts so as to maximize his expected profits, conditional upon both his private information, and the information that he deduces from observing the market price. After observing the market price, each participant has no desire to re-contract, or submit a different demand or supply than the one which he originally submitted to the market. Each agent also has rational expectations, in that his beliefs about the relevant prices and private information, turn out to be correct. Finally, the total market demand equals the total market supply, so that the market clears.

Fully-Revealing Models

As Admati (1989: 351) notes, in some REE models prices are 'so effective as information signals that they wipe out any informational asymmetry which may have existed initially among agents'. Each individual agent's private information about the future is then totally aggregated into the single market price. In such so-called 'fully revealing' models, the outcome is identical to that which would occur in a similar but artificially constructed Walrasian model, in which all agents share their private signals before any bids or offers are submitted to the Walrasian auctioneer. As in the Walrasian outcome, all relevant information is revealed in the price. In fully revealing REE models, however, all private information about the future is incorporated in the price, in addition to the relevant information about tastes, technologies, and endowments. As in the Walrasian outcome, the equilibrium allocation is Pareto efficient.

Despite the advantages of fully-revealing REE models when compared with the Walrasian paradigm, there are several problems with such models that limit their applicability to real financial markets. Two concern the realism of the models' assumptions. They do not allow for the possibility that traders might be differentially informed at, and beyond, the time of submission of their orders to the market, nor can they incorporate the likelihood that such differences in information might give rise to trading. These two factors appear to be key elements of real financial markets.

There are also several conceptual weaknesses in the theory of fully revealing models. The first, as identified by Grossman and Stiglitz (1980), arises because there is a trade-off between the informational efficiency of a market and the incentive to acquire information. They show that when the acquisition of information is costly, as is likely to be the case, then prices cannot fully reflect all the available information and markets cannot be informationally efficient. If prices did fully reflect all the available information and markets were informationally efficient, then those market participants who spent resources to obtain the information would receive no compensation for having done so. Other market participants would not be prepared to pay for any information because they could simply look at the relevant fully revealing prices. If market participants do not receive any compensation for acquiring information, however, they will have no incentive to acquire the information in the first place. Prices will then not be fully revealing. There is therefore a limit on the extent to which prices can aggregate information, or put another way, it is logically impossible for financial markets to be informationally efficient with costly information acquisition.

A second theoretical problem with fully revealing REE models concerns the nature of agents' demand functions. In the classical equilibrium, there are two effects that determine how an agent's demand for an asset will vary as its price changes: the substitution effect and the income effect. The substitution effect is such that if the price of a good rises, then consumers will demand relatively less of the good, and substitute their consumption of it by the consumption of other goods. The income effect is such that if the price of a good rises, then this will adversely affect the total purchasing power of the consumer, and in most circumstances, the consumer will again consume less of the relevant good.

In REE models, there is another effect that influences a consumer's demand function: the so-called information effect. This arises because when the price of a risky asset rises, consumers buy more of it because they believe that there must be some good news about its future price. In fully revealing rational expectations equilibria, the substitution and income effects are exactly counterbalanced by the information effect, so that an agent's demand for an asset is independent of the price of the asset. This independence puts into question, however, the very role of the market. If agents' demands are price-independent, then there is no need to have a market in order to find a price at which there is no excess demand or supply, and at which the market clears. Every price will clear the market.

Noisy and Partially Revealing Models

Some of the problems of fully revealing REE models can be alleviated in models in which prices are not fully revealing, but are either masked by the presence of so-called 'noise', or are 'partially revealing'. The essence of a noisy REE model is that one or more random variables, whose values are not known to market participants, are used as a mechanism in the model to stop prices from being fully revealing. Market participants then no longer know whether a higher price is indicative of the fact that some other agent has good news about the relevant asset, or is due to a fluctuation in a random variable. In such circumstances, private information once again becomes valuable, the collectors of costly information are able to earn a rate of return on their investment, and it is possible for there to be trade between market participants who hold different beliefs.

Grossman and Stiglitz provide one of the first examples of a noisy REE. They model a world in which there is one safe asset which yields a known return, and one risky asset which has a return that varies. Part of this random return may be observed at a specified cost, while the other part is unobservable. Agents in the market have a choice either of becoming informed by buying the signal of the future price of the asset or of remaining uninformed. Prices in the market do not fully reveal the information collected by the informed traders, due to the presence of an additional random variable that affects the supply of the risky asset. Uninformed traders cannot distinguish between price movements that are due to changes in the informed traders' information, from changes that are due to variations in the supply of the risky asset.

In equilibrium, the supply of traders with information adjusts to make prices sufficiently noisy that information collecting and processing are adequately rewarding at the margin. Three implications of the model are particularly relevant: first, the greater the number of informed individuals, the more informative the price system is; second, the higher the cost of information, the smaller the equilibrium percentage of individuals who are informed; and third, the greater the magnitude of noise, the less informative the price system is, and hence the lower the expected utility of uninformed individuals. This last implication also means that in equilibrium the greater the magnitude of noise, the larger the proportion of informed individuals.

A range of noisy REE models that extend Grossman and Stiglitz's analysis have been constructed. In Diamond and Verrechia (1981) and Hellwig (1980), for example, all agents develop their expectations using both the equilibrium price and private information. These models also examine a world with one safe asset and one risky asset, and lead to the following three intuitive results: first, increases in the payoff of the risky asset, and decreases in its supply, both lead to increases in the price of the risky asset; second, both the equilibrium price and private information have positive coefficients in agents' expectation functions; and third, the demand for the risky asset strictly decreases as its equilibrium price rises.[4]

These conclusions do not always hold, however, as shown by Admati (1985), in an REE model with many assets. In this model, the price of one asset typically contains information about the future value of other assets as well as about its own future payoff. There may then be instances where if the price of one good rises, but that of another remains the same, market participants are able to infer that the payoff of the first good is likely to be lower, because the lack of change in the price of the second good may contain important adverse information about the future price of the first good. Other models have been developed to explain the extent to which participants in a market should decide whether to acquire information or not.[5]

A relatively small number of partially-revealing REE models have been developed. The essence of such models is that in equilibrium there remains a level of asymmetric information between market participants. Some agents are informed about relevant information, others are not, and the information revealed in equilibrium prices does not eliminate the differences between these individuals. Ausubel (1990) proves the existence of a robust set of partially-revealing REE equilibria for a class of economies.[6] He resolves the problem of reconciling prices that reveal information with costly information acquisition. Different classes of agents in the market may choose endogenously how much information they wish to purchase, and such an allocation of information may be consistent with the REE that obtains in the model.

Notwithstanding the benefits of noisy and partially-revealing REE models, several problems with attempting to use rational expectations to model the determination of prices in real financial markets remain. The first is intractability: REE models are very complicated to build. A second is the difficulty of modelling dynamic or multi-period environments. A third problem arises in the implementation of rational expectations models. Such models essentially provide an abstract description of how prices are formed, and do not specify the institutional structure of a market or equivalently the game, which could effect or implement this abstract description. In order to apply the lessons learnt from an REE model, it is therefore necessary to specify a game which could implement the model. This is difficult. Furthermore, even if a particular REE model is implementable under a certain market structure, this structure may be very unlike the real market that the model is attempting to describe.

Informational Efficiency and the Social Value of Information

There has been much confusion both over the meaning of the term 'efficiency' when applied to markets, and over the question of whether it is socially desirable that markets be efficient or not. Although one particular application of the term, in the so-called 'efficient markets hypothesis', has gained wide acceptance in financial markets, and has been used to justify much regulatory policy concerning the dissemination of prices and quotes, it has a narrower relevance than is commonly assumed.[7]

The efficient markets hypothesis was introduced by Fama (1970). He characterized a market as being efficient when the prices in the market fully and instantaneously reflected all available relevant information. When such informational efficiency obtained in a capital market, it was then claimed that the prices in the market were 'accurate signals for capital allocation'.[8] Given that informational efficiency was viewed as a necessary condition for allocational or Pareto efficiency, the achievement of efficient capital markets was therefore seen as a socially desirable goal.

The pivotal mechanism which Fama assumed would lead to informational efficiency in a market was that of arbitrage. Individual agents would trade so as to maximize their profits, and by doing so they would ensure that prices were fully revealing, and that the best estimate about the future value of an asset was reflected in the current price of that asset. If it were not, namely if there were any information about the future price of the asset which was not incorporated in the current price, then it would be possible to make a profit by entering an order against that side of the market which did not fully reflect the relevant information, and then reversing the position when the information did get incorporated into the price. Given that the current price should be the best estimate for the future price in an efficient market, prices should follow a random walk. If they did not, they would then follow some pattern, and once again any such pattern would be observable by market participants who could then profit by it.

In order to test whether a market was efficient or not, Fama examined the time-series structure of price paths in the market. In particular, he assessed whether the current price in the market was the best estimate for the future price, or whether there was any extra information in a pre-specified set of information that could help provide a better predictor. Three different sets of information were examined.[9] In particular, under 'weak-form' efficiency, the relevant information was defined to be solely the set of historical price and return information; under 'semi-strong-form' efficiency, the relevant information was defined to be the set of all publicly available information; and under 'strong-form' efficiency, the relevant information was defined to be the set of all information, whether publicly available or not.

Fama's notion of efficient markets has come to underpin much regulation concerning the dissemination of price and quote information in financial markets. Most commonly, the notion of efficient markets is used to support the following argument. Without the publication of prices and quotes, it is claimed that market participants will not have sufficient information to be adequately informed, that the prices of the assets traded in the market will therefore not be informationally efficient, and that allocative efficiency will therefore not obtain.

There are several flaws, however, in attempting to use the notion of informational efficiency to draw inferences concerning the value of disseminating prices and quotes. First, as Grossman and Stiglitz showed, there is a theoretical trade-off between the informational efficiency of a market and the incentive to acquire information. Given that information is costly to obtain, markets logically cannot be informationally efficient. To predicate any arguments based on the fact that they are informationally efficient, therefore, may lead to false conclusions.

Independent of this theoretical concern, a second weakness arises because it is extremely difficult to ascertain empirically whether informational efficiency obtains in a market or not, and if so, to what extent. There is a large and contested literature examining both how efficient stock prices are in reflecting information, and the associated issue of whether they exhibit excessive volatility.[10] Even if it were possible to show empirically that the prices in a market did follow a random walk, this would not confirm that the market was informationally efficient. Indeed, many of the rational expectations models predict that prices will follow such a time-series path, even though they do not deliver informational efficiency. A further problem arises because there appears to be a range of regularities in market data indicating that prices typically do not follow a random walk.[11]

A third flaw in the argument about the value of efficient capital markets, concerns the perceived relationship between informational efficiency and allocational efficiency. Given that there is a tension between the informational efficiency of a market and the acquisition of information, it is not easy to judge how to balance the two opposing goals in order to best maximize social welfare. Indeed, there has been little economic analysis of the wider question of how the release of information may influence social welfare.[12]

Three instances of such analysis are commented on here. Hirschleifer (1971) notes that the pursuit of information may have purely distributional effects, and may not necessarily be in the social interest. While a group of participants in a market might have a private incentive to invest in technology to obtain price and quote information before other participants, for example, such an investment would have no social benefit. It would simply affect which participants in the market were relatively better informed first, and thereby influence the distribution of profits in the market. Orosel (1993) examines the relationship between informational efficiency and welfare within an 'overlapping generations' model of the stock market. He provides an example in which the market may be informationally efficient, but in which the allocation of goods is not Pareto-efficient and public dissemination of information about future stock returns may be harmful.

Dow and Gorton (1997) explicitly investigate whether there is a connection between informational efficiency and allocational efficiency. They develop a complex model of an economy in which managerial decisions at the firm level and stock price formation are linked, information acquisition is costly, and prices are partially revealing. Managers can choose what investments to make, and may have private information about the future prospects of the firms at which they work, as a result of their past investment decisions. Stock market traders may have material information that managers do not have about the value of future investment opportunities. Share prices may therefore transmit information both from managers to market traders, and vice versa. Shareholders wish to induce managers to take account of both their private information, and to react to the information contained in stock prices. In order to do so, they may need to design compensation packages for managers that are linked to share prices, given that managers' employment horizons are short compared to the horizons over which their decisions affect their firms. A link is thus established between informational efficiency and allocational efficiency.

This link is, however, tenuous. Dow and Gorton prove the existence of an equilibrium in which prices exhibit strong-form efficiency, but investment decisions are not optimal. Managers may choose not to produce information because they believe stock prices are not informative, and this belief may be self-fulfilling. Informational efficiency is thus not sufficient for economic efficiency. Dow and Gorton also suggest that informational efficiency may not be necessary for economic efficiency, by considering a banking system that may serve as an alternative to the stock market for the efficient allocation of investment resources.

A further problem in attempting to relate informational efficiency with allocational efficiency arises when market participants do not take prices as given, but have sufficient market power to affect the prices in the market. The assumption of perfect competition lies at the basis of the determination that informationally efficient equilibria are allocationally efficient. Once non-competitive behaviour is allowed, however, any link between informational efficiency and allocational efficiency may break down.

The key conclusion that should be drawn from this discussion is that the commonly assumed view that the efficient markets hypothesis can justify regulatory intervention to require the dissemination of prices and quotes is false. There is no clear basis in the economics literature for concluding that informational efficiency in markets does obtain, and if so to what extent. Nor is it possible to conclude that informational efficiency is required in order to obtain a Pareto-efficient outcome. Nor is it possible to conclude that informational efficiency is a socially desirable outcome. Our ignorance on these issues does not, however, mean that it is possible to draw the opposite conclusions. The claim that a lack of informational efficiency is desirable, therefore, can also not be justified.

MICROSTRUCTURE

The microstructure literature attempts to assess how the detailed structural attributes of markets affect their performance. A range of studies that investigate the implications of disseminating different types of price and quote information in various market structures, is summarized in this section. The studies are grouped together according to whether they employ a theoretical, empirical, or experimental approach. A brief comment on the lessons that can be drawn from the literature is also presented.

Theory

Seven theoretical examinations of the effects that different amounts of transparency have in a range of market contexts are outlined in this part. The environments include: (i) a competitive dealer market; (ii) an auction market; (iii) a comparison of four auction and dealer market structures; (iv) a competing dealer market with consolidation and fragmentation of information; (v) a market in which anonymity is possible; (vi) a fragmented multiple dealer market compared with a centralized one with inventory risk; and finally (vii) a competitive dealer market with inventory risk.

Competitive Dealer Market

Kyle and Roëll (1989) investigate the effects of implementing last-sale publication in a dealer market in which there are strategic interactions between market makers who have different information about the order flow. A two-period model is constructed, in each of which an agent comes to the market to trade one unit of a security. At the end of the second period the price of the security may take one of two values, and this value is revealed to all market participants.

Three types of market participants are assumed to exist: market makers, liquidity traders, and informed traders. Market makers make a market in both periods. Liquidity traders deal for reasons determined exogenously to the model. Informed traders know which of the two values the security will take at the end of the second period, and trade with the market maker according to whether the prices at which he is offering to deal differ sufficiently from the end-of-horizon price. They are assumed to profit maximize. Both market makers and liquidity traders know that the security may take one of the two prices at the end of the second period, but not which price. Both liquidity and informed traders deal with the market maker, but he is unable to distinguish between them.

The model predicts that last-sale publication will lead dealers to widen their bid–ask spreads in order to protect themselves from their competitors when taking on a large position. When there is no transparency, dealers compete to invest in information by dealing with an insider, and therefore their spreads are relatively tight when dealing initially with potentially informed traders. Once a dealer has dealt, however, he has an informational advantage over both his competitors and the liquidity traders, and they will lose out in subsequent trading. The publication of transactions in the market has two effects. On the one hand bid–ask spreads decrease because information about transactions reaches all market participants. On the other hand, bid–ask spreads widen because market makers have less incentive to pay to capture the information which a trade with the informed trader will bring. If averaged over all transactions, liquidity traders benefit from mandatory trade reporting, while informed traders lose.

In a similar model, Roëll (1988) studies the effect of allowing off-exchange dealers or dealers in less-regulated markets, who are not required to publish details of their trades, to compete with the on-exchange market makers who are required to do so. The less regulated dealers are always able to under-cut the more regulated exchange market makers in the first period. They are then able to use the confidential knowledge gained from dealing with the informed trader, to withdraw from the loss-making side of the market in the second period. This option is not, however, open to the more regulated exchange market makers.

Auction Market

The extent to which the dissemination of information about orders affects the performance of a batch auction market has been investigated by Madhavan (1996). He compares two market structures in which both liquidity and informed traders are assumed to participate. The first is one in which traders do not receive any information about order-flow composition, and the market is thus defined as being opaque. Traders submit orders for simultaneous execution at a single price, and may only submit price-contingent limit orders or market orders, which will be executed at the market clearing price. In the second 'transparent' market, traders are allowed to see changes in the order-flow, and can thus submit orders that are contingent both on the clearing price, and on the volume transacted at that price.

In some circumstances, enhanced transparency about the order-flow may both increase volatility and decrease liquidity. It reduces the effective amount of noise, giving traders higher quality information about the value of the asset being traded than without such disclosure. If there is only a small amount of liquidity trading, informed traders may be less willing to trade because by doing so they reveal more of their information to others. Although transparency encourages stabilizing speculation which helps absorb order-flow imbalances, it thus also exacerbates traders' strategic behaviour towards each other. Given the possibility that some traders are informed, market participants tend to increase their orders on seeing that another trader is increasing his order, and vice versa. Informed traders profit from the difference between the expected and the actual price, and are aware that if they attempt to trade to take advantage of a difference between the actual and the expected price, other traders will follow suit, thereby reducing the expected difference. They may therefore reduce their order size so as to maintain a wider differential between the expected and the actual price. In extreme circumstances, this may lead to a market failure. Madhavan does, however, show that transparency always leads to more informative prices, as long as there is no market failure. In addition it always reduces price volatility and increases liquidity as long as the market is sufficiently large and liquid.

Comparison of Four Types of Auction and Dealer Markets
Pagano and Roëll (1996) compare the liquidity that obtains on four different market structures, each with a different level of transparency. The four market structures are: first, a transparent batch auction in which all orders are submitted to a central mechanism, and in which the price and size of each order is publicly visible; second, a batch auction in which all orders are submitted to a central mechanism, and in which only the aggregate order flow is publicly visible; third, a continuous auction in which all past orders and trades are visible, but in which each order is executed separately; and last, a continuous dealer market in which each order submitted to the market is executed separately by a single dealer, and in which there is no publication of trades within a trading period, and thus dealers do not know anything about orders received by other dealers.

A partial ranking of the four market structures in terms of transparency is possible. The batch auction, in which the price and size of each order is publicly visible, is more transparent than both the batch auction in which only the aggregate order flow is visible, and the continuous auction in which all past orders and trades are visible. The continuous auction is functionally equivalent to a dealer market with immediate trade publication, and is more transparent than the dealer market without publication of trades. It is not, however, possible to rank the dealer market without publication against the batch auction with only the aggregate order flow visible, because the size of a single order may or may not be more informative than the sum of all orders.

An environment with potentially one informed trader, and potentially several uninformed traders is modelled, and the liquidity of the various market structures is examined in two contexts. In the first, the trading strategy of the informed trader is assumed to be exogenous, and thus identical in all the different types of market. In the second, the trading strategy of the informed trader is assumed to be endogenous, and thus conditioned on the type of market in which he is trading.

When the trading strategy of the informed trader is given irrespective of the type of market, the trading costs for uninformed traders for all possible trade sizes are lower in the transparent batch market than in the dealership market. The intuition behind this result is that in the transparent auction market, the market price is based on the greatest amount of information, and therefore informed traders have less opportunity to hide behind the actions of liquidity traders. Liquidity in the relatively un-transparent batch auction cannot unequivocally be compared with the two other market structures. Pagano and Roëll do not examine the characteristics of the continuous auction market when the strategy of the insider is exogenous, given that this artificially requires the insider to disregard any information he could see about the past history of quotes.

The performances of the various markets are also examined when the insider is allowed to follow one of two types of endogenous trading strategies. In the first he can pre-commit to a given trading strategy, and in the second such pre-commitment is not allowed. Pre-commitment means that the informed trader chooses what trading strategy he will follow before observing what the value of the security will be in the final period, and commits to follow such a strategy even if he would have chosen not to on observing what the final value will be. With such pre-commitment, the expected trading costs of liquidity traders are higher on average in the dealer market than in the transparent auction market. Although this is true on average, there may be a range of trade sizes for which the dealer market provides better prices for liquidity traders.

Without pre-commitment, a range of different scenarios is considered by Pagano and Roëll. If all noise traders' orders are of the same size, transparency unambiguously enhances market performance. The transparent batch market is more liquid than the continuous auction market, which in turn is more liquid than the dealership market. In the special situation where there is only a single noise trader and where the distributions of his trade size and of the insider's information are similar, the liquidity of all the different types of markets is identical. In an environment where the optimal strategy of the informed trader differs between markets, the liquidity of the auction market may, however, no longer be better for all noise traders. In particular, if two trade sizes are allowed, transparency may not enhance liquidity for all noise traders, regardless of trade size. A noise trader placing a small order may prefer the dealership market over the transparent auction. The transaction costs of noise traders averaged across all trade sizes, however, are lower in the transparent auction than in the dealership market.

'Consolidation' and 'Fragmentation'

Madhavan (1995) studies the effects of the publication of information about trades on price formation and market fragmentation. He constructs a two-period model in which investors have different motives for trading and in which dealers compete to attract order flow. There are four types of market participants: 'noise' traders who wish to trade one unit of the asset, 'large liquidity' traders who wish to trade two units of the asset and who must deal in both periods of the model, 'informed' traders, and dealers. Noise traders submit their orders to the dealer with the highest bid or lowest offer. Large liquidity traders place their orders strategically to obtain the best overall expected execution, taking into account the disclosure policy of dealers. Informed traders profit maximize, given their knowledge about the future price of the asset. Dealers update their beliefs rationally, given the optimal strategies of the other market participants and the information available to them, and set their bid and offer prices so as to maximize profits. They cannot distinguish between liquidity and informed traders.

In the market with full trade publication all dealers have the same information and therefore quote identical prices. Such a market is referred to as 'consolidated'. Without trade publication, however, they do not have the same information, and therefore act in a strategic manner that depends on the information they have. The fact that they quote different prices makes the market 'fragmented'.

A key implication of the model is that if dealers are given a choice as to whether to disclose their trading information or not, they will not naturally do so, even if there are potential economies of scale in consolidating order flow. This is because fragmentation serves dealers by reducing price competition: non-disclosing dealers can selectively participate in future trading to profit from their private information on past trades. Fragmentation also benefits both large liquidity traders and informed traders. Both their execution costs are larger in a consolidated than a fragmented market, because the initiation of their trades makes the market move against them before their trades have been completed. The effects of non-disclosure on noise traders are ambiguous. Without disclosure, bid–ask spreads are narrower in the first period of trading, but wider than they would be in a transparent market in the second period.

Madhavan also considers a market in which trade disclosure is mandatory for at least one dealer, but voluntary for the rest. Once again the unconstrained dealers will choose not to disclose trading information in equilibrium. The expected trading volume of such dealers is larger than for the constrained dealers, as the constrained dealers are not able to match the quotes of the dealers who do not disclose their trading information. The imposition of transparency on some, but not all, competing dealers can widen bid–ask spreads and lower market efficiency.

The relaxation of transparency rules can also improve the market's performance, for example by lowering spreads, as it may increase competition between non-disclosing dealers to attract order flow. The fragmentation which arises as a result of a lack of trade reporting does lead, however, to various types of inefficiencies compared to what would occur in a fully transparent market. There is higher price volatility because less information is incorporated into prices. In addition prices are inefficient, in that there are deviations between transaction prices and the full-information value of the asset, even though prices follow a martingale path. These effects are most pronounced for thinly traded assets, for assets with high underlying volatility, and for assets with a large amount of informed trading.

Anonymity

Forster and George (1992) examine the question of what are the effects of relaxing the assumption of anonymity in financial markets.[13] They model a market in which liquidity traders are allowed to advertise either the direction of the orders they submit to the market, namely whether they are net buyers or sellers, or the magnitude of their orders. Four degrees of anonymity are examined in which information about liquidity trades is revealed: first, to all market participants, second, only to those participants making the market, third, only to those agents trading for profit, and last, the fully anonymous case, in which no information is revealed to anybody. The model contains no analysis of the specific trading mechanism that might allow agents to disclose the relevant information.

The disclosure of the net direction of liquidity orders to all market participants in advance of trading decreases the expected transactions costs paid by liquidity traders. Their losses are greatest when neither the market maker nor profit-seeking participants know the direction of their trades, less when only the profit-seeking participants know this information, and less again when only the market maker is aware of it. If the market maker does not know the direction of trade of liquidity traders' orders, the liquidity traders lose out because the market maker's price does not reflect the direction of their trades. The average sensitivity of prices to order flow, and thus liquidity, is not influenced by the disclosure of the net direction of liquidity trades. Similarly, the informativeness of prices, namely the extent to which the equilibrium price reflects the security's fundamental value, is independent of whether, and to whom, information about the net direction of liquidity trades is revealed. Such revelation does, however, reduce the incentive for private information acquisition, provided that there is at least one privately informed trader.

The disclosure to all types of market participants of the size of liquidity traders' orders decreases their transaction costs only if there is enough competition between market participants with private information about the security's fundamental value. It does not, however, affect the average price informativeness. Disclosure of the magnitude of liquidity trades increases the incentive for acquiring costly private information that is possessed by only a few traders, but decreases the incentive for acquiring inexpensive private information that is widely known.

Forster and George argue that the model's results have several implications for market structure. A centralized market, for example, may provide lower execution costs for liquidity traders than a decentralized market, if competition between informed traders is more intense in the centralized market. If, on the other hand, private information is held monopolistically, a decentralized market structure that releases no information about agents' willingness and motivation for dealing, might deliver lower execution costs for liquidity traders. Another implication is that an open limit order book might allow all traders to estimate the volume of orders at different prices, and might therefore encourage the production of new costly information.

'Centralized' versus 'Fragmented' Dealer Markets with Inventory Risk
Biais (1993) analyses the performance of two types of dealer markets which he characterizes as 'centralized' and 'fragmented', and which have different levels of transparency. In the centralized market, dealers compete to attract order flow, and can observe the quotes and transactions of their competitors. Each dealer can thus also infer the positions held by his competitors. In the fragmented market, transactions arise as a result of bilateral negotiations, and market makers cannot observe their competitors' quotes. They can therefore only indirectly assess competitors' positions. Dealers are assumed to be risk-averse, and thus to incur a cost when they take on some inventory. They face no costs arising from asymmetric information, however, as there are no informed traders in the market.

The quote-setting behaviour of dealers is shown to be dependent both on their own inventories, and on the information that they have about their competitors' quotes and inventories. In the fragmented market, market makers take advantage of the lack of transparency to post wider bid–ask spreads, and to earn monopolistic profits. While the average market bid–ask spread is equal in both market structures, it is more volatile in the centralized market than in the fragmented one.

Competitive Dealer Market with Inventory Risk
Lyons (1996) examines what level of post-trade transparency a group of competing dealers will choose to establish in a market similar to the foreign exchange market. The market analysed consists of two types of participants: customers and dealers. Customers are atomistic and behave competitively, while dealers, in contrast, behave strategically. The market operates for two periods, in each of which four events take place sequentially.

First, each dealer quotes a single price that is observable and available to all customers and competing dealers. Second, each dealer satisfies all customer market-orders at this price. As information about customer–dealer trades remains confidential to the counter-parties to each trade, and as these trades are informative, dealers thus become differentially informed. Third, dealers trade among themselves. To the extent that it is observable, the order-flow in period one influences the determination of the quotes in period two. Fourth, some information is made public. In period one, a signal of the inter-dealer order-flow is published, and in period two the full-information value of the asset being traded is revealed. In order to model the optimal amount of transparency, a variable amount of noise may be added to the signal of the inter-dealer order-flow that is released at the end of period one.

The model attempts to capture the bursts of customer activity that occur in the foreign exchange market by ensuring that in period one each dealer receives random customer orders that both disturb the dealer's position and provide information. In period two, however, customers only trade if the risky asset yields a sufficient return conditional on the information available to them.

Lyons identifies two opposing effects of transparency: on the one hand it accelerates the revelation of true prices, while on the other it impedes dealers' management of their inventory risk. At one extreme, too noisy a public signal about inter-dealer order-flow provides customers too little incentive to trade in period two, and if they do not trade, they cannot share in the risk that would otherwise be borne entirely by dealers. At the other extreme, full transparency ensures that the interim price reveals all order-flow information. In this case all price risk has been absorbed by the dealers already, so customer risk-sharing in period two is irrelevant. Dealers prefer an environment with incomplete transparency. A moderately noisy signal slows price adjustment and allows time for customers to trade, thereby sharing the dealers' risk.

Empirical Analysis

Various empirical studies have attempted to assess how the amount of information disseminated in different market structures influences the performance of markets. Evidence about the following contexts is described here in turn: (i) improvements in price and quote dissemination technology arising as a result of the establishment of the US domestic telegraph, the trans-Atlantic cable and the Consolidated Tape Association; (ii) an information asymmetry in the US Treasury securities market; (iii) the value of the quotes of competing dealers to each other in the US Government National Mortgage Association (GNMA) pass-through securities market; (iv) the last-sale reporting for NASD stocks implemented under the NMS; (v) pre- and post-trade transparency on the London Stock Exchange; and (vi) order-book transparency on the Toronto Stock Exchange. A brief summary is also provided of the evidence on two topics with important implications for transparency, namely the price formation processes in markets and linkages between markets.

US Domestic Telegraph, the Trans-Atlantic Cable and the CTA

The effects of improving the means of price and quote dissemination in a historical context have been investigated by Garbade and Silber (1978). They study the consequences of three advances in information technology on the integration of various geographically separated markets. In particular, they investigate the impact of the establishment of the US domestic telegraph system during the

1840s on the New York and Philadelphia stock markets and on the New York and New Orleans markets for foreign exchange; the impact of the opening of the trans-Atlantic cable in 1866 on the New York and London markets for US Treasury debt; and the impact of the implementation of the Consolidated Tape Association in 1975 on the New York and regional stock exchanges for NYSE-listed stocks. The behaviour of the price differentials between the various markets are examined before and after the introductions of these technological advances.

The differences in prices between the New York and Philadelphia stock markets narrowed significantly following the introduction of the domestic tele-graph. The narrowing occurred immediately, and there was no evidence that inte-gration between the two markets improved during the year following the technological advance. A similar narrowing in price differentials between the New York and London bond markets took place following the opening of the trans-Atlantic cable. Again, there was no evidence that further integration occurred in subsequent years. The introduction of the CTA, however, did little to reduce price differentials between the New York and the regional stock exchanges. Garbade and Silber argue that there were two reasons for this. First, although the tape allowed traders in New York to see details of trades undertaken on the regional exchanges, the regional exchanges were already able to see prompt details of trades undertaken on the NYSE via the NYSE's ticker tape system. A more important reason, however, arose because of a distinction between the CTA and the domestic and international telegraphic communication technology employed in the other two advances. The CTA speeded up the flow of information to potential traders as with the other two innovations. Unlike the tele-graph, however, it did not speed up the possibility of traders transmitting their orders back to the markets for execution. Such orders still had to be transmitted by telephone following the introduction of the CTA.

Garbade and Silber note that the first two innovations were established by the private sector in the pursuit of profit opportunities, while the CTA, in contrast, was implemented as a result of a regulatory initiative. They contend that without such regulatory intervention, the consolidated tape would not have been estab-lished, because it would have been thought unnecessary given the already-existing relatively short time of information transfer, and the minimal economic benefits that were obtainable.

US Treasury Dealer Market

Umlauf (1990) examines the empirical effects of an informational asymmetry in the market for US Treasury securities, which arose because of the existence of two different types of dealers in the market. Primary dealers were allowed to trade through all Inter-Dealer Brokers (IDBs) operating in the market, while secondary dealers were only allowed to trade through a subset of the full group of IDBs. The secondary dealers were therefore at a disadvantage to the primary dealers, in that they did not have access to the full set of trading information relayed on all the IDBs' screens. Umlauf finds that this informational asymmetry affected the transactional characteristics of the market in two ways. First, secondary dealers' price expectations lagged those of primary dealers by an esti-mated 2.2 minutes and 4.3 minutes in the two-year note and in the long-bond series, respectively. Second, the bid–ask spreads of secondary dealers were wider than the corresponding ones of the primary dealers.

US GNMA Market

Garbade, Pomrenze and Silber (1979) investigate the extent to which the quotes of competing dealers held information of value to each other in the US GNMA pass-through securities market. Three propositions concerning the value to one dealer of the information contained in other competing dealers' quotes were tested: first, that the prices of other dealers never contained any new information; second, that the mean observed price of other dealers' quotes always contained all relevant information; and third, that other dealers' quotes might contain some information, but that the quality of that information was an increasing function of the number of competing dealers and a decreasing function of the relative disper-sion of the prices.

Both the first and the second propositions were rejected. Although dealers were found to acquire new information from their competitors, they did not consistently treat their own quotes as redundant information once they had observed those of their competitors. The quality of the information carried in a particular set of observed quotes depended on the dispersion of those quotes. In particular, the more compact the distribution of competing dealers' prices was observed to be, the more dealers revised their estimates of the equilibrium price towards the mean price of this observed distribution.

NASDAQ

Following the 1975 amendments to the Securities and Exchange Act and the establishment of the NMS, a set of NASDAQ OTC stocks were voluntarily desig-nated as NMS securities.[14] On 8 February 1983 these 'Tier 2' securities began trading under NMS conditions, the most important of which was full last-sale reporting. In order to assess whether NMS designation had any adverse effects, the NASD examined how the trading characteristics of these securities behaved over the period from 8 February 1983 to 29 March 1983.[15] Measures of the trad-ing volumes, bid–ask spreads, and price volatilities, for these securities were compared for the periods before and after their change in status. They were also compared with similar measures for two control groups of stocks to see whether there were any significant differences between the different groups.

The volume of trading increased significantly for most of the stocks that were upgraded to NMS status. It could not be concluded, however, that this result arose unequivocally as a result of the changes in reporting rules. The reasons for this were investigated for a sub-sample of five stocks. It was noted that actual NMS volume was often less than that called for by the last-sale rule. In addition to such under-reporting of NMS trades, however, instances of over-reporting were also found. These inconsistencies in last-sale reporting prevented the drawing of any conclusions concerning the effects of transparency. No significant changes in bid–ask spreads were observed for the upgraded stocks before and after their change of status, and similarly there appeared to be no apparent pattern in the changes of volatility.

A similar analysis has been undertaken by Seguin (1992), using more sophisticated statistical techniques. He examines the trading characteristics of the 2,639 NASDAQ securities that joined the NMS system from its inception up until September 1987, and studies the effects of transaction reporting on daily returns volatilities, bid–ask spreads, and required rates of return (betas).

Daily returns volatilities were found to decline by 8–10% immediately upon the inception of transaction reporting, bid–ask spreads were roughly 3.5% lower in the post NMS period, and required rates of return also declined. Seguin's cross-sectional analysis indicates that transaction reporting effects were not homogenous. In particular, they were most pronounced for those firms where information about transactions was dispersed among many market makers, and where the information content per trade was high. The information content per trade was proxied by the log of the ratio of returns volatility to volume. This proxy was chosen because it was assumed that price changes in a stock arose as a result of new information, and that information was brought to the market by trades—the larger the value of the proxy, therefore, the larger the information content per trade.

London Stock Exchange I

This part describes the findings of three of the initial studies that examined the effects and implications of different transparency regimes on the London Stock Exchange. The first is by the International Stock Exchange (1989), as the LSE was then called. It summarizes a study the exchange undertook concerning some stocks which had been promoted from beta to alpha status, a change in status that brought with it publication of the prices and sizes of all trades within five minutes. No significant increase in turnover for the promoted shares was found. Few details of the study were, however, provided.

In the second study, MacIntyre (1991) examines the effects of the LSE's 1991 rule changes governing transparency on 'quote quality', turnover, and depth. For the most liquid stocks, the rule changes led to an increased amount of information about trading volume being published, but a decreased amount about transaction prices being disseminated. For the medium-sized stocks, price and size transparency was increased, while for the smaller stocks it remained the same. The effects of the new transparency regime were mixed. For the more liquid stocks, the spreads and touches (i.e. market bid–ask spreads) remained relatively constant, while for the stocks for which transparency increased, spreads and touches declined. For the larger stocks there was a decline in total trading volume, while for the smaller stocks there was an increase. For those stocks for which transparency improved, there was a significant decrease in the number of large trades undertaken. Although note was made of the potential effects of changes in trading volume in the various stocks on the measures of market quality, no formal account of the importance of this effect was undertaken in the study.

In the third study, Franks and Schaefer (1990) investigate the effects of block trading on the LSE. Although they do not undertake any empirical analysis concerning the effects of transparency, they note several differences between the publication requirements for NASDAQ and for SEAQ. In particular, on NASDAQ dealers were allowed to incorporate a 'markup', 'markdown', or 'service charge', in the price that they reported to the NASD. Different dealers apparently had different policies concerning such markups, markdowns, and service charges. On SEAQ, in contrast, market makers were required to report the net price at which they transacted business. A second difference was that many of the large trades on NASDAQ were matched, implying that the participating dealer had taken no position risk. In contrast, on SEAQ market makers frequently took blocks of stock on to their own books, thus assuming the market risk of the position. A third difference was that trading appeared to be concentrated on SEAQ in a smaller number of dealers than on NASDAQ. Franks and Schaefer argue that this might have made it easier to identify which market maker had taken a position on SEAQ than on NASDAQ.

London Stock Exchange II

A further study of the effects of transparency on the LSE was undertaken by Gemmill (1996). He explores the way in which share prices on the LSE reacted to large trades under three different trade publication regimes: when publication of large trades was immediate over the period 1987/8, when publication of large trades was delayed for twenty-four hours over the period 1989/90, and when publication of large trades was delayed for ninety minutes (after the exchange's rule changed on 14 January 1991). He tests five hypotheses each of which, if supported by the evidence, would support delaying publication. They were: first, that there is no permanent impact of a large trade on price, only a temporary one; second, that delayed publication leads to narrower transactions spreads for block trades; third, that delayed publication does not affect the permanent price impact of a given size of trade, if any, but only the temporary price impact; fourth, that delayed publication leads to smoother price transitions, and thus less volatility, following large trades; and fifth, that delayed publication does not slow the response of prices in reaching a new permanent level after a large trade.

Gemmill found that the first four hypotheses could be rejected, but that the fifth could not. His findings may be summarized as follows. First, block purchases were found to have a permanent and significant impact on price level, with a value of about one third of the buying spread, while block sales had a permanent impact which only bordered on significance and averaged about one sixth of the value of the selling spread. This implied that there was an advantage in knowing about the existence of large trades. Second, there was no consistent reduction in transaction spreads for large trades when publication was delayed.

Although spreads were narrower for large trades than for small trades in three of the four years with delayed publication, in the other year the opposite was true. Third, there was no clear relationship between delayed publication and the price effects following a block trade. This was observed for both the temporary and the permanent effects. Fourth, there was no reduction in returns volatilities associated with delayed publication. Fifth, the price responses to large trades were similar under all three publication regimes, and thus delayed publication did not slow down the attainment of permanent price levels following block trades.

Gemmill concluded that delayed publication had little impact on spreads, speed of adjustment, smoothing or the ultimate price level. He did note, however, that although there was an advantage to knowing that a large trade occurred, the information of the existence of a transaction leaked out so rapidly after its occurrence, that the potential advantage could not be exploited.

London Stock Exchange III

The most detailed empirical investigation of the effects of transparency on the LSE has been undertaken by Board and Sutcliffe (1995). They examine all the prices and quotes for forty-two stocks over a two-year period. Twenty-four of the forty-two stocks had associated traded options contracts (designated alpha stocks), while the other eighteen (designated beta stocks) did not.[16] After describing the characteristics of their data set in detail, they investigate four main issues: the manner in which prices for large and small trades varied, the extent to which market makers adjusted their trading books before and after a big trade, the price impact of large trades, and the relationship between equity market transparency and traded options volume.

Board and Sutcliffe summarized their main conclusions about transparency on the LSE as follows:

The major benefit claimed for [the transparency] arrangements is that market makers can reduce their risks, and so allow institutional customers to trade immediately in size at good prices. The costs are that the information asymmetries, which must arise if the system is to be successful, mean that the counterparties to the offsetting trades are at a disadvantage. In addition, the lack of transparency resulting from delayed publication means that markets which depend on information about the stock price (in particular the traded options market) may be adversely affected. Given this, and since restricting information is in principle undesirable, publication should only be delayed when demonstrably beneficial to investors.[17]

Their key findings are as follows.

Descriptive Statistics: On average almost 70% of the value of trading in each stock was accounted for by the five largest market makers in that stock, and 62% of the number of deals by the three largest market makers. Board and Sutcliffe took this to mean that market-making and off-setting excess inventory were less likely to be anonymous than if larger numbers of firms were involved. IDB business represented 13% of the value of trading, and so order-driven IDB trading was seen as forming a significant part of equity trading in London. Nearly half of all trading by value was subject to delayed publication, and for the beta stocks, this figure rose to three-quarters. Publication of 56% of customer trades by value was delayed under the 90 minute rule.

Relative Prices Paid by Small and Large Trades: On average, customer trade prices were slightly inside the quoted touch, IDB trades were further inside (by 0.33%), while inter-market maker trades were outside the touch by a very small amount. In addition, depending on the trade size, IDB systems offered better prices than those available on SEAQ. There was some evidence that trade prices improved as trade size increased. Thus very large trades took place at better prices than did smaller ones. Board and Sutcliffe thought that this could imply that delayed publication over-compensated market makers for the risk of such trades.

Trade Positioning: The evidence Board and Sutcliffe found, and the key conclusions they drew, about the behaviour of market makers adjusting their books in response to large trades, were as follows:

Of the volume of large trades, 26% was pre-positioned, while 15% of volume was post-positioned. In addition, no positioning took place for 26% of trades, while only 11% of trades were fully positioned. These results strongly suggest that market makers do not consistently use the opportunity offered by the transparency regime to offset the excess inventory acquired as a result of a large trade.

The degree of positioning tends to fall as trade size rises. This surprising result implies that market makers do not perceive that very large trades are riskier than smaller ones; in which case the justification for delayed publication is weakened.

Market makers complete such positioning as they undertake in less than 45 minutes. Since trade publication is delayed by 90 minutes, this suggests that the current publication delay is unnecessarily long.[18]

Price Impact: A permanent effect of large trades on prices was found in the alpha stocks to be 0.23% for customer buys, and − 0.18% for customer sells. Although much of the price response occurred in the first trade, the full impact was found to occur only after about twelve subsequent trades, after an average period of about forty-five minutes. This suggested to Board and Sutcliffe that market efficiency might be improved if large trades were published immediately.

LIFFE—Traded Options: In general, only a small amount of options trading was found to occur. A positive correlation was observed between the volume of small equity trades and the volume of options traded. No such association was seen, however, between the volume of large equity trades, whose publication was delayed, and options volume. This was taken to imply that large equity trades were not hedged with options, and that there was no evidence of substantial options trading on the basis of superior information. Board and

Sutcliffe put forward two reasons why this might occur. First, because there might be,

a lack of interest in the use of options by equity market participants. [Alternatively it might be because] options market makers are reluctant to trade at times when they believed that large equity trades at unobservable price or volume are occurring, and that it is likely that their counter party will have superior information about recent equity trades. The result of this will be wide spreads on the options market, with a consequent lack of volume.[19]

London Stock Exchange IV

Following the implementation of an enhanced transparency regime for the LSE in January 1996, Board and Sutcliffe (1996) undertook a further study to analyse the effects of these rule changes. The main rule changes were: first, that immediate publication (within three minutes) would be required of trades of 3–6 times the Normal Market Size (NoMS), unlike before where there had been a ninety minute delay; second, that IDB trades had also to be published immediately, again without the ninety minute delay; and third, that the period of delay for trades larger than six times NoMS was reduced from ninety to sixty minutes.

Board and Sutcliffe's findings were as follows. There was a major reduction (of 43%) of the value of trading for which publication was delayed. There was not, however, any change in the size distributions of trades, so that traders did not appear to be avoiding the 3–6 times NoMS range for which immediate publication was required. The bid–ask spread for trades of 3–6 times NoMS narrowed slightly, contrary to the expectations of market makers. There was a slight decline in inter-market maker business for the FT-SE 100 stocks. The inventory management of market makers for trades of larger than three times NoMS appeared to be little changed. Board and Sutcliffe therefore concluded that the enhanced transparency regime had increased the information published about trades without leading to any adverse effects.

Toronto Stock Exchange

Porter and Weaver (1996*a*) examine how the quality of the market on the Toronto Stock Exchange was affected by the implementation of a new 'Market-by-Price' system that increased pre-trade transparency for a subset of the stocks traded on the exchange. The new system delivered real-time dissemination of the quotes and associated volumes for the current inside market, as well as the volume and limit order prices for up to four price levels above and below the current market. Various measures of market quality were identified, and it was assessed whether their values changed following the enhanced transparency regime. The evidence was mixed. On the one hand, dollar spreads, percentage spreads, effective dollar spreads, and effective percentage spreads, all exhibited significant increases implying a decrease in market quality. On the other, there was a significant increase in the depth of the market. There were no notable changes in measures of market efficiency or execution costs.

Price Formation Processes and Market Linkages

In addition to the empirical literature that directly addresses the effects of disseminating price and quote information, work on two other topics has indirect implications for assessing the consequences of transparency. The first relates to the formation of prices in a market, and the role that information plays in this process. The second concerns the relationship between the prices on two associated markets. The significance of the literature on both topics is briefly outlined here.

Economic models of price formation processes attempt to explain how prices evolve in a market. Some of these studies examine specific events, for example by focusing on the price behaviour surrounding large trades, as undertaken by Gemmill, and Board and Sutcliffe, while others examine the behaviour of prices on a continuous time basis. Typically these studies attempt to gauge whether price changes occur after trades, and if they do whether such changes are temporary or permanent in nature. If they are permanent, it is assumed that new information is incorporated into the price. The importance of these analyses in the context of transparency is that if trades do convey information, then without full transparency only the market participants who participate in trades will be aware of the information which these trades reveal. This may have several effects including distorting competition.

Several studies have examined the time series behaviour of prices on the LSE. Breedon (1993), for example, draws three tentative conclusions. First, small trades contained no relevant information, in contrast to medium-sized trades for which the information effects were quite apparent. Second, large buy orders appeared to contain more information than large sell orders. Third, although the information contained in trades appeared to increase with order size, large sell orders often had less information than medium size sell orders—possibly because the large trades were index trades. Breedon also finds that the price response to trades was extremely rapid. In contrast, both Lee (1989) and Neuberger and Roëll (1991) find that the amount of informationally based trading was relatively small. The extent to which large trades convey information and lead to permanent price changes has also been the subject of many American studies.[20]

The manner in which the prices on two markets trading the same or associated assets are related may also affect the value of transparency. One form of *a priori* reasoning suggests that unless full information about the prices and quotes on one market is released, any associated markets will not have the relevant information to price properly the contracts or assets which are associated with those trading on the primary market. Without this information, arbitrage may not eliminate the pricing differences between the different centres. The little analysis that there is on the effects of information dissemination on the links between associated markets, however, paints a more complex picture.

Pagano and Roëll (1991) find that the London Stock Exchange had derivative pricing with respect to the Paris and Milan bourses in those shares which were traded both in London and respectively Paris or Milan. Prices in London tended to follow the prices obtaining on the domestic continental markets. Prices were, however, very tightly arbitraged despite the lack of any post-trade transparency on SEAQ International. Garbade and Silber (1979) similarly find that the pricing on the regional stock exchanges in the USA had derivative pricing with respect to the NYSE. As noted above, they also found that the introduction of the CTA did not markedly improve price differentials between the NYSE and the regional exchanges.

Although the links between trading on a cash market and an associated derivative market have been investigated in depth, the effects of transparency on such links have not been much explored.[21] There has been considerable debate over whether prices in the cash market lead those of associated derivative markets or vice versa, whether the presence of derivatives markets enhances the efficiency of the cash markets, and whether the presence of derivatives markets leads to greater volatility or volume in the cash markets. Answers to all these questions might affect how the effects of transparency are viewed. If the prices on a derivatives market do follow those in the cash market, for example, then transparency in the cash market may be important for ensuring efficiency in the derivatives market.

Grünbichler, Longstaff and Schwartz (1994) examine the extent to which the prices for a futures index contract traded on an electronic screen trading system, lead or lag the prices of the index's component stocks, which are traded on a floor-based exchange. They find that the futures prices of the index lead those of the component stocks by nearly twenty minutes. Although they observe that this finding may be due to many reasons, they note that it is consistent with several hypotheses about the relative transparencies of the two trading systems. It may be because the automated system accelerates the price discovery process, as the price and quote information disseminated from such a system is collected and published much more quickly than is possible from a floor-based exchange. Alternatively, it may be because the automated system is less transparent than the floor-based exchange, in that it is easier to maintain anonymity on a screen than on a pit. Informed traders may therefore choose to trade on the automated system to protect their identities, and this may lead to more informative trading on this system than on the floor-based one.

Board and Sutcliffe claim that the traded options market in London has not developed as a result of the opacity on the LSE. Various other reasons have also, however, been put forward for the perceived illiquidity in the London traded-options market, including a dearth of local traders, restrictions on stock-borrowing, the costs of a floor-based trading system, a lack of demand, and excessive taxation. The relative merits of these different conjectures have not been confirmed empirically.

Kofman and Moser (1996) investigate the nature of the competition between two futures exchanges, the DTB and LIFFE, which both trade the same contract but which have different amounts of transparency. The DTB is characterized as a more anonymous and less transparent automated system, while LIFFE is deemed a less anonymous and more transparent pit-based exchange. Two key issues are examined: whether quote setting is related to the transparency of the trading system, and whether the transparency of the trading system influences the lead/lag relationship between the two markets.

The evidence confirms that the realized spreads on both systems are virtually identical, but that the components of these spreads are quite different at the two exchanges. An order processing costs component is found to be significantly lower on the automated DTB than on LIFFE, while in contrast the costs that arise as a result of information asymmetries and time-varying expected returns are significantly higher on the DTB. Kofman and Moser argue that market makers on the more anonymous system, the DTB, might widen their bid–ask spreads in order to protect themselves from the likelihood that informed traders will choose to trade there rather than on LIFFE, given the greater facility for hiding their identity on the DTB. This reduction of liquidity may counterbalance the increase in cost efficiency created by the informed traders seeking to trade on DTB. The difference in transparency between the two systems appears to have no effect on the lead/lag relationship in pricing. Both markets appear informationally efficient, and there is an instantaneous feedback of news from each market to the other.

Experimentation

Five studies that use laboratory experiments to investigate how transparency affects different elements of a market's performance are described here. They examine, in turn: (i) a transparent dealer market, and a similar market that operates in addition with a non-transparent bilateral search process; (ii) a market with two competing market makers under different transparency settings; (iii) quote transparency in a multiple-dealer market; (iv) post-trade transparency in a multiple-dealer market; and (v) competition between transparent and opaque markets.

A Transparent Dealer Market, and a Transparent Dealer Market with Opaque Bilateral Search

Lamoureux and Schnitzlein (1997) compare, in an experimental setting, a transparent market where all trading is channelled centrally to a group of competing dealers, with a similar market where traders may also trade with another via an opaque process of bilateral search. In each experiment, trading in a risky asset is conducted over a series of periods. There are three types of agents in both types of markets: a single insider who knows the value of the risky asset at the end of each trading period, three competing market makers, and four liquidity traders who trade to satisfy an exogenously determined motive. The insider is chosen at random each period from amongst the five players who are not dealers, and is anonymous.

The structure of the dealer market is as follows. Each trading period is composed of two trading intervals. Before each trading period, each dealer sets a bid and an ask price for a single unit of the risky asset without seeing other dealers' prices. Once the first trading interval opens, all market participants can see all dealers' bid and offer prices. The liquidity traders and the insider may deal with the dealer(s) with the inside quotes, whenever, and as often, as they wish. Dealers may revise their quotes whenever they wish. When a trade is executed, details of its price, but not the identities of the counterparties, are publicly disseminated. Each trading interval lasts for two minutes, after which there is a halt, and then a second trading interval takes place. The market with the search alternative operates in exactly the same manner, except that bilateral trading between liquidity traders and the insider may take place during the trading halt (lasting eight minutes). During the period of bilateral search, traders may send bids and offers to other traders, who may in turn accept or reject such proposals. Information about both any proposed bids and offers during this period, and about any trades executed during the period, is not publicized. Dealers are excluded from trading in the halt between trading intervals.

The main results of the experiments are as follows. When there is no bilateral search alternative, both dealer profits and liquidity trader losses are large. When bilateral search is allowed, liquidity traders do much better, and dealer profits are close to zero. The narrowest bid–ask spreads obtain in the first trading interval in the market with the bilateral search process. Dealers thus compete more aggressively against the search alternative than they do against each other in markets without a search process. Lamoureux and Schnitzlein argue that this is probably because 'while liquidity demand is exogenous in the pure dealer market and post search in the dealer-cum-search market, it is endogenous prior to search in the dealer-cum-search markets'. In order to attract order flow from liquidity traders, spreads must be small. Insider profits are, however, greatest when opaque trading is allowed. Market efficiency is not harmed by the introduction of the bilateral search process. Search trades tend to be set at prices close to those obtaining in the dealer market prior to its close. Trades in the market with the search alternative are closer to the asset's true value during the search process than in the trading intervals before and after the halt. They are also generally closer to the asset's true value than at any time in the market without the search alternative.

Two-Dealer Markets

Bloomfield and O'Hara (1996) undertake two experiments to investigate how different amounts of transparency affect the performance of a market with competing dealers. Each market consists of a sequence of trading rounds for a particular security. In the first experiment, the market contains four types of participants: two informed computerized traders which know the true value of the security being traded, two computerized noise traders which buy and sell an arbitrary number of shares in each round of trading, two uninformed active human traders who must make or invest a predetermined amount of the laboratory currency before trading closes in each security, and two human market makers. The performance of the market is compared under three transparency settings. In the most transparent, both market makers' quotes and trades are publicly disclosed after each round of trading. In the semi-opaque market, dealers' quotes are disseminated after each round of trading, but their trades are not. In the opaque setting, market makers do not see each others' quotes or trades after trading, and traders do not see market makers' trades. In all three settings, traders see the market makers' quotes before trading.

Three main results are obtained. First, the dissemination of information about trades significantly improves the informational efficiency of the market. In particular, the mid-point of the market bid and ask prices converges to the security's true value more quickly than in the opaque markets. Second, trade disclosure causes opening spreads to widen dramatically. Bloomfield and O'Hara argue that this is because market makers do not need to compete for order-flow to obtain information about the value of the security with post-trade transparency in the first round. Trade disclosure has little effect on spreads in later rounds, which rapidly decline to zero. Bloomfield and O'Hara posit that this is because sufficient information is already contained in market prices, and fewer rounds of trading remain in which to recoup any costs of purchasing order flow. Quote disclosure has no effect on opening spreads, which are the same in the semi-opaque and opaque settings. The third key result is that trade disclosure benefits market makers at the expense of both informed traders and liquidity traders who cannot time their trades. Such transparency, however, has no welfare effect on active traders who can wait until spreads narrow sufficiently to undertake their trades.

In their second experiment, Bloomfield and O'Hara model a market with a 'high-visibility' market maker and a 'low-visibility' market maker. Trades with the former are revealed to all participants, while those with the latter are not. The market this time is composed of computerized liquidity traders, human informed traders, human active but uninformed traders, and the two market makers. Traders can choose the market maker with whom they wish to deal.

The main result of the experiment is that the low-visibility market maker tends to set wider opening spreads than his high-visibility counterpart. Bloomfield and O'Hara contend that this is done in order to charge a premium to informed and active traders who prefer to conceal their trading behaviour. Consistent with this hypothesis, informed traders often trade with the low-visibility market maker at prices that are less favourable than those quoted by the high-visibility market maker. In contrast, they rarely trade with the high-visibility market maker at prices less favourable than those quoted by the low-visibility dealer. The low-visibility dealer therefore faces a greater adverse selection problem than the high-visibility dealer, in that informed traders choose to deal more often with him. The costs of this higher adverse selection problem tend to offset the bid–ask premium that the low-visibility dealer is able to charge, so that both market makers earn comparable trading gains.

Quote Transparency in a Multiple-Dealer Market
The issue of how quote transparency affects the informational efficiency of an experimental multiple-dealer market has been investigated by Flood *et al.* (1996).

They construct a continuous market with two types of participants: uninformed human market makers and informed computerized traders. There are no noise traders. Dealers set prices at which both the computerized traders and the other market makers can trade. No trade information is publicly displayed, and market makers are thus aware only of their own trades. Three market structures with varying amounts of quote information made public are examined. In the first, the 'centralized' market, live quotes from all market makers appear continuously on a trading screen. In the second, the 'modified centralized' market, only the best bid and ask quotes from all the market makers are displayed. In the 'decentralized' market, no quote information is publicly disseminated. Instead, prices and transactions are communicated on a bilateral basis, with customers calling dealers, and dealers calling other dealers. In all three markets, the caller who initiates a transaction decides the size of the trade, and the quoting dealer then sets the price.[22]

An unexpected result is that price discovery is faster, in a certain sense, when dealers have less information about the quotes of others. In real time, there are no clear differences in the informational efficiency of the centralized and decentralized markets. However, in 'transaction' time, a scaling of time in which a unit of time passes after each transaction, transaction prices converge significantly more quickly to their fundamental values in the decentralized market than in the centralized markets. Flood *et al.* attribute this to what they call 'arbitrage avoidance' behaviour. They argue that if dealers rigidly follow the law of one price, prices will not change until the most reluctant dealer changes his quote. The speed of price discovery is therefore constrained by the problem of coordinating the simultaneous quote changes of multiple dealers. As arbitrage between dealers is easier when quotes are public information, dealers adhere more rigidly to consensus pricing, and it is therefore more difficult for them to change their prices all together towards what is believed to be the true value of the security.

Post-Trade Transparency in a Multiple-Dealer Market
Flood *et al.* (1997) study how the dissemination of information about transactions affects the performance of an experimental multiple-dealer market. The market comprises nine competing uninformed human market makers, and two computerized traders, each of which may be informed with a publicly pre-specified probability. Flood *et al.* compare two markets with different levels of post-trade transparency, both of which have minimal quote transparency. In one, each dealer only has access to information about the transactions in which he is involved, and in the other, details of all trades are disseminated to all market makers. The information published about each trade consists of the two identities of the parties to the trade, and the size and price of the trade. In both markets, dealers only know about their own quotes, and those of any other dealers with whom they trade.

A key result is that post-trade transparency significantly improves the informational efficiency of price quotes. Flood *et al.* argue that this is because the enhanced transparency reduces profit opportunities for informed traders, as their information is more rapidly transmitted to uninformed market participants. Uninformed traders, be they dealers or customers, thus gain at the expense of informed traders. On average, traders also face significantly smaller effective dealing spreads in the transparent market, as good prices are easier to find. In contrast, opening spreads are wider in the transparent market than in the opaque one. This difference disappears, however, over time. Flood *et al.* contend that this occurs because dealers compete more vigorously for order flow in opaque markets than in transparent ones, in order to obtain price information. As trading proceeds more information is progressively revealed, and the information differences between opaque and transparent markets disappear.

Competition between Transparent and Opaque Markets
Bloomfield and O'Hara (1997) investigate whether trading on opaque markets dominates trading on transparent markets. They examine two experimental environments. In the first, there are five categories of participants: two dealers who must publish information about the trades they execute, two dealers who do not publish such information, one informed trader, one active trader, and two computerized liquidity traders. Trading takes place in a series of rounds. The informed trader knows at the beginning of each round what the value of the security being traded will be at the end of the round. His identity is not known by the other market participants. The active trader is given a monetary target to raise or invest over the different rounds of trading. The liquidity traders provide a significant source of uninformed order flow. Prior to each round, the dealers set bid and ask prices independently of each other. Once a trading round starts, all quotes are visible to all market participants. During each round, the three types of traders (i.e. the market participants other than the dealers) choose whether, and with which of the dealers, they wish to deal. Each trader can submit one order to any number of the dealers in any one round, and may therefore hit multiple quotes. Each order may vary in size from one to ten shares.

In this market structure, low transparency dealers are able to outcompete their more transparent rivals in several ways, including profitability and the ability to set narrower spreads. Bloomfield and O'Hara investigate three non-exclusive reasons why this might be so: first, low-visibility dealers may be more aggressive because they receive more benefit from capturing order-flow in early rounds; second, low-visibility dealers may set their prices more competitively because they have better information, and therefore face less adverse selection; and third, low-visibility dealers may have more market power and so are able to influence their mix of orders better than their high-visibility counterparts. Bloomfield and O'Hara note that high transparency dealers do have an informational advantage over low transparency dealers, in that both informed traders and large uninformed traders generally choose to trade in an opaque fashion so as to protect the value of their information. They conclude, however, that this advantage does not outweigh the advantage of low transparency dealers in setting their prices more efficiently, and in dealing more profitably at the inside spread.

In the second experimental environment, the operation of the market is exactly the same as in the first structure, except that each dealer is allowed endogenously to select whether to be transparent or not. Dealers make this choice in the following manner. The first dealer chooses whether to be transparent or not. The second dealer then learns of the first dealer's decision, and makes his own choice. The other two dealers then make similar consecutive choices. Once all the choices have been made, all dealers are told the total number of both types of dealers.

The key results of the second experiment were as follows. First, there was striking evidence that dealers have a preference for being opaque. Second, the low transparency dealers do not drive out their more transparent competitors. While dealers gravitate towards less transparency, there are advantages to being the only transparent dealer in an otherwise opaque market. Some informed traders may intentionally engage in loss-making visible trades in order to mislead other market participants. In addition, when there are many low-visibility dealers, no one of them has a significant informational advantage over the high-visibility dealer, as the informed trader may spread his trades more evenly among the competing low-visibility dealers. This reduces the losses that high-visibility traders incur as a result of adverse selection.

Summary and Comment

The microstructure literature examining the effects of transparency has had two critically important successes. It has provided a rigorous foundation on which it is possible to draw firm conclusions in specific settings based on well specified assumptions. Without such analysis, be it in a theoretical, empirical, or experimental context, there is no rational basis for evaluating the implications of transparency for market performance. Second, it has identified a range of themes that better our understanding of the effects of disseminating price and quote information on the quality of markets. The key ones are as follows. Transparency may improve informational efficiency. It may reduce the advantages of informed traders over liquidity traders with various consequences. Bid–ask spreads may widen because market makers have less incentive to pay to capture the information that a trade with an informed trader will bring. Alternatively spreads may decrease because information about transactions reaches all market participants, or because dealers are aware of each others' positions and compete more strongly with each other. Transparency may encourage stabilizing speculation that helps absorb order flow imbalances and reduce volatility. Alternatively it may exacerbate market participants' strategic behaviour towards each other, with the possibility of increasing volatility.

Notwithstanding the successes of the microstructure literature, however, many aspects of it are confusing. First, and as is self-evident from the above list, several of the themes developed in the literature are contradictory. Second, generalizations from the various microstructure models are extremely difficult. There are many types both of transparency and of order execution mechanisms, and it is hard to compare the effects either of similar forms of transparency on different order execution mechanisms, or of different forms of transparency on similar order execution mechanisms. Third, it is difficult both theoretically and experimentally to model complex dynamic environments, to judge how robust the conclusions of such models are to slight changes in the assumptions on which they are based, and to assess what are realistic values of the parameters in such models. Fourth, the effects of transparency may differ for different types of stocks or traders. Fifth, the results of many of the studies indicate that transparency may enhance one measure of market performance while simultaneously diminishing other measures. It is therefore impossible to assess the value of transparency without first specifying a set of preferences over these different measures of market performance. Most of the microstructure also does not directly address the issue of whether a market can effect a Pareto-efficient allocation.[23]

Sixth, many of the theoretical studies are based on the over-simplistic assumption that markets may be divided into informed traders, who know what the future price of a market asset will be, and liquidity traders, who do not. It is more realistic, however, to expect both that each participant in a market has some information of his own, and that the quality of different participants' information cannot be ranked against each other.[24] Seventh, a further weakness of the theoretical literature is that it is extremely hard to build 'general equilibrium' models in which all relevant variables are endogenously determined. For instance, although the volume of trading on a market is widely accepted as a key determinant of the market's performance, with for example narrower bid–ask spreads associated with greater volume, the role that transparency plays in determining trading volume is not well understood.

In sum, despite the advances made in the microstructure literature, and accepting the extreme nature of the demand that it address the problems identified here, it is nevertheless still difficult to draw robust conclusions from the literature concerning the effects or the merits of transparency.

CONCLUSION

Although it is widely accepted that the dissemination of prices and quotes plays a central role in the functioning of markets, the nature of that role is the subject of much controversy and ignorance. The current state of knowledge on this topic, as examined in the economics literature, is surveyed in this chapter which is composed of two sections.

In the first, the informational role of prices in equilibrium models is discussed. Such models attempt to explain how goods are allocated and prices are determined in an economy. The role of prices in them is critical. In the Walrasian or classical model they show the terms of trade between goods, and in equilibrium also reflect the various marginal rates of substitution and production in the economy. All relevant information about the tastes, endowments, and technology of other market participants, is incorporated in the price. The allocation of goods in the Walrasian model is Pareto-efficient. Walrasian prices do not, however, signal individual agents' information about future states of the world, and do not therefore necessarily contain all relevant information needed to effect a Pareto-efficient outcome in a world with uncertainty and asymmetric information. Although fully revealing rational expectations equilibrium models are able to effect this, they cannot incorporate the need for market participants to have an incentive to acquire information. Not only are the noisy rational expectations and partially revealing equilibrium models that can do this intractable, it is also difficult to specify an appropriate institutional structure in which such models can be implemented in a realistic setting.

The concept of informational efficiency is fraught with difficulty. The view commonly held by regulators that the efficient markets hypothesis can justify regulatory intervention to achieve the dissemination of prices and quotes is false. There is no clear basis in the economics literature for concluding that informational efficiency in markets does obtain, and if so to what extent. Nor is it possible to conclude that informational efficiency is required in order to obtain a Pareto-efficient outcome. Nor is it possible to conclude that informational efficiency is a socially desirable outcome. Our ignorance on these issues does not, however, mean that it is possible to draw the opposite conclusions. The claim that a lack of informational efficiency is desirable, therefore, can also not be justified.

In the second section of the chapter, the effects of different amounts of transparency in different market contexts are examined. The microstructure literature provides a range of insights into the consequences of disseminating price and quote information on market performance. Transparency may improve informational efficiency. It may reduce the advantages of informed traders over liquidity traders with various consequences. Bid–ask spreads may widen because market makers have less incentive to pay to capture the information that a trade with an informed trader will bring. Alternatively spreads may decrease because information about transactions reaches all market participants, or because dealers are aware of each others' positions and compete more strongly with each other. Transparency may encourage stabilizing speculation that helps absorb order flow imbalances and reduce volatility. Alternatively it may exacerbate market participants' strategic behaviour towards each other, with the possibility of increasing volatility.

Many aspects of the microstructure literature are, however, confusing. Several of the broad themes identified in the literature are contradictory. Broad generalizations are difficult. It is difficult both theoretically and experimentally to model complex dynamic environments, to judge how robust the conclusions of such models are to slight changes in the assumptions on which they are based, and to assess what are realistic values of the parameters in such models. Given that many studies indicate that transparency affects more than one measure of market performance, no evaluation of transparency is possible without a specification of preferences over the competing measures of market performance. Many of the theoretical studies are based on the over-simplistic assumption that markets may be divided into informed traders, who know what the future price of a market asset will be, and liquidity traders, who do not. It is extremely hard to build 'general equilibrium' models in which all relevant variables are endogenously determined. In sum, it is difficult to draw any unequivocal conclusions concerning either the effects or the merits of transparency from the microstructure literature.

11

Information and Competition: Policy

INTRODUCTION

Many legal and regulatory issues concerning the dissemination of price and quote information have been, and remain, extremely contentious. Most of these questions—including those arising from the law and regulation on intellectual property, *sui generis* rights, misappropriation, and confidentiality—are not unique to the financial markets. Their resolution in the context of exchanges and trading systems will therefore depend on how they are answered in the wider commercial arena. There are, nevertheless, certain issues that are specific to the financial markets, either because of their nature or because the relevant law and regulation may preempt other legal or regulatory authorities. Attention is focused here on these topics, and most importantly on the law and regulation governing certain aspects of competition and the securities markets.

The chapter is composed of three sections. In the first, some general comments are presented on the nature and role of regulation in financial markets, and in particular on the function that competition policy should play in the regulation of exchanges and trading systems. In the next two sections, two broad questions are respectively addressed: Should the dissemination of price and quote information be mandated by regulation? and, How, if at all, should the price of such information be regulated?

THE NATURE AND ROLE OF REGULATION

All prescriptions for the regulation of exchanges, trading systems, and markets, are based on a series of assumptions, be they explicit or implicit, about the nature and role of regulation. Disagreement about the need for a particular regulatory proposal may therefore arise, not only because of discord about the likely effects of the regulation itself, but also because of differences in the assumptions underlying its proposal. In order to discuss the merits of any substantive regulatory policy, there are three areas related to the general characteristics of regulation where a specification of assumptions is particularly important. These concern the goals regulation should seek to effect, the way it is implemented, and the character of competition policy. A brief exposition of the nature of these assumptions is presented in this section.

Goals

The central reason why regulation is proposed is that it is thought a means of achieving objectives that are in the public interest, but that would not be achieved in its absence. Unsurprisingly, however, the character of the public interest is not always clearly identifiable. Indeed, so controversial is it that most participants in most regulatory debates claim that their position is coincident with the public interest. Differences in the objectives either chosen by, or imposed on, a regulator may imply that different regulatory policies are optimal. The broad goals that regulators of financial and commodity markets are typically asked to follow in the public interest are investor protection, economic efficiency, fairness, market integrity, and the minimization of systemic risk. The interpretation of all these objectives is subject to much debate.

A range of questions need to be addressed in order to clarify the notion of investor protection, including: What level of fraud is acceptable? Do different classes of investors need different levels of protection? To what extent can traders be assumed to have sufficient experience and knowledge to take their own investment decisions? and, How much regulatory intervention into the activities of financial intermediaries is acceptable?

The concept of economic efficiency is also unclear. It normally refers to the minimization of costs or analogously the maximization of social welfare. A specification of the costs arising from trading on a market may, however, be controversial. The most important such costs are typically thought to include insufficient liquidity, excessive volatility, and adverse price discovery or equivalently a lack of informational efficiency. Not all market participants, however, view these attributes of a market as costly. Furthermore, even if it can be agreed what the relevant costs are, the definition and measurement of these concepts is itself extremely difficult. The notion of social welfare is similarly enigmatic. The simplest definition of it is the sum of consumer and producer surplus. This takes no account of the distribution of resources, however, and other more sophisticated yardsticks may thus be deemed more appropriate. Even if the meaning of social welfare can be agreed, direct measures of it are also difficult to obtain. Indirect proxies, normally again those of informational efficiency and liquidity, are therefore evaluated.

Amongst the many questions raised in assessing whether a market operates in a manner that is fair or not, are: Should traders be allowed to trade wherever they desire? Should equal access be granted to all market participants to the three key functions of the market, namely information dissemination, order routing, and order execution? Should the same regulatory outcome obtain for different categories of market participants that are functionally equivalent? and, To whom should the property rights associated with the products traded on a dealing system, and the price and quote information arising from the system, be assigned?

The notions of both market integrity and systemic risk are also particularly elusive. Two central activities that are frequently believed to undermine the integrity of a market are insider trading and manipulation. Both concepts are, however, fraught with ambiguity.[1] The difficulty in assessing the integrity of a market is mirrored in the difficulty of assessing the confidence participants have in the operations of a market. It is nevertheless commonly believed that a lack of confidence in a market frequently causes participants to withdraw from the market. Definitions of systemic risk have also been problematic.[2] It has been taken to refer to the existence of extreme price movements, to the possibility of a contagious rash of bankruptcies amongst financial intermediaries, or to the like-lihood of a break-down, a breach of security, or a lack of capacity, on a trading system.

In order to decide on appropriate regulatory policies, not only must the nature of these individual regulatory goals be specified, it is also necessary to determine how conflicts between them should be resolved. In many circumstances, the reso-lution of such conflicts is essentially a matter of preferences. The statutory authorities that standardly mandate the existence of a regulator must simply lay out the goals it is required to pursue. While no amount of logical analysis can force changes in such preferences, it is still crucial to understand the implications of making particular choices, as there are frequently complicated trade-offs between the realization of different regulatory goals. Several involve balances between the maximization of economic efficiency and the other socially desirable goals.

The attempt to deliver a market in which investors are protected, for example, may give rise to several concerns regarding the delivery of efficiency. The first is that of moral hazard. An important instance of this is when investors do not take sufficient care to monitor the risks associated with their investments, in the knowledge that they will be compensated for any investments that go seriously wrong or for any fraud to which they are subject. Promoting investor protection by establishing a compensation scheme may therefore inappropriately distort the incentives faced by investors. A second problem is that of cross-subsidy. Although it is typically institutional investors who fund investor compensation schemes, it is they who have the least need of such protection given their ability to monitor the risks that they incur. Institutional investors also have relatively low costs of switching their business to environments in which they are not required to fund such compensation funds. Unless there is uniform investor protection in different jurisdictions, promoting investor protection may therefore occur at the expense of liquidity, given that institutional business may migrate to the cheapest location for trading. A further problem is that the promotion of investor protec-tion may be used as a front merely to restrict competition.

The pursuit of fairness may also affect the realization of efficiency. If it is stip-ulated, for example, that all market participants should receive the same infor-mation, the incentive for traders to seek out and create information will be reduced. Another difficulty may arise because it is frequently argued that in order to be fair, exchanges should ensure that small retail trades receive the same execution prices as large institutional trades. If large trades do receive better execution prices than small trades, however, it may be because there are different costs of effecting them.[3] If so, the only way for an exchange to guarantee that all orders be executed at the same prices is again to require that the trading of retail investors be subsidized by that of institutional traders. Given the intense competition between trading systems for institutional business, and the fact that most small investors are represented in the market by major institutions, via their insurance policies and pension funds, such a subsidy may, however, have the perverse result of indirectly harming the very interests of the retail traders the policy sought to serve.

Apart from any effects that the realization of the goals of fairness and investor protection may have on the delivery of economic efficiency, there may also be a causal relationship in the other direction. Most importantly, efficiency may be viewed as the best antidote to any perceived unfairness or lack of investor protection in a market. The narrower and the deeper the bid–ask spread, for example, the fewer the problems that will arise as a result of orders of different sizes receiving different execution prices, and the smaller the opportunity financial intermediaries will have to set inappropriate prices for customer transactions.

No attempt is made here either to present or to justify in full an ideal set of assumptions to govern the determination of regulatory policies for exchanges and markets. Nevertheless, the pursuit of economic efficiency is taken to be a key regulatory goal, only to be overridden by other objectives in exceptional circumstances. The reason is simple: the benefits of doing so are believed larger, not least in the delivery of other desired goals, and the costs smaller, than any alternative can deliver.

Implementation

Even if there is unanimity both about what is in the public interest and about the regulatory policies necessary to achieve this, the decision as to whether to ask a regulator to implement such policies may be affected by perceptions of how the regulatory regime actually works in practice. There are two main views of how regulators operate, in addition to being simply agents of the public interest, both of which, if valid, imply that regulators may pursue different goals from those believed socially desirable.[4]

A regulator may first be perceived as an arbiter between different constituencies in the market. Under such circumstances the regulatory regime adopted will then be the outcome of a political process. It may be a compromise to satisfy competing demands, or it may reflect the interests of an especially powerful or persuasive group of market participants. In the USA, for example, the protection and promotion of the retail investor has been an important goal in the development of the legislation and regulation governing the securities markets. In contrast, and notwithstanding any political rhetoric to the contrary, the regulatory structure in the UK has primarily sought to attract institutional business. Another view of regulation is that regulators have their own private objectives which they seek to maximize at the expense of the public interest. These might include their power, status, future earnings, the enlargement of their jurisdiction, the maximization of their budget, or the avoidance of blame for any scandals that occur.

Competition Policy

A critical assumption made here is that the maximization of economic efficiency should be the goal of competition policy. This may be contentious. As discussed in Chapter 4, the notion of competition has been used to mean many things. It may imply that there is a rivalry between market participants, that a market is fragmented in some manner, that the participants in a market are each individually too small to affect the prices established in the market and that they do not act in concert to achieve such an effect, that there is a lack of restrictions on market participants, or that different constraints are not placed on different participants who undertake the same activities. In many circumstances, if a market exhibits any or all of these characteristics, economic efficiency will be advanced. Use of economic efficiency as a yardstick to determine competition policy, however, has a crucial and sometimes controversial implication. It is possible that the behaviour of a market participant may not satisfy some or all of these characteristics, namely that it may reduce rivalry, or be monopolistic, restrictive, or discriminatory, but that at the same time the action may be judged not to obstruct competition policy because it maximizes economic efficiency.

This implication is vital in the context of exchanges and markets for two reasons. The first depends on the fact that although the market for exchanges and trading systems on the one hand, and the market for securities on the other, are closely associated, the two are not identical. Structural aspects in one market may affect structural aspects in the other. This occurs, for example, where in order for all orders in a particular security to compete against each other, it may be necessary that they be consolidated on a single trading system. Were this to happen, however, there would obviously be no possibility of rivalry between more than one trading system. Even if a particular set of characteristics of a market could be identified as pro-competitive, therefore, it would still not be clear *a priori* in which of the relevant markets, namely that for trading systems or that for securities, these characteristics should be promoted. Use of economic efficiency as the yardstick for assessing competition policy can, however, help resolve such conflicts.

The notion that economic efficiency should be the measure of competition is important also because it may challenge several commonly held views. In particular, there are four reasons why the activities of an exchange concerning the dissemination of its price and quote information are frequently thought anti-competitive. First, an exchange may be granted a statutory monopoly for the trading of particular assets, or similarly it may be thought to be a 'natural' monopoly due to the tendency for order flow to attract order flow. Given that one exchange is thus typically either the sole or the dominant forum for the trading in a particular commodity, it thus also becomes the sole or the dominant source of information about the trading in the commodity. Second, most exchanges claim property rights in the price and quote data that they produce in order to constrain the actions of other market participants with regard to their use of such data. Third, all exchanges specify a series of rules to govern the behaviour of the market participants trading on their system. Such rules are again restrictive. Finally, exchanges often provide differential access to different groups of market participants to their price and quote information. Contrary to received wisdom, the question of whether any of these types of exchange behaviour should be viewed as anti-competitive is *a priori* moot. It depends on whether they do or do not enhance economic efficiency.

Two seminal statements of the view that restraints on commercial agents are not necessarily anti-competitive are noteworthy. The first is a general comment made by Brandeis, who notes that,

the legality of an agreement or regulation cannot be determined by so simple a test, as whether it restrains competition. Every agreement concerning trade, every regulation of trade, restrains. To bind, to restrain, is of their very essence. The true test of legality is whether the restraint imposed is such as merely regulates and perhaps thereby promotes competition or whether it is such as may suppress or even destroy competition. To determine that question the court must ordinarily consider the facts peculiar to the business to which the restraint is applied; its condition before and after the restraint was imposed; the nature of the restraint and its effect, actual or probable.[5]

The second is a comment made specifically about exchanges by Coase (1988: 9), who argues that,

economists observing the regulations of . . . exchanges often assume that they represent an attempt to exercise monopoly power and restrain competition. They ignore, or at any rate, fail to emphasize an alternative explanation for these regulations: that they exist to reduce transaction costs and therefore to increase the volume of trade.

The issue of when a trading system's actions in disseminating its price and quote data are anti-competitive is the main focus of the rest of the chapter.

MANDATORY TRANSPARENCY

The question of whether the dissemination of price and quote information should be mandated by regulation is discussed in this section. The main arguments for and against imposing transparency are examined in turn, and a brief personal judgement about the merits of mandatory transparency is then provided. While attention is focused on the American arena, issues from other jurisdictions are discussed.

Justification

It is in the USA that a policy of mandatory transparency has been promoted for the longest period, and it is there too, that many of the strongest supporters of such a policy are to be found. Since the creation of the NMS in 1975, registered exchanges and national associations have been required to publish immediately details of almost all trades, and also the best quotes, for most securities. Over the years, and apart from a few exceptions, this policy has been progressively extended, by enlarging the range of securities for which transparency is obligatory, and by widening the types of trading systems required to publish price and quote information. Congress, the SEC and the SEC's staff, most importantly in its Division of Market Regulation, all now view full price and quote transparency as a fundamental cornerstone of the appropriate way of regulating exchanges and markets. The reason why is simple. They believe it enhances the delivery of almost all the regulatory goals they view as important, including investor protection, competition, fairness, market efficiency, liquidity, market integrity, and investor confidence.[6]

Transparency is believed to improve investor protection because investors are more easily able to monitor the quality of the executions they receive from their intermediaries with it than without it. It helps them assess whether their trades are being executed at the best prices in the market, what mark-ups their brokers are charging, whether their orders are being front-run, what the direction of trading activity is, and whether there is significant trading between, or outside, the displayed quotes.[7] Transparency is also thought vital for fair markets because it ensures that all investors, brokers, and other market participants, are provided with the same market information.

A key goal of transparency is to allow,

buyers and sellers of securities, wherever located, . . . [to] make informed investment decisions and not pay more than the lowest price at which someone is willing to sell, or not sell for less than the highest price a buyer is prepared to offer.[8]

Transparency is thus believed to enhance informational efficiency, and also to allow traders to select which dealer on a market is quoting the best price, and which of a group of competing trading systems is offering the best price. It therefore supposedly facilitates competition both between market intermediaries and between markets. In addition, even if investors do not have access to real-time market information, the combination of transparency and competition is thought to assure best execution for their orders, given that brokers have a fiduciary duty to search the competing quotes in order to obtain the best available prices. Transparency also facilitates arbitrage between trading systems thus reducing the possibility of different prices obtaining on different markets. This is believed to help unite dispersed markets without costly electronic or order-routing linkages, and again to enhance informational efficiency.[9]

The SEC has repeatedly maintained that it is for market participants themselves to determine market structure, stating, for example, that its mandate is 'to facilitate the development of the national market system by allowing competitive forces to shape market structure within a fair regulatory field'.[10] Transparency is thought to allow different trading systems the possibility of offering different market structures while still encouraging competition between them. It therefore supposedly has 'the advantage of counterbalancing the effects of market fragmentation while preserving competition among multiple markets'.

Transparency is also believed to enhance the liquidity of markets. The Division of Market Regulation has claimed, for example, that the liquidity for both listed and OTC equities increased following the adoption of the quote and trade transparency rules, despite the initial resistance of both the exchanges and the NASD. The Division thus dismisses the claim that transparency increases the position risk of dealers, and thereby forces them to quote wider spreads to protect themselves. Transparency is also thought to increase the integrity of the securities markets and foster investor confidence, thereby encouraging greater participation by investors, which in turn increases liquidity.

A further key justification has been made to support the claim that a lack of transparency decreases liquidity. A segmentation of the market into a relatively opaque institutional sector and a relatively transparent retail sector, has been argued as being likely to lead to higher dealing costs in the retail sector, with an attendant loss in volume. More generally, and as noted by Mendelson (1990: 24–30, 64), with no displacement of orders between an opaque system and other more transparent ones, there may be a disincentive to place orders on the transparent ones. Subscribers to the opaque system would have access to more information about prices and quotes than non-subscribers, and traders on the transparent systems might therefore widen their quotes in order to protect themselves from dealing with better informed traders. Furthermore, if one market sanctioned opacity, other markets might not be able to assess the overall supply and demand for securities, and thus the determination of the optimal price for the securities could be inaccurate.[11]

Three other aspects of transparency discussed by the SEC (1/1994: IV-3 to IV-5) are notable. First, the Division of Market Regulation has argued that increased transparency has led to meaningful innovations in the distribution of market information, and therefore benefited the exchanges and markets by providing them with a significant source of revenue. Second, in 1994 the Division accepted that an important cost associated with transparency was that of establishing the systems and procedures necessary to report and disseminate quotes and prices. It noted, however, that this cost had already been mostly met in the USA, and was therefore only of historical significance. Finally, the SEC has noted that although there are mechanisms besides transparency for enhancing investor protection and ensuring best execution, it did not believe that they were better alternatives than transparency. One such option would be if investors had sufficient access to markets to ensure the best execution of their orders. Unrestricted access in some markets was, however, thought unlikely to be feasible, most crucially for individual investors who would be too numerous and might lack the necessary sophistication, credit standing, and market power to ensure such access.[12] Another alternative was that of regulatory reporting. Sole reliance on regulatory reporting was, however, believed to require greater governmental and self-regulatory oversight than was necessary with transparency.

The SEC's views about transparency were most recently expounded in its discussion of its Electronic Communications Network (ECN) rules (discussed in Chapter 7). The Commission argued that the development of electronic trading systems that were not regulated as exchanges and that allowed market makers to display different prices to different customers, created the existence of 'two-tiered' markets. Market makers were thereby able to quote one price to public investors while quoting better prices on private 'hidden' systems with limited access. This was believed to have a range of adverse implications.

The Commission maintained that when exchange specialists and OTC dealers failed to display quotes that improved the published best bid and offer (BBO) prices, the BBO would not convey the real quotation spread and thus might present an inaccurate picture of trading interest. The Commission stated that,

[it] firmly believe[d] that all investors should have an opportunity to have their orders filled at the best prices made available by market makers. Consistent with Congress's goals for a NMS, these opportunities must be made available to all customers, not just those customers who, due to size or sophistication, may avail themselves of prices in ECNs not currently linked with the public quotation system.[13]

Another concern of the SEC was that many brokers used the BBO as the benchmark for the automated execution of retail customer orders, and for the starting point in negotiating execution prices with institutional investors. Narrowing the quoted BBO, an effect the SEC believed probable following the implementation of the ECN rules, was therefore thought likely to enhance the quality of executions both types of traders received. The Commission stressed that retail customers typically depended on their brokers for information and access to the market, as monitoring the relevant information was difficult and costly for them. Such customers expected prompt executions at the best prices reasonably available, and the SEC believed they should be able to rely on the public quotes for an accurate picture of the market. The Commission also asserted that if order flow was routed on a basis other than quote competition, the transparency and competitiveness of the American markets might suffer.

The SEC claimed the ECN rules facilitated the best execution of customer orders in a manner that preserved the maximum flexibility for the markets themselves to design and implement trading and communication systems that were consistent with the objectives of the NMS. It maintained that integrating the prices market makers quoted on ECNs into the consolidated quote should also significantly limit many types of anti-competitive practices, without limiting the usefulness of these systems as efficient alternative mechanisms for negotiating transactions. While the Commission accepted that private ECNs might increase intermarket competition, it believed that the consolidation of quotations and their dissemination to the public continued to be important elements of the NMS. Competition based on fragmented quotations was thought likely to reduce efficient pricing.

The Commission noted two ways in which the ECN rules would continue to favour non-exchange regulated ECNs. The first arose as a result of the ECN 'display alternative' the Commission had created. This allowed ECNs, rather than the market makers quoting prices on them, to disseminate information about the market makers' quotes. The display alternative was believed to provide ECNs an opportunity to generate additional order flow from non-subscribers, in that such traders' orders could now automatically be routed to ECNs unlike the situation before. The second advantage that ECNs would continue to have was that orders from investing institutions placed on ECNs, as opposed to those from market intermediaries, would still stay outside the SEC's regulatory ambit, and therefore not be required to be disseminated. The presence of these institutional orders on an ECN would therefore remain an incentive for market participants to keep on trading on ECNs.

The SEC also maintained that its development of the ECN display alternative countered the argument that if brokers were required to revise their public quotes upon changing an anonymous quote on an ECN, their anonymity would be compromised. The Commission accepted that such anonymity might be crucial to a market participant concerned not to impact adversely market liquidity while attempting to acquire or liquidate large positions. The display alternative was also thought to eliminate the risk that a market maker or specialist could be exposed to multiple executions at the ECN price.

Rebuttal

Notwithstanding the strength of Congress's, the SEC's, and other regulators', conviction about the rightness of a policy of mandatory transparency, there are many arguments against such an approach. Six closely linked themes run through the reasons disputing the need for mandatory transparency. The first, and most important, is that private incentives are normally sufficient for the establishment of the optimal level of transparency. The second is that there are various weaknesses in some of the arguments put forward to support mandatory transparency. The third is that the costs of successfully enforcing transparency rules may not outweigh the benefits. The fourth is that while mandatory transparency may deliver the goals that Congress and the SEC seek to attain, other jurisdictions may choose to follow different regulatory objectives for which such a policy is not desirable. The fifth is that nobody, including regulators, knows what many of the economic effects of mandating transparency actually are. The risk of creating regulations that do not deliver the intended consequences or that establish the wrong incentives may therefore be high.[14] The final theme is that in order to require all trading systems to publish details of their prices and quotes, it is necessary to define what a trading system is. This, however, is difficult to do in a consistent manner.

Various arguments substantiating the first three of these themes are examined in this section. The fifth theme, namely the difficulty of drawing unequivocal conclusions about many of the economic effects of transparency, was analysed in the previous chapter, while the sixth theme, concerning the problems of classifying trading systems, is explored in the next. The section is composed of three parts. In the first, the role of private incentives in information dissemination is examined, and some comments on the appropriate manner of implementing competition policy are presented. Various weaknesses in the arguments justifying mandatory transparency are then explored. Finally, some difficulties with enforcing transparency are discussed.

Private Incentives and Competition Policy

A fundamental motif running through the arguments against the need for mandatory transparency is that private incentives are normally sufficient for the establishment of the optimal level of transparency. This implies that the desired regulatory goals will be realized as a result of private activity, even in the absence of regulation requiring transparency. The key justification for this claim is the belief that in most circumstances market participants will seek to agree between each other a series of contractual relationships the effect of which is to minimize transactions costs.

The likelihood of market participants generally being able to negotiate an efficient, namely transactions-cost minimizing, assignment of property rights is dependent on several factors.[15] Amongst these are, first, there must be no significant information asymmetries between the various parties negotiating the contracts, otherwise the better informed parties may be able to negotiate contracts that are in their favour but not economically efficient. Second, there must be few sunk costs associated with such contracts, or if there are such costs, they must be appropriately recognized or internalized in some manner. Otherwise, even if the negotiating parties are able initially to agree to act in a certain manner, once a deal has been struck, some of the participants may not do what they originally agreed to do. The other participants may then have little choice but to continue dealing with their counter-parties on terms that they would not have agreed to at the initial stage, and that are not transaction-costs minimizing.

A third factor normally necessary for participants to be able to negotiate between themselves efficient assignments of property rights is that they each have sufficient market power to be able to negotiate on relatively equal terms. Otherwise, the dominant party may simply impose its will concerning the relevant assignment of property rights, again contrary to the interests of economic efficiency. While a general evaluation of when competition is impaired is not easy, and while there may be instances where it is believed that efficient levels of transparency cannot be negotiated, the merit of private incentives in delivering appropriate levels of transparency is evident in a wide range of contexts.

In an environment in which there is rivalry between trading systems, it is hard to conceive of any exchange or trading system, whatever its governance structure, that might not seek to attract order flow. The pursuit of this goal is likely to lead to the optimal provision of the desired regulatory objectives. Any action by an exchange that adversely affects the quality of its market increases the possibility that competing trading systems will be able to attract order flow away from the exchange. An exchange will therefore have an incentive to adopt whatever level of transparency best enhances market quality. This does not imply, however, that an exchange will always choose a market architecture with full transparency.

Indeed, as noted in Chapter 6, the strategic non-disclosure of prices and quotes is a central element of all markets' architectures. An exchange may also choose to restrict transparency in an attempt to let its members obtain better information than other market participants, and thus enhance liquidity on the exchange. Any cross-subsidies that arise from such a market structure, such as from retail to institutional traders, will, however, generally be unsustainable, if it is possible for alternative trading systems to cater solely to the groups of market participants that are being exploited.

The determination of whether a particular configuration of property rights is not efficient is particularly difficult when an exchange faces little competition from alternative trading systems, and the exchange is the dominant or sole source of information for the relevant prices and quotes. Mulherin, Netter, and Overdahl (1991*a*; 1991*b*) have analysed whether exchanges' restrictions on the activities that the purchasers of their prices and quotes are allowed to undertake are anti-competitive.[16] An exchange is viewed as 'a firm that creates a market in financial instruments', and the product of such a firm is seen as being 'accurate information, as reflected in the prices of the instruments traded on the exchange'. Mulherin, Netter, and Overdahl argue that given that price discovery is expensive, exchanges should be perceived as organizations that exist to reduce the transactions costs necessary to create prices. Without some protection for the information which it produces, they claim that an exchange would have little incentive to develop new products as it would not be able to capture the benefits of its investment. The creation of property rights by an exchange in its prices and quotes is therefore seen as a central function of an exchange.

Since property rights are by their very nature restrictive, Mulherin, Netter, and Overdahl accept that it is hard to distinguish between the establishment of a property right that enhances efficiency, and the creation of an anti-competitive restriction. They therefore argue that the issue of whether such rules hinder or help the use of advanced technology and promote market efficiency is an empirical question, and examine some historical evidence to assess the merits of the property rights approach.

The behaviour of various American exchanges during and after the second half of the nineteenth century is evaluated. This period is chosen because it was at this time that the stock price ticker and related technology were invented, which together allowed exchanges to disseminate their prices and quotes via telegraph. In addition, the second half of the nineteenth century was a period in which there was little regulation of either the cash or the futures markets. The effects of the creation by exchanges of their newly claimed property rights can therefore be assessed in the knowledge that there were no outside regulatory influences. The technological advances of the time gave rise to the standard effects of increased dissemination: they expanded the geographic market for potential customers of the exchanges, but simultaneously made it easier for market participants to trade off the exchanges. In response, the exchanges developed a series of new contractual arrangements to protect their perceived property rights, and in turn, these new contractual arrangements were challenged in various court cases.

Two central and related questions were addressed by the courts. Did exchanges have any public duty to disseminate their prices and quotes, a duty that the exchanges denied as having? and, Could prices and quotes be considered the property of exchanges, as the exchanges claimed? In *Wilson v. Telegram Co.*, the issue of whether the NYSE had a public duty to disseminate the prices of securities traded on its floor was considered.[17] The court ruled that the exchange was a voluntary private institution, and that as such it did not have a public duty to disseminate the quotes. The exchange was viewed as being no more than the sum of its members, and they were seen as having the right to keep the prices to themselves. The definitive ruling during this period on whether an exchange had any property rights in its prices and quotes was in *Board of Trade of the City of Chicago v. Christie Grain and Stock Company*.[18] The Supreme Court accepted that the exchange had a right to do what it wanted with its quotes, saying that they were similar to a trade secret.

Mulherin, Netter, and Overdahl summarize the historical evidence they study as follows: '(1) Technological innovation is often accompanied by stricter definition of property rights. (2) Financial innovation arises from stronger definition of property rights. (3) There is an interaction between monitoring the behavior of exchange members and limiting off-exchange trading of members.'[19] They then argue that 'technology, by itself, will not lead to lower transaction costs. Instead, new technology, combined with well-defined and well-enforced property rights, can lead to cost-reducing innovations.'[20] Far from being anti-competitive practices, therefore, they conclude that exchanges' restrictions on who could have access to their price and quote information, and on what terms this could be done, were the very mechanisms that led to increased levels of trading and the use of advanced technology.

A distortion to competition is often thought to arise when an exchange provides more information about prices and quotes to a designated group of market participants, typically its members, than it does to other market participants. This may occur, for example, when members are given information about the full book of buy and sell orders, while details of only the best bid and ask prices are disseminated to the public.[21] Although such conduct is clearly discriminatory, the question of whether or not it is inefficient is again *a priori* uncertain. Such a policy may re-distribute profits in favour of the exchange's members at the expense of non-members, it may obstruct competition by non-members of the exchange with members' activities, and it may also impede competing trading systems from using the exchange's information to establish and develop their own competing systems. In contrast, however, a policy of discriminatory release of information may also be transactions-cost minimizing. It may enhance market liquidity, and it may allow an exchange to stop other trading systems from obtaining its data without contributing to the costs of producing them, thereby increasing the incentive for the exchange to publish the data in the first place.

One example of how competition policy should not be implemented in the context of transparency is evident in the regulatory analysis by the OFT in 1995 of the then Rule 4.18 of the LSE.[22] This rule stipulated that members of the LSE were not allowed to quote prices on dealing systems away from the exchange that were better, either in price or size, than those that they input on SEAQ. The rule was applicable both to systems run by members of the exchange, such as Instinet, and to non-members' systems, such as Tradepoint, but not to IDBs. Tradepoint and Instinet argued that the rule was anti-competitive because it restricted the extent to which market makers on the LSE were able to use their dealing systems instead of SEAQ. The OFT agreed, and identified two key factors that it believed supported its view that the rule restricted competition.[23]

The first was the 'collective dominance' of the market makers in the market for domestic UK equities. Given that market makers were party to one or both sides of most trades, the OFT concluded that 'order matching systems must be left at a competitive disadvantage when such a large proportion of their potential trading volume is foreclosed to them'.[24] The other factor that the OFT maintained supported the view that the rule distorted competition, was the OFT's belief that, given that market makers used IDBs extensively, they would be likely to wish to use order-matching systems if only they were allowed to do so by the exchange.

Neither of these factors, however, did in fact support the OFT's position. While Rule 4.18 obviously did restrict the actions of the exchange's members, it placed no constraints on non-members who were free to trade on any trading systems they wished. Should a member not have wanted to follow the relevant rule, therefore, it could always have stopped being a member of the exchange. To complain that the exchange was dominant in its market, though true, is not sufficient to determine that the exchange was abusing its position. If a financial intermediary were to have quoted a better price on a trading system that competed with the LSE, investors could easily have directed their order flow to the alternative system, given that their switching costs were relatively low. Indeed, the OFT itself noted the existence of a range of alternative mechanisms via which quotes could be disseminated. More importantly, the fact that the market makers dominated the then-existing levels of trading did not imply that there were barriers to entry for the provision of liquidity. The very real possibility of disintermediation, an outcome occurring elsewhere, prevented the market makers from exploiting their position.

The other factor supposedly supporting the OFT's position similarly did not do so. The claim that market makers might have wished to trade on order-matching systems, if only they had been allowed to do so by the exchange, is based on two false assumptions. The assertion did not recognize that it was the market makers themselves who determined the rules of the exchange. Should they have been unhappy with any particular rule it was within their power to change it. More importantly, however, the OFT did not justify why the OFT itself was better able than the market makers to determine what was good for the liquidity of the market. The OFT dismissed the market makers' argument that the rule ensured that price formation was efficient because it consolidated the best market maker quotes on one screen, by claiming that there were a range of non-automated mechanisms for disseminating prices which could be better than those quoted on SEAQ, and also that many transactions were executed within the SEAQ touch. This argument does not acknowledge, however, that the relaxation of Rule 4.18 would effectively have sanctioned the possibility of the exchange not providing as liquid a market as it could. Given that its members would be allowed to quote better prices off the exchange than on it, bid–ask spreads on SEAQ would necessarily not be as narrow as they could be.

Weaknesses

There are a range of weaknesses with the arguments put forward to support mandatory transparency. Several of the most important concern efficiency and competition. The SEC's claim that without mandatory transparency markets will be informationally inefficient, in the sense that different prices will be quoted on different trading systems, is difficult to sustain. There are a few jurisdictions where private incentives have reportedly not been sufficient to stop what are believed to be excessive price differentials obtaining between competing trading systems.[25] This may, however, be self-correcting in that investors will choose not to deal on the relevant markets until they believe sufficient price and quote information becomes available.

More importantly, the markets on many exchanges trading the same assets appear to be tightly arbitraged even in the absence of enforced last-sale data.[26] This is unsurprising as there is a strong private incentive to ensure that prices are arbitraged between different trading systems, up to the point where the costs of doing so are not prohibitive. If the prices on different trading systems were not so arbitraged, risk-free profits would be available. Such arbitrage may be effected either by the behaviour of individual financial intermediaries operating on all the respective markets, or alternatively by private advances in telecommunications technology. As already noted, many price and quote publication mechanisms have been developed in the absence of regulatory intervention. Given that there are few technological or financial constraints on the development of such technology any longer, a regulatory response to co-ordinate industry action, as occurred with the development of the CTA and CQS, is normally unnecessary.

Contrary again to what the SEC has maintained, a policy of mandatory transparency is not neutral with regards to market structure. It restricts the types of order execution algorithms that trading systems are free to adopt, and thus implicitly imposes a regulatory view as to what are the optimal types of market structure. It is therefore simply false to argue that transparency has 'the advantage of counterbalancing the effects of market fragmentation while preserving competition among multiple markets'.

The fear that competition between trading systems may lead to a 'flight to opacity' and a subsequent decline in market quality has also yet to be confirmed.[27] In very few circumstances has such a move to restrict transparency been observed. Where it has occurred, most notably when several European stock exchanges changed their rules to become less transparent following the success of SEAQ International on the LSE, the issue of how their actions should be interpreted is debatable.[28] It may be seen as an instance of a flight to opacity that is not in the public interest and that can only be resisted by regulatory intervention requiring all markets to publish prices and quotes. In contrast, it may be seen as a response by the continental exchanges to the successful architecture of the LSE's trading system, in their goal of enhancing the liquidity on their own markets. Only empirical evidence and experience can determine which is correct, and to date there is none showing that the quality of the European markets has been damaged by such moves.

Despite the various regulatory assertions concerning the merits of mandatory post-trade transparency on the LSE, neither the theoretical nor the empirical evidence unequivocally supports the argument that a lack of such transparency has adversely affected market performance. Consider first, the OFT's claim that without transparency small market makers will be at an informational disadvantage to large market makers and that they will widen their spreads accordingly. If a large market maker were to take on a large trade and then trade with a small market maker to hedge his position, he would typically only be able to hedge a small part of this position. By trading directly with the small market maker, however, he would also reveal information about which side of the market he was interested in being on, information which the small market maker himself could then exploit. While the option of trading through an IDB if an appropriate order is available will allow the market maker to hide his identity, he will still reveal to the market the same information about the side of the market on which he is interested in trading. A large market maker, rather than being able to exploit any information which he gained by undertaking a large trade, would therefore be likely to move the market against himself if he attempted to unwind his position by dealing with a small market maker.

The evidence that large trades lead to permanent price changes on the LSE, and that this conveys sufficient information to large market makers to allow them to exploit small traders is mixed. Furthermore, even if the evidence were convincing that permanent price changes did occur following large trades, it is also not clear that the large market makers who undertook such trades could exploit these circumstances so as to deal at wider spreads on small trades in order to cross-subsidize large trades. Consider the situation of a market maker who has just made a large sale, details of which are not available to the public. In order both to cover his position and to exploit the information signalled by his sale, the market maker would have to purchase a series of small orders in the market from ignorant traders. In order to attract this business, typically he would have to raise his quotes so as to have the highest bid. By doing so, however, he may again reveal information about the sale he has just made. If he does not raise his bid, it is just as likely that the market maker will be required to sell stock as purchase it, given that he is obliged to deal on both sides of the market, and in such circumstances he is clearly not exploiting small traders. Therefore, either the market maker will attempt to take advantage of his superior information by trading with small incoming orders, in which case the information contained in the large trade may be inferred from his actions, or he will not be able to take advantage of the information.

The OFT's claim concerning the relative merits of trading on SEAQi and the Paris Bourse is both suspect, and also insightful in a way unnoticed by the OFT and antithetical to its views. The OFT noted both that small trades were executed at relatively narrower spreads on the relatively transparent Paris Bourse than on the LSE which was relatively non-transparent, and that patient traders achieved lower transactions costs in Paris whatever their trade size. These facts do not, however, indicate either that it was the presence of transparency that led to the spreads in Paris being smaller in London, or that there were other factors bringing trades to London. Although there were too many other differences in market architecture for this evidence to be determinative, as noted by the OFT, if anything it belies one of the SEC's key claims. This was that a segmentation of the market into a relatively opaque institutional sector and a relatively transparent retail sector was likely to lead to higher dealing costs in the retail sector. For those stocks traded in both London and Paris, there were effectively two markets: one relatively opaque, namely SEAQ International, and one relatively transparent, namely the Paris Bourse. Trading on the relatively opaque one did not appear to have led to a widening of spreads on the relatively transparent one.

The claim by Board and Sutcliffe that because market makers took advantage of the lack of transparency to hedge their positions to only a very small extent, they would incur few costs if transparency were instituted, needs to be interpreted with care. Board and Sutcliffe may be right. If so, however, the fact that market makers were unwilling to sanction increased transparency must be explained. There may have been a series of non-economic reasons for market makers' behaviour on this issue. For example, given that transparency formed one part of a larger raft of privileges to which market makers were entitled at the time, they may have been unwilling to give it up without attempting to protect their other privileges. The fact that market makers had supported transparency so vociferously for so long, may also have made it difficult for them to argue that it meant nothing to them without loss of face. Alternatively, Board and Sutcliffe could be wrong, and market makers could have used the transparency regime to hedge their positions, but not in ways that Board and Sutcliffe recognized. For example, market makers might have used the futures market, other shares or OTC options to hedge their positions, and have done so in the time sanctioned by the transparency rules. None of these options were examined by Board and Sutcliffe.

Furthermore, even if market makers did not hedge their positions in the time available under the then-current transparency rules, it might still have been the case that liquidity would have decreased with an increase in transparency. The existence of the transparency rules may have been the very reason why market makers did not hedge their positions. A requirement that market makers should publicize any large trades they effected, might have meant that they were much more inclined to hedge immediately any positions they took on, and thus have made them less willing to take on the positions in the first place.

Two of the arguments the SEC put forward in favour of transparency in its discussions of the ECN rules also have weaknesses.[29] As noted by Instinet (1996: 50), if a broker that operates an automated trading system is required to publish the trades and quotes arising from its system while non-automated brokers, who cannot readily disseminate information electronically about the orders they receive and trades they execute, are not so obliged, the automated broker will be at a disadvantage. Rather than encouraging broker-dealers to seek superior prices through non-traditional trading methods, the ECN rules may therefore induce them to use less automated and possibly less efficient methods.

A key goal of the ECN rules was to ensure that automated institutional trading systems provided the same access to individual investors that they offered to institutional traders, primarily through enforced linkages between such systems and the automated retail order execution systems. The SEC's concern was that the retail systems set their execution prices off the BBO, while the institutional systems allowed trading in-between the market spread. Once again, however, there is a strong private incentive for the operators of retail systems to ensure that price differences between their systems and institutional ones are arbitraged away. Firms that operate retail facilities should compete more successfully with each other if they are able to deal at finer prices with the institutional systems. The SEC did not explain, however, why such incentives had been insufficient for the noted price differences to disappear. The better prices on institutional systems might simply have reflected the lower cost of doing business on them for a range of possible reasons. If so, a requirement that the prices on both institutional and retail systems should be identical would require some form of cross-subsidy from the institutional to the retail systems.

Paradoxically, the best argument the SEC could have made to support the introduction of the ECN rules would have shown that the rules were both a solution to a problem of the SEC's own making in the past, and a likely source of a similar problem in the future. The CQS was established at the prompting of the SEC to ensure that quotes on the exchanges and the NASDAQ market were aggregated and disseminated. Over time, the prices and quotes published on the CQS have gained a further stamp of regulatory approval, as the SEC has progressively used the BBO, published on the CQS, as a key factor in determining whether brokers execute their customers' orders in the best manner possible. The fact that the CQS was intended to disseminate the quotes solely from the exchanges and the NASD, and indeed has been run by a committee composed solely of representatives of these institutions, however, has meant that other non-exchange participants who might have wished to have information about their orders put on to the CQS have not been allowed to do so. The very rules creating the CQS and sanctioned by the SEC, therefore established the barrier stopping non-exchange market participants from placing their quotes on the CQS. The purported solution devised by the SEC, namely to require quotes by market makers placed on an ECN to be incorporated into the CQS raises, however, two further problems.

The first, as noted above, is that a requirement that market makers incorporate their quotes on ECNs into the CQS, as opposed to a licence to allow them to do so, prejudges the cost/benefit analysis of them doing so, a judgement that can be better made by the private sector. The second problem is that in the ECN rules the SEC expressly states that it would not require orders presented to ECNs by investors, as opposed to those presented by market makers, to be incorporated into the CQS.[30] If the ECN rules do not allow this, and whether they do or not is debatable, the SEC will in all likelihood have to revise its ECN rules again in the name of competition, to fix a further barrier which it itself has created.

Other aspects of the SEC's defence of the need for mandatory transparency are also weak. The claim that mandatory transparency is a good policy because it benefited the exchanges and markets by providing them with a significant source of revenue, is wrong. The very fact that enhanced transparency did increase revenues might well have been sufficient incentive for the exchanges and markets themselves to undertake the same actions imposed by the SEC, without any regulation forcing them to do so. In addition, the SEC's argument, in its 'Market 2000' report, that the main costs associated with the delivery of transparency are historical is both false, and inappropriately assumes that the SEC is the best agent for determining the costs of regulation. Market participants have complained about the cost of satisfying the transparency requirements in the ECN rules that the SEC imposed subsequent to the Market 2000 report. More importantly, they have a better incentive than the SEC to understand what the costs of any regulatory policy are, given that it is they who will be incurring them. Finally, the SEC's dismissal of the value of other mechanisms besides mandatory transparency for enhancing investor protection and ensuring best execution, most importantly unrestricted access and regulatory reporting, is short-sighted. As noted above, the development of efficiency and liquidity greatly furthers the goals of investor protection and best execution.

Enforcement

If a particular regulatory regime for transparency cannot be enforced, there is little point in establishing it. In order for information disseminated about quotes and trades to be accurate and timely, quotes must show the best prices at which it is possible to effect a transaction, and trade reports must show the actual prices and sizes of transacted orders as soon as possible. There are, however, several problems with ensuring the comprehensiveness, timeliness, and accuracy of this information.

Not only may market participants have an incentive not to report information, it is also difficult to monitor whether they do so on an accurate and timely basis. As the SIB (1994: 12) notes, a requirement in a dealer market that details of large trades should be published immediately, for example, may lead dealers to 'find ways of reducing the resulting position risk, including techniques to enable them to defer reporting a trade for publication until the position risk had been laid off'. This has been evident at the LSE where several practices may have been used in the past to delay the publication of trades, some within the rules of the exchange and some against them.[31] A market maker could agree a trade with a client on condition that they both booked the trade at a later time, an action clearly against the rules of the exchange. Details of trades reported after the close of the market would not be published until the beginning of the next trading day. A trade could be done on a 'protected' basis, so that execution was guaranteed but the price could be improved if the market moved in the right direction, this time within the exchange's rules.[32] A customer could be sold a short maturity option, for example one with a duration of ten minutes, to buy a particular stock in the knowledge that the customer would execute the option. The market maker was thus given time to hedge his position. Trades could also be booked in another market.

Similar activity has also occurred in other markets. At different times, dealers on NASDAQ and on the Toronto Stock Exchange have had the option of reporting a price which differs from the actual price at which they execute a transaction with their client, through their 'markup' and 'markdown' rules. It is also generally possible to split or combine orders so that the sizes of reported trades are not the sizes of the trades which are actually executed. Many market makers have not consistently reported their trades on time or appropriately designated them as late as required by NASD rules.[33] Even on automated trading systems, it is possible to manipulate information about the times and sizes of trades, frequently within the operating rules of such systems.[34] The rules governing the placing of quotes on an exchange may also be difficult to enforce. For example, in order to be able to execute orders against any quotes, the quotes need to be firm. Although a dealer may place some quotes on a screen, however, he may simply refuse to answer the phones to deal on them and so avoid being held to his quotes.

An important problem with transparency rules is that they themselves are not as transparent as they appear to be. There is frequently a gap between what they promise and what they actually deliver. The situation in America provides an example of this. The explicit aim of the CQS is to provide full public information about all the relevant quotes for the most liquid equities. It is, however, standard practice in the upstairs block-trading market for dealers to seek out and agree the counter-parties to a trade before any information about the trade, including the originating counter-party's order or quote, is published. The notion that the public may participate in, or trade against, such quotes is therefore a myth.

That any rules on transparency may be hard to enforce, does not mean that they are not worth implementing. The costs of enforcement may be worth the benefits. If, however, market participants have a strong incentive not to follow the rules, the costs of enforcement may be high. Furthermore it is difficult to gauge the effectiveness of any enforcement policy. Board and Sutcliffe's claim, for example, that during the period when immediate transparency was required on the LSE, this policy was successfully enforced is suspect.[35] Even during that period, there are indications that dealers were reporting their transactions after the closing of the market, so that information about trades would not be released until the next day.[36]

Summary Judgement

The proponents of mandatory price and quote transparency, the most influential of which has been the SEC, believe in essence that it promotes almost all the key goals that regulation of the securities markets should seek to deliver, namely investor protection, fairness, competition, market efficiency, liquidity, market integrity, and investor confidence. They therefore argue that mandatory price and quote transparency should be a fundamental and universal cornerstone of the regulation of exchanges and markets. It is argued here, in contrast, that such a policy is inappropriate.

Contrary to what the SEC implicitly claims, there may be significant trade-offs between the attainment of different regulatory goals. An assessment of the relative importance of such objectives is therefore necessary. While the SEC has not explicitly stated a preference between different regulatory goals, and indeed is statutorily required to follow competing objectives, many of its statements and its actions indicate that foremost amongst all the goals it pursues is that of investor protection, and particularly the protection of retail investors.[37] Not only is this a worthy goal, mandatory transparency may further its realization, by helping retail investors monitor the quality of their executions, and by reducing the inequalities in access to information that they face compared to other types of market participants.

Despite this, mandatory transparency is generally thought here to be an inappropriate regulatory policy for the central reason that it can compromise the delivery of the two key regulatory goals of efficiency and liquidity. Private incentives as opposed to regulatory fiat, will normally lead to the level of transparency that best furthers these goals. Of course, if other regulatory goals, such as those of investor protection and fairness, are thought more important than efficiency and liquidity, or if it is believed that there are no significant trade-offs in the attainment of these different goals, a policy of mandatory transparency may be viewed as optimal.

Different regulators have taken opposing views on this issue. There is a variance, for example, in the relative political importance placed on retail traders and on institutional investors in the USA and the UK, with greater stress being placed on the larger market participants in the UK. Although a debatable simplification, this difference is likely to have meant that the SEC has focused on investor protection, a major concern of retail investors, whereas the SIB has concentrated on efficiency, the primary concern of institutional investors. Not unexpectedly, therefore, there has been conflict between the two regulatory agencies over the merits of transparency.[38] Although the positions of both agencies have both changed and at times been opaque, the SEC has for the most part promoted full and mandatory transparency at the international level, while the SIB has defended the need for lower levels of transparency. To the extent that such differences of opinion have arisen solely as a result of the respective regulators having incompatible goals, no easy resolution between them is possible. If, in contrast, the differences have arisen because the two regulators have differing beliefs about the effectiveness of mandatory transparency in delivering efficiency and liquidity, further evidence should help reduce the differences.

Given the difficulties of enforcing a regulatory regime against the interests of market participants, the problems of achieving regulatory consistency,[39] the ignorance and confusion we have about the effects of transparency, and most importantly given the private incentives that exist to disseminate information, it is argued here that market participants themselves should normally be left to decide the appropriate level of transparency. Contrary to what the SEC and others argue, therefore, price and quote transparency should be viewed as a mechanism that may or may not deliver the desired regulatory goals, rather than being seen as a regulatory objective *per se*. In most circumstances it should not be mandated.

THE SALE OF INFORMATION

Two forms of activity by exchanges concerning the prices they charge for their price and quote information are frequently believed to be anti-competitive: monopolistic pricing where the price is set greater than marginal cost, and price discrimination. An analysis of each of these issues is examined here.

Monopolistic Pricing

The standard argument against monopolistic pricing is that it leads to economic inefficiency because the sum of consumer and producer surplus is not maximized.[40] The price–quantity combination that maximizes a monopolist's profits occurs when his marginal cost equals his marginal revenue. When this occurs, the price charged by the monopolist is greater than the marginal cost he faces, the difference being a function of the price elasticity of demand. The less consumers are sensitive to changes in price, namely when they have a low price elasticity of demand, the more the monopolist will charge over marginal cost.

The price–quantity combination chosen by the monopolist may be contrasted with that which would occur in a perfectly competitive market, where no individual firm can affect the price by changing the amount of the good it produces. In equilibrium in the competitive world, the price of the good, namely its marginal cost, is lower than that which obtains in the monopolistic environment, and the amount produced is higher than that produced by the monopolist. The reason why the competitive outcome is thought preferable to the monopolistic one, and indeed socially optimal, is that the competitive outcome maximizes the sum of consumer and producer surplus.

In order to apply the above analysis to the situation of an exchange disseminating its data, several extra factors must be incorporated into the model. Account must first be taken of the fact that the marginal cost to the 'producer' (in this instance the exchange) of supplying an extra unit of the 'good' (in this instance the information) is typically very low, and thus the average cost which the producer faces declines with the total amount of the good produced. Once a digital feed containing the relevant information has been constructed, it is relatively cheap to deliver the feed to whomsoever wants it. The socially optimal outcome in such circumstances would still be when the producer sets the price for the good at the marginal cost of producing it, in this case close to zero.[41] Unfortunately if a producer were to do this, the total revenues which he received would not cover his total costs of production, and he would therefore incur losses. In a first-best world, in which all forms of taxation are allowed, it is typically advocated that the resulting deficit should be financed by charging consumers some form of lump-sum fee or tax. Such fees are 'non-distortionary' in that they do not affect the marginal costs which consumers face, and therefore still allow for the possibility of achieving an efficient outcome.

In most jurisdictions, however, the idea of charging a lump-sum fee and marginal cost pricing to support the operations of an exchange is unacceptable, and some other form of financing for the exchange must therefore be found. In such a second-best world, the best outcome in terms of output produced and price charged may not be close to that obtaining in the first-best world. One way of asking the question of what price an exchange should charge is to view the exchange as a public utility, and to require it to maximize social welfare, subject to the constraint that it not operate with a deficit.

Under these circumstances, the price the exchange should charge is inversely related to the elasticity of demand for information. The extent to which the exchange should set its price above marginal cost depends on the budget constraint, namely on the amount of losses it would incur if it did price the information at marginal cost, and on the extent to which these losses could be financed by lump-sum charges. When the constraint is non-binding, in particular when lump-sum fees may be charged, the price should be set at marginal cost to achieve the first-best outcome. If the required profit approaches the maximum possible in order to finance a large loss, and no lump-sum charges are allowed, the price the constrained producer should charge approaches the price that the monopolist will charge. Once again this is when marginal revenue equals marginal cost.

A further complication in the context of an exchange disseminating its price and quote information, is that this information is a joint product. It can only be 'produced' by an exchange which operates a trading system. The service of converting orders into trades, which is delivered by all trading systems, necessarily produces information about both the orders routed to the trading system, the quotes, and the prices and volumes of the executed trades. In these circumstances, the optimal price an exchange should charge for its information is thus also dependent on the sale of its trading services. As with the single good situation, if the exchange is required to maximize social welfare while still not making a loss, it can be shown that it should charge a price for each good which is inversely related to the elasticity of demand for that particular good.[42] The intuitive reason for this is that if consumers are relatively insensitive to changes in the price for one of the goods, they will still buy that good at a relatively high price, and the producer will be able to charge a relatively low price for the other good, for which consumers are relatively sensitive to changes in price.

The analysis should also be extended to allow for the possibility that the demands for the two products are interdependent, so that for example, the more trading that market participants undertake, the more they wish to buy information about the market on which they are trading. The optimal prices for each of the services offered by an exchange will then depend in addition on the cross-elasticities of demand, namely on how sensitive consumers' demands for each of the goods are to changes in the price of the other good.

Account may also need to be taken of the possibility that a multi-product monopolist may try to price its products so as to entrench its position against potential entrants, thus reducing the intensity of competition. If a monopolist produces a range of goods, and seeks to obtain a lower rate of return for those of its products which are subject to competition than for those which are not, the monopolist may be able to restrict competition in the production of the goods subject to competition, while still reaping monopoly profits for those goods which are not. In the context of exchanges, it is likely that the transaction services which an exchange provides are more open to competition than the information services it provides. While alternative trading systems can offer transaction services even if they attract only a small number of the orders flowing to an already-existing exchange, the information arising from their systems is likely not to be valuable to market participants unless a relatively large amount of trading is executed on their systems. An exchange may therefore seek to charge relatively low fees for transactions services, and relatively high fees for its information, in order to prevent rivals from providing competing trading systems.

The model outlined above provides useful insights into some of the factors that are important in determining what should be the optimal price for an exchange's information. To apply the model to a real exchange, however, would be difficult if not impossible. Full numerical specifications of the exchange's costs of production, of the demand for information, of the demand for trading services, and of the cross-elasticities of demand, would all be required. There are various other conceptual and practical issues which the model does not incorporate but which would nevertheless also affect the optimal price in a real environment.

The first is that no account is taken of uncertainty. The second is that the model describes the socially optimal pricing decision of a monopolistic exchange. In most real environments, however, the market participants trading on an exchange have a choice as to where they can send their orders, and thus exchanges operate in some form of competitive environment. From a theoretical point of view, the optimal pricing decisions of an exchange depend on the precise structure of the game in which competing exchanges are assumed to operate. In these circumstances, no simple general conclusions can be drawn about what is the socially optimal price for information.

The third weakness of the model is that it takes no account of the fact that most exchanges are required to undertake regulatory activities which have to be funded in some manner. In the past, exchanges were willing to subsidize these functions at the expense of their profitable activities. Given that most exchanges' revenue-producing activities are now subject to competition, however, they may be financially less able to do this to the same extent in the future. If an exchange is not allowed to finance both its public duties and the other costs it incurs, by charging appropriately for its information sales and other services, these public duties will have to be funded by resources external to the exchange.

Finally, the model does not take into account the facts that the members of an exchange may form an important subset of the market participants who receive the exchange's price and quote information, and that they may also have governance rights at the exchange. They will normally have an incentive to ensure both that the volume traded on the exchange is maximized, and that any fees charged for its information are limited. In these circumstances the information pricing strategy of the exchange is likely not to harm the interests of its members, and this may mean that even if there is only one exchange on which trading may take place, the exchange may still charge the socially optimal price.

The approaches that different jurisdictions have taken to the competitive regulation of an exchange's dissemination of its price and quote data may be assessed in light of the above discussion. The most explicit formulation a jurisdiction has placed on what an exchange should charge for its information is in Belgium, where the law requires that the dissemination of price and quote data 'be carried out at cost price and without any form of discrimination'.[43] The SEC has similarly argued that in disseminating its information, the NASD should recover only the costs of collecting, validating, and preparing the information for shipment. Costs related to the NASD's inquiry system, such as storing quotations for inquiry purposes and responding to actual inquiries, should not be considered in developing a subscriber charge. The SEC also stated that it believed that 'value-of-service ratemaking is a price-discrimination device, used either to maximize [a monopolist's] profit or to subsidize certain interests'.[44]

Although neither the Belgian nor the American positions specify precisely what fee should be charged, they both explicitly focus on the costs of production of the information, and reject the possibility that an exchange should exploit any elasticity of demand. They also take no account of any other complicating issues. Given the discussion presented above, it is concluded here that such policies would generally not lead to the socially optimal pricing decision by an exchange for its data.

Different approaches have been taken in deciding how the costs of a multi-product exchange should be apportioned in assessing whether it is making an unreasonable profit in the production and sale of its information. Two paradigms have been proposed. In the first, an exchange is viewed primarily as a trading system. As such, the production of price and quote information is seen as an incidental result of its primary function, and the cost of producing the information is seen as marginal. This was the view of one judge in the Pont Data case,[45] and also of a past executive of the CME who stated,

We sell two things: we sell transaction services and we sell clearing services. Information is a by-product.[46]

Alternatively, an exchange may be viewed as an organization for making prices. As such, the cost of producing the information is the total cost of running the exchange. Bronfman and Overdahl (1992: 1) argue, for instance, that,

a financial exchange is effectively a firm whose main line of business is the production and dissemination of information in the form of real-time prices, quotes, and transaction volumes.

Neither of these approaches is valid. The attempt to apportion costs, on the one hand to the production of trading services, or on the other to the production of information, is flawed. The allocation of joint operating expenses cannot be made on anything other than an arbitrary basis, given that information and trading services are joint products.

Apart from the SEC's actions and arguments against the NASD concerning what it should charge Instinet for its data, the SEC has notably attempted to avoid becoming a rate-making body. This was evident in its ruling on the OPRA case. Although the SEC ruled that an SIP was allowed to charge vendors a fixed access fee for receiving information about transaction reports, it expressly stated that it had not addressed whether the costs incorporated in the access fee represented permitted limitations on access under the Securities and Exchange Act, nor whether the level of the fee charged was reasonable, nor whether any particular alternative fee structure would have been more appropriate than the fixed access fee actually chosen.[47] Similarly the SEC has not interfered in the pricing of data arising out of the operations of the CTA.

Price Discrimination

Following Scherer and Ross (1990: ch. 13), the phrase 'price discrimination' is taken to refer to situations in which different market participants are offered services at price differentials which do not directly correspond to the differences in the costs of supplying the services. Many different types of such price discrimination are possible. The issue of whether discriminatory conduct is anti-competitive or not is *a priori* indeterminate. It depends on how such discrimination affects the level of social welfare.

Three conditions must be satisfied for a seller to be able to practise price discrimination profitably. The first is that the seller must have some monopoly power. If a seller operated in a competitive market, he could choose to sell at a price lower than his competitors, but would lose money doing so, given that price equals marginal cost. The second condition is that the seller must be able to separate different customers into different groups according to their reservation price, or their elasticity of demand. Only by doing so will a seller find different consumers who are willing to pay different prices for the same thing. Finally the seller must be able to stop arbitrage between customers. In particular, he must be able to restrict those customers to whom he sells the product at a relatively cheap price, from re-selling the product to those customers to whom the seller wishes to charge a relatively expensive price. If this is not possible, the seller will always be under-cut in his attempts to sell at the expensive price.

Exchanges' attempts to exploit the value of their information have meant that to a greater extent than before they are now trying to discriminate between different customers. Previously the most common way this was done was to charge a customer according to the number of devices on which he received the exchange's information, and further, to charge the larger customers proportionally less per device than the smaller ones. Such conduct may be classified as price discrimination as there is essentially only a fixed cost in delivering a data-feed to a single customer location—the marginal cost to an exchange of a customer using the information on progressively larger numbers of devices is close to zero. Although not widespread yet, the possibility of an exchange charging lower fees to its members than to other market participants, has also been the subject of discussion in the USA.

Three paradigms of price discrimination may be identified: first, second, and third degree discrimination. First degree discrimination is defined as occurring when each consumer pays his reservation price for each unit of production sold. The seller is thus able to charge a different price to every customer. Second degree discrimination is the same except that the seller is only able to partition consumers into ten groups, to each of which he is able to offer a different price. Third degree discrimination is defined as occurring when a seller can divide all customers into two or more independent segments, each of which has its own demand curve. The seller may then charge each group a single price, and may choose to charge different groups different prices. It is the third type of discrimination that exchanges have mostly attempted to employ. Although the precise effects of price discrimination depend on the specific manner in which it is applied, it generally has three major economic effects: on income distribution, on efficiency, and on market structure.

The first two of these effects may be illustrated by comparing three hypothetical environments: a monopolist who charges a single price, a monopolist practising first degree price discrimination, and a competitive environment. The amount of goods produced under the perfectly discriminating or first-degree monopolist and in the competitive world are identical. Furthermore, the sum of consumer and producer surplus is also the same in both environments. The essential difference between the two situations is that while consumers appropriate much of the surplus in the competitive world, it is the monopolist who gains this surplus in the first-degree discrimination world. Economics *per se* can make no judgement on who should have these profits. In contrast, however, the monopolistic world without the possibility of price discrimination is unequivocally worse, in terms of the sum of consumer and producer surplus and the output produced, than both the competitive and the first-degree discrimination world.

The welfare effects of third-degree price discrimination are more ambiguous than those arising from the other two types of discrimination. Assuming that a monopolistic producer is able to segment consumers into two groups with different elasticities of demand, the monopolist will typically charge the group with the higher elasticity of demand, namely the group which is more sensitive to price changes, a lower price than that it charges the group with the lower elasticity of demand. The question of whether total output will be lower in a situation with a third-degree discriminating monopolist than with a monopolist who charges a single price to all consumers depends on the specification of the demand curves of the different groups of consumers. Third-degree discrimination may also allow a producer in an industry with declining average costs the possibility of offering services to market segments which would not be served if only a single price could be charged, something which is beneficial for social welfare. An example of this may be when exchanges set a relatively low fee for the use of their data by retail subscribers.

If all participants were required to pay the same cost for receiving an exchange's information, an exchange might not be able to fund itself adequately, depending on the price it set. There are two reasons why exchanges are likely to consider charging their members less for their data than other market participants. The first is to re-distribute profits from non-exchange members to exchange members. Although this is a politically charged subject, economics *per se* has once again nothing to say about the merits of doing so. Given, however, that the re-dissemination of data is both relatively cheap and difficult to monitor, if an exchange does discriminate in favour of its members, it may not be able to stop them from re-disseminating its data, and thus competing directly with the exchange in selling the data to non-members of the exchange. The extent to which copyright law allows an exchange to forbid such re-dissemination will influence the extent to which it employs price discrimination.

The second reason why an exchange may wish to charge its members less for its data than other market participants, is that its members may be less willing to establish trading systems which compete with the exchange than would other market participants. As one of the central aims of an exchange is the enhancement of the wealth of its members, they may find it less profitable to establish a competing trading system than other participants. By charging non-members more than members for its data, an exchange may therefore seek to recoup money from actual or potential competitors. This may be deemed in the public interest in that without this possibility, other trading systems may use the prices an exchange disseminates in order to attract orders away from the exchange, without paying for the production of the information. Were this to occur, the exchange would have a reduced incentive to publish the information in the first place.

In a world of potential competitors, an exchange will seek to segment the market for its data into those who do or might provide competing trading systems to the exchange on the one hand, and non-competitors on the other. A segmentation of the market into members and non-members, however, is unlikely to deliver this goal successfully. Many non-members will not wish to compete with the exchange, and some members may wish to do so.

CONCLUSION

The aim of this chapter is to address a series of legal and regulatory issues concerning the dissemination of price and quote information that have been, and remain, contentious, and that are specific to the financial markets. It is composed of three sections. In the first, some general comments are presented on the nature and role of regulation in financial markets, and in particular on the function that competition policy should play in the regulation of exchanges and trading systems. A range of assumptions about four areas related to the general characteristics of regulation is examined. These concern the way regulation is implemented, the goals it should seek to effect, the manner in which conflicts between such goals should be resolved, and the nature of competition policy. It is argued that the maximization of economic efficiency should be the goal of competition policy.

In the next section, the broad question of whether the dissemination of price and quote information should be mandated by regulation is discussed. After presenting the arguments in favour and against full mandatory transparency, a judgement is made against it. There are essentially four sets of reasons for doing so: the difficulties of enforcing a regulatory regime against the interests of market participants, the problems of achieving regulatory consistency, the ignorance and confusion we have about the effects of transparency, and most importantly the private incentives that exist to disseminate information. Given these factors, it is argued that in most circumstances market participants themselves should be left to decide appropriate levels of transparency. Price and quote transparency should be viewed as a mechanism that may or may not deliver the desired regulatory goals, rather than being seen as a regulatory objective *per se*.

In the last section, two issues related to the pricing by exchanges of their price and quote information are examined. These are when exchanges charge prices that are greater than their marginal costs, and when they price-discriminate between different groups of customers. Contrary to the commonly-held view, it is shown to be difficult in many sets of circumstances to determine that either activity is anti-competitive.

12

Classification and Governance: Policy[1]

INTRODUCTION

The statutory distinction between exchanges and brokers has operated for over sixty years in the USA, and underpins the entire fabric of the regulatory structure governing not only the American securities markets but also that of many other jurisdictions.[2] The aim of this chapter is nevertheless to argue that the distinction is no longer viable in the face of the development of automated trading systems, and to propose an alternative approach. A critical element of this approach relates to the governance and self-regulation of trading systems. Although attention is focused on the American experience in the securities markets, and in particular on the SEC's manner of regulating exchanges and trading systems, the analysis and conclusions are more widely relevant both for other jurisdictions and for other types of markets.[3]

Confusion and controversy have been characteristic of the regulatory concerns about automated trading systems since their inception. The latest and most radical attempt at clarifying and resolving these worries has been by the SEC in a 'Concept Release' it issued in 1997.[4] This was issued following a Congressional sanction in 1996 that gave the SEC the right to exempt any person, security, or transaction from any provision of the Securities and Exchange Act or any rules made under it, if the exemption was 'necessary or appropriate in the public interest and was consistent with the protection of investors'.[5] In the Concept Release, the SEC discussed what it believed to be the problems of the past and present approach of regulating exchanges, and also proposed what it thought were appropriate responses. The nature and merits of the SEC's proposals are examined here.

The chapter is composed of three sections. In the first, the criteria that the SEC has historically used to identify whether a trading system should be classified as an exchange or a broker are evaluated. In the second, various flaws with the exchange/broker distinction are identified and discussed. While some are believed important, others, and in particular some of those raised by the SEC, are argued as being either inappropriate or themselves flawed. In the third section, various alternative approaches to regulating exchanges and trading systems, including the newest suggestions by the SEC, are analysed. A joint approach of separating the regulation of market structure from the regulation of other areas of public concern, and of employing competition policy to regulate market structure, is recommended as the best way of classifying and regulating trading systems.

THE HISTORICAL MEANING OF AN 'EXCHANGE'

An assessment of what the concept of an 'exchange' has signified in America prior to the introduction of the SEC's Concept Release, is complex for at least five reasons. First, the statutory definition is both broad and ambiguous. This was highlighted in a court case in 1991 concerning whether the Delta trading system was an exchange or not, in which the Court of Appeals confirmed that the wording of the definition was not 'crystal clear'.[6]

Second, constraints on the types of trading systems which may be designated exchanges arise not only from the statutory definition, but also from the duties that are imposed on institutions which satisfy the definition and register with the SEC. If a trading system were to fall within the statutory definition but not be able or willing to fulfil the duties that would be placed on it as a result of being registered as an exchange, the SEC would not allow the institution to register as an exchange. The various statutory and regulatory duties that an institution registered as an exchange is required to undertake are discussed in Chapters 7–9.

Third, the ambiguity in the definition has meant that in order to decide whether a particular trading system should be registered as an exchange, the SEC has sought to determine whether exchange registration would further the purposes of the SEA. There are, however, substantial difficulties in doing so. The Act mandates the pursuit of many goals, some of which clash. Also, a determination of the most appropriate way of interpreting the definitions laid out in the Act in order to help realize the statutory goals, is controversial.

Fourth, the SEC's policy concerning the registration of automated trading systems has responded to a series of initiatives in the markets, and has therefore evolved on a case by case basis. Prior to the SEC's Concept Release, no formal specification of either necessary or sufficient conditions for deciding what is, or what is not, an exchange had been developed. Instead, a basket of requirements has emerged over time, the importance of each of which is somewhat imprecise. The SEC has indeed stated that,

[no trading system] can avoid exchange registration simply by omitting particular characteristics of traditional exchange markets such as affirmative market making obligations or a limit order book. Instead, exchange registration will depend on an analysis of all the facts and circumstances relating to a particular system or marketplace.[7]

Finally, the legislative history of the SEA indicates that the SEC should have considerable leeway in interpreting which organizations should be classified as exchanges. In 1934 Congress noted that,

so delicate a mechanism as the modern stock exchange cannot be regulated efficiently under a rigid statutory program. Unless considerable latitude is allowed for administrative discretion, it is impossible to avoid, on the one hand, unworkable 'strait-jacket' regulation and, on the other, loopholes which may be penetrated by slight variations in the method of doing business.[8]

A series of judicial decisions have confirmed the SEC's flexibility by inviting it to re-interpret the definition over time,[9] and by deferring to its interpretation of what the term should mean.[10]

Notwithstanding these difficulties, this section attempts to identify the criteria by which the SEC has historically determined whether a trading system satisfies the statutory definition of an 'exchange'. A range of rules and judgements is examined, including most importantly: the proposal, withdrawal, re-proposal, and second withdrawal, of Rule 15c2-10 for regulating so-called 'proprietary trading systems' (PTSs) (as defined below); the application by the AZX (then called Wunsch Auction Systems Inc.) to obtain a limited volume exemption for its trading system from exchange registration, and the SEC's approval of this application; and the legal conflict concerning whether Delta should be classified as an 'exchange'. The market structure of the Delta system is described in Appendix 1.

It was in the Delta conflict that the SEC presented for the first time a seminal interpretation of how the 'exchange' definition should be understood, stating that,

what distinguishes an exchange from brokers, dealers and other statutorily defined entities is its fundamental characteristic of centralizing trading and providing purchasers and sellers, by its design (whether through trading rules, operational procedures or business incentives), buy and sell quotations on a regular or continuous basis so that those purchasers and sellers have a reasonable expectation that they can regularly execute their orders at those price quotations. The means employed may be varied, ranging from a physical floor or trading system (where orders can be centralized and executed) to other means of intermediation (such as a formal market making system or systemic procedures such as a consolidated limit order book or regular single price auction).[11]

Where exact specification of the criteria the SEC has employed to determine the regulatory status of a trading system proves difficult, the various options that the SEC might have used are discussed. Three sets of criteria used by the SEC are analysed, concerning: first, centralization; second, two-sided quotes, liquidity and volume; and third, trade execution and price discovery.

Centralization

The first of the two elements of the SEC's seminal 'exchange' interpretation relates to 'centralization'. The SEC's use of the concept of 'centralization' has not, however, been clear, and answers to any combination of the following five questions might be material in determining whether a trading system is centralized or not.

Do all orders compete against each other on a particular trading system? The SEC's decisions concerning Delta and the AZX support this version of what 'centralization' means. The Delta system was not required to register as an exchange, partially because it was possible on Delta for participants to trade directly with each other without exposing their orders to competition from the orders of other participants. Conversely, the fact that all orders on the AZX were funnelled through one order execution mechanism, was seen by the SEC as one indication that the AZX should be deemed an exchange. Use of the criterion that all orders should compete against each other on a particular trading system to determine that the system is an exchange, may imply that dealer markets are not exchanges. Typically in such markets, although the bids and offers of all the dealers do compete against each other, the orders submitted by investors to these dealers do not. Thus a sell order from one investor may go to one dealer and be executed while that from another investor, with a lower offer price attached to it, may go simultaneously to another dealer and not be executed.

Does price priority obtain on the system? Price priority holds when the order in which the bids and offers in a market are executed is dependent on the prices at which they are set. Although most trading systems do exhibit price priority, there are systems, such as Instinet, which do not. To date, all trading systems regulated as exchanges do exhibit price priority.

Are participants required to deal on the system if they deal in the assets traded on the system? Only a trading system with a monopoly in the trading of a particular set of assets can fulfil this requirement of centralization. No exchange in the USA has a legal monopoly for the trading in any stock.

Does most of the trading undertaken in the assets traded on the system take place on the system? The fact that the major volume of the trading in the stocks dealt on the regional exchanges is executed on the NYSE, means that this criterion cannot be what 'centralization' means. If it did, the regional exchanges could not be classified as exchanges.

Need a trading system have a physical location or floor to allow transactions to be negotiated? Both in its seminal interpretation and in several of its other decisions, the SEC has maintained that the lack of a trading floor does not obstruct the classification of a trading system as an exchange. This is evident in its statement that a trading system may employ 'varied means' to deliver centralization, and in its recognition of the CSE and the AZX as exchanges. One court has, however, suggested that the lack of a trading floor was an indication that a particular trading system was not what was generally understood to be a stock exchange.[12] The SEC has also not required a trading system to have negotiation facilities for it to be classified as an exchange: the AZX did not allow traders to negotiate with each other, but was classified as an exchange. One court has again, however, determined that an exchange is in part defined as a place to negotiate transactions.[13]

Two-Sided Quotes, Liquidity and Volume

The second part of the SEC's key 'exchange' interpretation was that in order to be classified as an exchange a trading system had, by its design, to provide two-sided quotes on a regular or continuous basis so that buyers and sellers had a reasonable expectation that they could regularly execute their orders at those quotes. There are several significant implications of this requirement.

Despite stating that the 'means employed [to deliver two-sided quotes] may be varied', the SEC has closely identified the provision of two-sided quotes with the mandated participation in a market of some form of financial intermediary, be it a specialist, a market maker, or a dealer.[14] The SEC expressly noted, for example, that one reason why the Delta system should not be classified as an exchange was that,

[there was] no formal requirement or expectation that System participants will undertake to maintain a fair and orderly market in the options they trade, by providing both the bid and offer side of a given market irrespective of their actual buying or selling interest.

In the case of the AZX, in contrast, the Commission did relax the requirements both that two-sided quotes be provided, and that some form of financial intermediation be present.

The SEC's use of the phrase 'by its design' implies that if a trading system attempts to mandate two-sided quotes so that buyers and sellers have a reasonable expectation that they can regularly execute their orders at those quotes but fails, it should be classified as an exchange; while conversely, if a trading system succeeds in having such two-sided quotes, but does not do so *by design*, then it need not be classified as an exchange. The SEC has, however, indicated in several contexts that it believes the second scenario is impossible, arguing that in order for a trading system to deliver continuous two-sided quotes, the system would have to do so by design.[15]

A further component of the interpretation is that two-sided quotes be provided 'on a regular or continuous basis'. The SEC found that Delta, a system which exhibited a low percentage of two-sided quotes relative to the overall number of buy and sell quotes, and on which prices and quotes were only displayed episodically, should not be classified as an exchange.[16] The Commission did, however, also relax the requirement that two-sided quotes be provided on a continuous basis in the case of the AZX, which operated a batch auction.

Although not mentioned in its seminal interpretation, the SEC has closely linked the 'two-sided quotes' provision with the production of liquidity in a market, stating that,

'Liquidity' goes to the participant's expectation that it can readily, if not immediately, execute its order due to the presence of regular or continuous two-sided quotations (bids and asks).[17]

Other characteristics of a market have also been associated with liquidity by the SEC, including immediacy, depth, and continuity.[18] No formal tests of whether trading systems deliver immediacy, depth or continuity have, however, been applied by the SEC. Furthermore, the markets on several of the registered exchanges, including the AZX, do not exhibit some or all of these characteristics.

The SEC has expressly avoided equating liquidity with trading volume, stating that the two are not equivalent. It has claimed, for example, that,

it is not difficult to envision a trading system that provides a centralized, liquid marketplace to its participants for the particular securities traded on the system, but, due either to limitations on the class of individuals that may participate or to the subset of securities that may be traded on the system, has a limited overall volume of trading and a <u>de minimis</u> impact on the securities market as a whole.[19]

As noted in a dissenting opinion in the Delta case, the presence of the 'limited volume' exemption in the statute implies that trading volume cannot be a determinant of exchange classification, because if it were it would not be possible to apply the limited volume exemption, given that low volume trading systems would not be classified as exchanges.[20]

The statute provides no standard as to what level of volume on a trading system would justify an exemption from exchange registration. A guideline used in the AZX ruling was the volume executed on the smallest of the registered national exchanges at the time.[21] Other yardsticks have also been proposed by the SEC, including: the dollar volume or number of transactions executed through a trading system expressed as a percentage of all trading done in the market of which that particular system is a part; the number and characteristics of participants or subscribers permitted to trade in the system; and the characteristics of the instruments traded, or transactions allowed, in the system.[22]

Trade Execution and Price Discovery

A system that does not provide trade execution does not satisfy the statutory definition of an exchange. Execution facilities, automated or otherwise, are not, however, sufficient to require that a trading system register as an exchange. Many execution systems have been regulated as broker-dealers under the no-action approach.[23]

To date all passive-pricing trade execution mechanisms have been classified as broker-dealers rather than exchanges. In addition, although the concept of a PTS has no formal bearing on how the SEC regulates trading systems, a lack of price discovery was put forward as a factor distinguishing PTSs from exchanges.[24]

The fact that a trading system does engage in price discovery is, however, not determinative that the system should be classified as an exchange. Many of the trading systems regulated as broker-dealers do engage in price discovery. On the other hand, the SEC did state that the AZX should be an exchange, in part because its automated procedures set an equilibrium price for securities, and therefore that its facilities were 'designed to create a liquid market where buyers and sellers have a reasonable expectation that they can regularly execute orders'.[25]

Summary

Despite the difficulties inherent in attempting to ascertain how the SEC has historically determined whether a trading system should be classified as an exchange, it is nevertheless possible to identify the main criteria which the SEC has employed. In particular, to be classified as an exchange, a trading system must: (i) provide trade execution facilities; (ii) engage in price discovery; (iii) centralize trading, which seems to imply that all orders on a trading system should compete with each other; and (iv) ensure, by design, the entry of buy and sell quotations on a regular basis, such that both buyers and sellers have a reasonable expectation that they can regularly execute their orders at those quotes. In most circumstances, this last criterion seems to imply the participation of some form of financial intermediation, although a single price auction market without such intermediation has been classified an exchange.

The SEA also contains many criteria which a trading system, once classified as an exchange, must satisfy in order to be registered as an exchange. The most important of these are that the trading system: (v) have members who are only broker-dealers; (vi) provide fair representation in its management to these members; (vii) act as a competent SRO, and ensure that its members comply with the securities laws; and (viii) participate in the NMS, first by publicly disseminating price and quote information, via the CTA and the CQS, and second by linking up with other exchanges and the NASD, via the ITS.

PROBLEMS

A range of flaws with the exchange/broker distinction is identified and analysed in this section. It is composed of seven parts. In the first five, various difficulties are discussed under the respective headings of ambiguity, re-classification, competition, self-regulation and governance, and incoherence. In the sixth part, the weaknesses perceived by the SEC with the exchange/broker distinction in its 1997 Concept Release are evaluated. While some of the points made by the SEC are believed persuasive, others are themselves viewed as flawed. The defects in these arguments, and in the supposed solutions the SEC has proposed to resolve them, are discussed in the next section. In the last part, some problems with the exchange/broker distinction in an international context are identified.

Ambiguity

All statutory language is ambiguous, and it is precisely to resolve such ambiguity that regulatory and judicial institutions are mandated to exist. Nevertheless, the confluence of developments in technology together with the opacity of both the statutory definition of an 'exchange' and of the SEC's key 'exchange' interpretation, mean that the definition is no longer useful for determining whether a particular institution should be classified as an exchange or not.

Many elements of the definition are confusing. The SEC itself has noted that an expansive reading of the statute would capture most PTSs, brokers, block trading desks and even quotation vendors.[26] This may be seen by considering the phrase 'facilities for bringing together purchasers and sellers of securities', which could apply to institutions traditionally categorized either as exchanges or as brokers. The argument that an expansive reading of the definition would be inappropriate given the existence of other relevant statutory categories, such as brokers and dealers, does not help clarify how the definition should be interpreted. It merely highlights that the interpretative puzzle requires a resolution of the definitions of these other categories, which are also very broad, as well as that of an 'exchange'.

Several problems arise as a result of the phrase 'a market place or facilities . . . for otherwise performing with respect to securities the functions commonly performed by a stock exchange as that term is generally understood'. The self-referential inclusion of the term 'stock exchange' makes the definition circular, and thus potentially meaningless. Identification of the functions that have been 'commonly performed by a stock exchange' is also not an easy process. Many functions have traditionally been undertaken by exchanges, and it is not self-evident which should be the criteria to determine whether an institution is an exchange or not. Furthermore, a prime consequence of the advance of cheap automation has been that many of the functions traditionally undertaken by exchanges are being disaggregated, and performed by new and separate institutions.[27] A historical analysis of what are the 'commonly performed' functions is therefore unlikely to be useful in assessing whether present automated trading systems should be classified as exchanges, precisely because many of them have non-traditional institutional structures. A historical analysis may also imply that institutions which were once classified as exchanges should no longer be so categorized, as they shed some of their traditional activities.

Use of the phrase 'as is generally understood' adds to the confusion. If the phrase is placed in a historical context, it may be interpreted as referring only to auction markets, given both that they were the standard type of exchanges operating when the statute was created, and that a separate statutory category was specifically created for an association of dealers.[28] In contrast, however, it is obvious but important to note that there is now no generally accepted understanding about what the various aspects of the definition mean. It is in addition debatable whether the 'as is generally understood' phrase should be interpreted as modifying solely the 'commonly performed functions' language, or should also modify the 'bringing together' language.[29]

The judgement that the SEC's exchange 'interpretation' should triumph in the Delta case, did not clarify the ambiguities in the statutory definition. The essence of the ruling was that as the definition was ambiguous, the SEC's interpretation should prevail given that it was the agency specifically created by government for the purpose of regulating the securities markets and adjudicating such ambiguities. The merits of the SEC's interpretation *per se*, as opposed to the SEC's power to make and enforce the interpretation, were therefore adjudged of secondary importance.

The SEC's interpretation of the statutory definition is in any event also open to attack. One of the two planks of the interpretation was that for an institution to be classified as an exchange it had to 'centralize' trading.[30] As noted above, this criterion is not unambiguous. Any combination of the following five questions might be important in addressing the issue of centralization: Do all orders compete against each other? Does price priority obtain on the system? Do other secondary priorities obtain on the system? Are participants required to deal on the system if they deal in the commodities traded on the system? And finally, Does all trading take place at a single location? Different combinations will imply that different mechanisms are to be classified as exchanges.

Re-Classification

There are two ways in which the issue of re-classifying automated trading systems may expose flaws with the exchange/broker distinction. The first may arise if the AZX, currently the only exempted exchange, captures an amount of business equal to that obtained by the smallest of the registered exchanges. Whatever the likelihood of such an event, the SEC has said that if this did occur it would revisit the issue of whether the AZX should be required to register as an exchange. If AZX were obliged to register as an exchange, it would become subject to the full panoply of exchange regulation, and in particular would be required to admit only brokers as members, and to provide them fair representation on its board. The intention of the AZX, however, is exactly to avoid the need for financial intermediation. The requirements that it grant only brokers access to its trading system and that it ensure that they are represented on its board, when its goal is their elimination, would therefore be perverse.

It may be possible for the SEC to interpret the Act in a creative manner such that the AZX would not be required to implement the 'access' and 'fair representation' obligations. For example, when the SEA defines the membership of an exchange, it does so with reference to the trading floor of an exchange. In particular, a 'member' of an exchange is specified as 'any natural person permitted to effect transactions *on the floor of the exchange* without the services of another person acting as broker'.[31] Although far outside the standard interpretation of the Act, it might therefore be feasible for the SEC to register the AZX as an exchange, while at the same time not requiring that it have any members, because it did not have a trading floor. Given that the AZX would have no members, it would not need to offer such members fair representation on its board.

While this approach would have the merit of allowing the AZX to function without undue interference, it would have the cost of undermining the standard interpretation of the SEA. It would reduce the value of the 'exchange' definition as a filter for assessing how different types of automated trading systems should be regulated. It might also lead market participants to question other aspects of the SEC's traditional interpretation of the Act. If such a principal statutory component as the set of membership criteria is not sacrosanct, what else could be open to re-interpretation by the SEC?

The second manner in which re-classification might pose problems concerns the possibility that a system classified as a broker might need to be re-classified as an exchange in order to further the goals of the SEA. The Commission has noted on several occasions the possibility that this might occur.[32] The problem is that, given the currently regulatory position, the SEC is unlikely to have any useful criteria by which to determine whether and when a broker-dealer operated trading system should be re-classified as an exchange.

Consider the situation where a system that does not mandate the provision of two-sided quotes and is not centralized, as per the SEC's key interpretation, starts capturing a significant amount of trading volume. The SEC would not then be able to use the statutory definition or its key interpretation to insist on classification of the system as an exchange. It would also not be able to employ the amount of trading executed on the system as a criterion for determining that the system should be re-classified, because of the existence of the low volume exemption.

This issue is not merely of hypothetical concern. In 1996, the SEC noted that the trading volume on Instinet amounted to 15% of total NASDAQ volume, and 20% of total volume for the 250 NASDAQ stocks with the highest median dollar volume.[33] Although Instinet has made some marginal modifications to the rules for dealing on its system since its inception, these could not be regarded as constituting sufficient change to warrant re-interpretation by the SEC that its rules now ensured the creation of two-sided quotes or centralization by design, whereas before they did not. Theoretically, therefore, even if Instinet were to capture all the trading away from NASDAQ, the SEC would still have no statutory basis to re-classify it as an exchange.

Competition

The exchange/broker distinction has given rise to several problems concerning the realization of competition. A critical one is that the distinction constrains the extent to which exchanges can determine their own market structure, in particular by requiring them to participate in the NMS. It is believed here that in most circumstances market participants face appropriate private incentives to deliver the socially optimal arrangements for all three facets of market structure, namely order routing, order execution, and, as argued in the last chapter, information dissemination. Although the SEC has repeatedly maintained that it is for market participants themselves to determine market structure, it does not accept that the NMS restraints are problematic. Instead, it argues that one of the ways of best delivering the desired regulatory objectives is for all market participants, including trading systems, to be appropriately integrated into the NMS. The nature and the merits of this view are explored below.

A second competitive problem arising from the exchange/broker distinction is that some key constraints placed on exchanges are not imposed on broker-regulated trading systems. This has meant that automated trading systems that are functionally similar have had different regulatory obligations imposed on them as a result of obtaining differing statutory classifications. These disparities give a competitive advantage to systems regulated as brokers over those regulated as exchanges, independent of any functional aspects of the systems themselves. The SEC has argued, however, that the 'level of regulation [of a trading system] should be tailored to the functions being performed by an entity and the corollary need for regulation'.34 Similarly its Division of Market Regulation has stated that 'the regulatory responsibilities of the primary markets versus their competitors should be examined to determine if the responsibilities are commensurate with the functions the various markets perform'.35 Prior to its issuance of the Concept Release, the Commission and the Division of Market Regulation also argued that 'in many respects PTSs do not perform the same functions as SROs and do not need a commensurate level of regulation'.36

The British approach of offering the operators of trading systems a choice as to what regulatory status they may adopt has not solved the problem of functionally similar systems being required to undertake different regulatory duties. Institutions that function as, what are believed to be, typical brokers are still expected to apply for authorization as such, and institutions that function as, what are believed to be, typical exchanges are expected to apply for exemption as Recognized Investment Exchanges. Neither the regulators nor the Financial Services Act, however, have any rules which delineate the types of institutions which may apply for authorization or exemption. The choice of which systems fit into which categories has therefore been a mixture of regulatory discretion and individual trading systems' preferences. Functionally similar dealing mechanisms have therefore been regulated in different ways with different associated regulatory duties and costs. A further problem arises in the UK because institutions placed in different regulatory categories have historically been supervised by different regulators.37 This makes it difficult to realize regulatory objectives which require concerted market-wide action, impedes the delivery of consistent regulation across regulatory categories, and may lead to regulatory gaps.

Another key set of burdens imposed on exchanges but not on brokers in the USA are the self-regulatory activities exchanges are required to undertake. As previously noted, it may be unsustainable for regulators to require of exchanges that they undertake certain public duties, and at the same time to deprive them of the means of doing so, by allowing non-exchange-regulated trading systems to compete away the revenues which the exchanges need to subsidize their regulatory activities. Furthermore, exchanges, as SROs, are subject to a lengthy rule-filing process requiring public comment on any rule changes they propose, while broker-regulated trading systems are not. Some exchanges have claimed that this process has hampered their efforts to provide prompt, flexible, and innovative order-entry and trading services to their members and the investing public. They note that broker-regulated trading systems may add new services or procedures to their systems instantaneously without SEC approval. The exchanges have argued that either their competitors should be subject to the same review process as they are, or that they should be relieved from the review requirement for their system changes. The NYSE has further recommended that only rule filings that present genuine investor protection concerns should be subject to the review process.38

Self-Regulation and Governance

A central difficulty that some automated trading systems pose for self-regulation is that they are not membership owned or operated institutions. The separation between the people who own and operate the market on the one hand, and the people who trade on and use the market on the other hand, means that the notion of self-regulation is no longer easily applicable. There is no single identifiable group of people who have the greater knowledge, experience, and interest in maintaining the integrity of the markets that self-regulation is meant to promote. To require market users to regulate the activities of market managers, or vice versa, may bring the two groups into conflict in ways that would damage the public interest.

An important instance of this may arise as a result of the fair representation requirements imposed on exchanges. To impose constraints on the manner in which trading systems should be governed may be to undermine the very factor which leads to their efficiency and innovativeness. As previously noted, an exchange whose members are financial intermediaries, for example, is frequently unwilling to allow investors direct access to its trading system. A non-member-owned system, on the other hand, does not have to satisfy the needs of the financial intermediaries, and this may therefore allow it to deliver trading mechanisms that are more preferable to investors than those that can be delivered by a membership exchange.

While the statutory membership and governance requirements, and the SEC's historical stress on the presence of some form of financial intermediation in its 'exchange' interpretation, may lead to efficient market structures, there is no *a priori* reason that they should do so. The imposition of a specified form of governance and membership structure is likely to obstruct market developments, and once again restrict competition.[39] In a market with rivalry between trading systems, regulation of the governance of exchanges that is imposed in order to influence their market structure is unnecessary. If, as a result of its governance structure, an exchange takes a decision concerning its market that is not in the interests of the traders using its systems, they can divert their order flow to a competing exchange. The owners of an exchange therefore face the correct incentive to create a suitable governance structure, even if this means giving up some of the rights associated with the control of the exchange to other market participants. Any regulatory constraints on governance can therefore only restrict an exchange's freedom to deliver an optimal governance structure. Even when trading systems do not face competitors, market participants will normally have appropriate incentives to agree a governance structure that maximizes efficiency. Only if they do not, is regulatory interference warranted.

Incoherence

The SEC has recognized that there is a tension between developing a regulatory structure for trading systems, and encouraging the development of such systems.[40] The Commission has also stressed that the determination of whether a trading system is an exchange or not is a judgemental, as opposed to a formulaic, process. It has noted, in particular, that,

in developing its [exchange] interpretation, the Commission was cognizant of the understanding of Congress when it delegated authority to the Commission to regulate exchanges that the concept of an exchange does not 'present a static situation susceptible to fixed standards'. Thus, there are no mathematical formulas that will definitively resolve all ambiguities with respect to what Congress referred to as a 'highly dynamic, ever-changing picture, subject to untold and unknown possibilities and combinations'.[41]

These observations, however, do not obviate the need for a consistent approach to the classification and regulation of trading systems. An inconsistent approach is likely to lead to at least three undesirable consequences. First, regulatory decisions may be reversed as a result of judicial review. Second, their consequences are likely to be unknown, and potentially harmful. Third, arbitrariness in the regulatory process, and the concomitant uncertainty, is likely to discourage market participants from developing new systems. Yet the combination of the SEC's 'exchange' interpretation and its various rulings are so full of inconsistencies as to be incoherent.

Consider first the logical status of the various elements of the SEC's 'exchange' interpretation. Although only one fundamental 'characteristic' of an exchange is specified, it is defined as being composed of two criteria, concerning respectively centralization and the provision of two-sided quotes. Use of the word 'and' in the phrase the 'fundamental characteristic of centralizing trading *and* providing purchasers and sellers . . .' implies that both criteria must be satisfied for an institution to be classified an exchange.[42] In its decision that the AZX was an exchange, however, the SEC did not require that both criteria be satisfied, given that the AZX did not provide two-sided quotes by design.

If the two criteria are together not necessary, the mere existence of the interpretation implies at a minimum that each criterion must by itself be sufficient, for a trading system to be classified an exchange. Again, however, the SEC has not implemented this implication in the decisions it has taken. If it is accepted that the centralization criterion requires that all orders on a trading system compete against each other, the SEC's decision to allow Instinet to be a broker is open to question. All quotes on the Instinet system are disclosed on the Instinet screen, but Instinet is not classified as an exchange.

Use of the phrase 'by its design' in the 'two-sided quotes' criterion is problematical. As noted above, the SEC has confirmed that it is concerned to regulate a trading system on the basis of the functions it undertakes. If so, it is irrelevant whether a system provides 'purchasers and sellers buy and sell quotations . . . on a regular or continuous basis so that those purchasers and sellers have a reasonable expectation that they can regularly execute their orders at those price quotations' *by design* or not. What matters is whether purchasers' and sellers' expectations are actually fulfilled or not.[43]

The SEC's stress on liquidity as a determinant of exchange classification also conflicts with the presence of the statutory low volume exemption.[44] Recognizing this problem, the SEC has claimed that it is quite possible to envisage a market which is liquid in the sense that two-sided quotes are provided by design, but which has a low trading volume. It is true that liquidity is a slippery concept, which may be assessed by reference to several, sometimes competing, yardsticks, including bid–ask spreads, immediacy, depth, continuity, and resiliency. Typically, however, improvements in all these measures, for example reductions in bid–ask spreads or increases in depth, show a strong correlation with increases in the volume traded on a market. Furthermore, the direction of causality between liquidity and volume is unclear. A liquid market, namely one with narrow bid–ask spreads and great depth is likely to attract a large amount of trading because of the low costs of dealing on the market. Conversely, a high volume market is likely to be one with low bid–ask spreads and great depth, because there are many orders competing with each other to determine the best prices. The SEC's attempt to separate liquidity from volume considerations is therefore unsustainable.

Further inconsistencies arise as a result of the SEC's approach to the imposition of regulatory costs. The Division of Market Regulation has accepted that the primary markets provide benefits to the whole of the market as a result of their self-regulatory obligations, including the maintenance of the integrity of the markets at large, the assurance of fair and orderly markets, and the provision of price discovery.[45] In addition, the Division has argued that the costs associated with these externalities are to a large extent offset by the revenues obtained by the primary markets—including membership fees, consolidated tape revenues, and listing fees—which are not available to other market centres. This view implies that if an institution classified as an exchange were to face reduced revenues as a result of competition by other non-exchange-automated trading systems, the regulatory costs and burdens placed on the institution should be re-allocated to the other more successful trading systems.[46] Whatever the merits of such a regulatory approach, however, it is inconsistent with current statutory requirements which do not allocate regulatory burdens and costs to different trading systems according to the amount of revenues they receive. On the contrary, the current statute imposes the major regulatory duties on trading systems classified as exchanges.

The ambiguity of the exchange definition has exposed yet another flaw in the regulatory structure. The Division of Market Regulation has maintained that a broad reading of the definition would have the distorted effect of punishing efficiency. It has argued that the more efficient and automated a broker-dealer's operations, the more it would be likely to bring together purchasers and sellers, and therefore, perversely, the more it would be likely to fall within the exchange category and be required to assume the corresponding regulatory burdens.[47] The implication is that a narrow reading of the statute should therefore be employed, so as not to punish any successful automation implemented by brokers. If appropriate for brokers, however, this argument is equally applicable to exchanges: the more automated an exchange becomes, the less the need for regulatory burdens to be placed on it. The problem is that this approach contradicts the statutory basis for regulating trading systems which mandates an all-or-nothing imposition of regulatory burdens on institutions registered as exchanges (apart from the limited volume exemption).

The SEC's Concerns

In its Concept Release discussing the appropriate way of regulating exchanges, the SEC identified two significant unintended effects arising from the exchange/broker distinction:

(1) it has subjected alternative trading systems to a regulatory scheme that is not particularly suited to their market activities; and (2) it has impeded effective integration, surveillance, enforcement, and regulation of the U.S. markets as a whole.[48]

The phrase 'alternative trading system' was used to refer to:

automated systems that centralize, display, match, cross, or otherwise execute trading interest, but that are not registered with the Commission as national securities exchanges or operated by a registered securities association.[49]

Amongst the conditions imposed on broker-dealer regulated systems, and noted by the SEC as being unsuitable, were that broker-dealers were required to protect customers' funds and securities, but that few alternative trading systems actually held such funds or securities. In addition, the SEC observed that the requirement for a broker-dealer to be member of an SRO, when such SROs frequently operated markets that competed for order flow with the broker, meant that there was 'an inherent conflict between SROs' competitive concerns as markets and their regulatory obligations to oversee alternative trading systems'.[50]

The SEC's second concern was very broad in nature. It stated that because the traditional broker-dealer regulation was 'not designed to apply to markets such as alternative trading systems, gaps have developed in the structures designed to ensure marketwide fairness, transparency, integrity and stability'.[51] The Commission summarized the principal effects of these gaps as follows:

alternative trading systems are not fully integrated into the national market system. As a result, activity on alternative trading systems is not fully disclosed to, or accessible by, public investors. The trading activity on these systems may not be adequately surveilled for market manipulation and fraud. Moreover, these trading systems have no obligation to provide investors a fair opportunity to participate in their systems or to treat their participants fairly; nor do they have an obligation to ensure that they have sufficient capacity to handle trading demand. These concerns together with the increasingly important role of alternative trading systems, call into question the fairness of current regulatory requirements, the effectiveness of existing NMS mechanisms, and the quality of public secondary markets.[52]

In its discussion of market access and fairness, the SEC stressed that although institutional participation in the US securities markets had grown enormously, there was still a very large participation, both direct and indirect, by individuals in the markets. Given that the needs of different types of investors differed at times, the SEC noted that a range of aspects of the regulatory structure imposed on exchanges was intended to ensure that 'diverse investors are treated fairly and have fair access to investment opportunities'.[53] These included that exchanges are required to consider the public interest in administering their markets, to set reasonable fees, to allocate them equitably, to establish rules designed to admit members fairly, and to establish rules to assure fair representation of members and investors in selecting their directors and administering their organizations. The current market regulation was also seen as being designed to remove bar-riers to competition by prohibiting exchange rules from being anti-competitive, and by requiring the Commission to review them.

In contrast, the SEC argued that,

under the current regulatory approach . . . there is no regulatory redress for unfair denials or limitations of access by alternative trading systems, or for unreasonably discriminatory actions taken against, or retaliatory fees imposed upon, participants in these systems.[54]

The Commission accepted that,

the availability of redress for such discriminatory actions may not be critical when alternative trading systems disclose any discriminatory practices to their participants and when market participants are able to substitute the services of one alternative trading system with those of another.[55]

It maintained, however, that,

when an alternative trading system has no other serious competitor, such as when it has a significantly large percentage of the volume of trading, discriminatory actions may be anti-competitive because market participants must use such trading system to remain competitive.[56]

The Commission was similarly concerned about anti-competitive situations arising from the lack of a mandatory regulatory review of the rules and operational structure of alternative trading systems.

The SEC's worries about market transparency and coordination mirrored the concerns it raised in its discussion of the ECN rules. It noted the increasing inter-dependence of markets, as a result of the 'opportunities technology provides to link products, implement complex hedging strategies across markets, and trade on multiple markets'.[57] While these factors were accepted as benefiting many investors, the SEC claimed, however, that 'they can also create misallocations of capital, widespread inefficiency, and trading fragmentation if markets do not coordinate. Moreover, a lack of coordination among markets can increase system-wide risks.' The development of the NMS was seen, partially, as a response 'to address the potential negative effects of a proliferation of markets'.

The existence of two-tiered markets was again taken to be evidence that a failure to coordinate fully the trading on alternative trading systems into NMS mechanisms had impaired the quality and pricing efficiency of secondary equity markets. While the Commission argued that this had been partially resolved by its ECN rules, it noted that these were not intended to coordinate fully all trading on alternative trading systems with public market trading. In particular, the ECN rules did not require that the quotes submitted by participants other than market makers and specialists be integrated in the CQS. Furthermore, the ECNs themselves, as opposed to the dealers trading on them, were under no obligation to integrate any of the orders submitted to them into the CQS. The SEC also claimed that, 'because a majority of trading interest on alternative trading systems is not integrated into the national market system, price transparency is impaired and dissemination of quotation information is incomplete'.[58]

Two major faults in the current regulatory structure with regards to market surveillance were identified by the SEC. The first was that because the broker-regulated alternative trading systems were not SROs, they did not have the same market-wide enforcement and surveillance obligations that the registered exchanges and the NASD did. The second was that the SROs' programmes of surveillance for fraud, insider trading and manipulation, did not adequately cover the trading activity undertaken on the alternative trading systems operated by the SROs' members. The SEC noted, in particular, that the NASD only received information about trades executed on members' trading systems after they had been executed, and that in some instances participants trading on alternative trading systems could not be identified, given that only the trading systems themselves were identified as the counter-parties to all trades executed between participants on their systems.

The SEC was also anxious that aspects of the exchange/broker distinction meant that there was insufficient regulation to ensure market stability and prevent systemic risks. It noted that each exchange was required to have an ongoing programme to monitor its system's capacity, integrity, and security, whereas alternative trading systems had no such responsibilities. The SEC believed this jeopardized its efforts to 'ensure that all trade execution centers will remain operational during periods of market stress'.[59]

International Issues

Any analysis of the international regulation of securities markets must answer the question of how regulatory costs, responsibilities, and powers should be allocated internationally. Various approaches have been proposed to address this issue.[60] These include national treatment, namely the identical treatment of all institutions in a particular jurisdiction, whether they are domestic or foreign; international harmonization; mutual recognition; identical international standards; a lead-regulator approach; the formation of a supranational regulatory authority; and regulatory competition and arbitrage. Although the merits of these various approaches are not examined here, two aspects of the ISD, to date the only supranational law that does determine how cross-border trading systems should be regulated within a specified set of jurisdictions, are discussed.[61] Both illustrate the difficulties in agreeing appropriate international legislation for the regulation of trading systems, and both have particular relevance for the exchange/broker distinction.

The first general difficulty highlighted by the ISD is that the development of such legislation, however pro-competitive in intention, may paradoxically entrench protectionist tendencies.[62] The Treaty of Rome establishes the fundamental European freedoms of movement and of establishment, and also requires that competition in the EU not be inhibited in an inappropriate manner. Furthermore, a key intention of the EU's Single Market legislative programme, of which the ISD is an important part, is to further the pro-competitive goal of economic liberalism. Nevertheless, throughout the negotiations in which the ISD was discussed, various attempts were made to create a law that restricted competition between the markets of the EU, all in the name of enhancing fairness and investor protection.[63] A non-competitive outcome could therefore easily have occurred. Even now that what appears to be a pro-competitive Directive has been agreed, various elements of the Directive may still allow national authorities to establish national law in a manner which suits their national markets, but not any competing markets from other Member States.

An important example of this, in the context of securities trading systems, arises from an ambiguity in the ISD about how the 'remote access' provision in the Directive should be interpreted.[64] This provision states that a Member State must allow the regulated markets of other Member States to provide 'appropriate facilities' within its jurisdiction, in order to enable its investment firms to become remote members of, or have access to, the other Member States' regulated markets. A trading system classified as a regulated market that operates without the need for a physical presence, should therefore be allowed to place its automated facilities in Member States of the EU other than the one in which it is based, without the need for any regulatory recognition other than that required by its home Member State.

The problem is that it is unclear whether it is the 'regulated' market itself, or the competent authority in the host Member State in which the 'regulated' market wishes to operate, that has the right to decide what is 'appropriate'. If it is the competent authority in the host Member State, an automated trading system classified as a regulated market may want to provide facilities which it deemed appropriate, but which the relevant competent authority did not. Regulators in some European countries may seek to halt the success of trading systems not based in their jurisdiction, and the benefits sanctioned by the 'remote access' provision may thus be unavailable to such trading systems. There is also a risk to an automated trading system of not being classified as a 'regulated' market. One French regulator has stated, for example, that the delivery of a European passport to non-'regulated' electronic markets was 'clearly inconsistent with the objectives of the ISD'.[65]

A second problem with the ISD is that it maintains a conceptual difference analogous to that between 'brokers' and 'exchanges', in the dichotomy it draws between 'investment firms' and 'regulated markets'. Those automated trading systems that are able to gain approval as investment firms will be required to undertake significantly fewer regulatory duties than those classified as regulated markets, while still being able to take advantage of the European 'passport'. Problems similar to those which have arisen as a result of the exchange/broker distinction, are therefore also likely to arise as a result of the investment firm/regulated market dichotomy. Harmonization between the securities laws of different jurisdictions, by itself, is thus not sufficient to resolve the questions associated with the international regulation of automated trading systems.

ALTERNATIVE REGULATORY STRATEGIES

While there is now wide agreement that the exchange/broker distinction has lead to serious flaws in the regulatory structure for exchanges and trading systems, the lack of unanimity about the nature and importance of these defects has meant that different reforms have been thought optimal. An evaluation of various alternative approaches to the classification and regulation of exchanges and trading systems is presented in this section. The costs and benefits of three general strategies are examined first of all. These strategies are to change the definition of an exchange, to employ purely 'functional regulation', and to extend the 'limited volume' approach. The two proposals put forward by the SEC in its Concept Release are then analysed, and finally, a joint strategy of separating the regulation of market structure from that of other areas of concern, and of employing competition policy to regulate market structure, is discussed. This last approach is recommended as the best policy.

Change the 'Exchange' Definition

The purpose of having an exchange definition is to be able to identify and classify institutions according to the regulation which it is believed that they require. If the definition is ambiguous, any regulatory commission implementing it will have great leeway as to how to interpret it. At the same time, however, the more ambiguous the definition is, the more likely will it be that the relevant commission's interpretations come under legal threat. The chief effect of an ambiguous definition will therefore be to increase the uncertainty surrounding the control of the financial markets. If a regulatory commission's decisions are questioned in the courts, two judicial responses are probable. The first, as in the Delta case, is to recognize the flexibility in the definition, and reinforce the commission's power to interpret the definition as it sees fit. The second is to attempt to prescribe the limits within which the agency must operate. Given that most courts do not have the expertise required to do this, they are likely to follow the first path.

Any attempt to define some form of intermediate institution between an exchange and a broker, and to apply some intermediate regulatory requirements to any institutions satisfying this new definition, is likely to fail. This was tried by the SEC in 1989 in its proposed rule 15c2-10.[66] The SEC proposed the rule because it believed that the exchange definition was unsatisfactory as it encompassed too wide a range of trading systems. While it believed that imposing the full panoply of exchange obligations on to PTSs was inappropriate, it also believed that more was needed than merely the standard broker-dealer requirements. The proposed rule did not contain a definition of the term 'proprietary', but did define a trading system to be:

any system providing for the dissemination outside the sponsor and its affiliates of indications of interest, quotations, or orders to purchase or sell securities, and providing procedures for executing or settling transactions in such securities.

Three exceptions to the definition were also proposed. In particular, it was not to apply to systems that were operated by broker-dealers solely for their own use or for the use of their own retail customers, to certain systems operated by brokers' brokers for non-equity (primarily government and municipal) securities, and to trading and information facilities operated by registered exchanges.

The proposed rule was finally retracted in 1994.[67] Although not stated explicitly, one reason why was because the proposed definition was ambiguous in the very area which it hoped to clarify, namely in the definition of what a PTS should be. Given the first exclusion in the definition, it is likely that most brokers would not have fallen within the scope of the definition had it ever been implemented. In addition, a comparison of the definitions of a PTS, an exchange, and a broker shows that it is hard to find any substantive differences between them. What is the provision of a 'market place' (a criterion from the exchange definition), if it is not the provision of 'indications of interest, quotations, or orders to purchase or sell securities', and of 'procedures for executing or settling transactions in such securities' (a criterion from the PTS definition)? Similarly, what is it that 'any person engaged in the business of effecting transactions in securities for the account of others' does (a criterion from the broker definition), other than disseminate 'indications of interest, quotations, or orders to purchase or sell securities', and provide 'procedures for executing or settling transactions in such securities'?

There are several problems with attempting to clarify the 'exchange' definition by making it more precise. The first is that the attempt will fail, in that many of the criteria which might be employed in such a definition are as difficult to assess objectively as those in the current definition. The notion of liquidity, for example, is controversial. A further problem is that it may become easier for a trading system which the commission believes should be regulated as an exchange, to escape falling within the definition by implementing appropriate but minor functional changes.

'Functional' Regulation

Almost all the analyses of how to regulate automated trading systems have suggested that 'functional' regulation may be the most appropriate method to employ.[68] The functional approach is to impose a level of regulation on a trading system that is dependent on the functions it undertakes. It is self-evident that some form of functional regulation must be employed in order to identify those activities that a regulator deems are of public concern. At a minimum, a regulator needs to identify those institutions which operate in the securities market, and of these it may need to select those which provide mechanisms for the execution of trades. Both these characteristics are functional attributes of the institutions in question. A pure functional approach does, however, have several shortcomings.

The prime reason used to support functional regulation is that it is believed that what a trading system does, rather than what it is called, should determine how the system should be regulated. It is argued that functional regulation is able to deliver this objective, in contrast to institutional regulation. This purported advantage of the functional over the institutional approach is, however, exaggerated as the distinction between functional and institutional regulation is blurred at best. Under an institutional approach, the definitions of the relevant institutions are typically written in terms of the functions they undertake. What an exchange is, in particular, is defined in terms of what it does. At least conceptually, therefore, it would be possible to create a different category of institution for each relevant set of functions undertaken by a trading system. The regulatory outcomes under both institutional and functional regimes would then be indistinguishable. It is true that having once created a set of institutional definitions, they may be difficult to change. While advances in technology may then make these historical definitions redundant or unstable, it is questionable whether any functional definitions could be any more relevant or stable over time than their institutional counterparts.

A second hoped-for benefit of functional regulation is that it might be able to delineate precisely the distinction between brokers and exchanges, something that institutional regulation has signally failed to do. This hope is unlikely to be realized, however. The ambiguities inherent in the institutional definitions of exchanges and brokers will not be avoided by using a functional approach. This is evident in the uncertainties that have arisen in the SEC's analysis of the statutory exchange definition, and in the two criteria it developed in its exchange interpretation. Both the definition and the SEC's interpretation turn on the functions that exchanges are believed to undertake. The hope also ignores the reality that brokers and exchanges do actually compete with each other in the provision of trading services. Although the development of automated broker-operated trading systems has brought awareness of this competition to the fore, it is not a new phenomenon. Brokers have always competed with exchanges. In the past, however, such competition used merely to be called internalization.

A further unfulfillable promise of a functional approach is that it may provide a solution to the difficulties that have arisen in reaching agreement on the best way of regulating market structure. It is sometimes implied that because the determination of the functions that a trading system undertakes is essentially a technical activity, it may be possible to adopt a similarly neutral approach to the determination of the regulation relevant to each function. This is an illusion. Agreement that a functional approach should be employed is not sufficient to determine what regulation should be implemented. At a minimum, this requires a specification of the objectives that regulation should aim to deliver, an analysis of the way in which the functioning of trading systems in the absence of regulation restricts the attainment of these objectives, and a determination of the regulation needed to deliver the chosen objectives. Functional regulation by itself contains no assessment of the risks or costs arising from the operation of different trading systems.

A 'Limited Volume' Approach

A third general strategy for the classification and regulation of trading systems is to extend the 'limited volume' approach specified in the SEA, and define a trading system to be an exchange as soon as it attracts a pre-specified minimum volume of trading. An advantage of this approach is that once the definition of what 'limited volume' consists of has been specified, it may be relatively clear which institutions will fall within the exemption and which not.[69] Furthermore, such an approach explicitly recognizes the fact that the existence of a large amount of volume on a trading system is an important factor increasing public pressure for appropriate regulation to be put in place concerning the trading on the system, not least in stopping anti-competitive activity.

The employment of such a definition would have several implications. It would tend to encourage start-up trading systems, but to penalize the success of a trading system. If a trading system attracted relatively large amounts of business, it would then be required to undertake more regulatory responsibilities, and this might constrain its future growth. This might in turn lead to a proliferation of small exchanges, each of which is established in response to the growing size of existing exchanges. There would also be an incentive to hide the amount of trading conducted on particular trading systems so as to avoid the need to register as an exchange. Finally, and obviously, it would foster the development of small-volume trading systems which were more lightly regulated than the major centres. This could be seen as an unfair competitive advantage to such small systems, and also socially undesirable because investors would not be so well protected on them as elsewhere.

The SEC's Proposals

The prime aim of the SEC's 1997 Concept Release was to provide responses to what it perceived to be the problems with the exchange/broker distinction. Central to the Commission's proposals was its view that,

within the existing regulatory framework, the issues currently associated with alternative trading systems could be addressed in large part by integrating alternative trading systems more effectively into national market system mechanisms.[70]

The Commission put forward two alternative and exclusive ways of doing this: first, by enhancing the current broker-dealer regulatory framework, and, second, by re-interpreting the exchange definition, and simultaneously establishing an exchange tiering strategy. The second policy was preferred by the SEC. Both options are described here, and then their merits and weaknesses are assessed.

Enhanced Broker-Dealer Regulation
The first approach suggested by the SEC to integrate alternative trading systems into the existing regulatory structure for market oversight was to enhance the current broker-dealer regulatory framework. A raft of changes were believed necessary to do so. The voluntary approach of the ECN rules would have to be changed, so that broker-dealers that operated alternative trading systems would be obliged to provide information about the orders on their systems to the CQS, rather than merely being permitted to do so. In addition, broker-dealer alternative trading systems would be obliged to disseminate information about all orders on their systems, and not just those submitted by dealers. They would also have to provide public access to all orders entered on their systems.

The surveillance of alternative trading systems would have to be more closely linked with those of their SROs, in particular by providing more timely and fuller audit trails to the SROs. The identities of all counter-parties to all trades on alternative trading systems would have to be released to the relevant SROs. Information provided by alternative trading systems to their SROs about non-listed, and other less standard, securities would also have to be increased. Real-time transmission of information about executed trades from alternative trading systems to their SROs would also have to be effected. An alternative trading system's SRO would also have to be provided with information about its operations, including its order execution algorithm, to a much greater extent, than currently obtained. Finally, alternative trading systems would have to demonstrate that they had sufficient systems capacity, security, and safety procedures.

The SEC identified three problems with this suggestion of broadening the broker-dealer regulatory framework so as to integrate alternative trading systems into the NMS. The first was that alternative trading systems would still not be subject to any requirements designed to ensure the fair treatment of investors. In particular, the SEC noted there was no regulatory redress for any unreasonably discriminatory rule of an alternative trading system. The greater the overall trading volume that such systems captured, especially if there were no viable alternatives to trading on them, and the more that they consistently displayed better prices than exchange systems, the more this was viewed as being problematic. The second difficulty was that broker-dealers operating alternative trading systems would still be subject to potentially inapplicable regulation, and still be subject to oversight by their SROs, namely potential or actual competitors. This problem would probably be exacerbated with the more intrusive examination by SROs of broker-dealer systems that would be necessary. The SEC did note, however, that it could be solved by having an association of brokers establish an

SRO that did not operate a market. The last concern was that alternative trading systems would still be free to engage in anti-competitive activities.

Re-Interpretation of the Exchange Definition and Exchange Tiering

The second approach proposed, and indeed recommended by, the SEC as being able to integrate alternative trading systems more fully into the NMS was to re-interpret the definition of an 'exchange', and to establish an exchange tiering (ET) policy. The SEC proposed broadening its interpretation of the definition to include,

any organization that both: (1) consolidates orders of multiple parties; and (2) provides a facility through which, or sets material conditions under which, participants entering such orders may agree to the terms of a trade.[71]

The SEC also noted that,

the term 'orders' . . . is intended to be read broadly, to include any firm trading interest. This would include both limit orders and market maker quotations.[72]

The Commission then suggested that three tiers of exchanges be identified, and that different regulatory obligations be imposed on institutions classified in each of the tiers. The first tier was to include those trading systems that either had a limited trading volume, such as start-up systems, or that operated wholly or primarily passive pricing mechanisms. These systems would not be required to register as exchanges, and would thereby gain exemption from the majority of exchange obligations, being subject to only a limited set of duties. Such duties might include guaranteeing that they had sufficient system capacity, confidentiality, and integrity. If an exempted exchange gained a sufficient amount of trading, it would, however, be required to register and be fully regulated in one of the other two regulatory categories.

The second tier of exchanges the SEC proposed establishing was to include those alternative trading systems with both a large volume of trading and active price discovery. The Commission proposed that these systems, which the SEC also referred to as 'proprietary' and 'non-traditional', register as exchanges, and be subject to the fundamental statutory requirements currently applicable to national securities exchanges. These would include that they be required to file for registration, to comply and enforce compliance with the appropriate federal laws, to prevent fraudulent and manipulative activity, to promote just and equitable principles of trade, to refrain from anti-competitive activity, to assure regulatory oversight of their participants, to participate in the NMS, and to take the public interest into account in administering their markets.

The SEC did observe, however, that many alternative trading systems did not fit well into the statutory framework which was aimed primarily at nonprofit membership exchanges. It accepted that many alternative trading systems 'had adopted different corporate structures than the traditional non-profit membership exchanges and . . . [had] entered into primarily commercial relationships with their participants'.[73] In order not to constrain such trading systems from adopting innovative means of furthering the exchange obligations, the SEC proposed that they be exempted from specific requirements not believed critical for the achievement of the objectives of the SEA. Two were particularly important. The Commission first proposed that alternative trading systems be allowed to provide direct access to their institutional customers, as opposed to being allowed to provide access only to broker-dealers, as the statutory membership constraints would require. While there were several statutory ways in which this might be accommodated, each would effectively allow the Commission to continue imposing the same obligations on broker-dealers with access to such systems, as it did on broker-dealers trading on traditional exchanges. Each of the options would also allow the Commission to apply whatever regulatory requirements it believed necessary on those institutional investors granted direct access to alternative trading systems.

The second area where the Commission believed that the imposition of traditional constraints on alternative trading systems might be inappropriate concerned the 'fair representation' requirements. If such governance requirements were imposed on alternative trading systems, the SEC argued it could require substantive changes both in the way in which alternative trading systems operated, and in their relationships with their participants. The Commission therefore suggested that alternative trading systems should be allowed to meet these requirements in non-traditional ways. It noted that the fair representation of members on a traditional exchange did not necessarily mean that all members had to be given equal rights at the exchange, and also that clearing agencies employed several methods to comply with the fair representation requirement. The Commission then argued that,

other [non-traditional] structures may also provide independent, fair representation for an exchange's constituencies in its material decisionmaking process, for exchanges that are not owned by their participants. For example, an alternative trading system that registers as an exchange might be able to fulfill this requirement by establishing an independent subsidiary that has final, binding responsibility for bringing and adjudicating disciplinary proceedings and rule making processes for the exchange, and ensuring that the governance of such subsidiary equitably represents the exchange's participants.[74]

The third tier of exchanges the SEC proposed establishing was to include the traditional exchanges, with non-profit and membership structures, which would continue to be regulated in the same way as before.

A central implication of the ET policy was that both the tier two and tier three exchanges, namely the alternative trading systems and the traditional exchanges, would have to be fully integrated into the NMS mechanisms, specifically the CQS, the CTA, and the ITS.[75] The SEC stated that the NMS would have to be reorganized to achieve this, noting its belief that,

integrating newly registered national securities exchanges into the NMS mechanisms should not cause the homogenizing of all markets—to the contrary, it is as important today as it was in 1975 to cultivate an atmosphere in which innovation is welcome and possible. Such integration therefore could require revision of NMS mechanisms so that they could accommodate diverse and evolving markets.[76]

The SEC claimed that,

participation in these transaction reporting plans should not seriously impair the function-ing of most alternative trading systems.[77]

The Commission noted several key rules of the ITS that alternative trading systems would have to follow, including the 'trade-through' rules, which require that members of participant markets avoid initiating a purchase or sale at a worse price than that available to another ITS market, the 'locked market' rules, govern-ing how trades are executed when a bid price is input that is higher than the high-est offer price (and vice versa), and the rules governing block trades.[78] The SEC did accept that,

some practices of alternative trading systems would undoubtedly conflict with the current provisions of the ITS plan, or would be incompatible with participation in ITS. For ex-ample, many alternative trading systems allow participants to trade in smaller increments than those available on current plan participants. Similarly, many alternative trading systems have institutional participants who may prefer to trade at an inferior price in order to trade in a larger size, resulting in a locked or crossed market.[79]

The Commission also commented on its policy of reviewing the rules of SROs. This was stated as being essential to stop anti-competitive activities, and to ensure that the SROs carried out their regulatory obligations vigilantly and effectively. The Commission did acknowledge, however, that the time required for solicita-tion and review of public comments could delay the implementation of innova-tive proposals. It therefore raised the possibility of exempting SROs from the need to submit certain rules designed to implement new trading systems during the development and initial operating stages of such systems.[80]

Comments

Some of the problems the SEC identified with the current regulatory structure are indeed very awkward. A number of the solutions the SEC proposed to resolve these problems are appropriate, but there is, nevertheless, a sufficient range of significant shortcomings both in the SEC's interpretation of what the problems with the exchange/broker distinction are, and in its responses to these problems, to mean that the broad thrust of its proposals in the Concept Release are funda-mentally flawed.

Recognize first the merits of some of the SEC's claims and proposals. It argued that the current regulatory structure was unsuitable with regards some of the activities of alternative trading systems, and responded by suggesting that unnecessary obligations on broker-dealers operating such systems be removed. The Commission maintained that the current structure provided inadequate surveillance to prevent market manipulation and fraud on alternative trading systems, and proposed that they be required to provide full real-time information about details of their quotes and trades, and the identities of relevant participants, to their SROs. The Commission claimed that it had insufficient legal backing to ensure market stability and prevent systemic risks on alternative trading systems, unlike on exchanges, and responded that greater scrutiny be undertaken of alternative trading systems' capacity, security, and safety procedures. Disregarding the question of whether the Commission should generally ensure that trading systems have sufficient capacity and security, rather than whether it should do so merely of exchanges, these three concerns are accepted as valid here, and the responses to them are believed appropriate.[81]

The Commission also noted that the current regulatory framework gave it insufficient power to ensure that alternative trading systems did not engage in anti-competitive behaviour, such as unfair denials and limitations of access, or unreasonably discriminatory actions taken against, or retaliatory fees imposed upon, participants. In response, the Commission suggested that more power be granted to it to prevent such activities. While it is once again accepted that the Commission should have sufficient legal backing to prevent such anti-competitive activity, this does not imply, as discussed below, that the fair representation requirements or similarly the rule review procedures should be imposed on alternative trading systems.

An acceptance of the validity of the above arguments and proposals of the Commission does not imply the necessity of supporting the thrust of either its enhanced broker-dealer regulatory strategy or its ET approach. There are too many problems with them to do so. Consider first the critical issue of ambiguity, an inescapable implication of the ET strategy that is problematic in two ways. The first concerns the distinction between alternative trading systems, or tier two exchanges, and institutions traditionally not categorized as exchanges. Unlike the past policy of the SEC when it attempted to identify and define a PTS as a regulatory category between an exchange and a broker, the SEC explicitly tried in the Concept Release to make its new 'exchange' definition cover a broad range of trading systems, including both traditional exchanges and alternative trading systems, while still excluding the traditional regulatory categories of broker-dealers, securities associations, IDBs, information vendors, and bulletin boards.[82] The SEC argued in particular that there was a difference between broker-dealer activities and those undertaken by exchanges, identifying three distinguishing characteristics. These were, first, that,

unlike organized markets, traditional broker-dealer activities do not involve the systematic interaction of customer orders where the customers themselves are informed of and have an opportunity to agree to the terms of their trades (or agree to the priorities under which the terms will be set).[83]

Second, broker-dealers traditionally retain discretion in determining how to handle customer orders. Finally, the SEC excluded from the exchange definition single market maker systems that 'merely provided a more efficient means of communicating the trading interest of separate customers to one dealer', and thus did not aim to centralize, cross or match customer orders between each other. Notwithstanding the hope of the SEC, significant ambiguity between the classification of traditional brokerage activities and alternative trading systems still, however, remains. The Commission did indeed accept this, noting that,

much of this analysis [i.e. of the functions undertaken by traditional broker-dealers] assumes that these activities are being engaged in 'systematically,' or in a 'traditional' or 'typical' fashion. The Commission recognizes that these concepts are not easily defined and that this approach will leave many issues and gray areas to be resolved.[84]

Similar problems were accepted by the SEC in distinguishing bulletin boards and IDBs from alternative trading systems. The key issue is whether such ambiguity is sufficiently important to lead to regulatory problems. There are two reasons to believe that it will be.

The first is that brokers operating trading systems will strive not to be classified as tier two exchanges. Those trading systems the SEC hopes to capture within its new definition may therefore be able to change their modes of operation in marginal ways so as to avoid the definition while still carrying out much the same type of functions. The second reason is that the SEC's approach will continue to penalize those brokers that operate automated systems to the advantage of those that do not. A cynical view of the ET approach is that it aims to ensure that full information is published by, and access provided to, only those systems for which the SEC can enforce such obligations, precisely because they are automated and can thus relatively easily provide appropriate information and access. The policy is not designed to apply to those systems that would find it difficult to provide information and access, namely the traditional non-automated brokers, even when the internal logic of the SEC's arguments dictated that they too provide the relevant information and access. Indeed, this logic will inevitably put pressure on the Commission to extend its policy and itself test the validity of the tier two definition. If the Commission believes that investors should have information about and access to the best orders in the market, why does it matter that the orders are submitted to what it terms a 'single market maker' system or to an IDB? The SEC should require that these prices and trades should also be publicly available.

The other area where ambiguity will play a crucial role is in the fundamental assumption underlying the ET strategy that alternative trading systems and traditional exchanges can be separated into different tiers. Both the consistency and the economic rationale of this assumption are flawed. The SEC's distinction between the two types of prospective exchanges turns on the term 'proprietary'. There has been much controversy about what this term signifies. The term is generally used to refer to the ownership rights associated with a trading system or exchange. The most important such rights on any single system include the right to trade on the system, the right to view the price and quote information it generates, the right to its residual profits or dividends, management rights, and governance or control rights. These various rights are often confused.

Three common usages of the term 'proprietary' may be identified. It has been used to refer to trading systems that are not operated by a regulated exchange or an SRO.[85] It has been used to denote systems operated by an individual intermediary, as opposed to those operated by an exchange, defined variously as a grouping of many market intermediaries, an association, or a membership organization.[86] In this context, it has also been used to describe the goals of the owners of a trading system as being self-interested, in contrast to those of membership-operated trading systems that are said to have as their goal the advancement of the public interest. Finally, it has been used to designate systems that are run on a for-profit basis.

None of these definitions are useful in determining which systems should fall within which of the SEC's proposed exchange tiers. The first is tautological and thus cannot be employed to identify whether a proprietary trading system should itself be an SRO. As for the second usage, there is no clear link between the number of owners of a trading system and the extent to which regulation of the system is necessary. Furthermore, the distinction between the private interest and the public interest supposedly identified in this definition is too simplistic to be a practical criterion for classifying trading systems. Not only may the pursuit by a trading system of its private interest be in the public interest, membership-operated trading systems are as liable to pursue their own private interests as are trading systems with other governance structures. More importantly, the separation between membership and non-membership exchanges is breaking down, as the various rights associated with membership, such as the trading, dividend, and governance rights, are progressively unbundled and allocated to different groups of market participants at different exchanges.

The third criterion of the profitable status of a trading system is a similarly inappropriate criterion. The only unequivocal way of categorizing trading systems by profitable status is their corporate legal status. This legal status, however, has little relevance for the economic behaviour of an exchange. The SEC implicitly assumes that if a system operates under a non-profit legal status it will require different regulatory oversight than if it does not. There is, however, no easy correlation between the behaviour of exchanges and their corporate governance structures. So-called 'nonprofit' exchanges, for example, may seek to maximize profits and disburse these by reducing exchange and information fees rather than handing out dividends.

The distinction between tier two and tier three exchanges, namely between alternative trading systems and traditional membership exchanges, is important because the SEC proposed applying different regulatory obligations on the different tiers, specifically concerning fair representation and direct access by institutional investors. There is, however, no rational basis for applying such different regulatory regimes. No answer has been provided, and no economically justifiable answer could be provided, for why traditional systems should be subject to different governance and access constraints than those imposed on alternative trading systems. Put differently, if such constraints are invalid for alternative trading systems, why should traditional exchanges be subject to them?

There is a further problem with the SEC's fair representation proposals for alternative trading systems. The Commission proposed that such systems be required to ensure some form of fair representation requirements, even if in a non-traditional way. It argued that if they were obliged to do so, it would still be possible for them to operate commercially on a for-profit basis and with a non-membership structure. The Commission noted, for example, that the fair representation requirements might be satisfied if an alternative trading system established a subsidiary on which fair representation was guaranteed. The SEC's optimism on this issue is, however, unwarranted.

Only two organizational outcomes are possible. On the one hand, a trading system may be free to adopt whatever corporate structure it chooses and take decisions on whatever commercial grounds it believes appropriate. This does not imply that the trading system would not take account of the views of all the diverse participants on its market; indeed not to do so is likely to lead to a loss in business. It does imply, however, that the system would not be obliged to take such views into account. On the other hand, a trading system may be required to provide some form of fair representation to the various participants on its market. This does not imply that all decisions relevant for the management of the trading system would be taken on a non-commercial basis. It does imply, however, that there may be circumstances when as a result of the fair representation requirements, the trading system would be required to pursue a course of action that it would not choose to undertake on commercial grounds. The problem is that either the governance constraints imposed on a trading system bind, or they do not. The SEC's suggestion that an alternative trading system could satisfy the fair representation requirements while still retaining the power to take decisions on commercial grounds, for example by creating an appropriately governed subsidiary, merely pushes the conflict between the two goals to a different level of the organization. The proposal does not, and cannot, resolve the conflict between binding and non-binding constraints.

The most important flaw with the SEC's approach is one that was noted in the previous chapter, and is discussed in more detail below. It is the falsehood of the key premise on which its proposals are based, namely that 'within the existing regulatory framework, the issues currently associated with alternative trading systems could be addressed in large part by integrating alternative trading systems more effectively into national market system mechanisms'. Unless competition is impaired, private incentives are believed to be best able to deliver an appropriate market structure. Given this, the ambiguities in the ET strategy, and the difficulties in justifying why alternative trading systems should be treated in a different regulatory manner from traditional exchanges, it is argued here that the SEC's proposed approaches in its Concept Release are fundamentally flawed.

Separation and Competition

The final regulatory strategy examined, and indeed recommended, here as the best way of regulating trading systems, is composed of two prongs: the separation of the regulation of market structure from the regulation of other areas of public concern, and the employment of competition policy to regulate market structure. Given the frequent confusion that exists about the meaning of the phrase 'market structure', it is worth repeating that the phrase is used here to refer to the combination of the three key market functions of order routing, order execution, and information dissemination. The nature of, and justifications for, the proposed joint strategy, are discussed. Two important sets of implications of the approach are then analysed. They concern, respectively, the desirability and possibility of separating market structure from other regulatory concerns, and the effects of simultaneous competition and cooperation between trading systems. The approach recommended here obviously aims to address the problems both with the current exchange/broker distinction, and with the SEC's proposed, but flawed, solutions.

Nature and Justification

The first prong of the joint strategy proposed here is that the regulation of market structure should be separated from the regulation of other areas of public concern. The most significant of these are market conduct, in particular the activities of financial intermediaries and other market participants, and market integrity, which relates to issues such as price manipulation and insider trading. The second prong is that competition policy should be employed to regulate market structure. The reason for proposing this joint strategy is to accommodate two beliefs that are thought central in determining the most appropriate way of regulating and classifying trading systems. They are, first, that competition is the single most important factor in effecting a market structure that will best deliver the desired regulatory goals, and second, that the regulation of competition between trading systems cannot be well executed via a self-regulatory process.

As previously discussed, the claim that competition is the most important factor in effecting an optimal market structure is controversial. There is first of all debate as to whether private incentives are best placed to deliver the goal of efficiency. A full examination of their merits in effecting optimal market structure is not presented here. The value of rivalry between trading systems has been discussed at length elsewhere.[87] The advantages of allowing market participants to determine appropriate levels of transparency have been highlighted in previous chapters. The key reason why there is no need for a mandated order-routing system, such as the ITS, is based on similar arguments. There are sufficient private incentives for market participants to create and sell private order-routing facilities, as by doing so they enhance the possibility of achieving better executions and facilitate arbitrage.

A further controversial aspect of using competition as a regulatory policy is that even if it is accepted that private incentives do deliver efficiency, there is debate about the extent to which other regulatory goals should be sacrificed in the pursuit of efficiency. No logical resolution of this issue is possible, as it is essentially a matter of preferences. Unlike what is believed by the SEC, however, it is believed here that significant trade-offs between the attainment of different regulatory goals are commonplace. In order to select any regulatory policy, it is therefore critical to make a ranking by importance of the different regulatory goals. Efficiency is taken to be a key goal here, not least because its delivery is thought to enhance that of fairness and the other desirable goals.

The justification for the second belief underlying the proposed separation, namely that the regulation of competition between trading systems cannot be well monitored via a self-regulatory process, is that the conflict between the interests of the owners and operators of one trading system and those of other trading systems is deemed too direct for self-regulation to be effective. It is certainly possible that an increased amount of trading in one asset on one system may lead to increased trading volume in that asset on other competing systems. More commonly, however, trading systems are viewed as substitutes rather than complements, implying that if one trading system does not compete as aggressively as possible, orders will flow away from it to its competitors.[88] The operators of a trading system therefore typically have an incentive to act anti-competitively, if such an option is available, in order to attract order-flow. Self-regulation is thus insufficient to enforce fair competition between trading systems.

The costs and benefits of employing competition as a regulatory policy to supervise market conduct and market integrity are not examined here. As noted by the SEC, however, past experience is taken to be sufficient evidence that the private incentives facing market participants are not adequate to ensure that unacceptable lapses in market conduct and in market integrity do not occur.[89] Regulatory intervention in these areas is therefore believed warranted, and indeed may be undertaken in much the same manner as it has been done in the past in both the securities and futures markets, namely via a process of self-regulation with appropriate governmental agency oversight.

Although the separation strategy proposed here has no implications for how such self-regulation should be organized, it is evident that such a policy will remain subject to the criticism that the members of an SRO whose duty is to further the public interest, may in fact regulate the markets the exchange operates to their own advantage. Two main strategies have been used to minimize the harmful effects of such conflicts: the imposition of constraints on the composition of the governing boards of exchanges, and the judicial response of developing a conduct for directors of exchanges according to which they are presumed to have obligations to the public, and must therefore not act in 'bad faith' contrary to these obligations.

As discussed in Chapter 9, conflicts of interests occur in a particularly acute form on futures exchanges when they are confronted with an emergency situation. Notwithstanding some vociferous complaints, both the courts and the CFTC have concluded that the actions of exchange boards in such situations have rarely been contaminated by inappropriate director behaviour. Nevertheless, in 1992 Congress passed a requirement aimed at reducing the presence of conflicts of interests on the governing boards of futures exchanges. It stipulated that exchange directors abstain from voting on any significant exchange action that would not be submitted to the CFTC for its prior approval, if they knowingly had a direct and substantial financial interest in the result of the vote. It is believed here that such an attempted reduction of conflicts of interest on exchange boards should only be undertaken in extreme conditions, given that the precise aim of self-regulation is to provide participation by knowledgeable and interested observers.[90] A requirement for such people to abstain would exclude the very participants the policy of self-regulation sought to promote.[91] Excessive bias on exchange boards should in most circumstances therefore continue to be prevented by ensuring a diversity of representation on such boards and by a general stipulation that directors act in bad faith.

A central implication of the separation approach proposed here is that there should be no distinction in the regulation of any market structure questions between institutions which are now classified as exchanges and those which are now classified as brokers. If the approach were implemented, ambiguities in the 'exchange' definition with regards to market structure would no longer matter because the definition would no longer be applicable. Problems concerning market structure arising from the re-classification of trading systems, from the incoherence of both the SEC's past approach for classifying trading systems and of the enhanced broker-dealer framework and the ET strategy it has proposed for the future, from any competitive advantages accruing to broker-dealers that arise as a result of regulatory diversity, and from the regulatory rigidities placed on exchanges, would also all no longer be relevant.

The proposed joint strategy does not specify how the regulatory responsibilities currently placed on SROs other than for issues related to market structure should be allocated. Three problems have been identified with the allocation of these responsibilities. The first arises because the costs of exchange regulation appear not to decrease linearly with volume, and there are large fixed costs of compliance especially for new systems that handle institutional order-flow.[92] If the provision of self-regulatory activities is tied with the provision of market facilities, the presence of economies of scale in the regulation of trading systems may act as a deterrent to the establishment of new markets. This need not be a problem in the USA, however, as long as trading systems are allowed to register with the NASD. This has effectively become the residual regulator, namely the regulator of all market participants who do not trade through the registered exchanges. A new trading system will thereby be able to take advantage of any economies of scale that exist in regulating a market, by operating its system under the regulatory umbrella of the NASD. While most new trading systems have been allowed by the SEC to follow this regulatory strategy, the case of the AZX, which was required to be classified as an exchange, shows that it has not been available to all such systems.

A second problem is that regulatory activities may cross-subsidize the provision of trading systems or vice versa, and this can distort competition between trading systems.[93] One example of this is when an SRO uses the revenues it obtains from undertaking its regulatory activities to subsidize the markets it provides. A remedy for this is to allow any regulatory activities which are profitable to be open to competition, as indeed is presently the case with the listing of securities. Another example may arise when an SRO's regulatory activities are loss-making and thus subsidized by the revenues the SRO receives from the markets it provides, and when at the same time the SRO is required to oversee a trading system not owned by the SRO. Unless the trading system is obliged to pay the SRO transaction-related fees, the SRO will be subsidizing the operations of one of its competitors, through its regulatory activities.

A third problem is that if an automated trading system is required to join an SRO which operates its own market, the SRO oversight of the trading system may be unsatisfactory because the automated trading system is subject to surveillance by a competitor. The operators of trading systems may, nevertheless, still prefer being regulated by a competitor with adequate safeguards of confidentiality, rather than being regulators themselves.[94] Alternatively, as discussed by the SEC, a new SRO that operates no markets could be established.[95]

Two approaches for allocating those regulatory responsibilities apart from market-structure concerns that are currently assigned to SROs may be considered. The first, which is similar to the *status quo*, would maintain an institutional definition of an SRO, possibly still called an 'exchange', and would assign appropriate regulatory duties to any institutions satisfying the definition. Trading systems that did not satisfy the definition would be required to join one of the statutorily defined SROs. Depending on the nature of the definition, the various classificatory difficulties identified above with the current exchange definition may still, however, continue to arise. One way of minimizing them would be to define an SRO using some form of limited volume terminology. Not only would this yield the advantage of reducing ambiguity about the definition, it would also not have any of the disadvantageous effects on market structure noted above with classifying an exchange using the current limited volume approach.

A second more radical approach would be to allow a trading system the freedom to choose which organization should act as its regulator, but to require it to be regulated by one SRO. This would place competitive pressure on competing regulators to provide cheap and efficient regulatory services to the competing markets they served. There would need to be SEC oversight of any institution choosing to be a regulator of trading markets in order to ensure minimum regulatory quality, in much the same manner as the current SEC oversight of existing SROs. Given the economies of scale associated with regulation, both approaches are likely in practice to lead to much the same result.

Desirability and Possibility of Separation

Two problems are frequently perceived to arise with the separation in the proposed regulatory strategy. The first is that it is undesirable because the costs of implementing it outweigh the benefits. Such a view often arises because of a confusion over exactly what the separation implies. At issue here is whether the operator of a market should be free of regulatory constraints in determining the market's structure. This type of separation is quite distinct from another type of regulatory separation in which the regulation of the conduct of market participants is separated from the regulation of the market's integrity.

Various considerations are important when assessing the merits of this second type of separation. As noted by the SEC, the responsibilities for market supervision and for regulating market conduct may overlap, and this could lead to jurisdictional conflicts between the two types of regulators if such a separation were ever implemented.[96] Examples of this may include the monitoring of whether dealers honour their quotes, and of the enforcement of trade reporting rules. Any synergy that exists when a single institution oversees both a market and the traders operating on the market, may also be lost if the two functions are separated. Whatever the merits of these arguments, however, they say nothing about whether the operator of a market should be free of regulatory constraints in determining the market's structure.

Similarly, it is frequently argued that separating regulatory from market structure concerns might undermine the self-regulatory role that SROs currently fulfil. If such a separation were effected, it is certainly possible that regulatory functions might not be properly performed by third party providers, namely participants other than the owners or operators of the market. There might also be co-ordination problems in contracting-out regulatory functions, and other advantages of self-regulation may be undermined.[97] Allowing the operator of a market to determine the structure of the market does not, however, necessarily imply that the regulation of the market could not be undertaken by a self-regulatory process, with similar governance constraints as those currently in operation. On the contrary, the governance of the market could be determined by commercial imperatives, while the governance of the SRO could still be determined in the same manner as at present. In particular, there could be fair representation of market participants, sufficient representation of the public, and appropriate participation by the operator of the market. The two governance structures would simply not be the same, and it would not be within the reach of the SRO to examine market structure issues.

Regulatory concern that the preferences of market participants not represented on the governance structures of trading systems would be inadequately considered is in most circumstances unnecessary. If a trading system did not take sufficient account of the desires of a group of its users, be they investors or issuers for example, they could respectively either re-direct their order-flow away from the trading system or re-list on another trading system, assuming that the one in question did not hold any monopolistic power in the market.

A second problem with the proposed separation is that market structure may be thought to be so inextricably linked with other regulatory concerns that no real separation is possible. As stated by a Senate Subcommittee, 'in the securities business, at least, every ethical question has economic aspects and every economic question has ethical aspects'.[98] Two instances of this belief are notable.

A central plank of the SEC's justification for transparency is that the publication of prices and quotes helps investors monitor the execution of their orders in order to assess whether they are obtaining best execution. Regulation of the dissemination of price and quote information, one of the three key elements of market structure, is therefore thought necessary for the protection of investors. Similarly, particular types of order execution algorithms may be viewed as unfair, particularly if they adversely discriminate against retail traders. Once again the supervision of a central element of market structure, this time that of the order execution mechanism, is thought essential to deliver a desired regulatory goal, namely fairness.

There are, however, two strong counter-arguments to the view that because no real separation between market structure and other regulatory concerns is possible, more intrusive regulation of market structure is required than merely that of competition policy. The first is that competition between trading systems will mean that any system on which investor protection appears compromised, or which offers what is believed to be an unfair order execution algorithm, as a result of its market structure, is likely to lose business. Competition will therefore provide an appropriate incentive for a trading system itself to create a market structure which delivers a suitable balance of liquidity and other regulatory goals. The second counter-argument is that the enhancement of liquidity, a key effect of competition between trading systems, is the best method for protecting investors and the best antidote to any perceived unfairness in markets. Any regulation which adversely affects its provision is therefore likely to be undesirable.

Further weight to the proposal that a separation between market structure and other regulatory concerns is appropriate, is the implicit support given to this position in an argument put forward by the SEC. Although its statements on this issue were inconsistent, one aspect of them nevertheless indirectly provides support for the separation proposed here. The Commission claimed on the one hand that the exchange/broker distinction meant that alternative trading systems could be, and in many instances were, regulated by an SRO that also operated a trading system, and that was therefore in competition with them at the same time as being their regulator.[99] Such a conflict of interest was viewed by many alternative trading systems as being unacceptable, and by the SEC to be avoided if possible. On the other hand, the Commission also proposed that it might consider allowing the smaller exchanges to outsource their regulatory responsibilities to bigger exchanges, who might thus be able to take advantage of economies of scale in their regulatory duties.[100] Were the smaller exchanges to do this, however, they too would become subject to regulation by a competitor, a situation the SEC precisely stated it wanted to avoid. While the SEC's inconsistency is not insignificant, the notion that trading systems or exchanges might appropriately seek to outsource their regulatory duties is much more important, as it explicitly sanctions the possibility that the regulation of market structure can reasonably be separated from the regulation of other areas of concern.

Simultaneous Competition and Cooperation

Much regulation, excluding that of market structure, requires cooperation between different regulatory agencies. When attempting to ascertain whether any market manipulation or insider trading has occurred, for example, it is essential to have information about all the trades that have taken place in the relevant assets, independent of where they were executed. In order to facilitate such information-sharing at the domestic level, regulatory commissions have encouraged the various SROs and markets under their purview to establish institutions, or declarations of intent, to share the relevant information. In the USA, for example, the SEC has promoted a range of inter-market regulatory coordinating groups, including the Intermarket Surveillance Group, the Intermarket Financial Surveillance Group, and the Intermarket Communications Group. In the UK, the SIB required the London Stock Exchange and Tradepoint to sign a memorandum of understanding (MOU) with each other which obliges them to share regulatory information on a confidential basis, when needed. At the international level, bilateral MOUs have also been signed between various regulatory commissions themselves, and in the EU a multilateral agreement has been created in the ISD to require the 'competent authorities' in Member States to share relevant information when necessary.[101]

The possibility of the exchange of information amongst securities market regulators, as envisaged in the various declarations which have been signed, does not, however, guarantee the full and immediate exchange of such information.[102] The effectiveness of these agreements will depend on the extent to which the regulators party to them are willing to work together. If the aims of the regulators are congruent, then both institutions are likely to comply with the agreement. The fight against fraud, for example, is likely to be a key goal of most regulators. If the exchange of information impinges on other objectives of the regulators, about which they may have differing views, the effectiveness of the relevant declarations could, however, be in doubt.

The most likely area in which this will be a problem is where there is competition between trading systems or between different national markets. A regulatory agency in one jurisdiction, for example, could believe that by handing over certain information to a regulatory agency in another jurisdiction, it might harm the prospects of the financial centre which it supervised. It may then not hand over the information on a full or timely basis. Similarly, if an SRO both regulates and manages a market, it may be hesitant about handing over confidential information which it believes may harm its market's prospects. The separation of the regulation of competition between trading systems from the regulation of other goals may help reduce such conflicts of interest.

CONCLUSION

The statutory distinction between exchanges and brokers has operated for over sixty years in the USA, and underpins the entire fabric of the regulatory structure governing not only the American securities markets but also that of many other jurisdictions. The aim of this chapter is nevertheless to argue that the distinction is no longer viable in the face of the development of automated trading systems, and to propose an alternative approach. A critical element of the proposed strategy relates to the governance and self-regulation of trading systems.

The chapter is composed of three sections. In the first, three sets of criteria used historically by the SEC to determine whether a trading system should be classified as an exchange or a broker are identified and analysed. They concern: first, centralization; second, two-sided quotes, liquidity and volume; and third, trade execution and price discovery.

In the second section, various flaws with the exchange/broker distinction are identified and discussed. Some difficulties are examined, first of all, under the respective headings of ambiguity, re-classification, competition, self-regulation and governance, and incoherence. The weaknesses perceived by the SEC with the exchange/broker distinction in its 1997 Concept Release are evaluated next. While some of the arguments made by the SEC are believed persuasive, others are themselves viewed as flawed. Two problems with the exchange/broker distinction in the international context of the EU are then identified.

In the third section, five alternative approaches to regulating exchanges and trading systems are analysed and criticized. These are: first, changing the 'exchange' definition; second, using solely 'functional regulation'; third, extending the 'limited volume' approach; fourth, adopting the SEC's enhanced broker-dealer approach or its exchange tiering (ET) strategy proposed in its 1997 Concept Release; and finally, implementing the joint strategy of separating the regulation of market structure from the regulation of other areas of public concern, and employing competition policy to regulate market structure. This last strategy is recommended as being the best way of classifying and regulating exchanges and trading systems.

APPENDIX 1 TRADING SYSTEMS

There is a wide variety in the types of trading systems currently operating, and an even greater potential diversity in the types of systems that could be built.[1] No attempt is made here to summarize, let alone describe, the full range of existing systems. The market structures of many traditional exchanges have been described at length elsewhere, and information about most of the new non-traditional trading systems remains confidential.[2] Instead, some ways of categorizing trading systems are briefly outlined, and then the market architectures of three specific trading systems are described. They are the Arizona Stock Exchange (AZX), Delta Government Options Corporation (Delta), and Instinet.

These systems are chosen for two reasons. First, each one has played an important role in various regulatory developments. Second, they illustrate three common types of trading systems, namely those of a single price call auction, an OTC bulletin board, and a continuous limit order book. For the most part, the market structure of both the AZX and Instinet are similar today to the way in which they operated in the period around 1990, during which some key decisions concerning their regulatory status were taken. In contrast, while the analysis of Delta's regulatory status was also undertaken at the same time, the structure of the Delta system has changed significantly since then. The description of the Delta system presented here is of the way in which it operated when the seminal regulatory decisions about it were taken.

TAXONOMY

Following the taxonomy devised by Domowitz (1993*a*), a range of different types of trading algorithms may be identified.[3] The order execution algorithm of a trading system is the set of rules that determines both how orders submitted to the system are to be ranked for execution, and the manner and price of any executions that may occur. The primary priority of an algorithm is the first criterion by which competing orders are ranked so as to determine which of them are to be executed first. The most common primary priority employed, that of 'price' priority, stipulates that higher bids and lower offers are executed respectively before lower bids and higher offers. Once the primary priority of an algorithm has been applied, other secondary priorities may be used to provide a further ranking of competing orders. For example, if price is used as the primary priority, any secondary priorities employed will specify which of the orders with the same price associated with them should be executed first.

Many possible secondary priorities may be employed. These include: 'price with market maker exposure', which stipulates that specified market makers are allowed to match or improve on the prices quoted elsewhere in a market; 'time', which requires that orders submitted earlier to a system are executed before those submitted later; 'order type', which stipulates that certain types of orders are executed before other types of orders, for example when market orders take priority over limit orders; 'quantity', which requires that larger orders are executed before smaller orders; 'quantity allocation', which specifies how orders with the same price are to be executed if a countervailing order comes on to the other side of the market, for example by allotting an equal number of shares to all orders at the same price; 'modified time' is a form of quantity allocation, which allots shares to the largest order which was input first into a trading system; 'display', which specifies that those orders about which more information is publicly displayed take precedence over those orders for which some information remains hidden; 'trader class', which specifies that the orders of specified types of traders should be executed before those from other types of traders, for example by giving retail investors precedence over financial intermediaries; 'preferencing', which specifies that a particular customer's orders should be routed to a particular financial intermediary; and 'hit and take', which allows any trader to deal with any quote in the market, and thus implies that there are no rules determining which orders should be executed first in a trading system.

Some trading systems determine the prices at which trades are executed by explicit reference to the pricing and sales activity in other markets. Such trading systems, which have no independent price discovery mechanism, are referred to as 'passive' or 'derivative' pricing systems. Some of these systems allow for the possibility of price improvement, by assessing market conditions in the underlying market, and then pricing their trades at a price better than the best quote on the underlying market available at the time of order entry. Prices may vary through the trading session, if the system operates at the same time as its associated primary market, or may be fixed at a single level, such as the closing price for an after-hours trading session. Trade execution on passive trading systems may be based on different secondary priorities than those present on the primary market.

A wide spectrum of order types may be allowed on a trading system, including: 'limit' orders, which have a price and volume attached, but need not be executed immediately; 'market' orders, which have a volume but no price attached, and which must be executed immediately; 'day' orders, which are good till the end of the trading day; 'good-till-cancelled' orders; 'all-or-none' orders, for which partial executions are not allowed; 'minimum fill' orders, which require the execution of a pre-specified minimum volume; and 'market on opening/closing' orders, which are to be executed at the opening/closing of the trading day. Some characteristics of some of these different types of orders can be associated in the same order. A limit order, for example, can also be an all-or-none order. Others are mutually exclusive. A trader cannot, for example, specify the price at which he would like his business transacted, namely submit a limit order, and require simultaneously that the transaction be executed immediately, namely submit a market order.

Many order types are contingent on the satisfaction of pre-specified conditions before they may be executed. These include: 'last-sale price' orders, which must be executed at a price equal to, or better, than the last-sale price; 'mid-market' orders, which must be executed at the middle of the most recent bid–offer spread; basket orders, in which the purchase or sale of a particular security may only be executed in tandem with the sale or purchase of another security; and index-related orders, where the execution price of a particular order must be related to the value of a specified market index. There are many other types of both contingent and non-contingent orders.

AZX[4]

The AZX allows institutional investor and broker-dealer participants to trade US stocks directly with each other at a single price determined through a call auction process. Customers of AZX may enter limit orders (specifying the name of the share, the volume, the price at which they wish to deal, and whether the desired trade is a buy or a sell) through terminals linked to a central computer over a period of time up until a previously established cut-off time. It is also possible to enter orders into a so-called 'reserve book'. These orders are not shown to other traders on the system, unless they match against an appropriate order on the other side of the market. The orders in each share on each side of the market are ranked first by price, second by time, and third by whether they are placed in the reserve book or not, in order to derive a demand and a supply schedule.

Immediately after each auction cut-off time, the system calculates the auction price by maximizing the total volume traded over the range of possible transaction prices, given the bids and offers resting in the system. This price is the price at which the demand and supply schedules intersect, and thus at which the volume of buying interest equals, or is most nearly equal to, the volume of selling interest. If the demand and supply schedules are such that a unique price but no unique volume is determined at their intersection, the limit orders equal to the auction price will be filled on the basis of time priority to the extent that counter-parties are available. If the demand and supply curves are such that a unique volume but no unique price is determined by their crossing, the price is normally set mid-way between the two prices between which the two curves are congruent.[5] Customers who entered bids above, and offers below, the auction price receive executions at the auction price.

Prior to the auction cut-off time, customers may at any time cancel or replace orders already entered. Customers may replace orders with more aggressive orders (i.e. higher bids or lower offers) without penalty, but are penalized for replacing an order with a less aggressive one (i.e. a lower bid or higher offer). Replaced orders are ranked in the order book according to the time of replacement, not the original entry time. In order to discourage the cancellation of orders, the AZX charges customers two commissions, on both the buy and sell side, for each cancelled order—even though no order is executed. The commission rate also increases as the time to the auction cut-off time decreases, thus providing an incentive for early submission of orders, and for not cancelling orders just before the auction cut-off time.

The information available to customers is dynamically updated with each new order entered into the system. Customers are able to see the full order book for any security, including bids and offers, their prices and volumes, both separately and in the aggregate. The expected auction price and trading volume based upon orders already entered in the system are also displayed. When established, only customers of the AZX could see information about the order book. All trading is anonymous.

DELTA[6]

In the period around 1990, the Delta system provided a trading mechanism, brokerage services and a central clearing facility for over-the-counter trading of options on US Treasury securities. Participation in Delta was limited to the major dealers in the US Treasury securities market and large institutional investors. Participants were linked via a continuously-updated automated communications network with video display terminals in each of their offices. The system was composed of three firms: RMJ Options Trading Corporation (RMJ), Delta Government Options Corporation (DGOC), and Security Pacific National Trust Company (SPNTCO). Each firm undertook a specific and different role in the operation of the system.

RMJ was a government securities broker, and owned and maintained the software, hardware, data transmission network, and communication interfaces of the system.[7] It also acted as an intermediary between participants trading on the system. DGOC performed a range of functions, including issuing the options traded on the system, settling all transactions, standardizing several aspects of the terms of all the option contracts, admitting participants into the system, enforcing the system's rules and procedures, and setting participants' margin requirements. SPNTCO cleared the trades executed on the system, and also undertook several administrative functions.

There were two ways in which trading could be conducted on Delta. A participant could firstly instruct RMJ by telephone to place a bid or an ask order on the system, information about which was then disseminated to other participants via the video display network. The premium, the exercise price, the expiration month, and the yield and maturity of the underlying securities, were chosen by the participant. Once a quote was on the screen, another participant could trade against it by telephoning RMJ with instructions either to hit the bid or lift the offer. In such trades, RMJ acted as a 'blind broker' between the two participants—traders could not disclose their identities when entering quotations, or trading against a bid or ask quote, through RMJ. When a participant hit a bid or lifted an offer, information about the trade was broadcast to all participants, again via the screen. The second manner of dealing was for participants to communicate and negotiate directly with each other via telephone, without using RMJ as an intermediary. Information about trades conducted directly between participants was not disseminated to other participants. It was possible to take a position using one of the trading methods, for example by direct negotiation with another participant, and then dispose of the position using the other method, for example by advertising the position on the screen via RMJ. All orders and information had to be delivered to RMJ by telephone.

INSTINET[8]

Instinet is a screen-based computer network for trading the major equities of a range of leading international markets.[9] It operates a continuous limit order book, in which bids and offers may be submitted and transactions may occur at any time (effectively twenty-four hours per day).

Two types of information are displayed on the Instinet screen: that coming from publicly available sources external to Instinet, and the prices or orders entered by Instinet customers. The raw quote data received from external sources are consolidated to form the 'Quote Montage'. This is a display in which all the bids and offers from the different external sources are ranked according to price priority. The size of each such bid and offer is also shown when available, as is the exchange or market maker from where the quote originated. Each security has its own Quote Montage. The information is dynamically updated, so that changes in quotes on the markets are instantaneously and automatically reflected as changes on the screen. It is not possible for Instinet customers to deal through the Instinet system directly with the prices relayed on the Quote Montage.

Each security traded on Instinet also has its own internal order book, which consists of a listing of all live orders, some orders which have expired, and some which have already been executed.[10] These different types of orders are ranked first by price and then by time. The price associated with each order is revealed on the screen, as is information about the order's size. Neither the identity of the user, nor the time the order was input, nor the period for which the order is good, however, is revealed on the screen. If a customer desires, dissemination of the order can be restricted.[11] As discussed in Chapter 7, recent regulatory developments in the USA now require Instinet, as an ECN, to publish the best-priced orders on its system. Information about the other contents of the internal order book for each stock, however, is not released to non-subscribers.

To trade on the system, a participant either responds to an order already placed on the internal order book, or initiates and places an order on to the book himself. The simplest orders which may be entered into the system are limit orders, in which a participant specifies the name of the share, the amount of shares he wants to transact, his desired price of execution, whether he is a buyer or a seller, and the time at which he wants his order to expire. If no expiration time is entered, the system automatically enters a default expiration time of three minutes. There are several extra conditions which a participant may impose on the manner in which his order is executed. An order may be pegged to the last sale price (in which case the price at which the order will be executed is protected to be equal or better than the continuously updated last-sale price on a particular exchange); it may be pegged to the middle of the bid/offer spread (in which case the price at which the order will be executed is continuously updated to be middle of the bid/offer spread); it may require a minimum fill (in which case a partial execution of the order will only be allowed if a pre-specified minimum amount of the order is executed); or it may be non-negotiable as to price (so that it will only match against other orders which satisfy its price constraint).

If there is a bid or offer in the Instinet book, and a participant enters a contra-side order at the same price or better, and there are no impeding conditions attached to either order, the orders are automatically and immediately executed by the Instinet system. In-coming orders can be matched against more than one existing order, and can also be matched against those orders not shown on the screen, although placed on the order book.

As well as transacting directly against orders on the Instinet book, participants can also negotiate with each other directly, anonymously, and electronically. The Instinet book not only contains all orders currently alive, but also some which have expired, and some which have already been executed. Any one of these types of orders may be selected by a participant, who may transmit a message to the person who originally submitted the order, in the hope of resuscitating the previous interest and negotiating a further order. A series of commonly-used pre-formatted messages are available such as: 'Are you still alive?', 'This is my best price', 'Could you do more?', 'Yes, I am interested', etc. When negotiating, there is no requirement for customers to respond to any specific order, and in particular no need to observe price priority. This means, for example, that if a participant is a buyer and wants to negotiate a transaction, he is not required to approach the participant quoting the lowest offered price.

APPENDIX 2 DEFINITIONS

In order to gauge the generally accepted meanings of the terms 'exchange', 'stock exchange', 'futures exchange',[1] and 'market', a survey was undertaken of their definitions in four general and traditional dictionaries, and seven more modern specialist finance and economics dictionaries.[2]

Eight significant points emerged in the generalist dictionaries:

(1) All of them have more than one definition for all the terms—so that there is no single exclusive meaning for any of the words.

(2) All the dictionaries define an 'exchange' and a 'stock exchange' as a building or place for buying and selling, or for the transacting of business.

(3) All the dictionaries refer to the items which are traded on a 'stock exchange' as stocks, shares, or securities, but none of the dictionaries puts any restriction on the things which may be traded on an 'exchange'.

(4) All the dictionaries define a 'stock exchange' as some form of association of people for the buying and selling of stocks.

(5) Three dictionaries make reference to an 'exchange' being centralized in some manner.[3]

(6) Two dictionaries refer to a 'stock exchange' as being a market or marketplace.[4]

(7) All the dictionaries define a 'market' as: first, a meeting of people for buying and selling; second, a place or building used for such meetings; and third, as buying and selling.

(8) Two dictionaries refer to a 'market' as being a 'stock exchange'.[5]

There was both less uniformity and a wider range of meanings for the four terms in the specialist dictionaries. Eighteen significant points emerged:

(1) All but one of the dictionaries define an 'exchange' or a 'stock exchange' as a physical location for buying and selling.[6]

(2) All the dictionaries refer to the items which are traded on a 'stock exchange' as stocks, shares or securities, but none of the dictionaries puts any restriction on the things which may be traded on an 'exchange'. Only futures contracts are traded on a 'futures exchange'.[7]

(3) Several dictionaries characterize an 'exchange' or a 'stock exchange' as being organized or formal, as opposed to being informal, decentralized, or over-the-counter.[8] Forms of organization included the standardization of contracts, and the creation of membership rules, listing rules, and a constitution.

(4) Several dictionaries characterize an 'exchange' or a 'stock exchange' as being authorized.[9]

(5) Several dictionaries note that an 'exchange' or a 'stock exchange' might operate electronically.[10]

(6) Several dictionaries note that an 'exchange' or a 'stock exchange' could be closed, meaning that only members are allowed to trade on it.[11] One dictionary notes that 'futures exchanges', like 'stock exchanges', are membership organizations.[12]

(7) Several dictionaries note that an 'exchange' or a 'stock exchange' organizes trade on a regular basis.[13]

(8) Several dictionaries mention that a 'stock exchange' centralizes trading in securities.[14]

(9) One dictionary says an 'exchange' ensures fairness of the pricing or auction process.[15]

(10) One dictionary says an 'exchange' provides fast price disclosure.[16]

(11) Several of the dictionaries say that an 'exchange' provides safe settlement, delivery, and clearing.[17]

(12) Several of the dictionaries say that an 'exchange' provides liquidity.[18]

(13) Several dictionaries refer to a 'futures exchange' as being an institution for providing a regulated market for trading in futures contracts.[19]

(14) Several of the dictionaries refer to an 'exchange' and a 'stock exchange' as a market.[20]

(15) Many of the dictionaries define a 'market' as a physical location for trading.[21]

(16) One dictionary specifically states, however, that a 'market' should not be thought of as a locality, but rather as buying and selling.[22] Many of the other dictionaries also identify a 'market' as buying or selling, as a medium for exchanges between buyers and sellers, or as the process of transacting.[23]

(17) One dictionary refers to a 'market' as those who participate in trading.[24]

(18) Several dictionaries refer to a 'market' as being an exchange or a stock exchange.[25]

Endnotes

1 INTRODUCTION

1. The term MONSTER was first used in Lee (1992). The definition here has been marginally changed from the original one which was a 'Market-Oriented New System for Terrifying Exchange Regulators'.
2. As stated by Humpty Dumpty, 'When I use a word . . . it means just what I choose it to mean—neither more nor less.' 'The question is,' said Alice, 'whether you can make words mean so many different things.' 'The question is,' said Humpty Dumpty, 'which is to be master—that's all.' Carroll (1872, reprinted 1958: 220).
3. See Mondo Visione (1997).
4. There are various other important parts of the trading cycle, such as custody in the equity markets, and delivery in the futures markets.
5. A fuller examination of the definitions of quotes and trades is presented in Chapter 6.
6. For definitions of these functions, see Moles and Terry (1997).
7. For discussions of various aspects of the clearing and settlement functions of exchanges, see Baer, France and Moser (1995; 1996), Hanley, McCann and Moser (1995), Kyle and Marsh (1993), Madhavan, Mendelson and Peake (1988), McGaw (1997), and Moser (1994).
8. For such evaluations, see O'Hara (1995) and Schwartz (1991).
9. As Powell and Friedkin (1987: 183) note, 'the methodology of case studies is typically used in research when the issues under investigation are complex, multi-faceted, nonrepetitive, and highly contextual, making more formal analysis impossible'.
10. Including barley, canola, cattle, copra, corn, cotton, dairy products, feed peas, flax, hogs, mung beans, oats, oranges, palm oil, peanuts, pork bellies, potatoes, rapeseed, red beans, rice, soya beans, sunflowers, sweet potatoes, wheat, wool, and yarn.
11. Including crude oil, fuel oil, gas, gasoline, propane, and electricity.
12. Including all the major and many of the minor currencies, interest rates, and many equity, commodity, and other forms of indices.
13. Including aluminium, antimony, copper, lead, magnesium, nickel, tin, and zinc.
14. Including gold, palladium, platinum, and silver.
15. Including cocoa, coffee, and sugar.
16. Including chemicals, cocoons, freight, insurance, plywood, pulp, rubber, seafood, silk, and timber.

2 GOVERNANCE

1. See Holmstrom and Tirole (1989: 63, 104–5), and Cunning (1988).
2. See Kreps and Spence (1985: 374–5).
3. See Kanter and Summers (1987: 155).
4. For general summaries of the theory of the firm, see Holmstrom and Tirole (1989)

and Hart (1989). For descriptions of the transaction cost methodology, see Coase (1937), and Williamson (1990; 1993; 1996).

5. See, respectively, Abolafia (1996) and chs. 5–7, Greising and Morse (1991).
6. This definition is not intended to prejudge the appropriate definitions of ownership and membership which are themselves controversial.
7. See also Chambers and Carter (1990).
8. Other sources of income to an exchange from other types of market participants, such as listing fees or payments for the use of the exchange's data, are ignored in this section.
9. Other groups of patrons who exercise some control are ignored in this section.
10. This ignores the possibility that losses may be intentionally made in one period if compensating future gains are expected. Consumer surplus is defined as the difference between the amount consumers are prepared to pay for something minus the amount they actually pay.
11. See Packel (1970) quoted in Sedo (1987: 378, footnote 6).
12. See Porter and Scully (1987).
13. See Hansmann (1980: 890, footnote 146).
14. Producer surplus is defined as profits, i.e. revenues minus costs. If the joint maximization of consumer and producer surplus leads to the same result as the maximization solely of consumer surplus subject to the breakeven constraint, the actions taken by a consumer cooperative and a nonprofit firm will be identical. This will occur if the maximization of the joint surplus yields zero profits. See Ben-Ner (1986: 95).
15. The role of nonprofit firms as producers of public goods is not believed important in the context of exchanges. For a summary of the literature on this topic, see James and Rose-Ackermann (1986: 27–9).
16. See, for example, the Buttonwood Agreement of the NYSE (1792) reproduced in Loss and Seligman (1990: 2852).
17. Their work was extended in Hart and Moore (1997).
18. Italics added.
19. Hart and Moore (1990: 1133) provide a formal definition of indispensability.
20. See, for example, Marsh (1993), notwithstanding the large literature on the indifference owners should have between capital gains and dividends initiated by Modigliani and Miller (1958).
21. See Hansmann (1981: 510, 553–6).
22. This occurs in some American states.
23. For discussions of developments in the law on nonprofit corporations, see Hansmann (1988) and *Harvard Law Review* (1992).
24. For example, the precursor to the CME, the Chicago Butter and Egg Board, submitted a certificate of intention to form a corporation 'not for pecuniary profit' on 1/2/1898.
25. Such as the LSE.
26. Such as the SSE.
27. As at LIFFE or the CME.
28. As at the CME.
29. As at the CBT.
30. See paras. (1)–(8), Clause 3, LSE (1997*d*).
31. See para. 27.02, LSE 'Articles of Association' (1997*d*). This can be changed by vote.

32. See LSE 'Articles of Association' (1997*d*). Although there are currently two types of shares issued by the Exchange, 'A' and 'B' shares, the 'A' shares are ignored here as they will be cancelled over time. All references to shares or shareholders therefore refer to 'B' shares or 'B' shareholders.

33. The 'share Trustee', a subsidiary of the Stock Exchange, may also be a shareholder of the Exchange, although it has no voting rights. It is ignored here. There may be a time lag between becoming a member and being put on to the share register, and similarly between resigning membership and being taken off the share register.

34. As of 1997 there were about 300 members, each with a share, with the possibility of issuing 14,399 shares.

35. So that if a member resigns he must transfer his shares back to the share Trustee.

36. This information comes from LSE (1997*a*), and discussions with exchange officials.

37. One other main category is that of being a stock borrowing and lending intermediary. The need for this category has, however, recently changed.

38. There is in fact a category of membership called a 'designated fund manager'. See LSE (1996*c*: 111). This category was created, however, solely to accommodate certain firms with specific legal or corporate structures. For example if a full service broker-dealer has within it a fund management division which does not, however, have a different legal status from that of the broker-dealer side of the firm, the fund management division would be required to follow certain of the exchange's rules which would place it at a competitive disadvantage versus other non-member fund managers. The firm may then become a designated fund manager to avoid this problem. There is also a membership category for firms undertaking corporate finance. Although previously this was important as only members of the exchange could sponsor new listings, this is now no longer relevant. Corporate finance firms retaining such membership therefore typically do so for the status of being a member of the exchange.

39. Italics in original.

40. Not least by regulators who have shown much concern about who is represented at board level, as discussed in Chapter 8.

41. See, for example, Crawford (1994*b*).

42. Booz Allen & Hamilton Inc. (1994: V-1).

43. Young (1987: 177).

44. Sir Nicholas Redmayne, quoted in Treasury Committee (1996: 30*b*).

45. As discussed in Chapter 5.

46. See, for example, Newhouse (1970). Chambers and Carter (1990) characterize a nonprofit futures exchange as a firm that seeks to expand its output, subject to breaking even.

47. See, for example, Maguire (1997).

48. See, for example, SSE (1996: 2).

49. This and the next two quotes are in CBT (1993*c*: 9–10).

50. For general discussions of collective choice rules, see McLean (1990) and Ordeshook (1985).

51. See, for example, Ben-Ner (1986).

52. By more skewed, Hart and Moore refer to the extent to which the median characteristic of the membership differs from its mean.

53. Discussion of the median voter theorem is presented in Ordeshook (1992: 104).

54. Although there are limits to rolling over leases, so that voting rights are not entirely separable from trading rights.

55. This section draws in part on the summary of the literature on principal agent problems presented in Holmstrom and Tirole (1989).
56. See Alchian and Demsetz (1972).
57. See, for example, Franks and Mayer (1993).
58. This argument does not claim, however, that the nonprofit form is beneficial because it reduces the possibility that management may attempt to sell low quality services, given that the purchasers of the services cannot easily monitor their quality. This may arise when the recipient of a service is not the same as the service's purchaser. See, for example, Hansmann (1980), Williamson (1979), and Easley and O'Hara (1983; 1988).
59. See Amsterdam Exchanges (1997), Australian Stock Exchange (1996), Consiglio di Borsa (1997*a*; 1997*b*), Copenhagen Stock Exchange (1996), Fédération Internationale des Bourses de Valeurs (1995), Helsinki Stock Exchange (1995); Stockholm Stock Exchange (1992), and Tradepoint Financial Networks plc (1992; 1994; 1995).
60. See Davey (1994*a*). The issue of the governance of exchanges is, however, frequently revisited.
61. For example in the EU and the USA.
62. If a central clearing house for futures contracts were developed, this would change markedly the nature of competition between futures exchanges.
63. See Barton (1991: 5).
64. This point is taken from *Futures and Options World* (1994*e*).
65. New technology, such as the introduction of hand-held computers, may also, however, enhance the services provided by financial traders and intermediaries.
66. See Rathore (1994).
67. See Gorham (1997).
68. I am indebted to Jim Moser for pointing out that the value of voting rights at a particular exchange could be estimated by capitalizing the rental income from a seat at the exchange and then subtracting this imputed value from the price paid for seats.
69. As of March 1996, OM owned 21% of the SSE—see SSE (1997: 22). Subsequently OM merged with the SSE—see OM and SSE (1997).
70. See Gapper (1996), Cohen (1996), and Warner (1996).

3 GOVERNANCE: CASE STUDIES

1. The term 'companization' was used by the exchange to describe the process of transformation it was undergoing.
2. See the introduction to Courtney and Thompson (1996).
3. For a discussion of the impossibility of finding the truth in such contexts, see Lee (1997*b*).
4. *Svensk forfattningssamling* (17/6/1992: 543).
5. This legal form was in fact unique to the exchange. Although it was a self-owned private entity, it was also viewed in some ways as a public authority.
6. Article 11, Articles of Association, SSE (1992: 29).
7. For this, and subsequent quotes by the President, see Rydén (1995).
8. See Umlauf (1993) and Froot and Campbell (1993).
9. SSE (1992: 4).

10. Ibid.

11. See, for example, OM Group (1993).

12. Rosenthal (1994).

13. For this and subsequent quotes by the Board of the CBT, see CBT (1994).

14. *Futures and Options World* (1994*f*).

15. See, for example, Davey (1994*a*).

16. *Futures and Options World* (1994*f*).

17. See CME (1994*a*: 4–5).

18. As specified by the board.

19. There was apparently some flexibility to this rule, such that it might be possible to be a clearing member with only one CME membership.

20. There would also be a transitional period of voting.

21. There were additional proposals concerning future elimination of any of the four trading 'quadrants' at the exchange (namely interest rate, equity, currency, and agricultural contracts), and also concerning liquidation rights.

22. CME (1994*b*: 4). Although this amount was initially subject to availability of funds, the exchange later agreed to guarantee to pay it in full.

23. Linton (1994).

24. For this and subsequent quotes by the CME, see CME (1994*a*: 5–6).

25. Pendley (1994).

26. *Dow Jones News* (1994).

27. CME (1994*b*: 5).

28. Linton (1994).

29. Fritz (1994).

30. Crawford (1994*a*).

31. The 'ag pits' being the group of agricultural traders. Smith (1994).

32. CME (1994*b*: 7).

33. A two-thirds majority was not obtained in each of the three divisional voting groups.

34. Botswana Share Market (1992).

35. Botswana Stock Exchange Act (1994) and Botswana Stock Exchange Regulations (1995).

36. Treasury Committee (1996*d*: 78).

37. LSE (1996*a*).

38. The exchange in fact only released publicly details of about 150 of the 180 responses, but stated that the rest were available from the Treasury Committee to which they had apparently also been submitted. The statistical analysis of the responses is in LSE (1996*b*).

39. This question had been controversial at the exchange for some time. See Stock Exchange (1984).

40. Cohen (1995*b*).

41. Cohen (1995*d*).

42. Eisenhammer (1995).

43. LSE (1996*a*: 9).

44. The exchange sought responses to the following eleven sets of questions: Which securities should be traded on the new system? What form of interaction should there be between orders and quotes? How should block trades be executed? What level of counterparty identification or anonymity should be sanctioned? How should partial fills be taken into account? What pilot method should be used to implement any new

system? When would be an appropriate time to start the new system from an IT point of view? What new facilities should be added to the exchange's international services? Should a 'central dealer service' similar to that of an IDB be established? Should a netting facility be created? and, What other services should be established?

45. See, for example, SBC Warburg (12/2/1996), quoted in Treasury Select Committee (1996*c*: 125),
46. See, for example, Stewart and Ivory (1996: 1).
47. Raphael Zorn Hemsley Limited (1996: 1).
48. See, for example, Salomon Brothers (1996: 1).
49. See, for example, Merrill Lynch (1996).
50. Schroder Securities (1996).
51. Schroder Investment Management (1996: 1).
52. Treasury Committee (1996*b*: 27).
53. See, for example, ibid. (29).
54. See Treasury Committee (1996*c*: 66).
55. See Treasury Committee (1996*d*: 84).
56. See ibid. (84).
57. See ibid. (80–1).
58. See ibid. (80).
59. See ibid. (94).
60. See First Equity (1996) and Openshaw (1996).
61. Treasury Committee (1996*a*: 13).
62. Treasury Committee (1996*e*: 143).
63. The quotes in this paragraph are in ibid. (144). It should be noted that these quotes are written reports of oral testimony, and that the last quote of Plenderleith, although not correct English, is quoted exactly as reported.
64. Press Conference, LSE (4/1/1996).
65. See Treasury Committee (1996*a*: 6), and Treasury Committee (1996*e*: 125).
66. See, for example, Cohen (1995*c*), Hellier (1996), *Independent* (1996), Marckus and Murray (1996), Milner (1996), and Treasury Committee (1996*b*: 31).
67. See, for example, Treasury Committee (1996*c*: 59).
68. See, for example, Stevenson (1996), *Independent* (1996), and Tehan (1996).
69. See Treasury Committee (1996*d*: 85).
70. Treasury Committee (1996*e*: 133).
71. See Treasury Committee (1996*d*: 86).
72. See ibid. (85).
73. Treasury Committee (1996*e*: 125).
74. Ibid. (132).

4 COMPETITION AND COOPERATION

1. The concept of liquidity is discussed in O'Hara (1995: 216–23) and in ch. 11, Schwartz (1988).
2. Further difficulties are noted in FSEEC (1992).
3. Tradepoint Financial Networks plc (1992).
4. Wolman (1997).

5. See Amihud and Mendelson (1986) and Macey and Kanda (1990).
6. See EASDAQ (1996) and LSE (1995).
7. This was called for by OMLX in 1993. See Corrigan (1993). The legal possibility of changing the Competent Authority is discussed in Section 157, FSA (1986).
8. See Cohen (1994).
9. See Drummond (1996).
10. See OFT (1990*b*).
11. See DTI (1991).
12. Waters (1993).
13. See OFT (1988: 3).
14. For discussions about fragmentation, see ch. 8, Cohen *et al.* (1986), ch. 13, Schwartz (1988), ch. 9, Schwartz (1991), and SEC (14/7/1992).
15. See National Legal Research Group (1996: 1–3 to 1–4).
16. Liebowitz and Margolis (1995) discuss the fact that much of the literature examining network externalities views them to be market failures, a position not taken here.
17. See Weber (1991).
18. See Pagano (1989).
19. See for example, Amsterdam Stock Exchange (1990), Bourse de Genève (1986), and Lurie (1979).
20. See, for example, Openshaw (1996).
21. This is normally only possible for stock exchanges. A futures exchange typically requires all members' trades to be executed through the exchange's execution systems.
22. CBOE (1993*a*; *b*).
23. See Wilson (1997), Young (1995), SEC Releases No. 34-32481 (16/6/1993), No. 34-33911 (15/4/1994), and No. 34-36573 (12/12/1995), and SEC (12/12/1995*a*).
24. For a description of the repurchase markets, see Corrigan, Georgiou, and Gollow (1995).
25. See Arnold *et al.* (1997).
26. This was intended, for example, in the merger between LIFFE and the LCE. See LIFFE (1996*b*: 1) and also EURO.NM (1996).
27. One reason why a link between the NYMEX and the SFE was established was precisely because their trading systems, SYCOM and ACCESS, were both based on a common technological platform, a relatively rare occurrence. See NYMEX (1994: 2) and (1995: 1, 7), and SFE and NYMEX (1995).

5 COOPERATION: CASE STUDIES

1. All of the projects examined in this chapter were proposed by exchanges themselves, and not as a result of any regulatory initiatives. The participating exchanges' actions may thus be viewed as arising purely to attain their own objectives, and not to deliver any regulatory goals.
2. DuBroeucq (1990*b*: 4) and Canolle (1990).
3. The name of the association changed from the FSEEC to the Federation of European Stock Exchanges (FESE) in 1993. The name of the European Community subsequently changed to the European Union.

4. See, for example, Bacot, DuBroeucq, and Juvin (1989), DuBroeucq (1990*a*), Istituto per la Ricerca Sociale (1991), Pagano and Roëll (1990*a*; 1990*b*; 1991), and Tonks and Webb (1989).
5. The measurement of how much trading SEAQi did in fact attract was controversial. See Jacquillat and Gresse (1995).
6. Commission of the European Communities (1985: 29).
7. FSEEC (1989).
8. FSEEC (1991: 2).
9. Waters (1991*a*).
10. The insertion of this 'commercial viability' phrase was at the request of the LSE.
11. FSEEC (1991: 3).
12. Ibid. (1).
13. FSEEC (1990: 5).
14. Waters (1990*a*).
15. Hall (1990).
16. von Rosen (1990: 12).
17. van Ittersum, quoted in FSEEC (1991).
18. Bennett, quoted in ibid.
19. Hall (1990).
20. Waters (1990*b*).
21. Montier, Knight and Nicoll (1990), and Montier (1990).
22. Waters and Graham (1990).
23. See Waters (1991*b*), Dobie (1991), Waters (1991*c*), and Cook (1991).
24. Waters (1991*b*). TOPIC stands for Teletext Output of Price Information by Computer.
25. von Rosen (1991: 1).
26. See OFT (1990*b*).
27. See AMEX (1985*a*; *b*; *c*; *d*), and SEC Releases No. 34-22001 (8/5/1985) and No. 34-22442 (20/9/1985).
28. See AMEX (1985*a*: 3) and TSE (1985: 14; 1986: 12).
29. In fact the Canadian Depository Service became a member of the National Securities Clearing Corporation in 1984 for this purpose.
30. This was proposed in SEC Release No. 34-22136 (12/6/1985), and approved in SEC Release No. 34-23075 (7/4/1986).
31. 137,000 shares were traded on the AMEX/TSE link in the fourth quarter of 1985, and 239,000 shares were traded in the fourth quarter of 1986.
32. See TSE (1988: 3–4).
33. This was proposed by the BSE in SEC Release No. 34-21324 (14/9/1984), and approved in SEC Release No. 34-21449 (1/11/1984).
34. See SEC Release No. 34-21925 (8/4/1985).
35. BEACON stands for Boston Stock Exchange Automated Communication and Order-routing Network.
36. See Montreal Exchange (1992). Two earlier links between the ME and the BSE had been established and then discontinued.
37. See SEC Release No. 34-35116 (19/12/1994).
38. For background on the proposed linkage, see SEC Release No. 34-22343 (21/8/1985). See also SEC Releases No. 34-22354 (30/8/1985) and No. 34-22847 (30/1/1986).

39. As discussed in Bernard (1987: 336).
40. Proposed in SEC Release No. 34-23022 (14/3/1986), and approved in SEC Release No. 34-23158 (21/4/1986). As discussed in Chapter 5, the NASD is formally not classified as an exchange in the USA, but rather as a 'national securities association'.
41. Approval was initially given for six months, and then extended because of anti-competitive complaints by Instinet. See SEC Release No. 34-24292 (2/4/1987).
42. This was Singapore time. See CME (1984; 1993*b*: 41–6), and Melamed and Tamarkin (1996: 317–20). Similar mutual off-set links have also been established between LIFFE and CBT—see LIFFE (1995), and between LIFFE and TIFFE—see LIFFE (1996*a*).
43. Kynaston (1997: 326). Although the CME's currency contracts were also listed on the mutual-offset link initially, they were not successful, however, and were subsequently de-listed due to a lack of liquidity. Since March 1996, the CME's Euroyen contract has also been eligible for mutual off-set via the link.
44. See Davey (1994*b*).
45. Tattersall (1990).
46. See CFTC (1989*a*: 76).
47. See ibid. (4, footnote 2).
48. Melamed and Tamarkin (1996: 337).
49. See CFTC (1989: 87–90).
50. This access was established by creating a separate category of member to the exchange, called a GLOBEX Institutional Access member. See Rule 106.J, CME (1997).
51. Vaughan (1993).
52. CBT (1990: 34–7).
53. During the period of negotiation, both exchanges apparently agreed not to make their system available to other exchanges, apart from the CME/MATIF link which had already been finalized. This was to stop the rivalry between the two exchanges in searching for potential partners. During this period, NYMEX reportedly approached the CME to join GLOBEX. The CME did not allow it to do so, however, because of its prior agreement with the CBT. NYMEX then developed its own automated trading system—ACCESS.
54. Globex Joint Venture L.P. (1992).
55. See CFTC (1989*a*: 87).
56. Melamed and Tamarkin (1996: 425).
57. Rules 151 and 574, CME (1997).
58. There are differences in the number of terminals reportedly live at the launch. Durr and Corrigan (1992) state there were 140, while Kynaston notes there were 224.
59. Melamed and Tamarkin (1996: 411).
60. Horne (1993*a*).
61. Davey (1992).
62. BTP stands for 'Buoni del Tesoro Poliennali'.
63. See Kynaston (1997: 280), and also Corrigan and Morse (1993). The discussions were re-instigated at a later date.
64. Davey and Hunter (1992).
65. *Futures and Options World* (1993*a*).
66. Davey (1993*b*).
67. Kynaston (1997: 281).
68. For this quote and the next point, see Burns (1992).

69. Kynaston (1997: 278).
70. Horne (1993*b*).
71. Melamed and Tamarkin (1996: 425–6).
72. Morse and Corrigan (1993).
73. In December 1993, daily volume for the two Chicago exchanges was 4,400 contracts, as compared to the contractual requirement of 50,000. See *Futures and Options World* (1994*b*).
74. See *Futures and Options World* (1993*c*; 1994*a*; *d*).
75. Morse (1994). The CBT apparently also stipulated that it would not list these products until GLOBEX could quote prices in quarters and eighths of a dollar, a condition which Reuters stated could be met.
76. *Futures and Options World* (1994*a*).
77. Morse (1993).
78. Wilson (1994).
79. As of March 1996, there were 284 dedicated CME terminals, 99 dedicated MATIF terminals, and 74 terminals accessing both exchanges' contracts.
80. SBF and MATIF (1997).
81. Davey (1997).
82. CME, MATIF, NYMEX, and SBF (1997).
83. See Wilson (1993*a*), and DTB/MATIF Press Release (1993*b*).
84. See DTB/MATIF (1993*a*; 1994*a*; *b*; *c*), *Futures and Options World* (1993*b*), Reierson (1993), and Loumeau (1993).
85. DTB/MATIF (1994*c*: 8).
86. Horne (1994: 57).
87. Rathore (1994).
88. Reierson (1993).
89. It did in fact open 12,000 square feet of new trading space at a cost of US $30 million, at the same time as beginning phase 1 of the link.
90. See SBF, MATIF, MONEP, and Deutsche Börse AG (1996).
91. See MATIF, MONEP, SBF, Deutsche Börse AG, and Swiss Exchange (1997).
92. The OM group has initiated other links with the Oslo Stock Exchange and the Finnish derivatives exchange, SOM.
93. OM Group (1993: 4).
94. Bradbery (1992*a*).
95. OMLX The London Securities and Derivatives Exchange (1993: 4).
96. *Futures and Options World* (1992).
97. Davey (1993*a*).
98. This and the next quote are on OM (1992: 2). The punctuation has been altered slightly.
99. Wilson (1993*b*).
100. See EOE (1993*a*; *b*).
101. Bradbery (1992*b*).
102. See Davey (1993*a*), Wilson (1993*c*), and Davey (1994*c*).
103. The Eurotop 100 was an index created to match the performance of the 100 top European traded equities.
104. The old COMEX contracts were to be replaced by similar ones deemed 'Replacement Contracts'.
105. Where 'New Metals Contracts' meant any new contracts not based on gold, silver,

copper, or platinum/palladium.

106. Where 'New Products Contracts' meant any new contracts which were not New Energy Contracts, Replacement Contracts, or New Metals Contracts. See next footnote.

107. Where 'New Energy Contracts' meant any new contracts based on alternative energy sources to those then being traded.

108. This and the other payments would be subject to an upwards or downwards adjustment, dependent on whether the adjusted liquid net worth of COMEX at the time of the merger was more or less than $15 million.

109. See NYMEX and COMEX Inc. (1994: 72–3).

110. The MRRP was the 'Merger Recognition and Retention Plan', a pension scheme.

111. This and the next quote are in NYMEX and COMEX Inc. (1994: 74–6).

112. A similar concern was also raised over a petition process established to appeal decisions by the COMEX Governors' Committee.

113. See, for example, *Futures and Options World* (1994c).

6 INFORMATION

1. As discussed below, most exchanges do not *sell* their data in their contracts, but rather *license* their use.

2. Regulatory distinctions between quotes and orders are ignored here.

3. The 'symbology' problem arises because there is a lack of standardization in the symbols used by vendors and exchanges to refer to the same information, and this has lead to a range of costs for the market data industry. See FISD, IIA (1996a).

4. This list reproduces and enlarges on those presented in Domowitz (1993a) and IOSCO (1990).

5. As described in Appendix 1.

6. See Feller (1987), SEC (28/7/1987), and Investment Technology Group (1997).

7. Described in Appendix 1.

8. Unless it is of a most unusual structure.

9. See Mendelson (1990: 25–7, 64).

10. Hasbrouck (1995), for example, argues that a preponderance (92.7%) of price discovery takes place on the NYSE, notwithstanding the long-standing competition offered to the NYSE by the regional exchanges.

11. See, for example, Garbade and Silber (1979) and Pagano and Roëll (1991).

12. See Barclays de Zoete Wedd (1990) and Bernard L. Madoff Investment Securities (1990; 1997).

13. See Schwartz (1991: 27). Although details of the order book were released, the exchange subsequently decided against such a policy. See Association for Investment Management and Research (undated), and SEC Release No. 34-28375 (30/8/1990).

14. See OFT (1994: 44, footnote 1).

15. An e-mail survey of 38 exchanges was conducted asking them what proportion of their total income arose from information sales in 1996. Seventeen exchanges responded usefully. Other sources of information on this issue are difficult to obtain. The three used here are: (i) various exchanges' annual reports; (ii) discussions with different exchanges' managements; and (iii) Gidel (1997: 12).

16. These figures are rounded to the nearest full percentage point. The figure for LIFFE

includes course fees and computer services as well as revenue from information sales. The only available information from the NASDAQ market is that 40% of its revenues comes from a combination of information fees and transaction services. The information from the Winnipeg Commodity Exchange includes fees for 'quotation data and communication fees'.

17. See Figure 2, Bronfman and Overdahl (1992).
18. A checklist of the standard provisions which may be found in a typical vendor contract is provided in Bull (1993),
19. The exchanges (and references) included the Association Tripartite Bourses (1992), Beursdata (1993), Bourse Data Beurs (1993), Canadian Exchange Group (Montréal, Toronto, and Vancouver Stock Exchanges) (1994*a*; *b*), Chicago Board of Trade (1993*a*), Chicago Mercantile Exchange (1993*a*), Commodities Exchange Center (NY, USA) (1993), Copenhagen Stock Exchange (1990; 1993*a*; *b*; *c*), Deutsche Börse (1992), Deutsche Terminbörse (1993), European Options Exchange (1994), International Petroleum Exchange (1993), London International Financial Futures Exchange (1993*a*; *b*; *c*), Commodity Market Services (London Commodities Exchange) (1993), London Stock Exchange (1992, 1993*a*; *b*), Marché À Terme Internationale de France (1993), MEFF Renta Fija (1993), National Association of Securities Dealers (19989*a*; *b*), New York Stock Exchange (1992), Oslo Børs Informasjon (A/S) (1993), Sociedad de Bolsas (1991), Société des Bourses Françaises (1989), Stock Exchange Information Services (Hong Kong Stock Exchange) (1993), Stockholm Stock Exchange (1993), and the Sydney Futures Exchange (1994). Although a vendor contract from the Tokyo Stock Exchange (1993) was not obtained, relevant portions of the contract were described in associated material. The contracts were in force in 1995.
20. See Bremner (1994) and Bull (1994) for a discussion of these other issues.
21. For example, the Stockholm Stock Exchange (1993) charged no fees for data which were delayed by sixty minutes or more.
22. See, for example, Sections 2 and 3, Beursdata (1993), and Section 3, Sociedad de Bolsas (1991).
23. Tokyo Stock Exchange (1993: 6).
24. See Sections 14(a) and (b), NYSE (1992).
25. See Articles, 1.1–1.3, Preamble, and Article 7.1, SBF FIM (1993).
26. Law no. 57-298 of 11 March 1957.
27. 10.1, SEIS, Hong Kong Stock Exchange (1993).
28. Article 4, Bourse Data Beurs Data (1993).
29. 3.1 London Stock Exchange (1993*b*). This right was subject to a minor exception.
30. 3.5.6 London Stock Exchange (1993*a*).
31. 3.5.8 London Stock Exchange (1993*a*). Different rules were however applicable to the non-UK shares traded on SEAQ International.
32. Article 3, Stockholm Stock Exchange (1993).
33. Article II, Section 3.01.(d) NASD (1989*a*; *b*).
34. Beursdata (1993).
35. 10.3, SEIS, Hong Kong Stock Exchange (1993).
36. Section 7, LIFFE (1993*a*).
37. 12, LIFFE (1993*b*).
38. Article 3, Stockholm Stock Exchange (1993).
39. 4.2 (iv) SEIS, Hong Kong Stock Exchange (1993).

40. SEIS, Hong Kong Stock Exchange (1993: 2).
41. Section 8, Appendix 1, Copenhagen Stock Exchange (1993*c*).
42. This section draws on anecdotal evidence and also on FISD, IIA (1992).
43. Section 11, Appendix 1, Copenhagen Stock Exchange (1993*c*).
44. Addendum 1, Association Tripartite Bourses (1992).
45. For example, the NYSE (1992) and the NASD (1989).
46. Section 2.2.b., Beursdata (1993). See also section 13.2, Sydney Futures Exchange (1994).
47. Section 13.2.3, Sydney Futures Exchange (1994). Underlines are in the original.
48. Tokyo Stock Exchange (1993: 10).
49. See #5, SIA and FISD, IIA (1992).
50. I am indebted to Jim Overdahl for the following example of this. In *Wall Street Letter* (3/5/1993), it was reported that Quotron Systems 'bowed to the Chicago Board of Trade last week and paid an undisclosed sum the CBOT claimed Quotron owed it. The payment—which had reportedly been disputed by Quotron—allows the company to continue disseminating CBOT quotes to its customers, confirmed an exchange spokesman. Although the spokesman would not elaborate on the proceedings, sources said Quotron pays the exchange millions each year—about $100 per month for each machine—to supply its customers with commodity quotes.' The dispute arose apparently because the CBOT did an on-site audit of Quotron customers and discovered a significant undercounting due to retransmission restrictions being ignored. The CBOT sent Quotron a bill (rumoured to be around $20 million) for use of data over a several year period.
51. See McPartlin, IPUG (1994).
52. See Waters Information Services (1990). Apparently no formal complaint was registered.
53. See *National Association of Securities Dealers Inc. v. SEC and Institutional Networks Corporation* 801 F.2d 1415 (D.C. Circ. 1986).
54. See *Cantor Fitzgerald and Co. and Ontario Securities Commission, et al.* Statement of Claim, Ontario Court (General Division) Commercial List (25/8/1993).
55. See Tattersall (1990).
56. See Sundel and Blake (1991: 758).
57. See FISD, IIA (1996*b*).
58. CBT (1997*b*).
59. Pricing Attachment to Schedule 1, CBT (1997*c*).

7 CLASSIFICATION AND MARKET STRUCTURE: LAW AND REGULATION

1. For a summary of the SEC's regulatory approach prior to 1996, see Becker *et al.* (1991).
2. See SEC Release No. 34-38672 (23/5/1997).
3. Section 3(a)(1), SEA (1934).
4. Section 3(a)(2), SEA (1934).
5. Section 3(a)(4), SEA (1934). Although the nature of what a broker consists of is not examined here, the SEA definition has proved ambiguous in many circumstances, as analysed by Lipton (1987).
6. Section 3(a)(5), SEA (1934).

7. Section 15A, SEA (1934).
8. Section 3(a)(26), SEA (1934).
9. Section 15A(b)(1)–(8), SEA (1934).
10. Section 5, SEA (1934).
11. In 1996 Congress gave the SEC the right to exempt any person, security or transaction from any provision of the Exchange Act or any rules made under it, if the exemption was 'necessary or appropriate in the public interest and was consistent with the protection of investors'. Section 105, National Securities Markets Improvement Act of 1996. The ways in which the SEC proposed to take advantage of this rule were in the proposals it put forward in 1997, discussed in Chapter 12.
12. See SEC Release No. 34-28899 (20/2/1991). The name the AZX operated under at that time was Wunsch Auction Systems, Inc. (WASI).
13. Section 6(b)(1), SEA (1934).
14. Section 6(b)(2), SEA (1934).
15. Section 6(b)(3), SEA (1934).
16. Section 6(b)(4), SEA (1934).
17. Quotes in this para. are from Section 6(b)(5), SEA (1934).
18. Section 6(b)(6) and (7), SEA (1934).
19. Section 6(b)(8), SEA (1934).
20. Section 19(b)(3), SEA (1934).
21. Sections 19(b)(1) and (2), SEA (1934).
22. SEC Releases No. 34-27445 (16/11/1989) and No. 34-29185 (15/5/1991).
23. Section 10(a), SEA (1934).
24. Section 12(f), SEA (1934).
25. Section 11(a)(1), SEA (1934).
26. Section 17, SEA (1934).
27. For example, a dealer must disgorge short-swing profits on both registered and exempt exchanges. Sections 16(b), (c), and (d), SEA (1934).
28. Section 15(b), SEA (1934).
29. SEC Release No. 34-27611 (12/1/1990: 45).
30. Section 15(b)(4), SEA (1934).
31. Rules 15c3-1, 15c3-3, SEA (1934).
32. Rule 10b-10, SEA (1934).
33. Section 15(c)1-3, SEA (1934), and Rules 15c1-1 to 15c2-12.
34. See Domowitz (1993*a*).
35. See SEC, Rule 17a-23, Release No. 34-33605 (9/2/1994). The definition of a BDTS was made intentionally broad so as to capture information about many new automated trading systems.
36. See Brooks (1986) and SEC (8/8/1986).
37. SEC Release No. 34-26708 (18/4/1989).
38. See Brooks (1986).
39. See SEC (8/8/1986).
40. Section 2, SEA (1934).
41. Section 11(A)(a)(2), SEA (1934).
42. Section 11(A), SEA (1934).
43. Section 11(A), SEA (1934).
44. SEC (10/3/1971).
45. SEC (2/2/1972).

46. SEC Release No. 34-14416 (26/1/1978*b*).
47. US Senate (1975: 7).
48. US Senate (1975: 8–9).
49. US Senate (1975: 16).
50. Section 11A(c)(3), SEA (1934).
51. For this and the next quote, see SEC Release No. 34-14416 (26/1/1978*b*).
52. Section 240.11Aa3-1, C.F.R. This rule was first designated as rule 17a-15, in SEC Release No. 34-9850 (8/11/1972).
53. For a full definition of what securities the three rules apply to, see Sections 240.11Aa2-1, 240.11Aa3-1(a)(4), 240.11Aa3-1(a)(3), C.F.R., CQS (1995), and CTA (1995).
54. Section 240.11Ac1-1, C.F.R. The publication of real-time quotes was originally approved in SEC Release No. 34-14415 (26/1/1978*a*).
55. SEC Release No. 34-37619 (29/8/1996).
56. Ibid. (186).
57. Or to an associated exclusive securities information processor.
58. 240.11Ac1-2, C.F.R.
59. See CQS (1995).
60. The CQ Plan also allows for information about unlisted over-the-counter securities not eligible for the NMS to be disseminated on 'Network C'.
61. See CTA (1995). It started operating on 30 April 1976.
62. See Parker and Becker (1981).
63. See OPRA (believed 1978), and SEC Release No. 34-26780 (26/5/1989: 24–5).
64. See NASD (1990*a*).
65. See SEC Release No. 34-32019 (19/3/1993).
66. See MSRB (1993*a*: 3–5; 1993*b*: 37–42), and SEC (9/1993: 17–21).
67. The ITS arose as a result of Section 11A(a)(3)(B) of the Act and Rule 11Aa3-2—see ITS (1997). The ITS was originally approved in SEC Release 34-14661 (14/4/1978). Since its inception, it has been amended many times.
68. ITS (1991: 51).
69. See ibid. (39–46).
70. Ch. II, Section 3, FSA (1986).
71. S.I. 1995/3273 implements the ISD into the FSA.
72. See section 48, FSA, and orders made under it. A trading system may also be regulated by the Bank of England under Section 43, FSA (1986), if it carries out wholesale market dealings that are not regulated by the rules of an RIE.
73. SFA (1997: 18).
74. See BZW (1988; 1990), and Kleinwort Benson (1990).
75. Service companies must also not guarantee transactions. Rule 1.15 (1)a(ii), SIB (1990*b*: 20).
76. Rule 1.15 (4)a, ibid. (20). The SIB has provided a definition of an 'ordinary business investor' and a 'private customer' in its Core Rules—see Glossary, SIB (1991*b*).
77. These are specified in Rule 1.15 (3), SIB (1990*b*).
78. See Rules 2.10 and 2.11, ibid. (27–8).
79. See SIB (1990*a*; *b*).
80. See SIB (1995: 25–6).
81. Subsection (1), Section 37, FSA (1986).

82. Schedule 4, FSA (1986).
83. Section 119(1) and 119(2), Ch. XIV, FSA (1986).
84. Sections 124–126, Ch. XIV, FSA (1986), exempt the rules of an RIE from part or all of the Fair Trading Act (1973), the Restrictive Trade Practices Act (1976), and the Competition Act (1980).
85. Quotes in this para. come from Section 13, SIB (1987: 45–6).
86. See section 41, FSA (1986).
87. See Section 40, FSA (1986).
88. HMT (1992: 6–7).
89. Ibid. (7).
90. Ibid. (12).
91. Ibid. (3). See also Section 119(4), Ch. XIV, FSA (1986).
92. para. 25B(2), Schedule 1, FSA (1986).
93. para. 25B(2), Schedule 1, FSA (1986).
94. para. 25B(3), Schedule 1, FSA (1986).
95. ISMA was previously known as the Association of International Bond Dealers (AIBD).
96. See SIB (1991*a*; *c*).
97. Section 1(3)(a), FSA (1986).
98. para 26(1) and (2), Schedule 1, FSA (1986).
99. IBIS stands for Integriertes Börsenhandels- und Informations-System—the meaning of which in English is 'integrated stock exchange trading and information system'. The Frankfurt Stock Exchange is now part of Deutsche Börse.
100. See Waters (1991*d*) and Frankfurt Stock Exchange (1991).
101. Only informal sources for this information were available.
102. This is done via HypoBank's TRAX terminal—ISMA's trade confirmation mechanism.
103. The definition of 'investment business' was extended, following implementation of the Investment Services Directive, to include those listed services set out in Section C of the Annexe to the ISD, the most relevant of which for trading systems is 'receiving and transmitting orders on behalf of investors'. This is ignored here.
104. para. 12, Schedule 1, FSA (1986).
105. para. 13, Schedule 1, FSA (1986).
106. SIB (1994: 29).
107. For a general assessment of how European law affects national legislation, see Hartley (1988).
108. See Articles 59–66, Treaty of Rome (25/3/1957).
109. Articles 52–58, Treaty of Rome (25/3/1957).
110. Articles 56 and 66, Treaty of Rome (25/3/1957).
111. See *Rewe-Zentral AG v. Bundesmonopolverwaltung für Branntwein* [1979] ECR 649 Case 120/78, and Usher (1991).
112. Article 8a, Treaty of Rome (25/3/1957).
113. In order to avoid confusion, the term 'home' Member State is always used to apply to the country of origin of an investment firm.
114. Article 15(4), ISD (11/6/1993).
115. Article 1(13), ISD (11/6/1993).
116. Article 21(2), ISD (11/6/1993).

8 INFORMATION: LAW AND REGULATION

1. See Bull (1994) and Geller (1994). The owner of a copyright has the right to restrict copying of the relevant work for a period of the author's life plus seventy years. Berne Copyright Convention (as revised 1886).
2. See, for example, Wolfsen (1996) and National Conference of Commissioners on Uniform State Laws (1996).
3. See, for example, US House of Representatives (1996), and Moorhead (1996). Discussion about a *sui generis* right at the international level is also under way. See WIPO (1997).
4. For an evaluation of the tension between US contract law, which is enacted at the state level, and US copyright law, which is a federal concern, see *ProCD, Inc. v. Zeidenberg* 86 F.3d 1447 (7th Cir. 1996).
5. See Berne Convention 1886, GATT TRIPs 1994, Correa (1994) and Worthy (1994).
6. The definition of what a 'work' means varies across jurisdictions.
7. This section draws on Skone James *et al.* (1991) and Cornish (1989).
8. Section 1.(1), CDPA (1988). Dramatic and musical works are not literary works. 'Computer generated' works may also be relevant for the price and quote data emanating from automated exchanges. See section 178, CDPA (1988).
9. Section 3.(1), CDPA (1988).
10. Section 16.(1), CDPA (1988).
11. Section 16.(2), CDPA (1988).
12. Section 16.(3), CDPA (1988).
13. Section 90.(4), CDPA (1988).
14. *University of London Press Ltd. v. University Tutorial Press Ltd.* [1916] 2 Ch. 601 @ 608.
15. *University of London Press Ltd. v. University Tutorial Press Ltd.* [1916] 2 Ch. 601.
16. *Interlego A.G. v. Tyco Industries* [1988] 3 All E.R. 949.
17. See, for example, *MacMillan & Co. Ltd. v. Cooper* (K. & J.) (1923) 40 T.L.R. 186.
18. *Cramp (G.A.) & Sons Ltd. v. Smythson (Frank) Ltd.* [1944] A.C. 329.
19. See Skone James *et al.* (1991: 20–1).
20. For all quotes in this section, see *Exchange Telegraph Co. Ltd. v. Gregory and Co.* [1896] 1 Q.B. 147.
21. This section draws on Geller (1991), Ginsburg (1990; 1992), Gupta (1992), Miller (1991), Schwarz (1991), and Yen (1991).
22. Article 1, Section 8, Clause 8, Constitution of the USA (4/3/1789).
23. Section 102(a), Copyright Act (1976).
24. Section 103(a), Copyright Act (1976).
25. Section 101, Copyright Act (1976).
26. Section 103(b), Copyright Act (1976).
27. A definition of 'derivative works' is provided in section 101, Copyright Act (1976).
28. *Jeweler's Circular Publishing Co. v. Keystone Publishing Co.* 281 F. 83 (2d Cir. 1922).
29. There has been much uncertainty in the copyright decisions following *Feist*. See IIA (1995: 4–14).
30. *Feist Publications v. Rural Telephone Service Co. Inc.* 111 S.Ct. 1282 @ 1290 (1991).
31. Ibid. @ 1289.

32. Ibid. @ 1296.
33. Ibid. @ 1297.
34. CME (1996*c*: 4), quoting *National Telegraph News Co. v. Western Union Telegraph Co.* 119 F. 294 @ 298 (7th Cir. 1902), that quote data failed to rise to the 'plane of authorship'.
35. The Nasdaq Market, for example, expressly requires broker-dealers who input quotes into Nasdaq workstations to transfer to the NASDAQ Market all ownership rights in these data. See NASDAQ Stock Market (1996*a*: 8).
36. See Reichman and Samuelson (1997), and United States, House of Representatives (1996).
37. Recitals 1–4, Preamble, European Parliament and Council (11/3/1996).
38. Recital 6, Preamble, European Parliament and Council (11/3/1996).
39. Recital 14–15, Preamble, and Article 3(1), European Parliament and Council (11/3/1996).
40. Article 3(2), European Parliament and Council (11/3/1996).
41. Recital 47, European Parliament and Council (11/3/1996).
42. Recital 41, Preamble, and Article 7(1), European Parliament and Council (11/3/1996).
43. Article 10(1), European Parliament and Council (11/3/1996).
44. Article 10(3), European Parliament and Council (11/3/1996).
45. Recital 47, European Parliament and Council (11/3/1996).
46. This is discussed at greater length in Chapter 9.
47. Commission of the European Communities (1992: 51).
48. See Overdahl (1997: 27) who refers to American Law Institute (1993) and Myers (1996).
49. *National Basketball Association v. Sports Team Analysis and Tracking Systems Inc.* 931 F.Supp. 1124 (S.D.N.Y. 1996) and *National Basketball Association v. Sports Team Analysis and Tracking Systems, Inc.* 939 F.Supp. 1071 (S.D.N.Y. 1996).
50. *National Basketball Association v. Motorola, Inc.* 105 F.3d 841 (2nd Cir. 1997).
51. See Mulherin, Netter, and Overdahl (1991*a*; *b*) for a discussion of these cases.
52. *Board of Trade of the City of Chicago v. Christie Grain and Stock Company* 25 Sup.Ct. 637 (1905). The next quote is at 25 Sup. Ct. 637 @ 639.
53. *International News Service v. Associated Press* 248 U.S. 215 (1918).
54. Although INS also obtained the information by bribery, this was not a key factor in the judgment.
55. *International News Service v. Associated Press* 248 U.S. 215 @ 235 (1918).
56. This and the next quote are at ibid. @ 239–40.
57. Subsequent cases extended a similar property right to non-competing firms. See *Dow Jones & Company, Inc. v. Board of Trade of the City of Chicago* 546 F.Supp. 113 (1982), *Board of Trade of the City of Chicago vs. Dow Jones & Company, Inc.* Ill. App. 439 N.E.2d 526 (1982), and *Board of Trade of the City of Chicago vs. Dow Jones & Company, Inc.* 456 N.E.2d 84 (Ill. 1983).
58. Section 301, Copyright Act (1976).
59. H.R. Rep. No. 94-1476 (94th Cong. 2d Sess.) @ 132, reprinted in Nimmer and Nimmer (1990: Appendix 4).
60. See *Computer Associates International, Inc. v. Altai, Inc.* 982 F.2d 693 @ 716 (2d Cir. 1992) and Nimmer and Nimmer (1990: Section 1.01[B]).

61. *National Basketball Association v. Sports Team Analysis and Tracking Systems Inc.* 939 F.Supp. 1071 @ 1098, footnote 24 (S.D.N.Y. 1996).
62. Quotes from this case are at 101 N.Y.S.2d 483 @ 488–92 (Sup.Ct.N.Y.Co. 1950).
63. *National Basketball Association v. Motorola, Inc.* 105 F.3d 841 @ 848–849 (2nd Cir. 1997).
64. Ibid. @ 849.
65. *Financial Information, Inc. v. Moody's Investors Service, Inc.* 808 F.2d 204 (2nd Cir. 1986).
66. *National Basketball Association v. Motorola, Inc.* 105 F.3d 841 @ 851 (2nd Cir. 1997).
67. Ibid. @ 845.
68. Ibid. @ 853.
69. As discussed in Chapter 11.
70. CME (1996*c*: 7).
71. This section draws on Gurry (1985) and ch. 8, Cornish (1989).
72. These were established in *Coco v. Clark (A.N.) (Engineers) Ltd.* [1969] R.P.C. 41 @ 47–48.
73. *Saltman Engineering Co. Ltd. v. Campbell Engineering Co. Ltd.* (1948) 65 R.P.C. 203.
74. See, for example, Gurry (1985: 117, footnote 45).
75. See *Franchi v. Franchi* [1967] R.P.C. 149.
76. *Dunford and Elliott Ltd. v. Johnston and Firth Brown Ltd.* [1978] F.S.R. 143.
77. See *Coco v. Clark (A.N.) (Engineers) Ltd.* [1969] R.P.C. 41.
78. *Exchange Telegraph Co. Ltd. v. Central News Ltd.* [1897] 66 L.J. Ch. 672. All quotes in this section are from the judgment.
79. This section draws on Whish and Sufrin (1993: ch. 19).
80. para. f, Article 3, Treaty of Rome (25/3/1957).
81. Article 86, Treaty of Rome (25/3/1957).
82. See *Hugin Kassaregister A.B. and Hugin Cash Registers v. EC Commission* [1979] ECR 1869 @ 1899 Case 227/78.
83. See *United Brands Co. & United Brands Continental B.V. v. EC Commission* [1978] ECR 207 Case 27/76.
84. See *Nederlandsche Banden-Industrie Michelin NV v. EC Commission* [1983] ECR 3461 Case 322/81.
85. See *United Brands Co. & United Brands Continental B.V. v. EC Commission* [1978] ECR 207 Case 27/76.
86. *Van den Haar (Jan) and Kaveka de Meern BV* [1984] ECR 1797 Cases 177 and 178/82.
87. This section draws on Bonet (1993), Feer Verkade (1996), Flynn (1992), Forrester (1992), Hermitte (1992), Myrick (1992), Reindl (1993), Smith (1992), Subiotto (1992), Van Kerckhove (1995), and Vinje (1992; 1995).
88. There have been Directives on computer software and on the term of a copyright.
89. For this and the next quote, see Article 36, Treaty of Rome (25/3/1957).
90. As discussed below, there were in fact three cases joined together.
91. *Hoffmann-La Roche & Co. A.G. v. Centrafarm* [1978] ECR 1139 Case 102/77.
92. Reindl (1993: 66).
93. *Deutsche Grammophon v. Metro* [1971] ECR 487 Case 78/70.
94. *Volvo A.B. v. Erik Veng (UK) Ltd.* [1988] ECR 6211 @ 6235 Case 238/87.

95. *Volvo A.B. v. Erik Veng (UK) Ltd.* [1988] ECR 6211 Case 238/87. A similar result was found in *CICRA and Maxicar v. Renault* [1988] ECR 6039 Case 53/87.

96. *Volvo AB v. Erik Veng (UK) Ltd.* [1988] ECR 6211 Case 238/87, recital 9.

97. The BBC did in fact allow third parties to publish its listing schedule in the Netherlands and Belgium, where they did not compete with the BBC's own magazine.

98. Dated 26/7/1989.

99. Commission of the European Communities (1988).

100. The appeal cases are *RTE v. EC Commission* [1991] ECR II-485 Case T-69/89, *BBC and BBC Enterprises v. EC Commission* [1991] ECR II-535 Case 70/89, and *ITP Ltd. v. EC Commission* [1991] ECR II-575 Case T-76/89.

101. *RTE v. EC Commission* [1991] ECR II-485 @ 519–520 Case T-69/89.

102. The two cases were joined together for the purposes of oral procedure.

103. *RTE and ITP Ltd. v. EC Commission* [1995] ECR I-747. For analyses of the Advocate General's Opinion, see Haines (1994), Miller (1994), and Van Kerckhove (1994). Subsequent quote is at [1995] ECR I-747 @ 752.

104. The Court examined a range of other issues, including: the effects of the appellants' actions on trade between Member States, whether the Berne Convention was applicable in the case, the powers conferred on the Commission, and the extent to which the Commission exhibited a lack of reasoning.

105. *RTE and ITP Ltd. v. EC Commission* [1995] ECR I-808 @ 822 Joined Cases C-241/91 P and C-242/91 P.

106. Ibid. @ 822.

107. Ibid. @ 824.

108. Ibid. @ 825.

109. ASX made a cross-claim against Pont, which was dismissed in court and is ignored here.

110. This section draws on Pont Data (1990).

111. In 1987, this was augmented with a fee of A$5,000 per information vendor.

112. *Pont Data Australia v. ASX Operations and Another* (1990) 93 ALR 523 @ 528.

113. These quotes are taken from ibid. @ 535–6. The information was that previously carried in Signal C.

114. Ibid. @ 533.

115. Ibid. @ 549.

116. Quotes in this and the next three paragraphs come from ibid. @ 549–54.

117. Ibid. @ 557.

118. Ibid. @ 560.

119. Ibid. @ 562.

120. Ibid. @ 564.

121. For a full description of the sittings of the court, see Pont Data (1990). The judge did however allow the ASX to make an application to change the figure 'if the respondents felt able to demonstrate that they did in fact incur a cost in supplying Signal C over and above the costs which they would otherwise incur and the proceeds of a nominal charge'.

122. Federal Court of Australia (1990: 7).

123. See Pont Data (1990).

124. *ASX Operations and Another v. Pont Data Australia* (1991) 100 ALR 125 @ 135.

125. Italics in the rest of this section are added.

126. *ASX Operations and Another v. Pont Data Australia* (1991) 100 ALR 125.
127. Ibid. @ 137. The merits of the pre-9 September 1988 fee scale were not examined.
128. The discussion about the LSE could have been classified in this chapter under competition law and regulation, given that the prime aim of the OFT is to prevent anti-competitive activity.
129. Section 3(a)(22)(A), SEA (1934).
130. Section 3(a)(22)(B), SEA (1934).
131. Section 11A(b)(1), SEA (1934).
132. Section 11A(b)(3), SEA (1934).
133. Section 11A(b)(5)(A) and (B), SEA (1934).
134. United States Senate (1975).
135. Section 11A(c)(1)(A)–(F), SEA (1934).
136. All quotes in this section come from SEC Release No. 34-15372 (29/11/1978).
137. The NQDS initially only contained information about NASDAQ/NMS stocks. At a later stage, the NASD agreed to supply information about all NASDAQ securities.
138. Section II, part G.1.b, SEC Release No. 34-20874 (17/4/1984).
139. Section I, part E, ibid.
140. Section II, part G.2.b, ibid.
141. Quoted from *New York, New Haven and Hartford Railroad v. US* 199 F.Supp. 635 @ 643 (D.C. Conn. 1961).
142. Section 11A(b)(5), SEA (1934).
143. SEC (30/10/1985: 37).
144. Ibid. (36).
145. *NASD Inc. v. SEC and Instinet* 801 F.2d 1415 @ 1419 (D.C. Cir. 1986).
146. Ibid. @ 1421.
147. Ibid. @ 1422.
148. See SEC Releases No. 34-28639 (21/11/1990*a*) and No. 34-28640 (21/11/1990*b*). The SEC approved an exemption from the exchange fee in Release No. 34-29238 (28/5/1991). Subsequent to the ruling, the NYSE revised the publication requirements for trading on its OHT facilities in 1993. See NYSE (1993).
149. See SEC Release No. 34-29237 (24/5/1991). All quotes in this section come from this release.
150. See NASD (undated—believed 1987; 1990*b*; 1991), and further references therein.
151. See SEC Release No. 34-29812 (11/10/1991).
152. Ibid. (30).
153. Quotes in this paragraph are in ibid. (37–9).
154. Underlines are in the original.
155. For a summary of the SIB's views on transparency on the LSE, SIB (1996: 23).
156. See Council Notices 6/89, 9/89, 24/89 and 110/89, LSE.
157. See LSE (1989: 21–2).
158. para. 2.6, Appendix, Council Notice 6/89, LSE.
159. OFT (1990*a*: 9).
160. This and the next quote are on ibid. (18).
161. This and the next quote are on ibid. (19–20).
162. Ibid. (25).
163. See Council Notices 5/91 and 6/91, LSE. The initial discussion of the need to reform the transparency rules is in International Stock Exchange (1989; 1990).
164. See Council Notice 65/93, LSE.

165. OFT (1994: 22).
166. Ibid. (23).
167. This research is also reported in Gemmill (1996), and discussed in Chapter 10.
168. OFT (1994: 30).
169. See de Jong, Nijman, and Roëll (1995), Pagano and Roëll (1990*a*), and Roëll (1992).
170. See Breedon (1993).
171. OFT (1994: 41).
172. Ibid. (36).
173. Ibid. (37).
174. Ibid. (39).

9 GOVERNANCE: LAW AND REGULATION

1. One particular type of conflict of interest on exchange boards is ignored, namely when a board member takes advantage of his position by trading on the basis of non-public information obtained as a consequence of his being a board member. CFTC Regulation 1.59, for example, requires exchanges to adopt rules that prohibit the misuse and disclosure by governing members of material, non-public information obtained in the course of their duties, but does not prohibit board participation by persons affiliated with a firm that trades commodities for the firm's accounts or its customers' accounts. See also CFTC (1984).
2. See, for example, CFTC (1976), (1977), and SEC Releases No. 34-32527 (28/6/1993) and No. 34-33901 (12/4/1994).
3. In the UK, for example, almost the only relevant regulatory statement on exchange governance has been a code of conduct on conflicts of interest in regulatory authorities. See SIB (1993). Judicial examination of exchange governance has been minimal. See, however, Frase (1993), *R. v. The International Stock Exchange ex parte Else* 1993 1 All E.R. 420, and *Shearson v. Maclaine* [1989] 2 Q.B. (Com. Ct.) 570.
4. All exchanges are incorporated under state corporation law, and their boards are thus subject to the state law provisions applicable to all company boards of directors. Company directors typically have fiduciary duties of care and loyalty to act on an informed basis, in good faith, in the honest belief that their actions are in the best interests of the company, and without self-interest.
5. The question of whether market participants should be required to regulate their own markets has long been debated in the USA. See Loss and Seligman (1990: 2692–705), NASD (1995: II-5 to II-21), and Study VI, SEC (1/1994).
6. Douglas (1940: 82).
7. SEC (1/1994: VI-3).
8. Miller (1985).
9. Peake and Mendelson (1991).
10. Quoted in NASD (1995: II-14).
11. See, for example, CFTC (1985: 683), National Market Advisory Board (1976), and *Crimmins v. American Stock Exchange, Inc.* 368 F.Supp. 270 @ 281 (S.D.N.Y. 1973).
12. Section 6(b)(3), SEA (1934).
13. Quoted on SEC (1/1994: VI-7).

14. Section 6(c)(1), SEA (1934).
15. Section 3(a)(3)(A), SEA (1934).
16. Section 6(f)(1), SEA (1934).
17. See SEC Release No. 34-38672 (23/5/1997: 59, footnote 101).
18. See, for example, Loss and Seligman (1990: 2670–91) and SEC Release No. 34-26708 (18/4/1989, footnote 31).
19. *Board of Trade of the City of Chicago v. SEC* 923 F.2d 1270 @ 1272 (7th Cir. 1991).
20. Section 6(b)(5), SEA (1934).
21. SEC Releases No. 34-21439 (31/10/1984) and No. 34-34-22058 (21/5/1985).
22. SEC Release No. 34-21122 (6/7/1984*b*).
23. SEC Release No. 34-21121 (6/7/1984*a*).
24. SEC Release No. 34-16701 (26/3/1980).
25. SEC Release No. 34-21439 (31/10/1984: 6).
26. SEC Release No. 34-22058 (21/5/1985).
27. Ibid. (footnote 49).
28. SEC Release No. 34-22728 (19/12/1985).
29. SEC Release No. 34-24212 (20/3/1987).
30. SEC Release No. 34-24090 (12/2/1987).
31. SEC Release No. 34-24212 (20/3/1987).
32. SEC Releases No. 34-20221 (23/9/1983), No. 34-24212 (20/3/1987), No. 34-28936 (4/3/1991), and No. 34-31633 (22/12/1992).
33. See SEC Release No. 34-38672 (23/5/1997: 66–67, footnote 118).
34. SEC Release No. 34-36417 (25/10/1995). The quotes below come from this Release.
35. SEC Release No. 34-33737 (8/3/1994).
36. SEC Release No. 34-32541 (29/6/1993).
37. SEC Release No. 34-31850 (10/2/1993).
38. For example, SEC Releases No. 34-25448 (11/3/1988) and No. 34-30465 (11/3/1992).
39. See Blume, Siegel, and Rottenberg (1993: 128–42).
40. See NASD (1995) and SEC (8/8/1996: 44).
41. See SEC (3/1/1962).
42. Martin (1971: 7).
43. For this and the next quote, see section 206, Futures Trading Practices Act (1992).
44. CFTC (1993*a*: 13566).
45. Ibid. (13567).
46. CFTC (1995: 8–9).
47. Section 404, Futures Trading Practices Act 1992.
48. CME (1993*c*: 4).
49. CBT (1993*b*: 2).
50. COMEX (1993: 2).
51. Regulation 1.64, CFTC (1993*b*).
52. The introduction to this section, and the description of the judicial and regulatory analysis of conflicts of interests, draws in part on Committee on Commodities Regulation, New York Bar Association (1985). The CFTC's current rules on the issue of conflicts of interest on exchange boards develop its previous examination of this issue. See, for example, CFTC (1980*a*; *b*; 1982).
53. CFTC (1985: 688, footnote 5).

54. This a substantively modified version of a definition provided in Committee on Commodities Regulation, New York Bar Association (1985: 370).

55. Although accepted by the courts for many years, private rights of action against exchanges and their officers and directors for failure to enforce their rules and for violations of law committed in enforcing those rules, were only statutorily granted by Congress in 1989. Sections 22(b)(4) and 25(b) and (d), CEA.

56. A claim that the CEA should be pre-empted by the Sherman Act, regulating anti-trust activity, was dismissed in *American Agriculture v. Board of Trade of the City of Chicago* 977 F.2d 1147 (7th Cir. 1992).

57. Section 5(d), CEA.

58. Section 5(g), CEA.

59. Section 5, CEA 1982 and CFTC Regulation 1.41. If an exchange declares an emergency, it is required to notify the Commission as soon as possible of its actions responding to the emergency, and provide an explanation of why the actions were taken.

60. *Daniel v. Board of Trade of the City of Chicago* 164 F.2d 815 (7th Cir. 1947). The 'bad faith' standard was also applied in *Cargill v. Board of Trade of the City of Chicago* 164 F.2d 820 (7th Cir. 1947). The need to protect exchange board members from unspecified and insubstantial claims of self-interest was recognized in *Crowley v. Commodity Exchange Inc.* 141 F.2d 182 (2d. Cir. 1944).

61. *Daniel v. Board of Trade of the City of Chicago* 164 F.2d 815 @ 819–820 (7th Cir. 1947).

62. *Chicago Mercantile Exchange* [1977-1980 Transfer Binder] Commodities Futures Law Reports (CCH) Sect. 20,436 @ 21,786 (20/5/1977).

63. *P.J. Taggares Co. v. New York Mercantile Exchange* 476 F.Supp. 72 @ 76 (S.D.N.Y. 1979).

64. *Joy v. North* 692 F.2d 880 @ 886–887 (2d Cir. 1982) quoted in *Bishop v. Commodity Exchange* 564 F.Supp. 1557 @ 1561, footnote 3 (S.D.N.Y. 1983).

65. *Gordon v. Hunt* 551 F.Supp. 509 @ 510 (S.D.N.Y. 1982). See also *Ryder Energy Distribution Corp. v. Merrill Lynch Commodities, Inc.* 748 F.2d 774 (2d Cir. 1984).

66. *Gordon v. Hunt* 558 F.Supp. 122 @ 123 (S.D.N.Y. 1983).

67. *Bishop v. Commodity Exchange* 564 F.Supp. 1557 @ 1559 (S.D.N.Y. 1983).

68. Ibid. @ 1562. Further quotes from this case are on the same page.

69. Italics in original.

70. *Bishop v. Commodity Exchange* 564 F.Supp. 1557 @ 1561, footnote 3 (S.D.N.Y. 1983).

71. *Sam Wong and Son Inc. v. New York Mercantile Exchange* 735 F.2d 653 (2d Cir. 1984). The case was consolidated with another case, *Spinale v. New York Mercantile Exchange*.

72. *Sam Wong and Son Inc. v. New York Mercantile Exchange* 735 F.2d 653 @ 674 (2d Cir. 1984).

73. Ibid. @ 675.

74. Ibid. @ 677.

75. Ibid. @ 673.

76. *Jordon v. New York Mercantile Exchange* 571 F.Supp. 1530 @ 1538, footnote 2 (S.D.N.Y. 1983).

77. Ibid. @ 1548.

78. Ibid. @ 1539.

79. Ibid. @ 1552.
80. *Minpeco, S.A. v. Hunt* 693 F.Supp. 58 @ 61–62 (S.D.N.Y. 1988), quoting from *Brawer v. Options Clearing Corp.* 807 F.2d 297 @ 302 (2d Cir. 1986).
81. *Minpeco, S.A. v. Hunt* 693 F.Supp. 58 @ 64 (S.D.N.Y. 1988).
82. Again quoting from *Brawer v. Options Clearing Corp.* 807 F.2d 297 @ 303 n. 9 (2d Cir. 1986).
83. *Minpeco, S.A. v. Hunt* 693 F.Supp. 58 @ 66 (S.D.N.Y. 1988).
84. Ibid. @ 69.
85. For example, CFTC (1980*a*; 1989*b*).
86. All quotes from this report are in CFTC (1985: 681–7).
87. Underlines in original.
88. Section 217, Futures Trading Practices Act (1992).
89. CFTC (1996: 19870).
90. Proposed Regulation 1.69(b)(1).
91. CFTC (1996: 19872).
92. Proposed Regulation 1.69(b)(2).
93. CSCE (1996). Each exchange's commentary is only referenced once.
94. CBT (1996).
95. CME (1996*b*).
96. NYCE (1996).
97. NYMEX (1996).
98. Quote is from NYMEX (1996). See also FIA (1996).
99. CFTC (1998).
100. This and the next quote are in Committee on Commodities Regulation, New York Bar Association (1985: 373–4).

10 INFORMATION: ECONOMICS

1. This section draws on Varian (1984).
2. The original statement of Coasian bargaining is in Coase (1960).
3. This section draws on Admati (1989; 1991), Bray (1985), and Grossman (1989).
4. As identified in Admati (1989).
5. See Admati and Pfleiderer (1986; 1987), Diamond (1985), and Verrechia (1982).
6. References for other work examining partially-revealing REE are provided therein.
7. For examples of regulatory positions justified by reference to the efficient markets hypothesis, see GAO (1990: 77), OFT (1994: 23), and SIB (1994: 8).
8. Copeland and Weston (1983: 286).
9. The classification of the three information sets is ascribed to Roberts (1967) in Campbell, Lo, and MacKinlay (1997: 22).
10. See Campbell, Lo, and MacKinlay (1997: 20–6).
11. See, for example, Dimson (1988).
12. But see, for example, Danthine and Moresi (1993), Hakansson, Kunkel, and Ohlson (1982), and Hirschleifer and Riley (1979).
13. Other authors have also studied the importance of anonymity. See Admati and Pfleiderer (1991), Fishman and Longstaff (1992), Grossman (1992), Harris (1991), Miller (1990), and Roëll (1990).

14. For a description of how the upstairs market works, see ch. 3, Schwartz (1991).
15. See NASD (1983).
16. This designation of alpha and beta had nothing to do with the Stock Exchange's similar and earlier such designations.
17. Board and Sutcliffe (1995: 1).
18. Ibid. (2).
19. Ibid. (161).
20. A full list of references is in ibid. (44).
21. See Hodges (1994) for a summary of the links between cash and futures markets.
22. Flood *et al.* also varied the ratio of customers to market makers, using this as a proxy for the rate of flow of fundamental information.
23. See Bronfman *et al.* (1992) for some experimental results that do examine the effects of transparency on the allocational efficiency of different market structures.
24. Extensions of the literature that address these two concerns are beginning to be developed in games of incomplete information. See, for example, Morris and Shin (1994).

11 INFORMATION AND COMPETITION: POLICY

1. See, for example, Brazier (1996) on the topic of insider trading, and Pirrong (1995) on the topic of manipulation.
2. For discussions of the nature and difficulties of defining and assessing systemic risk, see, for example, Bingham (1989), Dale (1996), Davis (1995), and OECD (1990).
3. See, for example, Lee (1997*a*).
4. See, for example, Buchanan and Tullock (1962), Demsetz (1969), Peltzman (1976), and Stigler (1971). The question of whether it is useful to ascribe to a regulatory agency, as opposed to the individuals of whom the agency is composed, the desire to pursue particular goals is open to debate.
5. *Board of Trade of the City of Chicago v. USA* 246 U.S. 231 @ 238 (1918).
6. The SEC's two most extended defences of mandatory transparency are in SEC (1/1994: IV-1 to IV-5), and SEC Release No. 34-37619 (29/8/1996). All unreferenced quotes in this section come from the first reference.
7. SEC Release No. 34-37619 (29/8/1996: 86).
8. SEC (2/2/1972: 9-10).
9. See also Amihud and Mendelson (1991).
10. Statement by the SEC upon Release of the Market 2000 Report (27/1/1994).
11. A similar argument against a lack of transparency was made by the OFT in its examination of the rules of the LSE.
12. SEC (26/9/1991: 7).
13. SEC Release No. 34-37619 (29/8/1996: 92). Underlines in original.
14. See, for example, Steil (1994).
15. See ch. 11, Williamson (1996) for a discussion of the merits of the transactions cost approach to antitrust analysis.
16. Quotes in this paragraph come from Mulherin, Netter, and Overdahl (1991*a*: 594).
17. *Wilson v. Telegram Company* 18 N.Y. St. Repr. 78 (1888), tried in Superior Court of Kings County, NY.
18. *Board of Trade of the City of Chicago v. Christie Grain and Stock Company* 25 Sup. Ct. 637 (1905).

19. Mulherin, Netter, and Overdahl (1991*a*: 626).
20. Mulherin, Netter, and Overdahl (1991*b*: 109).
21. As previously noted, variants of this form of discrimination have been practised by the NYSE, the CME on GLOBEX, and the Brussels Stock Exchange.
22. OFT (1995: 38–43).
23. Following this pressure by the OFT, the LSE amended the rule. See Cohen (1995*a*).
24. OFT (1995: 42).
25. For example in the Czech republic. An initiative to make the market more transparent is described in Broker's Club, Prague Stock Exchange (1995*a*; *b*), and *World Securities Law Report* (1995: 14–15). Apparently the initiative failed.
26. See Garbade and Silber (1978), and Pagano and Roëll (1991).
27. See SEC Release No. 34-29812 (11/10/1991: 37–9).
28. In mid-1994 the Paris Bourse sanctioned the delay of information about large trades, and the Amsterdam Stock Exchange permitted information about large trades not to be published until the next day. See Conseil des Bourses de Valeurs (1994*a*; *b*), Société des Bourses Françaises (1994*a*; *b*; *c*), and Amsterdam Stock Exchange (1994*a*; *b*).
29. These, and many other, criticisms of the rules are discussed in SEC (1996).
30. SEC Release No. 34-37619 (29/8/1996: 106).
31. See, for example, Clemons and Weber (1989), ch. 4, Lee (1989) and Franks and Schaefer (1990).
32. A similar delay has been allowed in the 'worked principal agreements' rules. See LSE (1997*c*).
33. Porter and Weaver (1996*b*) and SEC Release No. 34-37542 (8/8/1996).
34. See Sundel and Blake (1991).
35. Board and Sutcliffe (1995: 16).
36. See Lee (1989: 57, 82–4).
37. See, for example, Levitt (1994), and the fact that as of May 1997 on the home page of the SEC on the Internet, the SEC quotes a statement from William Douglas, its first chairman, stating that 'We are the investors' advocate'.
38. For a summary of the international debate in the early 1990s, see IOSCO (1992), SEC (1/1994: IV-16, footnote 7), and SIB (1992). The SIB also promoted a relatively lax transparency regime in the discussions concerning the ISD. Since the early 1990s, however, there appears to have been a gradual convergence of the SIB's attitudes to those of the SEC.
39. Discussed in the next chapter.
40. See ch. 2.1, Varian (1984).
41. See ch. 7.6, ibid., and ch. 15.2, Atkinson and Stiglitz (1980).
42. It is assumed here that the demands for information and for trading market services are independent, and that there are no income effects.
43. Article 12, para. 11, Loi 4 Décembre 1990 Belgium (4/12/1990). A similar conclusion was reached in *Société des Bourses Françaises et Société Cote Desfossés c/Société Sarl Option Service*.
44. The SEC, itself, was quoting from *New York, New Haven and Hartford Railroad v. US* 199 F.Supp. 635 @ 643 (D.C. Conn. 1961).
45. *Pont Data Australia v. ASX and ASXO* (1990) 93 ALR 523 @ 545.
46. Quoted in *Futures Industry Magazine* (1995: 26).
47. See SEC Release No. 34-15372 (29/11/1978).

12 CLASSIFICATION AND GOVERNANCE: POLICY

1. This chapter draws on, reproduces, and extends, Domowitz and Lee (1996).
2. The problem of regulating automated trading systems has been discussed in Australia, see ASC (1995*a*; *b*); in Ontario, Canada, see OSC (1994*a*; *b*; *c*; *d*); in France, see COB, Champarnaud, and Perier (1994); and in the UK, see SIB (1995).
3. For a discussion of classificatory questions relating to the futures markets, see Domowitz (1990*b*; 1993*c*).
4. SEC Release No. 34-38672 (23/5/1997).
5. Section 105, National Securities Markets Improvement Act 1996.
6. *Board of Trade of the City of Chicago v. SEC* 923 F.2d 1270 @ 1273 (7th Cir. 1991). For a description of the Delta trading system and this case, see Lee (1992).
7. See SEC Release No. 34-27611 (12/1/1990: 50, footnote 100).
8. US Senate (1934: 5).
9. *Board of Trade of the City of Chicago v. SEC* 883 F.2d 525 @ 525 (7th Cir. 1989).
10. See *Board of Trade of the City of Chicago v. SEC* 923 F.2d 1270 (7th Cir. 1991).
11. SEC Release No. 34-27611 (12/1/1990: 19), and similar language in SEC (1/1994: III-12), where this 'characteristic' is described as the 'function' of an exchange.
12. *Board of Trade of the City of Chicago v. SEC* 923 F.2d 1270 @ 1272 (7th Cir. 1991).
13. *LTV v. UMIC Government Securities, Inc.* 523 F.Supp. 819 @ 835–6 (1981).
14. SEC Release No. 34-27611 (12/1/1990: 28–35).
15. This was, for example, stated by the Director of the Division of Market Regulation at the SEC. SEC (5/1/1989: 97).
16. SEC Release No. 34-27611 (12/1/1990: 34–6).
17. SEC (27/4/1990: 16, footnote 18). See also SEC Release No. 34-26708 (18/4/1989), and SEC Release No. 34-28899 (20/2/1991: 15, footnote 36).
18. SEC (27/4/1990: 16).
19. Ibid. (30–1). Underlines in original.
20. See *Board of Trade of the City of Chicago v. SEC* 923 F.2d 1270 @ 1275–1276 (7th Cir. 1991).
21. This was the CSE which had an average of 717 trades per day and an average daily share volume of 1,238,241.
22. See SEC Release No. 34-26708 (18/4/1989).
23. See for example, SEC (24/11/1992), (9/9/1993), and (1/10/1993).
24. See SEC Release No. 34-26708 (18/4/1989).
25. See SEC Release No. 34-28899 (20/2/1991: 15, footnote 36). Lee (1992: 25) discusses how the AZX decision can also, however, be viewed as a means of avoiding a regulatory problem by SEC.
26. See SEC (1/1994: III-12).
27. See Lee (1993*a*).
28. This is argued by Maynard (1992).
29. The correct parsing of the language was touched on in *Board of Trade of the City of Chicago v. SEC* 923 F.2d 1270 @ 1272 (7th Cir. 1991).
30. SEC Release No. 34-27611 (12/1/1990: 19).
31. Italics added. Section 3(a)(3)(A), SEA (1934).
32. See, for example, SEC Release No. 34-27611 (12/1/1990: 49–50), and SEC Release No. 34-33605 (9/2/1994: 3).
33. SEC Release No. 34-37619 (29/8/1996: 11).

34. See SEC Release No. 34-33605 (9/2/1994: 8,   footnote 10).
35. SEC (1/1994: III-11).
36. Ibid. (VI-9).
37. The amalgamation of all the SROs in 1997 changed this.
38. SEC (1/1994: VI-9).
39. See Bronfman, Lehn, and Schwartz (1994: 50–3).
40. In 1989, Commissioner Grundfest stated, for example, that 'we're trying to structure rules that foster innovation, which is a little bit of an oxymoron right there'. Hearing before the SEC (5/1/1989: 83).
41. SEC (27/4/1990: 13–14).
42. Italics added.
43. As remarked in the dissenting opinion in the 'Delta' judgment, the stock market crashes of 1987 and 1989 also confirmed that even in what are thought to be the most liquid markets, where two-sided quotes are provided by design, there are times when the ability to execute transactions disappears. *Board of Trade of the City of Chicago v. SEC* 923 F.2d 1270 @ 1275 (7th Cir. 1991).
44. As noted again in the dissenting opinion in the Delta judgment, ibid. @ 1275.
45. SEC (1/1994: III-3).
46. Ignoring the possibility that the exchange might lose such an amount of trading volume that it could seek a low volume exemption from registration.
47. SEC (1/1994: III-12).
48. SEC Release No. 34-38672 (23/5/1997: 20).
49. Ibid. (7, footnote 1).
50. Ibid. (21).
51. Ibid. (22).
52. Ibid. (7).
53. Ibid. (23).
54. Ibid. (25).
55. Ibid. (25).
56. Ibid. (25–6).
57. The quotes in this paragraph are in ibid. (26).
58. Ibid. (29).
59. Ibid. (32).
60. See, for example, Donohue and Van Zandt (1995), Hawes (1987), International Capital Markets Group (1989*a*; *b*; 1991), IOSCO (1994), Karmel (1986; 1993), Kübler (1987), and SEC (27/7/1987). The issue of whether competition between jurisdictions is beneficial has been examined in many places. See, for example, Buxbaum and Hopt (1988), and Buxbaum *et al.* (1991; 1996).
61. Outside the EU, there have been a number of cross-border trading systems for which dedicated inter-jurisdictional regulatory agreements have been established. For a discussion of inter-jurisdictional regulatory questions relating to GLOBEX, see CFTC (1989*a*). The SEC examined appropriate ways of regulating foreign automated trading systems in the USA in part VII, SEC Release No. 34-38672 (23/5/1997).
62. See Lee (1994) and Steil (1993).
63. This included, for example, attempting to require that all trades be 'concentrated' on 'regulated' markets, and then defining a regulated market specifically to exclude particular types of national markets. The most important such market was SEAQ

International, the London Stock Exchange's trading system which at the time was very successful in attracting order flow from the continental European stock exchanges.

64. As discussed in Chapter 7. See Article 15(4), ISD (11/6/1993).
65. See Perier (1994).
66. SEC Release No. 34-26708 (18/4/1989).
67. SEC Release No. 34-33621 (14/2/1994).
68. See, for example, International Capital Markets Group (1994), International Councils of Securities Associations (1993), IOSCO (1990; 1994), and Merton (1993).
69. For a discussion of the difficulties of measuring trading volume, see SEC Release No. 34-28577 (24/10/1990).
70. SEC Release No. 34-38672 (23/5/1997: 35).
71. Ibid. (48).
72. Ibid. (74, footnote 132).
73. Ibid. (57).
74. Ibid. (67).
75. Participation in OPRA and the NASDAQ/NMS/Unlisted Privileges would also be necessary where appropriate.
76. SEC Release No. 34-38672 (23/5/1997: 90).
77. Ibid. (92).
78. Ibid. (94).
79. Ibid. (94).
80. Ibid. (105).
81. For a discussion of the question of sufficient capacity, see NYSE (1989).
82. SEC Release No. 34-38672 (23/5/1997: 75).
83. Ibid. (75).
84. Ibid. (77).
85. IOSCO (1994: 1).
86. IOSCO (1990: 1).
87. See for example, Schwartz (1991) and Steil *et al.* (1996).
88. The managers of both the competing European stock exchanges, and the competing European futures exchanges, certainly do not believe that any success of their rivals in attracting order flow will rebound positively on their own exchanges.
89. See, for example, SEC Release No. 34-38672 (23/5/1997: 17, footnote 20; 66).
90. See Lee (1996).
91. Melamed (1989: 364).
92. See SEC Release No. 34-28899 (28/2/1991: 19).
93. This and the next problem are discussed in SEC, Division of Market Regulation (26/9/1991: 4, footnote 4).
94. A choice, for example, that Instinet has expressly made.
95. SEC Release No. 34-28899 (20/2/1991: 40).
96. For this and the next argument, see SEC, Division of Market Regulation (1/1994: VI-5). This is an argument against the separation recently undertaken by the NASD of its regulation of its members from the regulation of its market.
97. IOSCO (1994: 9–10).
98. US Senate (1973: 160).
99. SEC Release No. 34-38672 (23/5/1997: 20–1).

100. Ibid. (102–3).
101. For an example of an international MOU, see SEC and ASC (20/10/1993).
102. See Lee (1993*b*).

APPENDIX 1 TRADING SYSTEMS

1. For a list of trading systems not regulated as exchanges in the USA, see Appendix IV, SEC, Division of Market Regulation (1/1994). In 1997, the SEC reported that there were about 140 such systems in the securities markets in the USA—SEC Release No. 34-38672 (23/5/1997: 15, footnote 14). For various other lists of automated trading systems, see Domowitz (1993*b*), Grody and Levecq (1993), and Grody, Levecq and Weber (1994).

2. See, for example, Schwartz (1991).

3. See also Domowitz (1990*a*; 1993*b*; *d*), and IOSCO (1990).

4. The sources for this description are: AZX (1992*a*; *b*; 1997); Brooks (1990); SEC Release No. 34-28577 (24/10/1990), Release No. 34-28899 (20/2/1991), and (28/2/1991); WASI (1990*a*; *b*; *c*; *d*; *e*); Wunsch (1988), and discussions with AZX management. The priorities have been changed from those presented in the description, so that time is now the primary priority. Orders with worse prices that are submitted earlier, may thus now preempt orders with better prices that are submitted later.

5. A rule similar to the NYSE's trade-through rule determines the exact auction price in these circumstances.

6. The sources for this description are: SEC Release No. 34-27611 (12/1/1990); Delta excerpts in CBT/CME Petitioners' Appendix (1990); RMJ Options Trading Corp. (undated—believed 1989*a*; *b*). The term Delta is used here to refer to the whole system. All quotes in this section come from these sources.

7. The operational link between DGOC and RMJ Options was subsequently disbanded, and now many brokers can provide similar functions to those previously solely provided by RMJ Options.

8. The sources for this description are: Brooks (1986); SEC (8/8/1986), Instinet (1990*a*: Appendix B; 1990*b*; 1991; 1992), Instinet Canada Limited, Appendix B, (1990), OSC (1990), Reuters Australia (1988), Schedule 'A', Toronto Stock Exchange (1990), and discussions with Instinet management. Quotes in this section come from these sources.

9. Although the system described here is the major activity of the Instinet corporation, the company also runs another trading mechanism called the Crossing Network, which allows shares to be crossed at the closing prices of the NYSE.

10. The extent to which expired orders remain on the screen depends on the level of trading activity.

11. Broker-dealers, market makers and specialists are defined not to be institutions.

APPENDIX 2 DEFINITIONS

1. There were very few entries specifically under 'futures exchange'.

2. The four general dictionaries are the Macdonald, *Chambers Twentieth Century Dictionary* [CTCD] (1978), the *Oxford English Dictionary* [OED] (1975), Stein,

the *Random House College Dictionary* [RHCD] (1979), and Grove *Webster's Third New International Dictionary* [WTNID] (1961). The specialist finance and economics dictionaries are Collin (1996), Corben (1997), D'Andrea (1996), Economist Books (1994), Mahony (1997), Moles and Terry (1997), Rutherford (1995), Webber (1994), and Woelfel (1994). Dates are not put in subsequent references.

3. WTNID, CTCD, and RHCD.
4. OED and RHCD.
5. OED and WTNID.
6. Corben, Collin, D'Andrea, Economist, Mahony, Moles and Terry, and Rutherford.
7. Collin, Mahony, Moles and Terry, and Woelfel.
8. D'Andrea, Moles and Terry, Woelfel.
9. Moles and Terry.
10. Economist, Mahony, Moles and Terry, and Rutherford.
11. D'Andrea, Moles and Terry.
12. Woelfel.
13. D'Andrea and Rutherford.
14. Woelfel, and Moles and Terry.
15. Moles and Terry.
16. Mahony.
17. Mahony, and Moles and Terry.
18. Mahony, and Moles and Terry.
19. Collin, Mahony, and Moles and Terry.
20. Collin and Rutherford.
21. Collin, D'Andrea, Moles and Terry, and Rutherford.
22. Woelfel.
23. Moles and Terry, and Rutherford.
24. Moles and Terry.
25. Moles and Terry.

AUTHORITIES

AUSTRALIA

Trade Practices Act (1974) (Cth).

BOTSWANA

Botswana Stock Exchange Act, 1994. Act No. 11 of 1994.
Botswana Stock Exchange Regulations, 1995. Statutory Instrument No. 74 of 1995.

BELGIUM

Loi 4 décembre 1990 relative aux opérations financières et aux marchés financiers.

EUROPEAN UNION

Treaty Establishing the European Economic Community, as amended. (25/3/1957). (Treaty of Rome).
Council Directive 93/22/EEC of 10 May 1993 on Investment Services in the Securities Field.
Directive 96/9/EC of the European Parliament and of the Council on the Legal Protection of Databases.

FRANCE

Loi No. 57–298 du 11 Mars 1957 sur la propriété littéraire et artistique.

SWEDEN

Lag om bors- och clearingverksamhet. (17/6/1992). Svensk forfattningssamling. SFS 1992: 543.

UK

Competition Act (c.21) 1980.
Copyright, Designs and Patents Act (c.48) 1988.
Fair Trading Act (c.41) 1973.

Financial Services Act (c.60) 1986.
Restrictive Trade Practices Act (c.34) 1976.
Sale of Goods Act (c.54) 1979.
Supply of Goods and Services Act (c.29) 1982.
Unfair Contract Terms Act (c.50) 1977.
Investment Services Regulations 1995. Statutory Instrument 1995/3275, coming into force 1/1/1996, except for Regulations 27 and 31, coming into force 1/1/1997.

USA

Constitution of the United States of America. (4/3/1789).
Commodity Exchange Act 1936, as amended.
Copyright Act 1976.
Futures Trading Practices Act 1992. Pub.L. 102–546, (28/10/1992), 106 Stat. 3590.
National Securities Markets Improvements Act 1996. Pub.L. 104–290, (11/10/1996), 110 Stat. 3416.
Securities Exchange Act 1934, as amended.

WORLD

Berne International Copyright Convention, as revised (1886).
General Agreement on Trade and Tariffs: Agreement on Trade-Related Aspects of Intellectual Property Rights, Including Trade in Counterfeit Goods (1994).

CASES

Van den Haar (Jan) and Kaveka de Meern BV [1984] ECR 1797 Cases 177 and 178/82.
Volvo A.B. v. Erik Veng (UK) Ltd. [1988] ECR 6211 Case 238/87.

FRANCE

Société des Bourses Françaises et Société Cote Desfossés c/Société Sarl Option Service (2/6/1989) Tribunal de Grande Instance de Compiègne pp. 24–5.

UK

Coco v. Clark (A.N.) (Engineers) Ltd. [1969] R.P.C. 41.
Cramp (G.A.) and Sons Ltd. v. Smythson (Frank) Ltd. [1944] A.C. 329.
Dunford and Elliot Ltd. v. Johnston and Firth Brown Ltd. [1978] F.S.R. 143.
Exchange Telegraph Co. Ltd. v. Gregory and Co. [1896] 1 Q.B. 147.
Exchange Telegraph Company (Ltd.) v. Central News (1897) 66 L.J. Ch. 672.
Franchi v. Franchi [1967] R.P.C. 149.
Interlego A.G. v. Tyco Industries [1988] 3 All E.R. 949.
MacMillan and Co. Ltd. V. Cooper (K. and J.) (1923) 40 T.L.R. 186.
R. v. International Stock Exchange of the United Kingdom and the Republic of Ireland Ltd, ex parte Else (1982) Ltd and another [1993] 1 All E.R. 420.
Saltman Engineering Co. Ltd. v. Campbell Engineering Co. Ltd. (1948) 65 R.P.C. 203.
Shearson v. Maclaine [1989] 2 Q.B. 570.
University of London Press Ltd. v. University Tutorial Press Ltd. [1916] 2 Ch. 601.

USA

American Agriculture Movement, Inc. v. Board of Trade of the City of Chicago 977 F.2d 1147 (7th Cir. 1992).
Bishop v. Commodity Exchange, Inc. 564 F.Supp. 1557 (S.D.N.Y. 1983).
Board of Trade of the City of Chicago v. Christie Grain and Stock Company 25 Sup.Ct. 637 (1905).
Board of Trade of the City of Chicago v. SEC 883 F.2d 525 (7th Cir. 1989).
Board of Trade of the City of Chicago v. SEC 923 F.2d 1270 (7th Cir. 1991).
Board of Trade of the City of Chicago v. United States of America 246 U.S. 231 (1918).
Board of Trade of the City of Chicago vs. Dow Jones and Company, Inc. Ill. App. 439 N.E.2d 526 (1982).
Board of Trade of the City of Chicago vs. Dow Jones and Company, Inc. 456 N.E.2d 84 (Ill. 1983).
Brawer v. Options Clearing Corp. 807 F.2d 297 (2d Cir. 1986).
Cargill v. Board of Trade of the City of Chicago 164 F.2d 820 (7th Cir. 1947).
Chicago Mercantile Exchange [Transfer Binder 1977–1980] Comm. Fut. L. Rep. (CCH) Sect. 20,436. @ 21,769.
Computer Associates International, Inc. v. Altai, Inc. 982 F.2d 693 (2nd Cir. 1992).
Crimmins v. American Stock Exchange, Inc. 368 F.Supp. 270 (S.D.N.Y. 1973).

Crowley v. Commodity Exchange 141 F.2d 182 (2d Cir. 1944).

Daniel v. Board of Trade of the City of Chicago 164 F.2d 815 (7th Cir. 1947).

Dow Jones and Company, Inc. vs. Board of Trade of the City of Chicago 546 F.Supp. 113 (1982).

Feist Publications Inc. v. Rural Telephone Service Company Inc. 111 S.Ct. 1282 (1991).

Financial Information, Inc. v. Moody's Investors Service, Inc. 808 F.2d 204 (2nd Cir. 1986).

Gordon v. Hunt 551 F.Supp. 509 (S.D.N.Y. 1982).

Gordon v. Hunt 558 F.Supp. 122 (S.D.N.Y. 1983).

International News Service v. Associated Press 248 U.S. 215 (1918).

Jeweler's Circular Publishing Co. v. Keystone Publishing Co. 281 F. 83 (2d Cir. 1922).

Jordon v. New York Mercantile Exchange 571 F.Supp. 1530 (S.D.N.Y. 1983).

Joy v. North 692 F.2d 880 (2d Cir. 1982).

LTV Federal Credit Union v. UMIC Government Securities, Inc. 523 F.Supp. 819 (1981).

Metropolitan Opera Association v. Wagner-Nichols Recorder Corp. 101 N.Y.S.2d 483 (Sup.Ct.N.Y.Co. 1950).

Minpeco, S.A. v. Hunt 693 F.Supp. 58 (S.D.N.Y. 1988).

National Association of Securities Dealers, Inc. v. SEC and Institutional Networks Corporation 801 F.2d 1415 (D.C. Cir. 1986).

National Basketball Association v. Motorola, Inc. 105 F.3d 841 (2nd. Cir. 1997).

National Basketball Association v. Sports Team Analysis and Tracking Systems, Inc. 931 F.Supp. 1124 (S.D.N.Y. 1996).

National Basketball Association v. Sports Team Analysis and Tracking Systems, Inc. 939 F.Supp. 1071 (S.D.N.Y. 1996).

National Telegraph News Co. v. Western Union Telegraph Co. 119 F. 294 (7th Cir. 1902).

New York, New Haven and Hartford Railroad v. United States 199 F.Supp. 635 (D.C.Conn. 1961).

P.J. Taggares Co. v. New York Mercantile Exchange 476 F.Supp. 72 (S.D.N.Y. 1979).

ProCD, Inc. v. Zeidenberg 86 F.3d 1447 (7th Cir. 1996).

Ryder Energy Distribution Corp. v. Merrill Lynch Commodities, Inc. 748 F.2d 774 (2d Cir. 1984).

Sam Wong and Son, Inc. v. New York Mercantile Exchange 735 F.2d 653 (2d Cir. 1984).

Wilson v. Telegram Company 18 N.Y.St.Repr. 78 (1888), tried in Superior Court of Kings County, NY.

REFERENCES

Abolafia, M.Y. (1996) *Making Markets: Opportunism and Restraint on Wall Street.* Cambridge, MA: Harvard University Press.

Admati, A.R. (1985) 'A Noisy Rational Expectations Equilibrium for Multi-Asset Securities Markets'. *Econometrica*, 53: 629–57.

Admati, A.R. (1989) 'Discussion—Information in Financial Markets: The Rational Expectations Approach', in U. Bhattacharya and G.M. Constantinides (eds.), *Financial Markets and Incomplete Information: Frontiers of Modern Financial Theory.* Volume 2, Lanham, MD: Rowman & Littlefield.

Admati, A.R. (1991) 'The Informational Role of Prices: A Review Essay'. *Journal of Monetary Economics*, 28: 347–61.

Admati, A.R. and Pfleiderer, P. (1986) 'A Monopolistic Market for Information'. *Journal of Economic Theory*, 39: 400–38.

Admati, A.R. and Pfleiderer, P. (1987) 'Viable Allocations of Information in Financial Markets'. *Journal of Economic Theory*, 43: 76–115.

Admati, A.R. and Pfleiderer, P. (1991) 'Sunshine Trading and Financial Market Equilibrium'. *Review of Financial Studies*, 4: 443–81.

Alchian, A.A. and Demsetz, H. (1972) 'Production, Information Costs, and Economic Organization'. *American Economic Review, Papers and Proceedings*, 62: 777–95.

American Law Institute. (1993) *Restatement (Third) on Unfair Competition.*

American Stock Exchange. (1985*a*) *Letter to Michael Cavalier, SEC, re: File No. SR-AMEX-85-8 Pursuant to Rule 19b-4 under the Securities Exchange Act of 1934*, 3 April.

American Stock Exchange. (1985*b*) *Form 19b-4: Proposed Rule Change by American Stock Exchange*, 3 April.

American Stock Exchange. (1985*c*) *Letter to Michael Cavalier, SEC, re: File No. SR-AMEX-85-8 Pursuant to Rule 19b-4 under the Securities Exchange Act of 1934 concerning AMEX-TSE link*, 4 April.

American Stock Exchange. (1985*d*) *Letter to Brandon Becker, SEC, re: File No. SR-AMEX-85-8*, 21 June.

Amihud, Y. and Mendelson, H. (1986) 'Asset Pricing and the Bid–Ask Spread'. *Journal of Financial Economics*, 17: 223–49.

Amihud, Y. and Mendelson, H. (1991) 'How (Not) To Integrate The European Capital Markets', in A. Giovannini and C. Mayer (eds.), *European Financial Integration.* Cambridge: Cambridge University Press.

Amsterdam Exchanges. (1997) *AEX Amsterdam Exchanges nv: Offering of 50,000 B Shares*, 20 February.

Amsterdam Stock Exchange. (1990) *A century of stocks and shares: A historical sketch of the Vereniging voor de Effectenhandel (Stock Exchange Association) and the Amsterdam Stock Exchange.*

Amsterdam Stock Exchange. (1994*a*) *The New Trading-Systems on the Amsterdam Stock Exchange*, July.

Amsterdam Stock Exchange. (1994*b*) *Omzettelling en Publicatie.* Circulaire S94-199, 28 October.

Arizona Stock Exchange. (1992*a*) *Fact Sheet*, 2 January.

Arizona Stock Exchange. (1992*b*) *Bulletin of Corporate Events and Developments*, 14 February.

Arizona Stock Exchange. (1997) World-wide web page—http://www.azx.com/intro.html, 30 July.

Arnold, T., Hersch, P., Mulherin, J.H., and Netter, J. (1997) 'Merging Markets', Working Paper, University of Georgia, Wichita State University, and Penn State University.

Association for Investment Management and Research. (undated) *Question and Answer Session with NYSE executives*.

Association Tripartite Bourses. (1992) *SMF (Swiss Market Feed) Data Distribution Agreement*, 17 September.

Atkinson, A.B. and Stiglitz, J.E. (1980) *Lectures on Public Economics*. New York: McGraw-Hill.

Australian Securities Commission. (1995*a*) *Policy Statement 100, Stock Markets*, 18 September.

Australian Securities Commission. (1995*b*) *Guidelines for Stock Market Applications*, 20 September.

Australian Stock Exchange Ltd. (1996) *Circular to Member Organisations re: ASX Governance Proposal*. 310/96, 29 July.

Ausubel, L.M. (1990) 'Partially-Revealing Rational Expectations Equilibrium in a Competitive Economy'. *Journal of Economic Theory*, 50: 93–126.

Bacot, F., DuBroeucq, P.-F., and Juvin, H. (1989) *Le Nouvel Age des Marchés Français*. Paris: Les Djinns, Collection Médiances, September.

Baer, H.L., France, V.G., and Moser, J.T. (1995) 'What does a Clearinghouse Do?'. *Derivatives Quarterly*, Spring: 39–46.

Baer, H.L., France, V.G., and Moser, J.T. (1996) 'Opportunity Cost and Prudentiality: An Analysis of Futures Clearinghouse Behavior', Working paper, Chicago, 15 August.

Barclays de Zoete Wedd. (1988) *TRADE: The Automated Dealing and Order Routing System*, June.

Barclays de Zoete Wedd. (1990) *TRADE <2.0> NMW Version: User Guide*, 1 May.

Barton, R. (1991) 'Recent Product Launches on LIFFE', London Business School, Trading Markets Seminar, Eynsham Hall, 17 December.

Becker, B., Adkins, A., Fuller, G., and Angstadt, J. (SEC, Division of Market Regulation). (1991) *The SEC's Oversight of Proprietary Trading Systems*, 11 April.

Ben-Ner, A. (1986) 'Non-Profit Organizations: Why Do They Exist in Market Economies?', in S. Rose-Ackermann (ed.), *The Economics of Nonprofit Institutions: Studies in Structure and Policy*. Oxford: Oxford University Press.

Bernard L. Madoff Investment Securities. (1990) *Bernard L. Madoff, Investment Securities*.

Bernard L. Madoff Investment Securities. (1997) World-wide web page—http://www.madoff.com/company/OrderHandlingContent.htm, 17 October.

Bernard, R.P. (1987) 'International Linkages between Securities Markets: "A Ring of Dinosaurs Joining Hands and Dancing Together?"' *Columbia Business Law Review*, No. 2: 321–38.

Beursdata B.V. Amsterdam Stock Exchange. (1993) *Information Contract*.

Biais, B. (1993) 'Price Formation and Equilibrium Liquidity in Fragmented and Centralized Markets'. Journal of Finance, 48: 157–85.

Bingham, T.R.G. (1989) *Securities Markets, Systemic Stability and Regulation*. Special Paper, Financial Markets Group, London School of Economics.

Black, D. (1986) *Success and Failure of Futures Contracts: Theory and Empirical Evidence*. Salomon Brothers Center for the Study of Financial Institutions, New York University, Monograph Series in Finance and Economics.

Bloomfield, R. and O'Hara, M. (1996) 'Market Transparency: Who Wins and Who Loses?', Working paper, Cornell University, October.

Bloomfield, R. and O'Hara, M. (1997) 'Can Transparent Markets Survive?', Working paper, Cornell University, May.

Blume, M.E., Siegel, J.J., and Rottenberg, D. (1993) *Revolution on Wall Street: The Rise and Decline of the New York Stock Exchange*. New York and London: Norton.

Board, J. and Sutcliffe, C. (1995) *The Effects of Trade Transparency in the London Stock Exchange*. Commissioned by London International Financial Futures and Options Exchange and the London Stock Exchange, January.

Board, J. and Sutcliffe, C. (1996). 'The Proof of the Pudding: The Effects of Increased Trade Transparency in the London Stock Exchange', Working paper, Financial Markets Group, London School of Economics.

Bonet, G. (1993) 'Propriétés Intellectuelles: Chronique'. *Revue Trimestrielle de Droit Européen*, 29: 525–44.

Booz Allen and Hamilton Inc. (1994) *Report of the Implementation Committee: Chicago Board of Trade (Final Report)*, 8 March.

Bork, R.H. (1978) *The Antitrust Paradox: A Policy at War with Itself*. New York: Basic Books.

Botswana Share Market. (1992) *Botswana Share Market Information*, 28 January.

Bourse Data Beurs. (1993) *Data Transmission Agreement*.

Bourse de Genève. (1986) *Geneva Stock Exchange*.

Bradbery, A. (1992a) 'Clearing the decks'. *Futures and Options World*, June, No. 253: 37.

Bradbery, A. (1992b) 'Going Dutch'. *Futures and Options World*, July, No. 254: 47–51.

Bray, M. (1985) 'Rational Expectations, Information and Asset Markets: An Introduction'. *Oxford Economic Papers*, 37: 161–95.

Brazier, G. (1996) *Insider Dealing: Law and Regulation*. London: Cavendish.

Breedon, F.J. (1993) 'Intraday Price Formation on the London Stock Exchange', Discussion Paper No. 158, London School of Economics, March.

Bremner, J.P. (1994) *Guide to Database Distribution: Legal Aspects and Model Contracts* (2nd. edition). Philadelphia: National Federation of Abstracting and Indexing Services.

Broker's Club, Prague Stock Exchange. (1995a) 'Reporting Initiative Agreed: Increased Transparency for Direct Trades', 3 August.

Broker's Club, Prague Stock Exchange. (1995b) *Convention among Independent Securities Dealers for Immediate Public Disclosure of Direct Trades*. Final Draft (before Prague Stock Exchange legal comments), 20 May.

Bronfman, C.M. and Overdahl, J.A. (1992) 'Would the Invisible Hand Produce Transparent Markets?', CFTC Working Paper No. 92-10, 2 June.

Bronfman, C.M., Lehn, K., and Schwartz, R.A. (1994) 'U.S. Securities Markets Regulation: Regulatory Structure', in B. Steil (ed.), *International Financial Market Regulation*. Chichester: John Wiley and Sons.

Bronfman, C.M., McCabe, K., Porter, D., Rassenti, S., and Smith, V. (1992) 'An Experimental Examination of the Walrasian Tatonnement Mechanism', Working paper, CFTC, University of Arizona, and elsewhere.

Brooks, D. (1986) *Letter to Richard Ketchum, Director, Division of Market Regulation, SEC re: Statutory Classification of Instinet*, 23 April.

Brooks, D. (1990) *Letter to John Ramsay, SEC re. No Action request on Behalf of Wunsch Auction Systems, Inc., BT Brokerage Corporation and a Single Price Auction System*, 28 August.

Buchanan, J. and Tullock, G. (1962). *The Calculus of Consent*. Ann Arbor, Michigan: University of Michigan Press.

Bull, G. (1993) 'Information Provider Agreements: Checklist'. Unpublished.

Bull, G. (1994) 'Licensing and Distribution of Market Data'. *Computer Law & Security Report*, 10: 50–5.

Bull, G. (1997) 'Data Law: Market Data Rights Bingo'. *Computer Law & Security Report*, 13: 75–86.

Burns, G. (1992) 'Globex: up, but not yet running'. *Futures and Options World*, August, No. 255: 13.

Buxbaum, R.M., Hertig, G., Hirsch, A., and Hopt, K.J. (eds.). (1991) *European Business Law: Legal and Economic Analyses on Integration and Harmonization*. Berlin and New York: Walter de Gruyter.

Buxbaum, R.M., Hertig, G., Hirsch, A., and Hopt, K.J. (eds.). (1996) *European Economic Business Law: Legal and Economic Analyses on Integration and Harmonization*. Berlin and New York: Walter de Gruyter.

Buxbaum, R.M. and Hopt, K.J. (eds.). (1988) *Legal Harmonization and the Business Enterprise: Corporate and Capital Market Law Harmonization Policy in Europe*. Berlin and New York: Walter de Gruyter.

Campbell, J.Y., Lo, A.W., and MacKinlay, A.C. (1997) *The Econometrics of Financial Markets*. Princeton: Princeton University Press.

Canadian Exchange Group. (1994*a*) *Application Agreement for Receipt of Canadian Exchange Group Market Data*.

Canadian Exchange Group. (1994*b*) *Canadian Exchange Group Market Data Distribution Agreement*.

Canolle, M. (1990) 'The Modernization of the French Stock Exchange', in Fédération Internationale des Bourses de Valeurs conference proceedings, 3 October.

Carroll, L. (1872, reprinted 1958) *Through the Looking-Glass and What Alice Found There*. London: Macmillan and Co.

Chambers, S. and Carter, C. (1990) 'US Futures Exchanges as Nonprofit Entities'. *Journal of Futures Markets*, 10: 79–88.

Chicago Board of Trade. (1990) *Task Force for the Exchange Business Plan: Special Report to the Membership*, 18 July.

Chicago Board of Trade. (1993*a*) *Vendor Agreement*.

Chicago Board of Trade. (1993*b*) *Letter to CFTC re: Proposed Rule Concerning Composition of Various Self-Regulatory Organization Governing Boards and Major Disciplinary Committees*, 12 April.

Chicago Board of Trade (Strategic Planning Committee). (1993*c*) *A Strategic Framework for the Chicago Board of Trade: A Report to the Board of Directors*, July.

Chicago Board of Trade. (1994) *Notice of Ballot Vote*, 18 August.

Chicago Board of Trade. (1996) *Letter to CFTC re: Rulemaking on Voting by Interested Members of Self-Regulatory Organization Governing Boards and Committees and Concerning the Publication of Broker Group Memberships*, 2 July.

Chicago Board of Trade. (1997*a*) Chicago Board of Trade Open Datafeed/Network Environment Reporting Flow Chart, April.

Chicago Board of Trade. (1997*b*) *Letter from Daniel Rooney, Vice President, Market Data Services, to Market Data Subscribers*, 1 April.

Chicago Board of Trade. (1997*c*) *Chicago Board of Trade Market Data Vendor/Subvendor Agreement*, 1 April.

Chicago Board of Trade and Chicago Mercantile Exchange. (1990) Petitioners' Reply Brief: 'Petition for Review of Order of the SEC before US Court of Appeals for the Seventh Circuit—CBT and CME Petitioners v. SEC, Respondent, and Delta Government Options Corporation, Intervenor-Respondent'. No. 90-1246, 14 May.

Chicago Board Options Exchange. (1993*a*) *FLEX Options—Supplement to the Booklet Entitled 'Characteristics and Risks of Standardized Options'*.

Chicago Board Options Exchange. (1993*b*) *FLEX Options—FLexible EXchange Options*, February.

Chicago Mercantile Exchange. (1984) The SIMEX Connection: An Operating Guide to Inter-Exchange Trade Clearing.

Chicago Mercantile Exchange. (1993*a*) *Vendor Agreement*.

Chicago Mercantile Exchange. (1993*b*). 'Inter-Exchange Trades', in *Clearing House Manual of Operations*, March: 41–6.

Chicago Mercantile Exchange. (1993*c*) *Letter to CFTC re: Proposed Rule Concerning Composition of Various Self-Regulatory Organization Governing Boards and Major Disciplinary Committees*, 12 April.

Chicago Mercantile Exchange. (1994*a*) *CME/IMM Consolidation Plan*, 10 October.

Chicago Mercantile Exchange. (1994*b*) *CME and IMM Merger Questions and Answers*, 10 October.

Chicago Mercantile Exchange. (1996*a*) *CME/SIMEX Mutual Offset System: The World's Most Successful Trading Link*.

Chicago Mercantile Exchange. (1996*b*) *Letter to CFTC re: Proposed CFTC Regulation 1.69—Voting by Interested Members of SRO Governing Boards and Various Committees*, 2 July.

Chicago Mercantile Exchange. (1996*c*) 'National Basketball Association and NBA Properties, Inc., vs. Motorola, Inc. d/b/a Sports Trax and Sports Team Analysis and Tracking Systems, Inc., d/b/a STATS, Inc.: Brief of Amicus Curiae Chicago Mercantile Exchange in support of Appellees National Basketball Association and NBA Properties, Inc.'. US Court of Appeals for the Second Circuit 96-7975, 96-7983, 96-9123, 26 September.

Chicago Mercantile Exchange. (1997) *Rulebook*. World-wide web page—http://207.250.124.101/folio.pgi/cmerule?, 19 November.

Chicago Mercantile Exchange, Marché à Terme International de France SA, New York Mercantile Exchange, Société des Bourses Françaises-Bourse de Paris. (1997) 'Exchange of Technology agreed between French and American Markets'. Press Release, 20 February.

Clemons, E.K. and Weber, B.W. (1989) 'International Stock Exchange: Assessment and Recommendations'. Prepared for ISE, 15 August.

Coase, R.H. (1937) 'The Nature of the Firm'. *Economica*, 4: 386–405.

Coase, R.H. (1960) 'The Problem of Social Cost'. *Journal of Law and Economics*, 3: 1–44.

Coase, R.H. (1988) *The Firm, the Market, and the Law*. Chicago: University of Chicago Press.

Coffee, Sugar and Cocoa Exchange. (1996) *Letter to CFTC re: Proposed Rulemaking Concerning Voting by Interested Members of Self-Regulatory Organization Governing Boards and Committees and Concerning the Publicizing of Broker Association Memberships*, 2 July.

Cohen, K.J., Maier, S.F., Schwartz, R.A., and Whitcomb, D.K. (1986) *The Microstructure of Securities Markets*. Englewood Cliffs, NJ: Prentice-Hall.

Cohen, N. (1994) 'Exchange to take big stake in Crest'. *Financial Times*, 28 May: 6.

Cohen, N. (1995*a*) 'Stock exchange set to drop restrictive share trading rule'. *Financial Times*, 23 September: 20.

Cohen, N. (1995*b*) 'Stock Exchange rejects trading shake-up'. *Financial Times*, 23 October: 22.

Cohen, N. (1995*c*) 'Stock Exchange may create own rival service'. *Financial Times*, 1 November: 24.

Cohen, N. (1995*d*) 'Day of reckoning for stock exchange'. *Financial Times*, 30 November: 15.

Cohen, N. (1996) 'The trouble with being three things at the same time. . .' *Financial Times*, 21 February: 10.

Collin, P.H. (1996) *Dictionary of Banking and Finance*. Teddington: Peter Collin Publishing.

Commission des Opérations de Bourse, Champarnaud, F., and Perier, F. (1994). 'Identification of a Market: The COB Discussions', Marchés 2001, Entretiens de la COB, 3rd Round Table, 17 November.

Commission of the European Communities. (1985) *Completing the Internal Market: White paper from the Commission to the European Council*, June.

Commission of the European Communities. (1988) 'Commission Decision 89/205/EEC of 21/12/1988 relating to a proceeding under Article 86 of the EEC Treaty (IV/31.851— Magill TV Guide/ITP, BBC and RTE)'. *Official Journal of the European Communities*, L78/43.

Commission of the European Communities. (1992) *Proposal for a Council Directive on the legal protection of databases: Explanatory Memorandum*. COM (93) 24 final— SYN 393, Brussels, 13 May.

Committee on Commodities Regulation, Bar Association of New York. (1985) *Conflicts of Interests on Commodity Exchanges*, 22 January.

Commodities Exchange Center. (1993) *Standard Vendor Agreement*. CEC Form 6-031286.

Commodity Exchange. (1993) *Letter to CFTC re: Proposed Rule Concerning Composition of Various Self-Regulatory Organization Governing Boards and Major Disciplinary Committees*, 15 April.

Commodity Futures Trading Commission. (1976) 'Policy Statement on Indemnification of Exchange Directors'. *Federal Register*, 16 July, 41: 29,474.

Commodity Futures Trading Commission. (1977) 'Standards for exchange directors and control committees', Memorandum from the Division of Trading and Markets to the Commission, 7 November.

Commodity Futures Trading Commission. (1980*a*) 'Standards for the Prevention of Conflicts of Interest in Actions Authorized by the Governing Boards of Contract Markets', Memorandum from the Office of the General Counsel to the Commission, 8 December.

Commodity Futures Trading Commission. (1980*b*) 'Conflicts of Interest on Governing Boards and Committees of Contract Markets', Memorandum from the Division of Trading and Markets to the Commission, 10 December.

Commodity Futures Trading Commission. (1982) 'Contract Market Rules and Practices Governing Conflicts of Interest; Request for Public Comment'. *Federal Register*, 15 July, 47: 31703.

Commodity Futures Trading Commission. (1984) *A Study of the Nature, Extent and Effects of Futures Trading by Persons Possessing Material, Nonpublic Information.* Submitted to Committee on Agriculture, House of Representatives, and Committee on Agriculture, Nutrition and Forestry, Senate, September.

Commodity Futures Trading Commission. (1985) *The Silver Market of 1979/1980: Actions of the Chicago Board of Trade and the Commodity Exchange, Inc., Investigative Report of the Division of Trading and Markets.*

Commodity Futures Trading Commission. (1989a) *Chicago Mercantile Exchange's Proposed Globex Trading System*, 25 January.

Commodity Futures Trading Commission (Division of Trading and Markets). (1989b). *Review under Commission Regulation 1.41(f) of the Chicago Board of Trade's Temporary Emergency Action of July 11, 1989 Ordering the Liquidation of Positions in the July 1989 Soybean Futures Contract*, 7 September.

Commodity Futures Trading Commission. (1993a) 'Proposed Rule Concerning Composition of Various Self-Regulatory Organization Governing Boards and Major Disciplinary Committees'. *Federal Register*, 12 March, 58: 13565-71.

Commodity Futures Trading Commission. (1993b) 'Final Rule and Rule Amendments Concerning Composition of Various Self-Regulatory Organization governing Boards and Major Disciplinary Committees'. *Federal Register*, 13 July, 58: 37644-55.

Commodity Futures Trading Commission. (1995) *Report on Diversity of Representation on Self-Regulatory Organization Governing Boards*, 19 September.

Commodity Futures Trading Commission. (1996) 'Proposed Rulemaking Concerning Voting by Interested Members of Self-Regulatory Organization Governing Boards and Committees and Concerning the Publicizing of Broker Association Memberships'. *Federal Register*, 3 May, 61: 19869-78.

Commodity Futures Trading Commission. (1998) 'Proposed Rulemaking Concerning Voting by Interested Members of Self-Regulatory Organization Governing Boards and Commitees'. *Federal Register*, 23 January, 63: 3492–505.

Commodity Market Services (London Commodities Exchange). (1993) *CMS Vendor Contract.*

Conseil des Bourses de Valeurs. (1994a) *Modifications du Règlement Général du Conseil des Bourses de Valeurs*, July.

Conseil des Bourses des Valeurs. (1994b) *Décision Général No. 94-06 Relatives aux Applications, À La Contrepartie sur Actions et Aux Opérations Portant sur des Blocs d'Actions Structurants*, July.

Consiglio di Borsa. (1997) *Decree of the Ministry of the Treasury of July 4th, 1997 containing the terms and conditions of the sale of the shares of the Borsa Italiana SPA*, 4 July.

Consiglio di Borsa. (1997) *Collocamento privato dell'intero capitale sociale della Borsa Italiana SPA—Documento informativo*, 18 July.

Consolidated Quotation System. (1995) *Plan Submitted to Securities and Exchange Commission for the Purpose of Implementing Rule 11Ac1-1 Under the Securities and Exchange Act of 1934.* (July 1978, As Restated December 1995).

Consolidated Tape Association. (1995) *Second Restatement of Plan Submitted to the*

Securities and Exchange Commission Pursuant to Rule 17a-15 under Securities and Exchange Act of 1934. (May 1974, As Restated March 1980, and December 1995).

Cook, S. (1991) 'European share-trading hopes dashed'. *Independent on Sunday*, 23 June: 8.

Copeland, T.E. and Weston, J.F. (1983) *Financial Theory and Corporate Policy.* Reading, MA: Addison Wesley.

Copenhagen Stock Exchange. (1990) *Appendix 4: Agreement on Stock Exchange Information Redistribution*, December.

Copenhagen Stock Exchange. (1993*a*) *Nordquote: Copenhagen Stock Exchange Market Information.*

Copenhagen Stock Exchange. (1993*b*) *Stock Exchange Information Agreement.*

Copenhagen Stock Exchange. (1993*c*) *Appendix 1: Conditions for the Receipt and Redistribution of Information from the Copenhagen Stock Exchange.*

Copenhagen Stock Exchange. (1996) *Prospectus 1996 Copenhagen Stock Exchange A/S*, 12 March.

Corben, E.R. (1997) *Corben's Glossary of Financial and Investment Terms* (6th. edition). London: Corben's Financial Publications Limited.

Cornish, W.R. (1989) *Intellectual Property: Patents, Copyrights, Trade Marks and Allied Rights* (2nd. edition). London: Sweet and Maxwell.

Correa, C.M. (1994) 'TRIPs Agreement: Copyright and Related Rights'. *International Review of Industrial Property and Copyright Law*, 25: 543–52.

Corrigan, D., Georgiou, C., and Gollow, J. (1995). *NatWest Markets Handbook of International Repo.* London: IFR.

Corrigan, T. (1993) 'OMLX plans trade in both securities and derivatives'. *Financial Times,* 31 March: 3.

Corrigan, T. and Morse, L. (1993) 'Liffe and CBOT end plans for link'. *Financial Times,* 28 June: 17.

Courtney, C. and Thompson, P. (1996) *City Lives: The changing voices of British finance.* London: Methuen.

Crawford Jr., W.B. (1994*a*) 'Merc members reject chairman's seat-consolidation plan'. *Chicago Tribune*, 26 October, Section III: 1.

Crawford, W. (1994*b*) 'Report calls for CBOT reforms'. *Futures and Options World*, March, No. 274: 19.

Cunning, S.W. (ed.). (1988) *Black Box: The Worldwide Report on Automated Trading Systems.* Waters Information Services.

D'Andrea, A. (ed.). (1996) *Capital Markets Glossary.* London: IFR.

Dale, R.S. (1996) *Risk and Regulation in Global Securities Markets.* Chichester: John Wiley and Sons.

Danthine, J.-P. and Moresi, S. (1993) 'Volatility, Information, and Noise Trading'. *European Economic Review*, 37: 961–82.

Davey, E. (1992) 'Liffe's new man in at the deep end'. *Futures and Options World*, December, No. 259: 12.

Davey, E. (1993*a*) 'Link and be merry'. *Futures and Options World*, June, No. 265: 35–41.

Davey, E. (1993*b*) 'Globex partners parade unity at Bürgenstock . . .' *Futures and Options World*, October, No. 269: 16.

Davey, E. (1994*a*) 'Nymex and CME go one more step along road to for-profit exchanges'. *Futures and Options World*, May, No. 276: 28.

Davey, E. (1994*b*) 'Simex and CME rejoin hands'. *Futures and Options World*, May, No. 276: 19.

Davey, E. (1994*c*). 'Join together'. *Futures and Options World*, June, No. 277: 47–9.

Davey, E. (1997) 'GLOBEX is dead. . .' *Futures and Options World*, April, No. 311: 42–4.

Davey, E. and Hunter, K. (1992) 'Globex joins the record-breakers'. *Futures and Options World*, December, No. 259: 13–14.

Davidson III, J.P. (1994) 'DisIntermediated, DisAggregated and DisSatisfied: A Financial Intermediary's Perspective on Unbundling', 17th Chicago Kent Conference, Chicago, 3 November.

Davis, E.P. (1995) *Debt, Financial Fragility, and Systemic Risk*. Oxford: Clarendon Press.

de Jong, F., Nijman, T. and Roëll, A. (1995) 'A Comparison of the Costs of Trading French Shares on the Paris Bourse and on SEAQ International'. *European Economic Review*, 39: 1277–301.

Demsetz, H. (1968) 'The Cost of Transacting'. *Quarterly Journal of Economics*, 82: 33–53.

Department of Trade and Industry. (1991). 'John Redwood agrees Changes to the Stock Exchange's Arrangements for Company News'. Press Notice P/91/595, 31 October.

Deutsche Börse (1992) *Real-Time Price Marketing Contract (Real-Time-Kursvermarktungs-Vertrag)*, 22 December.

Deutsche Terminbörse. (1993) *Contract*.

Deutsche Terminbörse and Marché à Terme International de France. (1993*a*) 'DTB and MATIF plan to Link Markets'. Press Release, 13 January.

Deutsche Terminbörse and Marché à Terme International de France. (1993*b*) 'MATIF and DTB finalize Agreement to Link Trading'. Press Release, 29 July.

Deutsche Terminbörse and Marché à Terme International de France. (1994*a*) 'DTB–MATIF Cooperation gets under way: First MATIF Members to be Connected in Paris'. Press Release, 14 September.

Deutsche Terminbörse and Marché à Terme International de France. (1994*b*) *Trading Across Europe*, November.

Deutsche Terminbörse and Marché à Terme International de France. (1994*c*) *TRADEUS: Trading Across Europe*, November.

Diamond, D. (1985) 'Optimal Release of Information by Firms'. *Journal of Finance*, 40: 1071–94.

Diamond, D. and Verrechia, R. (1981) 'Information Aggregation in a Noisy, Rational Expectations Economy'. *Journal of Financial Economics*, 9: 221–35.

Dimson, E. (1988) *Stock Market Anomalies*. Cambridge: Cambridge University Press.

Dobie, C. (1991) 'Plan for rival to Reuters scrapped'. *Independent*, 25 May: 21.

Domowitz, I. (1990*a*) 'The Mechanics of Automated Trade Execution Systems'. *Journal of Financial Intermediation*, 1: 167–94.

Domowitz, I. (1990*b*) 'When is a Marketplace a Market? Automated Trade Execution in the Futures Markets', in D. Siegel (ed.), *Innovation and Technology in the Markets—A Reordering of the World's Capital Markets*. New York: McGraw-Hill.

Domowitz, I. (1993*a*) 'A Taxonomy of Automated Trade Execution Systems'. *Journal of International Money and Finance*, 12: 607–31.

Domowitz, I. (1993*b*) 'Automating the Price Discovery Process: Some International Comparisons and Regulatory Implications'. *Journal of Financial Services Research*, 6: 305–26.

Domowitz, I. (1993*c*) 'Equally Open and Competitive: Regulatory Approval of Automated Trade Execution in the Futures Markets'. *Journal of Futures Markets*, 13: 93–113.

Domowitz, I. (1993*d*) 'Automating the Continuous Double Auction in Practice:

Automated Trade Execution Systems in Financial Markets', in D. Friedman and J. Rust (eds.), *The Double Auction Markets: Institutions, Theories and Evidence*. Reading, MA: Addison Wesley.

Domowitz, I. (1994) 'Electronic Derivatives Exchanges: Implicit Mergers, Network Externalities and Standardization', Working paper, Department of Economics, and Center for Urban Affairs and Policy Research, Northwestern University, October.

Domowitz, I. and Lee, R. (1996) 'The Legal Basis for Stock Exchanges: The Classification and Regulation of Automated Trading Systems', Working paper, Northwestern University and Oxford Finance Group, May.

Donohue, J. and Van Zandt, D.E. (1995) 'Four Models of Deregulation in International Capital Markets', Conference on Communications Technology and National Sovereignty in the Global Economy, Northwestern University, 16 April.

Douglas, W.O. (1940) *Democracy and Finance*. New Haven, CT: Yale University Press.

Dow Jones News. (1994) 'Move to Change Non-Profit Status Put on Back-Burner'. 15.09, 1 September.

Dow, J. and Gorton, G. (1997) 'Stock Market Efficiency and Economic Efficiency: Is There a Connection?' *Journal of Finance*, 52: 1087–129.

Drummond, H. (1996) *Escalation in Decision-Making*. Oxford: Oxford University Press.

Dubroeucq, P.-F. (1990*a*) 'Automation of Trading Systems of the Paris Bourse', Speech to London School of Economics conference, 8 May.

DuBroeucq, P.-F. (1990*b*) 'Eurolist, Euroquote, Wholesale Market: Les Projets Boursiers Européens, Quelle Démarche pour La France'. Société des Bourses Françaises, 20 September.

Durr, B. and Corrigan, T. (1992) 'The future comes into focus on screen'. *Financial Times*, 26 June: 21.

EASDAQ. (1996) *An Introduction to EASDAQ*.

Easley, D. and O'Hara, M. (1983) 'The Economic Role of the Nonprofit Firm'. *Bell Journal of Economics*, 14: 531–8.

Easley, D. and O'Hara, M. (1988) 'Contracts and Asymmetric Information in the Theory of the Firm'. *Journal of Economic Behaviour and Organization*, 9: 229–46.

Economist Books. (1994) *Pocket Finance*. London: Profile Books.

Eisenhammer, J. (1995) 'Revolution in share dealing to hit City'. *Independent*, 1 December: 24.

EURO.NM (1996) *EURO.NM: The Gateway to European Stockmarkets for Growth Companies*.

European Options Exchange. (1993*a*) *Letter to all Members re: Trading and Clearing link between EOE/EOCC and OM-London*. EOE/M/93-05 Amsterdam, 22 January.

European Options Exchange. (1993*b*) *Trading Link EOE-Optiebeurs—OM-Londen*. EOE/M/93-05 Amsterdam, 29 January.

European Options Exchange. (1994) *Data-vendor Agreement*.

Fama, E.F. (1970) 'Efficient Capital Markets: A Review of Theory and Empirical Work'. *Journal of Finance*, May, 25: 383–417.

Federal Court of Australia, New South Wales District Registry, General Division. (1990) *Supplemental Reasons for Judgment between Pont Data Australia and ASX, and ASXO No. NG485 of 1989*. Coram: Wilcox J. 18 May.

Fédération Internationale des Bourses de Valeurs. (1995) *Focus*, May.

Federation of the Stock Exchanges of the European Community. (1989) *Business Proposal*, 5 September.

Federation of the Stock Exchanges of the European Community. (1990) *Background Document: The PIPE Project*, February.

Federation of the Stock Exchanges of the European Community. (1991) *Euroquote*, 1 February.

Federation of the Stock Exchanges of the European Community (Economics and Statistics Sub-Committee, Ad-Hoc Group). (1992) *Towards Comparable EC Stock Market Turnover Statistics?* Interim Report, November.

Feer Verkade, D.W. (1996) 'Comment: Magill Judgment'. *International Review of Industrial Property and Copyright Law*, 27: 94–8.

Feller, L. (1987) *No-Action Letter concerning POSIT to SEC*, 2 June.

Financial Information Services Division, Information Industry Association. (1992) 'Guideline: Billable Units of Measure Document'. Draft Version 6.

Financial Information Services Division, Information Industry Association. (1996*a*) 'Symbology Conflicts: Definition and Proposed Solution'. Report to the Securities Industry prepared by the Symbology Task Force, Discussion Draft, January.

Financial Information Services Division, Information Industry Association. (1996*b*) 'Model Policies and Procedures for Market Data Administration'. Vendor Committee submission to 1996 Market Data Administration Conference, May.

Financial Times. (1996) 'Conflicts on the exchange'. 5 January: 15.

First Equity Limited (S. Cowan). (1996) 'New electronic trading service: consultation feedback—Response', London Stock Exchange no. 076, 16 February.

Fishman, M.J. and Longstaff, F.A. (1992) 'Dual Trading in Futures Markets'. *Journal of Finance*, 47: 643–71.

Flood, M.D., Huisman, R., Koedijk, K.G., and Mahieu, R.J. (1996) 'Price Discovery in Multiple Dealer Financial Markets: The Effect of Pre-Trade Transparency', Working paper, Concordia University, Maastricht University, and Erasmus University, December.

Flood, M.D., Huisman, R., Koedijk, K.G., Mahieu, R.J., and Roëll, A. (1997) 'Post-Trade Transparency in Multiple Dealer Financial Markets', Working paper, Concordia University, Maastricht University, Erasmus University, and ECARE, March.

Flynn, J. (1992) 'Intellectual Property and Anti-trust: EC Attitudes'. *European Intellectual Property Review*, February, 14: 49–54.

Forrester, I.S. (1992) 'Software Licensing in Light of Current EC Competition Law Considerations'. *European Competition Law Review*, 13: 5–20.

Forster, M.M. and George, T.J. (1992) 'Anonymity in Securities Markets'. *Journal of Financial Intermediation*, 2: 168–206.

Frankfurt Stock Exchange. (1991) *IBIS: Integrated Stock Exchange Trading and Information System*.

Franks, J.R. and Mayer, C.P. (1993) 'Corporate Control: A Synthesis of the International Evidence', Working Paper No. IFA 165–92, London Business School.

Franks, J.R. and Schaefer, S.M. (1990) 'Large Trade Publication on the International Stock Exchange', for Department of Trade and Industry, 12 November.

Frase, A.R.G. (1993) 'The Role of the Exchange', in H. Parry, E. Bettelheim, and W. Rees (eds.), *Futures Trading Law and Regulation*. London: FT Law and Tax.

Fritz, M. (1994) 'Merc worlds converge'. *Crain's Chicago Business*, 5 September: 42.

Froot, K.A. and Campbell, J.Y. (1993) *Securities Transaction Taxes: What about International Experiences and Migrating Markets*. A Catalyst Institute Research Project, Harvard and Princeton, July.

Futures and Options World. (1992) 'Fex breaks new European ground'. June, No. 253: 12.

Futures and Options World. (1993*a*) 'Summer madness'. September, No. 268: 9.

Futures and Options World. (1993*b*) 'MATIF/DTB forge ahead'. September, No. 268: 14.

Futures and Options World. (1993*c*) 'Reuters attacks CBOT'. December, No. 271: 10.

Futures and Options World. (1994*a*) 'Globex summit stand-off'. January, No. 272: 13.

Futures and Options World. (1994*b*) 'CBOT/Globex—split over restructuring'. February, No. 273: 13.

Futures and Options World. (1994*c*) 'Comex board approves merger with Nymex'. March, No. 274: 17.

Futures and Options World. (1994*d*) 'Globex takes yet another blow as LIFFE gives a no'. March, No. 277: 10.

Futures and Options World. (1994*e*) 'Profits aren't everything'. July, No. 278: 9.

Futures and Options World. (1994*f*) 'CBOT rejects "for profit"'. October, No. 281: 11.

Futures Industry Association. (1996) *Letter to CFTC re: Voting by Interested Members of Self-Regulatory Organization Governing Boards and Committees*, 30 July.

Futures Industry Magazine. (1995), January.

Gapper, J. (1996) 'Tamer required for lions' den'. *Financial Times*, 5 January: 15.

Garbade, K.D. and Silber, W.L. (1978) 'Technology, Communication and the Performance of Financial Markets 1840–1975'. *Journal of Finance*, 33: 819–32.

Garbade, K.D. and Silber, W.L. (1979) 'Dominant and Satellite Markets: A Study of Dually-Traded Securities'. *Review of Economics and Statistics*, 61: 455–60.

Garbade, K.D., Pomrenze, J.L., and Silber, W.L. (1979) 'On the Informational Content of Prices'. *American Economic Review*, 69: 50–9.

Geller, P.E. (1991) 'Copyright in Factual Compilations: U.S. Supreme Court Decides the Feist Case'. *International Review of Industrial Property and Copyright Law*, 22: 802–8.

Geller, P.E. (1994) 'The Universal Electronic Archive: Issues in International Copyright'. *International Review of Industrial Property and Copyright Law*, 25: 54-69.

Gemmill, G. (1994) *Transparency and Liquidity: A study of large trades on the London Stock Exchange under different publication rules.* Office of Fair Trading, Research paper 7, November.

Gemmill, G. (1996) 'Transparency and Liquidity: A Study of Block Trades on the London Stock Exchange under Different Publication Rules'. *Journal of Finance*, 51: 1765–90.

General Accounting Office. (1990) *U.S. Government Securities: More Transaction Information and Investor Protection Measures are Needed.* GAO/GGD-90-114, 14 September.

Gidel, S.A. (1997) 'The Business of Exchanges'. *Futures Industry*, 8 September: 11–14.

Ginsburg, J.C. (1990) 'Creation and Commercial Value: Copyright Protection of Works of Information'. *Columbia Law Review*, 90: 1865–938.

Ginsburg, J.C. (1992) 'No "Sweat"? Copyright and Other Protection of Works of Information After Feist v. Rural Telephone'. *Columbia Law Review*, 92: 339–88.

Globex Joint Venture L.P. (1992) *GLOBEX: Report*, 8 June, Vol. 1, No. 1.

Gorham, M. (1997) 'Exchange Subsidiaries Proliferate'. *Futures Industry*, 8 September: 15–18.

Gove, P.B. (ed.) (1961) *Webster's Third New International Dictionary.* London: George Bell & Sons.

Greising, D. and Morse, L. (1991) *Brokers, Bagmen, and Moles: Fraud and Corruption in the Chicago Futures Market.* New York: John Wiley and Sons.

Grody, A.D. and Levecq, H. (1993) 'Past, Present and Future: The Evolution and

Development of Electronic Financial Markets', Department of Information Systems, Stern School of Business, New York University, November.

Grody, A.D., Levecq, H., and Weber, B.W. (1994) 'Global Electronic Markets: A Preliminary Report of Findings', New York University, 31 May.

Grossman, S.J. (1989) *The Informational Role of Prices*. Cambridge, MA: MIT Press.

Grossman, S.J. (1992) 'The Informational Role of Upstairs and Downstairs Trading'. *Journal of Business*, 65: 509–28.

Grossman, S.J. and Hart, O.D. (1986) 'The Costs and Benefits of Ownership: A Theory of Vertical and Lateral Integration'. *Journal of Political Economy*, 94: 691–719.

Grossman, S.J. and Stiglitz, J.E. (1980) 'On the Impossibility of Informationally Efficient Markets'. *American Economic Review*, 70: 393–408.

Grünbichler, A., Longstaff, F.A., and Schwartz, E.S. (1994) 'Electronic Screen Trading and the Transmission of Information: An Empirical Investigation'. *Journal of Financial Intermediation*, 3: 166–87.

Gupta, P.R. (1992) 'Recent Developments in US Copyright Litigation'. *European Intellectual Property Review*, 14: 100–3.

Gurry, F. (1985) 'Breach of Confidence', in P. Finn (ed.), *Essays on Equity*. London: Sweet and Maxwell.

Haines, S. (1994) 'Copyright Takes the Dominant Position: The Advocate General's Opinion in Magill'. *European Intellectual Property Review*, 16: 401–3.

Hakansson, N.H., Kunkel, J.G., and Ohlson, J.A. (1982) 'Sufficient and Necessary Conditions for Information to have Social Value in Pure Exchange'. *Journal of Finance*, 37: 1169–81.

Hall, M. (1990) 'London's Approach to the Year 2000', Frankfurt SEMA Finance Symposium on 'European Stock Markets Heading Towards 2000', 22 November.

Hanley, W.J., McCann, K., and Moser, J.T. (1995) 'Public Benefits and Public Concerns: An Economic Analysis of Regulatory Standards for Clearing Facilities', Michigan Working Paper Series (WP-95-12), Federal Reserve Bank of Chicago, September.

Hansmann, H.B. (1980) 'The Role of Nonprofit Enterprise'. *Yale Law Journal*, 89: 835–98.

Hansmann, H.B. (1981) 'Reforming Nonprofit Corporation Law'. *University of Pennsylvania Law Review*, 129: 497–623.

Hansmann, H.B. (1988) 'Ownership of the Firm'. *Journal of Law, Economics and Organization*, 4: 267–304.

Hansmann, H.B. (1996) *The Ownership of Enterprise*. Cambridge, MA: Harvard University Press.

Harris, L.E. (1991) *Liquidity, Trading Rules, and Electronic Trading Systems*. Salomon Center, New York University, Monograph Series in Finance, No. 1990-4.

Hart, O.D. (1989) 'An Economist's Perspective on the Theory of the Firm'. *Columbia Law Review*, 89: 1757–74.

Hart, O.D. (1991) 'Incomplete Contracts and the Theory of the Firm', in O. Williamson and S. Winter (eds.), *The Nature of the Firm: Origins, Evolution, and Development*. New York: Oxford University Press.

Hart, O.D. and Moore, J. (1990) 'Property Rights and the Nature of the Firm'. *Journal of Political Economy*, 98: 1119–58.

Hart, O.D. and Moore, J. (1994) 'The Governance of Exchanges: Members' Cooperatives versus Outside Ownership', Working paper, Harvard University and London School of Economics, April.

Hart, O.D. and Moore, J. (1997) 'Cooperatives vs. Outside Ownership', Working paper, Harvard University, and London School of Economics and University of St. Andrews, 16 October.

Hartley, T.C. (1988) *The Foundations of European Community Law: An Introduction to the Constitutional and Administrative Law of the European Community* (2nd. edition). Oxford: Clarendon Press.

Harvard Law Review. (1992) 'Developments in the Law: Nonprofit Corporations'. 105: 1578–699.

Hasbrouck, J. (1995) 'One Security, Many Markets: Determining the Contributions to Price Discovery'. *Journal of Finance*, 5: 1175–99.

Hawes, D.W. (1987) 'Internationalization Spreads to Securities Regulators'. *University of Pennsylvania Journal of International Business Law*, 9: 257–63.

Hellier, D. (1996) 'Outsider was under fire from the start'. *Independent*, 5 January: 16.

Hellwig, M.T. (1980) 'On the Aggregation of Information in Competitive Markets'. *Journal of Economic Theory*, 22: 477–98.

Helsinki Stock Exchange. (1995) 'Helsinki Stock Exchange to Change Company form'. Press Release L/58/95, 21 September.

Her Majesty's Treasury. (1992) *Guidance for Applicants for Recognition as an Overseas Investment Exchange or Overseas Clearing House* (3rd. edition), June.

Hermitte, M.-A. (1992) 'Concurrence'. *Journal du Droit International*, 191: 471–7.

Hirschleifer, J. (1971) 'The Private and Social Value of Information and the Reward to Inventive Activity'. *American Economic Review*, 61: 561–74.

Hirschleifer, J. and Riley, J.G. (1979) 'The Analytics of Uncertainty and Information—An Expository Survey'. *Journal of Economic Literature*, 17: 1375–421.

Hodges, S.D. (1994) 'Equity Derivatives and the Underlying Asset Markets', June.

Holmstrom, B.R. and Tirole, J. (1989) 'The Theory of the Firm', in R. Schmalansee and R. Willig (eds.), *Handbook of Industrial Organization*. Amsterdam: North Holland.

Honoré, A.M. (1961) 'Ownership', in A.G. Guest (ed.), *Oxford Essays in Jurisprudence*. Oxford: Clarendon Press.

Horne, J. (1993a) 'Globex's regulatory headaches'. *Futures and Options World*, April, No. 263: 13.

Horne, J. (1993b) 'Famous for LIFFE?' *Futures and Options World*, No. 269: 44-51.

Horne, J. (1994) 'Les Liasons Dangereuses'. *Futures and Options World*, No. 275: 56-61.

Independent. (1996) 'Big mistakes that upset all sides at the Exchange'. 5 January: 17.

Information Industry Association. (1995) 'Database Protection: An Industry Perspective on the Issues', Discussion Paper, August.

Instinet. (1990a) *INSTINET: The World At Your Fingertips*.

Instinet. (1990b) *INSTINET: Quick Reference Guide*. Version 4.0, May.

Instinet. (1991) *INSTINET: Changing the Way the World Trades*.

Instinet. (1992) *Description of Instinet Corporation: Automated Brokerage Services, in letter to Brandon Becker, SEC*, 7 February.

Instinet. (1996) *Letter to SEC re: Securities Exchange Release N0. 36310 (Proposed Order Handling and Exposure Rules)*, 16 January.

Instinet Canada Limited. (1990) *Submission by Instinet Canada to the Ontario Securities Commission*, 15 January.

Intermarket Trading System. (1991) *Plan for the Purpose of Creating and Operating an Intermarket Communications Linkage Pursuant to Section 11(A)(a)(3)(B) of the Securities and Exchange Act of 1934*. (April 1978, As Restated May 5 1991).

Intermarket Trading System. (1997) *Plan for the Purpose of Creating and Operating an Intermarket Communications Linkage Pursuant to Section 11(A)(a)(3)(B) of the Securities and Exchange Act of 1934*. (April 1978, As Restated May 30 1997).

International Capital Markets Group (Fédération Internationale des Bourses de Valeurs, Section on Business Law—International Bar Association, and International Federation of Accountants). (1989*a*) *International Regulatory Issues—Part 1: An Inventory of the Issues raised by the Application of National Securities Laws and Regulations in Other Countries*, 24 April.

International Capital Markets Group (Fédération Internationale des Bourses de Valeurs, Section on Business Law—International Bar Association, and International Federation of Accountants). (1989*b*) *International Regulatory Issues—Part 2: Analysis of Alternative Solutions to International Regulatory Issues*, 20 December.

International Capital Markets Group (Fédération Internationale des Bourses de Valeurs, Section on Business Law—International Bar Association, and International Federation of Accountants). (1991) *International Regulatory Issues—Part III: Recommendations*, March.

International Capital Markets Group (Fédération Internationale des Bourses de Valeurs, Section on Business Law—International Bar Association, and International Federation of Accountants). (1994) *The Regulation of Electronic Securities Markets: Generally Accepted Principles and Regulatory Actions and Policies*, August.

International Councils of Securities Associations. (1993) *Regulation of Electronic Cross-Border Trading Systems*, 26 May.

International Organization of Securities Commissions. (1990) *Screen-Based Trading Systems for Derivative Products*, June.

International Organization of Securities Commissions (Technical Committee, Working Party on the Regulation of Secondary Markets). (1992) *Transparency on Secondary Markets: A Synthesis of the IOSCO debate*, December.

International Organization of Securities Commissions. (1994) *Report on Issues in the Regulation of Cross-Border Proprietary Screen-Based Trading Systems*, October.

International Petroleum Exchange. (1993) *Quote Vendor Agreement*, 18 January.

International Stock Exchange. (1989) *Review of the Central Market in UK Equities: A Consultative Document from the Council of the International Stock Exchange*, May.

International Stock Exchange. (1990) *Review of the Central Market in UK Equities: Report of the Special Committee on Market Development*, March.

Investment Technology Group. (1997) World-wide web page—http://www.itginc.com/products/posit/html, 24 November.

Istituto per la Ricerca Sociale. (1991) *Rapporto IRS sul Mercato Azionario 1991*.

Jacquillat, B. and Gresse, C. (1995) 'The Divergence of Order Flow on French Shares from the CAC Market to the SEAQ International: An Empirical Investigation', Université Paris Dauphine, Second Version, June.

James, E. and Rose-Ackermann, S. (1986) *The Nonprofit Enterprise in Market Economies*. Fundamentals of Pure and Applied Economics 9. Harwood Academic Publishers.

Jensen, M.C. and Meckling, W. (1976) 'Theory of the Firm: Managerial Behavior, Agency Costs, and Capital Structure'. *Journal of Financial Economics*, 3: 305–60.

Kanter, E.M. and Summers, D.V. (1987) 'Doing Well while Doing Good: Dilemmas of Performance Measurement in Nonprofit Organizations and the Need for a Multiple-Constituency Approach', in W. Powell (ed.), *The Nonprofit Sector: A Research Handbook*. New Haven, CT: Yale University Press.

Karmel, R.S. (1986) 'Can Regulators of International Capital Markets Strike a Balance Between Competing Interests'. *Boston University International Law Journal*, 4: 105–10.

Karmel, R.S. (1993) 'National Treatment, Harmonization, and Mutual Recognition—The Search for Principles for the Regulation of Global Equity Markets', reprinted in S. Revell (1994) (ed.), *Capital Markets Forum Yearbook Volume 1*, 1993. London: Graham & Trotman and International Bar Association.

Klein, B., Crawford, R.G., and Alchian, A.A. (1978) 'Vertical Integration, Appropriable Rents, and the Competitive Contracting Process'. *Journal of Law and Economics*, 21: 297–326.

Kleinwort Benson. (1990) *BEST*.

Kofman, P., and Moser, J.T. (1996) 'Spread, Information Flows and Transparency Across Trading Systems', Working paper, March.

Kreps, D., and Spence, M. (1985) 'Modelling the Role of History in Industrial Organization and Competition', in G. Feiwel (ed.), *Issues in Contemporary Microeconomics and Welfare*. London: MacMillan.

Kübler, F. (1987) 'Regulatory Problems in Internationalizing Trading Markets'. *University of Pennsylvania Journal of International Business Law*, 9: 107–20.

Kyle, A.S., and Marsh, T.A. (1993) 'On the Economics of Securities Clearing and Settlement', Working paper, Duke University and University of California, Berkeley, 27 December.

Kyle, A.S. and Roëll, A. (1989) 'Comments on recent developments and proposals concerning dealing practices in the UK equity market', Special Paper No. 17, Financial Markets Group, London School of Economics.

Kynaston, D. (1997) *LIFFE: A Market and its Makers*. Cambridge: Granta Editions.

Lamoureux, C.G. and Schnitzlein, C.R. (1997) 'When It's not the Only Game in Town: The Effect of Bilateral Search on the Quality of a Dealer Market'. *Journal of Finance*, 52: 683–712.

Lee, R. (1989) 'Market-Making in the UK Equity Market'. D.Phil. Thesis, Nuffield College, Oxford University, June.

Lee, R. (1992) 'What is an Exchange?', reprinted in S. Revell (1994) (ed.), *Capital Markets Forum Yearbook Volume 1, 1993*. London: Graham & Trotman and International Bar Association.

Lee, R. (1993*a*) 'Public Virtues, Private Vices? or Vice Versa? Competition and Regulation of Trading Systems'. *London Stock Exchange Quarterly*, Summer: 19–23.

Lee, R. (1993*b*) 'Enforcement Issues in Securities Markets'. XVIII Annual Conference of IOSCO, Mexico, 28 October.

Lee, R. (1994) 'The Legal Foundation for Competition in EC Capital Markets: The Gap Between Rhetoric and Reality'. *International Review of Law and Economics*, 14: 163–73.

Lee, R. (1995) *The Ownership of Price and Quote Information: Law, Regulation, Economics and Business*. Oxford: Oxford Finance Group, February.

Lee, R. (1996) 'In good faith'. *Financial Times*, 17 December: 17.

Lee, R. (1997*a*) 'The Future of the London Stock Exchange', reprinted in Treasury Committee, House of Commons, *The Prospects for the London Stock Exchange*. Fifth Report, HC311 (17/3/1997), 7 January.

Lee, R. (1997*b*) 'Now, time for the truth'. *London Financial News*, 3–9 November: 9.

Levitt, A. (1994) 'Putting Investors First'. XIX Annual Conference of IOSCO, Tokyo, 19 October.

Liebowitz, S.J. and Margolis, S.E. (1995) 'Are Network Externalities a New Source of Market Failure'. *Research in Law and Economics*, 17: 1–22.

Linton, C. (1994) 'Talk of IMM and CME Seat Merger Highlights Inequities'. *Agence Presse-Dow Jones*, 14.28 (06277), 14.30 (06279), 14.32 (06282), 14.34 (06283), 4 August.

Lipton, D.A. (1987) 'A Primer on Broker-Dealer Registration'. *The Catholic University Law Review*, 36: 899–985.

London International Financial Futures Exchange. (1993*a*) *Approved Subscriber Agreement*.

London International Financial Futures Exchange. (1993*b*) *Quote Vendor Agreement*.

London International Financial Futures Exchange. (1993*c*) *Sub-Vendor Agreement*.

London International Financial Futures Exchange. (1995) *Formal Link Agreement with the Chicago Board of Trade*. Circular No. 95/112, 28 December.

London International Financial Futures Exchange. (1996*a*) *Euroyen Three Month Interest Rate Contract Clearing Arrangements*. Circular No. 96/18, 1 March.

London International Financial Futures Exchange. (1996*b*) *Offer by LIFFE (Holdings) plc for the whole of the issued share capital of The London Commodity Exchange (1986) Limited*, 26 June.

London Stock Exchange. (undated) 'A History of the London Stock Exchange'.

London Stock Exchange. (various) 'Council Notices'.

London Stock Exchange (1989) *Quality of Market Quarterly Review*, Spring.

London Stock Exchange. (1992) *CRS-LYNX: License Agreement*. CRSLIC-03/92, March.

London Stock Exchange. (1993*a*) *CRS-LYNX: License Agreement*. CRSLIC-05/93, May.

London Stock Exchange. (1993*b*) *CRS-LYNX: Order Form*. CRS34-07/93, July.

London Stock Exchange. (1995) *AIM: A New Opportunity*, February.

London Stock Exchange. (1996*a*) *New electronic trading services: Implementation of a public limit order book*. Consultation document, 12 January.

London Stock Exchange. (1996*b*) *New Electronic Trading Services: Analysis of Consultation Feedback*. Prepared by PA Consulting Group, March.

London Stock Exchange. (1996*c*) *Regulatory Guide: Domestic Equity Market, Traditional Options Market and AIM*, December.

London Stock Exchange. (1997*a*) *Membership Application Pack*.

London Stock Exchange. (1997*b*) *Share Ownership for All*, April.

London Stock Exchange. (1997*c*) *Amendments to Rules: Rules for the Stock Exchange Electronic Trading Service*. Stock Exchange Notice N21/97, 18 April.

London Stock Exchange. (1997*d*) *Memorandum and Articles of Association of London Stock Exchange (as amended by special resolution passed on 10 July 1997 and effective on that date)*, 10 July.

Loss, L. and Seligman, J. (1990) *Securities Regulation* (3rd. edition). Boston: Little, Brown and Company.

Loumeau, P. (1993) 'DTB-MATIF Cooperation', Presentation before the Networked Markets Study Group, Prométhée, 30 September.

Lurie, J. (1979) *The Chicago Board of Trade 1859–1905: The Dynamics of Self-Regulation*. Urbana, Illinois: University of Illinois Press.

Lyons, R.K. (1996) 'Optimal Transparency in a Dealer Market with an Application to Foreign Exchange'. *Journal of Financial Intermediation*, 5: 225–54.

Macdonald, A.M. (ed.). (1978) *Chambers Twentieth Century Dictionary*. Edinburgh and London: W. and R. Chambers.

McGaw, I.W.T. (1997) *The World's Clearing Houses* (3rd. edition). London: Futures and Options World.

MacIntyre, D. (1991) 'Review of the January 14th Rule Changes'. *Stock Exchange Quarterly with Quality of Markets Review*, Summer: 35–7.

McLean, I. (1990) *Public Choice: An Introduction*. Oxford: Blackwell Publishers.

McPartlin, N. (Information Providers User Group). (1994) 'The User's View', The Ownership of Real-Time Data in the Financial Markets, ICG Conference, London, 7 July.

Macey, J.R. and Kanda, H. (1990) 'The Stock Exchange as a Firm: The Emergence of Close Substitutes for the New York and Tokyo Stock Exchanges'. Cornell Law Review, 75: 1007–52.

Madhavan, A. (1995) 'Consolidation, Fragmentation, and the Disclosure of Trading Information'. *Review of Financial Studies*, 8: 579–603.

Madhavan, A. (1996) 'Security Prices and Market Transparency'. *Journal of Financial Intermediation*, 5: 255–83.

Madhavan, A., Mendelson, M., and Peake, J.W. (1988) 'Risky Business: The Clearance and Settlement of Financial Transactions', Working Paper, Rodney L. White Center for Financial Research, Wharton, 14 October.

Maguire, F. (1997) 'The Price is Right?' *Futures and Options World*, June, No. 313: 61–2.

Mahony, S. (1997) *A–Z of International Finance: The Essential Guide to Tools, Terms and Techniques*. London: FT Pitman Publishing.

Marché à Terme International de France. (1993) *MATIF Vendor Agreement*.

Marché à Terme International de France, Marché des Options Négociables de Paris SA, Société des Bourses Françaises-Paris Bourse, Deutsche Börse AG, and Swiss Exchange. (1997) 'Frankfurt, Paris and Zürich Exchanges Extend their Alliance Developing a Single Range of Fixed Income Derivatives Extension to Cash Markets Planned'. Press Release, 17 September.

Marckus, M. and Murray, A. (1996) 'London stock market chief is dismissed'. *Times*, 5 January: 1.

Marsh, P. (1993) *Short-Termism on Trial* (3rd impression). Institutional Fund Managers' Association, November.

Martin Jr., W.M. (1971) *The Securities Markets: A Report with Recommendations*. Submitted to the Board of Governors of the New York Stock Exchange, 5 August.

Maynard, T.H. (1992) 'What is an "Exchange?"—Proprietary Electronic Securities Trading Systems and the Statutory Definition of an Exchange'. *Washington and Lee Law Review*, 49: 833–912.

MEFF Renta Fija. (1993) *Provisional Agreement for the Delivery of the MEFF Renta Fija Data Signal to Quote Vendors*.

Melamed, L., Chairman of the Executive Committee and Special Counsel to the Board of the Chicago Mercantile Exchange (1989) *Testimony before the U.S. Senate, Committee on Agriculture, Nutrition and Forestry*. Futures Trading Practices Act of 1989 S. 1729, S.Hrg. 101-1052: 355–72, 17 October.

Melamed, L. and Tamarkin, B. (1996) *Leo Melamed: Escape to the Futures*. New York: John Wiley and Sons.

Mendelson, H. (1990) 'On the Impact of Computer-Based Market Access Systems on the Ontario Capital Market: An Economic Analysis', in Dealer Group, *Submission to the Ontario Securities Commission*, 15 January, 2: 1–70.

Merrill Lynch (M. Marks). (1996) 'New electronic trading service: consultation feedback—Response', London Stock Exchange no. 108, 16 February.

Merton, R.C. (1993) 'Operation and Regulation in Financial Intermediation: A Functional Perspective', in P. Englund (ed.), *Operation and Regulation of Financial Markets*. Stockholm: The Economic Council.

Middleton, M. (1987) 'Nonprofit Boards of Directors: Beyond the Governance Function', in W. Powell (ed.), *The Nonprofit Sector: A Research Handbook*. New Haven, CT: Yale University Press.

Miller, C.G. (1994) 'Magill: Time to Abandon the "Specific Subject-matter" Concept'. *European Intellectual Property Review*, 16: 415–21.

Miller, M. (1990) 'International Competitiveness of U.S. Futures Exchanges'. *Journal of Financial Services Research*, 4: 387–408.

Miller, P.H. (1991) 'Life after Feist: Facts, the First Amendment, and the Copyright Status of Automated Databases'. *Fordham Law Review*, 60: 507–39.

Miller, S.S. (1985) 'Self-Regulation of the Securities Markets: A Critical Examination'. *Washington and Lee Law Review*, 42: 853–87.

Milner, M. (1996) 'A case of order driven out'. *Guardian*, 5 January: 14.

Modigliani, F. and Miller, M.H. (1958) 'The Cost of Capital, Corporation Finance and the Theory of Investment'. *American Economic Review*, 48: 261–97.

Moles, P. and Terry, N. (1997) *The Handbook of International Financial Terms*. Oxford: Oxford University Press.

Mondo Visione. (1997) *The IFR Handbook of World Stock and Commodity Exchanges 1997*. London: IFR.

Montier, B. (1990) 'European List', conference, Centre for European Policy Studies, Brussels, 29 November.

Montier, B., Knight, J.R., and Nicoll, S. (1990) 'Technical Integration', Centre for European Policy Studies, Brussels, 29 November.

Montreal Exchange. (1992) *The Montreal Boston Link: An Efficient Trading Service for U.S. Securities*, October.

Moorhead, Hon. Carlos J. (1996) 'The Database Investment and Intellectual Property Antipiracy Act of 1996'. Congressional Record, E890–E891, 23 May.

Morris, S. and Shin, H.S. (1994) 'Impact of Public Announcements on Trade in Financial Markets', CARESS discussion paper #94-16, University of Pennsylvania, June.

Morse, L. (1993) 'Reuters attacks its partners in Globex system'. *Financial Times*, 12 November: 27.

Morse, L. (1994) 'First price manipulation charges filed by CFTC'. *Financial Times*, 12 January: 32.

Morse, L. and Corrigan, T. (1993) 'Globex backers split over withdrawal of Liffe from talks'. *Financial Times*, 18 August: 25.

Moser, J.T. (1994) 'Origins of the Modern Exchange Clearinghouse: A History of Early Clearing and Settlement Methods at Futures Exchanges', Working Paper (WP-94-3), Federal Reserve Bank of Chicago, April.

Mulherin, J.H., Netter, J.M., and Overdahl, J. (1991a) 'Prices are Property: The Organization of Financial Exchanges from a Transaction Cost Perspective'. *Journal of Law and Economics*, 34: 591–644.

Mulherin, J.H., Netter, J.M., and Overdahl, J. (1991b) 'Who Owns the Quotes? A Case Study into the Definition and Enforcement of Property Rights at the Chicago Board of Trade'. Review of Futures Markets, 10: 108–29.

Municipal Securities Rulemaking Board. (1993a) MSRB Reports: Vol. 13.

Municipal Securities Rulemaking Board. (1993*b*) *Report of the Municipal Securities Rulemaking Board on Regulation of the Municipal Securities Market*, 3 September.

Myers, G. (1996) 'The Restatement's Rejection of the Misappropriation Tort: A Victory for the Public Domain'. *University of South California Law Review* 47: 673–706.

Myrick, R.E. (1992) 'Will Intellectual Property on Technology still be Viable in a Unitary Community?' *European Intellectual Property Review*, September, 14: 298–304.

NASDAQ Stock Market (1996*a*) *Nasdaq Workstation II Subscriber Agreements*.

NASDAQ Stock Market (1996*b*) *Vendor Agreement for Level 1 Service and Last Sale Service*.

National Association of Securities Dealers. (1983) 'Analysis of the Impact of Last-Sale Reporting on Market Characteristics of Tier 2 NASDAQ Securities', discussion paper, June.

National Association of Securities Dealers. (undated—believed 1987) *Application of NASDAQ International Limited for Recognition as an Overseas Investment Exchange Pursuant to Section 37 of the Financial Services Act of 1986*.

National Association of Securities Dealers. (1989*a*) *NASDAQ, Inc.: Level I Service Vendor Agreement*, July.

National Association of Securities Dealers. (1989*b*) *NASD Market Services, Inc.: Last Sale Information Vendor Agreement*, July.

National Association of Securities Dealers. (1990*a*) *OTC Bulletin Board User Guide*, May.

National Association of Securities Dealers. (1990*b*) *Form 19b-4 Proposed Rule Change*. File No. SR-NASD-90-33, Amendment No. 1, 3 October.

National Association of Securities Dealers. (1991) *Letter from Frank J. Wilson, NASD, to Christine Sakach, SEC, re: Technical Amendment to the Transaction Reporting Plan for the NASDAQ International Service*, 10 June.

National Association of Securities Dealers. (1995) *Report of the NASD Select Committee on Structure and Governance to the NASD Board of Governors*, 15 September.

National Conference of Commissioners on Uniform State Laws. (1996) 'Uniform Commercial Code (Private), Article 2B, Licenses'. Draft, 3 May.

National Legal Research Group (T.J. Snider). (1996) *Regulation of the Commodities Futures and Options Markets*. (Release #1, 10/96) Deerfield, Illnois: Clark-Boardman Callaghan (2nd. Ed.), October.

National Market Advisory Board. (1976) *The Possible Need for Modifications of the Scheme of Self-Regulation in the Securities Industry so as to Adapt it to a National Market System*. Report to Congress, 31 December.

Neuberger, A. and Roëll, A. (1991) 'Components of the Bid–Ask Spread: A Glosten-Harris Approach', Working paper No. IFA-137-91, London Business School.

New York Cotton Exchange (1996) *Letter to CFTC re: Proposed Rulemaking with Respect to Conflicts of Interest, et al.*, 28 June.

New York Mercantile Exchange. (1994) 'NYMEX, Asia-Pacific Exchanges plan Electronic Trading Links'. *This Month at NYMEX*, November, 94: 2.

New York Mercantile Exchange. (1995) 'The Exchange Signs Strategic Alliance Agreement with Sydney Futures Exchange'. *Barrels, Bars and BTUs*, February, 95: 1, 7.

New York Mercantile Exchange. (1996) *Letter to CFTC re: Proposed Rulemaking Concerning Voting by Interested Member of Self-Regulatory Organization Governing Boards and Committees and Concerning the Publicizing of Broker Association Memberships*, 11 July.

New York Mercantile Exchange, and Commodity Exchange Inc. (1994) *Joint Proxy Statement*, 26 March.

New York Stock Exchange. (1989) *NYSE: 1989 and Beyond—An Overview of an Academic Seminar*, 5 May.

New York Stock Exchange. (1992) *Exhibit A: Agreement for Receipt and Use of Market Data*.

New York Stock Exchange. (1993) 'Reporting of Crossing Session II Trade Details', Information Memo to Members and Member Organizations, 15 September.

Newhouse, J. (1970) 'Towards a Theory of Nonprofit Institutions: An Economic Model of a Hospital'. *American Economic Review*, 60: 64–74.

Nimmer, M. and Nimmer, D. (1990) *Nimmer on Copyright*. New York: Matthew Bender & Co..

O'Hara, M. (1995). *Market Microstructure Theory*. Oxford: Basil Blackwell.

Office of Fair Trading. (1988) The International Stock Exchange, April.

Office of Fair Trading. (1990*a*) *Financial Services Act 1986: Trade Publication and Price Transparency on the International Stock Exchange*, April.

Office of Fair Trading. (1990*b*) *Financial Services Act 1986: The International Stock Exchange: dissemination of company news*, June.

Office of Fair Trading. (1994) *Trade Publication Rules of the London Stock Exchange*, November.

Office of Fair Trading. (1995) *Rules of the London Stock Exchange relating to Market Makers*, March.

OM. (1992) 'Distribution of Financial Products through Exchange Linkage: A Discussion Paper', 12 May.

OM Group. (1993) *Annual Report 1992*.

OM Group and Stockholm Stock Exchange. (1997) 'OM merges with the Stockholm Stock Exchange'. Joint Press Release, 28 November.

OMLX—The London Securities and Derivatives Exchange. (1993). *A World of Opportunity*.

Ontario Securities Commission. (1990) *In the matter of the Securities Act, R.S.O. 1980, Chapter 466, as amended; and of a Report by the Rule Review Committee of the TSE on the Operation of the Auction Market; and of INSTINET Canada Limited*, 27 March.

Ontario Securities Commission (Capital Markets Branch). (1994) 'Electronic Trading Systems in Ontario'. *Ontario Securities Commission Bulletin*, 27 May, 17: 2512–50.

Ontario Securities Commission. (1995*a*) 'Dealer Electronic Services'. *Ontario Securities Commission Bulletin*, 24 March, 18: 1347–50.

Ontario Securities Commission. (1995*b*) *Electronic Trading Systems: OSC Forum Proceedings*, 29 June.

Ontario Securities Commission. (1995*c*) 'Registration of Instinet Corporation (Instinet) as an International Dealer—Registration Staff Notice'. *Ontario Securities Commission Bulletin*, 22 September, 18: 4302–3.

Ontario Securities Commission. (1995*d*) *Decision: In the Matter of the Securities Act, R.S.O. 1990, c.S.5, as amended; and In the Matter of Instinet Corporation; and In the Matter of Applications by the Toronto Stock Exchange, the Alberta Stock Exchange, the Investment Dealers Association of Canada, the Montreal Exchange, and the Vancouver Stock Exchange, for a Hearing and Review Under Sections 8, 127 and 144*, 15 November.

Openshaw, C.D. (1996) 'New electronic trading service: consultation feedback—Response', London Stock Exchange no. 054, 13 February.

Options Price Reporting Association. (undated—believed 1978) *Plan for Reporting of Consolidated Options Reports and Quotation Information*.

Ordeshook, P.C. (1985) *Game Theory and Political Theory*. Cambridge: Cambridge University Press.

Ordeshook, P.C. (1992) *A Political Theory Primer*. New York: Routledge.

Organisation for Economic Cooperation and Development. (1990) 'Systemic Risks in Securities Markets'. *Financial Market Trends*, 7 December.

Orosel, G.O. (1993) 'Informational Efficiency and Welfare in the Stock Market', Discussion Paper No. 176, London School of Economics, December.

Oslo Bors Informasjon (A/S). (1993) *Customer Agreement*.

Overdahl, J.A. (1997) 'The Licensing of Financial Indexes: Implications for the Development of New Index-Linked Investment Products', in A. Neubert (ed.), *Indexing for Maximum Investment Management Results*. Chicago: Glenlake Publishing (forthcoming).

Oxford English Dictionary. (1971) Oxford: Oxford University Press.

Packel, I. (1970) *The Law of the Organization and Operation of Cooperatives* (4th. edition). Philadelphia: Joint Committee on Continuing Legal Education of the American Law Institute and the American Bar Association.

Pagano, M. (1989) 'Trading Volume and Asset Liquidity'. *Quarterly Journal of Economics* 104: 254–74.

Pagano, M. and Roëll, A. (1990*a*) 'Shifting Gears: An Economic Evaluation of the Reform of the Paris Bourse', Working paper, London School of Economics, July.

Pagano, M., and Roëll, A. (1990*b*) 'Trading Systems in European stock exchanges: current performance and policy options'. *Economic Policy*, October: 65–115.

Pagano, M., and Roëll, A. (1991) 'Dually-traded Italian equities: London vs. Milan', Working paper, March.

Pagano, M. and Roëll, A. (1996) 'Transparency and Liquidity: A Comparison of Auction and Dealer Markets with Informed Trading'. *Journal of Finance*, 51: 579–611.

Parker, S.L. and Becker, B. (1981) 'Unlisted Trading Privileges'. *Review of Securities Regulation*, 14: 853–60.

Peake, J.W. and Mendelson, M. (1991) 'Who Should Guard the Hen House? Regulating Market Centers'. XVI Annual Conference of IOSCO, Washington, 11 September.

Peltzman, S. (1976) 'Towards a More General Theory of Regulation'. *Journal of Law and Economics*, 19: 211–40.

Pendley, K. (1994) 'CME Faces Redistributing Power Through Seats'. *Knight Ridder Financial News* 20.39 CDT, 27 July.

Perier, F. (1994) 'The Investment Services Directive and the European Capital Market in Securities', European Capital Markets Institute conference, 3 March.

Pirrong, S.C. (1995) 'The Self-Regulation of Commodity Exchanges: The Case of Market Manipulation'. *Journal of Law and Economics*, April, 38: 141–206.

Pont Data Australia. (1990) *Summary of court case: Pont Data vs. ASX*.

Porter, D.C. and Weaver, D.G. (1996*a*) 'Pre-Trade Transparency and Market Quality', Working paper, University of Wisconsin and Marquette University.

Porter, D.C. and Weaver, D.G. (1996*b*) 'Do NASDAQ Market Makers "Paint the Tape"?', Working paper, University of Wisconsin and Marquette University, 19 October.

Porter, P.K. and Scully, G.W. (1987) 'Economic Efficiency in Cooperatives'. *Journal of Law and Economics*, 30: 489–512.

Powell, W.W. and Friedkin, R. (1987) 'Organizational Change in Nonprofit

Organizations', in W. Powell (ed.), *The Nonprofit Sector: A Research Handbook*. New Haven, CT: Yale University Press.

Raphael Zorn Hemsley Ltd (W.K. Sharp). (1996) 'New electronic trading service: consultation feedback—Response', London Stock Exchange no. 082, 15 February.

Rathore, S. (1994) 'Sitting on a fortune'. *Futures and Options World*, October, No. 281: 19.

Reichmann, J.H. and Samuelson, P. (1997) 'Intellectual Property Rights in Data?' *Vanderbilt Law Review*, 50: 51–166.

Reierson, A. (1993) 'Europe mulls Franco-German axis'. *Futures and Options World*, October, No. 269: 21.

Reindl, A. (1993) 'The Magic of Magill: TV Program Guides as a Limit of Copyright Law?' *International Review of Industrial Property and Copyright Law*, 24: 60–82.

Reuters Australia Pty. Ltd. (1988) *Submission regarding Designation by the Ministerial Council to conduct an Exempt Stock Market*, 3 March.

RMJ Options Trading Corp. (undated—believed 1989*a*) *The Over-the-Counter Trading System*.

RMJ Options Trading Corp. (undated—believed 1989*b*) *The Over-the-Counter Trading System: Procedures*.

Roberts, H. (1967) 'Statistical versus Clinical Prediction of Stock Market Prices', Unpublished manuscript, Center for Research in Security Prices, University of Chicago, May.

Roëll, A. (1988) 'Regulating Information Disclosure among Stock Exchange Market Makers', Discussion Paper No. 51, Financial Markets Group, London School of Economics, October.

Roëll, A. (1990) 'Dual Capacity and the Quality of the Market'. *Journal of Financial Intermediation*, 1: 105–24.

Roëll, A. (1992) 'Comparing the Performance of Stock Exchange Trading Systems', in J. Fingleton and D. Schoenmaker (eds.), *Internationalisation of Capital Markets*. London: Graham and Trotman.

Rosenthal, L. (1994) 'Membership Share Plan'. 25 May.

Rutherford, D. (1995) *Routledge Dictionary of Economics*. London: Routledge.

Rydén, B. (1995) 'The Reform of the Stockholm Stock Exchange: Background and Experiences'. November.

Salomon Brothers (G. Lawson and R. O'Hare). (1996) 'New electronic trading service: consultation feedback—Response', London Stock Exchange no. 020, 6 February.

Saloner, G. (1984) 'Self-Regulating Commodity Futures Exchanges', in R. Anderson (ed.), *The Industrial Organisation of Futures Markets*. Lexington, MA: Lexington Books.

Scherer, F.M. and Ross, D. (1990) *Industrial Market Structure and Economic Performance* (3rd. edition). Boston: Houghton Mifflin Company.

Schroder Investment Management (N.T. Ralston). (1996) 'New electronic trading service: consultation feedback—Response', London Stock Exchange no. 153, 19 February.

Schroder Securities (P. Augar). (1996) 'New electronic trading service: consultation feedback—Response', London Stock Exchange no. 034, 12 February.

Schwartz, R.A. (1988) *Equity Markets: Structure, Trading and Performance*. New York: Harper and Row.

Schwartz, R.A., assisted by Cohen, L.M. (1991) *Reshaping the Equity Markets: A Guide for the 1990s*. New York: Harper and Row.

Schwarz, M. (1991) 'Copyright in Compilations of Facts: Feist Publications, Inc. v Rural Telephone Service Co., Inc.'. *European Intellectual Property Review*, 13: 178–82.

Securities and Exchange Commission (Division of Trading and Exchanges). (1962) *Staff Report on Organization, Management, and Regulation of Conduct of Members of the American Stock Exchange*. Special Study of Securities Markets, Appendix XII-A.

Securities and Exchange Commission. (10/3/1971) *Transmittal Letter to Accompany Institutional Investor Study Report of the Securities and Exchange Commission*.

Securities and Exchange Commission. (2/2/1972) 'Statement of the Securities and Exchange Commission on the Future Structure of the Securities Markets'. *Federal Register*, 37: 5286.

Securities and Exchange Commission. (8/11/1972) *Adoption of Rule 17a-15*. Release No. 34-9850.

Securities and Exchange Commission. (26/1/1978*a*) *Rule 11Ac1-1 Composite Quotation System*. Release No. 34-14415.

Securities and Exchange Commission. (26/1/1978*b*) *Development of a National Market System*. Release No. 34-14416.

Securities and Exchange Commission. (14/4/1978) *In the Matter of AMEX Inc., BSE Inc., NYSE Inc., PSE Inc., PHLX Inc., Application pursuant to Section 11A(a)(3)(B) Temporary Order*. Release No. 34-14661, File No. 4-208.

Securities and Exchange Commission. (29/11/1978) *In the Matter of Bunker Ramo Corporation, GTE Information Systems Incorporated, Options Price Reporting Authority*. Release No. 34-15372, File No. 4-280.

Securities and Exchange Commission. (26/3/1980) *Termination of the Options Moratorium*. Release No. 34-16701.

Securities and Exchange Commission. (23/9/1983) *In the Matter of the Full Registration as Clearing Agencies of: The Depository Trust Company; Stock Clearing Corporation of Philadelphia; MidWest Securities Trust Company; The Options Clearing Corporation; Midwest Clearing Corporation; Pacific Securities Depository Trust Company; Pacific Clearing Corporation; National Securities Clearing Corporation; and Philadelphia Depository Trust Company*. Release No. 34-20221, File Nos. 600-1, 600-4, 600-7, 600-8, 600-9, 600-10, 600-11, 600-15, and 600-19.

Securities and Exchange Commission. (17/4/1984) *In the Matter of Institutional Networks Corp., and NASD, Inc.: Order Announcing Commission Findings, Modifying Interim Relief, and Instituting Proceedings*. Release No. 34-20874, File No. 4-256.

Securities and Exchange Commission. (6/7/1984*a*) *Notice of Filing of Proposed Rule Change and Amendment to Proposed Rule Change by the Chicago Board Options Exchange, Inc.*. Release No. 34-21121, File No. SR-CBOE-84-16.

Securities and Exchange Commission. (6/7/1984*b*) *Notice of Filing of Proposed Rule Change and Amendment to Proposed Rule Change by the Chicago Board Options Exchange, Inc.*. Release No. 34-21122, File No. SR-CBOE-84-15.

Securities and Exchange Commission. (14/9/1984) *Notice of Filing of Proposed Rule Change by Boston Stock Exchange, Inc.*. Release No. 34-21324, File No. SR-BSE-84-5.

Securities and Exchange Commission. (31/10/1984) *Chicago Board Options Exchange, Inc.; Order Instituting Proceedings to Determine Whether to Disapprove Rule Change*. Release No. 34-21439, File Nos. SR-CBOE-84-15 and SR-CBOE-84-16.

Securities and Exchange Commission. (1/11/1984) *Boston Stock Exchange, Inc.; Order Approving Proposed Rule Change*. Release No. 34-21449, File No. SR-BSE-84-6.

Securities and Exchange Commission. (8/4/1985) *Self-Regulatory Organizations; Boston*

Stock Exchange, Inc.; Order Approving Proposed Rule Change. Release No. 34-21925, File No. SR-BSE-84-8.

Securities and Exchange Commission. (8/5/1985) *Self-Regulatory Organizations; Proposed Rule Change by American Stock Exchange, Inc.; Relating to Amex/Toronto Trading Linkage.* Release No. 34-22001, File No. SR-AMEX-85-8.

Securities and Exchange Commission. (21/5/1985) *Self-Regulatory Organizations; Chicago Board Options Exchange, Inc.; Order Disapproving Proposed Rule Change SR-CBOE-84-16 and Approving Proposed Rule Change SR-CBOE-84-15.* Release No. 34-22058, File Nos. SR-CBOE-84-15 and SR-CBOE-84-16.

Securities and Exchange Commission. (12/6/1985) *Self-Regulatory Organization; Proposed Rule Change by Midwest Stock Exchange, Incorporated, Relating to an Electronic Trading Link Between Midwest Stock Exchange and the Toronto Stock Exchange.* Release No. 34-22136, File No. SR-MSE-85-4.

Securities and Exchange Commission. (21/8/1985) *Self-Regulatory Organizations; Proposed Rule Change by the Philadelphia Stock Exchange, Inc.; Relating to Foreign Currency.* Release No. 34-22343, File No. Phlx-85-24.

Securities and Exchange Commission. (30/8/1985) *Self-Regulatory Organizations; the Options Clearing Corporation; Notice of Proposed Rule Change.* Release No. 34-22354, File No. SR-OCC-85-13.

Securities and Exchange Commission. (20/9/1985) *Self-Regulatory Organization; American Stock Exchange, Inc., Order Approving Proposed Rule Change.* Release No. 34-22442, File No. SR-AMEX-85-8.

Securities and Exchange Commission. (30/10/1985) 'NASD (Petitioner) v. SEC (Respondent) and Institutional Networks Corporation, (Intervenor): On petition for Review of Order of the SEC—Answering Brief of the SEC'. No. 85-1012, US Court of Appeals, District of Columbia Circuit.

Securities and Exchange Commission. (19/12/1985) *Self-Regulatory Organizations; Philadelphia Stock Exchange, Inc.; Order Approving Proposed Rule Change.* Release No. 34-22728, File No. SR-PHLX-85-23.

Securities and Exchange Commission. (30/1/1986) *Self-Regulatory Organizations; the Options Clearing Corp.; Amendments to Proposed Rule Change.* Release No. 34-22847, File No. SR-OCC-85-13.

Securities and Exchange Commission. (14/3/1986) *Self-Regulatory Organizations; Request for Approval by National Association of Securities Dealers, Inc. of a Pilot Program with the Stock Exchange, London England for the Exchange and Distribution of International Securities Information.* Release No. 34-23022, File No. SR-NASD-86-4.

Securities and Exchange Commission. (7/4/1986) *Self-Regulatory Organizations; Midwest Stock Exchange, Inc.; Order Approving Proposed Rule Change.* Release No. 23075, File No. SR-MSE-85-4.

Securities and Exchange Commission. (21/4/1986) *Self-Regulatory Organizations; National Association of Securities Dealers, Inc.; Order Approving Proposed Rule Change.* Release No. 34-23158, File No. SR-NASD-86-4.

Securities and Exchange Commission. (8/8/1986) *Letter from Richard Ketchum, to Daniel Brooks re: Request for no-action position regarding Instinet's non-registration with the SEC as an exchange, an association, or a clearing agency.*

Securities and Exchange Commission. (12/2/1987) *Self-Regulatory Organizations; Order Approving Proposed Rule Change by the Cincinnati Stock Exchange Relating to an*

Affiliation with the Chicago Board Options Exchange. Release No. 34-24090, File No. SR-CSE-86-6.

Securities and Exchange Commission. (20/3/1987) *Self-Regulatory Organizations; Order Granting Accelerated Approval to Proposed Rule Change by American Stock Exchange, Inc., Relating to Classification of Exchange Floor Governors and Structure of Nominating Committee*. Release No. 34-24212, File No. SR-AMEX-86-30.

Securities and Exchange Commission. (2/4/1987) *Self-Regulatory Organizations; Granting Accelerated Approval to Proposed Rule Change by National Association of Securities Dealers, Inc., to extend the period of effectiveness of the Pilot Program with the Stock Exchange of the UK and Republic of Ireland, Ltd., for the Exchange and Distribution of International Securities Information*. Release No. 34-24292, File No. SR-NASD-87-15.

Securities and Exchange Commission. (27/7/1987) *Internationalization of the Securities Markets*. Report of the Staff of the U.S. Securities and Exchange Commission to the Senate Committee on Banking, Housing and Urban Affairs, and the House Committee on Energy and Commerce.

Securities and Exchange Commission. (28/7/1987) *No-Action Letter from Brandon Becker concerning POSIT*.

Securities and Exchange Commission. (11/3/1988) *Order Granting Accelerated Approval to a Proposed Rule Change by the Philadelphia Stock Exchange Relating to Continuity of the Office of the Chairman and Vice Chairman of the Board of Governors*. Release No. 34-25448, File No. SR-Phlx-87-41.

Securities and Exchange Commission. (5/1/1989) 'Hearing of January 5, 1989 Before the Securities and Exchange Commission'.

Securities and Exchange Commission. (18/4/1989) *Proprietary Trading Systems*. Release No. 34-26708, File No. S7-13-89.

Securities and Exchange Commission. (26/5/1989) *Multiple Trading of Standardized Options*. Release No. 34-26870, File No. S7-25-87.

Securities and Exchange Commission. (16/11/1989) *Automated Systems of Self-Regulatory Organisations*. Release No. 34-27445.

Securities and Exchange Commission. (12/1/1990) *Self-Regulatory Organizations; Delta Government Options Corporation; Order Granting Temporary Registration as a Clearing Agency*. Release No. 34-27611, File No. 600-24.

Securities and Exchange Commission. (27/4/1990) 'Answering Brief of the SEC, Respondent before US Court of Appeals for the Seventh Circuit: CBT and CME Petitioners v. SEC, Respondent, and Delta Government Options Corporation, Intervenor-Respondent'. No. 90-1246.

Securities and Exchange Commission. (30/8/1990) *Self-Regulatory Organizations; Proposes Rule Change by New York Stock Exchange, Inc. Relating to a System Whereby the Exchange Would Make Available a Specified Portion of the Limit Orders for Securities Included on the Display Books*. Release No. 34-28375, File No. SR-NYSE-90-33.

Securities and Exchange Commission. (24/10/1990) *Self-Regulatory Organizations; Wunsch Auction Systems, Inc.; Application for Limited Volume Exemption from Registration as an Exchange under Section 5 of the SEC Act; . . . Request for Comments*. Release No. 34-28577, File No. 10-100.

Securities and Exchange Commission. (21/11/1990a) *Self-Regulatory Organizations; Notice of Filing of Proposed Rule Change by the NYSE relating to the NYSE's*

Aggregate-Price Session of its Off-Hours Trading Facility. Release No. 34-28640, File No. SR-NYSE-90-53.

Securities and Exchange Commission. (21/11/1990*b*) *Self-Regulatory Organizations; Notice of Filing of Proposed Rule Change by the NYSE relating to the NYSE's Closing-Price Session of its Off-Hours Trading Facility.* Release No. 34-28639, File No. SR-NYSE-90-52.

Securities and Exchange Commission. (20/2/1991) *Self-Regulatory Organizations; Wunsch Auction Systems, Inc.; Order Granting Limited Volume Exemption from Registration as an Exchange under Section 5 of the SEA.* Release No. 34-28899, File No. 10-100.

Securities and Exchange Commission. (28/2/1991) *Letter from John Ramsay to Daniel Brooks, re. Non-registration of WASI as a National Securities Exchange.*

Securities and Exchange Commission. (4/3/1991) *Self-Regulatory Organizations; Boston Stock Exchange, Inc.; Order Approving Proposed Rule Change Relating to the Composition of its Audit Committee.* Release No. 34-28936, File No. SR-BSE-90-19.

Securities and Exchange Commission. (15/5/1991) *Automated Systems of Self-Regulatory Organisations.* Release No. 34-29185, File No. S7-12-91.

Securities and Exchange Commission. (24/5/1991) *Self-Regulatory Organizations; NYSE Inc.; Order Granting Temporary Approval to Proposed Rule Changes Relating to the NYSE's Off-Hours Trading Facility.* Release No. 34-29237, File Nos. SR-NYSE-90-52 and SR-NYSE-90-53.

Securities and Exchange Commission. (28/5/1991) *Securities Transactions Exempt from Transaction Fees.* Release No. 34-29238.

Securities and Exchange Commission (Division of Market Regulation). (26/9/1991) *Automated Securities Trading: A Discussion of Selected Critical Issues.* XVI Annual conference of IOSCO, Washington.

Securities and Exchange Commission. (11/10/1991) *Self-Regulatory Organizations; Order Approving Proposed Rule Change by the National Association of Securities Dealers, Inc. Relating to the NASDAQ International Service.* Release No. 34-29812, File No. SR-NASD-90-33.

Securities and Exchange Commission. (11/3/1992) *Self-Regulatory Organizations; Philadelphia Stock Exchange, Inc.; Order Approving Proposed Rule Change Relating to the Election of Chairman and Vice Chairman of its Board.* Release No. 34-30465, File No. SR-Phlx-91-49.

Securities and Exchange Commission. (14/7/1992) *U.S. Equity Market Structure Study* (Market 2000 Concept Release). Release No. 34-30920, File No. S7-18-92.

Securities and Exchange Commission. (24/11/1992) *Letter from Larry Bergmann to Larry Fondren: Re Crosscom Trading Network.*

Securities and Exchange Commission. (22/12/1992) *Self-Regulatory Organizations; Midwest Stock Exchange, Inc.; Order Approving Proposed Rule Changes and Notice of Filing and Order Granting Accelerated Approval of Amendment No. 1 to Proposed Rule Changes Relating to its Organization and Governance.* Release No. 34-31633, File Nos. SR-MSE-92-12 and SR-MSE-92-13.

Securities and Exchange Commission. (10/2/1993) *Self-Regulatory Organizations; American Stock Exchange, Inc.; Order Approving Proposed Rule Change Relating to the Number of Consecutive Terms Which an Exchange Governor May Serve.* Release No. 34-31850, File No. SR-AMEX-92-27.

Securities and Exchange Commission. (19/3/1993) *Self-Regulatory Organizations;*

National Association of Securities Dealers; Order Approving Proposed Rule Change and Amendment No. 1 relating to the Proposed Operation of a Pricing System for Certain High Yield Fixed Income Securities. Release No. 34-32019, File No. NASD-92-45.

Securities and Exchange Commission. (16/6/1993) *Self-Regulatory Organizations; Clearing Corporation for Options and Securities; Notice of Filing of Application for Exemption from Registration as a Clearing Agency.* Release No. 34-32481, File No. 600-27.

Securities and Exchange Commission. (28/6/1993) *Self-Regulatory Organizations; MBS Clearing Corporation; Order Approving Proposed Rule Change Relating to the Limitation or Elimination of a Director's Liability in Certain Circumstances.* Release No. 34-32527, File No. SR-MBS-92-04.

Securities and Exchange Commission. (29/6/1993) *Self-Regulatory Organizations; Cincinnati Stock Exchange, Inc.; Order Granting Approval to Proposed Rule Change Amending its By-Laws to Permit Simultaneous Service as Chairman and President.* Release No. 34-32541, File No. SR-CSE-92-06.

Securities and Exchange Commission (Division of Market Regulation). (9/1993) *Staff Report on the Municipal Securities Market.*

Securities and Exchange Commission. (9/9/1993) *Letter from Brandon Becker to Lloyd Feller: The Lattice Network.*

Securities and Exchange Commission. (1/10/1993) *Letter from Larry Bergmann to Deborah Tuchman, Skadden Arps Slate Meagher and Flom re: Cantor Fitzgerald G.P.*

Securities and Exchange Commission (Division of Market Regulation). (1/1994) *Market 2000: An Examination of Current Equity Market Developments.*

Securities and Exchange Commission. (27/1/1994) *Statement upon Release of Market 2000 Study.*

Securities and Exchange Commission. (9/2/1994) *Recordkeeping and Reporting Requirements for Trading Systems operated by Brokers and Dealers.* Release No. 34-33605, File No. S7-3-94.

Securities and Exchange Commission. (14/2/1994) *Proprietary Trading Systems.* Release No. 34-33621.

Securities and Exchange Commission. (8/3/1994) *Self-Regulatory Organizations; National Association of Securities Dealers, Inc.; Order Approving a Proposed Rule Change to the By-Laws and Rules of Fair Practice Relating to Rule Approval Procedures.* Release No. 34-33737, File No. SR-NASD-93-48.

Securities and Exchange Commission. (12/4/1994) *Self-Regulatory Organizations; Chicago Stock Exchange, Inc.; Order Granting approval to Proposed Rule Change and Notice of Filing and Order Granting Accelerated Approval to Amendment No. 1 to Proposed Rule Change Relating to Corporate Governance Issues.* Release No. 34-33901, File No. SR-CHX-93-28.

Securities and Exchange Commission. (15/4/1994) *Self-Regulatory Organizations; Clearing Corporation for Options and Securities; Notice of Filing of Amendment to Application for Exemption from Registration as a Clearing Agency.* Release No. 34-33911, File No. 600-27.

Securities and Exchange Commission. (19/12/1994) *Self-Regulatory Organizations; Boston Stock Exchange, Inc.; Order Granting Approval to Proposed Rule Change and Notice of Filing and Order Granting Accelerated Approval to Amendment No. 1 to*

Proposed Rule Change Relating to the Boston–Montreal Linkage. Release No. 34-35116, File No. SR-BSE-94-01.

Securities and Exchange Commission. (25/10/1995) *Self-Regulatory Organizations; Boston Stock Exchange, Inc.; Order Granting Approval to Proposed Rule Change and Notice of Filing and Order Granting Accelerated Approval of Amendment No. 1 to Proposed Rule Change Relating to Specialist Concentration.* Release No. 34-36417, File No. SR-BSE-95-12.

Securities and Exchange Commission. (12/12/1995a) *Letter from Richard Lindsay to Mark Young re. Chicago Board Brokerage, Inc. and Clearing Corporation for Options and Securities.*

Securities and Exchange Commission. (12/12/1995b) *Self-Regulatory Organizations; Clearing Corporation for Options and Securities; Order Approving Application for Exemption from Registration as a Clearing Agency.* Release No. 34-36573, File No. 600-27.

Securities and Exchange Commission (Division of Market Regulation). (1996) *Summary of Comments: Order Execution Obligations, Securities Exchange Act.* Release No. 34-36310, File No. S7-30-95.

Securities and Exchange Commission. (8/8/1996) *Report Pursuant to Section 21(a) of the Securities Exchange Act of 1934 regarding the NASD and the NASDAQ Market.* Release No. 34-37542.

Securities and Exchange Commission. (29/8/1996) *Order Execution Obligations.* Release No. 34-37619, File No. S7-30-95, RIN 3235-AG66.

Securities and Exchange Commission. (23/5/1997) *Regulation of Exchanges: Concept Release.* Release No. 34-38672, File No. S7-16-97.

Securities and Exchange Commission and Australian Securities Commission. (1993) *Memorandum of Understanding concerning Consultation and Cooperation in the Administration and Enforcement of Securities Laws.* 20 October.

Securities and Futures Authority. (1997) *Annual Report 1997.*

Securities and Investments Board. (1987) *SIB's Approach to its Regulatory Responsibilities*, February.

Securities and Investments Board. (undated—believed 1990a) *Service Companies: Requirements for Authorisation.*

Securities and Investments Board. (1990b) *The Financial Services (Conduct of Business) Rules 1990.* Release 90, 18 October.

Securities and Investments Board. (1991a) *Recognised Investment Exchanges and Designated Investment Exchanges and Designated Investment Exchange Questionnaire.* DIE/291191.

Securities and Investments Board. (1991b) *Principles and Core Rules for the Conduct of Investment Business*, 31 January.

Securities and Investments Board. (1991c) *Designated Investment Exchanges, and Designated Investment Exchange Questionnaire.* NM/047 290791 and NM/048 010791, July.

Securities and Investments Board. (1992) *Letter to the SEC re Market 2000 Study*, 1 December.

Securities and Investments Board. (1993) *Conflicts of Interest in Regulatory Authorities: A Code of Conduct*, August.

Securities and Investments Board. (1994) *Regulation of the United Kingdom Equity Markets: Discussion paper*, February.

Securities and Investments Board. (1995) *Regulation of the United Kingdom Equity Markets*, June.

Securities and Investments Board. (1996) *Maintaining Enhanced Market Liquidity*. Consultative Paper 97, May.

Securities Industry Association, Telecommunications and Information Management Committee, and Financial Information Services Division, Information Industry Association. (1993). *Market Data Survey*.

Sedo, K.J. (1987) 'Cooperative Mergers and Consolidations: A Consideration of the Legal and Tax Issues'. *North Dakota Law Review*, 63: 377–403.

Seguin, P.J. (1992) 'The Value of Transaction Reporting', Working Paper 92-16, Mitsui Life Financial Research Center, University of Michigan, September.

Skone James, E.P., Copinger, W.A., Mummery, J.F., Rayner James, J., and Garnett, K.M. (eds.). (1991) *Copinger and Skone James on Copyright* (13th. edition). London: Sweet and Maxwell.

Smith, J. (1992) 'Television Guides: The European Court Doesn't Know "There's So Much In It" '. *European Competition Law Review*, 13: 135–8.

Smith, W. (1994) 'Merc Mulls Expanded Financial Trade Role'. *Chicago Sunday Times*, 25 October: 47.

Sociedad de Bolsas. (1991) *Contract for the Continuous Provision of Information from the Stock Exchange Link-Up System*, September.

Société des Bourses Françaises. (1989) *Distributor Agreement FIM, Right of Distribution*, March.

Société des Bourses Françaises. (1994a) *New rule for block trades in Paris*, July.

Société des Bourses Françaises. (1994b) 'La création d'un marché de blocs', Dossier de Presse, July.

Société des Bourses Françaises. (1994c) 'Avis relatif aux Tailles Normales des Blocs (TNB) des valeur éligibles aux opérations de négociation de blocs'. No. 94-2568, 28 August.

Société des Bourses Françaises and Marché à Terme International de France. (1997) 'MATIF opts for NSC for Off-Hours Trading'. Press Release, 24 January.

Société des Bourses Françaises, Marché à Terme International de France, Marché des Options Négociables de Paris, and Deutsche Börse. (1996) 'French and German Exchanges will Create Steering Committees to Link Markets'. Press Release, 11 April.

Steil, B. (1993) *Competition, Integration and Regulation in EC Capital Markets*. Royal Institute of International Affairs, International Economics Programme, September.

Steil, B. (1994) 'Whither International Regulation? To Better Our Markets or Beggar Our Neighbours'. XIX Annual Conference of IOSCO, Tokyo, 21 October.

Steil, B. (1996) 'Equity Trading IV: The ISD and the Regulation of European Market Structure', in B. Steil *et al.*, *The European Equity Markets*. A Report of the European Capital Markets Institute, Royal Institute of International Affairs.

Steil, B. *et al.* (1996) *The European Equity Markets*. A Report of the European Capital Markets Institute, Royal Institute of International Affairs.

Stein, J. (ed.). (1979) *Random House College Dictionary*. New York: Random House.

Stevenson, T. (1996) 'Stock Exchange chief gets the sack'. *Independent*, 5 January: 16.

Stewart & Ivory (M. Brooks). (1996) 'New electronic trading service: consultation feedback—Response', London Stock Exchange no. 052, 14 February.

Stigler, G.J. (1971) 'The Theory of Economic Regulation'. *Bell Journal of Economics and Management Science*, 3: 3–21.

Stock Exchange. (1984) The Choice of a New Dealing System for Equities. *Stock Exchange Quarterly*, September: 10–28.

Stock Exchange Information Services, Hong Kong Stock Exchange. (1993) *Standard Realtime Digital Data Service Agreement*, 10 June.

Stockholm Stock Exchange. (1992) *Invitation to Members of the Stockholm Stock Exchange and Issuers to Subscribe for the 1992 Issue of New Shares in Stockholms Fondbörs AB*, 13 October.

Stockholm Stock Exchange. (1993) *Agreement (for Value Line)*.

Stockholm Stock Exchange. (1996) *Annual Report 1995*.

Stockholm Stock Exchange. (1997) *Annual Report 1996*.

Subiotto, R. (1992) 'The Right to Deal with Whom One Pleases Under EEC Competition Law: A Small Contribution to a Necessary Debate'. *European Competition Law Review*, 13: 234–44.

Sundel, M.B. and Blake, L.G. (1991) 'Good Concept, Bad Executions: The Regulation and Self-Regulation of Automated Trading Systems in United States Futures Markets'. *Northwestern University Law Review*, 85: 748–89.

Sydney Futures Exchange, Australian Futures Exchange Information Services Pty. Ltd.. (1994) *Market Information Distribution Agreement*.

Sydney Futures Exchange and New York Mercantile Exchange. (1995) *The Link*, 21 August.

Tattersall, P.A. (1990) 'The Future of Financial Markets and the Role of Technology: The Impact of the GLOBEX System', in D. Siegel (ed.), *Innovation and Technology in the Markets—A Reordering of the World's Capital Markets*. New York: McGraw-Hill.

Tehan, P. (1996) 'City bankers lambast sacked Exchange chief'. *Times*, January: 19.

Tokyo Stock Exchange. (1993) *Utilization of the Tokyo Stock Exchange Market Information Service*.

Tonks, I. and Webb, D. (1989) 'The Reorganisation of the London Stock Market: The Causes and Consequences of "Big Bang" ', Discussion Paper No. 20, Financial Markets Group, London School of Economics, July.

Toronto Stock Exchange. (1985) *Annual Report 1985*.

Toronto Stock Exchange. (1986) *Annual Report 1986*.

Toronto Stock Exchange. (1988) *AMEX-MIDWEST Links Report*.

Toronto Stock Exchange. (1990) *Submission of the Toronto Stock Exchange to the Ontario Securities Commission concerning the Report of the Rule Review Committee on the Operation of the Auction Market and Computer Based Market Access Systems in Ontario and concerning Instinet Canada Limited*, 15 January.

Tradepoint Financial Networks plc. (1992) *Initial Public Offering: Prospectus*, 29 December.

Tradepoint Financial Networks plc. (1994) 'Statement of Material Facts'. Notice (#53/94), Superintendent of Brokers and Vancouver Stock Exchange, 24 July.

Tradepoint Financial Networks plc. (1995) 'Statement of Material Facts'. Notice (#39/95), Superintendent of Brokers and Vancouver Stock Exchange, 21 September.

Treasury Committee, House of Commons. (1996*a*) *The Stock Exchange: Minutes of Evidence—Mr. John Kemp-Welch, Mr. Ian Plenderleith, Mr. Giles Vardey & Ms. Christine Dann (The London Stock Exchange)*. Session 1995–96, 237-i, 19 February.

Treasury Committee, House of Commons. (1996*b*) *The Stock Exchange: Minutes of Evidence—Sir Nicholas Redmayne and Mr. Mark Potashnick (Kleinwort Benson), Mr. Gordon Lawson & Mr. Richard O'Hare Salomon Brothers International Ltd.)*. Session 1995–96, 237-ii, 21 September.

Treasury Committee, House of Commons. (1996c) *The Stock Exchange: Minutes of Evidence—Mr. John Cobb and Mr. Geoffrey Turner (Association of Private Client Investment Managers and Stockbrokers—APCIMS), Mr. David Wenman, Mr. Philip Ellick, Mr. John Woodman & Ms. Abigail Harvey (SBC Warburg)*. Session 1995–96, 237-iii, 26 February.

Treasury Committee, House of Commons. (1996d) *The Stock Exchange: Minutes of Evidence—Mr. Michael Lawrence*. Session 1995–96, 237-iv, 28 February.

Treasury Committee, House of Commons. (1996e) *The Stock Exchange: Minutes of Evidence—Mr. Donald Brydon (BZW), Mr. John Kemp-Welch, Mr. Ian Plenderleith, Mr. Ian Salter, Mr. Giles Vardey & Mr. Richard Kilsby (The London Stock Exchange)*. Session 1995–96, 237-vi, 30 March.

Umlauf, S.R. (1990) 'Information Asymmetries and Security Market Design: An Empirical Study of the Secondary Market for US Government Securities'. LBS Discussion paper, IFA-131-90, August.

Umlauf, S.R. (1993) 'Transaction taxes and the Behavior of the Swedish Stock Market'. *Journal of Financial Economics*, 33: 227–40.

United States, House of Representatives. (1996) *A Bill to amend title 15, United States Code, to promote investment and prevent intellectual property piracy with respect to databases*. H.R. 3531, 104th Congress, 2d Session, 23 May.

United States Senate, Committee on Banking and Currency. (1934) *Securities Act*. S.Rep. 792, 73rd Congress, 2d Session, 17 April.

United States Senate, Committee on Banking, Housing and Urban Affairs, Subcommittee on Securities (1973) *Securities Industry Study*. 93rd Congress, 1st Session, 89-135 [93-13], 6 April.

United States Senate, Committee on Banking, Housing and Urban Affairs, Subcommittee on Securities (1975) *Report to Accompany S. 249*. S.Rep. No. 94-75, 94th Congress, 1st Session.

Usher, J. (1991) '1992 and the Implications for Banking and Finance: An Overview', in R. Cranston (ed.), *The Single Market and the Law of Banking*. London: Lloyds of London Press.

Van Kerckhove, M. (1994) 'The Advocate General Delivers his Opinion on Magill'. *European Competition Law Review*, 15: 276–9.

Van Kerckhove, M. (1995) 'Magill: A Refusal to License or a Refusal to Supply'. *Copyright World*, June–July, 51: 26–30.

Varian, H.R. (1984) *Microeconomic Analysis* (2nd. edition). W.W. Norton and Co..

Vaughan, L. (1993) 'Exchange alliances fall into disarray'. *Independent*, 13 September: 25.

Verrechia, R. (1982) 'Information Acquisition in a Noisy Rational Expectations Economy'. *Econometrica*, 50: 1415–30.

Vinje, T.C. (1992) 'Magill: Its Impact on the Information Technology Industry'. *European Intellectual Property Review*, November, 14: 397–402.

Vinje, T.C. (1995) 'The Final Word on Magill: The Judgment of the ECJ'. *European Intellectual Property Review*, 17: 297–303.

von Rosen, R. (1990) 'The Future of the European Stock Exchanges—The German Perspective', conference at London School of Economics, 8 May.

von Rosen, R. (1991) 'Creating the Infrastructure to Support Cross-Border Share Trading', conference, London, 22 April.

Warner, J. (1996) 'A City crusader who lost the battle'. *Independent*, 6 January: 17.

Waters Information Services (1990) 'Legal Moves Set Exchange Alarm Bells Ringing'. *Dealing with Technology*, 3 August, 2: 3–4.

Waters, R. (1990*a*) 'Stock exchanges fail to bury the hatchet'. *Financial Times*, 22 May: 30.

Waters, R. (1990*b*) 'Stalemate in the marketplace'. *Financial Times*, 15 November: 38.

Waters, R. (1991*a*) 'Euroquote charts an ambitious course'. *Financial Times*, 13 March: 34.

Waters, R. (1991*b*) 'Euroquote christening may become its funeral'. *Financial Times*, 23 May: 21.

Waters, R. (1991*c*) 'Europe extends the fuse leading to Big Bang'. *Financial Times*, 29 May: 21.

Waters, R. (1991*d*) 'Frankfurt gains a foothold'. *Financial Times*, 4 October: 32.

Waters, R. (1993) 'SE in move to sell information wholesale'. *Financial Times*, 15 March: 15.

Waters, R. and Graham, G. (1990) 'Birth of a market needs burial of differences'. *Financial Times*, 27 November: 27.

Webber, A. (1994) *Dictionary of Futures and Options*. Cambridge: Probus Publishing.

Weber, B.W. (1991) 'Information Technology and Securities Markets: Feasibility and Desirability of Alternative Electronic Trading Systems'. Ph.D. Thesis, London Business School.

Whish, R. and Sufrin, B.E. (1993) *Competition Law*. London: Butterworths.

Williamson, O.E. (1975) *Markets and Hierarchies: Analysis and Antitrust Implications*. New York: Free Press.

Williamson, O.E. (1979) 'Transaction-Cost Economics: The Governance of Contractual Relations'. *Journal of Law and Economics*, 22: 233–61.

Williamson, O.E. (1985) *The Economic Institutions of Capitalism*. New York: Free Press.

Williamson, O.E. (1990) 'The Firm as a Nexus of Treaties: an Introduction', in M. Aoki, B. Gustafson, and O.E. Williamson (eds.), *The Firm as a Nexus of Treaties*. London: Sage.

Williamson, O.E. (1993) 'The Logic of Economic Organization', in O. Williamson and S. Winter (eds.), *The Nature of the Firm: Origins, Evolution, and Development*. New York: Oxford University Press.

Williamson, O.E. (1996) *The Mechanisms of Governance*. Oxford: Oxford University Press.

Wilson, N. (1993*a*) 'The Matif–DTB connection'. *Futures and Options World*, February, No. 261: 13.

Wilson, N. (1993*b*) 'EOE and OML connect first FEX link'. *Futures and Options World*, March, No. 262: 16–17.

Wilson, N. (1993*c*) 'A rocky road ahead?' *Futures and Options World*, September, No. 268: 51–3.

Wilson, N. (1994) 'Brawling for FCM Business'. *Futures and Options World*, January, No. 272: 38–41.

Wilson, N. (1997) 'How Big a Deal is CBB going to Be?' *Futures and Options World*, March, No. 310: 49.

Woelfel, C. (ed.). (1994) *Encyclopedia of Banking and Finance* (10th. edition). Chicago: Probus Publishing.

Wolfsen, J.R. (Associate General Counsel, The Nasdaq Stock Market). (1996) 'The Legal and Business Issues of Electronic Contracts', slides for Financial Information Services Division, Information Industry Association, conference, 20 May.

Wolman, C. (1997) 'IDBs and Tradepoint face doom'. *London Financial News*, 10–16 November: 1.

World Intellectual Property Organization. (1997) *Governing Bodies of WIPO and the Unions administered by WIPO: Thirtieth Series of Meetings: General Information—Memorandum of the International Bureau*, 20 January.

World Securities Law Report. (1995) 'Czech Republic: Brokers Plan Self-Regulation, Disclosure of Off-Market Trades'. February: 14-15.

Worthy, J. (1994) 'Intellectual Property Protection after GATT'. *European Intellectual Property Review*, 16: 195–8.

Wunsch Auction Systems Inc. (1990) *Supplemental Statement to Application for Exemption from Registration as a National Securities Exchange under the Securities Exchange Act of 1934*. Exhibit N to the SEC, 3 October.

Wunsch Auction Systems Inc. (1991*a*) *SPAworks—The Single Price Auction*.

Wunsch Auction Systems Inc. (1991*b*) *SPAworks User's Guide*. Equities 1.2.

Wunsch Auction Systems Inc. (1991*c*) *Letter from Steve Wunsch to Alden Adkins, Office of Automation and International Markets, SEC*, 25 January.

Wunsch Auction Systems Inc. (1991*d*) *SPAworks—Commission Rate Schedule*, 3 June.

Wunsch Auction Systems Inc. (1991*e*) *Auction Countdown*, 10 June.

Wunsch, S. (1988) 'The Single Price Auction', in Wayne Wagner (ed.), *The Complete Guide to Securities Transactions: Controlling Costs and Enhancing Investment Performance*. New York: John Wiley and Sons.

Yen, A.C. (1991) 'The Legacy of Feist: Consequences of the Weak Connection Between Copyright and the Economics of Public Goods'. *Ohio State Law Journal*, 52: 1343–78.

Young, D.R. (1987) 'Executive Leadership in Nonprofit Organizations', in W. Powell (ed.), *The Nonprofit Sector: A Research Handbook*. New Haven, CT: Yale University Press.

Young, M. (Kirkland & Ellis). (1995) *Letter to Richard Lindsey, Division of Market Regulation re: Request for No-Action Determination relating to Chicago Board Brokerage, Inc. and Clearing Corporation for Options and Securities*, 11 December.

Zusman, P. (1992) 'Constitutional selection of collective-choice rules in a cooperative enterprise'. *Journal of Economic Behaviour and Organization*, 17: 353–62.

INDEX

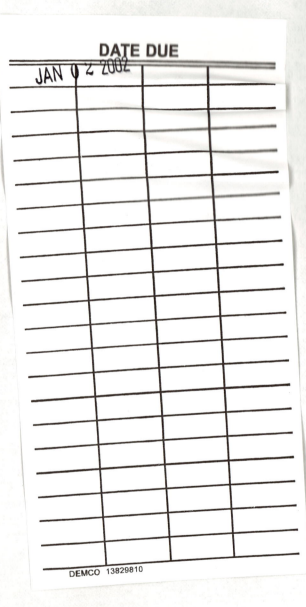

DATE DUE

JAN 0 2 2002